# RESEARCH DESIGN EXPLAINED

# RESEARCH DESIGN EXPLAINED
## *Third Edition*

**Mark Mitchell**
*Clarion University*

**Janina Jolley**
*Clarion University*

**Harcourt Brace College Publishers**

Fort Worth   Philadelphia   San Diego   New York   Orlando   Austin   San Antonio
Toronto   Montreal   London   Sydney   Tokyo

| | |
|---|---|
| Publisher | Ted Buchholz |
| Editor in Chief | Christopher P. Klein |
| Project Editor | Jeff Beckham |
| Senior Production Manager | Ken Dunaway |
| Production Manager | Carlyn Hauser |
| Senior Art Director | David A. Day |

Cover Image: © Akira INOUE/Photonica

ISBN: 0-15-502828-6

Library of Congress Catalog Card Number: 95-79985

*Address for Editorial Correspondence:* Harcourt Brace College Publishers, 301 Commerce Street, Suite 3700, Fort Worth, TX 76102.

*Address for Orders:* Harcourt Brace & Company, 6277 Sea Harbor Drive, Orlando, FL 32887-6777. 1-800-782-4479, or 1-800-433-0001 (in Florida).

Printed in the United States of America

5  6  7  8  9  0  1  2  3  4  039  9  8  7  6  5  4  3  2  1

*To Anna, Glen, and Neal*

# PREFACE

This textbook began as a search for a textbook. When we first began teaching research design, we looked around for a textbook that conveyed the excitement that accompanies scientific discovery. We also wanted a user-friendly book that could engage our students while offering practical advice about how to read, conduct, and write up research.

Unfortunately, we couldn't find such a book. Existing books conveyed one of two messages: "Research design is easy—just memorize these terms and research studies" or, "Research design is hard—it's something so complicated to understand that it should be left to the professionals."

We wanted to replace the sense of mystery and confusion that students bring to scientific psychology with an appreciation of science's excitement and relevance to psychology. To enable students to explore uncharted psychological frontiers, we wanted a book that explained fundamental concepts so clearly and with so many real-life analogies and examples that students would understand these ideas rather than simply memorize terms.

In short, we discovered we were going to have to write the textbook ourselves. And, once we got started, we discovered that all those frustrations that we—and our students—had experienced in the past were actually helpful. We were able to translate these difficulties into a textbook that explained research concepts in a way that was easy to grasp. Here are some of our methods (methods that you probably use in your teaching):

- We make a concerted effort to stimulate students interest in the course. For example, we show students how understanding scientific psychology can make them more sophisticated consumers and more marketable job/ graduate school applicants.
- We use numerous, clear examples—especially for concepts with which students have trouble, such as statistical significance and interactions.
- We show the logic behind the process of research design so that students know more than just terminology—they learn how to think like research psychologists.
- We let students see the relationships among different designs—how else can they choose the right design?
- We explain statistical concepts (not computations) because statistics need to be considered *before* doing research, not afterward.

- We use a large number of summary tables to help drive home main points. (We think that at least one research text should employ pedagogical techniques that research has shown to be effective.)

## DISTINCTIVE CHAPTERS & APPENDICES

The goal of this book is to encourage students to value, read, and conduct ethical research. Therefore, we:

- Introduce ethical issues in Chapter 1 and discuss ethics throughout the book. In addition, we have a separate appendix on ethical issues.
- Give the practical advice a novice needs. (We even have a special appendix on how to conduct a study.)
- Have an entire chapter on how to read research (and an appendix on how to search the literature.)
- Have an entire chapter on generating research ideas (Chapter 2.)
- Offer an entire chapter on survey research—the research method that students will most likely use after they leave school.
- Include an entire chapter on how to write research proposals and articles in APA style.
- Provide a glossary at the end of each chapter that not only defines key terms, but shows the inter-relationships between the terms.
- Supply an appendix on how understanding research can help students' careers.

## FLEXIBLE ORGANIZATION

Although it's perfectly acceptable to cover the chapters in order, chapters are relatively self-contained modules. Indeed, we know that some professors start at Chapter 5 and others start at Chapter 10. Even we do not always cover all the chapters in order. Because each chapter focuses on ethics, construct validity, external validity, and internal validity, it's easy to skip chapters or cover them in different orders.

## THE THIRD EDITION

As in previous editions, we help students by:

- Focusing on important, fundamental concepts;
- Showing students why those concepts are important;
- Relating those concepts to what students already know;
- Dealing directly with common misconceptions about those concepts;
- Giving students numerous examples;

- Using graphic organizers such as tables and diagrams to help students see relationships among associated concepts and between steps in a decision-making process; and
- Using a conversational style and avoiding unnecessary terms, mathematical notation, and complex computations.

## CHANGES INCORPORATED IN THIS EDITION

In this edition, we have made major changes to both the book and the Instructor's Manual.

### The book now has:
- Shorter chapters;
- An even clearer writing style;
- Chapters that are more self-contained. Consequently, as explained in the Instructor's Manual, chapters can be covered in a wide variety of orders;
- Improved figures and tables; and
- End-of-chapter "glossaries" that define key terms and explain the inter-relationships among those terms.

### The Instructor's Manual includes:
- A class-tested Test Bank;
- Sample lectures;
- Lab exercises; and
- Detailed answers to the end-of-chapter exercises.

# ACKNOWLEDGMENTS

Writing *Research Design Explained* was a monumental task that required commitment, love, effort, and a high tolerance for frustration. If it had not been for the support of our friends, family, publisher, and students, we could not have met this challenge.

Robert Tremblay, a Boston journalist, has our undying gratitude for the many hours he spent critiquing the first two editions of this book. We are also grateful to Lee Howard, a Connecticut journalist, for his work on this edition of the text. We also give special thanks to Michael Cobb, Christina Oldham, Susan Pierce, Susan Meyers, Kirsten Olson, and the rest of the folks at Harcourt Brace for sharing and nurturing our vision. In addition to thanking Bob, Lee, and Harcourt Brace, we would like to thank three groups of dedicated reviewers.

First, we would like to thank the competent and conscientious professors who shared their insights with us. The following people were actually co-authors of this book: Louis Banderet, Quinsigamond Community College; James H. Beaird, Western Oregon State College; John P. Brockway, Davidson College; Tracy L. Brown, University of North Carolina—Asheville; Edward Caropreso, Clarion University; Walter Chromiak, Dickinson College; James R. Council, North Dakota State University; Helen J. Crawford, University of Wyoming; Raymond Ditrichs, Northern Illinois University; Patricia Doerr, Louisiana State University; Linda Enloe, Idaho State University; Mary Ann Foley, Skidmore College; George L. Hampton III, University of Houston—Downtown; Robert Hoff, Mercyhurst College; Lynn Howerton, Arkansas State University; John C. Jahnke, Miami University; Randy Jones, Utah State University; Scott A. Kuehn, Clarion University; Kenneth L. Leicht, Illinois State University; Charles A. Levin, Baldwin-Wallace College; Joel Lundack, Peru State College; Kenneth B. Melvin, University of Alabama; Stephen P. Mewaldt, Marshall University; John Nicoud, Marion College of Fond du Lac; David Pittenger, Marietta College; Ray Reutzel, Brigham Young University; Anrea Richards, University of California—Los Angeles; Margaret Ruddy, Trenton State College; James J. Ryan, University of Wisconsin—La Crosse; Rick Scheidt, Kansas State University; Sylvia Stalker, Clarion University; Sandra L. Stein, Rider College; Russ A. Thompson, University of Nebraska; Benjamin Wallace, Cleveland State University; Paul Wellman, Texas A&M University; and Christine Ziegler, Kennesaw State College.

Second, we would like to thank our student reviewers, especially Susanne Bingham, Shari Custer, Chris Fenn, Kris Glosser, Melissa Gregory, Barbara Olszanski, Rosalyn Rapsinski, and Melissa Ustik.

Third, we would like to thank the English professors who critiqued our book: William Blazek, Patrick McLaughlin, and John Young. In addition to improving the writing style of the book, they also provided a valuable perspective—that of the intelligent, but naive, reader.

Finally, we offer our gratitude to Vivian, Liona, and Max for allowing us the time to complete this project.

# About the Authors

After graduating summa cum laude from Washington and Lee University; Mark L. Mitchell received his M.A. and Ph.D. degrees in psychology at The Ohio State University. He is currently an Associate Professor at Clarion University.

Janina M. Jolley graduated with "Great Distinction" from California State University at Dominguez Hills and earned her M.A. and Ph.D. in psychology from The Ohio State University. She is currently a consulting editor of *The Journal of Genetic Psychology* and *Genetic Psychology Monographs*. Her previous book was *How to write psychology papers: A student's survival guide for psychology and related fields,* which she wrote with J. D. Murray and Pete Keller. She is currently a Professor of Psychology at Clarion University and director of Clarion University's Honors Program.

Drs. Mitchell & Jolley are married to research, teaching, and each other— not necessarily in that order. You can write to them at the Department of Psychology, Clarion University, Clarion, PA 16214; or send e-mail to them at Mitchell@vaxa.Clarion.edu. or Jolley@vaxa.Clarion.edu.

# CONTENTS

PREFACE     VII


*CHAPTER 1    Psychology and Science*     1
OVERVIEW     2
WHY PSYCHOLOGY USES THE SCIENTIFIC APPROACH     2
 The Characteristics of Science     2
 The Characteristics of Psychology     8
 Conclusions about the Importance of Science to Psychology     14
QUESTIONS ABOUT APPLYING TECHNIQUES FROM
PHYSICAL SCIENCES TO PSYCHOLOGY     15
 Internal Validity Questions     16
 Construct Validity Questions     17
 External Validity Questions     20
 Ethical Questions     20
 Conclusions about the Questions that Researchers Face     25
WHY YOU SHOULD UNDERSTAND RESEARCH DESIGN     26
CONCLUDING REMARKS     32
SUMMARY     33
KEY TERMS     34
EXERCISES     35


*CHAPTER 2    Generating Research Hypotheses*     41
OVERVIEW     42
GENERATING RESEARCH IDEAS BY CHALLENGING COMMON SENSE     42
GENERATING RESEARCH IDEAS FROM THEORY     43
 Why Scientists Like Theories     44
 Using "Good" Theories to Generate Research Ideas     47
 Conclusions about Generating Research Ideas from Theory     54
GENERATING RESEARCH IDEAS FROM PREVIOUS RESEARCH     55
 Specific Strategies     55
 Conclusions about Generating Research Ideas from Previous Research     58
CONVERTING AN IDEA INTO A RESEARCH HYPOTHESIS     59
 Make It Testable     59
 Be Sure to Have a Rationale     61

Demonstrate Its Relevance    61

Make Sure that Testing It Is Practical and Ethical    61

Changing Impractical and Unethical Ideas into Research Hypotheses    61

CONCLUDING REMARKS    64

SUMMARY    65

KEY TERMS    66

EXERCISES    67


CHAPTER 3    *Measuring and Manipulating Variables*    69

OVERVIEW    70

MEASUREMENT    71

Where Observers Can Go Wrong    71

Minimizing Observer Errors    72

Errors in Administering the Measure    74

Errors Due to the Participant    75

Reliability    77

Beyond Reliability: Establishing Construct Validity    87

MANIPULATING VARIABLES    92

Common Threats to a Manipulating's Validity    92

Evidence Used to Argue for Validity    93

Tradeoffs among Three Common Types of Manipulations    95

Manipulating Variables: A Summary    97

CONCLUDING REMARKS    98

SUMMARY    98

KEY TERMS    99

EXERCISES    101


CHAPTER 4    *Beyond Reliability and Validity: Choosing the Best Measure for Your Study*    105

OVERVIEW    106

SENSITIVITY: WILL THE MEASURE BE ABLE TO DETECT THE DIFFERENCES YOU NEED TO DETECT?    107

Achieving the Necessary Level of Sensitivity    107

Sensitivity: Conclusions    112

SCALES OF MEASUREMENT: WILL THE MEASURE ALLOW YOU TO MAKE THE KINDS OF COMPARISONS YOU NEED TO MAKE?    112

The Different Scales of Measurement    113

Why Our Numbers Do Not Always Measure Up    116

Which Level of Measurement Do You Need?    116

Conclusions about Scales of Measurement    121
**ETHICAL AND PRACTICAL CONSIDERATIONS**    121
**CONCLUDING REMARKS**    122
**SUMMARY**    123
**KEY TERMS**    123
**EXERCISES**    124


*CHAPTER 5    Internal Validity*    127
**OVERVIEW**    128
**WHY WE CANNOT GET TWO IDENTICAL GROUPS: SELECTION**    129
Self-Assignment to Group as a Source of Selections Bias    129
Researcher Assignment to Group: An Obvious Source of Selection Bias    131
Arbitrary Assignment to Group as a Source of Selection Bias    131
Matching: A Valiant, but Unsuccessful Strategy for Getting Identical Groups    132
Problems with Matching on Pretest Scores    135
**PROBLEMS WITH THE PRETEST–POSTTEST DESIGN**    139
Three Reasons Participants May Change between Pretest and Posttest    140
How Measurement Changes May Cause Scores to Change between
Pretest and Posttest    142
**CONCLUSIONS**    146
Ruling Out Extraneous Variables    146
The Relationship between Internal and External Validity    148
**SUMMARY**    150
**KEY TERMS**    151
**EXERCISES**    152


*CHAPTER 6    The Simple Experiment*    155
**OVERVIEW**    156
**CAUSALITY: THE SIMPLE EXPERIMENT'S PURPOSE**    156
The Logic of Causality    156
The Variability Problem    157
**BASIC TERMINOLOGY**    162
Experimental Hypothesis    162
Null Hypothesis    162
Administering the Independent Variable    163
Experimental and Control Groups    164
Collecting the Dependent Variable    168
The Statistical Significance Decision    168
Summary of the "Ideal" Simple Experiment    170

## ERRORS IN DETERMINING WHETHER RESULTS ARE STATISTICALLY SIGNIFICANT    171

Type 1 Errors    171

Type 2 Errors    172

Tradeoffs between Type 1 and Type 2 Errors    173

How to Prevent Type 2 Errors    174

How Designing a Simple Experiment Is Affected by Statistical Considerations: A Summary    178

## NONSTATISTICAL CONSIDERATIONS    179

External Validity versus Power    179

Construct Validity versus Power    179

Ethics versus Power    181

## ANALYZING DATA FROM THE SIMPLE EXPERIMENT: THE t-TEST    181

Estimating What You Want To Know    182

Inferential Statistics    185

Executing the t-Test    194

Questions Raised by Results    196

## CONCLUDING REMARKS    197

## SUMMARY    198

## KEY TERMS    200

## EXERCISES    205


## CHAPTER 7    *Expanding the Simple Experiment: The Multiple Group Experiment*    209

## OVERVIEW    210

## THE ADVANTAGES OF USING MORE THAN TWO VALUES OF AN INDEPENDENT VARIABLE    210

Comparing More than Two Kinds of Treatments    210

Comparing Two Kinds of Treatments with No Treatment    212

Comparing More than Two Levels (Amounts) of an Independent Variable to Increase External Validity    212

Using Multiple Levels to Improve Construct Validity of Experiments    219

## ANALYSIS OF MULTIPLE GROUP EXPERIMENTS    224

Analyzing the Multiple Group Experiments: An Intuitive Overview    225

A Closer Look at the Analysis of a Multiple Group Experiment    227

## CONCLUDING REMARKS    237

## SUMMARY    237

## KEY TERMS    238

## EXERCISES    240

*CHAPTER 8    Expanding the Simple Experiment: Factorial Designs*    243
OVERVIEW    244
THE 2 × 2 FACTORIAL DESIGN    244
    How One Experiment Can Do as Much as Two    245
    How One Experiment Can Do More than Two    245
    Potential Results of a 2 × 2 Experiment    253
ANALYZING THE RESULTS FROM A 2 × 2 EXPERIMENT    264
    Interpreting the Results of an ANOVA Table    266
    Interactions    267
PUTTING THE 2 × 2 TO WORK    276
    Adding a Replication Factor to Increase Generalizability    277
    Using an Interaction to Find an Exception to the Rule: Looking at a Potential
        Moderating Factor    278
    Using Interactions to Create New Rules    278
    Studying Non-Experimental Variables    279
CONCLUDING REMARKS    284
SUMMARY    284
KEY TERMS    285
EXERCISES    287

*CHAPTER 9    Within-Subjects Designs*    289
OVERVIEW    290
THE MATCHED PAIRS DESIGN    291
    Procedure    291
    Considerations in Using Matched Pairs Designs    292
    Analysis of Data    295
    Summary of the Matched Pairs Design    296
PURE WITHIN-SUBJECTS DESIGNS    296
    Procedure    296
    Considerations in Using Within-Subjects Designs    298
    Dealing with the Order Problem    303
    Analysis of Data    305
    Summary of Pure Within-Subjects Designs    306
COUNTERBALANCED WITHIN-SUBJECTS DESIGNS    306
    Procedure    307
    Advantages and Disadvantages of Counterbalancing    307
    Conclusions about Counterbalanced Designs    312
CHOOSING DESIGNS    313
    Choosing Designs: The Two Conditions Case    313
    Choosing Designs: When You Have More than One Independent Variable    314

**CONCLUDING REMARKS**    318
**SUMMARY**    318
**KEY TERMS**    319
**EXERCISES**    321

*CHAPTER 10    Reading and Evaluating Research*    323
**OVERVIEW**    324
**READING FOR UNDERSTANDING**    324
    Choosing an Article    324
    Reading the Abstract    325
    Reading the Introduction    325
    Reading the Method Section    329
    Reading the Results Section    330
    Reading the Discussion    333
**DEVELOPING RESEARCH IDEAS FROM EXISTING RESEARCH**    334
    The Direct Replication    337
    The Systematic Replication    339
    The Conceptual Replication    342
    The Value of Replications    343
    Extending Research    344
**CONCLUDING REMARKS**    345
**SUMMARY**    345
**KEY TERMS**    346
**EXERCISES**    347

*CHAPTER 11    Single-n Experiments and Quasi-Experiments*    349
**OVERVIEW**    350
**INFERRING CAUSALITY IN RANDOMIZED EXPERIMENTS**    350
    Establishing Covariation    350
    Establishing Temporal Precedence    351
    Controlling for Irrelevant Factors without Keeping Everything Constant    351
**SINGLE-N EXPERIMENTS**    352
    Keeping Nontreatment Factors Constant: The A–B Design    352
    Variations on the A–B Design    356
    Evaluation of Single-n Experiments    360
    Conclusions about Single-n Experiments    364
**QUASI-EXPERIMENTS**    365
    The Problem: Accounting for Nontreatment Factors    365

The Pretest–Posttest Design    369

Time Series Designs    370

The Non-Equivalent Control Group Design    378

Conclusions about Quasi-Experimental Designs    382

**CONCLUDING REMARKS**    383

**SUMMARY**    384

**KEY TERMS**    386

**EXERCISES**    389


*CHAPTER 12    Introduction to Descriptive Methods*    391

**OVERVIEW**    392

**USES FOR DESCRIPTIVE METHODS**    393

Descriptive Research and Causality    393

Description for Description's Sake    395

Description for Prediction's Sake    396

Why Do We Need Science to Describe Behavior?    397

Conclusions about the Need for Descriptive Research    399

**SOURCES OF DATA**    400

Ex Post Facto Research: Data You Have Already Collected    400

Archival Data    401

Observation    405

Tests    407

**DESCRIBING YOUR DATA**    408

Graphing Your Data    408

Correlation Coefficients: When a Number May Be Worth a Thousand Points    411

Summary of Describing Correlational Data    418

**MAKING INFERENCES FROM DATA**    418

Analyses Based on Correlation Coefficients    420

Analysis Not Involving Correlation Coefficients    421

Interpreting Significant Result    425

Interpreting Null Results    428

**A LOOK AHEAD**    430

**SUMMARY**    430

**KEY TERMS**    431

**EXERCISES**    433


*CHAPTER 13    Survey Research*    435

**OVERVIEW**    436

DECIDING WHETHER TO DO SURVEY RESEARCH          437
    Applications    437
    Considerations    437
THE ADVANTAGES AND DISADVANTAGES OF DIFFERENT SURVEY
INSTRUMENTS    441
    Questionnaires    441
    Psychological Tests    442
    Interviews    443
PLANNING A SURVEY    446
    What Is your Hypothesis?    446
    Format of Questions    446
    Format of Survey    452
    The Art of Asking Good Questions    453
SAMPLING    459
    Random Sampling    459
    Stratified Random Sampling    460
    Convenience Sampling    461
    Quota Sampling    462
    Conclusions about Sampling Techniques    462
ADMINISTERING THE SURVEY    462
ANALYZING SURVEY DATA    463
    Summarizing Data    463
    Summarizing Interval Data    464
    Summarizing Ordinal and Nominal Data    464
    Using Inferential Statistics    466
    Using Inferential Statistics with Nominal Data    468
CONCLUDING REMARKS    469
SUMMARY    469
KEY TERMS    470
EXERCISES    473


CHAPTER 14    Putting It All Together: Writing Research Proposals
and Reports    475
OVERVIEW    476
AIDS TO DEVELOPING YOUR IDEA    476
    The Research Journal    476
    The Proposal    477
WRITING THE INTRODUCTION TO YOUR RESEARCH PROPOSAL    478
    The Elements of an Introduction    478
    Justifying Specific Types of Studies    482

**WRITING THE METHOD SECTION**    487

    Participants    488

    Design    489

    Apparatus and Materials    489

    Procedure    489

**WRITING THE RESULTS SECTION**    490

**WRITING THE DISCUSSION SECTION**    491

**PUTTING ON THE FRONT AND BACK**    492

    Title and Title Page    492

    Abstract    492

    References    493

**WRITING THE FINAL REPORT**    493

    What Stays the Same or Changes Very Little    493

    Writing the Results Section    494

    Writing the Discussion Section    496

**CONCLUDING REMARKS**    497

**SUMMARY**    502

**KEY TERMS**    503

**APPENDIX A: ETHICS**    505

**APPENDIX B: LIBRARY RESOURCES**    519

**APPENDIX C: CONDUCTING A STUDY**    529

**APPENDIX D: MARKETING YOUR RESEARCH SKILLS IN THE REAL WORLD**    547

**APPENDIX E: STATISTICS AND RANDOM NUMBERS TABLES**    555

**APPENDIX F: SAMPLE RESEARCH PAPER**    569

**APPENDIX G: THE FIELD EXPERIMENT**    589

**GLOSSARY**    601

**REFERENCES**    615

**INDEX**    619

# RESEARCH DESIGN EXPLAINED

RESEARCH DESIGN EXPLAINED

# CHAPTER 1

———

# Psychology and Science

*Overview*

*Why Psychology Uses the Scientific Approach*

THE CHARACTERISTICS OF SCIENCE

THE CHARACTERISTICS OF PSYCHOLOGY

CONCLUSIONS ABOUT THE IMPORTANCE OF SCIENCE
TO PSYCHOLOGY

*Questions about Applying Techniques from Physical Sciences to Psychology*

INTERNAL VALIDITY QUESTIONS

CONSTRUCT VALIDITY QUESTIONS

EXTERNAL VALIDITY QUESTIONS

ETHICAL QUESTIONS

CONCLUSIONS ABOUT THE QUESTIONS THAT
RESEARCHERS FACE

*Why You Should Understand Research Design*

*Concluding Remarks*

*Summary*

*Key Terms*

*Exercises*

# *Chapter 1*

# PSYCHOLOGY AND SCIENCE

*"The whole of science is nothing more than the refinement of every-day thinking."*

—ALBERT EINSTEIN

*"Since the beginning of the 20th century, people's innate desire to understand themselves—and the human condition—has found a new avenue toward the answer: the scientific method."*

—JACQUELINE SWARTZ

## OVERVIEW

In this chapter, you will learn why psychologists embrace scientific research. Then, you will learn about the problems psychologists encounter when they try to apply traditional scientific techniques to the study of human behavior. Finally, you will learn how you will benefit from understanding research design.

## WHY PSYCHOLOGY USES THE SCIENTIFIC APPROACH

Since humans were first able to reason, they have asked themselves: "Why are people the way they are?" A little more than 100 years ago, a few individuals tried a novel approach to answering this question—the scientific approach. As a result, psychology was born.

Today, thousands of psychologists believe in the scientific approach. What is it about the scientific approach that psychologists find so attractive?

### The Characteristics of Science

Psychologists find the scientific approach attractive because it is a useful tool for getting accurate answers to important questions. Detectives have used the scientific approach to solve crimes; biologists have used the scientific approach to track down the genes responsible for inherited disorders; and behavioral scientists use the scientific approach to unravel the mysteries of the human mind.

What is it about the scientific approach that makes it such a useful tool for people who want answers to important questions? As you will soon see, the strengths of the scientific approach are that it

1. finds general rules
2. collects objective evidence
3. makes verifiable statements
4. adopts a skeptical, questioning attitude about all claims, yet still remains open-minded about new claims
5. is creative
6. is public
7. is productive

## GENERAL RULES

Just as detectives assume that crimes have motives, scientists assume that events happen for reasons. Furthermore, scientists are optimistic that they can find general rules that will allow us to better understand the world. Their hope is that by finding the underlying reasons for events, they will find simplicity, order, and predictability in what often seems a complex, chaotic, and random universe. Thus, contrary to what happens in some science classes, the goal of science is not to make the world more complex and confusing. Instead, science's goal is to make the world more understandable. One way to make the world more understandable is to find simple rules that explain, describe, and predict behavior.

## OBJECTIVE

Scientists must be careful, however, not to be blinded by the desire to see the world as a simple and predictable place. We all know people who, in their desire to see the world as simple and predictable, "see" rules and patterns that reflect their prejudices and biases, rather than fact. For example, some people think they can "size up" a person based on the person's race, astrological sign, attractiveness, handwriting, body build, or some other superficial characteristic. However, when we objectively test the ability of these people to predict other people's behavior, they fail miserably—as more than 100 studies have shown (Dawes, 1994).

Scientists believe in objective facts because they know from past experience that we can't always accept people's subjective opinions. In the past, physicians believed that scalding patients with hot water and destroying parts of their brain (lobotomies) made patients "better." Some even issued reports about the percentage of patients who were "better off"—but "better off" was based on their subjective judgment, rather than on an objective report of observable changes in their patients (such as returning to work).

To avoid being swept away by either unfounded speculations or biased perceptions, scientists *collect observable evidence.* That is, they compile concrete data that can be verified by independent observers, as well as by skeptics. Thus, the scientific laws of gravity, magnetism, and operant conditioning were discovered through objective observation of physical evidence (Ruchlis & Oddo, 1992).

## VERIFIABLE

Although we have attacked unsupported speculation, we are not saying that scientists don't speculate—they do. Like detectives, scientists are encouraged to make bold, specific predictions, and then to find evidence that either supports or refutes their speculations.

Scientists welcome studies that test their hypotheses because, whether or not their ideas are disproven, scientific knowledge has been enhanced. To reiterate: Scientists are not concerned about having their ideas disproven.

Scientists are not concerned about having their ideas disproven for at least two reasons. First, a major goal of science is to identify false beliefs. Second, one of science's major strengths is that it allows scientists to learn from mistakes.

Scientists are, however, concerned when people make statements that no amount of evidence can disprove. As you will see, such untestable statements can never be changed, refined, or corrected by the discovery of new facts. Because scientists are concerned about untestable statements, scientists avoid making vague statements and avoid blindly accepting after-the-fact explanations.

***Scientists avoid vague statements.***    Vague statements are both unverifiable and useless. For example, a detective who claims that the murderer lives in this galaxy will neither be proven wrong nor given credit for solving the case. Vague statements are often the province of "sucker bets" and of pseudosciences, such as palmistry and astrology. For example, suppose a stranger bets you that Wednesday will be a good day, but doesn't define what a good day is. No matter what happened on Wednesday, the stranger may come back on Thursday, demanding payment because Wednesday, by the stranger's definition, was a great day. Similarly, one of the authors' horoscopes once read: "Take care today not to get involved with someone who is wrong for you and you for him or her. Trouble could result." This horoscope tells us nothing. No matter what happens, the astrologer could claim to have predicted it.

One reason the astrologer can be so slippery is because he used vaguely defined terms. For example, the astrologer does not give us a clue as to what "wrong for you" means. Thus, if trouble had resulted, the astrologer could say, "The person was wrong for you." If trouble had not resulted, the astrologer could say, "The person was right for you." Note that because the horoscope doesn't tell us anything, it cannot be proven wrong. But because it doesn't tell us anything, it is also useless.

One way that scientists avoid making vague statements is by defining their concepts in precise and objective terms. Instead of talking only in terms of vague, invisible, and hard-to-pin-down abstractions such as "love," psychologists talk in terms of the specific, observable procedures they use to measure love.

More technically, scientists use **operational definitions:** descriptions of variables in terms of the specific, observable, concrete steps that are involved in measuring or manipulating that variable. Thus, researchers are not limited to talking about psychological concepts such as stress, love, and intelligence in vague, abstract ways. Instead, researchers can also talk about a psychological concept in terms of the specific recipes they have invented for measuring that variable.

As you will see in Chapter 3, these recipes may range from measuring brain wave activity to scoring a multiple-choice test. Some of these recipes will be clever and do a good job of capturing the psychological variable they are supposed to measure, others may not be quite so good. But no matter what the recipe, it is a recipe that other scientists can follow. Because of the objective nature of the recipe, there is no disagreement about what each participant's score is.

When researchers phrase their predictions in such clear, concrete, and objective terms, they can objectively determine whether the evidence supports their predictions. That is, no matter what their biases, they can objectively establish whether scores on a given happiness test are correlated with scores on a certain IQ test.

You have seen that vague statements do not lead to testable predictions. You have also seen that one way of making a vague statement is to avoid using operational definitions. By not using operational definitions, "quacks" can avoid being pinned down about what they really mean. Scientists, on the other hand, want to make testable predictions so that they can change their views if they are wrong. To better understand why scientists like testable predictions, let's contrast testable predictions with after-the-fact explanations.

***Scientists question after-the-fact explanations.***    After-the-fact explanations, like vague statements, are difficult to prove wrong. For example, if we say that a person committed a murder because of some event in his childhood, how can we be proven wrong? Most people would accept or reject our claim based on whether it sounded reasonable. However, the problem with accepting "reasonable-sounding" explanations is that after something happens, almost anyone can generate a plausible-sounding explanation for why it happened. Although these explanations may seem reasonable, they may be incorrect.

To dramatize the fact that plausible-sounding explanations may be wrong, psychologists have asked people to explain numerous "facts," such as why "opposites attract," and why changing your original answer to a multiple-choice test question usually results in changing from a right answer to a wrong answer. Participants were able to generate logical, persuasive reasons for why those "facts" were true—*even though all of those "facts" are false* (Dawes, 1994; Myers, 1990; Slovic & Fischoff, 1977; Stanovich, 1990; Weiten, 1990).

## SKEPTICAL

Scientists are not just skeptical about after-the-fact explanations. Scientists, like detectives, are so skeptical that they want evidence before they believe even the most "obvious" of statements. For example, Galileo tested the obvious "fact" that heavier objects fall faster—and found it to be false. Thus, like the detective, scientists' approaches range from "show me," to "let me see," to "let's take a look," to "can you verify that?" Neither detectives nor scientists accept notions merely because an authority says it's true or because everyone is sure that it's true. Instead, both detectives and scientists demand objective evidence.

However, even after scientists have evidence, they continue to be skeptical. They realize that evidence is not the same thing as proof. In other words, like detectives, scientists ask themselves, "What other explanations are there for these facts?" Consequently, scientists are experts at considering alternative explanations for events. For instance, malaria means "bad air" ("mal" means bad as in "malpractice," "aria" means air) because people thought malaria was caused by breathing the bad-smelling air around swamps. People pointed out that malaria cases were more common around swamps and that swamps contained foul-smelling marsh gas. Scientists countered by pointing out that the presence of marsh gas is not the only difference between dry areas and swampy areas. For instance, there are more insects, such as mosquitoes, in swamps. As we now know, it is mosquitoes—not marsh gas—that cause people to contract malaria.

Being skeptical also means realizing that "convincing proof" may merely be the result of a coincidence. A suspect may be near the victim's house on the night of the murder for perfectly innocent reasons; a patient may suddenly get better even after getting a "quack" treatment; a volcano may erupt exactly 20 years after an atomic bomb went off; and we can have one very warm summer for reasons having nothing to do with the "greenhouse effect."

## OPEN-MINDED

Despite being so skeptical, good scientists are extremely open-minded. Just as they are reluctant to accept an idea because everyone believes it, they are reluctant to rule out an idea simply because nobody believes in it. That is, just as a good detective initially considers everyone a suspect, scientists are willing to entertain all possibilities. Consequently, scientists will not automatically dismiss anything as nonsense, not even ideas that seem to run counter to existing knowledge, such as telepathy. The willingness to test odd ideas has led scientists to important discoveries, such as the finding that certain jungle plants have medicinal properties.

## CREATIVE

To test such ideas, scientists have to be creative. Unraveling the mysteries of the universe is not a boring, unimaginative, or routine task. For good reason, scientific giants such as Marie Curie (the discoverer of radium), Charles Darwin, and Friederich Kekule (who, while dreaming, solved the riddle of how carbon molecules are structured) are referred to as *creative* geniuses.

We should point out, however, that you don't need to be "naturally creative" to think in a creative way. Indeed, Darwin, Einstein, and Edison did not attribute their creative success to natural creative ability, but to persistence.

## PUBLIC

Although science owes a great debt to individual geniuses like Einstein, science does not depend on the secret knowledge possessed by one individual. Instead, science produces and relies on publicly shared knowledge.

By making knowledge public, biases and errors can be spotted—and corrected. Thus, if a researcher publishes a biased or flawed study, rival investigators may repeat that study or challenge the researcher's conclusions.

Furthermore, by being public, researchers can build on each other's work. By building on each other's work, scientists can accomplish much more than if each had worked alone.

Without such open sharing of information, science doesn't work, as the debate on cold fusion illustrates. In 1989, two physical scientists called a press conference to announce that they had invented a way of creating nuclear fusion, a potential source of safe electric power, without heating atoms to extreme temperatures. (Before the scientists' announcement, all known ways of producing nuclear fusion used more energy to heat atoms than the fusion reaction produced. Thus, nobody could seriously consider using nuclear fusion to produce electricity commercially.) However, the two scientists did not submit their research to peer-reviewed journals, and they failed to give details of their procedures.

All these actions worked against science's self-corrective and *unbiased* nature. By not sharing their work, they removed the checks and balances that make science the reliable source of evidence that it is. Instead of letting others verify their findings, the two scientists expected people to accept their findings only on the basis of a press conference. Fortunately, scientists refuse to accept statements, whether from astrologers or physical scientists, without objective evidence.

Thus far, we have skeptically assumed that cold fusion did not really happen. But what if it did? The researchers' lack of openness would still be tragic because science flourishes only in the open. The reason science is so powerful is that people can build on one another's work. Each individual scientist does not have to reinvent the wheel. By sharing their findings, scientists discover more than if they worked in isolation. Indeed, by combining their efforts, ideas and facts multiply to such an extent that the knowledge in some fields doubles every five to 10 years.

## PRODUCTIVE

The power of science to make discoveries and advance knowledge is obvious. The technology created by science has vaulted us a long way from the Dark Ages or even the pre-VCR, pre-personal computer, pre-microwave early 1970s.

The progress science has made is remarkable considering that it is a relatively new way of finding out about the world. As recently as the 1400s, people were punished for studying human anatomy and even for trying to get evidence on such basic matters as the number of teeth a horse has. As recently as the early 1800s, the scientific approach was not applied to medicine or psychology. Until that time, people were limited to relying on tradition, common sense, intuition, and logic for medical and psychological knowledge.

Once science gained greater acceptance, people used the scientific approach to test and refine commonsense notions, as well as notions derived from intuition, tradition, and logic. As a result of supplementing and complementing other ways of knowing, science helped knowledge progress at an explosive rate.

## The Characteristics of Psychology

Most people agree that science has allowed physics, chemistry, and biology to progress at a rapid rate. However, many wonder whether the scientific approach can have the same benefits for psychology. Indeed, some people question whether psychology can even be a science.

### GENERAL RULES

Perhaps the most serious question about psychology as a science is, "Can psychologists find general rules that will predict, control, and explain human behavior?" Skeptics argue that whereas finding rules to explain the behavior of molecules is possible, finding rules to explain the behavior patterns of people is not.

Critics claim that, unlike molecules, people are not all alike. Psychologists respond by saying that even though people are not all alike, all humans are quite similar genetically. Perhaps because of this similarity, most of us share many traits in common, from using language to trying to repay those who help us.

Skeptics also claim that, unlike molecules, humans may spontaneously do something for no reason. Psychologists argue that most behavior does not just spontaneously appear. Instead, there usually are reasons why a behavior occurs.

Although both skeptics and psychologists make logical arguments for their position, psychologists have evidence to back up their arguments. Specifically, psychologists argue that if human behavior is not governed by rules, psychologists will not find any rules. However, the fact is that psychologists have found general rules that explain a wide variety of human behaviors (Kimble, 1990). For example, psychologists have discovered laws of operant and classical conditioning, laws of perception, laws of memory (Banaji & Crowder, 1989), and even laws of emotion (Frijda, 1988). (If you doubt that emotions follow rules, then ask yourself why people have fairly predictable reactions to certain movies. For example, most people cry or come close to tears the first time they see *Bambi,* whereas most people feel a nervous excitement the first time they see *Speed.*)

Resistance to the idea that human behavior follows general rules has affected not only psychology, but medicine. Until recently, people believed that no general rules applied to illness. One person's flu was caused by circumstances that were completely different from another's. "Each patient regarded his own suffering as unique, and demanding unique remedies" (Burke, 1984). Consequently, one patient's treatment was totally different from another's. Partly because what cured one person was supposed to be totally ineffective for curing anyone else, knowledge about cures was not shared. As a result, medicine did not progress and many people died unnecessarily. It was only after physicians started to look for general causes of disease that successful cures (such as antibiotics) were found.

Nevertheless, *general* rules do not always work. A treatment that cures one person may not cure another. For example, one person may be cured by penicillin, whereas another may be allergic to it. However, it would be wrong to say that reactions to drugs do not follow any rules. It's simply that how an individual will respond to a drug is affected by many rules. Predicting a person's reaction to a drug would require knowing at least the following: the individual's weight, family history of reactions to drugs, when they last ate, condition of their vital organs, other drugs they are taking, and level of dehydration.

Like human physiology, human behavior is governed by many factors. Because there are so many rules that may come into play in a given situation, predicting what a given individual will do in that situation would be difficult even if you knew all the rules. Thus, psychologists agree with cynics that predicting and explaining an individual's behavior is difficult. However, psychologists disagree with the cynic's assumption that there are no rules underlying behavior. Instead, psychologists know that there are rules that are useful in predicting the behavior of many of the people much of the time. As Sherlock Holmes said, "You can never foretell what any man will do, but you can say with precision what an average number will be up to. Individuals may vary, but percentages remain constant."

Some people argue that if you can't predict an individual instance of behavior, then the behavior does not follow general rules. Although this argument sounds convincing, think about trying to predict the outcome of a coin flip. We can't predict the outcome of a coin flip. Why not? Is it because the outcome of a coin flip does not follow any rules? No, it follows very simple rules: The outcome depends on what side was up when the coin was flipped and how many times the coin turned over. Nevertheless, since we do not know how many times the coin will turn over, we cannot predict the outcome of a single coin toss. Similarly, most would agree that the weather is determined by specific events. However, because there are so many events and since we do not have data on all events, we can't predict the weather with perfect accuracy.

In short, just because a given behavior in a given situation cannot be predicted, we should not conclude that the behavior does not follow rules. The behavior might be perfectly predictable—if we knew the rules and could precisely measure the relevant variables.

## OBJECTIVE EVIDENCE

A second question people raise about psychology's ability to be a science is, "Can psychologists collect objective evidence about the human mind?"

Even though we cannot see the mind, we can collect objective evidence about it. That is, although we can't directly measure abstract concepts such as love, aggression, and memory, we can develop observable operational definitions of these concepts.

In the effort to measure the unobservable objectively, psychology can follow the lead of the physical sciences. The physical sciences have a long history of studying things they could not see. Genetics was well advanced before anyone had seen a gene; physicists and chemists were discussing electrons long before electrons were seen; and nobody has yet seen gravity, time, temperature, pressure, or magnetism. Unobservable events can be inferred from observable events: gravity can be inferred from observing objects fall, and psychological variables such as love can be assessed by observable indicators such as how long a couple gazes into each other's eyes, pupil dilation at sight of partner, physiological arousal at sight of partner, and passing up the opportunity to date attractive others.

One indication that psychologists have succeeded in making unbiased observations is that when psychologists repeat another's study, they are very likely to get the same pattern of results that the original investigator obtained. In fact, psychological research is just as reliable as physics research (Hedges, 1987; Stanovich, 1990).

## VERIFIABLE

A third question people have about psychology is, "Can it make verifiable statements?" If it cannot, then it would share the weaknesses of astrology. Fortunately, most published research articles in psychology make verifiable predictions. Indeed, our journals are full of articles in which predictions made by the investigators were disconfirmed. For example, to his surprise, Charles Kiesler (Kiesler, 1982; Kiesler & Sibulkin, 1987) found that many mentally ill individuals are hurt, rather than helped, by being put in mental institutions.

## SKEPTICAL

A fourth question about psychology is, "Can psychologists be as skeptical as other scientists?" Some people were concerned that psychologists would not test ideas that "made sense." They needn't have worried. Psychologists test even the most "obviously true" of ideas. For example, Greenberger & Steinberg (1986) did a series of studies testing the "obviously true" idea that teenagers who have jobs better understand the value of hard work. They found that, contrary to conventional wisdom, teenagers who work are more cynical about the value of hard work than non-working teens. Similarly, Shedler and Block (1990) tested the "obviously true" idea that drug use is the cause of psychological problems. Their evidence suggested that conventional wisdom was wrong—heavy drug use was a symptom, rather than a cause, of psychological problems.

In addition to questioning conventional wisdom, psychologists question observable evidence. For example, psychologists may question the degree to which mental tests or other measures of behavior truly capture the psychological concepts that those instruments claim to capture. Psychologists are not easily convinced that a set of questions labeled as a "love scale" actually measures love or that an "intelligence test" measures intelligence. Instead, psychologists would need evidence documenting that these tests really measure what the tests claim to measure.

Psychologists are skeptical about measures because they realize that we never have a direct pipeline into a person's mind. We cannot see the mind; we can see only behavior. From observing behavior, we may be able to make inferences about what is going on in the mind. Unfortunately, our inferences about what is going on inside a person's head could be incorrect. Consequently, we should never assume that we know what a behavior really means. In other words, there is often a gap between the operational definition of a concept and the concept. Therefore, we should always question how well the operational definition really matches the label that the investigator gives it.

Psychologists are also very skeptical about drawing cause-effect conclusions. They realize that it is hard to isolate the one factor that may be causing a certain behavior. Therefore, if they find that better students have personal computers, they do not leap to the conclusion that computers cause academic success. Psychologists realize that academic success may lead to obtaining a computer. For example, some students may have been given a computer because they were doing well in school. Furthermore, psychologists realize that the computer-owning students may be doing better than other students because the computer-owning students went to better preschools, had better nutrition, or received more parental encouragement. Until these and other explanations are eliminated, psychologists would not assume that computers cause academic success.

Finally, many psychologists are skeptical about the extent to which results from a study can be generalized to the real world. They do not assume that a study done in a particular setting with a particular group of people can be generalized to other kinds of participants in a different setting. For instance, they would not automatically assume that a study originally done with gifted 10-year-olds at a private school would obtain the same results if it were repeated with adult participants studied in the workplace.

## OPEN-MINDED

Paralleling the concern that psychologists would not test "obvious facts" is the concern that psychologists would not be open to ideas that run counter to common sense. These concerns are groundless. Psychologists have tested all sorts of counter-intuitive ideas, such as the idea that subliminal, backward messages (back-masking) on records can lead teens to Satanism (Custer, 1985); the idea that people can learn in their sleep; and the idea that ESP can be reliably used to send messages (Swets & Bjork, 1990). Although psychologists found no evidence for any of those ideas, psychology's willingness to try to test virtually anything has led to tentative acceptance of some novel concepts, such as the idea that acupuncture may be effective in relieving pain and the idea that meditating causes people to live longer (Langer et al., 1989).

## CREATIVE

Whereas psychologists' open-mindedness has been questioned, few have questioned psychologists' creativity. Most people realize that it takes creativity to come up with research ideas. In fact, a few people even believe that they lack the creativity required to generate research ideas. However, they are wrong—anyone who follows the tips on idea generation in Chapter 2 can come up with a research idea.

The need for creativity doesn't end with generating the research idea. Creativity is also needed to test the idea. For example, creativity is needed to develop accurate measures of the concepts the researcher plans to study. Imagine the challenge of developing measures of such concepts as love, intelligence, and helpfulness. Fortunately, to measure key variables, the individual researcher doesn't always have to rely on his or her own creativity. As you will see in Chapter 3, the researcher can often rely on the creativity of others. After all, why reinvent the wheel when creative psychologists have already developed ways of measuring all kinds of concepts—from practical intelligence (Sternberg, 1990) to level of moral reasoning (Kohlberg, 1968) to need for exciting stimulation (Zuckerman, 1992)?

Even after finding ways of measuring key concepts, researchers may need to use their creativity to develop a situation that will permit them to test their research idea. Like the inventors of the wind tunnel, they may need to create a scaled-down model of a real-life situation that is simpler and more controllable than real life, yet still captures the key aspects of the real-life situation. For example, to study real-life competition, social psychologists have developed competitive games for participants to play. Similarly, to model the situation in which nothing you do seems to matter, Martin Seligman (1992) had people try to solve unsolvable puzzles.

## PUBLIC

Psychologists have also been very good at sharing their ideas and findings with others in the field, as shown by the hundreds of journals in which they publish their work. Indeed, psychologists may enjoy more candor and cooperation than scientists in other fields because psychologists usually gain little by keeping results secret. For example, if you wanted to be the first to patent a new technology, it would pay to keep secrets from competitors. In such a race, if you were first, you might make millions. If you were second, you would make nothing. Although such "races for dollars" are common in chemistry, they are rare in psychology because we produce few patents or inventions.

## PRODUCTIVE

Perhaps because of this candor, psychologists have made tremendous progress in the last 100 years. To see the effect of research on the teaching and practice of psychology, compare introductory textbooks published in 1910, 1930, 1950, 1970, and 1990. Even a cursory examination of these texts will dramatize two facts. First, research has radically increased the amount of knowledge in every field of psychology. Second, the rate of research discovery is rapidly accelerating—especially in the fields of counseling, developmental, personality, cognitive, physiological, social, and applied psychology.

Because research has contributed to every area of psychology, even former opponents of research now praise it. For example, Abraham Maslow (1970), the founder of the "Third Force," an approach that initially rebelled against scientific psychology and openly questioned whether scientific psychology was relevant to human concerns, later wrote: "Clearly, the next step for this psychology . . . is research, research, research. . . " (p. 1).

Today, because the questions and challenges facing modern society are ever-changing, scientific research is as relevant as ever. To take just a few examples, researchers have identified ways of getting people to behave in ways that will stop the spread of the AIDS virus (O'Keeffe et al., 1990), ways of increasing volunteerism (Omoto & Snyder, 1990), ways of encouraging energy conservation (Aronson, 1990), and ways of understanding and helping married couples get along (Gottesman, 1994; Holmes & Boon, 1990). No wonder people outside psychology, professionals in areas such as education, communication, marketing, economics, and medicine, now adopt the same research methods that psychologists use.

## Conclusions about the Importance of Science to Psychology

Not only is the scientific method responsible for the tremendous progress in psychology, but it is also largely responsible for psychology's uniqueness. Whereas many other fields—from astrology to philosophy—are concerned with the thoughts and behaviors of individuals, only psychology studies individuals scientifically (Stanovich, 1990). Thus, it is no accident that every definition of psychology starts out, "the science of . . . ." Indeed, without the scientific method, psychology might simply be a branch of astrology (Stanovich, 1990).

The success of psychology as a science depends, in part, on discovering the rules that guide human behavior. Like all sciences, psychology has had to contend with people who argued that its subject matter followed no rules. Since the beginning of recorded history, there have been people who have argued that finding rules or laws that govern nature is impossible. For centuries, most people believed the stars followed no pattern. Not that long ago, it was believed that diseases follow no patterns. Even today, some people believe that human behavior follows no discernible pattern. Yet, each of these assumptions has been disproven. The stars, the planets, diseases, and humans behave for reasons that we can understand. Admittedly, the rules determining human behavior may be complex and numerous—and it may even be that some behaviors do not follow rules. However, to this point, searching for rules of behavior has been fruitful (see Table 1-1).

Despite the success of scientific psychology, we should point out that the scientific approach has its limitations. If scientists become corrupt, overly arrogant, or stop being skeptical, science's ability to be objective would suffer. Furthermore, science, even at its best, is only one way of obtaining information.

Although science is only one way of knowing, science can work in concert with a variety of other ways of knowing. It can verify knowledge passed down by tradition or from an authoritative expert. It can test knowledge obtained by intuition or common sense. By anchoring speculation in reality, psychology can create, refine, or verify common sense and eliminate superstitions (Kohn, 1988). For example, consider the following five findings from research:

1. Punishment is not very effective in changing behavior.
2. Having teens work in low-wage jobs does not instill the "work ethic."
3. Drug use is often a symptom rather than a cause of psychological problems.
4. Absence makes the heart fonder only for couples who are already very much in love.
5. If you tell somebody what happened, they will tend to think they could have predicted the event, that "they knew it all along."

**TABLE 1–1**
**Psychology as a Science**

| CHARACTERISTIC | EXAMPLE |
| --- | --- |
| Finds general rules | Helps us understand human behavior through rules such as: laws of operant and classical conditioning, laws of memory (meaningless information is hard to remember, memorizing similar information, such as Spanish and Italian, leads to memory errors), and a wide range of theories from social learning theory to cognitive dissonance theory. |
| Collects objective evidence | Tests whether beliefs and theories are consistent with objective evidence. Obtains objective evidence by recording participants' behaviors: number of words written down on memory test, ratings made on an attitude scale, responses on personality test, reaction times, etc. One index of how effective we are at being objective is that our research findings are as replicable as research findings in physics. |
| Makes verifiable statements | Makes specific testable predictions that are sometimes found to be wrong (rewarding someone for doing a task will always increase their enjoyment of that task). That is, we use evidence to correct wrong beliefs. |
| Skeptical | Demands evidence for almost any statement. Challenges common sense and traditional notions. Does not take evidence (participants' statements or ratings) at face value. Considers alternative explanations for evidence (group given memory pill may do better than another on memory task because they had naturally better memories, because they were tested later in the day, or because they believed the pill would work). |
| Open-minded | Entertains virtually any hypothesis, from acupuncture relieving pain to meditation prolonging life. |
| Creative | Measures psychological concepts, generates hypotheses, and devises studies that rule out alternative explanations for findings. |
| Public | Allows scientists to check and build on each other's work because research is presented at conferences and published in journals. |
| Productive | Increases psychological knowledge at a dramatic rate. |

All of these findings are refinements of the "common sense" of a few years ago. All of these findings are, or will soon become, part of the common sense of the 1990s.

In short, science is a powerful tool that can be used to solve human problems. If we have such a tool, why shouldn't we use it—especially when it does not rule out the use of other tools?

## QUESTIONS ABOUT APPLYING TECHNIQUES FROM PHYSICAL SCIENCES TO PSYCHOLOGY

Although psychologists are excited about using a tool that has been so successful in the physical sciences, they are not blind to the fact that there are problems with applying the scientific method to humans. To appreciate how sensitive psychologists are to the unique challenges and responsibilities involved in studying the behavior of living things, let's see how a psychologist would react if someone ignored those challenges and responsibilities. For instance, suppose that a novice investigator tried to model his psychological research after the following chemistry experiment:

> A chemist has two test tubes. Both test tubes contain a group of hydrogen and oxygen molecules. She leaves the first test tube alone. She heats the second over a flame. She observes that water forms only in the second test tube. Because there was only one difference between the two test tubes (the flame), she concludes that the flame caused the group of molecules in the second test tube to behave differently than the molecules in the first tube. She then concludes that heat always causes hydrogen and oxygen to combine.

Instead of filling two test tubes with hydrogen and oxygen, the novice investigator fills two rooms with people. He treats both groups identically, except that he makes the second group's room 10 degrees warmer than the first group. He then compares the behavior of the two groups and observes more "aggression" in the second room. Consequently, he concludes that "feeling warmer" makes people more "aggressive."

Because of the vast differences between humans and molecules, an experienced research psychologist would have four sets of questions about the novice investigator's study. The first three deal with the validity of our novice investigator's conclusions: (1) Did the treatment manipulation really *cause* the differences in *behavior?* (2) Did the investigator really measure and manipulate the variables that he thought he did? (Did the manipulation make participants feel warm and did the participants' behavior really reflect aggression?); and (3) Would the results *generalize* to other settings and participants? The fourth set of concerns is the most serious: Was it moral and ethical to perform the study?

## Internal Validity Questions: Did the Treatment Cause a Change in Behavior?

The first set of questions deals with the study's **internal validity:** the degree to which the study demonstrates that the treatment *caused* a change in behavior. If the study establishes that putting the participants into different rooms *caused* the one group to behave differently from the other group, the study has internal validity. If something else could be causing the groups to differ, then the study does not have internal validity.

For the chemist, establishing internal validity is fairly simple. If the flame condition yields water and the no-flame condition does not, the flame manipulation must be responsible. The chemist does not have to worry that the oxygen molecules in one tube were more likely to combine with hydrogen than were the molecules in the other tube. That is, since all oxygen molecules are basically alike, she knows she would have gotten the same results if she had applied the flame to the second tube rather than to the first. Similarly, she does not worry that other factors may be responsible for the change in the oxygen's behavior because, by doing her study in a test tube, she can isolate the oxygen from any unwanted influences. Thus, isolating the cause of a change in molecular behavior is relatively easy.

In psychological research, on the other hand, it is not easy to determine whether a particular treatment is the only *cause* of a change in behavior. In the novice investigator's study, for example, there may have been many more aggressive individuals in the warm-room group than there were in the normal-room group. Since we do not know that the groups were the same at the start of the study, finding a difference between groups at the end of the study is not conclusive evidence that the room manipulation caused the groups to differ. Furthermore, even if the groups were initially equivalent, they might not be equivalent at the time of testing. For example, suppose that the novice tested the "normal room" group in the morning and the "warm room" group at night. In this case, many events completely unrelated to the room manipulation might cause the "warm room" participants to behave differently from the "normal room" participants. For instance, during the early evening, the "warm room" group may have had a few drinks or heard some bad news. Although neither the alcohol nor the bad news have anything to do with what happened to participants inside the warm room, the alcohol or bad news might affect the participants' behavior.

To reiterate, if we cannot be sure that the *manipulation* is *the only systematic difference* between our participants, we cannot determine that the manipulation is the cause of a difference in behavior. That is, if we cannot be sure that the groups were equivalent in every respect except that one group was placed in one room and the other was placed in another room, it would be careless to conclude that being in the different rooms caused the difference in the groups' behavior.

## Construct Validity Questions

As we have seen, the novice investigator carelessly assumed that the room manipulation *caused* the participants to behave differently. However, that was not the only questionable assumption he made. He also presumed that his manipulation made warm room participants "feel warm" and that he accurately measured "aggression." In other words, the novice assumes that he can accurately measure psychological **constructs:** mental states that cannot be directly observed, such as love, intelligence, hunger, feeling warm, and aggression.

The experienced researcher would point out that the novice investigator did not see participants "feel warm." Rather, the novice investigator only manipulated the external, physical environment by raising the thermostat. Similarly, the novice investigator did not see participants "feel aggressive." He only observed their outward behavior. Yet, despite not directly manipulating or directly observing participants' psychological states, the novice investigator is talking about psychological states. He is labeling his room manipulation as a manipulation of "feeling warm" and he is labeling participants' behavior as "aggressive." How can he justify using those arbitrary levels?

The novice investigator might respond that most scientists go beyond talking about the procedures they use. That is, physical scientists' conclusions do not deal with the actual actions they performed, but with the underlying variables that they manipulated. For example, the chemist's conclusions would not deal with the effects of "a lit Bunsen burner," but rather with the effects of the underlying variable—heat.

The experienced researcher would point out that the leap from assuming that the Bunsen burner manipulates the heat of molecules in a test tube is relatively safe and short. It is unlikely that the burner has any other effects. The molecules do not notice the flame's color, are not terrified by its intensity, do not care if it discolors the test tube, and do not smell it. On the other hand, people may be annoyed by the noise or the smell coming from the heater. Thus, manipulating the temperature of molecules is simpler than manipulating how people feel. Furthermore, the chemist makes virtually no inference when it comes to observing the results of the reaction: Water is easy to observe and measure. In contrast, it is difficult to measure "aggression" accurately.

In short, the experienced research psychologist realizes that measuring and manipulating people's thoughts and feelings is more difficult than measuring and manipulating the behavior of molecules. If you are not careful, going from objective, observable, physical events to inferring invisible, subjective, psychological concepts may involve jumping to conclusions. For instance, some people are quick to infer that a person who works slowly is unintelligent. However, the truth may be that the individual is cautious, ill, lazy, or unfamiliar with the task.

Because the possibility of error is so great, psychologists are extremely cautious about inferring private mental states from publicly observable behavior. Therefore, the research psychologist would question the temperature study's **construct validity:** the degree to which the study measures and manipulates the underlying psychological elements that the researcher claims to be measuring and manipulating. Specifically, the research psychologist would have four major reasons to doubt that the novice investigator's aggression study had adequate construct validity.

### WHAT DOES THE TREATMENT REALLY MANIPULATE?

First, turning up the thermostat is not necessarily a "pure" manipulation of room temperature, much less of "feeling warm." For example, turning up the thermostat in the "warm" room might not only make the room hotter, but also make the room noisier (if the heater was noisy) or decrease the room's air quality (if the heater's filter was dirty). If turning up the thermostat is a temperature manipulation, a noise manipulation, *and* an air quality manipulation, how can the novice justify calling it a "warmth" manipulation?

Second, even if the novice had a pure manipulation of heat, he might still fail to have a pure manipulation of "feeling warm." In other words, it is impossible to manipulate a participant's thoughts or feelings directly. To reiterate, the only way we can try to manipulate participants' mental states is *indirectly*—by changing their physical environment. For our indirect manipulation to work, participants must mentally react to the research situation in the way we expect them to. Unfortunately, participants may interpret the research situation or manipulation differently from how the researcher intended. Consequently, the participants in the hotter room may not *feel* warm. That is, participants may take off jackets and sweaters to cool off or they may find the room's temperature "comfortable." But even if the novice investigator succeeded in making the "warm room" participants feel warm, he may have also made them feel frustrated about being unable to open the windows to cool off the room or he may have made participants feel angry with him for putting them in such an uncomfortable room. Thus, in addition to being a manipulation of feeling warm, the treatment may have had the additional side effect of making people frustrated and angry. So, how can the novice justify calling the room manipulation a "warmth" manipulation when it may actually be a frustration or anger manipulation?

## WHAT DOES THE PARTICIPANT'S BEHAVIOR REALLY MEAN?

Third, unlike molecules, people know they are in a research project and may act accordingly. In the novice investigator's study, warm-room participants may realize that they have been (1) deliberately placed in an abnormally warm room and then (2) given a questionnaire that asks them how aggressive they feel. If they like the investigator, they may *act* aggressive for the investigator's benefit. The investigator may misinterpret this acting as genuine aggression.

Fourth, unlike the amount of water produced by a chemical reaction, psychological concepts such as aggression are abstract, invisible, and therefore impossible to measure directly. We can only indirectly assess inner reality from clues we find in outer reality. Because there is no direct pipeline to the mind, participants' behaviors and reactions may be mislabeled. For example, the novice investigator may have misinterpreted "kidding around" and attention-getting behaviors as aggression. Or, the novice investigator may have misinterpreted physiological reactions to being warm (sweating, flushed face) as signs of anger. In other words, it is reckless to assume that an operational definition will perfectly capture the construct that the researcher is trying to measure.

In conclusion, our novice wants both internal and construct validity. He wants to be able to conclude that warmth causes aggression. If his study had only internal validity, the only thing he could safely conclude would be that "turning up the thermostat *causes* a difference in how people fill in circles on a multiple-choice answer sheet." That is, because he didn't have construct validity, he could not say that he had made participants "feel warm" and that he had measured the construct of aggression. If, on the other hand, he had only construct validity, he could only conclude that "the group that felt warm was more aggressive." Without internal validity, he could not conclude that warmth *causes* aggression because it might be that individuals in the warm room group had more aggressive personalities than the people in the other group.

## External Validity Questions

Even if the novice researcher actually manipulated "feeling warm" and measured aggression (construct validity) and established that differences between the two groups in this particular study were caused by the room manipulation (internal validity), the experienced researcher would still question the study's **external validity:** the degree to which the results could be *generalized* to different participants, settings, or times. There are at least two reasons to question the aggression study's external validity.

### CAN THE RESULTS BE GENERALIZED TO OTHER PARTICIPANTS?

First, since people differ, a result that occurs with one group of people might not occur with a different group of people. The novice investigator might have obtained different results had he studied Russian sixth-graders instead of Midwestern college students; if he had studied people used to working in very warm conditions; or if he had studied less aggressive individuals. To maximize external validity, the novice should have tested a large, random sample of participants.

### CAN THE RESULTS BE GENERALIZED TO OTHER SETTINGS?

Second, since people's behavior may change depending on the situation, the results might not hold in another setting. For instance, suppose the novice investigator used a very sterile laboratory setting to eliminate the effects of non-treatment factors. By isolating the treatment factor, the novice investigator may have succeeded in establishing internal validity. However, results obtained under such controlled situations may not generalize to more complex situations, such as the workplace or the home, where other factors, such as frustration and pressure, come into play. Thus, the investigator may have achieved internal validity at the expense of external validity.

In short, even if temperature increased aggression in this particular lab with this particular group of participants at this particular time, the experienced researcher would not automatically assume that temperature would have the same effect in future studies conducted with different participants in different settings. Therefore, to maximize external validity, the experienced researcher might repeat the study, using different types of participants and different situations.

## Ethical Questions: Should the Study Be Conducted?

As you have seen, the novice failed to fully appreciate the differences between humans and molecules. The novice's failure to take into account the fact that

**TABLE 1–2**

**Common Threats to the Three Kinds of Validity**

| TYPE OF VALIDITY | MAJOR SOURCES OF PROBLEMS | MISTAKES TO AVOID | EXAMPLES OF PROBLEM IN REAL LIFE |
|---|---|---|---|
| **Construct:** The names we give to our measures and manipulations are accurate. That is, we are making accurate inferences about what our participants' behaviors mean and about the psychological states that our manipulations produce. | Faulty measures, resulting in mislabeling or misinterpreting behavior. Poor manipulations can also harm construct validity, as can participants figuring out and playing along with the hypothesis. | Accepting at face value that a test measures what its title claims it does. Anybody can type up some questions and call it an intelligence test—but that doesn't mean the "test" really measures intelligence. | Mislabeling a behavior. Thinking that a shy person is a snob, believing that what people *say* they think and feel is exactly what they think and feel, having complete confidence in lie detectors, "knowing" that a cat loves you because it sits in your chair after you get up. |
| **Internal:** Determining *cause-effect* relationship between manipulation and behavior *in* a given study. Establishing that a certain observable event caused (was responsible for, influenced) a change in behavior. | Allowing factors other than the manipulation to vary. For example, if the treatment and the no-treatment group differ before the study begins, we can't conclusively establish that the treatment caused the difference in the groups' behavior. | Failing to ask the question, "Isn't there something other than the treatment that could cause the difference in behavior?" | Misidentifying the causes of a problem. Giving a new president credit or blame for changes in the economy, blaming a new dentist for your existing dental problems, claiming that a parent's child-rearing methods are responsible for the child's autism. |
| **External:** The results of the study can be generalized *outside* the study to other situations and participants. | Artificial situations, testing an unusual group of participants, small number of participants. | Believing that any survey, regardless of how small or biased, has external validity. | Stereotyping—based on a very limited sample, people conclude that, "They are all like that. Seen one, seen them all." |

humans are more complex and individualized than molecules would force any research psychologist to question the validity of the novice's temperature study. But in addition to failing to understand that humans are more complex and individualized than molecules, the student also overlooked the two most important differences between molecules and humans:

**1.** Molecules do not have rights, whereas humans do, and
**2.** Chemists have no responsibility for the welfare of molecules involved in their studies, but psychologists have a responsibility for the welfare of their participants.

Therefore, in the researcher's mind, the most important question about the study is whether it was **ethical:** consistent with the American Psychological Association's principles of right and wrong. Indeed, no professional researcher would do a study without first determining whether the study could be conducted in an ethical manner. If the study can't be conducted ethically, it shouldn't be done.

In deciding whether the study was ethical, the researcher would consult the American Psychological Association's *Ethical principles of psychologists and code of conduct* (APA, 1992). A copy of these ethical guidelines, often referred to as the "*Principles*," is included in Appendix A. In addition to the *Principles*, the researcher might also consult the American Psychological Association's *Ethical principles in the conduct of research with human participants* (APA, 1982). By consulting both sources, the researcher should be able to make an informed decision about whether the participants' rights had been protected and whether the novice investigator had lived up to his responsibilities.

### HAS POTENTIAL HARM BEEN MINIMIZED?

As the *Principles* point out, participants have the right to know what will happen in the study, the right to refuse to be in the study, and the right to anonymity. Thus, according to the *Principles*, the novice should have told participants that the study would involve sitting in a warm room with a group of people. Knowing what the study was about, participants should have freely volunteered to be in the study. Once in the study, they should have been told that they could quit the study at any point. Furthermore, the novice should have taken extensive precautions to ensure that no one other than the investigator found out how each participant behaved during the study.

The *Principles* not only discuss participant rights, but also discuss investigator responsibilities (see Table 1–3). According to the *Principles*, the investigator's responsibilities begin well before the study begins. As part of the planning phase, the investigator should try to anticipate all possible risks to participants and then protect participants from these risks. In this study, the investigator should consult with physicians to be sure that the temperature was not too hot and to identify people who might have a bad physiological reaction to the heat. In addition, the investigator would have to determine how to make sure that the aggression induced by the heat would not get out of hand, leading to someone getting physically or psychologically hurt.

While the study is being conducted, the investigator is responsible for behaving in an ethical manner. Furthermore, under some circumstances, the investigator may also be responsible for ensuring that others behave ethically. For example, if the novice had others working on the aggression study, the novice would be responsible for their conduct. In other words, if the people working with or for the novice behaved unethically, the novice could not avoid responsibility by saying that he personally did not misbehave or that he did not know what the others were doing.

After each participant has finished taking part in the study, the investigator should actively look for evidence of harm. The investigator cannot merely

TABLE 1–3

**Selected Ethical Guidelines for Studies Involving Human Participants**

1. Participants should volunteer to be in the study. They should not be forced to participate.

2. Participants should have a general idea of what will happen to them if they choose to be in the study. In addition, they should be well-informed about anything that they might perceive as unpleasant. That is, they should know about anything that might cause them to decide not to participate.

3. Participants should be told that they can quit the study at any point and they should be encouraged to quit the study, if, at any point, they find the study upsetting.

4. Participants have the right to anonymity.

5. Investigators should keep each individual participant's responses confidential.

6. Investigators should make sure all people working for them behave ethically.

7. Investigators should try to anticipate all possible risks to participants and take steps to prevent these potential problems from occurring.

8. At the end of the study, investigators should probe participants for signs of harm and take steps to undo any harm detected.

9. At the end of the study, investigators should explain the purpose of the study and answer any questions participants may have.

10. Researchers should get approval from appropriate committees (such as the school's animal care and use committee, the institution's human participants committee) before conducting research.

assume that no one has been harmed. Of course, if he detected harm, he should have tried to undo that harm.

Finally, after people finish taking part in the study, the investigator should explain the study to them. Educating participants about the study is the least an investigator can do to compensate people for their participation. Furthermore, telling participants about the study may help participants by assuring them that their reactions are not unusual. For example, participants might think that they were anti-social or highly aggressive unless they were told that the study was designed to make them act and feel that way.

Unfortunately, the reader cannot determine that the novice's study was ethical merely by observing that the novice followed a few simple guidelines. Instead, as the introduction to the *Ethical principles in the conduct of research with human participants* (APA, 1982) states, "the decision to undertake research rests upon a considered judgment by the individual psychologist about how to *best contribute to psychological science and human welfare*" (emphasis added).

This statement has two important implications. First, it means that even if the novice fulfilled all his responsibilities to the participants, the study might still be unethical if the study were unlikely to contribute to psychological science and human welfare. Second, it means that even if the investigator violated certain participant rights (such not telling participants what the study is trying to find out), the study might still be ethical if the expected benefits of the study would compensate for those violations. Consequently, an important step in determining whether a study is ethical is determining the likelihood that the study will benefit humanity.

### HAVE POTENTIAL BENEFITS BEEN MAXIMIZED?

The researcher would begin to determine the likelihood that the study would benefit humanity by determining the importance of the research question. Unfortunately, determining the value of the research question is highly subjective. One person may find the idea very important, another may find it unimportant. In the aggression study, the novice may believe that determining the relationship between temperature and aggression is extremely valuable, arguing that it might lead to ways of preventing riots. Others, however, may disagree.

To further complicate the problem of assessing the potential value of a piece of research, no one knows what the researcher will discover. A study that looks promising may discover nothing. On the other hand, many scientific studies designed to answer one question have ended up answering a very important, but unrelated question (Burke, 1984; Coile & Miller, 1984). For example, Pavlov set out to discover the role of saliva in digestion, yet ended up discovering classical conditioning. Because it is so hard to judge the value of a research question, the researcher would probably acknowledge that the novice's research question has some merit.

As you have seen, judging the importance of a research question is difficult. Therefore, to estimate the potential value of the novice's study, the research psychologist would put less emphasis on her subjective impression of the importance of the research question and put more emphasis on the more objective judgment of how well the study would answer the research question. That is, she would ask, "Is the study likely to provide valid data?" However, she would not consider the study worthless if it failed to have high levels of all three types (internal, external, and construct) of validity. Indeed, few studies even attempt to have all three validities.

The important thing is that the study have the validity or validities necessary to answer the research question. To illustrate that different research goals require different validities, let's look at three examples.

First, suppose that an investigator wants to describe what most people do in a given situation. In that case, the researcher is **not** interested in the causes of behavior. Therefore, the investigator would not strive for internal validity. However, because the investigator is interested in generalizing the results to most people, the investigator would strive for external validity.

Second, suppose that an investigator is trying to develop a test of social intelligence. If the investigator's only goal is to show that the test accurately measures the construct of social intelligence, the investigator needs only construct validity.

Third, suppose that an investigator is trying to explain or control behavior. In that case, the investigator needs to discover the causes of a behavior. Therefore, such an investigator would need internal validity.

After carefully considering whether the study had the validity or validities necessary to answer the research question and after considering the importance of the research question, the research psychologist would have some sense of the potential value of the study. Then, the research psychologist would again consider the potential risks to participants. If steps had been taken to avoid harm and if the benefits outweighed the risks, the researcher would believe that conducting the study was ethical.

That does not mean, however, that the researcher would grant the novice permission to conduct the study. Indeed, even if the researcher wanted to conduct the study herself, she would not just go out and do it. Instead, she—like most researchers—would consult with others before doing the research.

Consulting with others is vital for two reasons. First, when weighing the benefits of one's own research against the costs to participants, it is hard to be fair and impartial. Second, consulting with others may lead to insights about how to protect participants from harm.

Because consulting with others is so important, some researchers will not do a research study until that study has been approved by their department's ethics committee. At many schools, researchers *must* obtain permission from a campus-wide ethics committee before conducting any study that involves human participants. In any event, a novice investigator should always get approval from a higher authority *before* conducting a study. To reiterate: *Never conduct a study without first obtaining approval from your professor!*

As you have seen, the psychological researcher's most important concerns about the novice's aggression study are ethical concerns. Indeed, since ethical concerns include concerns about validity and since the goal of research is human betterment, one could argue that ethical concerns are the researcher's only concerns (see Table 1–4).

But what if the novice's study had used animals instead of human participants? In that case, some might think that the psychologist would not have been concerned about ethics. As you can see from Table 1–5, nothing could be further from the truth. Indeed, in recent years, animal rights have received more attention from the American Psychological Association than human rights. If the aggression study had used animals as participants, the researcher would have consulted the ethical standards listed in Table 1–5 (APA, 1992) as well as APA's (1993) booklet, *Ethical principles for the care and use of animals,* a copy of which is included in Appendix A. If the study had been done unethically, the investigator would be severely punished.

## Conclusions about the Questions that Researchers Face

You have seen that research psychologists are aware of the responsibilities and challenges of studying human and animal behavior. What you have not seen is the wide range of methods psychologists use to meet these challenges and responsibilities. Investigators may use a single participant or thousands of participants, human participants or animal participants, laboratory studies or field

TABLE 1–4
**Determining Whether a Research Study Is Ethical**

**Does it maximize the potential benefits to psychological science and human welfare?**

1. Is the research question important?

2. Will the research study provide valid answers to the research question? The type of validity needed will depend on the research question.

   • If the research question concerns finding out whether a certain factor causes a change in behavior (Does a certain type of school environment increase student attendance?), the study should have internal validity. That is, the study should take steps to rule out the possibility that other factors may be responsible for the effect.

   • If answering the research question hinges on accurately measuring abstract psychological concepts, construct validity would be very important. That is, the researchers should be able to make a strong case that the psychological variables they are talking about are the variables they actually measured. Construct validity would be the main concern in a research study that was trying to develop a psychological test.

   • If the main purpose of the research is to provide results that can be generalized to the real world, external validity would be very important. In such a case, the researchers would want to show that their participants did not represent a limited sample of people. External validity is very important for polls because polls try to determine how most people would respond to certain questions.

**Does it minimize the potential for harm to participants?**

1. Does it conform to the Ethical Principles of the American Psychological Association?

   • Are participants volunteers?

   • Did they know what the study involved before they agreed to participate?

   • Were participants told they could quit the study at any point?

   • Were participants debriefed?

2. If participants will be subjected to stress,

   • Have less stressful alternatives been considered?

   • Has the amount of stress been minimized?

   • Have procedures for helping distressed participants been established?

studies, experiments or surveys—depending on ethical considerations, the type of validity the researcher is after, and the research problem.

# WHY YOU SHOULD UNDERSTAND RESEARCH DESIGN

Thus far, we have explained why professional psychologists are interested in scientific research. Psychologists see research as a useful tool to obtain answers to their questions. But why should you know how to use this tool?

## To Understand Psychology

The classic answer is that you cannot really understand psychology, the *science* of behavior, unless you understand its methods. Without understanding

**TABLE 1–5**
**Care and Use of Animals in Research**

The ethical standards below are considered enforceable rules of conduct. Violating these rules may result in being expelled from the American Psychological Association and/or being sued or arrested.

a. Psychologists who conduct research involving animals treat them humanely.

b. Psychologists acquire, care for, use, and dispose of animals in compliance with current federal, state, and local laws and regulations, and with professional standards.

c. Psychologists trained in research methods and experienced in the care of laboratory animals supervise all procedures involving animals and are responsible for ensuring appropriate consideration of their comfort, health, and humane treatment.

d. Psychologists ensure that all individuals using animals under their supervision have received instruction in research methods and in the care, maintenance, and handling of the species being used, to the extent appropriate to their role.

e. Responsibilities and activities of individuals assisting in a research project are consistent with their respective competencies.

f. Psychologists make reasonable efforts to minimize the discomfort, infection, illness, and pain of animal subjects.

g. A procedure subjecting animals to pain, stress, or privation is used only when an alternative procedure is unavailable and the goal is justified by its prospective scientific, educational, or applied value.

h. Surgical procedures are performed under appropriate anesthesia; techniques to avoid infection and minimize pain are followed during and after surgery.

i. When it is appropriate that the animal's life be terminated, it is done rapidly, with an effort to minimize pain, and in accordance with accepted procedures.

SOURCE: From Ethical Principles of Psychologists and Code of Conduct (1992), *American Psychologist, 47,* 1597–1611 by the American Psychological Association.

Reprinted with the kind permission of the American Psychological Association.

psychology's scientific aspects, you may know some psychological facts and theories, but you will not understand the basis for those facts and theories. Thus, to major in psychology without knowing about research would be like buying a car without looking at its engine or a house without inspecting its foundation. Furthermore, as a young science, psychology has not yet produced as much knowledge as some other sciences have. Consequently, in some complex, applied situations, the most useful thing psychology can offer is not a pre-packaged answer to the problem based on established facts, but rather its method of getting answers to problems (Levy-Leboyer, 1988).

## So You Can Read Research

When research gets answers to problems that interest you, you will want to take advantage of that research. Often, to take advantage of that research, you must be able to read and interpret scientific research reports. For instance, you may want to know something about the latest treatment for depression, the causes of shyness, factors that lead to better relationships, or new tips for improving workplace morale. If you need the most up-to-date information, if you want to draw your own conclusions, or if you want to look at everything that is known about a particular problem, you need to read research.

You cannot rely on reading *about* research in textbooks, magazines, or newspapers. Textbooks will give you only sketchy summaries of the few out-of-date studies selected by the textbook's authors. Magazine and newspaper articles, on the other hand, often talk about up-to-date research, but these reports may not accurately represent what happened. A knowledge of research terminology and logic will allow you to bypass second-hand accounts of research. Consequently, you will be able to read the original source and come to your own conclusions.

## So You Can Evaluate Research

If you understand research, you will not only be able to get recent, first-hand information, but you will also be in a position to evaluate that information. You may also be able to evaluate many second-hand reports of research in magazines and newspapers.[1] Thus, you will be able to take full advantage of the knowledge that psychologists are giving away, knowledge that is available to you free in libraries, in newspapers, and on television. Your critical abilities will also enable you to judge how much weight you should place on a particular research finding—a very useful skill, especially when you encounter two conflicting research findings.

## To Protect Yourself from Quacks

Perhaps more important than encountering conflicting research findings is the problem of identifying quacks. Free speech protects quacks, just as the free market protected "snake oil" salespeople in the days before the U.S. had the Food and Drug Administration. Back then, patent medicine vendors could sell the public almost anything, even pills that contained tapeworm segments. Today, "experts" are free to go on talk shows and push "psychological tapeworms." Common "psychological tapeworms" include unproven and sometimes dangerous tips on how to lose weight, quit smoking, discipline children, and solve relationship problems. Unfortunately, without some training in research, it is hard to distinguish which free information is helpful and which is potentially harmful.

## To Be a Better Thinker

Not only can understanding the scientific approach improve your access to psychological knowledge, but it can also improve your thinking. As you will see,

---

[1] Assuming, of course, that the articles provide you with enough information about the study's methodology. If they do not, you will have to go to the original scientific publication.

science is an elaboration of everyday thinking. The skills you learn in this course—problem-solving skills, decision-making skills, looking for objective information, and being able to judge and interpret information—are transferable to real life. Consequently, the same scientific thinking skills you will learn in this book are taught in books that purport to raise your practical intelligence (e.g., Lewis & Greene, 1982). Furthermore, those same skills are measured by some tests of "practical intelligence" (Frederikson, 1988) and are necessary for understanding certain real-life situations (Lehman, Lempert, & Nisbett, 1988). Finally, Lehman, Lempert, and Nisbett's (1988) research suggests that learning about research methodology in psychology transfers to understanding real life applications of methodological principles better than does learning about other sciences, such as chemistry (see Figure 1–1).

## To Be "Scientifically Literate"

Another reason students take psychological research methods courses is that taking such courses is a relatively easy way to learn about how science works. Intelligent people are supposed to be able to profit from experience, and in today's world, many of our experiences are shaped by scientific and technological changes. Yet many people do not know how science works.

Many argue that this scientific illiteracy threatens our democracy—and they have a point. How can we make intelligent decisions about the so-called "greenhouse effect" if we cannot properly interpret the data about global warming? We would like to rely on experts, but experts contradict each other on many important issues. Therefore, if we are going to make an informed decision about global warming, addressing the crime problem, or a host of other issues, we need to know how to interpret scientific research.

Regrettably, it appears that many people are not scientifically literate. Most high school students (and some high-ranking politicians) believe in astrology. Furthermore, many of astrology's skeptics can easily be made into believers (Glick et al., 1989). In addition to astrology, other scientifically invalid procedures such as handwriting analysis, foot reflexology, and numerology also enjoy surprising popularity (Lardner, 1994).

Given this low level of scientific literacy, perhaps it is not surprising that hype often seems to carry more weight than objective facts. Politicians, for example, often say, "We don't need to do research on the problem; we know what we need to do," or "I don't care what the research says, I feel. . . ." Similarly, many consumers are buying products that include "secret, ancient remedies" rather than products that have been proven to be effective through open, public, scientific testing.

With flagrant disregard for internal validity, people often make careless cause-effect statements. Leaders take credit for random or cyclical changes in the economy. Advertisers try to convince us that certain products cause professional models to be attractive. Even people who are not trying to sell us products use very weak evidence. For example, *Sports Illustrated* presented

**FIGURE 1–1**

## Changes in Reasoning Scores as a Function of Program of Study

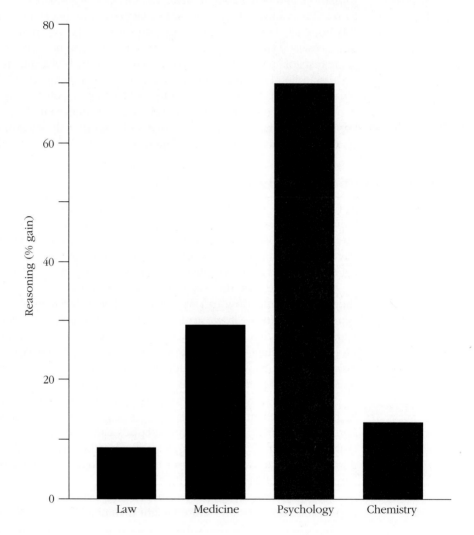

Reproduced from Lehman, D. R., Lempert, R. O., & Nisbett, R. E. (1988). Used with the kind permission of Darrin R. Lehman and the American Psychological Association.

the following evidence "proving" that teens are being killed for high-priced sneakers: a young man was found dead, and his money, cocaine, and shoes had been stolen. Couldn't it be that he was killed for the money, the drugs, or some other reason? Does it have to be the shoes alone?

With blatant disregard for internal, external, and construct validity, talk show hosts periodically parade a few people who claim "success" as a result of some dieting or parenting technique. Similarly, advertisers still successfully hawk products using testimonials from a few satisfied users, and political leaders "prove" what our country needs by telling us stories about one or two individuals rather than boring us with facts (Kincher, 1992). Unfortunately, research shows that, to the naive, these nonscientific and often misleading techniques are extremely persuasive (Nisbett, & Ross, 1980).

## To Increase Your Marketability

Besides making you a more informed citizen and consumer, knowing about research makes you more employable. In today's information age, you will probably *not* be hired for what technical information you know because such information is quickly obsolete and will soon be available at the punch of a keystroke from a computer database. Instead, you will probably be hired for your ability to evaluate and create information. That is, as you will see in Appendix D, you will be hired for your analytical abilities rather than your knowledge of facts. For example, even marketing majors are told that, at least for their first few years, their scientific skills, not their marketing intuition, is what will pave the way to future career success (Edwards, 1990). These same analytical skills will, of course, also be helpful if you plan to go to graduate school in business, law, medicine, or psychology.

## So You Can Do Your Own Research

To get into graduate school or enhance your marketability, you may do your own research. Or, you may do research as part of your job or graduate school experience. It seems that everyone is doing research these days. Some of our former students have been surprised that they ended up doing research to get government grants or get more staff for their social services agencies. Even movie moguls do research to determine such things as whether a movie's length, music, and ending are effective. As a result of such research, the endings for the movies *Fatal Attraction* and *Terminator 2—Judgment Day* were re-shot.

But beyond the employment angle, you may find that doing research is its own reward. Some students like research because it allows them to "do psychology" rather than read about it. Others enjoy the teamwork aspect of working with professors or other students. Still others enjoy the excitement of trying to get answers to questions about human behavior. Once you start an investigation into one of the many uncharted areas of the human psyche, we think you will understand what Carl Rogers (1985) meant when he said, "We need to sharpen our vision of what is possible . . . to that most fascinating of all enterprises: the unearthing, the discovery, the pursuit of significant new knowledge" (p. 1).

## CONCLUDING REMARKS

In conclusion, no matter what you do in the future, a knowledge of scientific research will be useful (see Table 1-6). The skills you learn will allow you to refine your critical thinking skills and become a scientifically literate citizen and consumer—almost necessities in our science-dominated world.

Similarly, no matter what you do in the future, you may find it necessary to read and evaluate the merit of specific psychological research findings. If you become a counseling psychologist, you will want to use the best, most up-to-date treatments with your clients. Partly for this reason, licensing exams for counseling psychologists include questions testing knowledge of research methods. If you become a manager, you will want to know the most effective management techniques. If you become a parent, you will want to evaluate the relative effectiveness of different child-rearing strategies. To get accurate answers in any of these areas, you will need to understand research. Unless you understand the research process, you may be limited by insufficient, out-of-date, or inaccurate information.

Finally, knowing about research will help you get the tools you need to get answers to your own questions. By reading this book, you will learn how to generate research ideas, manipulate and measure variables, collect objective data, ensure validity, choose the right design for your particular research question, treat participants ethically, interpret your results, and communicate your findings. We hope you will use this knowledge to join the most fascinating quest of our time—exploring the human mind.

**TABLE 1-6**

**Eight Reasons to Understand Psychological Research Methods**

1. To understand psychology better.
2. To keep up with recent discoveries by reading research.
3. To evaluate research claims.
4. To protect yourself from quacks and frauds.
5. To be a better thinker.
6. To be scientifically literate and thus a better-educated citizen and consumer.
7. To improve your marketability in our information age.
8. To do your own research.

## SUMMARY

1. Psychologists use the scientific approach to unearth observable, objective evidence that either supports or refutes their preconceived notions.

2. Because scientists make their evidence public, scientists can check each other's work, as well as build on each other's work. Because of the public, group-oriented nature of science, scientific progress can be rapid.

3. Because scientists make their evidence public, informed people can make use of new discoveries.

4. Science is both open-minded and skeptical. It is skeptical of any idea that is not supported by objective evidence; it is open-minded about any idea that is supported by objective evidence.

5. One goal of science is to find simple, general rules that will make the world more understandable.

6. One reason psychological research is objective is that psychologists use concrete, operational definitions of abstract concepts.

7. Not only do psychologists question the labels that people give to measures, but psychologists also question whether the evidence really proves that a certain treatment caused an effect. Psychologists realize that to prove that a treatment caused a change in behavior, you would have to show that no other factor was responsible for the change in behavior.

8. Psychologists also realize that what happens with one group of participants in one setting may not generalize to another type of participant or to a different setting. For example, they realize that a study done with one group of students in a lab setting may not apply to a group of people working in a factory. Therefore, they are appropriately cautious about generalizing the results of a study to real-world situations.

9. There is no psychology without science. Without science, psychology would have fewer facts than it does now and psychology would be little better than palmistry, astrology, graphology, and other pseudo-sciences. More specifically, using the scientific approach in psychology has allowed psychologists to (1) improve common sense, (2) disprove certain superstitions, and (3) make enormous progress in understanding how to help people.

10. Scientific research is a logical, proven, and ethical way of obtaining important information about human behavior.

11. If a study has internal validity, it establishes that a particular, observable, physical stimulus or manipulation *causes* a certain, observable response.

12. The study's external validity is the degree to which its findings can be generalized to other people, places, and times. Often, people question whether a result can be generalized to real-world situations.

13. When investigators are studying the psychological/mental states they claim to be studying, their research has construct validity.

14. Threats to construct validity include poor measures of variables, treatments that do not succeed in doing what they claim to do, and participants figuring out how the researchers want them to behave and then acting that way.

15. Human participants in research studies have many rights, including the right to decide whether they want to be in the study, the right to privacy, and the right to learn what the study's purpose is.

16. Do not conduct a study without the approval of your professor. In addition, obtain approval from the appropriate ethics committees. For example, if you are doing animal research, you may need approval from your school's animal care and use committee. If you are doing research with human participants, you may need approval from your school's internal review board (IRB).

17. If you are involved with a study that harms a participant, you cannot avoid responsibility by arguing that you did not know the rules, that you did not mean to harm the person, that you were just doing what the lead investigator told you to do, or that your assistant, rather than you, was involved in the harmful behavior.

18. According to APA's ethical principles, the potential benefits of a study should outweigh the study's potential for harm. Thus, there are two ways to increase the chances that your study is ethical: reduce the potential for harm and maximize the potential gains of your research.

19. If your research question is about whether something causes a certain effect, your study should have internal validity.

20. If your research question is about what percentage of people do some behavior, you need a study that has external validity. One key to having external validity is to have a large, random, representative sample of participants.

21. If your research question involves measuring or manipulating some state of mind (hunger, stress, learning, fear, motivation, love, etc.), then you need construct validity.

22. Depending on the research question, you may often be interested in only one of the three kinds of validity.

23. Skills learned in research design are transferable to real life.

## KEY TERMS

**construct:** a mental state that cannot be directly observed or manipulated, such as love, intelligence, hunger, feeling warm, and aggression (p. 17)

**operational definition:** a "recipe" for how you are going to measure or manipulate a construct; the specific, observable, concrete steps involved in measuring or manipulating that particular construct. (p. 5)

**construct validity:** the degree to which the study actually measures and manipulates the elements that the researcher claims to be measuring and manipulating. If the operational definitions of the constructs are poor, the study will not have good construct validity. For example, a test claiming to measure "aggressiveness" would not have construct validity if it really measured assertiveness. (p. 18)

**internal validity:** the degree to which the study demonstrates that the treatment *caused* a change in behavior. If a study lacks internal validity, the researcher may falsely believe that a factor causes an effect when it really doesn't. Most studies involving humans do not have internal validity because they cannot rule out the possibility that some other factor may have been responsible for the effect. Unfortunately, steps taken to increase internal validity (such as keeping non-treatment factors constant) could harm the study's external validity. (p. 16)

**external validity:** the degree to which the results of the study can be *generalized* to other places, people, or times. (p. 20)

**ethical:** conforming to a profession's principles of what is morally correct behavior. In the case of psychological research, the American Psychological Association has established guidelines and standards of morally appropriate behavior. To learn more about these guidelines and standards, see Table 1.3 and Appendix A. (p. 21)

## EXERCISES

1. Why is it important for scientists to make verifiable statements?
2. List at least two similarities between a scientist and a detective.
3. Physicists cannot accurately predict certain simple events. For example, physicists have trouble with such questions as, "If you drop a basketball from a table, how many times will it bounce—and what will be the pattern of those bounces?" Which characteristic of science is threatened by physicists' failure to answer this question? What implications, if any, does this failure have for psychology?
4. Some early psychologists studied and reported on their own thoughts. For example, a person would solve a mathematical problem and then report on everything that went on in his mind during the time that he worked on the problem. What quality of science was missing in these studies?
5. From what you know about astrology, grade it on a "pass/fail" basis on how well it does on the following characteristics of science:

| CHARACTERISTIC | GRADE |
|---|---|
| Makes verifiable statements | |
| Productive (knowledge refined, new discoveries made) | |
| Seeks objective, unbiased evidence to determine the accuracy of beliefs. | |

6. According to some, iridology is the science of determining people's health by looking at their eyes. Practitioners of this "science" learn it through secret, closed-door seminars; don't try to verify their diagnoses through other means; and different practitioners will diagnose the same patient very differently. What characteristics of science does iridology have? Where does it fall short?

7. Some claim that psychoanalysis is not a science. They attack it by claiming that it lacks certain characteristics of science. Below are three such attacks. For each attack, name the characteristic of science that psychoanalysis is being accused of failing to achieve.
   a. "Psychoanalytic explanations for a person's behavior often fit with the facts, but are generally made after the fact."
   b. "The unconscious is impossible to observe."
   c. "The effectiveness of psychoanalysis does not appear to have improved in the last 20 years."

8. Abraham Maslow and other humanistic psychologists have argued that psychologists have studied rats and neurotic individuals but have not studied exceptionally well-adjusted people. This is a criticism about the _____ validity of research.

9. The professor of a Psychology of Women class notes that a study used only male participants. The professor is probably attacking the _____ validity of that study.

10. The professor of a Psychology of Women class notes that a study claiming that women are more conforming than men could be interpreted as showing that women are more cooperative than men. The professor is probably attacking the _____ validity of that research.

11. A survey finds that Diet Coke drinkers are less irritable than Diet Pepsi drinkers. The investigator concludes that consuming Diet Pepsi causes enhanced irritability. This conclusion lacks _____ validity.

12. Don and Julie are engaged to be married this summer. However, upon taking a "couple compatibility" test in a popular magazine, they find they are not compatible. Before breaking off their engagement, Don and Julie should determine the _____ validity of the test.

13. A medical school asks people to volunteer for a "Study that involves taking drugs and undergoing psychological testing." The researchers conclude that the drug calms people down. Given the participants used in this study, the _____ validity of the research could be questioned.

14. Near the end of the last lecture before the exam, a professor asks two students whether they have any questions. Both say "no." As a result, the professor concludes that those two students know and understand everything that was covered in class. The professor's measure of "knowing and understanding everything" may lack ———— validity.

15. Match the criticism to the type of validity (internal, external, or construct) being questioned.

| CRITICISM | VALIDITY BEING QUESTIONED |
| --- | --- |
| Two groups differ, not because of treatment, but by chance. | |
| Participants studied are not typical of an average cross-section of people. | |
| Measure used is not very good. | |
| Participants only included gifted 10-year-olds. | |
| Groups were not the same before treatment was introduced. | |
| Participants' reports of their feelings may be inaccurate. | |
| Only males were used. | |
| Participants may have guessed hypothesis and played along. | |
| Measure does not capture construct. | |
| Participants may have changed even without treatment so researcher should not conclude that treatment caused change. | |
| Results would not hold in a real-life situation. | |
| Task was boring and meaningless so participants were not psychologically involved in the study. | |
| Manipulation may not have produced intended effect on participants' psychological states. | |
| Measure is biased. | |

16. "A rose by any other name would smell as sweet." Perhaps. But if a scale that measured conservatism were relabeled "close-mindedness scale," there would be ———— validity problems with studies using this "close-mindedness" scale.

17. *Teen* magazine puts a survey form in a recent issue. Of those who reply, 40 percent claim to have used drugs. As a result, the magazine

concludes that 40 percent of teens have used drugs. Even assuming the respondents are honest, the study may lack _____ validity.

18. The author of the book, *The Hidden Life of Dogs,* claims that her dogs fell in love and got married, have moral fiber, and that a male dog told a female dog that he knew she was younger than he and inferior to him in every way that mattered to dogs, but he didn't care about that since he felt unrequited love for her. A psychologist might question the _____ validity of these observations. Why?

19. A police officer puts a drunk in a blue room. The prisoner acts in a way that the officer describes as "violent." Then, the officer moves the prisoner to a pink room. This prisoner then acts in a way that the officer describes as "less violent."

   a. A scientist doubts that the pink room changed the prisoner's behavior. Instead, she thinks the change in the prisoner's behavior in the pink room might just be a coincidence. The prisoner may have changed his behavior for reasons that have nothing to do with the pink room at all (for example, the prisoner has calmed down by the time he enters the pink room). Since the scientist is doubting that the pink room caused the effect, she is questioning the study's _____ validity.

   b. A second scientist believes that even if the pink room changed this prisoner's behavior (that is, the study had _____ validity), there would be serious doubts as to whether the pink room would change the behavior of sober prisoners. The second scientist is questioning the degree to which the results would generalize. Thus, this scientist is questioning the study's _____ validity.

   c. A third scientist agrees that the prisoner's behavior changed, but does not agree that the behavior became "less violent." Instead, the scientist thought that the prisoner was simply less active in the pink room. Since the scientist is disputing the way the behavior was labeled, the scientist is attacking the study's _____ validity. Specifically, the scientist is attacking the _____ validity of the study's measure of aggression.

20. What type of validity are chemists most interested in? Why don't chemists do more research in natural settings like bakeries? What implications does this have for psychological research?

21. Is it ethical to treat a patient with a method that has not been scientifically tested? Why or why not? Is it ethical to withhold a treatment that is believed to work in order to find out if it does indeed work? Why or why not?

22. What APA ethical principles (see Table 1–3) are violated by television shows such as "Candid Camera," "Totally Hidden Video," and "America's Funniest Home Videos"?

23. Would the studies done by the U.S. government in the 1950s to determine the effects of nuclear radiation—studies done without the

participants' knowledge—be ethical according to APA's ethical code? Why or why not?

**24.** Two of the most ethically questionable studies in the history of psychology are Milgram's obedience study (where participants were told to deliver dangerous shocks to an accomplice of the experimenter) and Zimbardo's prison study (where well-adjusted students pretended to be either prisoners or guards). In both of these studies, there would have been no ethical problems at all if participants had behaved the way common sense told us they would. No one would have obeyed the order to shock the accomplice and none of the "guards" would have mistreated the prisoners.

Points to ponder:

**a.** Does the inability to know how participants will react to a research project mean that research should not be done?

**b.** Does people's inability to know how they and others will react in many situations mean that certain kinds of research should be performed so we can find out the answers to these important questions?

**25.** From the brief description above, what ethical principles, if any, were violated in Milgram's shock experiment (see Table 1–3)?

**26.** From the brief description in No. 24, what ethical principles, if any, were violated in Zimbardo's prison study (see Table 1–3)?

**27.** Assume that a participant in a study in which you were involved suffered intense distress. According to the APA ethical guidelines, which of the following are legitimate excuses that would relieve you of responsibility? Explain your answers.

**a.** "I was just following orders."

**b.** "My assistant conducted the session and behaved inappropriately, not me."

**c.** "I didn't notice that the participant was upset."

**d.** "I just didn't think that we had to tell participants that they would get mild electrical shocks."

**e.** "I didn't think that asking questions about suicide would be upsetting—and for most of my participants it wasn't."

**f.** "When the participant got upset, it surprised me. I just didn't know what to do and so I didn't do anything."

**g.** "Our subjects were mice. We can cause mice whatever distress we want."

# CHAPTER 2

—

# Generating Research Hypotheses

*Overview*

*Generating Research Ideas by Challenging
Common Sense*

*Generating Research Ideas from Theory*

WHY SCIENTISTS LIKE THEORIES
USING "GOOD" THEORIES TO GENERATE RESEARCH IDEAS
CONCLUSIONS ABOUT GENERATING RESEARCH IDEAS
FROM THEORY

*Generating Research Ideas from Previous Research*

SPECIFIC STRATEGIES
CONCLUSIONS ABOUT GENERATING RESEARCH IDEAS
FROM PREVIOUS RESEARCH

*Converting an Idea into a Research Hypothesis*

MAKE IT TESTABLE
BE SURE TO HAVE A RATIONALE
DEMONSTRATE ITS RELEVANCE
MAKE SURE THAT TESTING IT IS PRACTICAL AND ETHICAL
CHANGING IMPRACTICAL AND UNETHICAL IDEAS
INTO RESEARCH HYPOTHESES

*Concluding Remarks*

*Summary*

*Key Terms*

*Exercises*

# Chapter 2

## GENERATING RESEARCH HYPOTHESES

*"If you do not ask specific questions, I cannot be responsible for your misinterpretation of the answer."*

—SOLITAIRE
"LIVE AND LET DIE"

*"Much of what we take to be true is seriously wrong."*

—GORE VIDAL

### OVERVIEW

Research does not begin with variables, equipment, or participants. It begins with questions. Thus, at one level, this is a book about how you can get answers to questions.

But where do you get questions? As you'll see in this chapter, you can get questions by challenging common sense, testing theory, and questioning the results of existing research.

### GENERATING RESEARCH IDEAS BY CHALLENGING COMMON SENSE

In trying to find out what is and isn't true, one place to begin is by testing common sense. As one scientist (Stern, 1993) put it, a major goal of psychology should be to "separate common sense from common nonsense."

Many psychologists have tested commonsense assumptions. For example, Stanley Schachter (1959) tested the saying that "misery loves company." Bob Zajonc (1968) found the saying, "familiarity breeds contempt," to be false in many situations. Ellen Berscheid and her colleagues (1971) found that "birds of a feather flock together." Don Byrne (1971) found that opposites don't attract. Latané, Williams, and Harkins (1979) found evidence for the idea that "too many cooks spoil the broth." Wohlford (1970) found that fathers who smoked were more likely to have sons who smoked. Thus, he found some support for the saying, "like father, like son."

If we mentioned a saying that you were planning to test, do not automatically abandon plans to test that saying. Clichés are usually broad enough that all aspects of them cannot be completely tested in a single study. For example, researchers still do not have definitive answers on the extent to which many of a son's behaviors (other than smoking) are modeled after his father's. Similarly, even though in 1971, Byrne found evidence that opposites (in terms of attitudes) don't attract, it wasn't until seven years later that researchers found that opposites—in the form of psychologically "masculine" males and psychologically "feminine" females—don't attract in short-term blind dates (Ickes & Barnes, 1978). And it wasn't until 12 years later that researchers discovered that psychologically "masculine" males and psychologically "feminine" females don't attract in long-term marriage relationships (Antill, 1983). However, if you want to test completely untested sayings, there are many from which to choose. Perhaps you could test hypotheses generated from common sense such as "the more, the merrier," "brevity is the soul of wit," or some other phrase you might find in a fortune cookie, in a package of Salada tea (Dillon, 1990), in a book of quotations, in a self-help or advice book such as *Life's Little Instruction Book,* in a song, in an ad, on a bumper sticker, or on a T-shirt.

Rather than trying to verify or refute old sayings, you might try to refine them. For example, you might ask yourself, "under what circumstances is the saying accurate—and when is it inaccurate?" That is, you might think of exceptions to the rule. For instance, although much research had shown support for the old saying, "people from a different race all look alike," Leslie Zebrowitz and her colleagues (Zebrowitz, Montepare, & Lee, 1993) found that, under certain conditions, people could do a good job of distinguishing between members of other racial groups.

Alternatively, you might try to reconcile the inconsistencies of common sense. For example, when does "like attract like" and when do "opposites attract"? Under what circumstances are "two heads better than one" and under what circumstances is it better to do it yourself (after all, "too many cooks spoil the broth" and "nothing is worse than a committee")? When does "absence make the heart grow fonder"—and when does absence mean "out of sight, out of mind"?

## GENERATING RESEARCH IDEAS FROM THEORY

In the previous section, we concentrated on generating ideas from common sense. However, testing common sense is not the only—or even the most preferred—method of generating ideas. As you will see in this section, many psychologists think it is better to derive research ideas from theory.

## Box 2–1
## Seven Ways to Tap Your Intuition

1. For "old sayings," assumptions/ predictions made in songs, assumptions made in classic or popular literature, and statements made by experts ask:
   a. Is it true?
   b. Is there anything I know that seems to contradict that?
   c. When isn't it true? When is it more likely to be true?
   d. Is it true only in moderation?
   e. Why is it true (what is the cause-effect relationship? what is the mediating variable?)
   f. Why do people believe it's true?
2. Collect data on your own behavior, try to find rules that govern your behavior, and then see if those rules apply to other people.
3. Transform an argument into a research idea—find facts to settle a battle between two opinions.
4. Ask five key questions about any interesting phenomenon:
   a. Who does the behavior? How do people who are high and low on the behavior differ?
   b. What precisely is the behavior?
   c. When is the behavior most likely to occur? What occurs before the behavior?
   d. Why do people engage in the behavior?
   e. What are the long- and short-term effects of the behavior?
5. Figure out why bad/irrational actions occur.
6. Attack a practical problem (ecology, illiteracy, prejudice, apathy, alcoholism, violence).
   a. Document that it exists
   b. Evaluate the effectiveness of potential cures for the problem.
7. Investigate factors that decrease your creativity.

## Why Scientists Like Theories

To understand why many psychologists prefer to derive research ideas from theory, you need to understand what a theory is. Unfortunately, theory is hard to define and may be confused with related terms (see Table 2–1).

### WHAT IS A THEORY?

Although no definition is perfect, we think that, for researchers, the most practical definition of theory is *an integrated set of principles that explain observations and that can be used to deduce a large number of hypotheses*. This definition highlights two important facts about good theories. First, theories use a *few* principles to explain and summarize a large number of facts. Second, because they are a source of hypotheses, they stimulate *new* discoveries. Thus, researchers used "germ theory" to discover the bacteria responsible for certain

Even psychologists do not always properly distinguish between hypotheses, theories, and laws. However, as you can see below, there are differences.

*Hypothesis:* A specific prediction that can be tested.

*Theory:* More complex than hypotheses because a theory is a *set of related propositions* that attempt to specify the relationship between a set of variables. Usually, a theory summarizes a body of empirical evidence. Theories may be used to derive hypotheses. Note, however, that theories are not facts or laws.

*Law:* A thoroughly documented relationship between two or more variables. Usually, the relationship specified by a law is a very strong one. For example, take the hypothesis that higher status people will start calling lower status people by first name before lower status people will call higher status people by first name. If research shows that this happens most of the time, the hypothesis would then be (tentatively) considered a fact. Furthermore, if this almost always happens, it could be considered a law. Similarly, if a theory has been substantially verified, it could be called a law. Thus, some behaviorists would argue that their theories of behavior are really laws of behavior.

diseases, "gene theory" to discover DNA, Newton's theory of gravity to discover Neptune, and social learning theory to discover ways of reducing aggression and shyness. In short, theory, like common sense, is a good source of research ideas.

## ADVANTAGES OF USING THEORY TO GENERATE IDEAS

But why do many psychologists prefer theory to common sense? As you can see from Table 2-2, there are at least eight reasons why scientists prefer theory to common sense.

First, theories tend to be more internally consistent than common sense. That is, a theory usually doesn't contradict itself. Common sense, on the other hand, often contradicts itself ("absence makes the heart grow fonder," but "out of sight, out of mind"). Researchers find it easier to make clear, consistent predictions from a consistent theory rather than from inconsistent common sense.

Second, theories tend to be more consistent with existing facts than common sense. Often, theories are constructed by systematically collecting data and carefully analyzing the data for patterns. But even when facts do not play a dominant role in giving birth to a theory, facts will usually shape the theory's development. Generally, if deductions from a theory are incorrect, the theory will be changed or abandoned. Thus, unlike common sense, theories do not ignore facts. Consequently, a hypothesis based on an established theory is a more educated guess and should have a greater chance of being correct than one based on common sense.

Third, theories are not restricted to making commonsense or intuitively obvious predictions. Theories can make predictions that are counter-intuitive. For example, social learning theory predicts that rewarding a child for a behavior could make the child like doing the behavior less (because the child may decide that he or she does the behavior because of the reward, rather than because the child likes it). Because theories are not limited to making predictions that are consistent with common sense, a theory may suggest controversial, new ways of viewing the world. For instance, Darwin's theory on evolution had us look at apes as relatives, Einstein's theory of relativity had us look at matter and energy as being the same thing, Freud's theory had us look at ourselves as being motivated by forces of which we weren't aware, and Watson's theory had us look at ourselves as a set of reflexes.

Fourth, theories summarize and organize a great deal of information. Just as the plot of a movie may connect thousands of otherwise unrelated images, theories connect individual facts and give them meaning. That is, theories try to explain facts. The ability of theories to connect facts means that theory-based research will not produce isolated bits of trivia. Instead, the findings will fit into a framework that connects many other studies. In other words, the facts revealed by theory-based research are not merely of interest for their own sake, but also for how they relate to the theory's explanation of how the world works. For example, consider the following fact: around age 7, children stop believing in Santa Claus. In its own right, this is a relatively trivial fact. However, when put in the context of Piaget's theory, which states that around age 7, children are able to think logically about concrete events (and thus realize that Santa Claus can't be everywhere at once and can't carry that many toys), the finding has deeper significance.

Fifth, in addition to giving individual facts a meaningful context, theories focus research. Because many researchers try to test theories, findings from theory-based research are not only relevant to the theory's explanation of events, but also to the findings of other researchers. Because progress in science comes from researchers building on each other's work, the importance of a theory's ability to coordinate individual scientists' efforts should not be underestimated.

Sixth, theories are often broad in scope. Because theories can be applied to a wide range of situations, researchers can generate a wide variety of studies from a single theory. For example, social learning theory can be applied to prisons, businesses, advertising, politics, schizophrenics, smokers, librarians, mad dogs, and Englishmen. Similarly, Freud's theory of the unconscious can be applied to virtually any situation.

Seventh, theories try to explain the facts with only a few core ideas. That is, they tend to be **parsimonious:** explaining a broad range of phenomena with a few principles. The value of parsimony is evident when you consider that a major function of science is to simplify our world. The parsimonious theory provides a few simple rules that summarize hundreds of observations. These general rules making existing knowledge easier to understand, remember, and use. Therefore, scientists prefer theories with a few far-reaching principles to theories that require a different principle to explain each new phenomenon. Thus, it should be no surprise that two theories that have enjoyed great popularity—evolutionary theory and social learning theory—possess only a few, broad-ranging principles.

**TABLE 2–2**
**Contrasting Theory and Common Sense**

| THEORY | COMMON SENSE |
|---|---|
| Internally consistent. | Makes contradictory statements. |
| Consistent with existing facts. | Not overly concerned with being consistent with existing knowledge. |
| May make novel, counter-intuitive predictions. | Makes intuitively obvious, commonsense predictions. |
| Summarizes and organizes information. | Summarizes, but not as extensively or accurately as theories. Furthermore, some studies derived from "intuition" yield results than cannot be integrated with existing knowledge. |
| Focuses research on a particular set of problems. | Rarely focuses research on a problem. |
| Broad in scope. | Broad in scope. |
| Parsimonious. | Parsimonious, often to the point of grossly oversimplifying reality. |
| Testable because it makes specific predictions and provides operational definitions of key variables. | Sometimes not testable because commonsense predictions predict all possible outcomes, are too vague, or key variables can't be measured. |

Finally, theories are often more testable than common sense. That is, by talking about variables that can be objectively measured and by making specific predictions, a *good* theory is easy to test.

## Using "Good" Theories to Generate Research Ideas

Despite their similarities, all theories are not equally good. Some are more parsimonious than others, some are broader than others, some are more logically consistent than others, some make more interesting predictions than others, and some are more consistent with the facts than others. However, if you are trying to develop a research hypothesis, the most important difference between theories is that some theories are more testable—and thus more useful—than others. Therefore, when choosing a theory, make sure that it is testable.

### CHARACTERISTICS OF A TESTABLE THEORY

To be testable, a theory must:

1. make predictions rather than rely entirely on after-the-fact explanations;
2. predict one outcome rather than several contradictory outcomes;
3. make a specific prediction, rather than an extremely vague one; and
4. make a prediction that can be verified through objective observation.

***Prediction rather than postdiction.***    To be testable, a theory must tell you about events that have not yet been observed. Unfortunately, not all theories make such predictions. Instead, some, such as McDougall's (1908) instinct theory, only explain what happened after the fact. For example, *after* a woman picked apples from her orchard, McDougall might say, "she picked apples because the instinct to pick apples from an orchard was activated." However, McDougall's theory could not make before-the-fact predictions because his theory didn't tell us when to expect instincts to be aroused or how to tell whether someone would inherit a high level of an instinct.

***Prediction rather than predictions.***    To be testable, a theory must be capable of making one and only one prediction about what would happen in a certain situation. To illustrate the problem of making more than one prediction, consider Freudian theory. According to Freudian theory, receiving a severe beating from one's father could result in any of the following outcomes:

1. no apparent effect (we try not to think about it: repression or suppression);
2. deep anger and resentment at people similar to our father (displacement);
3. great love for our father (reaction formation); or
4. hate for ourselves (internalization).

Given all these predictions, it is hard to imagine an outcome that would not agree with one of them. Freudian theory would be more testable if it made one prediction.

***Precision in prediction.***    Almost as useless as making many predictions about what would happen in a certain situation is making one extremely vague prediction. Some theories purport to make predictions about the future, but these predictions are so vague that they are untestable. An extremely vague prediction may remind us of the fortune cookies that read, "You will make a decision soon."

Precision is the reason we often like to see quantitative statements in theories. For instance, the statement, "People taking drug *A* will remember twice as much as those not taking *A*," is more precise than the statement, "People taking drug *A* will remember more than those not taking *A*."

***Operationalism.***    Even if a theory makes specific, unambiguous predictions about the future, these predictions must involve publicly observable events—if the theory is to be testable. That is, for the relevant variables, we must be able to provide **operational definitions**: publicly observable sets of procedures (operations) to manipulate or measure variables.

To illustrate the importance of operational definitions, consider the statement: "When you die, you will go to heaven." Although this is a prediction about future events, it cannot be scientifically tested because we cannot find any *publicly observable,* physical evidence that would help us determine whether a person has gone to heaven. Since religion makes such metaphysical (beyond the physical world) statements, science and religion usually do not mix. Analogously, a few scientists have argued that science and psychoanalysis do not mix because we cannot observe the unconscious. Such is the fate of theories whose variables cannot be operationalized.

We should caution, however, that not all variables in a theory must be *directly* observable. Many theories discuss **hypothetical constructs:** entities that we cannot, with our present technology, observe directly. Gravity, electrons, love, learning, and memory are all hypothetical constructs because they are invisible. Although hypothetical constructs can't be seen, we may be able to infer their presence from their traces or impact. With enough indirect, physical evidence, scientists can make a very convincing case for the existence of an invisible entity (a hypothetical construct). Thus, although no one has ever seen a quark, physicists have demonstrated that quarks exist.

In psychology, the challenge has not been to see inside the atom, but to see inside the head. Like quarks, mental states cannot be directly observed. For example, we cannot directly observe learning. However, we can see its effect on performance. That is, we can operationally define learning as an increase in performance. Thus, if we see someone improve their performance after practicing a task, we would conclude that learning has occurred. Similarly, we can provide operational definitions for such intangible hypothetical constructs as hunger, thirst, mood, love, etc.

You now know how to judge whether a theory can help you generate research ideas. But where do you find theories?

## FINDING A TESTABLE THEORY

To find a useful theory, start by reading textbook summaries of theories. Reading a textbook summary should at least acquaint you with some of the theory's propositions. Although these summaries will allow you to select a theory, do not rely exclusively on textbook summaries—such summaries may oversimplify the theory. Thus, the researcher who relies exclusively on textbook summaries may be accused of ignoring key propositions of the theory or of using a **straw theory:** an exaggerated, oversimplified caricature of the theory. Therefore, in addition to reading textbook summaries, you should also see how other researchers have summarized the theory. To find these summaries, consult journal articles that describe studies based on the theory (e.g., "Elation and Depression: A test of opponent process theory"). Usually, the beginnings of these articles include a brief description of the theory that the study tests.

Once you have selected a theory, read the original statement of the theory (the citation will be in the texts or articles that you read). Then, to keep up-to-date about changes in the theory, use *Psychological Abstracts* to find books and review articles devoted to the theory (see Appendix B).

## WAYS OF DEDUCING HYPOTHESES FROM THEORY

Once you understand the theory, your task is to apply your powers of deduction. You have these powers or you wouldn't have passed high school geometry and you wouldn't be able to write an essay. In fact, much of your everyday thinking involves deductive logic. For example, you may say, "The important thing about a college education is to learn how to think. This assignment doesn't help me learn how to think. Therefore, this assignment is not important to my college education." If your premises were sound, your statement would be an example of sound, deductive logic.

In deducing hypotheses from theory, you will use the same deductive logic illustrated above. That is, you will apply a general rule to a specific instance. The only difference is that the general rule comes from a theory instead of from the top of your head. To reassure yourself that you can apply deductive reasoning to propositions that were made up by someone else, try this deductive reasoning test:

1. All people treated like b turn out c.
2. Person a is being treated like b.
3. Person a will turn out _____.

1. All behavior can be changed by controlling its consequences.
2. Al's behavior is bad.
3. Al's bad behavior can be changed by _____.

As this "test" illustrates, if you know the premises and set them up correctly, deductive logic can be as simple as 1-2-3. Thus, because you know common sense's premises, you probably had no problem deducing research ideas from common sense. Consequently, once you know what a theory's premises are, your problem will not be *how* to think deductively, but *what* to think about. In the next few pages, we will give you some strategies that will help you focus your deductive reasoning.

***Apply it to solve a practical problem.***    Contrary to common stereotypes about theories, theories can be applied to practical situations. As Kurt Lewin said, "there is nothing so practical as a good theory." For example, social learning theory has been used to cure shyness, promote energy conservation, address speech problems, reduce violence, and improve studying behavior.

To take a closer look at how theory can help you attack a practical problem, consider cognitive dissonance theory (Festinger, 1957). According to cognitive dissonance theory, if a person holds two thoughts that he considers inconsistent, he will experience dissonance (see Table 2–3). Since dissonance is unpleasant, the person will try to reduce it, much as the person would try to reduce hunger, thirst, or anxiety (Aronson, 1990).

Let's see how dissonance theory was used to get people to conserve energy. After being told they would get their names in the paper if they conserved energy, people cut back on their energy use. Then, dissonance was induced by

**TABLE 2–3**

**Basic Propositions of Cognitive Dissonance Theory**

1. If a person has two thoughts that the person considers inconsistent, the individual will experience dissonance.
2. Dissonance is an unpleasant state, like anxiety or hunger.
3. A person will try to reduce dissonance.
4. Changing one of the thoughts to make it consistent with the other is one way of reducing dissonance.

telling them that their names would not be printed. This created dissonance between two inconsistent ideas: (1) I do things for a reason, and (2) I went without air conditioning for no reason. Participants resolved the dissonance by cutting energy use even more! That is, they decided: (1) I do things for a reason, and (2) I went without air conditioning because I believe in energy conservation (Pallak, Cook, & Sullivan, 1980). Similarly, Stone, Aronson, Crain, Winslow, and Fried (1994) applied dissonance theory to getting people to engage in safe sex. Specifically, they created dissonance by (1) having participants publicly advocate the importance of safe sex and then (2) reminding each participant about times when that participant had failed to use condoms. Stone and his colleagues found that participants reduced this feeling of dissonance by buying condoms.

***Use theory to understand a real life situation.***    Many researchers take advantage of the fact that a major purpose of theories is to explain what happens in the world. For example, researchers wanted to understand why fraternities engage in hazing (Aronson & Mills, 1959; Gerard & Mathewson, 1966). They wondered if cognitive dissonance theory could explain hazing. Consequently, they tried to induce dissonance in some participants by having them suffer electrical shocks as a requirement for being accepted into a "boring" group, whereas other participants were able to join the group without an "initiation." The researchers found that the participants who received shocks resolved the dissonance caused by the opposing thoughts, "I am a logical person," and, "I went through unpleasantness to join a boring group," by deciding that the boring group was a pretty interesting group after all.

***Look for moderator variables.***    Theories are general rules that, ideally, hold most of the time under specific conditions. Therefore, ask yourself, "under what situations or conditions, does the theory not apply?" That is, has the theory neglected to specify important **moderator variables:** variables that can intensify, weaken, or reverse the relationship between two other variables?

Because researchers asked this question about cognitive dissonance theory, we now know that people do not change their attitude every time they behave in a way that goes against their attitudes. Instead, the presence of certain moderator variables will determine whether performing a counter-attitudinal behavior will change participants' attitudes (Aronson, 1989; Brehm & Cohen, 1962; Festinger & Carlsmith, 1959). Specifically, if participants are going to change their attitudes after doing a counter-attitudinal behavior, the following conditions must be met:

1. participants must believe that they engaged in the behavior of their own free will (perceived freedom);
2. they do not receive a large reward for doing the behavior (insufficient justification); and
3. they view the attitude as important to their self-concept (self-relevance).

For example, if a smoker is forced at gunpoint to say smoking is bad, or given $10,000 for saying smoking is bad, or does not view smoking as important to his self-concept, the smoker will not change his or her attitude about smoking. That is, perceived freedom, insufficient justification, and self-relevance are all variables that moderate the relationship between doing a counter-attitudinal behavior and changing one's attitude. Can you think of other moderator variables that should be included in dissonance theory? To answer this question, think about factors, situations, or circumstances that might prevent people from trying to eliminate inconsistencies between their attitudes and actions.

When looking for moderating variables, ask yourself whether the theory might be too parsimonious. For example, operant conditioning theory's rule that a behavior reinforced under a partial reinforcement schedule is more resistant to extinction is too simple. A behavior reinforced under a partial reinforcement schedule is more resistant to extinction *only when* the person believes the reward is controlled by external forces, such as chance, fate, or the experimenter's whim. Partially reinforced behaviors are *not* more resistant to extinction when the participant believes that getting reinforcement depends on skill (Rotter, 1990). In other words, the relationship between reinforcement schedules and extinction is moderated by the variable of perceived control.

***Go for the jugular.***    Another way to generate research ideas from a theory is to design a study that tests the accuracy of the theory's core assumptions. Often, attacking the heart of the theory involves examining the physiological or cognitive events that are—according to the theory—the underlying causes (mediators) of a phenomenon. For instance, cognitive dissonance theory assumes that when people have two beliefs that they see as contradictory, they experience an unpleasant, anxiety-provoking state called dissonance. To reduce dissonance, people will reconcile the inconsistency. In other words, dissonance theorists assume that dissonance *mediates* attitude change.

To test this assumption, you might try to induce and maintain dissonance in participants and determine whether they do find dissonance an unpleasant, anxiety-provoking state (Elliot & Devine, 1994). If participants felt *decreased* arousal, it would seem that you had disproved a core assumption of the theory. That is, you would have cast doubt on the belief that the state of dissonance is a **mediating variable**—physiological process or mental state that is the mechanism for how an event has its effect—for attitude change.

In addition to trying to measure an alleged mediating variable, you may try to manipulate it. For example, suppose that a certain manipulation tends to cause attitude change, presumably because it creates a cognitive and physiological state of dissonance that people then reduce. If the psychological state of dissonance is really the mechanism by which attitude change occurs, interfering with that psychological state should reduce attitude change. Therefore, you might expose all your participants to the attitude change manipulation, but do something so that half of your participants would be less likely to experience the physiological arousal of the dissonance state. For example, you might reduce any feelings of dissonance-related arousal by giving one group a tranquilizing drug. If dissonance really is the mediating variable for attitude change, your tranquilized participants should experience less dissonance-related arousal and thus less attitude change than your other participants.

***Pit two theories against each other.***    Rather than trying to torpedo a theory, some researchers think the best hypotheses are those in which two theories make opposite predictions. Ideally, these studies, called **critical experiments,** try to settle the question of which theory's view of the world is more correct. One of the first critical experiments was simple but persuasive. Participants looked at two lights. Almost as soon as one went on, the other went off. According to structuralism, the person should see one light going on, another going off. However, according to Gestalt theory, participants should see the illusion of a single light moving back and forth. Gestalt theory was supported.

More recently, cognitive dissonance theorists have taken on psychoanalysis. Specifically, dissonance researchers tested the psychoanalytic position that if you express hostility towards a person, you'll release pent up anger and consequently feel better about the person. Dissonance theory, on the other hand, predicts that if people are mad at someone and then hurt that person, then people will justify their aggression by denigrating that person. Consequently, after expressing their aggression toward a person, people will feel more hostility toward that person. Experiments support the dissonance prediction (Aronson, 1990).

If you can devise a situation where two theories make different predictions, you have probably designed a study your professor will want to hear about. However, even if you perform a critical experiment, do not expect the "loser" of your study to be replaced. The loser has only lost a battle, not a war. There is usually enough vagueness in any theory for its arch-supporters to minimize the extent of the damage. That is, they may argue that their theory wouldn't necessarily make the prediction that you claimed it would. In other words, they may say that you put words in their theory's mouth. If they can't claim that you put words in their theory's mouth, they may concede that their theory applies to a more limited set of situations than they thought or they may modify the theory to account for the results (Greenwald, 1975). Because scientists usually respond to a damaging set of findings by modifying an established theory rather than "throwing the baby out with the bath water," Darwin's theory of evolution and Festinger's theory of cognitive dissonance survive today, but not in their original form. That is, by adapting to new data, theories evolve.

## Conclusions about Generating Research Ideas from Theory

As you have seen, theory is a very useful tool for developing research ideas and tying those ideas to existing knowledge. Without research based on theory, psychology would chaotically move in every direction with little purpose, like a chicken with its head cut off. Indeed, theory-based research is responsible for much of psychology's progress since 1892, when psychology was described by William James (p. 468) as:

> a string of raw facts; . . . but not a single law in the sense in which physics shows us laws, not a single proposition from which any consequence can causally be deduced . . . This is no science. . . .

Yet not everyone believes that theory-based research is always best (Greenwald et al., 1986; Kuhn, 1970; Skinner, 1956). (See Table 2–4 for pros and cons of theory-based research.) Thomas Kuhn (1970) argues that theories can serve as blinders, causing us to ignore problems that don't fit nicely into existing theory. Skinner (1956) also argues that sticking to a theory's narrow path may cause us to ignore interesting side streets. Specifically, Skinner's advice to investigators was "when you find something of interest, study it."

In addition to stopping us from seeking new facts, theories may also stop us from seeing old facts in new ways. Thus, we may fail to make the kind of discoveries Darwin, Freud, and Skinner made—the ones that result from seeing what everyone else has seen, but thinking what no one else has thought. As physicists learned when Newton's theory was largely overturned by Einstein, looking at things exclusively through one theory's perspective is especially dangerous when the theory has not been extensively tested. In other words, some experts (Greenwald et al., 1986; Kuhn, 1970; Skinner, 1968) would agree with Sherlock Holmes' statement about the danger of premature theorizing: "One begins to twist facts to fit theories rather than theories to fit facts."

Fortunately, as Aronson (1989) points out, science is like a big circus tent. Under the tent, there is room for research derived from theory, but there is also room in the tent for researchers who follow hunches.

Not only can hunch-based and theory-based research share the same circus tent, but they can sometimes share the same ring. For example, suppose that an intuitive hunch led you to predict that having pets would cause the elderly to be more mentally alert and healthy. You might then use theory to help you clearly articulate a logical rationale for your prediction—or even to help you refine your prediction. For example, according to learned helplessness theory, a lack of control over outcomes may cause depression. Therefore, having a pet,

**TABLE 2–4**
**Pros and Cons of Theory-Based Research**

| PROS | CONS |
|------|------|
| Theory focuses research on specific issues and problems. | Theory may divert attention away from other important issues and problems. |
| Theory provides a way of interpreting and explaining facts, a way of looking at the world. | Theory may provide an inaccurate way of looking at the world and may prevent us from finding more accurate ways of viewing phenomena. |

or even a plant, may give one more of a sense of control and thus make one less vulnerable to helplessness (Langer & Rodin, 1976).

# GENERATING RESEARCH IDEAS FROM PREVIOUS RESEARCH

The research circus tent not only has a ring for researchers using intuition and a ring for researchers using theory, but also a third ring for research based on previous studies. For a beginning researcher, basing an idea on previous research has at least three major advantages.

First, a hypothesis based on previous research is indeed an educated guess. Consequently, you have a reasonable chance of obtaining results that support your hypothesis.

Second, regardless of whether your hypothesis is supported, your study will be relevant to what other scientists have done. Consequently, your research will not produce an isolated, trivial fact.

Third, doing research based on other people's work is easier than starting from scratch. Rather than re-inventing the wheel, you can use the tools and plans that others have invented.

## Specific Strategies

You have seen that there are advantages to developing research ideas from previous research. But how can you take advantage of other people's work?

### REPEAT STUDIES

The simplest way to take advantage of other people's work is to repeat someone else's study. Since science relies on skepticism, you should repeat studies when you find the study's results hard to believe—especially if those results conflict with results from other studies, seem inconsistent with established theory, or have not been replicated.

***Do a study suggested by a journal article's author(s).***    Almost as simple as replicating a study is doing a study suggested by the article's authors. At the end of many research articles, the authors suggest additional studies that should be done. For example, they may point out that the research should be repeated using a different sample of participants or should be done in a different setting.

## IMPROVE THE STUDY'S EXTERNAL VALIDITY

Even if the researchers don't suggest it, you may decide to test the generality of their findings. For example, you might ask:

Should I redo a study, but include types of participants that were not adequately represented in the original sample? That is, are there reasons to believe that the original study's results would not apply to most people—or to most women or to most members of some other group?

Should I redo a lab study by taking the study outside of the lab into the real world? In other words, is there any important element of real life that was not only left out of the study, but that I think will moderate the relationship found in the original study?

Should I repeat the study using stimulus materials that are more like stimuli that people are exposed to in real life? That is, would it make sense to use less extreme amounts of the treatment or to use more complex and lifelike stimulus materials, such as having participants memorize information from a videotaped lecture rather than having them memorize a list of nonsense syllables?

Are there any other situations I can think of where the relationship between the variables that was observed in the original study may not hold?

## IMPROVE THE STUDY'S INTERNAL VALIDITY

Instead of improving a study's external validity, you may choose to improve its internal validity. As you learned in Chapter 1, establishing that one factor *caused* an effect is very difficult, partly because it is hard to control other factors. For example, Gladue & Delaney (1990) argued that a study (Pennebaker et al., 1979) finding that "girls get prettier at closing time" at bars left unanswered the question of whether time or alcohol consumption was responsible for increased perceptions of attractiveness. Therefore, they modified the original study to control for the effects of alcohol consumption.

Similarly, Frank and Gilovich (1988) found that teams switching to black uniforms get called for more penalties. However, they realized that it would be careless to say that this fact proves that wearing black causes a team to get more penalties. After all, it could be that aggressive coaches like to have their teams wear black. Therefore, as you can see in Appendix F, Frank and Gilovich devised a study that allowed them to make sure that uniform color was the only difference between their teams. Consequently, Frank and Gilovich were able to isolate black as the cause of the aggression effect.

## IMPROVE THE STUDY'S CONSTRUCT VALIDITY

Rather than improving a study's external or internal validity, you may choose to improve a study's construct validity. As you learned in Chapter 1, researchers may not really be measuring and manipulating the psychological constructs they think they are.

One threat to construct validity is participants figuring out what the hypothesis is and then playing along. Thus, when reading a study, you should ask, "If I were a participant, would I know what results the researcher expected?" If your answer to this question is "yes," you may decide to repeat the study but improve it by reducing the biasing effects of participants' expectations. One way to do this is to use the **double-blind technique,** in which neither the participants nor the research assistants who interact with the participants know what treatment the participants are getting. You are probably most familiar with the double-blind technique from studies examining the effects of new drugs. Such studies use the double-blind technique to make sure that a patient's improvement is due to the drug itself rather than to the patient's or physician's belief that the drug will work.

Another common threat to construct validity is that the study used an operational definition of a construct that does not truly reflect the construct. For example, the original study's construct validity may be harmed by poor measures or manipulations. Even when a measure is not poor, it is unlikely that any single measure of a broad construct such as intelligence, aggression, or memory will fully capture the entire construct. Therefore, if the original study finds a relationship between two constructs using one set of operational definitions and then you find the same relationship using different operational definitions, we can be more confident that a relationship really exists between those constructs. To illustrate, suppose a memory researcher finds that rehearsal strategy affects the order in which participants recall information. This finding might lead the researcher to believe that rehearsal strategy affects how information is organized in memory. However, to be more confident that rehearsal strategy affects memory organization, you might decide to repeat the study using a different measure of memory organization. For example, you might use a reaction time measure of organization (such as how much faster participants recognize a key word when they have been primed by exposure to a related word).

## MAP OUT THE FUNCTIONAL RELATIONSHIP

Even if you are satisfied with the original study's validity, the study will still leave many questions unanswered. For example, suppose that a study finds that exercise increases alertness. Although you are satisfied with the study's validity, the study only uses two amounts of exercise (none and one hour a day). As a practical matter, you would like to know the **functional relationship** between exercise and alertness: how much exercise produces what level of alertness. Can you get away with exercising for five minutes or do you need the full hour to get the full effect? Is exercising for two hours much better than exercising for one hour—or is it actually worse?

To answer these questions, it would be helpful to know the shape of the functional relationship between amount of exercise and level of alertness. To map the functional relationship, repeat the study using different amounts of exercise (for specifics, see Chapter 7).

### LOOK FOR PRACTICAL IMPLICATIONS OF THE RESEARCH

If the study involves basic (non-applied) research, determine whether the findings can be applied to a practical situation. For example, can a memory effect demonstrated in the lab be used to help students on academic probation? Similarly, if a study finds that a treatment affects the way people think, you could do a study to see if the same treatment also affects what people actually do. It is one thing to show that a treatment makes participants remember certain information, or stops participants from seeing the victim of a crime as being somehow responsible for his or her fate, or makes participants' brains produce more of a certain kind of chemical. However, it is something else to see that the treatment changes the way participants actually act in real life situations.

### TRY TO RECONCILE STUDIES THAT PRODUCE CONFLICTING RESULTS

When you find studies that produce conflicting results, there is obviously a need to reconcile the apparent contradiction. One strategy for resolving the contradiction is to look for subtle differences in how the studies were conducted. What do the studies that find one pattern of results have in common? What do the studies that find a different pattern have in common? In other words, what is a possible moderator variable?

Answering these questions is a creative and potentially productive task. For example, many studies found a "social facilitation" effect, such that the presence of an audience improved performance. However, many other studies found a "social inhibition" effect, such that the presence of others decreased performance.

Bob Zajonc (Zajonc, 1965; Zajonc & Sales, 1966) looked at all the studies and found how the two sets of studies differed: studies finding social facilitation involved tasks that were easy for participants to do whereas studies finding social inhibition involved tasks that were hard for participants to do. Zajonc then designed several studies where he varied both the presence of others and task difficulty. His results supported the hypothesis that task difficulty was a moderator variable. That is, the effect that other people's presence had on task performance *depended* on how difficult the task was.

## Conclusions about Generating Research Ideas from Previous Research

In conclusion, existing research is a rich source of research ideas. At the very least, you can always just repeat the original study. If you wish to modify the existing study, there are numerous ways you can go. You could improve its internal, construct, or external validity. Or, you may decide to pursue the practical applications of the study. Or, you may try to find situations where the findings would not hold. Or, you could try reconciling a study's findings with a study that obtained very different findings. Or, you could try to map more precisely the relationship between the variables. Or. . . .

Not only does using existing research make it relatively easy to come up with ideas, it also makes it relatively easy to test those ideas. For instance, if you decide to repeat a study, reading the original study will tell you almost everything you need to do. Even if you develop a spin-off study, reading the original article closely will help you figure out how to measure your variables, what to say to your participants, and so forth.

## CONVERTING AN IDEA INTO A RESEARCH HYPOTHESIS

If you used any of the strategies we have discussed thus far, you should have some research ideas. However, you may not have a research hypothesis. Although converting an idea into a workable research hypothesis can be difficult, it is absolutely essential. It is essential because the goal of all research is to test hypotheses.

Admittedly, different types of research may test different kinds of hypotheses. For example, laboratory experiments test causal hypotheses. That is, they try to find out whether a treatment causes a certain effect. Survey research, on the other hand, tries to test descriptive hypotheses. That is, rather than find out why the behavior occurs, survey research tries to focus on who does the behavior, how they do the behavior, or when and where the behavior is done. Thus, a lab experimenter's hypothesis may involve seeing whether a given intervention stops people from cheating, whereas a survey researcher's hypothesis may deal with finding out whether men are more likely to cheat than women. However, despite their differences, both researchers will have hypotheses.

Not only do all researchers have hypotheses, they have their hypotheses before they conduct their research. If they started their research without having a hypothesis to help them know what to look for, it is unlikely that they would have found anything. Consequently, most professors and many ethics committees require you to state the hypothesis you plan to test before they will even consider allowing you to do research. Because having a hypothesis is so important, the rest of this chapter is devoted to helping you generate a workable research hypothesis.

### Make It Testable

When converting an idea into a hypothesis, you must be sure that your hypothesis is testable. In general, a testable hypothesis has the same basic characteristics as a testable theory or a verifiable bet.

As with any bet, you must be able to define your terms. For example, if you bet that, "Gene will be in a bad mood today," you need some publicly observable way of ascertaining what a bad mood is. Similarly, if you hypothesize a relationship between two variables, you must be able to obtain operational definitions of your key variables. For example, if you plan to measure the effects of physical attractiveness on how much a person is liked, you must be able to measure liking objectively, and you must be able to define attractiveness according to publicly observable criteria.

Also, as with any bet, your prediction should be specific so that it is clear what patterns of results would indicate that your hypothesis "won" and what results would indicate that your hypothesis "lost." You do not want to do a study and then have to debate whether the results supported or refuted your hypothesis. Usually the easiest way to avoid such disputes is to make your hypothesis as specific as possible. Therefore, when stating your hypothesis, specify not only a relationship between two or more variables, but also the *direction* of that relationship. Thus, rather than saying aggression will vary with temperature, it would be better to say increases in aggression will correspond to increases in temperature. Ideally, you would be even more specific. For example, you might predict that increasing the temperature from 80 to 90 degrees Fahrenheit will increase aggression more than increasing the temperature from 70 to 80. To check that your prediction is precise enough, ask yourself, "What kind of result would disconfirm my prediction?" and "What kind of result would support my prediction?" Then, graph both of these patterns of results.

By being precise, you can avoid making predictions that are so vague that no pattern of results will disprove them. Unlike some fortune tellers and unscrupulous gamblers, you want to be fair by giving yourself the opportunity to be proven wrong.

Of course, you also want to give yourself the opportunity to be proven right. Consequently, you not only have to beware of making bets you can't lose, but also of bets you can't win.

You must be especially wary of one kind of bet you can never win—trying to prove the **null hypothesis:** a prediction that there is no relationship between your variables. No pattern of results can support the null hypothesis. To illustrate, suppose you hypothesize no relationship between attraction and liking. Even if you find no relationship, you can't say that there isn't a relationship. You can only say that you didn't find the relationship. Failing to find something—whether it be your keys, a murder weapon, a planet, or a relationship between variables—is hardly proof that the thing doesn't exist.

The fact that you can't prove the null hypothesis has two important implications. First, you can't do a study to prove that a treatment has no effect. That is, if you find no difference between your treatment group and no-treatment group, you can't say that your treatment has no effect: You can only say that you failed to find a treatment effect. Second, you can't do a study to prove that two treatments have the same effect. That is, if you find no difference between your two treatment groups, you can't say that the treatments have the same effect: You can only say that you failed to find a difference between them.

## Be Sure to Have a Rationale

In addition to making sure that your hypothesis is testable, you should make sure that you have a solid rationale for your hypothesis. If you can't think of a good reason why your hypothesis should be correct, your hypothesis is probably a "bad bet." For example, if you hypothesized, without giving any rationale, that people would be more creative after drinking seven glasses of water, it is doubtful that your prediction would pan out. Instead, it would appear that you were simply going on a hopeless fishing expedition, with little chance of catching anything. Therefore, always write out the reasons for making your prediction. Your rationale can come from theory, common sense, or the fact that related research has found similar findings.

## Demonstrate Its Relevance

In addition to giving yourself a reasonable chance of proving your hypothesis, you should explain how your research fits in with existing theory and research or how it solves a practical problem. Scientists frown on doing research to find isolated bits of trivia. For example, without any other rationale, doing a study to show that alcohol decreases Ping-Pong performance is meaningless, except possibly to people who bet on Ping-Pong.

## Make Sure that Testing It Is Practical and Ethical

If your hypothesis is testable, reasonable, and relevant, then you should still ask two additional questions. First, can *you* test it? Sometimes, you may not have the skills or the resources to test it. For example, testing some hypotheses in physiological psychology may require equipment or surgical skills that you do not possess. Second, should your hypothesis be tested? That is, can the hypothesis be tested in an ethical manner?

### GET APPROVAL FROM YOUR PROFESSOR

You have a serious obligation to make sure that your study is ethical. Clearly, you do not have the right to physically or psychologically harm another. Reading Appendix A can *help* you decide whether your study can be done in an ethical manner. However, because conducting ethical research is so important, do not make the decision to conduct research without consulting others. Specifically, before doing a study, you and your professor will probably need to have your project reviewed by an ethics committee. In any event, *never conduct a study without your professor's approval!* (See Table 2–5).

## Changing Impractical and Unethical Ideas into Research Hypotheses

In their present form, some of your ideas may be impractical or unethical. However, with a little ingenuity, many of your ideas can be converted into workable

**TABLE 2–5**

**Questions to Ask about a Potential Hypothesis**

1. Can it be proven wrong?
   - Can you obtain operational definitions of the variables?
   - Is the prediction specific?

2. Can it be supported?
   - Are you predicting that you will find an effect or a difference? (Remember, no pattern of results from your study will support the null hypothesis.)

3. Are there logical reasons for expecting the prediction to be correct?
   - Is it predicted by theory?
   - Is it consistent with past research findings?
   - Does it follow from common sense?

4. Would the results of the test of your prediction be relevant to:
   - previous research?
   - existing theory?
   - a practical problem?

5. Is it practical and ethical to test your prediction?
   - Do you have physical and financial resources to test this idea?
   - Would testing the hypothesis cause physical or psychological harm to the participants? (See Appendix A.)
   - Do you have approval from your professor?
   - If your school has a research review board, do you have approval from that board?

research hypotheses. Basically, many practical and ethical obstacles can be overcome by making the key variables more abstract, constructing a smaller scale model of the situation, toning down the strength of the manipulation, not using manipulations, or finding ways to operationalize the crucial variables.

To understand how these principles can turn even the most impractical and unethical idea into a viable research hypothesis, consider the following hypothesis: Receiving severe beatings causes one to be a murderer. How could we convert this idea into a workable research hypothesis?

### MAKE VARIABLES MORE GENERAL

One possibility is to make your key variables more abstract. That is, you might view murder as a more specific instance of *aggression.* Similarly, you might view beating as a specific instance of either aggression, pain, or punishment. Thus, you now have three research hypotheses that have been studied in controlled settings: "aggression leads to more aggression"; "pain causes aggression"; and "punishment causes aggression."

### USE SMALLER SCALE MODELS OF THE SITUATION

Of course, you are not going to have human participants hitting each other to measure aggression. Instead, you may give participants an opportunity to destroy something that supposedly belongs to the target of their anger, an opportunity to write a negative evaluation, an opportunity to press a button that supposedly—but doesn't really—delivers a mild shock to another person, etc. As you can imagine, working with a small scale model of aggressive situations is more ethical than manipulating real-life aggression.

Smaller scale models of the situation have not only ethical, but practical, advantages. For example, if you are interested in the effects of temperature on aggression, you can't manipulate the temperature outside. However, you can manipulate the temperature in a room. Similarly, you can't manipulate the size of a crowd at a college football game to see the effect of crowd size on performance. However, you can manipulate audience size at a dart contest that you sponsor. By using a dart contest, testing your audience-size hypothesis is not only possible, but also practical. For instance, if audience size has an effect, you could probably find it by varying the size of the audience from zero (when you are hiding behind a one-way mirror) to three (yourself and two friends).

Once you have a small scale model of a phenomenon, you can test all kinds of ideas that previously seemed impossible to test. For example, can you imagine using the dart contest situation to test the effects of audience involvement or size of reward on performance?

Because smaller scale models of situations are so valuable, researchers often do a literature review to find out if someone else has already made a smaller scale model of the phenomenon they wish to study. That is, just as an airplane designer may use a wind tunnel to test new airplane designs, researchers may use someone else's scale model of a situation to see if their ideas fly.

## CAREFULLY SCREEN POTENTIAL PARTICIPANTS

In some research, you might decrease the ethical problems by choosing participants who would be unlikely to be harmed by the manipulation. Therefore, if you were to do a frustration-aggression study, you might only use participants who:

1. were, according to a recently administered personality profile, well-adjusted;
2. were physically healthy;
3. volunteered after knowing about the degree of discomfort they would experience;
4. were fully aware that they could withdraw from the study at any time without any penalty.

## USE "MODERATE" MANIPULATIONS

Not only can you limit who will be in the study, you can also limit how much of the manipulation you use. By reducing the extent to which you use unpleasant stimuli, you reduce the harm to participants. Thus, if you were to induce frustration to see its effects on aggression, you might decide not to use a very high level of frustration. Even though a high level of frustration would be more likely to produce aggression, you might decide to use lower levels of frustration to lower the risks of harming your participants.

### DO NOT MANIPULATE VARIABLES

Finally, you may decide not to manipulate the variables at all. To understand the basic advantages and disadvantages of this approach, let's return to the original hypothesis: Receiving severe beatings causes one to be a murderer. You might pursue this idea by interviewing murderers and non-murderers to see whether murderers were more likely to have been beaten as children. Unfortunately, even if you found that murderers were more likely than non-murderers to have been beaten, your results would not necessarily mean that the beatings caused the murders. Beatings may have no impact on murders. Instead, murderers may have been beaten more than non-murderers because, even when they were younger, murderers were more aggressive and more disobedient than non-murderers. Although interviewing wouldn't allow you to discover whether beatings *cause* children to become murderers, it might allow you to address a related research hypothesis: "Are murderers more likely to be beaten by their parents than non-murderers?" [1]

## CONCLUDING REMARKS

In this chapter, you have learned how to generate research ideas from common sense, theory, and previous research. Consequently, if you spend a little time reviewing this chapter, you should be able to generate several hypotheses about how two or more variables are related. Once you have those ideas, you may want to test them. However, before you can test those ideas, you must find a way to obtain or generate operational definitions of your variables. Chapter 3 will help you do that.

---

[1] Unfortunately, even answering this question is difficult because murderers may exaggerate the extent to which they were beaten.

## SUMMARY

1. The purpose of scientific research is to test ideas. Thus, one way to get research ideas is to test commonsense ideas.

2. Like common sense, theories are good sources of ideas. Unlike common sense, theories are formally stated and internally consistent.

3. A theory, unlike a law, is not a documented fact. Consequently, theories may be disproven.

4. Hypothetical constructs are abstract variables that cannot be directly observed (love, learning, thirst, etc.). Researchers can deal with abstract constructs by devising "recipes" for these variables called *operational definitions:* concrete ways of manipulating or measuring abstract constructs.

5. Testable theories make specific predictions and have variables that can be operationalized.

6. You can generate hypotheses from a theory by testing the theory's core assumptions, applying the theory to novel or practical situations, or comparing two theories that make opposing predictions.

7. Scientists prefer theories that are broad in scope, parsimonious, and make counter-intuitive predictions.

8. Theories evolve and change as a result of adapting to new findings.

9. Building on other people's research is an easy way to get good research ideas.

10. Strategies for developing research ideas from previous research include: improving the original study's external, internal, or construct validity; repeating the study; seeing if the finding has any practical implications; and trying to determine why two studies produced conflicting findings.

11. You can sometimes improve a study's construct validity by using the double-blind technique.

12. Never do a study without first getting your professor's permission.

13. The null hypothesis is that there is no relationship between two variables. While it can be disproven, it can't be proven.

14. A research hypothesis must be testable and must be testable in an ethical manner.

15. Even the most impractical and unethical of ideas may be converted into a practical and ethical hypothesis if you carefully screen your participants, use a small scale model of the phenomenon you wish to study, make key variables more general or abstract, tone down the intensity of your manipulation, or don't use manipulations.

## KEY TERMS

**constructs:** entities that we cannot, with our present technology, observe directly. We can only infer constructs from participants' behavior. Hunger, happiness, and learning are all hypothetical constructs. (p. 49)

**operational definitions:** publicly observable set of procedures (operations) to manipulate or measure a construct. (p. 48)

**double-blind technique:** a strategy for improving construct validity that involves making sure that neither the participant nor the researcher who has direct contact with the participant knows what treatment the participant has received. (p. 57)

**functional relationship:** the shape of the relationship between variables. (p. 57)

**law:** a strong, consistent, documented relationship between two or more variables. (p. 45)

**null hypothesis:** a prediction that there is no relationship between your variables. (p. 60)

**hypothesis:** a testable prediction about the relationship between two or more variables. Unlike laws, hypotheses are not facts. (p. 45)

**theory:** an integrated set of principles that explain facts and from which a large number of *new* observations can be deduced. (p. 44)

**deduction:** applying a general rule to a specific situation. When you apply a theory to a specific situation, your deduction may be a hypothesis. (p. 50)

**parsimonious:** explaining a broad range of phenomena with a few principles. A good theory is parsimonious. (p. 46)

**straw theory:** an exaggerated or oversimplified view of the real theory. Some people claim to be attacking a theory when they are actually attacking a straw version of that theory. (p. 49)

**critical experiment:** a study that sets up a contest between two competing theories to try to settle the question of which theory's view of the world is more accurate. (p. 53)

**mediating variable:** when a stimulus causes a response, it does so by changing something inside the organism (such as a person's thoughts, feelings, or physiological reactions). In other words, the stimulus has its effect because it causes changes mediating variables, which, in turn, cause changes in behavior. Because knowing the mediating variables leads to understanding how a stimulus causes an effect, researchers are often interested in tracking down mediating variables. For example, not only have researchers found that smelling a certain fragrance (stimulus) improves performance on a task (response), but they have also tried to find the underlying mechanisms (the mediating variables) responsible for the fragrance's effect. Some have used brain imaging techniques to look for physiological mediators; others have used questionnaires to try to see if the fragrance has its effect on behavior by changing mood. (p. 53)

**moderator variables:** variables that can intensify, weaken, or reverse the effects of another variable. For example, the effect of wearing perfume may be moderated by gender: If you are a woman, wearing perfume may make you more liked; if you are a man, wearing perfume may make you less liked. (p. 51)

## EXERCISES

1. Look up a research study that tests a commonsense notion or proverb. What is the title of the article? What are its main conclusions?
2. Generate a research idea based on testing a commonsense notion.
3. How are the qualities of a good theory similar to the qualities of a good answer to an essay test?
4. Is theory or intuition more valuable in generating useful research? Support your conclusions by listing the strengths and weaknesses of each.
5. Why do scientists like theories?
6. What is the difference between a theory and a law?
7. Does psychology have more theories or more laws? Why?
8. What is the difference between a theory and a hypothesis? Are there more theories or more hypotheses? Why?
9. Why should a theory be testable?
10. What qualities make a theory testable? How do those same qualities make the theory useful?
11. List at least three ways to use a theory to generate research ideas.
12. Find a research article that tests a hypothesis derived from theory. Give the citation for the article and describe the main findings.
13. Evaluate sociobiology according to the text's criteria for a good theory.
14. Evaluate psychoanalysis according to the text's criteria for a good theory.
15. Evaluate astrology according to the text's criteria for a good theory.
16. Derive a research hypothesis from a theory. Theories you might use would include: Bandura's social learning theory, Skinner's theory of operant conditioning, Solomon's opponent process theory, learned helplessness theory, Piaget's theory, dual memory theory, cognitive dissonance theory, attribution theory, equity theory, reactance theory, or sociobiology.
17. What similarities are there between getting ideas from theory and getting ideas from existing research?
18. Design a study to improve the construct validity of the study reported in Appendix F.
19. Design a study to test the generalizability of the findings of the study reported in Appendix F.

20. The study reported in Appendix F finds a relationship between two variables. Design a study to map out the functional relationship between those two variables.

21. Design a study to test the practical implications of the findings from the study reported in Appendix F.

22. Generate five research ideas that are spin-offs of published research.

23. In terms of the null hypothesis, discuss what is wrong with the following research conclusions:

    - There is no difference in outcome among the different psychological therapies;
    - There is no difference in effectiveness between generic and brand name drugs;
    - Viewing television violence is not related to aggression;
    - Nutrasweet ® has no side effects;
    - There are no gender differences in emotional responsiveness.

# CHAPTER 3

---

# Measuring and Manipulating Variables

*Overview*

*Measurement*

WHERE OBSERVERS CAN GO WRONG
MINIMIZING OBSERVER ERRORS
ERRORS IN ADMINISTERING THE MEASURE
ERRORS DUE TO THE PARTICIPANT
RELIABILITY
BEYOND RELIABILITY: ESTABLISHING CONSTRUCT VALIDITY

*Manipulating Variables*

COMMON THREATS TO A MANIPULATION'S VALIDITY
EVIDENCE USED TO ARGUE FOR VALIDITY
TRADEOFFS AMONG THREE COMMON TYPES OF MANIPULATIONS
MANIPULATING VARIABLES: A SUMMARY

*Concluding Remarks*

*Summary*

*Key Terms*

*Exercises*

# Chapter 3

## MEASURING AND MANIPULATING VARIABLES

*"Science begins with measurement."*

—LORD KELVIN

### OVERVIEW

In the last chapter, you learned how to generate ideas about how two or more variables are related. But before you can test any of your ideas about those variables, you must generate **operational definitions** of those variables. For example, if you wanted to test the idea that "bliss causes ignorance," you would first have to define the vague, general, abstract, and invisible concepts "ignorance" and "bliss" in a clear, specific, concrete, and visible way. That is, you must spell out the exact procedures you would follow to create "bliss" and the exact procedures you would follow to measure "ignorance."

Operational definitions, because they are concrete recipes for your variables, allow you to do two things. First, they allow you to talk about your variables in concrete, specific, objective terms rather than in abstract, vague, poetic, subjective terms. That is, rather than saying, "My opinion is that they are happy," you can say, "They scored 94 on the happiness scale." By letting you talk about facts rather than opinions, operational definitions make it possible for you to test your hypothesis objectively. Second, by being specific and public, operational definitions allow others to repeat your study. Thus, operational definitions allow other scientists to check on, as well as build on, your research.

In short, to be a science, a field must produce publicly observable facts. Consequently, the science of psychology depends on psychologists being able to develop publicly observable ways to measure and manipulate variables.

Most people correctly believe that the ability of psychology to be a science depends on the ability of psychologists to measure psychological variables objectively and accurately. Unfortunately, most people also believe one of two myths about measuring psychological variables. Some people believe that psychological variables cannot be measured. These people think that psychology is not—and cannot—be a science. On the other hand, some people believe that psychological variables are easy to measure. People believing this myth believe that anyone who says they are measuring a psychological variable is really doing so. These gullible people are unable to distinguish between pseudo-scientific claims and scientific claims.

The truth is that measuring and manipulating psychological variables is not easy. However, measuring constructs as abstract and as subjective as love, motivation, shyness, religious devotion, or attention span is not impossible. Indeed, by the end of this chapter, you will not only know how to develop operational definitions of such abstract concepts, but also how to determine whether such operational definitions have a high degree of construct validity.

## MEASUREMENT

Although we might like to see abstract, invisible constructs like love, we cannot. However, we can see behavior. Thus, if we are to measure a variable objectively, we must measure behavior.

But what behavior should we observe? We need to choose a behavior that, according to theory, past research, or intuition, is an indicator of the concept we are trying to measure. Usually, operational definitions will involve measuring one of the following four types of behavior:

1. Verbal behavior: What participants say, write, rate, or report.
2. Overt actions: What participants do.
3. Nonverbal behavior: Participants' body language.
4. Physiological responses: Brain wave activity, heart rate, blood pressure, sweating, pupil dilation, etc.

### Where Observers Can Go Wrong

Fortunately, all these behaviors can be measured accurately. Unfortunately, just because a behavior can be measured accurately, doesn't mean that it will be measured accurately. When people observe, score, and record behavior, they tend to make two types of mistakes.

#### OBSERVER BIAS

The first, and by far the most serious, mistake is that people's subjective biases may prevent them from making objective observations. In other words, a measure of behavior may be victimized by **observer bias:** observers recording what they expect participants will do rather than what participants are actually doing. For example, after participants go through a "stop smoking" program, observers might become less likely to record that a participant was smoking. That is, before the "stop smoking" program, taking one puff from a cigarette might have been counted as smoking an entire cigarette, but now "only one puff" is not considered smoking. In such a case, observer bias would be systematically pushing cigarette smoking scores in a given *direction*—down. By decreasing the average smoking score, observer bias may lead us to believe that a smoking prevention program worked, even if it did not.

If we can't control observer bias, we can't do scientific research. After all, there is no point in doing a study if, regardless of what actually happens, you are just going to "see" the results you expect to see.

### RANDOM OBSERVER ERROR

The second type of mistake that people make in scoring behavior is caused by carelessness. These unsystematic, random mistakes will erratically increase some scores while decreasing others. Thus, unlike observer bias, *random observer error* may not change a group's overall, average score. However, random observer error does cause individual measurements to be less accurate than they would otherwise be.

## Minimizing Observer Errors

To get accurate information from our measures, we would like to reduce the influence of both observer bias and random observer error. However, it is more important for us to reduce observer bias than to reduce random error. To understand why observer bias is more of a problem than random error, let's consider two error-prone basketball referees. The first makes many random errors, the other is biased. Which would you want to referee your team's big game?

Your first reaction might be to say, "Neither!" After all, the referee who makes many random errors is aggravating. Who wants an inattentive, inconsistent, and generally incompetent ref? However, in the course of a game, those random errors will tend to balance out. Consequently, neither team will be given a significant advantage. On the other hand, a referee who is biased against your team will consistently give the opponent a several point advantage. Thus, if you had to choose between the two error-prone officials, which one would you pick? Most of us would pick the one who made many random errors over the one who was biased against us.

### REDUCING OBSERVER BIAS

Often, we don't have to choose between minimizing random error and minimizing observer bias because the steps that reduce observer bias also tend to reduce random observer error. For example, one way to eliminate observer bias is to replace human observers with scientific recording devices. Obviously, eliminating the observer eliminates both bias due to the observer and random error due to the observer.

If you can't eliminate observer bias and random observer error by eliminating the observer, you may still be able to limit observer bias and random

**TABLE 3–1**

**Techniques That Reduce Both Random Observer Error and Observer Bias**

**1.** Use machines (such as computers and automatic counters) rather than humans to observe and record behavior.

**2.** Simplify the observer's task by:

    **a.** using objective measures, such as multiple-choice tests rather than essay tests.

    **b.** replacing tasks that require observers to judge a behavior's intensity with tasks that merely ask observers to count how many times the behavior occurs.

    **c.** reducing the possibility for memory errors by making it very easy to immediately record their observations. For example, give your observers checklists so they can check off a behavior when it occurs, or counters that observers can click every time a behavior occurs.

**3.** Tell observers that they are to record and judge observable behavior rather than invisible psychological states.

**4.** Photograph, tape record, or videotape each participant's behavior so that observers can re-check their original observations.

**5.** Carefully define your categories so that all observations will be interpreted according to a consistent, uniform set of criteria.

**6.** Train raters and motivate them to be accurate.

**7.** Use only those raters who were consistent during training.

observer error by limiting the observer's role. For instance, rather than having observers interpret participants' answers to essay questions, you could limit the observer's role to recording participants' answers to multiple-choice questions.

As you might imagine, almost any time you make the observer's job easier, you reduce both observer bias and random observer error. Thus, if you follow the tips in Table 3–1 for making the observer's job easier, your measure will be less vulnerable to both observer bias and random observer error.

Although Table 3–1 includes a wide variety of strategies that will help reduce observer bias, those tactics may not eliminate observer bias. To understand why they won't, suppose you were having observers judge essays to determine whether males or females used more "aggressive" words. Even if you conducted a thorough training program for your raters, the raters might be biased if they knew whether the writer was a male or a female. Therefore, instead of letting your raters know whether an essay was written by a male or female, you should consider making your raters **blind:** unaware of the participant's characteristics and situation.

In essence, the tactics you would use to reduce observer bias are the same tactics a professor would use to avoid favoritism in grading. The professor who is concerned with avoiding favoritism in grading would certainly not determine students' grades solely by sitting down at the end of term and trying to recall the quality of each student's class participation. Instead, a professor who was solely concerned with avoiding favoritism would give multiple-choice tests that were computer-scored. If the favoritism-conscious professor were to give an essay exam, the professor would establish clear-cut criteria for scoring the essays, follow those criteria to the letter, and not look at students' names while grading the papers.

### REDUCING RANDOM OBSERVER ERROR

Making observers blind will reduce observer bias, but it will not eliminate random observer error. Blind observers can still be careless, inattentive, forgetful, or inconsistent about how they interpret behavior. For example, suppose a history professor grades 100 essay exams over the weekend. Even if the professor grades all those exams "blind," the professor's scoring may not be perfectly consistent from test to test: The amount of partial credit for a certain answer may change from hour to hour and errors may be made in totaling up all the points. Nevertheless, almost every step that you take to reduce observer bias will also tend to reduce random observer error.

## Errors in Administering the Measure

By using blind procedures and by eliminating or reducing the observer's role, you can reduce the amount of measurement error that is due to observers making mistakes when they score participants' behaviors. However, not all errors in measurement are due to the scorer. Some errors are also made in administering the measure. As was the case with scoring, there are two kinds of errors that people can make in administering the measure: bias and random error.

When you administer the measure, you hope to avoid introducing either bias or random error. However, to avoid both these errors completely, you would have to keep all of the factors that influence a participant's response constant. For example, if you were administering an IQ test, you would have to keep everything—the noise level, lighting, your instructions to participants, your facial expressions, voice inflections, and gestures—the same.

Keeping all these factors perfectly constant would be impossible. However, most researchers strive for a high level of **standardization:** treating each participant in the same (standard) way. Thus, you should try to test all your participants in the same soundproof, temperature-controlled setting. Furthermore, you should write out a detailed description of how you are going to test your participants and then you should stick to those procedures. For example, you might write down whatever instructions you were going to give participants and then read those instructions to every single participant. To further standardize procedures, you might put instructions and measures in a booklet, or you might even have a computer administer the measure.

Because perfect standardization is usually impossible, there will be some error in measurement due to imperfect standardization. If we must have error, we would prefer that this error be random error rather than bias. For example, it would be disastrous if the researcher was more attentive and enthusiastic when administering the test to the treatment group than to the no-treatment group. To avoid such biases, you should try to keep the person who administers the measure "blind." For example, you might have one researcher who administers the treatment and a second researcher—who is blind to what the first researcher did—administer the measure.

## Errors Due to the Participant

To this point, we have focused on two sources of measurement error: errors made by the person administering the measure and errors made by the person scoring the measure. We will now turn to a third source of both random error and bias—the participant. In other words, we will now discuss two reasons why participants may produce responses that don't reflect their true behavior or feelings.

### RANDOM PARTICIPANT ERROR

First, participants themselves are not perfectly consistent. Their behavior is variable. Some of this variability is random. Thus, one moment they may perform very well, the next moment they may perform very poorly. For example, participants may misread questions, lose their concentration, make lucky guesses, or make unlucky guesses. One way to overcome this random variability in participants' behavior is to get a large sample of their behavior. Thus, if you wanted to know how good a free throw shooter someone was, you wouldn't judge her based on two shots. Similarly, if you wanted to know how outgoing she was, you wouldn't base your conclusion on a two-item test. Instead, you might use a 50-item test so that random participant error would tend to balance out. In addition to giving random error more opportunities to balance out, you should also try to reduce random error. For example, refining your measure so that participants will be less likely to misunderstand questions would also make participants' responses less affected by random error.

### SUBJECT BIAS

The second, and more troublesome, reason why participants' actions may not reflect their true behavior is because participants' responses may be biased. That is, participants may change their behavior because they are being observed.

One of the earliest documented examples of the problem of participants reacting to being watched was the case of Clever Hans, the mathematical horse (Pfungst, 1911). Hans would answer mathematical problems by tapping his hoof the correct number of times. For example, if Hans' owner asked Hans what 3 times 3 was, Hans would tap his hoof 9 times. Hans' secret was that he would watch his owner. His owner would stop looking at Hans' feet when Hans had reached the right answer. Thus, although people interpreted Hans' hoof-tapping as evidence that Hans was mentally performing mathematical calculations, hoof-tapping really only meant that Hans was watching and reacting to his owner's gaze.

If animals can produce the "right" answer when they know what you are measuring, so can humans. In fact, for humans, there are two kinds of "right" (biased) responses.

***Social Desirability Bias.***    The first kind is the **socially desirable response:** answers that make the participant look good. Participants are quite willing to give socially desirable responses. For example, many studies have shown that people claim to be much more helpful (Latané, 1970) and less conforming (Milgram, 1974) than they really are. On most questionnaires, it is easy for participants to check the answer that makes them look good.

***Obeying Demand Characteristics.***    The second kind of "right" answer is the one that makes you, the researcher, look good by ensuring that your hypothesis is supported. Martin Orne (1962) believes that participants are very willing to give researchers whatever results the researcher wants. In fact, participants are so eager to please that they look for clues as to how the researcher wants them to behave. That is, participants look for hints about what the hypothesis is. According to Orne, if a participant finds a hint, the participant will follow that hint as surely as if the researcher had *demanded* that the participant follow the hint. Therefore, Orne refers to such hints as **demand characteristics.**

To see how demand characteristics might affect the results of a study, suppose you have participants rate how much they love their partner. Next, you give them fake feedback, supposedly from their partner, showing that their partner loves them intensely. Finally, you have participants rate how much they love their partner a second time. In this study, participants may realize that they are supposed to rate their love higher the second time. Therefore, if participants reported that they loved their partner more the second time, you would not know whether learning about their partner's devotion increased love or whether participants merely obeyed the study's demand characteristics.

How did participants know what you wanted them to do? Your measure made it obvious that you were measuring love. Once participants knew that you were measuring love, they were able to guess why you showed them their partners' ratings. You gave them all the clues they needed to figure out what you would consider a "good" response.

## REDUCING SUBJECT BIAS

Fortunately, you do not have to make it so easy for participants to figure out what you are measuring and then act accordingly (see Box 3-1). Specifically, you could make it harder for participants to fake their responses by:

1. Not letting participants know that you are observing them.
2. Letting participants know that you are observing them, but not letting them know what particular behavior you are observing.

## Box 3–1
## WAYS TO AVOID SUBJECT BIASES WHEN MEASURING LOVE

| Technique | Example |
| --- | --- |
| Measure participants in non-research settings | Observe hand-holding in the college cafeteria. |
| Unobtrusive observation | Observe hand-holding in the lab through a one-way mirror. |
| Unobtrusive measures (nonverbal) | Observe how much time partners spend gazing into each other's eyes. |
| Unobtrusive measures (physical traces) | Measure how close together the couple sat by measuring the distance between their chairs. |
| "Unexpected Measures" | Asking participant to repair the damage "caused" by his/her partner. |
| Disguised Measures | Asking participants to rate themselves and their partners on several characteristics. Then, inferring love from the extent to which they rate their partner as being similar to themselves. |
| Physiological Responses | Measure pupil dilation and blood pressure to see if they increase when their partner comes into the room. |
| Important Behavior | See if the participant passes up the opportunity to date a very attractive person. |

3. Letting participants know what behavior you are interested in, but not letting them know what construct the behavior is designed to measure.
4. Choosing a response that most participants couldn't or wouldn't change.

## Reliability

We have discussed three major sources of measurement error: errors due to the person scoring the measure, errors due to the person administering the measure, and errors due to the participant. We have also stressed that there are two types of measurement error: random error and systematic bias (see Figure 3–1).

**Figure 3–1**

## Sources and Types of Measurement Error

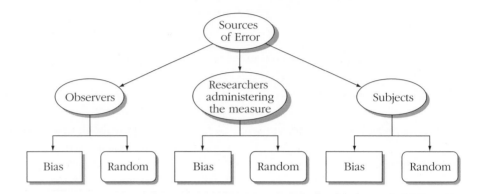

In the next section, we will discuss how to determine whether scores on your measure are too strongly influenced by random error.

But before discussing how to select a measure that is relatively free of random error, we should first be clear about why you want a measure that is free from random error. That is, why do you want a measure that is **reliable:** producing stable, consistent scores because it is not strongly influenced by random error?

The reason you want reliability is easy to understand. You think you are measuring some stable trait. You assume that a person's traits, such as intelligence, shyness, and height, don't change from minute to minute. Therefore, if you measure the same person at two different times, you should get basically the same results each time. If you don't get the same results each time, then you know that your measurements are being affected by something other than the stable trait that you are trying to tap. Specifically, your measurements are probably being affected by random error.

Clearly, you don't want your measurements to be wildly bounced around by the erratic winds of chance. Consequently, when deciding whether to use a measure, you want to know whether it is strongly contaminated by chance.

### ASSESSING OVERALL RELIABILITY

To find out to what extent your measurements are affected by random error, you should find out the measure's reliability. Perhaps the most straightforward way to find out the degree to which the measure produces consistent results is to obtain its **test-retest reliability.**

As the name suggests, test-retest reliability requires participants to be tested and then retested. The test-retest coefficient is based on how well participants' scores on the first measurement correspond to their scores on the second measurement. Usually, test-retest coefficients range between +.30 (poor reliability) to .98 (excellent reliability). However, it is conceivable to get any number from 0.00 to +1.00.[1]

A test-retest coefficient of zero would mean that there was absolutely no relationship between scores participants received the first time they took the test and the scores they received when they were retested. A coefficient of 1.00, on the other hand, would mean that there was a perfect correspondence between the first and second time of measurement—all those who scored high the first time also scored high the second time.

If you are examining a previously published measure, the test-retest reliability coefficient may have already been calculated for you. The measure's test-retest reliability coefficient may be cited in the original researcher report, in the test's manual, in *Mental Measurements Yearbook* (Kramer & Conoley, 1992), in *Test Critiques* (Keyser & Sweetland, 1984), in *Tests in Print* (Mitchell, 1983), or in *Directory of Unpublished Experimental Mental Measures* (Goldman & Mitchell, 1990). Normally, you would not choose a measure that had a test-retest reliability coefficient below .70.[2]

## ASSESSING OBSERVER RELIABILITY

What if your measure's reliability is below .70? Your measure's unreliability would have to be due to at least one of the following three sources:

1. Random error due to the observers.
2. Random error due to the way the measure is administered.
3. Random error due to the participant.

It would be nice if we could know how much of measure's unreliability is due to each of these sources. If we knew the source of a measure's unreliability, we might then be able to fix the problem at the source. Unfortunately, it is usually not easy to determine the source of a measure's unreliability. However, we can determine how much of the random error is due to the observer.

We can estimate how much of the random error is due to the observer by assuming that if two trained raters score the same behavior differently, they are doing so because of random error. For example, one is not noticing something

---

[1] The test-retest reliability coefficient is usually not a correlation coefficient. If it were, it could range from −1 to +1. However, it is usually the square of the test-retest reliability correlation (Anastasi, 1982). This squared term represents the percentage of variation that is *not* due to random error.

[2] Normally, the test-retest correlation is a square of the test-retest correlation coefficient. Since squaring the test-retest correlation gives the percentage of variation in scores that is *not* due to random observer error, a test-retest reliability coefficient of .70 means that 30% of the variation in scores is due to random error. A test-retest reliability coefficient below .70 would mean that more than 30% of the variation in scores was due to random error.

**FIGURE 3–2**

### Graph of How Rater 1's Ratings of Six Participants Might Relate to How Rater 2 Rated the Same Six Participants

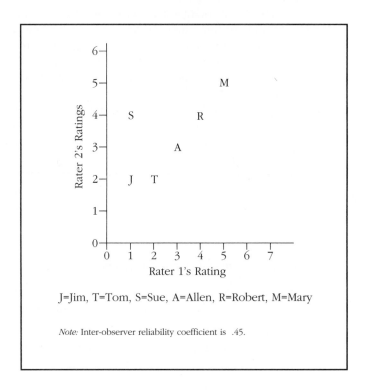

J=Jim, T=Tom, S=Sue, A=Allen, R=Robert, M=Mary

*Note:* Inter-observer reliability coefficient is .45.

important, one is forgetting something, one is guessing about which category to put the behavior in, or one is misreading the timer. Therefore, researchers often provide evidence of how reliable observers are by having two or more observers *independently* (without talking to one another) rate the same behaviors. The researchers would then compare how different raters judged the same behavior (see Figure 3-2). To express the extent to which observers agree, researchers use one of two indexes: inter-judge agreement and inter-observer reliability.

Sometimes, the researchers will simply report **inter-judge agreement:** the percentage of times the raters agree. For example, the researchers might report that the raters agreed 98% of the time.

Often, researchers will report another index of the degree to which different raters give similar ratings: **inter-observer reliability.** To obtain inter-observer reliability, researchers calculate a correlation coefficient between

FIGURE 3–3

### Graph Indicating a Near Zero Inter-Rater Reliability Coefficient between Rater 1's Ratings of Six Participants and Rater 2's Ratings of the Same Six Participants

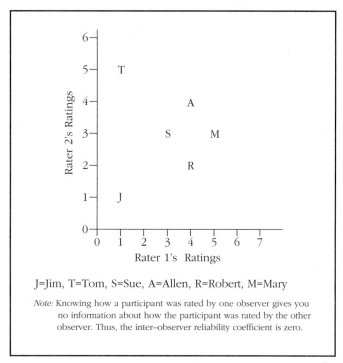

J=Jim, T=Tom, S=Sue, A=Allen, R=Robert, M=Mary

*Note:* Knowing how a participant was rated by one observer gives you no information about how the participant was rated by the other observer. Thus, the inter–observer reliability coefficient is zero.

the different rater's judgments of the same behaviors and then square that correlation.[3]

Like overall reliability coefficients, inter-observer reliability coefficients can range from 0 to +1. An inter-observer reliability coefficient around zero (0.00 to +.20) indicates that there is virtually no relationship between the observers'

---

[3] There are two main reasons for squaring the correlation coefficient. First, it allows researchers to directly compare observer reliability with the test-retest reliability (which is also a squared correlation coefficient). Second, squaring the correlation coefficient gives the percentage of variation in scores that is *not* due to random observer error. That is, subtracting these coefficients from 100% gives you the percentage of variation that is due to random error. Thus, inter-observer reliability of .80 tells you that 20% of the variation in scores is due to random observer error (100 − 80 = 20). Similarly, if you also know that test-retest reliability coefficient is .70, you realize that 30% of the total variations in scores are due to random error (100 − 70 = 30). Thus, without doing any sophisticated calculations, you realize that 2/3 (20%/30%) of the measure's unreliability is due to random observer error. Therefore, you would know that if you could substantially reduce random observer error, the measure would be fairly reliable.

FIGURE 3-4

**Graph Indicating a High Inter-Rater Reliability
Coefficient between Rater 1's Ratings of Six Participants
and Rater 2's Ratings of the Same Six Participants**

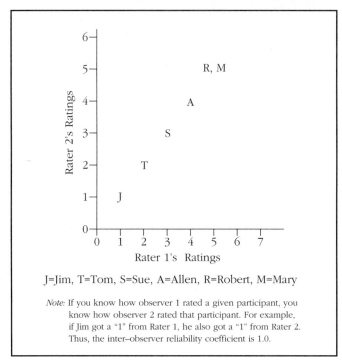

J=Jim, T=Tom, S=Sue, A=Allen, R=Robert, M=Mary

*Note:* If you know how observer 1 rated a given participant, you
know how observer 2 rated that participant. For example,
if Jim got a "1" from Rater 1, he also got a "1" from Rater 2.
Thus, the inter–observer reliability coefficient is 1.0.

ratings. Knowing how one observer rated a behavior gives you almost no idea about how the other observer rated the same behavior (see Figure 3-3).

Since observers usually agree to some extent, and since journals usually require a high degree of inter-rater reliability, you will almost never see a published study that includes an inter-observer reliability coefficient below + .6. Therefore, when reading a study, your question will not be: "Did the observers agree?" but "To what extent did the observers agree?" Generally, you will expect inter-observer reliability coefficients of around .90 (see Figure 3-4).

**ASSESSING RANDOM ERROR DUE TO THE PARTICIPANT**

Although it is relatively easy to assess observer reliability, it is difficult to assess how much random error is due to the participant. However, for tests, scales, and surveys that can be objectively scored, there is a way to get a rough index of the amount of random error due to the participant.

How can we do this? The key is to assume that each question on the test is measuring the same thing. For example, all questions on a shyness test are measuring shyness, and all questions of an IQ test are measuring IQ. If this assumption is correct, people who score shy on one question should score shy on all the other questions. Similarly, if a person does well on one IQ test question, he should do well on other IQ test questions. But what if he doesn't?

One possibility is that the person is being careless or inconsistent in how he answers the questions. Possibly, the inconsistency is due to random fluctuations in how the person thinks or feels. More often, the inconsistency is due to the person guessing at the answers or misreading some of the questions. Guessing and misreading questions are particularly likely if the test is long and the questions are not carefully worded.

Another reason that people may respond differently to the questions is that the questions are not all measuring the same thing. One way to correct this problem is to revise the test by eliminating the "bad" questions. For example, suppose that on a class exam, most of the people who did well on the exam got a certain question wrong, whereas the students who did poorly on the exam got that question right. The teacher would probably decide that there was something wrong either with that question or with how that question was scored. Thus, the teacher would be less likely to use that question in future tests. Put another way, each question can be viewed as a judge of whether participants have a certain characteristic. If one judge's scores are far apart from everyone else's, we would doubt that judge's competence. We might ask, "Was he watching the same thing everybody else was?" Similarly, if the scores that participants get from certain questions don't correspond with the scores participants get from the rest of the test, we doubt the value of those questions. Typically, researchers will throw out or rephrase the "deviant" questions, hoping to end up with a scale that has a high degree of **internal consistency:** the degree to which each item (question) correlates with the overall test score.

How do researchers establish that their measure is internally consistent? They use a wide range of indexes, but all of these indexes are designed to measure the degree to which answers to one item of the test correspond to answers given to other items on the test. As the name suggests, the *average inter-item correlation* is a very direct measure of the extent to which answers to one test item correlate with answers to other test items. Other indexes, such as the *split half correlation,* where participants' scores on one half of the test are correlated with their scores on the other half of the test, are less direct. However, regardless of whether researchers report inter-item correlations, Cronbach's alpha, split-half reliabilities, or Kuder-Richardson reliabilities, they are telling you the extent to which their measure is internally consistent.

Internal consistency seems like a good idea if you are measuring a simple construct that has only one dimension. But what if you are measuring a complex construct that you think has two separate aspects? For example, suppose you want to measure love and you think that love has two different dimensions (sexual attraction and willingness to sacrifice for the other). Furthermore, you believe that these dimensions are relatively independent. That is, you believe that a person could be high on sexual attraction, but low on willingness to sacrifice. In such a case, you don't expect a high level of internal consistency because you are measuring two different things.

One solution would be to make up a love scale that had two different subscales. You would then hope that the measure *as a whole* had a low degree of internal consistency, but that each of the individual subscales had a high degree of internal consistency. That is, all the responses to items related to sexual attraction should correlate with one another, and all the responses to items related to sacrifice should correlate with one another. However, the sexual attraction items should not correlate highly with the sacrifice items.

A more sophisticated solution—and one that is often reported in journals—is to do a factor analysis (Reis & Stiller, 1992). We can define **factor analysis** as a statistical technique designed to divide the many questions on a test into as few coherent groups as possible. Put another way, rather than explaining how participants answer the test by talking about how participants answer each individual question, factor analysis tries to explain participants' patterns of answers in terms of a smaller number of underlying hypothetical factors.

The logic behind factor analysis is fairly straightforward. We assume that if participants' answers to one group of questions correlate with each other, then those questions all measure the same factor. For example, imagine that we have a 10-item test. In that test, participants answered the first six questions similarly: If we know how they answered one of those questions, we can make a reasonable prediction about how they answered the other five. Similarly, their responses to the last four items were highly correlated. However, their responses to the first six questions did not correlate very well with their answers to the last four questions. In such a case, factor analysis would say that since the test seems to be composed of two groups of items, the test measures two factors. In technical terminology, the first six items of the test would *load* on one factor, the last four items would load on another factor. Each question's **factor loading** tells us the degree to which it appears to be measuring a given factor.

Factor loadings, like correlation coefficients, can range from $-1$ to $+1$. Ideally, questions designed to measure a certain factor would have a factor loading of 1.0. However, because of unreliability and other measurement error, a question's factor loadings will usually be well below 1.0. Indeed, a factor loading of $+.7$ is considered very high and many researchers are happy if a question has a factor loading above $+.3$.

You have seen that factor analysis tries to find out how many factors are being measured by a test and how well individual questions measure those factors. But what results would you want to obtain from a factor analysis of your love scale? In the case of your love scale, you would hope for two outcomes.

First, you would hope that the factor analysis supported the view that there were two different factors being measured by the test. You would be

**FIGURE 3–5**

### Determining Whether—And How—To Improve A Measure's Reliability

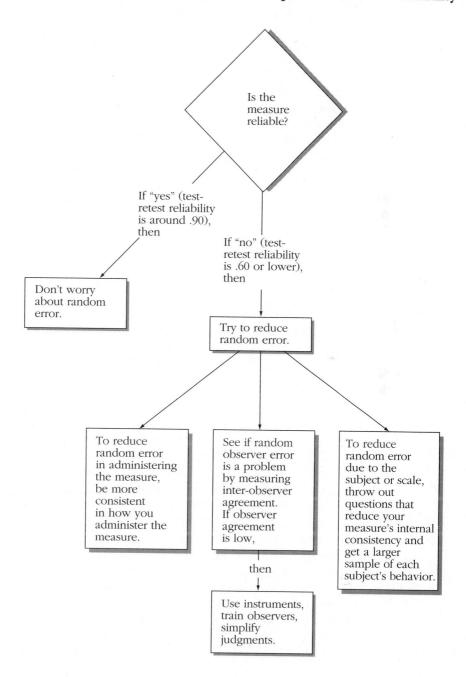

disappointed if the factor analysis reported that, based on participants' responses, your test seemed to be composed of three types of items. Similarly, you may read articles in which the authors hope that their measure is composed of two factors. If factor analysis supports this view, they may say something like, "the two factor solution accounts for a large amount (at least 60%) of the variability in participants' responses."

Second, you would hope that the factor analysis found that the items that you thought made up the sexual attraction subscale all corresponded to one factor and the items that made up the sacrifice subscale all corresponded to another factor. In technical terminology, you would hope that all the sexual attraction items loaded on one factor and all the sacrifice items loaded on a different factor. Specifically, since factor loadings are like a correlation between the test question and the factor, you would want all your sexual attraction items to have high loadings on the factor you want to label sexual attraction and near zero loadings on the factor that you want to label sacrifice. Conversely, you would want all your sacrifice items to have very low factor loadings on the factor that you want to label sexual attraction and high loadings on the factor you want to label sacrifice.

## CONCLUSIONS ABOUT RELIABILITY

In this section, we have shown you why reliability is important, how to determine if a measure has sufficient reliability, and how to determine where a measure's reliability is breaking down. We have stressed that you want measures that are highly reliable because getting inconsistent, unreliable measurements virtually guarantees inaccuracy. That is, reliability puts a ceiling on validity. For example, suppose a junior high student's measurements of your blood pressure are extremely unreliable—he measures it as 100 one day and 200 the next. In that case, you would suspect that at least one of the student's measurements was off by *at least* 50 points. On the other hand, suppose a professional's measurements of your blood pressure are extremely reliable—she measures you at 150 one day and 152 the next. In that case, you realize that each of her measurements *might* be within one point of your true blood pressure.

In a way, the relationship between random error and construct validity in a measure is similar to the relationship between ice and cola in a glass. Where there is ice, there can't be cola. Similarly, where there is random error, there cannot be validity. In other words, the more random error in your measure, the less opportunity there is for validity.

To appreciate how random error can prevent a measure from having validity, let's consider an extreme case. Specifically, let's imagine a measure that has no reliability whatsoever. Admittedly, it is hard to imagine a measure that is so horrible that the *only* reason that one participant would score differently from another would be random events such as carelessness in observing or scoring responses, guessing on the part of participants, etc. Indeed, to get such a measure, you might have to do something ridiculous like determining participants'

IQ scores based on how close they came to guessing next week's winning lottery number. Because such a measure would be completely dominated by random error, it could have no validity—just as there could be no cola in a glass that is full of ice. To reiterate, if scores on a measure were completely determined by random error, the measure would have no reliability and no construct validity. Therefore, if a measure is to have any chance of being valid, it must be reliable. Put another way, *a valid measure must be reliable.*

However, *a reliable measure is not necessarily valid.* A consistent, reliable measure could be consistently and reliably wrong. For example, a thoroughly incompetent person might always measure your blood pressure as 0.

The reason that reducing random error, by itself, does not guarantee construct validity is that random error is not the only source of measurement error. Random error is only one reason your measure might not have validity, just as having your glass full of ice is only one reason you might not have cola in your glass. Thus, just as the absence of ice in your glass doesn't mean the glass is completely full of cola, the absence of random error doesn't mean that the measure is completely valid.

In fact, in small quantities, random error may be the least serious of the many threats to construct validity. Random error is not as serious as some threats because it is inconsistent: Random error will not systematically or reliably bias your measurements in any given direction. That is, whereas a biased observer might give women lower scores than they deserve, random error will not systematically discriminate against any group. Similarly, whereas a biased observer might inflate the scores of participants who received the treatment, random error has no such bias. Thus, just as the ice dilutes—but does not poison—the cola, random error dilutes—but does not poison—validity. Therefore, even a measure with a moderate degree of reliability may have a moderate degree of construct validity and be relatively free of systematic bias.

In conclusion, reliability puts a ceiling on construct validity. An unreliable measure cannot be valid. However, reliability does not guarantee validity. Thus, the most reliable measure may not be the most valid. Indeed, a reliable measure may have no construct validity (see Table 3-2).

One reason that a reliable measure is not necessarily valid is that reliability has nothing to do with whether a measure is free from systematic biases. For example, a measure may have very good inter-rater reliability because both judges are extremely biased. Therefore, when evaluating a measure of behavior, don't get so dazzled by reliability coefficients that you don't look at the extent to which the measure is free from systematic biases.

## Beyond Reliability: Establishing Construct Validity

Unfortunately, it is not as easy to measure systematic error as it is to measure random error. For example, if the judges agree all the time, we know that there is no random observer error. However, their agreement doesn't tell us that

TABLE 3–2
**Key Points to Remember about Reliability**

1. Two major avoidable sources of unreliability are:
   a. random fluctuations in the measurement environment.
   b. random fluctuations in how observers interpret and code observations.
2. Reliability is necessary for validity: Valid measures are reliable.
3. Reliability does not guarantee validity: Reliable measures are not always valid.
4. Unreliability weakens validity, but does *not* introduce systematic bias into the measure.

there is no observer bias. Perhaps the judges agree because they share the same biases.

Despite the problems in showing that a measure is not biased, we should collect enough evidence to make an informed judgment about the degree to which the measure is biased. Usually, you would examine such evidence when evaluating the case for the measure's **construct validity:** the degree to which the measure is measuring what it claims to measure.

### DISCRIMINANT VALIDATION STRATEGIES: SHOWING THAT YOU AREN'T MEASURING THE WRONG CONSTRUCT

One step that would help build the case for a measure's construct validity (that the measure is measuring what you claim it measures) is to show that it is *not* measuring something else. For example, you might want to obtain evidence that would help you estimate the degree to which the measure is influenced by social desirability bias. In research that uses tests and questionnaires, the most common way of showing that your measure is not affected by social desirability is to correlate scores on your measure with scores on a social desirability scale.

As the name suggests, a social desirability scale is a scale that measures the degree to which a person tends to respond in the socially desired way. Basically, a social desirability scale includes questions that have two answers:

1. a socially desirable response (what you should do, according to society);
2. a correct response (what you really do).

An example of such a question would be: "True or False: I always help other people out." People who always lie by picking the socially correct response will score high on the social desirability scale. On the other hand, people who always pick the truthful, but less flattering, answer will score low in social desirability.

If scores on the social desirability scale correlate highly with responses on your scale, then your measure may be strongly affected by the social desirability bias. Thus, rather than measuring what people really think, you may just be measuring their willingness to make a good impression.

If, on the other hand, scores on your scale do not correlate with scores on the social desirability scale, then your measure is probably not affected by social desirability bias. Because researchers usually want to measure people's true feelings rather than people's willingness to make a good impression, most researchers hope that their measure does not correlate with social desirability. Thus, showing that their measure does not correlate with social desirability is often one of the first steps that researchers take in establishing **discriminant validity:** showing that the measure is *not* measuring the wrong construct by demonstrating that the measure does not correlate strongly with measures of other constructs.

Unfortunately, social desirability is only one of several constructs that you may have to show that you are not measuring. Thus, you may have to show that your measure has discriminant validity relative to a variety of constructs. For example, if you have a love measure, you may have to show that it does not correlate too highly with measures of related constructs such as liking, lust, loyalty, and trust.

To reiterate, if a measure has high reliability, it is measuring something other than random error. But the "something" that the measure is measuring is not necessarily the same thing that the measure claims to be measuring. For example, rather than love, the measure may be tapping social desirability. To make sure that the measure is not just tapping social desirability, most tests should be correlated with a test of social desirability. If the correlation is near zero, then discriminant validity in regard to social desirability is established.

Unfortunately, even if the measure isn't measuring social desirability, it may still be measuring something other than what the author claims it is. For example, a "love scale" may measure liking or an "ability" test may really measure experience. Consequently, if you are looking at a measure, you should ask two questions:

1. What else might this measure be measuring? and
2. Is there evidence that this measure does *not* measure those other constructs? That is, does the measure show a low correlation with measures of those other constructs?


## CONVERGENT VALIDATION STRATEGIES: SHOWING THAT YOU ARE MEASURING THE RIGHT CONSTRUCT

Showing that a measure is *not* measuring other constructs only goes so far in making the argument that your measure has construct validity. At some point, you must also present evidence suggesting that your measure *is* measuring the construct you claim it is. One way to convince people that your measure is valid is to show that it correlates with other indicators of the same construct, such as:

1. other measures of the construct;
2. membership in a group composed of individuals known to possess a high level of the construct;

3. membership in an experimental group that has been given a treatment that should cause the members to have a high level of the construct; and
4. behaviors known to correlate with the construct.

The process of getting evidence that your measure correlates with other indicators of the construct is called **convergent validation.** The general idea is that your measure and these other indicators correlate because they are all converging on the same thing—your construct.

Perhaps the most obvious step in convergent validation is to show that your measure correlates with other measures of the same construct. Thus, if you were measuring love, you might correlate your measure with another measure of love. Since both measures are supposed to be measuring the same thing, the two measures should correlate with one another. That is, participants scoring high on your measure should score high on the other measure and participants scoring low on your measure should score low on the other measure.

Another obvious tactic is to find two groups: one known to be high on the characteristic you want to measure, one known to be low on that characteristic. You would hope that participants in the first group would score higher on your measure than participants in the second group. This tactic is called the **known-groups technique.** Thus, in validating your love scale, you might give your scale to two groups—one that is known to be in love (dating couples) and one that is known to not be in love (strangers). You would hope to find, as Rubin (1970) did when he validated his love scale, that the two groups score differently on your scale.

In addition to looking at whether your measure distinguishes between two existing groups, you could determine whether your measure *predicts* whether participants will later belong to different groups. For instance, you might see if your measure could predict which dating couples would get engaged and which would soon split up (again, like Rubin, 1970).

You could also see if your measure distinguishes between two groups exposed to different experimental manipulations. For example, if you had an experimental group that was expecting a shock and a control group that was not, you would expect the experimental group to score higher on a measure of anxiety than the control group.

Finally, you could determine whether your measure correlated with other verbal or nonverbal indicators of the concept. Thus, you could correlate scores on the love scale with a behavior that lovers are supposed to do. For instance, Rubin (1970) showed that his love scale correlated with how long couples looked into each other's eyes.

## CONTENT VALIDITY: IS EVERYTHING REPRESENTED?

In addition to establishing discriminant and convergent validity, you might try to make a case for your measure's construct validity by establishing its **content validity:** the extent to which it represents a balanced and adequate sampling of

---

### BOX 3–2
### VALIDATING A LOVE MEASURE:
### RUBIN'S LOVE SCALE

**Reliability:**

Showing that measure was not excessively affected by random error:

Test-Retest Reliability of .85

**Content validity:**

All three dimensions of love are represented (predisposition to help, dependency, and possessiveness).

**Convergent validity:**

Predicts how much two individuals will gaze at each other.

Predicts probability that individuals will eventually get married.

People who are engaged score higher than people who are casually dating.

**Discriminant validity:**

Doesn't just measure friendship: Lovers score higher than friends.

---

relevant dimensions, knowledge, and skills. For example, if you defined love as, "feeling sexual attraction toward a person and a willingness to make sacrifices for that person," then you would make sure your measure had both kinds of items. As we mentioned earlier, you would probably want to have both a "sexual attraction" and a "sacrifices" subscale.

When evaluating classroom tests and other tests of knowledge or skills, content validity may be extremely important. For example, a test to assess everything you have learned about psychology should not consist of only one multiple-choice question. Beyond having many questions, such a test should cover all areas of psychology, not just one. For example, if such a test consisted of 500 questions about classical conditioning, it would not have content validity.

### SUMMARY OF CONSTRUCT VALIDITY

As you can see, building a strong case for your measure's construct validity is several research projects in itself. Often, researchers have to consult theory and past research to see what manipulations would affect their construct and then see if those manipulations affect scores on their own measure. Furthermore, they may need to consult theory and past research to see what behaviors correlate with high levels of the construct and then see if people scoring high on their measure exhibit those behaviors. Since validating a measure takes so much time and since most researchers are interested in finding out new things about a construct rather than finding new ways to measure it, most researchers do not invent their own measures. Instead, they use measures that others have already validated. (In fact, while reading about what it would take to validate your own love scale, you may have been saying to yourself, "Let's use Rubin's scale instead.")

# MANIPULATING VARIABLES

There are two reasons why we have devoted most of this chapter to measuring, rather than manipulating, variables. First, we have focused on measurement because although not all research involves manipulating variables, all research does involve measuring variables. Second, we have focused on measurement because many of the things you should think about when measuring variables also apply to manipulating variables—as you will soon see.

## Common Threats to a Manipulation's Validity

For example, when evaluating manipulations, you have the same concerns as you have when you measure variables:

1. Can we reduce random error?
2. Can we reduce bias due to the researcher?
3. Can we reduce bias due to the participant?
4. Can we provide evidence that the operational definition we are using is valid?

### RANDOM ERROR

Just as you want to minimize random error when measuring variables, you want to minimize random error when manipulating variables. Therefore, just as you standardized the administration of your measure, you want to standardize the administration of your treatment. That is, you want to administer the treatment the same way every time.

### EXPERIMENTER BIAS

Just as you were worried about researchers being biased in their observations, you will also be worried about **experimenter bias:** experimenters being biased when they administer the treatment. For example, researchers may be friendlier to the participants who are getting the treatment. As was the case with observer bias, the key is to use scientific equipment to administer the manipulations, to use paper and pencil instructions, to standardize procedures, or to make the researcher blind to what condition the participant is in.

### SUBJECT BIASES

Just as you were concerned that your measure might tip participants off to how they should behave, you should also be concerned that your manipulation might tip participants off as to how they should behave. One of the most frequently cited examples of how a treatment could lead to demand characteristics was a series of studies done in the 1920s at the Hawthorne Electric Plant. The investigators, Roethlisberger and Dickson, were looking at the effects of lighting on productivity. At first, everything seemed to go as expected. Increasing illumination increased productivity. However, when they reduced illumination, productivity continued to increase. The researchers concluded that the treatment group was reacting to the special attention, rather than to the treatment itself. This effect became known as the **Hawthorne Effect.**

Although many experts now believe that Roethlisberger and Dickson's results were not due to the "Hawthorne Effect," no one disputes that participants may act differently simply because they think they are getting a treatment. Therefore, researchers use a wide variety of techniques to avoid the "Hawthorne Effect." Some of these techniques are similar to the techniques used to make a measure less vulnerable to subject biases. For example, just as researchers may reduce subject biases by measuring participants in non-research settings, experimenters may reduce subject biases by manipulating the treatment in a non-research setting.

A more common way of offsetting subject biases is to give the "no-treatment" group a **placebo:** a treatment that is known to have no effect. For example, in drug studies, some participants may get a caffeine pill (the treatment), whereas others get a sugar pill (the placebo). If both groups improve equally, the researchers can conclude that the improvement was due to participants expecting to get better. If, however, the treatment group improves more than the placebo group, we know that the results were not due to participants' expectations.

## Evidence Used to Argue for Validity

As with measures, you would like to provide evidence that your treatment is doing what you claim it is. The difference is that making a case for the validity of a treatment is usually less involved than making a case for the validity of a measure.

The two most common ways of establishing validity are to (1) argue that your treatment is consistent with a theory's definition of the construct and to (2) use a **manipulation check:** a question or set of questions designed to determine whether participants perceived the manipulation in the way that the researcher intended.

### CONSISTENCY WITH THEORY

To illustrate the value of these two ways of establishing validity, suppose that you wanted to manipulate cognitive dissonance: a state of arousal caused when participants are aware of having two inconsistent beliefs. You would want to argue that your manipulation meets three general criteria that dissonance theory says must be met for dissonance to be induced:

1. participants must believe they are voluntarily performing an action that is inconsistent with their attitudes (a smoker writing an essay about why people shouldn't smoke);
2. participants should believe that the action is public and will have consequences (before writing the essay, they must know that others will read their essay and know that they wrote it); and
3. participants must not feel that they did the behavior for any reward (you didn't pay them for doing the behavior).

To make the case that the manipulation is consistent with dissonance theory, you might argue that:

1. you told participants their cooperation was voluntary and they could refuse;
2. you told them that their essay would be signed and that children who were thinking about smoking would read it; and
3. you did not pay participants for writing an anti-smoking essay.

## MANIPULATION CHECKS

Your procedures would seem to induce the mental state of dissonance—*assuming* that participants perceived the manipulation as you intended. To check on that assumption, you might use a manipulation check. For example, you might ask participants if they felt aroused and uncomfortable, if they felt that their attitudes and behavior were inconsistent, if they felt they were coerced, if they felt that their behavior was public, whether they foresaw the consequences of their behavior, etc. Many researchers believe that you should always use a manipulation check when doing research on human participants.

But what if giving people the manipulation check tips participants off to the study? In that case, manipulation check advocates would say to use the manipulation check, but only after the participant has responded to your measure. Or, you might conduct a mini-study in which the only thing that happens is that participants are given the manipulation and then they respond to the manipulation check.

But what if it's obvious that you are manipulating whatever you think you are manipulating (physical attractiveness, concrete versus abstract words, etc.)? Even then, manipulation check advocates would urge you to go ahead with a manipulation check for two important reasons. First, a manipulation check could establish the discriminant validity of your treatment. For example, wouldn't it be nice if you could show that your attractiveness manipulation increased perceptions of attractiveness, but did not change perceptions of age or wealth? Second, since you are doing research to test assumptions rather than make assumptions, you should be willing to test the assumption that you are manipulating what you think you are manipulating (see Table 3–3).

**TABLE 3-3**
**Similarities between Measuring and Manipulating Variables**

| MEASURE | MANIPULATION |
|---|---|
| Reduce random error by standardizing administration of the measure. | Reduce random error by standardizing administration of the manipulation. |
| Reduce observer bias by training, standardization, instruments, and making researcher "blind" about the participant's condition. | Reduce researcher bias by training, standardization, instruments, and making researcher "blind" about the participant's condition. |
| Participants may figure out what the measure is measuring and then act in such a way to make a good impression or give the researcher the "right" results. Sometimes, the problem of subject biases is dealt with by not letting participants know what the measure is or what the hypothesis is. | Participants may figure out what the manipulation is designed to do and then act in such a way as to make a good impression or give the researcher the "right" results. Sometimes, the problem of subject biases is dealt with by not letting participants know what the manipulation is or what the hypothesis is. |
| Show that your operational definition is consistent with theory's definition of the construct. | Show that your operational definition is consistent with theory's definition of the construct. |
| Convergent validity shown by correlating the measure with other measures of construct. | Convergent validity is sometimes demonstrated by showing that the manipulation has same effect that other manipulations of the construct have and that it has an effect on a simple, direct measure of the construct (the manipulation check). |

## Tradeoffs among Three Common Types of Manipulations

Choosing a manipulation usually involves making tradeoffs because there is no such thing as the perfect manipulation. Different manipulations have different strengths and weaknesses. Below, we will briefly highlight the strengths and weaknesses of three common kinds of manipulations: instructional manipulations, environmental manipulations, and stooge manipulations.

### INSTRUCTIONAL MANIPULATIONS

Perhaps the most common treatment manipulation is the **instructional manipulation:** manipulating the variable by giving written or oral instructions. The advantage of an instructional manipulation is that you can standardize your manipulation easily. All you have to do is give each participant the same xeroxed instructions or play each participant the same tape. This standardization reduces both random error and experimenter bias.

However, just because you can consistently *present* instructions to participants, don't assume that your instructions will be *perceived* the same way every time. Participants may ignore, forget, or misinterpret instructions.

To reduce random error due to participants interpreting your instructions differently, be sure to repeat and paraphrase your most important instructions. Many researchers advise you to "hit participants over the head" with your manipulation. Thus, if you were manipulating anonymity, you would tell "anonymous" participants that their responses would be anonymous, *and* confidential, *and* private, *and* that no one would know. Furthermore, you would also tell them not to write their name on the paper. In the public condition, you would do just the opposite. You would tell "public" participants that everyone would see their paper, that you were going to make copies of their paper, and you would make a big deal of their signing their names to the paper.

If participants do not understand or do not pay attention to the manipulation, the instructional manipulation will have little effect on your participants. However, by making the instructions clear, this problem can be overcome. Unfortunately, participants may understand your manipulation too well. That is, participants may figure out what you are trying to manipulate and then play along. Fortunately, you can reduce this threat to your study's construct validity by using placebo treatments, counterintuitive hypotheses, and clever ways of measuring your construct (see Box 3–1).

## ENVIRONMENTAL MANIPULATIONS

If you are concerned that participants will "play along" with an instructional manipulation, you may use an **environmental manipulation:** changing the participant's surroundings. Some environmental manipulations take the form of "accidents." For instance, smoke may fill a room, the participant may be induced to break something, or the participant may overhear some remark.

When considering an environmental manipulation, ask two questions. First, will participants notice the manipulation? Even when manipulations have involved rather dramatic changes in participants' environments (smoke filling a room), a sizable proportion of participants report not noticing the manipulation (Latané, 1969).

Second, can you present the manipulation the same way every time? Fortunately, many environmental manipulations can be presented in a consistent, standardized way. Most animal research, for example, involves environmental manipulations that can be consistently presented (food deprivation). Likewise, research in perception, sensory processing, cognition, and verbal learning usually involves environmental manipulations (presenting illusions or other stimuli). These manipulations vary from the routine—presentation of visual stimuli by computer, tachistoscope, memory drum, or automated slide projector—to the exotic. For example, Neisser and his associates have done studies in which the manipulation consists of silently moving the walls of the participant's cubicle.

## MANIPULATIONS INVOLVING STOOGES

A special kind of environmental manipulation employs **stooges:** confederates who pretend to be participants, but are actually the researcher's assistants. By

**TABLE 3–4**

**Comparing the Advantages and Disadvantages of Three Different Kinds of Manipulations**

| INSTRUCTIONAL | ENVIRONMENTAL | STOOGES |
|---|---|---|
| Easy to do. | Not as easy to do. | Not easy to do. |
| Easily standardized. | Not easily standardized. | Not easily standardized. |
| Reduces: | May lead to concerns about: | May lead to concerns about: |
| 1. Random error | 1. Random error | 1. Random error |
| 2. Potential for experimenter biases. | 2. Potential for experimenter biases. | 2. Potential for experimenter biases. |
| Vulnerable to subject biases. | Less vulnerable to subject biases. | Not very vulnerable to subject biases. |

using stooges, social psychologists and others get participants to respond openly, thus avoiding the demand characteristics that accompany instructional manipulations. Unfortunately, there are two problems with using stooges.

First, using stooges raises ethical questions because, by deceiving your participants, you are violating the principle of informed consent. Your attempt to reduce demand characteristics is coming at the cost of participants' rights. The decision to try to deceive participants should only be made after careful consideration of the alternatives. Thus, for ethical reasons, you or your professor may decide against using stooges.

Second, it's very hard to standardize the performance of a stooge. At best, inconsistent performances by stooges creates unnecessary random error. At worst, stooges may bias the results. Some researchers solve the standardization problem by having participants listen to tapes of actors rather than relying on stooges to give the exact same performance time after time. For example, both Aronson and Carlsmith (1974) and Latané (1968) made participants believe they were listening to people talking over an intercom when participants were actually listening to a tape-recording.

As you can see, choosing manipulations usually means making tradeoffs (see Table 3-4). To choose the right manipulation for your study, you must determine what your study needs most. Is experimenter bias your biggest concern? Then, you might use an instructional manipulation. Are you most concerned with demand characteristics? Then, you might use an environmental manipulation.

## Manipulating Variables: A Summary

When manipulating variables, you have many of the same concerns you have when measuring variables. However, when manipulating variables, you have one set of concerns that you don't have when measuring variables: How many levels of the treatment should you have and how different should your levels be? We will deal with the important decision of choosing treatment levels in Chapters 6 and 7.

## CONCLUDING REMARKS

In Chapter 2, you developed a research idea: a prediction about how two or more variables were related. In this chapter, you learned how to determine whether you had valid operational definitions of those variables. Now that you have the raw materials to build a research design, you can take advantage of the rest of this book.

## SUMMARY

1. Validity of a measure refers to whether you are measuring what you claim you are measuring.
2. A reliable measure is relatively free from random error.
3. Three major sources of unreliability are random errors in scoring the behavior, random variations in how the measure is administered, and random fluctuations in the participant's performance.
4. Correlation coefficients can range from $-1.00$ to $+1.00$. Since reliability coefficients are squared correlation coefficients (and squared numbers can't be negative), reliability coefficients range from 0 to 1.
5. An unreliable measure cannot be valid, but a reliable measure may be invalid.
6. A valid measure must have some degree of reliability and be relatively free of observer bias and subject biases.
7. Two common subject biases are social desirability (trying to make a good impression) and obeying the study's demand characteristics.
8. By not letting participants know what you are measuring (unobtrusive measurement), you may be able to reduce subject biases (see Box 3-1).
9. Establishing reliability, discriminant validity, convergent validity, and content validity are all ways of validating a measure.
10. Choosing a manipulation involves many of the same steps as choosing a measure.
11. Placebo treatments and unobtrusive measurement can reduce subject bias.
12. "Blind" procedures and standardization can reduce experimenter bias.
13. You can use manipulation checks to make a case for your manipulation's validity.

# KEY TERMS

**correlation coefficient:** an index that can vary from $-1.00$ to $+1.00$. The sign of the correlation coefficient indicates the kind of relationship that exists between two variables: Positive correlations indicate that the variables tend to go in the same direction (if a participant is low on one variable, the participant will tend to be low on the other). Negative correlations indicate that the variables tend to head in opposite directions (if a participant is low on one, the participant will tend to be high on the other). The farther the correlation coefficient is from zero, the more closely the two variables are related. Thus, $+.95$ and $-.95$ both indicate equally strong relationships, whereas $+.05$ and $-.05$ both indicate equally weak relationships. (p. 79)

**factor analysis:** a statistical technique designed to group together questions that seem to be measuring the same underlying hypothetical factor. (p. 84)

**factor loadings:** tells us the degree to which a given question appears to be measuring a certain factor. Factor loadings, like correlation coefficients, can range from $-1$ to $+1$. (p. 84)

**observer bias:** bias created by the observer seeing what the observer wants or expects to see. (p. 71)

**blind observer:** an observer who is unaware of the participant's characteristics and situation. Using blind observers reduces observer bias. (p. 73)

**operational definition:** a publicly observable way to measure or manipulate a variable; a "recipe" for how you are going to measure or manipulate your factors. (p. 70)

**reliability:** the extent to which a measure produces stable, consistent scores. Measures are able to produce such stable scores if they are not strongly influenced by random error. A measure can be reliable, but not valid. However, if a measure is not reliable, it cannot be valid. (p. 78)

**test-retest reliability:** a way of assessing the amount of random error in a measure by administering the measure to participants at two different times and then correlating their results. (p. 78)

**inter-judge agreement:** the percentage of times the raters agree. (p. 80)

**inter-observer reliability:** an index of the degree to which different raters rate the same behavior similarly. (p. 80)

**internal consistency:** the degree to which all the items on a measure appear to be measuring the same construct. Estimated by determining the degree to which answers to each item correlate (agree) with answers to the other items. (p. 83)

**subject biases:** ways the participant can bias the results (guessing the hypothesis and playing along, giving the socially approved of response, etc.). (p. 75)

**socially desirability bias:** participants acting in a way that make the participant look good. (p. 76)

**demand characteristics:** aspects of the study that allow the participant to figure out how the researcher wants that participant to behave. (p. 76)

**unobtrusive measurement:** recording a particular behavior without the participant knowing you are measuring that behavior. Reduces subject biases such as social desirability bias and obeying demand characteristics. (p. 77)

**Hawthorne Effect:** when the treatment group changes its behavior not because of the treatment itself, but because group members know they are getting special treatment. (p. 93)

**instructional manipulation:** manipulating the variable by giving written or oral instructions. (p. 95)

**environmental manipulation:** a manipulation that involves changing the participant's environment rather than giving the participant different instructions. (p. 96)

**stooges:** confederates who pretend to be participants, but are actually the researcher's assistants. (p. 96)

**construct validity:** the degree to which an operational definition reflects the concept that it claims to reflect. Establishing content, convergent, and discriminant validity are all ways of arguing that your measure has construct validity. (p. 88)

**content validity:** the extent to which a measure represents a balanced and adequate sampling of relevant dimensions, knowledge, and skills. (p. 90)

**convergent validity:** validity demonstrated by showing that the measure correlates with other measures, manipulations, or correlates of the construct. (p. 90)

**discriminant validity:** the extent to which the measure does not correlate strongly with measures of other constructs. (p. 89)

**known-groups technique:** determining the validity of a measure by seeing whether groups known to differ on a characteristic differ on a measure of that characteristic (e.g., ministers should differ from atheists on a measure of religious beliefs). A way of establishing convergent validity. (p. 90)

**experimenter bias:** experimenters being more attentive to participants in the treatment group or giving different nonverbal cues to treatment group participants than to other participants. (p. 92)

**standardization:** treating each participant in the same (standard) way. Standardization should reduce experimenter bias. (p. 74)

**manipulation check:** a question or set of questions designed to determine whether participants perceived the manipulation in the way that the researcher intended. (p. 93)

**placebo treatment:** a treatment that is known to have no effect. It is used to make sure that the treatment effect is not simply due to subject bias. (p. 93)

# EXERCISES

1. What is an operational definition? Give an example of an operational definition. How does an operational definition differ from a dictionary definition?
2. What two general types of errors may cause a measure of behavior to be inaccurate? If you were doing a study, which of these two factors would have the greater impact on the average score of your treatment group?
3. What is reliability?
4. Why do we want reliability?
5. Can you have a test-retest reliability coefficient of below zero? Why or why not?
6. What are two main sources of unreliability?
7. In which situation will inter-observer reliability be higher:
   a. scoring an essay exam
   b. scoring a multiple-choice test?
8. True or False: If the inter-observer reliability was 1.00, inter-judge agreement was 100%.
9. If your measure's test-retest reliability was .90, should you go try to discover what your inter-observer reliability was? Why or why not?
10. If your measure's test-retest reliability was .50, would you go about trying to discover what your inter-observer reliability was? Why or why not?
11. If your measure's inter-observer reliability is .70, can your test-retest reliability be .80? Why or why not?
12. Assume that test-retest reliability is .50 and inter-observer reliability is 1.00. What is the source of your measure's reliability problems? What would you do to increase reliability?
13. Assume that test-retest reliability is .50 and inter-observer reliability is .60. What is the main source of your measure's reliability problems? What would you do about it?
14. True or False: Reliability guarantees validity.
15. True or False: A measure's reliability puts a ceiling on validity.
16. True or False: Unreliability dilutes a measure's validity.
17. True or False: Unreliability poisons a measure's validity.
18. True or False: Validity guarantees reliability.
19. How would assessing inter-observer reliability differ from assessing test-retest reliability?
20. What are the two primary types of subject bias? What are the differences between these two sources?
21. List four basic tactics for reducing the possibility of subject bias.
22. Suppose you are interested in measuring procrastination. You have students write an essay on a computer. Unknown to them, the computer

measures how long it takes them to begin, how many breaks they take, and how long each of those breaks is. What would be the advantages of having the computer secretly record the information?

23. What is convergent validity? What are four basic ways of establishing convergent validity?

24. What is the flip side of convergent validity? Why is it necessary?

25. What is the value of internal consistency?

26. What is content validity? For what measures is it most important?

27. True or False: Shortening a test would probably harm its content validity.

28. True or False: Shortening a test would probably harm its internal consistency.

29. True or False: Internal consistency may be assessed by split-half reliability coefficients.

30. If lovers score higher on a "love" test than strangers, the love test has _____ validity, established by the _____ _____ technique.

31. If friends do not score higher on a "love" test than strangers, the test has _____ validity.

32. A test of empathy that did not correlate with intelligence would have _____ validity.

33. If therapists with high scores on an empathy test have better success rates than therapists with lower scores, then the empathy test has _____ validity.

34. If a test over Chapters 1–3 has 30 questions on Chapter 1, 15 questions on Chapter 2, and only 5 questions on Chapter 3, we might suspect that the test lacked _____ validity.

35. Why might it always be a good idea to correlate scores of a new personality test with a social desirability scale?

36. If researchers use an aggression scale to see if they have increased the participants' level of aggression, what two threats to validity should they particularly be concerned about?

37. What information about an aggression test would suggest that the test is a good instrument?

38. Measuring the degree to which someone is thinking is difficult. However, imagine that you are to try to measure thinking by using a measure of facial tension. How would you validate that measure?

39. A researcher wants to measure "aggressive tendencies." The researcher is trying to decide between a paper-and-pencil test of aggression and observing actual aggression.

    a. What problems might there be with participants' aggressive behavior?

    b. In evaluating the test, what should the researcher beware of?

    c. What information about the test would suggest that the test is a good instrument?

40. Define a construct that you would like to measure.

41. Locate two published measures of that concept (see Appendix B).

42. Develop a measure of that construct.

43. What could you do to improve or evaluate your measure's reliability?

44. If you had a year to try to validate your measure, how would you go about it? (Hint: Refer to the different kinds of validities discussed in this chapter.)

45. How vulnerable is your measure to subject and observer bias? Why? Can you change your measure to make it more resistant to these threats?

46. What factor would you like to manipulate? Define this factor as specifically as you can.

47. Find one example of this factor being manipulated in a published study (see Appendix B).

48. How would you manipulate that factor? Why?

49. How could you perform a manipulation check on the factor you want to manipulate? Would it be useful to perform a manipulation check? Why or why not?

50. Compare the relative advantages and disadvantages of using an instructional manipulation versus an environmental manipulation.

# CHAPTER 4

---

# Beyond Reliability and Validity: Choosing the Best Measure for Your Study

*Overview*

*Sensitivity: Will the Measure Be Able to Detect the Differences You Need to Detect?*

ACHIEVING THE NECESSARY LEVEL OF SENSITIVITY
SENSITIVITY: CONCLUSIONS

*Scales of Measurement: Will the Measure Allow You to Make the Kinds of Comparisons You Need to Make?*

THE DIFFERENT SCALES OF MEASUREMENT
WHY OUR NUMBERS DO NOT ALWAYS MEASURE UP
WHICH LEVEL OF MEASUREMENT DO YOU NEED?
CONCLUSIONS ABOUT SCALES OF MEASUREMENT

*Ethical and Practical Considerations*

*Concluding Remarks*

*Summary*

*Key Terms*

*Exercises*

# Chapter 4

---

# BEYOND RELIABILITY AND VALIDITY: CHOOSING THE BEST MEASURE FOR YOUR STUDY

*"When possible, make the decisions now, even if action is in the future. A reviewed decision usually is better than one reached at the last moment."*

—WILLIAM B. GIVEN, JR.

## OVERVIEW

When selecting a measure, you might think that you should always choose the most valid measuring instrument available. After all, you want to make sure that your instrument measures what it is supposed to measure. However, the best measure for your study is not always the most valid one.

For example, imagine that you find four measures that have slightly different levels of validity, but very different sources of invalidity. The first measure's validity is weakened by demand characteristics, the second measure's validity is weakened by social desirability bias, the third measure's validity is weakened by observer bias, and the fourth measure's validity is weakened by unreliability. Which measure should you choose? The answer depends on your particular study.

If you have a counter-intuitive hypothesis that participants probably won't figure out, you might not be concerned about a measure's vulnerability to demand characteristics. Thus, you might choose the measure that is vulnerable to demand characteristics.

If you are comparing a treatment group to a no-treatment group, you may not be concerned about social desirability because social desirability would influence both groups equally. Thus, because social desirability would not cause the treatment group to score differently than the no-treatment group, you might choose the measure that is vulnerable only to social desirability bias.

If you were able to keep observers "blind," you would not be concerned with observer bias. Consequently, you might choose the measure that is vulnerable to observer bias.

Finally, if you were very concerned about avoiding any type of bias, you would choose the measure that was strongly affected by random error. That is, even though the measure was unreliable, you would use it because at least it wasn't vulnerable to bias.

In short, even if validity were your only concern, you would not always choose the most valid measure. However, validity is never your only concern. For starters, ethical and practical concerns will always affect your choice of measure. Furthermore, you should also choose a measure based on whether it will allow you to answer your research question.

## SENSITIVITY: WILL THE MEASURE BE ABLE TO DETECT THE DIFFERENCES YOU NEED TO DETECT?

To understand how a measure could prevent you from answering your research question, imagine a cell biologist's reaction to being told that she could only use a magnifying glass. Obviously, she would be surprised. Without a microscope, the cell biologist could not determine the effect of different treatments or see how cells differed.

Like cell biologists, psychologists often look for subtle differences. Consequently, like cell biologists, psychologists usually want their measure to be **sensitive:** have the ability to detect differences among participants on a given variable.

### Achieving the Necessary Level of Sensitivity

How can you find or develop a sensitive measure? Often, you can evaluate or improve a measure's sensitivity by simply using common sense. For example, if participants must receive either a score of "1" or a score of "2," the measure will not be sensitive to subtle differences among participants. But beyond such common sense considerations, look at the measure's validity and reliability. A sensitive measure will also tend to be more valid and more reliable than an insensitive measure.

#### LOOK FOR HIGH VALIDITY

The desire for sensitivity is a major reason why researchers often insist on having the most valid measure available. That is, even though they have several valid measures to choose from, they want the most valid one because it will tend to be the most sensitive.

Why does the most valid measure tend to be the most sensitive? To answer this question, keep two facts in mind. First, the most valid measure is the one in which scores are least affected by random error, bias, and other factors that are irrelevant to what you are trying to measure. Second, the less a measure's scores are affected by irrelevant factors, the more it will be sensitive to changes in the relevant factor. For example, if you were weighing people to find out whether a diet had an effect, you would be more likely to find the diet's effect if participants were weighed unclothed rather than clothed. Both the clothed and unclothed measures could be valid. However, because the unclothed measure is not assessing the weight of the clothes, it is more valid and more sensitive to actual weight changes.

For similar reasons, measures that involve fewer inferences tend to be both more valid and more sensitive. That is, scientists would prefer to measure a person's weight on a scale rather than by the depth of the impression the person's footprint left in the sand. Similarly, they would prefer to measure body fat using calipers rather than by estimating it from overall body weight.

The following two steps will often increase a measure's validity and sensitivity. First, know precisely what it is you want to measure. Initially, you may have a general sense that you want to measure attraction. However, upon reflection, you may decide that you are really interested in measuring a specific type of attraction. For example, you may decide that you want to measure lust rather than liking. Similarly, you may start off thinking you want to measure memory. After giving your hypothesis more thought, you may determine that you are interested in a specific aspect of memory (size of short-term memory, organization of long-term memory, memory biases, etc.). Second, ask if there is a more direct way of measuring your construct. For example, if you are interested in measuring aggression in football, do not simply measure how many penalties a team gets. Instead, measure how many penalties they get for unsportsmanlike conduct. Similarly, rather than measuring fear by how closely children sit to each other, ask children how afraid they are.

## LOOK FOR HIGH RELIABILITY

As you have seen, the desire for sensitive measures is one reason why psychologists value validity. As you will soon see, the desire for sensitive measures is also a reason why psychologists value reliability. In our example of choosing among the four equally valid measures, you might have wondered why we did not suggest choosing the one that had only one weakness: poor reliability. After all, given a choice between a measure weakened by random error or one weakened by bias, it would seem that one should choose random error. However, in some cases, a researcher may decide to use a more reliable—but potentially biased—measure over a less reliable and less biased measure. Why? Because to the extent that a measure is varying because of random error, it is not sensitive to variations in participants' behavior.

Unreliability is to data what static is to television reception. With a little static, you can still listen to the television news. However, as the static increases, it becomes increasingly difficult to understand the news. Similarly, with a lot of random error in your measurements, it becomes hard to pick up the news your data is sending you. If your measures are very unreliable, even a large difference between your groups may be due to random measurement error. Therefore, if you see that your groups score differently on a measure, you don't know if these differences are due to measurement error or whether they represent actual differences. To illustrate this point, suppose you were measuring the time it took two different rats to run a maze. Suppose that Rat A and Rat B ran the maze four times each. Their actual times were:

|  | Trial 1 | Trial 2 | Trial 3 | Trial 4 |
|---|---|---|---|---|
| Rat A | 6 seconds | 6 seconds | 6 seconds | 6 seconds |
| Rat B | 5 seconds | 5 seconds | 5 seconds | 5 seconds |

If you had obtained these data, you could clearly see that Rat B was the faster rat. However, suppose your measuring system was unreliable. For example, suppose you were having some problems with the stopwatch or you weren't always paying close attention. Then, you might record the rats' times as follows:

|  | Trial 1 | Trial 2 | Trial 3 | Trial 4 |
|---|---|---|---|---|
| Rat A | 7 seconds | 6 seconds | 5 seconds | 6 seconds |
| Rat B | 8 seconds | 4 seconds | 6 seconds | 2 seconds |

Despite the random error in your measurements, you correctly calculated that Rat A averages six seconds to run the maze and Rat B averages five seconds to run the maze. Thus, random error does not bias your observations. However, because of the unreliable, erratic nature of your measuring system, it is hard to determine whether Rat B is really the faster rat. That is, the unreliability of the measuring system causes static that makes it harder to get a clear picture of the message the data should be sending you.

You have seen that too much random error in your measuring system can prevent you from detecting true differences between participants. In other words, all other things being equal, the more reliable the measure, the more sensitive. Therefore, if you want to have a sensitive measure, you should probably choose a measure that has a high (above .70) test-retest reliability coefficient.

## FIND MEASURES THAT PROVIDE A VARIETY OF SCORES

Thus far, we have discussed cases in which you could increase sensitivity by increasing validity and reliability. However, often a measure is insensitive not because it is invalid, but because—like a scale that will only measure you to the nearest 100 pounds—it fails to differentiate between participants.

If a measure is to be sensitive to subtle differences between participants, different participants must get different scores. Thus, if you measured a wide variety of participants, you should get a wide variety of scores. Some participants would get extremely low scores, others would get extremely high scores. Very few participants would get the exact same score.

What could prevent a valid measure from producing the wide variety of scores necessary to reflect the full extent of the variation among your participants? To answer this question, let's imagine that you are trying to detect small changes in how much a man loves a woman. What could stop you from detecting changes in the man's love?

***Avoid Behaviors That Are Resistant to Change.***    One reason why you might be unable to detect small changes in love is if you choose to measure a behavior that is very resistant to change. Measures based on such behaviors are insensitive. Therefore, if sensitivity is a big concern, you should not choose to measure a behavior that is resistant to change. But what behaviors are resistant to change?

Important behaviors, such as getting married or buying a car, and well-ingrained habits, such as smoking or cursing, are resistant to change. Consequently, these behaviors may not change as readily as the underlying construct they are supposed to measure. For instance, suppose your measure of love was whether a man asked a woman to marry him. Since a man would only ask a woman to marry him once his love had reached a high level, this measure would be insensitive to many subtle changes. For instance, it would not be able to detect a man's love changing from a near-zero level of love to a moderate level.

So, if you are interested in sensitivity, stay away from measures that cannot detect low levels of a construct. Don't use death as a measure of stress, tile erosion in front of a painting as a measure of the painting's popularity, or quitting smoking as a measure of willpower.

***Avoid Measures That Produce a Limited Range of Scores.***    A second thing that could prevent you from distinguishing between subtly different levels of the man's love is if your measure did not represent all these different levels. Consequently, a second reason that a marriage proposal is an insensitive measure is that there are only two scores the man could receive (asked or didn't ask). You are trying to distinguish between numerous subtly differing degrees of love, but you are only letting your participant respond in two different ways. If a measure is going to discriminate between many different degrees of love, participants must be able to give many different responses.

***Ask How Much Instead of Whether.***    One obvious way to allow participants to get a variety of scores on a measure is to add scale points to your measure. Adding scale points to your measure may increase its sensitivity just as adding 1/2 inch marks to a yardstick makes the yardstick more useful for detecting subtle differences in the length of boards. Therefore, if you are measuring generosity, don't just record *whether* someone gave to charity. Instead, record *how often* she donated, or *how much* she gave, or *how long* you had to talk to her before she was willing to give (**response latency**). Similarly, if you are using maze running to measure motivation, don't simply record whether or not the rat ran the maze. Instead, time the rat to determine *how fast* the rat ran the maze.

Scientific equipment can help you add scale points to your measure. For instance, with the proper instruments, you can measure reaction time to the nearest thousandth of a second. Or, by using a sound meter to measure how loudly a person is speaking, you can go beyond saying that the person was speaking softly or loudly: You can specify exactly *how many* decibels the person produced.

***Add Scale Points to a Rating Scale.***    You can also add scale points to self-report measures. For example, don't measure love by asking the question: "Are you in love? (1- yes, 2- no)." Instead, ask: "*How* in love are you? (1- not at all 2- slightly 3- moderately 4- extremely)." Similarly, rather than having an observer rate whether a child was aggressive, you could have the observer rate the extent to which the child was aggressive.

However, there comes a point where adding scale points to a measure will not enhance sensitivity. Asking people to report their weight to the nearest 1/1000th of a pound or asking them to report their love to the nearest 1/1000th will probably not boost sensitivity. That is, after a certain point, any apparent gains in precision are wiped out by the fact that responses are unreliable guesses. Besides, such questions may cause participants to be frustrated or to doubt your competence. Therefore, to boost sensitivity without frustrating your participants, you should not unnecessarily add scale points beyond a certain point. But what is that point?

According to conventional wisdom, the point at which you should stop adding scale points depends on both the kind of question you are asking and the kind of participant you are asking. If you are asking about something that your participants think about a lot and your participants are intelligent, you might be able to use an 11-point scale. If you are asking about an issue that they are relatively ignorant of (or apathetic toward) and they are not very intelligent, you may want to use a three-point scale. When in doubt, use either a five- or seven-point scale.

***Pilot Test Your Measure.***    If you have followed our advice, you now have a measure that *potentially* provides a range of scores. However, just because there are many possible scores a participant *could* get on your measure, that does not mean there are many different scores that your participants *will* get. To determine if scores will vary, pilot test your measure. That is, before conducting a full-blown study, try out your measure on a few participants. Often, you will find—or would have found—that participants' scores on the measure do not vary. For example, one investigator did an experiment to see if reading along with a videotape would help children remember more than if they just saw the videotape. To measure memory, she asked the children 24 questions about the story. Unfortunately, the questions were so hard that none of the children got any of the questions right. Thus, the results of her study were hard to interpret.

## Sensitivity: Conclusions

You have seen that if a measure is to be sensitive to differences between participants, participants must differ on the measure. However, for a measure to be sensitive, it is not enough that different participants get different scores. For example, random error (unreliability) should not be the reason for participants getting different scores. Instead, participants should get different scores because they differ in the degree to which they possess the behavior or construct you are trying to measure. In other words, all other things being equal, your measure should be as valid as possible. Consequently, you should minimize the extent to which participants' scores vary because of factors unrelated to your construct. Thus, if you use simple, anonymous behaviors as measures (such as self-rating scales), you may be more likely to detect differences between participants than if you observe complex, public behaviors that are influenced by many factors other than your construct.

As you can imagine, the goal of sensitivity sometimes conflicts with the goal of validity. For example, to avoid subject biases, you might want to use a complex, public behavior (sacrificing for one's partner) as your measure of love. However, to have a sensitive measure, you might want to use a simple rating scale. Do you choose the complex behavior that might be insensitive? Or, do you use the rating scale, even though it would be invalid if participants simply give you the ratings they think you want?

In certain situations, some researchers would choose the more sensitive rating scale. To understand why, realize that a sensitive measure can help you find small differences so that you can make discoveries. An insensitive measure, on the other hand, may stop you from making discoveries. Consequently, some scientists would use a sensitive measure that would first allow them to find differences, and then they would later debate what those differences mean (the construct validity question). They would prefer debating what their difference meant to doing a study that had virtually no chance of finding any differences at all.

In short, even though validity is important, it is not the only factor to consider when selecting a measure. Depending on the circumstances, having the ability to detect subtle differences may be equally important. After all, an insensitive measure may—by making sure that you fail to find anything—prevent you from being able to answer your research question.

## SCALES OF MEASUREMENT: WILL THE MEASURE ALLOW YOU TO MAKE THE KINDS OF COMPARISONS YOU NEED TO MAKE?

An insensitive measure is not the only kind of measure that can prevent you from answering your research question. Indeed, perhaps a more important aspect of the measure is whether it allows you to make the kind of comparison you need to make.

The kind of comparison you need to make is determined by your research question. For example, consider these four questions:

1. Do the two groups differ on the variable?
2. Does one group have *more* of the variable than the other?
3. *How much more* does one group have of the variable than the other group?
4. Does one group have more than three *times* as much of the variable than the other group?

These four questions could be answered by using numbers. All measures can provide numbers. However, very few measures could help you answer the fourth question. Why?

The answer lies in the fact that *not all measures produce the same kinds of numbers.* To repeat, not all numbers are alike. Just as some descriptive phrases are more informative and specific than others ("Joe doesn't look the same as Tom" versus "Joe is twice as attractive as Tom"), some numbers are more informative than others.

## The Different Scales of Measurement

Rather than saying that some numbers provide more specific information than other numbers, psychologists say that different numbers represent different *scales of measurement.* In the next few sections, we will show you:

1. how numbers representing different scales of measurement differ;
2. why some measures provide more informative numbers than others; and
3. how to determine what kind of numbers you need.

### NOMINAL NUMBERS: DIFFERENT NUMBERS
### REPRESENTING DIFFERENT STATES

The least informative numbers are **nominal** numbers: numbers that substitute for names. Like names, nominal numbers can be used to identify, label, and categorize things. That is, things having the same number are alike, things with different numbers are different. Also like names, nominal numbers cannot meaningfully be ordered. In other words, just as we do not say that Jane is a bigger name than Jim, we do not say that someone having the uniform number 36 is better than someone wearing number 35. In everyday life, we run into nominal numbers constantly—social security numbers, players' uniform numbers, charge card numbers, license plate numbers, and serial code numbers.

In psychological research, the best use of nominal numbers is when the participants can be clearly classified as either having a certain quality or not. For example, we may put people into categories such as male/female or student/ faculty. In other words, this most basic way of using numbers is perfect when you aren't interested in measuring different amounts, but *different kinds* or *types.* For example, someone scoring a "1" might think of love as an addiction, a person scoring a "2" might think of love as a business partnership, a person scoring a "3" might think of love as a game, and a person scoring a "4" might think of love as "lust" (Sternberg, 1994).

Sometimes, however, we have nominal scale measurement because our measurements are primitive and crude. This may happen in the early stages of developing a measure, especially if we only have a rough idea of what the measure is assessing. For instance, suppose that when participants see their partner, some participants produce one pattern of brain-waves whereas others produce a different pattern. Labeling the first brain-wave pattern "1" and the other pattern "2" is arbitrary. We could have just as easily labeled the first pattern "2" and the other pattern "1." Consequently, we have nominal scale measurement because we do not know whether "2" indicates a greater reaction than "1." We only know that "2" is a *different* pattern than "1." Once we find out that one pattern indicates more love than another, we can give that pattern the higher number. At that point, we have moved beyond nominal scale measurement.

## ORDINAL NUMBERS: WHEN BIGGER MEANS MORE

As you shall see, we often want to move beyond nominal scale measurement. Rather than always being limited to saying only that participants getting different numbers differ, we often want to say that participants receiving higher scores have more of a given quality. That is, beyond saying that people scoring "3" are similar to each other and different from people scoring "1," we want to also state that people scoring "3" have more of a certain quality than those scoring "1." In other words, we may want to be able to meaningfully *order* scores from lowest to highest. That is, we want *higher* scores to mean *more* of the quality. For example, people scoring a "5" feel more love than people scoring "4," who feel more love than people scoring "3," etc.

If you can assume that higher numbers indicate more love than lower numbers, your measure is producing at least **ordinal** scale numbers: numbers that can be meaningfully ordered from lowest to highest. When you assume that you have ordinal data, you are making a very simple assumption: The numbers are ordered. Note, however, that you are *not* assuming that the difference between "2" and "1" is the same as the difference between "3" and "2." To reiterate, you are assuming that "2" is bigger than "1" and "3" is bigger than "2," but you have no idea *how much* bigger "3" is than "2."

To illustrate what ordinal scaling does and does not assume, suppose you successfully ranked 10 couples in terms of how much they loved each other. Because the numbers can be meaningfully ordered from highest to lowest, these are definitely ordinal data. Yet, because they are ordinal data, the difference between "1" and "2" may be very different from the distance between "9" and "10." For example, there might be very little difference between the couple getting rank 1 and the couple getting rank 2, but there might be an enormous difference between the couple getting rank 9 and the couple getting rank 10.

## INTERVAL SCALE NUMBERS: KNOWING HOW MUCH MORE

Because of the limitations of ordinal numbers, you may decide you want a higher scale of measurement. For example, in addition to assuming that numbers can be ordered, you might also want to be able to assume that the psychological distance (the difference between what is happening in participants' minds) between a score of "1" and "2" is exactly the same as the difference between "2" and "3," which is the same as the psychological distance between any two consecutive whole numbers. In technical terminology, you are assuming that your numbers are on an **interval scale:** a scale for which equal numerical intervals represent equal psychological intervals.

Unfortunately, the assumption of equal intervals is not easy to defend—no matter what measure you use. As we have seen, ranked data are typically assumed not to be interval. Furthermore, if you use a measure of nonverbal behavior, you could still fail to meet the assumption of equal intervals. For example, suppose you had couples come into a lab for 10 minutes and recorded the total amount of time a couple stared into each other's eyes. It would be risky to assume that the difference in love between a couple who looks for 360 seconds and a couple who looks for 300 seconds is the same as the difference between a couple who looks for a total of 60 seconds and a couple who does not look at all.

Most psychologists assume that rating scales produce interval scale data. Yet, even if you use a rating scale, the assumption of equal intervals might be hard to justify. For example, suppose you had people rate how they felt about their spouse on a $-30$ (hate intensely) to a $+30$ (love intensely) scale. Would you be sure that someone who changed from $-1$ to $+1$ had changed to the same degree as someone who had changed from $+12$ to $+14$?

## RATIO SCALES: ZEROING IN ON PERFECTION

If you are extremely demanding, it may not be enough for you to assume that your measure's numbers can be meaningfully ordered from lowest to highest and that equal intervals between numbers represent equal psychological distances. You may want to make one last, additional assumption—that your measure has an absolute zero. In other words, you might assume that someone scoring a zero on your measure feels absolutely no love. If a score of zero on your love measure represented absolutely no love and you had equal intervals, then you could make ratio statements such as: "The couple who scored a '1' on the love measure was 1/2 as much in love as the couple scoring a '2.'" Because measures that have both an absolute zero and equal intervals allow you to make ratio statements, these measures produce **ratio** scale numbers.

The assumption of having an absolute zero is not automatic even when measuring physical reality. For example, zero degrees Fahrenheit doesn't mean no (zero) temperature. If it did, we could make ratio statements such as saying that 50 degrees is half as hot as 100 degrees.

As you have seen, meeting the assumptions of ratio scale measurement is not automatic even when measuring physical reality. Not surprisingly, then, it is hard to meet the requirements of ratio scale measurement when measuring a psychological characteristic. It is hard to say that a zero score means a complete absence of a psychological characteristic. Furthermore, it is hard to say that the numbers generated by a measure correspond perfectly to psychological reality. It's tough enough to have some degree of correspondence between scores on a measure and psychological reality, much less to achieve perfection. Indeed, most researchers do not even ask participants to try to make ratio scale judgments. For example, they often ask participants to rate on a 1 to 5 scale rather than on a 0 to 4 scale. Furthermore, even when participants rate on a 0 to 4 scale, participants are rarely asked to think of "2" as having twice as much of the quality as "1," "3" as three times "1," and "4" as four times as much as "1." Of course, even if participants were asked to make ratio scale judgments, there is no guarantee that participants would be able to do so successfully.

## Why Our Numbers Do Not Always Measure Up

But why don't you get ratio scale numbers from your behavioral measures? For example, why isn't time staring into each other's eyes a ratio scale measure? Isn't zero the complete absence of gazing? Isn't three seconds of gazing three times as much as one second? Yes and no. Yes, seconds of gazing is a ratio scale measure if you are interested in knowing about gazing. But you aren't measuring gazes for gazing's sake. You are using gazes to measure love. You are not trying to measure physical reality (gazes); you are trying to use physical reality to measure psychological reality (love). As an indirect, imperfect reflection of love, time of gaze is not a ratio scale measure (see Box 4-1).

To reiterate, you cannot measure love, or any other construct, directly. You can only measure constructs indirectly. It is unlikely that your indirect measure of a construct will measure that construct with the perfect accuracy that ratio scale measurement requires.

## Which Level of Measurement Do You Need?

You have seen that there are four different levels of measurement: nominal scale, ordinal scale, interval scale, and ratio scale. As you go up the scale from nominal to ordinal to interval to ratio scale measurement, the numbers become increasingly informative (for a review, see Table 4-1). Furthermore, as you go up the scale, it becomes harder to find a measure that provides that level of

## Box 4–1
## Numbers and the Toll Ticket

| TOLL BY VEHICLE CLASS (in dollars) | | | | |
| | 1 | 2 | 3 | 4 |
|---|---|---|---|---|

| Exit No. | # Miles | | | | |
|---|---|---|---|---|---|
| 1 | 3.0 | .25 | .35 | .60 | .35 |
| 2 | 10.0 | .40 | .45 | 1.00 | .60 |
| 3 | 40.0 | .50 | .60 | 1.35 | .80 |
| 4 | 45.0 | .80 | .90 | 2.15 | 1.30 |
| 5 | 49.0 | .90 | 1.10 | 2.65 | 1.55 |
| 6 | 51.0 | 1.45 | 1.65 | 3.65 | 2.15 |
| 7 | 117.0 | 3.60 | 4.15 | 9.95 | 5.85 |

The toll ticket show us many kinds of numbers in action. For example, the numbers representing vehicle class (1–4) at the top of the ticket (under toll by vehicle class) are nominal numbers. The only reason the toll people used numbers instead of names is that numbers take less room. So, instead of writing "car," "16-wheeled truck," "small truck," etc., they wrote 1, 2, 3, and 4. There's no particular order to these numbers as shown by the fact that a "3" is charged more than any other number.

The exits, when used as an index of distance, represent ordinal data. You know that if you have to get off at exit 4, you will have to go farther than if you get off at exit 5, but—without looking at the miles column—you don't know how much farther. Thus, missing exit 4 isn't too bad, the next exit is only four miles away. Missing exit 6, on the other hand, is terrible—the next exit is 66 miles farther down the road!

Money, as a measure of miles, is also an ordinal measure. That is, although you know that the more money you spend on tolls, the farther you have gone, you can't figure out how much farther you have gone merely by looking at how much money the toll was. For example, if you are vehicle class number 1, it costs you 25 cents to go three miles, 15 cents more to go seven additional miles, and only 10 more cents gets you 30 additional miles. That is, amount of money spent and number of exits passed are only ordinal measures when trying to estimate the amount of another variable (distance). Similarly, some behavioral and physiological measures (eye-gazing or blood pressure increases) may only be ordinal measures when used to estimate the amount of an invisible psychological state (such as love).

measurement. For example, a measuring system that ranks participants provides ordinal data, but not interval data. Therefore, if you need interval data to answer your research question, you cannot use a measure that involves ranking participants from lowest to highest. This is true no matter how valid the ranking system is.

TABLE 4–1

**The Meaning and Limitations of Different Scales of Measurement**

| SCALE | MEANING | LIMITATIONS |
|---|---|---|
| Nominal | Different scores represent different types of behavior or different amounts of the construct. ("3" is a *different* kind of love than "1" or a different level of love.) | Since there is no order to nominal numbers, we can't say that "3" indicates *more* love than "1." |
| Ordinal | Different scores indicate different amounts *and* higher scores represent greater amounts of what is being measured. ("3" is **more** love than "1.") | Since the distances between numbers do not correspond to psychological reality, we can't say *how much* more of a quality one participant has than another. |
| Interval | Higher scores represent more of the construct *and* equal distances between numbers represent equal psychological differences. Therefore, we can say *how much* more love one participant feels than another. ("3" is more love than "1" to the same extent that "5" is more love than "3.") | Since we do not have an absolute zero, we cannot say *how many more times* as much love one participant has than another. |
| Ratio | Higher scores represent more of the construct and equal distances between numbers represent equal psychological differences *and* zero means a complete absence of the construct. The mathematical ratio between two scores perfectly corresponds to reality. ("3" is 3 times as much love as "1.") | None. |

Thus, when choosing a measure for a study, you should ask two questions:

1. What scale of measurement do I need to answer the research question?
2. Which of the measures that I am considering will give me this level of measurement?

The next sections and Tables 4–2 and 4–3 will help you answer these questions.

### WHEN YOU NEED RATIO SCALE DATA

Suppose you want to find out whether engaged couples are *twice* as much in love as dating couples who are not engaged. Since you are hypothesizing a 2 to 1 ratio, you need a measure that gives you ratio scale numbers. As Table 4–3 indicates, there are very few measures that you can use if you need ratio scale numbers.

Fortunately, you only need ratio scale level of measurement if you are trying to make ratio statements like John is twice as attractive as Mike, or married women are twice as happy as widows.

**TABLE 4–2**

**Different Research Questions Require Different Levels of Measurement**

| RESEARCH QUESTION | SCALE OF MEASUREMENT REQUIRED |
|---|---|
| Are members of Group A more likely to be _____ *types* than members of Group B? | At least nominal |
| Is Group A *more* _____ than Group B? | At least ordinal |
| Is the difference between Group 1 and Group 2 *as much as* the difference between Group 3 and Group 4? | At least interval |
| Did Group A change *as much as* Group B? | At least interval |
| Is Group A three *times* more _____ than Group B? | Only ratio scale data will do |

**TABLE 4–3**

**Measuring Instruments and the Kind of Data They Produce**

| SCALE OF MEASUREMENT | MEASURING TACTICS ASSUMED TO PRODUCE THOSE KINDS OF NUMBERS |
|---|---|
| Ratio | Magnitude estimation |
| Interval | Rating scales <br> (Magnitude estimation) |
| Ordinal | Nonverbal measures <br> Physiological measures <br> Rankings <br> (Rating Scales) <br> (Magnitude estimation) |
| Nominal | Any valid measure <br> (All of the above) |

*Note:* Any measurement technique that provides data that meet a certain level of measurement also provides data that meet the less stringent requirements of lower levels of measurement. Thus, a measure that provides data that meet the requirements of interval scale measurement also provides data that meet the requirements of ordinal and nominal scale measurement.

## WHEN YOU NEED AT LEAST INTERVAL SCALE DATA

Since you will probably not be comparing groups to find out whether one group is twice as much in love as another group, you will rarely need to assume that your measure has ratio properties. However, you may have to assume that your measure does have interval properties. For example, suppose you are trying to estimate the effects of therapy on relationships. Before relationship counseling is offered on your campus, you measure the degree to which couples are in love. Next, you observe who goes to counseling and who doesn't. Finally, at the end of the term, you measure the couples' love again. Let's say that you got the following pattern of results:

|  | Beginning of term | End of term |
|---|---|---|
| Didn't go to counseling | 3.0 | 4.0 |
| Went to counseling | 5.0 | 7.0 |

(The higher the score, the more in love. Scores could range from 1 to 9.)

Did the couples who went for counseling change more than those who didn't? Don't say "yes" too soon! If you say "yes," you are assuming that the psychological distance between 3 and 4 is less than the psychological distance between 5 and 7. However, it could be that the psychological distance between 3 and 4 is much more than the psychological distance between 5 and 7. Thus, to answer the question of which group changed more, you must assume that your data conform to an interval scale. Therefore, to answer the research question, "Did couples who went for counseling change more than those who didn't?", you would have to use a measure that has interval properties, such as a self-rating scale.

## WHEN ORDINAL DATA ARE SUFFICIENT

Suppose you don't care how much more in love one group is than the other. Rather, all you want to know is which group is most in love. For example, suppose you want to be able to order these three groups in terms of amount of love:

| Didn't go to counseling at all | 3.0 |
|---|---|
| Went to counseling for 1 week | 5.0 |
| Went to counseling for 8 weeks | 7.0 |

(The higher the score, the more in love. Scores could range from 1 to 9.)

If you had ordinal data, you could conclude that participants who went to counseling for 8 weeks were most in love, those who went for 1 week were less in love, and those who didn't go to counseling were least in love. So, if you simply want to know which group is higher on a variable and which group is lower, then all you need is ordinal data. If all you need is ordinal data, you are in luck. As you can see from Table 4–3, most measures produce data that meet or exceed the requirements of ordinal level measurement.

## WHEN YOU ONLY NEED NOMINAL DATA

It's conceivable that you aren't interested in discovering which group is more in love. Instead, you might have the less ambitious goal of just trying to find out whether the different groups differ in terms of their love for each other. If that's the case, nominal data are all you need. Since you only need to make the least demanding and safest assumption about your numbers (that different numbers represent different things), any valid measure you choose will measure up.

## Conclusions about Scales of Measurement

As you have seen, different research questions require different scales of measurement. If you are only asking whether two groups differ, any scale of measurement will do. If, however, you are asking whether one group has more of a quality than another, you need at least ordinal level data. If your research question involves asking how much more of a quality one group has than another, then you need to use a measure that provides at least interval data. If you need to find out how many times more of a quality one group has than another, then you need ratio level data.

Just as different research questions require different levels of measurement, different measures produce different levels of measurement. Consequently, you may find that the type of data you need will dictate the measure you choose. That is, you may find that the only measure that will give you the type of data you want is not as sensitive or as free from biases as another measure.

Let's look at one example that illustrates this point. Measuring a nonverbal behavior may give you a measure of love that is less vulnerable to subject biases than a rating scale measure. However, suppose you want to know if a treatment is more effective for couples having relationship problems than it is for couples that are very much in love. If both types of couples will improve, your research question requires interval scale data.

To illustrate why you require interval data, imagine that the problem couple's score on the measure goes from a "1" to a "3" whereas the happy couple's increases from an "8" to a "9." To say that the problem couple actually *experienced* more improvement, you must assume that the difference between "1" and "3" is greater than the difference between "8" and "9." This is not an assumption you can make with either nominal or ordinal data. It is, however, an assumption you can make if you have interval data (because with interval data, the psychological distance between "1" and "2" is the same as the distance between "8" and "9."

Because your research question requires interval data, you must use a measure that provides interval data. Consequently, if the rating scale is the only measure that gives you interval scale data, you will have to use it—despite its vulnerability to subject bias—because it is the only measure that will allow you to answer your research question.

## ETHICAL AND PRACTICAL CONSIDERATIONS

There are times when you may decide not to use a certain measure even though that measure allows you to answer your research question. For example, suppose you have a measure that gives you the right scale of measurement and is more valid than other measures because it is not vulnerable to subject biases. However, it avoids subject bias by surprising or tricking participants. In that case, you may decide against using a measure because you believe participants should be fully informed about the study before they agree to participate. Similarly, you may reject field observation because you feel those tactics threaten participants' privacy.

Although you should always be concerned about ethical issues, you often have to be concerned about practical issues. You may have to reject a measure because it is simply too time-consuming or expensive to use. Or, you might choose a measure primarily because it has high **face validity**: the extent to which it looks, on the face of it, to be valid. Although there is nothing scientific about face validity,[1] face validity may be important to the consumer (or the sponsor) of your research. For example, how loud a person yells and how many widgets a person produces may be equally valid measures of motivation. But if you were going to get a manager to take your research seriously, which measure would you use?

## CONCLUDING REMARKS

In this chapter, you have seen that choosing a measure is a complex decision. It is not simply enough to pick the most valid measure. Instead, you need to pick the measure that will be most likely to answer your research question. To pick the best measure for your particular study, you must decide what threats to validity are most serious, decide how much sensitivity you need, decide what level of measurement your research question requires, and carefully weigh ethical, as well as practical, considerations.

Clearly, in designing a research project, choosing a measure is an important decision. However, it is only one of several decisions a researcher may make. For example, the researcher has to decide whether to do a survey, an experiment, or some other type of research. Then, if the researcher decides to do an experiment, the researcher must decide on what type of experiment to do. In the next few chapters, you will learn how to make these key design decisions.

---

[1] Face validity means that, on the surface (on the face of it), the measure appears to be valid. In other words, it means "unscientific validity." That is, in contrast to careful evaluation of evidence, people may take a superficial glance at a measure and come to a "conclusion" about the measure. A measure with face validity may have no scientific validity at all. For example, a measure with face validity could be vulnerable to social desirability bias. To prevent you from confusing face validity with scientific validity, we did not mention face validity in our chapter on the scientific validity of measures (Chapter 3).

## SUMMARY

1. Since no measure is perfect, choosing a measure involves making tradeoffs.
2. Sensitivity, reliability, and validity are highly valued in a measure.
3. Sensitivity is a measure's ability to detect small differences.
4. An unreliable measure cannot be sensitive, but a reliable measure may be insensitive.
5. By asking how much rather than whether, by knowing what you want to measure, by avoiding unnecessary inferences, and by using common sense, you may be able to increase a measure's sensitivity.
6. Different kinds of measures produce different kinds of numbers.
7. Nominal numbers only let you say that participants differ. However, they do not let you say that one participant has more of a characteristic than another. With nominal measurement, the number you give each group is arbitrary. For example, if you coded men as "1" and women as "2," that is entirely arbitrary. You could even go back and recode women as "1" and men as "2."
8. Ordinal numbers let you say that one participant has more of a quality than another. However, ordinal numbers do not allow you to talk about specific amounts of a quality. They only let you talk about having more of it or less of it, but not about how much more.
9. Interval and ratio numbers let you say how much more of a quality one participant has than another.
10. Ratio scale numbers let you say how many times more of a quality one participant has relative to another.
11. Depending on the research question, a measure's sensitivity and its level of measurement may be almost as important as validity.
12. You must always consider ethical and practical issues when choosing a measure.

## KEY TERMS

**face validity:** the extent to which a measure looks valid to the ordinary person. Face validity has nothing to do with scientific validity. However, for practical/political reasons, you may decide to consider face validity when comparing measures. (p. 122)

**nominal scale numbers:** numbers that substitute for names. Different numbers represent *different* types, kinds, categories, or qualities, but larger numbers do not represent more of a quality than smaller numbers. (p. 113)

**ordinal scale numbers:** numbers that can be meaningfully ordered from lowest to highest. With ordinal numbers, we know that the higher scoring participant has *more* of a quality than the lower scoring participant, but we don't know how much more of the quality the higher scoring participant has. (p. 114)

**interval scale data:** data for which equal numerical intervals represent equal psychological intervals. That is, the difference between scoring a "2" and a "1" and the difference between scoring a "7" and a "6" is the same not only in terms of scores (both are a difference of 1), but also in terms of the actual amount of the psychological characteristic being measured. Interval scale measures allow us to compare participants in terms of *how much* of a quality they have. (p. 115)

**ratio scale numbers:** numbers having all the qualities of interval scale numbers, but that also result from a measure that has an absolute zero (zero on the measure means the complete absence of the quality). As the name implies, ratio scale numbers allow you to make ratio statements about the quality that you are measuring. (p. 116)

**response latency:** how long it takes the participant to begin to act or to react. Perhaps the most familiar example is *how long* it takes participants to push a button on a reaction time task. Measuring response latency, rather than just whether or not the participant responded, can improve sensitivity. (p. 110)

**sensitivity:** a measure's ability to detect differences among participants on a given variable. (p. 107)

## EXERCISES

1. Researchers have used a measure to find small differences between groups. Based on this information, would you infer that the measure's reliability was low or high? Why?
2. Becky wants to know how much students drink.
   a. What level of measurement could Becky get? Why?
   b. Becky asks participants: How much do you drink:
      a) 0–1 drinks; b) 1–3 drinks; c) 3–4 drinks; d) more than 4 drinks? What scale of measurement does she have?
   c. Becky ranks participants according to how much they drink. What scale of measurement does she have?
   d. Becky assigns participants a "1" if they are a wine drinker, and a "2" if they are a beer drinker. What scale of measurement is this?
   e. Becky asks participants: How much do you drink:
      a) 0–1 drinks; b) 1–3 drinks; c) 3–4 drinks; d) more than 4; e) don't know?
      If she codes the data as follows: a=1, b=2, c=3, d=4, e=5, what scale of measurement does she have? Why?
3. Assume that facial tension is a measure of thinking.
   a. How would you measure facial tension?
   b. What scale of measurement is it on? Why?
   c. How sensitive do you think this measure would be? Why?

4. If an investigator wants to know whether one drug awareness program is more effective than another, what scale of measurement does the investigator need? What if the investigator wants to show that one program is better for informing the relatively ignorant than it is for informing the fairly well-informed?

5. Find or invent a measure.
   a. Describe the measure.
   b. Discuss how you could improve its sensitivity.
   c. What kind of data (nominal, ordinal, interval, or ratio), do you think that measure would produce? Why?

# CHAPTER 5

---

# Internal Validity

*Overview*

*Why We Cannot Get Two Identical Groups: Selection*

SELF-ASSIGNMENT TO GROUP AS A SOURCE OF SELECTION BIAS
RESEARCHER ASSIGNMENT TO GROUP: AN OBVIOUS
SOURCE OF SELECTION BIAS
ARBITRARY ASSIGNMENT TO GROUP AS A SOURCE
OF SELECTION BIAS
MATCHING: A VALIANT, BUT UNSUCCESSFUL STRATEGY
FOR GETTING IDENTICAL GROUPS
PROBLEMS WITH MATCHING ON PRETEST SCORES

*Problems with the Pretest–Posttest Design*

THREE REASONS PARTICIPANTS MAY CHANGE
BETWEEN PRETEST AND POSTTEST
HOW MEASUREMENT CHANGES MAY CAUSE SCORES TO CHANGE
BETWEEN PRETEST AND POSTTEST

*Conclusions*

RULING OUT EXTRANEOUS VARIABLES
THE RELATIONSHIP BETWEEN INTERNAL AND EXTERNAL VALIDITY

*Summary*

*Key Terms*

*Exercises*

# Chapter 5

# INTERNAL VALIDITY

*"All things are possible until they are proved impossible"*
—PEARL S. BUCK

## OVERVIEW

This chapter is about internal validity. As you may recall from Chapter 1, for a study to have internal validity, it must clearly demonstrate that a specific factor causes an effect. Thus, if you establish that turning on blue lights in a room *causes* higher scores on a happiness questionnaire, your study has internal validity.

The logic of establishing internal validity is simple. First, you determine that changes in a treatment (blue lighting) are *followed* by changes on a variable (increased happiness). Then, you determine that the treatment (blue lighting) is the *only* factor responsible for the effect (increased happiness). That is, you show that the results could not be due to anything other than the lighting. Or, as a psychologist would say, you rule out **extraneous factors:** factors other than the treatment.

The most direct way to rule out the possibility that your results are due to the effects of extraneous factors is to eliminate all extraneous factors from your study. If there are no extraneous factors in your study, extraneous factors obviously cannot be responsible for your results. In the abstract, there are two ways you can get rid of extraneous factors:

1) get two identical groups, treat them identically, except that you only give one of the groups the treatment, then compare the treatment group to the no-treatment group;
2) get some participants, measure them, make sure that nothing in their life changes except that they get the treatment, then measure them again.

In actual practice, however, neither of these methods succeed in eliminating extraneous variables. As a result, these approaches—contrary to what a naive person might believe—*cannot* prove that a treatment caused an effect.

In this chapter, you will learn why these two approaches fail to establish internal validity. Specifically, you will learn about Campbell and Stanley's (1963) eight general threats to internal validity:

1. selection,
2. selection by maturation interactions,
3. regression,
4. maturation,
5. history,
6. testing,
7. instrumentation, and
8. mortality.

In addition, you will know enough about these threats to:

1. be cautious about accepting a claim that a factor causes a certain effect;
2. detect their presence in research that erroneously claims to prove that a certain factor has an effect;
3. avoid using a design that is vulnerable to these threats; and
4. take steps to prevent these threats from affecting the results of your research.

## WHY WE CANNOT GET TWO IDENTICAL GROUPS: SELECTION

To begin our exploration of Campbell and Stanley's (1963) eight threats to validity, let's examine the first approach to ruling out extraneous variables: getting two identical groups. Specifically, suppose you get two groups of participants and treat them identically, except that only one of the groups gets the treatment (blue lighting). Then, you give both groups the happiness scale and note that they have different levels of happiness.

What do you conclude? If the groups were identical before you introduced the treatment, you would correctly conclude that the treatment caused the groups to differ. However, if the groups were not identical before you introduced the treatment, the effect could be due to **selection:** choosing groups that were different from one another before the study began.

### Self-Assignment to Group as a Source of Selection Bias

How can you avoid the selection error? That is, how can you get two identical groups? Obviously, one key to avoiding selection error is to prevent participants from choosing what condition they want to be in (self-selection). If your participants choose their own conditions, then you know that the groups will differ on at least one dimension: one group chose the treatment, the other chose to avoid the treatment. Furthermore, the groups probably differ in ways

**FIGURE 5–1**

An anti-health care demonstration organized by citizens who don't understand selection.

that you do not know about. As a result, if you let participants choose what condition they will be in, you will probably end up comparing apples and oranges.

Sometimes the effects of self-selection are obvious. For example, suppose you compare two groups—one group volunteers to stay after work to attend a seminar on "Helping Your Company," the other does not. If you find that the seminar group is more loyal to the company than the no-seminar group, you cannot conclude that the effect is due to the seminar. The groups obviously differed in loyalty before the study began.

Sometimes the effects of self-selection are not as obvious. For instance, what if you let participants choose whether they get blue lighting or no lighting? If you find that the blue lighting group is happier than the no-lighting group, you cannot conclude that the effect was due to the blue lighting. People who prefer blue lighting may be happier than people who prefer no lighting. You really do not know how participants who choose one condition differ from those who choose another condition. But you do know that they differ. And these differences may cause the groups to differ at the end of the study.

## Researcher Assignment to Group: An Obvious Source of Selection Bias

Obviously, letting participants assign themselves to a group creates unequal groups. However, if you assign participants to groups, you might unintentionally bias your study. For example, you might put all the smiling participants in the blue light condition and all the frowning participants in the no-treatment condition.

## Arbitrary Assignment to Group as a Source of Selection Bias

To avoid the bias of "picking your own team," you might assign participants to groups on the basis of some arbitrary rule. For example, why not assign students on the right-hand side of the room to the no-treatment group and assign students on the left side of the room to the treatment group? The answer is simple: "Because the groups are *not* equal." At the very least, the groups differ in that one group prefers the right side, while the other group prefers the left side. They probably differ in many other ways. For example, if the left side of the room is near the windows and the right side is near the door, we can list at least four reasons why "left-siders" might be happier and/or more energetic than "right-siders":

1) People sitting on the left side of the room may be more energetic because they walked the width of the room to find a seat.
2) People sitting on the left side of the room may be early-arrivers (students who came in late would tend to sit on the right side so they would not disrupt class by crossing the width of the room).
3) People sitting on the left side may be more interested in the outdoors since they chose to have access to the window.
4) People sitting on the left side may have chosen those seats to get a better view of the professor's performance (if the professor shows the typical right-hander's tendency of turning to the right, which would be the students' left).

You can probably come up with many other differences between left-siders and right-siders in a particular class. But the point is that the groups definitely differ in at least one respect (choice of side of room), and they almost certainly differ in numerous other respects (see Figure 5–2).

What's true for the arbitrary rule of assigning participants to groups on the basis of where they sit is true for any other arbitrary rule. Thus, any researchers who assign participants on the basis of an arbitrary rule (the first-arriving participants assigned to the treatment group, people whose last names begin with a letter between A and L in the treatment group, etc.) make their research vulnerable to selection bias.

**FIGURE 5–2A**

Every other person . . .

**The rule of choosing "every other person" to get the treatment is not random. The problem with this rule is most obvious when applied to situations where people are encouraged to line up "boy/girl."**

The reason that arbitrarily assigning participants to groups does not work is because you are assigning participants to groups based on their differences. Your groups can't be equal when you are deliberately ensuring that they are different on some variable (preference for side of the room, etc.).

## Matching: A Valiant, but Unsuccessful Strategy for Getting Identical Groups

If you can assign participants in a way that guarantees they are different, why can't you assign participants in a way that guarantees they are identical? In other words, why not use **matching:** choosing your groups so that they have identical characteristics?

**FIGURE 5–2B**

**The arbitrary rule of assigning the front of the class to one treatment and the back of the class to no treatment does not work. Ask any teacher! The two groups are definitely different.**

## THE IMPOSSIBILITY OF PERFECTLY MATCHING INDIVIDUAL PARTICIPANTS: IDENTICAL PARTICIPANTS DO NOT EXIST

In the abstract, matching seems like an easy, foolproof way of making sure that your two groups are equal. In practice, however, matching is neither easy nor foolproof. Imagine the difficulty of finding two people who match on every characteristic and then assigning one to the no-treatment condition and the other to the treatment condition. It would be impossible. Even identical twins would not be exactly alike—they have different first names, different injuries, and different experiences.

## THE DIFFICULTY OF MATCHING GROUPS ON EVERY VARIABLE: THERE ARE TOO MANY VARIABLES

Obviously, you cannot create the situation in which each member of the treatment group has an identical clone in the no-treatment group. Try as you might,

**FIGURE 5–2c**

**Assigning by left side vs. right side ruins an attention study's internal validity. Students on the window-side of the room are sitting there because they want to look out the window or at the clock. The students on the other side of the room may be sitting there to avoid distractions.**

there would always be some variable on which you had not matched—and that variable might be important. Thus, even if you created two groups that had the same average age, same average intelligence, same average income, same average height, and same average weight, there would still be thousands of variables on which the groups might differ. For example, the groups might differ in how they felt on the day of the experiment, how they were getting along with their parents, how many books they had read, their overall health, etc.

## TWO DIFFICULTIES WITH MATCHING GROUPS ON EVERY RELEVANT VARIABLE

Clearly, you cannot match your no-treatment and treatment groups on every single characteristic. However, making groups identical in every respect may be unnecessary. You only need them to be identical in respect to the variable you want to measure. For example, suppose you were studying happiness.

Then, all you would need to do is match your groups on every characteristic that will influence their score on your happiness measure.

Unfortunately, there are two problems with this "solution." First, matching only on those factors that influence the key variable may be impossible because there may be thousands of factors that influence happiness. Second, you probably do not know every single characteristic that influences happiness. If you knew everything about happiness, you would not be doing a study to find out about happiness.

## Problems with Matching on Pretest Scores

Instead of matching participants on every characteristic that affects the variable you want to measure, why not match participants on the variable you want to measure? In your case, why not match participants on the happiness scores? That is, before you assign participants to groups, test people on the happiness scale (what psychologists call a *pretest*). Next, match your groups so that the treatment group and no-treatment group have the same average pretest score. Finally, at the end of the study, test the participants again, giving participants what psychologists call a *posttest.* If you find a difference between your groups on the posttest, then you should be positive that the treatment worked, right? *Wrong!*

Even if the treatment had no effect whatsoever, there are two possible reasons why two groups that scored the same on the pretest could differ on the posttest: selection by maturation interactions and regression effects.

### SELECTION BY MATURATION INTERACTIONS: PARTICIPANTS GROWING IN DIFFERENT WAYS

The first reason is the **selection by maturation interaction:** The groups started out the same on the pretest, but afterwards developed at different rates or in different directions. That is, participants who start out the same on a dimension may grow apart because they differ in other respects.

To visualize the strong impact that selection by maturation interaction can have, imagine you found a group of fourth grade boys and girls. You put all the boys in one group. Then, you had them lift weights. You saw that the average weight they could lift was 40 lbs. You then picked a group of 4th grade girls who could also lift 40 lbs. Thus, your groups are equivalent on the pretest. Then, you introduced the treatment: strength pills. You gave the boys strength pills for eight years. When both groups were in the 12th grade, you measured their strength. You found that boys were much stronger than the girls. This effect might be due to the strength pills. However, the effect may also be due to the boys naturally developing strength at a faster rate than the girls. That is, the effect may be due to failing to match on a variable (gender) that influences muscular maturation.

You have seen that groups may grow apart because of different rates of physical maturation. Groups may also grow apart because of different rates of social, emotional, or intellectual maturation. To illustrate this point, let's examine a situation where the two groups are probably changing in different ways on virtually every aspect of development.

For example, suppose a researcher matched—on the basis of job performance—a group of 19-year-old employees with a group of 63-year-old employees. The researcher then enrolled the 19-year-olds into a training program. When the researcher compared the groups two years later, the researcher found that the 19-year-olds were performing better than the 63-year-olds. Why?

The difference may have been due to training. However, the difference may also have been due to the fact that 19-year-olds' productivity should increase even without training because they are just learning their jobs. The 63-year-olds' performance, on the other hand, might naturally decrease as this group anticipates retirement. Therefore, the apparent treatment effect may really be a selection by maturation interaction.

You may be saying to yourself that you would never make the mistake of matching 19-year-olds and 63-year-olds on pretest scores. If so, we are glad. You intuitively know that you cannot make groups equivalent by merely matching on pretest scores. We would caution you, however, to realize that age is not the only—or even the most important—variable that might affect maturation.[1] Many factors, such as intelligence, motivation, and health, might affect maturation. Thus, if you are going to match on pretest scores, you must also match on all of the variables that might affect maturation. Otherwise, you run the risk of a selection by maturation interaction.

In reiteration, matching on pretest scores is incomplete. Pretest scores are a good predictor of posttest scores, but not a perfect predictor. Many factors affect how a participant does on the posttest. If the groups are not matched on these other relevant variables, two groups that started out the same on the pretest may naturally grow apart. Thus, what looks like a treatment effect may really be a selection by maturation interaction.

If you were somehow able to match on pretest scores and all other relevant variables, you would be able to rule out selection by maturation. However, even then, your matched groups may not be equal.

## THE REGRESSION EFFECT

How could your groups not be equal if you measured them and made sure that they were equal? The problem is that you cannot measure them to make sure

---

[1] Note that, contrary to ageist stereotypes, we might find that the older workers improved more than the younger workers. That is, older workers are much more productive and involved than they are often given credit for. Indeed, this ageism is probably why our poor researcher was forced to do such a flawed study. The researcher was able to get management to invest in training for younger workers but not for the older workers. That is, the researcher used the older workers as a comparison group because management gave her no choice—not because she wanted to.

they are equal. In other words, measuring them as equal does not mean they are equal.

Even though you tend to assume that measurement is perfect, it is not. For example, if a police officer stops you for speeding, the officer might say, "You were going 75." Or the officer might say, "I clocked you at 75." The officer's two statements are very different. You may have been going 40 and the radar mis-timed you (radars have clocked trees at over 100 miles per hour) or you may have been going 95. In any event, you probably were not going at exactly the speed that the officer recorded. Even in this age of advanced technology, something as simple as measuring someone's height is not immune to measurement error. In fact, one of the authors fluctuates between 5'5" and 5'8", depending on who measures her. Needless to say, if measurements of variables as easy to measure as height are contaminated with random error, measurements of psychological variables—variables that are not as easy to measure as height—are probably also victimized by random measurement error.

You can capitalize on measurement error to make two groups that are very different *appear* to be very similar and later *appear* to become very different. For example, suppose you were offered $1,000 to find and take pictures of a white sheep and a black sheep that are the same color. Then, you were asked to take another picture that would make the two sheep differ in terms of color. What would you do?

To get a photo of a black sheep that looks like a white sheep, you would take hundreds of pictures of white sheep and hundreds of pictures of black sheep. Eventually, due to some random measurement error (overexposure, underexposure, mis-timed flash, error in developing film, etc.), you would get at least one photo of a white sheep that looks black, or a black sheep that looks white, or a black sheep and a white sheep that both look gray. You got the results you wanted by selectively taking advantage of measurements that were heavily contaminated by random measurement error.

After you have a photo of a white sheep and a black sheep that appear to be the same color, it is easy to make the sheep "become" different colors. You would simply re-photograph the two sheep. The second time you photograph the two sheep, the white one would probably look white and the black one would probably look black. The photographic illusion you created was temporary because extreme amounts of random measurement error rarely strike the same measurements twice in a row. In other words, to create the illusion of change, you took advantage of **regression to the mean:** the tendency for scores that are extremely unusual to revert back to more normal levels on the retest.

Regression toward the mean occurs because unusual scores tend to be unusually affected by chance. As a result, when participants receiving unusual scores are retested, their scores tend to be affected by chance to a more usual (and lesser) degree the second time around.

In the example above, you intentionally took advantage of the erratic nature of random measurement error. That is, you "matched" two groups on a factor in which they differed. Then, when they scored differently on the posttest, it *looked* like the groups had changed. Unfortunately, a researcher might *unintentionally* rely on measurement error to match two groups on a factor in which they differ. For instance, suppose a researcher working at an institution for the mentally retarded wants to see whether a specially developed training program can increase intelligence. The researcher wants to have two groups that are identical in intelligence, give one group the training program, and see whether the training program group does better on a second intelligence test than the no-training group. However, the researcher also wants both groups to have near-normal intelligence. Unfortunately, after testing all the patients, the researcher only finds eight patients who score between 85 and 95 on the IQ test.

The researcher decides that eight participants are only enough for the treatment group. Therefore, he still needs to find a no-treatment group, preferably one that has the same IQ as his treatment group. As he drives by your school, he has an idea: use some of your school's students as participants. After clearing it with your school and taking precautions so that no one will be harmed by his procedures, he begins work. He sets up an office at your school and offers $25 to anyone who will take the IQ test.

After testing many people, he finds eight college students who score around 90 on the IQ test. He makes this group his no-treatment group. At the end of the study, he gives both groups IQ tests. When he looks at his results, he's horrified. He finds that the eight college students score much higher on the second IQ test (the posttest) than the institutionalized people. On closer examination, he finds that the college students' IQ scores increased dramatically from the pretest to posttest while the institutionalized patients' IQ scores dropped from pretest to posttest.

What happened? Did the true intelligence of the college students increase even though the researcher did nothing? Did the training program shrink the true intelligence of institutionalized patients?

What happened was that the investigator selected scores that were likely to be heavily contaminated with measurement error. To understand how this occurred, think about what would cause your classmates to score 90 on an IQ test. They certainly would not score a 90 because that was their true level of intelligence. Instead, they must have scored so low because of some factors having nothing to do with intelligence. Perhaps pulling an all-nighter, being hung-over, or suffering from the flu would cause such poor performance. If they did score a 90 on an IQ test because they were very ill, would it be likely that they would score a 90 the second time? No, chances are that they would not be as ill the second time they took the test. As a result, their second score should be higher because it would probably be a closer reflection of their true intelligence.

Likewise, the investigator chose those retarded patients' scores that were most likely to be loaded with measurement error. Consider how a retarded person could score 90 on the IQ test. What could account for a person scoring so far above their true score? Probably some form of luck would be involved. That is, just as you might have found yourself getting lucky on a multiple-choice test for which you were unprepared, a retarded person might get lucky the first time the test was administered. That is, if you test 8,000 retarded people, eight might score fairly high due to chance. But would these same eight be as lucky the next time? It's a good bet that they would not. Instead, their second score should be a more accurate reflection of their true score. Consequently, they would get lower scores than they did the first time.

### CONCLUSIONS ABOUT MATCHING ON PRETEST SCORES

In conclusion, there are two reasons why matching on pretest scores does not make your groups equal. First, you match on scores rather than on actual characteristics—and *scores* are flawed indicators of actual *characteristics.* Consequently, because of measurement error, it's possible to get two groups that match on pretest scores but that are actually very different. That is, random error may create the mirage that two dissimilar groups are similar. As convincing as this mirage may be, it is only temporary. Often, the mirage will vanish on the posttest, as chance exerts less of an influence on scores so that the extremely deviant scores revert back to more typical levels (regression to the mean). If the mirage disappears during the posttest, two groups that *appeared* to be similar on the pretest may reveal their true differences during the posttest. Although the change in scores is only due to changes in measurement error, you can understand how people could mistakenly interpret these changes as a treatment effect.

Second, matching on pretest scores is incomplete. It is incomplete because the pretest performance is not a perfect indicator of posttest performance. Many factors determine how participants will change from pretest to posttest. Therefore, to predict a participant's posttest score, you need to match not only on the pretest score, but on every other variable that might affect how participants will change. If you do not, you may have two groups that started out the same, but naturally grew apart—no thanks to the treatment. In other words, you may have what appears to be a treatment effect, but is really a selection by maturation effect.

# PROBLEMS WITH THE PRETEST–POSTTEST DESIGN

No matter how much we match, we cannot form two identical groups of participants. The only way we could get two identical groups of participants would be to have the same participants in both groups. That is, each participant could be in both the no-treatment group and in the treatment group. For instance, we might use a **pretest–posttest design,** where we give each

**TABLE 5–1**
**Why the Selection Problem Is Difficult to Eliminate**

1. Self-assignment causes selection bias.

2. Researcher assignment can cause selection bias

3. Arbitrary assignment to group causes selection error by making the groups differ in at least one respect.

4. We cannot match participants on every single variable.

5. We cannot even match participants on all relevant variables. Therefore, "matched" groups may differ from each other in terms of "unmatched" variables. These "unmatched" variables may cause the groups to behave differently at the posttest.

6. We have to worry about the effects of "unmatched" variables even when we match on pretest scores. As cases of *selection by maturation interactions* demonstrate, just because participants scored the same at pretest, it does not mean they will score the same at posttest.

7. Even if there were no selection by maturation interactions, matching on pretest scores is imperfect because *scores* may be heavily influenced by random error. The groups may only *appear* to be similar because one or both groups' pretest scores are heavily influenced by random error.

participant the pretest, administer the treatment, then give the posttest. If we make sure that the participants in the treatment group are the same participants that were in the no-treatment group, we have eliminated the threat of selection.

At first glance, the pretest–posttest design seems to be a perfect way to establish internal validity. However, for the pretest-posttest design to have internal validity, the treatment must be the only reason why posttest scores differ from pretest scores.

Unfortunately, the treatment is not the only reason why scores may change from pretest to posttest. For example, posttest *scores* may differ from pretest scores because of changes in scoring accuracy or scoring method. Thus, even if participants do not change from pretest to posttest, their scores may change.

## Three Reasons Participants May Change between Pretest and Posttest

Participants may, however, change from pretest to posttest. Indeed, even without the treatment, participants may change over time. For instance, a participant's mood may change by the minute. To be more specific, besides the treatment, there are at least three reasons why participants may change from pretest to posttest: maturation, history, and testing.

### MATURATION

A participant may change between the time of the pretest and the time of the posttest as a result of becoming more mature. For example, suppose you instituted a weight lifting program for high school sophomores. You find that—as

**FIGURE 5–3**

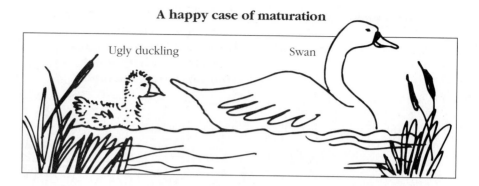

**A happy case of maturation**

Ugly duckling                    Swan

seniors—they can lift 40 pounds more than they could as sophomores. Your problem is that you do not know whether the weight training or natural development is responsible for the change. Similarly, if you give a baby 10 years of memory training, you will find that her memory improves. However, this difference may be due not to the training, but to **maturation:** changes due to natural development.

## HISTORY

A participant may change between pretest and posttest because the participant's environment has changed between pretest and posttest. These environmental changes are called **history.** To understand the effects of history, suppose two social psychologists have a treatment they think will change how Americans feel about space exploration. However, between pretest and posttest, a spacecraft explodes. Or, suppose an investigator was examining the effect of diet on maze-running speed. However, between pretest and posttest, the heat went off in the rat room and the rats nearly froze to death. Obviously, events that happen in a participant's life (*history*) between the pretest and the posttest can have a powerful effect on a participant's posttest score.

## TESTING

One event that always occurs between the start of the pretest and the start of the posttest is the pretest itself. If the pretest changes participants, you have a **testing effect.** For example, if your instructor gave you the same test twice, you would score better the second time around. However, your improvement might not be due to better studying habits, but rather to remembering some of the questions. People who have taken many intelligence tests (for example, children of clinical psychologists) may score very high on IQ tests, regardless of their true intelligence.

**FIGURE 5–4**

The testing effect is not limited to knowledge tests. Rather, the testing effect can occur with virtually any measure. To illustrate, let's choose a pretest that has nothing to do with knowledge. For instance, suppose we were to ask people their opinions about Greenland entering the World Bank. Would we get another answer the second time we asked this question? Yes, because the very action of asking for their opinion may cause them to think about the issue more and to develop or change their opinion. In short, by measuring something, you may change it.

## How Measurement Changes May Cause Scores to Change between Pretest and Posttest

Obviously, participants' scores may change over time because participants have changed. What is less obvious is that participants' *scores* may change over time even if participants themselves have not changed. Instead, participants' scores may change because of changes in how participants are measured. Specifically, scores may change because of instrumentation, mortality, and regression.

## CHANGES IN HOW PARTICIPANTS ARE MEASURED: INSTRUMENTATION

An obvious reason for a participant's score changing from pretest to posttest is that the measuring instrument used for the posttest is different from the one used during the pretest. If the difference between pretest and posttest scores is due to changes in the measuring instrument, you have an **instrumentation** effect.

Sometimes, changes in the measuring instrument are unintentional. For example, suppose you are measuring aggression using the most changeable measuring instrument possible: the human rater. As the study progresses, raters may broaden their definition of aggression. Consequently, raters may give participants higher posttest scores on aggression, even though participants' behavior has not changed. Unfortunately, there are many ways that raters could change between pretesting and posttesting. Raters could become more conscientious, less conscientious, more lenient, less lenient, etc. Any of these changes could cause an instrumentation effect.

Often, changes in the instrument occur because the researcher is trying to make the posttest better than the pretest. Thus, the researcher may get rid of typographical errors, bad questions, make the scales neater, etc. Unfortunately these changes, no matter how minor they may seem and no matter how logical they may be, are changes. And these changes may cause instrumentation effects.

We are not saying that you should not administer the best measure possible. Of course, you should. But you should refine the measure *before* beginning the study.

## CHANGING THE EXTENT TO WHICH MEASUREMENT IS AFFECTED BY RANDOM ERROR: REGRESSION REVISITED

Even if the measuring instrument is the same for both the pretest and posttest, the amount of chance measurement error may not be. In other words, with a pretest-posttest design, you still have to deal with regression toward the mean. To show that you do not get away from regression toward the mean by using the pretest-posttest design, think back to the researcher who was investigating the effects of a training program on intelligence. Suppose that he had decided not to compare the eight highest-scoring patients with a group of college students. Instead, after having the eight highest-scoring patients complete the training program, he administered a second IQ test as his posttest. What would he observe?

As before, he would have observed that the patients' IQ scores dropped from pretest to posttest. This drop is not due to the training program robbing patients of intelligence. Rather, the posttest scores more accurately reflect the patients' true intelligence. The posttest scores are lower than the pretest scores only because the pretest scores were inflated with random measurement error.

The pretest scores were destined to be inflated with measurement error because the investigators selected only those participants whose scores were extreme. Extreme scores tend to have extreme amounts of measurement error. To understand why, remember that a participant's score is a function of two things: the participant's true characteristics and measurement error. Thus, an extreme score may be extreme because measurement error is making the score extreme. To take a concrete example, let's consider how a student might get a perfect score on a quiz. There are three basic possibilities for the perfect score:

1) the student is a perfect student;
2) the student is a very good student and had some good luck;
3) The student is an average or below average student but got incredibly lucky.

As you can see, if you study a group of people who got perfect scores on the last exam, you are probably studying a group of people whose scores were inflated by measurement error. If participants were measured again, random error would probably be less generous. (After all, random error could not be more generous. There's only one place for scores to go—down.) Therefore, if you were to give them a treatment (memory training) and then look at their scores on the next exam, you would be disappointed. The group that averaged 100% on the first test might average "only" 96% on the second test.

In the case we just described, regression's presence is relatively obvious because it's taking advantage of a rather obvious source of measurement error— error in test scores. But regression may take advantage of less obvious sources of random measurement error.

The subtlest form of measurement error seems more like an error in sampling than an error of measurement. For example, suppose you are trying to make inferences about a participant's typical behavior from a sample of that participant's behavior. If the behavior you observe is not typical of the participant's behavior, you have measurement error. Even if you measured the behavior you observed perfectly, you have measurement error because you have not measured the participant's *typical* behavior perfectly. This measurement error can lead to regression toward the mean.

To illustrate how a sample of behavior may not be typical of normal behavior, let's look at a coin's behavior. Suppose you find a coin that comes up heads six times in a row. Although you have accurately recorded that the coin came up heads six times in a row, you might be making a measurement error if you concluded that the coin was biased towards heads. In fact, if you were to flip the coin 10 more times, you probably would not get 10 more heads. Instead, you would probably get something close to five heads and five tails.

Coins are not the only things to exhibit erratic behavior. Virtually every behavior is inconsistent and therefore prone to atypical streaks. For example, suppose you watch someone shoot baskets. You accurately observe that she made 5/5 shots. Based on these observations, you may conclude that she is a great shooter. However, you may be wrong. Perhaps if you had observed her shooting on a different day, you would have seen her make only 1/5 shots.

To illustrate how this subtle form of measurement error can lead to regression toward the mean, suppose a person who has been happy virtually all of her life feels depressed. This depression is so unlike her that she seeks therapy. Before starting the therapy, the psychologist gives her a personality test. The test verifies that she is depressed. After a couple of sessions, she is feeling better. In fact, according to the personality test, she is no longer depressed. Who could blame the psychologist for feeling proud?

But has the psychologist changed the client's personality? No, the patient is just behaving in a way consistent with her normal personality. The previous measurements were contaminated by events that had nothing to do with her personality. Perhaps her depressed manner reflected a string of bad fortune: getting food poisoning, her cat running away, and being audited by the IRS. As this string of bad luck ended and her luck returned to normal, her mood returned to normal.

Regression toward the mean is such an excellent impersonator of a treatment effect that regression fools most of the people most of the time. Many people swear that something really helped them when they had "hit bottom." Thus, the baseball player who recovers from a terrible slump believes that hypnosis was the cure; the owner whose business was at an all-time low believes that a new manager turned the business around; and a man who was at an all-time emotional low feels that his new girlfriend turned him around. What these people fail to take into account is that things are simply reverting back to the norm (regressing to the mean). When listening to stories about how people bounced back due to some miracle treatment, remember comedian Woody Allen's line: "I always get well, even without the leeches."

## CHANGES IN HOW MANY PARTICIPANTS ARE MEASURED: MORTALITY

The last, and perhaps most obvious, reason that you could find differences between pretest and posttest scores would be that you were measuring fewer participants at posttest than you were at pretest. In other words, your study may fall victim to **mortality:** participants dropping out of the study before it is completed.

To illustrate how much of an impact mortality can have, imagine that you are studying the effect of diet on memory in older adults. You pretest your participants, give them your new diet, and test them again. You find that the average posttest score is higher than the average pretest score. However, if the pretest average is based on 100 participants and the posttest average is based on 70 participants, your results may well be due to mortality. Specifically, the reason posttest scores are higher than pretest scores may be that the people who scored very poorly on the pretest are no longer around for the posttest.

Although death is a dramatic way to lose participants, death is not the only way to lose participants. In fact, mortality usually results from participants deciding to quit the study, participants moving away, or from participants failing to follow directions.

## CONCLUSIONS

We tried to create a situation where we manipulated the treatment, while keeping everything else constant. However, nothing we tried worked.

When we tried to compare a treatment group versus a no-treatment group, we had to worry that our groups were not identical before the study started. Even when we matched our groups, we realized that the groups might not be identical because:

1) we could not match on every single characteristic;
2) we could not match on participants' true characteristics, so we had to match based on imperfect measures of these characteristics.

Because we could not get equivalent groups at the start of the study, we did not even bother to dwell on the problems of keeping them equivalent. That is, we did not discuss the mortality problem that would result if, for example, more participants dropped out of the treatment group than out of the no-treatment group.

Because of the problems with comparing a treatment group against a no-treatment group (see Table 5–2), we tried to measure the same group before and after giving them the treatment. Although this before-after tactic got rid of some threats to validity, it introduced others. As Table 5–3 shows, participants may change from pretest to posttest for a variety of reasons having nothing to do with the treatment. Participants may change as a result of:

1. natural development (maturation);
2. other things in their lives changing (history); and
3. learning from the pretest (testing).

Furthermore, participants may *appear* to change from pretest to posttest as a result of:

1. the posttest measure being different from the pretest measure (instrumentation);
2. their pretest scores being unduly influenced by chance (setting up regression to the mean); and
3. participants dropping out of the study so that the posttest group is not the same as the pretest group (mortality).

### Ruling Out Extraneous Variables

Why couldn't we eliminate extraneous variables? Was it because we used improper designs? No, as you will see in later chapters, matching participants

**TABLE 5–2**

**Questions to Ask When Examining a Two-Group (Treatment vs. No-Treatment) Study**

**Selection:** Were groups really equal before the study began?

**Selection by maturation interaction:** Would the groups have naturally grown apart, even without the treatment?

**Regression effects:** Even if the groups *appeared* equivalent before the study began, was this apparent equivalence merely a temporary illusion created by random measurement error?

**Mortality:** Did more participants drop out of one group than the other?

---

**TABLE 5–3**

**Questions to Ask When Examining a Pretest–Posttest (Before–After) Study**

**Maturation:** Could the before–after (pretest-posttest) differences have been due to natural changes resulting from participants becoming older?

**History:** Could other events in the participants' lives have caused the pretest-posttest differences?

**Testing:** Could participants score differently on the posttest as a result of the practice and experience they got on the pretest?

**Instrumentation:** Were participants measured with the same instrument, in the same way, the second time?

**Regression:** Were participants selected for their extreme pretest scores? Participants who get extreme scores have a tendency to get less extreme scores the second time around.

**Mortality**: Did everyone who took the pretest stick around for the posttest? Or, were the pretest group and the posttest group really two different groups?

---

and testing participants before and after treatment are useful research techniques.

We couldn't eliminate extraneous variables because it can't be done. Keeping everything the same is impossible. Imagine, in our ever-changing world, trying to make sure that only one thing (amount of blue lighting) in a participant's life changed!

## ACCOUNTING FOR EXTRANEOUS VARIABLES

Fortunately, you do not have to eliminate extraneous variables to rule out their effects. Instead of eliminating extraneous variables, you can rule out their *effects*. That is, you could try to track down a treatment's effect the way a detective tracks down a murderer. The detective is confronted with more than one suspect for a murder, just as you are confronted with more than one suspect for an effect. The detective cannot make the suspects disappear, just as you cannot eliminate extraneous factors. However, like the detective, you can use logic to rule out some suspects and implicate others.

Of course, before you can begin to account for the actions of every suspicious extraneous variable, you have to know "who" each of these variables is. At first glance, identifying all the thousands of variables that might account for

**TABLE 5–4**
**Campbell and Stanley's Eight Threats to Internal Validity**

**History:** Things other than the treatment that have changed in the participants' environments.

**Testing:** Changes resulting from the practice and experience participants got on the pretest.

**Instrumentation:** The way participants were measured changed from pretest to posttest.

**Regression effects:** If participants are chosen because their scores were extreme, these extreme scores may be loaded with extreme amounts of random measurement error. On retesting, participants are bound to get more normal scores as random measurement error decreases to more normal levels.

**Mortality:** Differences between conditions are due to participants dropping out of the study.

**Maturation:** Apparent treatment effects are really due to natural development.

**Selection:** Treatment and no-treatment groups were different before the treatment was administered.

**Selection by maturation interaction**: Treatment and no-treatment groups were predisposed to grow apart.

the relationship between the treatment and the effect seems as impossible as eliminating all those variables.

### IDENTIFYING EXTRANEOUS VARIABLES

Fortunately, identifying the extraneous variables is not as difficult as it first appears because every one of these thousands of factors falls into eight categories: Campbell and Stanley's (1963) eight threats to validity. Thus, you really only have eight suspects (See Table 5-4). If you can show that selection, history, maturation, testing, regression, mortality, instrumentation, and selection by maturation were not responsible for the effect, then you can conclude that the treatment was responsible.

## The Relationship between Internal and External Validity

If you rule out these threats, you have established **internal validity.** That is, you have demonstrated that a factor causes an effect in a particular study. But you have not demonstrated that you can generalize your results outside your particular study. Internal validity alone does not guarantee that an investigator doing the same study, but with different participants (depressed patients instead of college students), or using a different setting (a library instead of a lab) would obtain the same results. If you want to *generalize* your results, you need **external validity.**

If internal validity does not guarantee external validity, why bother with establishing internal validity? One answer is that you may not care about external validity. Some researchers do not care about generalizing their results; they may only want only to show that a certain treatment causes a certain effect in a certain setting. For example, therapists may want to show that with their patients, in their hospital, giving the patients an exercise program reduces patients'

**TABLE 5–5**

**Classic Conflicts between the Goals of Internal and External Validity**

| TACTIC USED TO HELP ESTABLISH INTERNAL VALIDITY | TACTIC'S IMPACT ON EXTERNAL VALIDITY |
|---|---|
| Use participants who are very similar to each other to reduce the effects of selection. For example, only study twins or only study rats. | Studying a limited group raises questions about the degree to which the results can be generalized to different participant populations. Do the results hold for people who are not twins? Animals that are not rats? |
| Study participant in a highly controlled environment, such as a lab, to reduce the effects of extraneous factors, such as history. | Studying participants in an isolated, controlled, laboratory setting raises questions about the extent to which the results might generalize to more complex, real-life settings. |

alcohol consumption. The therapists may not care whether the treatment would work with other kinds of patients at other hospitals (external validity). They only care that they have a method that works for them.

However, few people are so single-minded that they are totally unconcerned with external validity. But unfortunately, it often seems that things you would do to improve your study's internal validity would reduce its external validity (see Table 5-5). For example, to reduce the problem of selection bias, you might use twins as your participants. Although using twins as participants could increase internal validity by reducing differences between your treatment and no-treatment groups, it might hurt the generalizability of your study. Your results might only apply to twins. Similarly, you might reduce the threat of history by testing your participants in a situation (a lab) where they are isolated from nontreatment factors. This highly controlled situation may increase internal validity because the treatment was one of the only things to change during the study. However, you would have to wonder whether the treatment would have the same effect outside this artificial, laboratory situation. Would the results generalize to real life, where the factors from which you isolated your participants come into play?

As you have seen, internal validity and external validity are *sometimes* in conflict. The same procedures that increase internal validity may decrease external validity. Fortunately, however, internal validity and external validity are not incompatible. As you will see in future chapters, you can have studies that have both internal and external validity.

If you want to establish both internal and external validity, many would argue that you should first establish internal validity. After all, before you can establish that a factor causes an effect in most situations, you must show that the factor causes an effect in at least one situation.

But how can you establish internal validity? In the next chapter, you will learn the easiest and most automatic way: the simple experiment.

## SUMMARY

1. If you observe an effect in a study that has internal validity, you know what caused that effect.
2. Campbell and Stanley (1963) described eight major threats to internal validity: selection, selection-maturation interaction, regression, maturation, history, testing, mortality, and instrumentation.
3. When you compare a treatment group to a no-treatment group, beware of the selection bias: differences in the groups before you administer the treatment.
4. To reduce selection bias, participants should never get to choose what amount of treatment they get. In addition, participants' characteristics, attitudes, or behaviors should have nothing to do with what group (treatment or no-treatment) they are put in.
5. It is impossible to match two groups of participants so that they are identical in every respect. Participants simply differ in too many ways.
6. Even matching participants on pretest scores is not perfect because of the problems of selection by maturation interactions and regression.
7. Selection by maturation occurs when your two groups mature at different rates or in different directions.
8. The fact that extreme scores tend to be a little less extreme the second time around is called regression toward the mean. Regression toward the mean can cause two groups that appear to be matched on a pretest to score differently on the posttest.
9. In the pretest–posttest design, you measure a group, administer the treatment, and measure the group again.
10. Using the pretest–posttest method is not as perfect as it first appears. It is vulnerable to testing, history, regression, maturation, mortality, and instrumentation effects.
11. Regression can occur in the pretest–posttest design because the person may have gotten the treatment when he or she had "hit bottom." There was no place to go but up.
12. Maturation refers to biological changes that occur in people merely as a result of time. In some cases, becoming more mature—not the treatment—accounts for pre-post differences.
13. Events having nothing to do with the treatment, but that occur in a participant's life between pretest and posttest (history) can cause changes in a participant's posttest score.
14. Testing bias refers to the fact that taking a pretest may affect performance on a posttest.
15. The instrumentation bias occurs when the posttest measure is different from the pretest measure.
16. External validity is the degree to which the results from a study can be generalized.
17. Internal and external validity are not necessarily incompatible.

# KEY TERMS

**external validity:** the degree to which the results of a study can be *generalized* to other places, people, or times. (p. 148)

**internal validity:** the degree to which the study demonstrates that the treatment *caused* a change in behavior. If a study lacks internal validity, the researcher may falsely believe that a factor causes an effect when it really doesn't.

Most studies do not have internal validity because they cannot rule out the possibility that some other factor may have been responsible for the effect. Unfortunately, steps taken to increase internal validity (such as keeping non-treatment factors constant) could harm the study's external validity. (p. 148)

**extraneous factors:** factors other than the treatment. If we cannot control or account for extraneous variables, we can't conclude that the treatment had an effect. That is, we will not have internal validity. History, instrumentation, maturation, mortality, regression, testing, selection, and selection by maturation interactions are all potential sources of extraneous variables. (p. 128)

**history:** events other than the treatment that have changed in the participants' environments. (p. 141)

**instrumentation:** the way participants were measured changed from pretest to posttest. In instrumentation, the actual measuring instrument changes or the way it is administered changes. (p. 143)

**testing:** participants score differently on the posttest as a result of what they learned from taking the pretest. Practice effects could be considered a type of testing effect. (p. 141)

**maturation:** apparent treatment effects are really due to natural growth or development. (p. 141)

**mortality:** differences between conditions are due to participants dropping out of the study. (p. 145)

**selection:** treatment and no-treatment groups were different before the treatment was administered. (p. 129)

**selection by maturation interaction:** treatment and no-treatment groups, although similar at one point, would have grown apart (developed differently) even if no treatment had been administered. (p. 135)

**regression:** if participants are chosen because their scores were extreme, these extreme scores may be loaded with extreme amounts of random measurement error. On retesting, participants are bound to get more normal (average) scores as random measurement error's effects decrease to more normal levels. (p. 137)

**matching:** choosing your groups so that they are identical (they match) on certain characteristics. Matching reduces, but does not eliminate, selection bias. Because of regression and selection by maturation effects, two groups that were matched on the pretest may score differently on the posttest. (p. 132)

**pretest–posttest design:** a before-after design in which each participant is given the pretest, administered the treatment, then given the posttest.

The pretest–posttest design is not vulnerable to selection and selection by maturation interactions. It is, however, extremely vulnerable to history, maturation, and testing effects. (p. 139)

## EXERCISES

1. What questions would you have of a researcher who said that the no-treatment and treatment groups were identical before the start of the study?

2. In all of the following cases, the researcher wants to make cause-effect statements. What threats to internal validity is the researcher apparently overlooking?
   a. Employees are interviewed on job satisfaction. Bosses undergo a three-week training program. When employees are re-interviewed a second time, dissatisfaction seems to be even higher. Therefore, the researcher concludes that the training program caused further employee dissatisfaction.
   b. After completing a voluntary workshop on improving the company's image, workers are surveyed. Workers who attended the workshop are now more committed than those in the "no-treatment" group who did not make the workshop. Researcher's conclusion: The workshop made workers more committed.
   c. After a six-month training program, employee productivity improves. Conclusion: Training program caused increased productivity.
   d. Morale is at an all-time low. As a result, the company hires a "humor consultant." A month later, workers are surveyed and morale has improved. Conclusion: The consultant improved morale.

3. A hypnotist claims that hypnosis can cause increases in strength. To "prove" this claim, the hypnotist has participants see how many times they can squeeze a hand-grip in two minutes. Then, he hypnotizes them and has them practice for two weeks. At the end of two weeks, they can squeeze the hand-grips together many more times than they could at the beginning. Other than hypnosis, what could have caused this effect?

4. How could a quack psychologist or doctor take advantage of regression to the mean to make it appear that certain phony treatments actually worked?

5. How could a participant's score on an ability test change even though the person's actual ability had not?

6. A memory researcher administers a memory test to a group of residents at a nursing home. He finds grade school students who score the

same as the older patients on the memory pretest. He then administers an experimental memory drug to the older patients. A year later, he gives both groups a posttest.

   **a.** If the researcher finds that the older patients now have a worse memory than the grade school students, what can the researcher conclude? Why?

   **b.** If the researcher finds that the older patients now have a better memory than the grade school students, what can the researcher conclude? Why?

7. What is the difference between history and maturation?

8. What is the difference between testing and instrumentation?

9. A psychologist's daughter scores much higher on an IQ test than you expect. The score seems extremely inconsistent with the child's grades and your general impressions of the child. What is one possible explanation for the unusually high score?

10. A researcher reports that a certain argument strategy has an effect, but only on those participants who hold extreme attitudes. Why might the researcher be mistaken about the effects of the persuasive strategy?

11. What is the difference between internal and external validity? Can you have internal validity without external validity? Can you have external validity without internal validity?

# CHAPTER 6

---

# The Simple Experiment

*Overview*

*Causality: The Simple Experiment's Purpose*

*Basic Terminology*

*Errors in Determining Whether Results Are Statistically Significant*

*Nonstatistical Considerations*

*Analyzing Data from the Simple Experiment: The t-Test*

*Concluding Remarks*

*Summary*

*Key Terms*

*Exercises*

# Chapter 6

---

# THE SIMPLE EXPERIMENT

*"What you have is an experience, not an experiment."*

—R. A. FISCHER

## OVERVIEW

Why do people behave the way they do? How can we help people change? To answer these questions, we must be able to isolate the underlying causes of behavior. To be able to isolate the underlying causes of behavior, we must design a study that has **internal validity:** the ability to determine whether a factor *causes* an effect.

This chapter introduces you to one of the easiest ways to establish that a factor causes an effect: the simple experiment. You'll start by learning what a simple experiment is and how it establishes internal validity. Next, you'll learn how to make intelligent and ethical decisions about how to conduct a simple experiment. Finally, you will learn how to use the t-test to analyze the results of a simple experiment.

## CAUSALITY: THE SIMPLE EXPERIMENT'S PURPOSE

The purpose of the **simple experiment** is *not* to describe what people typically think or do. Instead, the simple experiment's purpose is to determine whether a treatment causes an effect.

### The Logic of Causality

To establish that a treatment causes an effect (that is, to establish internal validity), you must create a situation where you establish that

1. participants' behavior changes *after* the treatment is administered; and
2. the change in behavior is due to the treatment, rather than to some other factor.

Thus, any internally valid experiment must involve administering a treatment. Therefore, the simple experiment differs from field observation and the survey method, two nonexperimental research methods that do not involve administering a treatment. For example, whereas field observation involves watching people to find out what typically happens, the simple experiment involves introducing a treatment to see if we can make something happen.

However, administering a treatment is not enough to guarantee that you have an internally valid experiment. You must also rule out the possibility that something other than the treatment is responsible for the change in the behavior.

In an ideal world, you could rule out the possibility that something other than the treatment was responsible for the change in behavior by keeping everything in the world constant except the treatment. Specifically, you would find two identical groups of participants, treat them identically except that only one group would receive the treatment, test them under identical conditions, measure them perfectly, and then compare the behavior of the two groups. Under these ideal conditions, if you found any difference between the groups, you would know that the only possible cause of this difference was the treatment.

## The Variability Problem

Unfortunately, you cannot create these ideal, constant conditions. You cannot find two identical groups of participants. You usually cannot test each subject under identical conditions. Furthermore, you cannot eliminate random measurement error. Thus, although you would like to keep all nontreatment factors constant, the reality is that nontreatment factors will vary. Because the treatment isn't the only thing varying, if your treatment group scores differently than your no-treatment group, you have to accept the *possibility* that this difference may be due to something other than the treatment.

### A SOLUTION: ACCOUNT FOR VARIABILITY

Since you cannot eliminate the possibility that the difference between your groups could be due to nontreatment factors, you'll have to settle for the next best thing: determining how unlikely this possibility is. If it's very unlikely that nontreatment variables are entirely responsible for the differences between the two groups, then you could be reasonably confident that at least some of the difference between the groups is due to the treatment. You might be wrong occasionally, but you would be playing the percentages.

### ACCOUNTING FOR RANDOM VARIABILITY

How can you set up a situation that allows you to determine the odds that the difference between groups is due—at least in part—to the treatment? You first need to set up a situation where there can be only two possible reasons for differences between your groups:

1. they got different amounts of the treatment; and
2. random error.

Then, you need to use statistics to estimate the odds that the entire difference between your groups could be due to random error. If statistics told you that it was very unlikely that such a difference could be entirely due to chance, you would conclude that at least some of the difference was due to the treatment.

But how you set up a situation where the only two possible reasons your groups could differ are (1) the treatment and (2) random error? By using **independent random assignment:** randomly determining, for each individual participant, whether that participant gets the treatment. For example, you might flip a coin for each participant. If the coin comes up heads, the subject gets the treatment; if the coin comes up tails, the participant does not get the treatment.[1] Or, you might assign participants to condition based on the random numbers table (see Box 6-1).

To get a general idea of how random assignment mixes and scatters non-treatment factors, imagine a large mixing bowl. Into the bowl you put a variety of ingredients. By the time you are done mixing, the mixture on the right side of the container is remarkably similar to the mixture on the left side. Like the electric mixer, random assignment scatters nontreatment variables fairly equally between the groups. More importantly, random assignment ensures that any differences between the groups in terms of height, weight, IQ, or any other nontreatment variable you could name will not follow any systematic, predictable pattern. There will not be any systematic differences between the groups because every participant—regardless of that participant's characteristics—has an equal chance of being assigned to each condition. In other words, thanks to random assignment, all non-treatment differences between your groups are due to random error. This is good news because we can use statistics to factor out the effects of random error.

To better understand what random assignment does, imagine what would happen if there were no treatment effect. In that case, your two groups would both be random samples of the same "parent" population—the population consisting of all the subjects who were in your study. Consequently, the only reason that the two groups could differ would be random error. In that case, we could use the science of random error—inferential statistics—to predict the degree to which the groups would differ.

---

[1] As you will see in Box 6-1, psychologists usually do not use pure independent random assignment. They typically use independent random assignment with the restriction that an equal number of subjects is in each group.

# BOX 6-1
# RANDOMLY ASSIGNING PARTICIPANTS
# TO TWO GROUPS

There are many ways to randomly assign participants to groups. Your professor may prefer another method. However, following these steps guarantees random assignment and an equal number of participants in each group.

**STEP 1**  On the top of a sheet of paper, make two columns. Title the first "Control Group." Title the second "Experimental Group." Under the group names, draw a line for each participant you will need. Thus, if you were planning to use eight participants (four in each group), you would draw four lines under each group name.

| CONTROL GROUP | EXPERIMENTAL GROUP |
|---|---|
| _____ | _____ |
| _____ | _____ |
| _____ | _____ |
| _____ | _____ |

**STEP 2**  Turn to a random numbers table, like the one tabled below. Roll a die to determine which column in the table you will use.

RANDOM NUMBERS TABLE

| | COLUMN | | | | | |
|---|---|---|---|---|---|---|
| LINE | 1 | 2 | 3 | 4 | 5 | 6 |
| 1 | 10480 | 15011 | 01536 | 02011 | 81647 | 69179 |
| 2 | 22368 | 46573 | 25595 | 85393 | 30995 | 89198 |
| 3 | 24130 | 48360 | 22527 | 97265 | 76393 | 64809 |
| 4 | 42167 | 93093 | 06243 | 61680 | 07856 | 16376 |
| 5 | 37570 | 39975 | 81837 | 76656 | 06121 | 91782 |
| 6 | 77921 | 06907 | 11008 | 42751 | 27756 | 53498 |
| 7 | 99562 | 72905 | 56420 | 69994 | 98872 | 31016 |
| 8 | 96301 | 91977 | 05463 | 07972 | 18876 | 20922 |

*(continued)*

*(continued from previous page)*

**STEP 3** Assign the first number in the column to the first space under Control Group, the second number to the second space, etc. When you have filled all the spaces for the control group, place the next number under the first space under Experimental Group and continue until you have filled all the spaces. Thus, if you rolled a "5," you would start in the fifth column and your sheet of paper would look like this:

| CONTROL GROUP | EXPERIMENTAL GROUP |
|:---:|:---:|
| 81647 | 06121 |
| 30995 | 27756 |
| 76393 | 98872 |
| 07856 | 18876 |

**STEP 4** At the end of each control group score, write down a "C." At the end of each experimental group score, write down an "E." In this example, our sheet would now look like this:

| CONTROL GROUP | EXPERIMENTAL GROUP |
|:---:|:---:|
| 81647C | 06121E |
| 30995C | 27756E |
| 76393C | 98872E |
| 07856C | 18876E |

**STEP 5** Rank these numbers from lowest to highest. Then, on a second piece of paper, put the lowest number on the top line, the second lowest number on the next line, and so on. In this example, your page would look like this:

06121E
07856C
18876E
27756E
30995C
76393C
81647C
98872E

*(continued)*

*(continued from previous page)*

**STEP 6** Label the top line, "Participant 1," the second line "Participant 2," etc. The first participant who shows up will be in the condition specified on the top line, the second participant who shows up will be in the condition specified by the second line, and so forth. In this example, the first participant will be in the experimental group, the second in the control group, the third and fourth in the experimental group, the fifth, sixth, and seventh in the control group, and the eighth in the experimental group. Thus, our sheet of paper would look like this:

| | |
|---|---|
| Participant Number 1 = | 06121E |
| Participant Number 2 = | 07856C |
| Participant Number 3 = | 18876E |
| Participant Number 4 = | 27756E |
| Participant Number 5 = | 30995C |
| Participant Number 6 = | 76393C |
| Participant Number 7 = | 81647C |
| Participant Number 8 = | 98872E |

**STEP 7** To avoid confusion, recopy your list, but make two changes. First, delete the random numbers. Second, write out "Experimental" and "Control." In this example, your recopied list would look like this:

| | |
|---|---|
| Participant Number 1 = | Experimental |
| Participant Number 2 = | Control |
| Participant Number 3 = | Experimental |
| Participant Number 4 = | Experimental |
| Participant Number 5 = | Control |
| Participant Number 6 = | Control |
| Participant Number 7 = | Control |
| Participant Number 8 = | Experimental |

But what if, in addition to differing because of nontreatment factors, the groups differed because one got an effective treatment whereas the other received no treatment? In that case, the groups should differ by more than would be predicted if chance (random error) alone were at work. Consequently, if the average scores of your two groups differ by much more than would be expected by chance alone, then you could conclude that the difference is due to the one factor that varied systematically: the treatment.

But what if the difference between your treatment and no-treatment groups is not more than could be expected by chance alone? Then, you can't conclude anything.

You can't conclude that the difference is due to the treatment. After all, the difference between your groups could be due to chance alone. For example, the differences could be due to random sampling error.

Yet, you can't conclude that the difference *is* due to chance alone. After all, just because something *could* be a coincidence doesn't mean that it *is* a coincidence. Thus, a difference that might possibly be due to chance could actually be due to the treatment.

In summary, when the difference between your groups is not larger than would be expected by chance alone, you don't know whether the difference is due to chance or to the treatment. Thus, to repeat a key principle of research: When the difference between your groups is not larger than could reasonably be expected by chance alone, your results are *inconclusive.*

## BASIC TERMINOLOGY

Now that you understand the logic of random assignment, let's look at the simplest application of independent random assignment: the simple experiment. In the simple experiment, subjects are independently and randomly assigned to one of two groups. Often, half the subjects are assigned to a treatment group whereas the other half are assigned to a no-treatment group.

### Experimental Hypothesis

Although the first step in doing a simple experiment is randomly assigning your subjects to groups, the first step in designing the simple experiment is generating an **experimental hypothesis:** a prediction that the treatment will *cause* an effect. In other words, you must predict that the treatment and no-treatment group will differ because of the treatment's effect. For example, you might hypothesize that people getting three hours of full-spectrum light will be happier than those getting no full-spectrum light because full-spectrum light causes increases in happiness.

### Null Hypothesis

The experimental hypothesis is pitted against the **null hypothesis:** the hypothesis that the treatment has *no* effect. In other words, the null hypothesis is that any difference you observe between the treatment and no-treatment group scores could be due to chance. Thus, the null hypothesis would be:

"Getting three hours of full-spectrum lighting will have no demonstrated effect on happiness."

If your results show that the difference between groups is probably not due to chance, you can reject the null hypothesis. By rejecting the null hypothesis, you tentatively accept the experimental hypothesis. You conclude that the treatment had an effect.

But what happens if you fail to demonstrate conclusively that the treatment has an effect? Can you say that there is no effect for full-spectrum lighting? *No,* you can only say that you failed to prove beyond a reasonable doubt that full-spectrum lighting causes a change in happiness. In other words, you're back to where you were before you began the study: You do not know whether full-spectrum lighting causes a change in happiness.[2]

We cannot overemphasize the point that *the failure to find a treatment effect doesn't mean that the treatment has no effect.* If you had looked more carefully, you might have observed the effect. Put another way, the null hypothesis is a "maybe" hypothesis, stating that the difference between conditions may be due to chance. Note that saying, "The difference *may be* due to chance" is not the same as saying, "The difference *is* due to chance."

## Administering the Independent Variable

Once you have your hypotheses, your next step is to administer (assign) the treatment to some subjects and withhold it from others. In the full-spectrum lighting experiment we've been discussing, you need to vary the amount of full-spectrum light people get. Furthermore, the amount of full-spectrum light that you give a subject should be independent of the individual's personal characteristics, as well as independent of both the subject's and experimenter's preferences. Specifically, the amount of full-spectrum light subjects receive should be determined by independent random assignment. Since the amount of full-spectrum light *varies* between the treatment group and the no-treatment group, since the amount of full-spectrum light varies *independently* of each participant's characteristics, and since the amount of full-spectrum lighting a participant gets is determined by *independent* random assignment, full-spectrum lighting is the **independent variable.**

In simple experiments, the independent variable will always vary between two amounts or **levels.** In this example, participants are randomly assigned to

---

[2] Those of you who are intimately familiar with confidence intervals may realize that null results do not necessarily send the researcher completely back to square one. Admittedly, we do not know whether the effect is greater than zero, but the data do allow us to estimate a range in which the effect may fall. That is, before the study, we may have no idea of the potential size of the effect. We might think the effect would be anywhere between −100 units and +100 units. However, based on the data collected in the study, we could estimate, with 95% confidence, that the effect is between a certain range. For example, we might find, at the 95% level of confidence, that the effect is somewhere in the range between −1 units and +3 units.

one of the following two levels of the independent variable: (1) three hours of full-spectrum lighting, and (2) no full-spectrum lighting.

## Experimental and Control Groups

The participants who are randomly assigned to get the higher level of the treatment (three hours of full-spectrum light) are called the **experimental group.** The participants who are randomly assigned to get a lower level of the treatment (in this case, no treatment) are called the **control group.** Thus, in this case, the experimental group is the treatment group and the control group is the no-treatment group.

Please note that the control group and the experimental group should be roughly equivalent at the start of the experiment. There should not be any systematic difference between them until the experimenter gives them different levels of the independent variable. Therefore, if the groups differ at the end of the experiment, the difference may be due to the independent variable. In other words, the *control* group is a *comparison* group—by comparing the experimental group with the control group, we can determine whether the treatment made participants behave differently than they would have behaved if they hadn't received the treatment.

As the terms experimental *group* and control *group* imply, you should have several participants in each of your conditions. The more participants, the more opportunities random assignment has to spread nontreatment factors equally between your groups. Thus, the more participants, the more likely it is that your two groups will be similar at the start of the experiment. Conversely, the fewer participants you have, the less likely it is that your groups will be similar. For example, if you are doing an experiment to evaluate the effect of a strength pill and only have two participants (a 6′4″, 280-pound offensive tackle and a 5′1″, 88-pound person recovering from a long illness), random assignment will not have the opportunity to make your groups equivalent. Consequently, your control group would not be a fair comparison group.

### THE VALUE OF INDEPENDENCE

Although we have noted that the experimental and control groups are groups in the sense that there should be several participants in each "group," that is the only sense in which these "groups" are groups. To conduct an experiment, you do not find two groups of subjects and then randomly assign one group to be the experimental group and the other to be the control group.

To see why not, suppose you were doing a study involving 10,000 janitors at a Los Angeles company and 10,000 managers at a New York company. You have 20,000 people in your experiment—one of the largest experiments in history. Then, you flip a coin and—on the basis of that single coin flip—assign the LA janitors to no treatment and the New York managers to treatment. Even though you have 10,000 participants in each group, your treatment and no-treatment groups differ in a systematic way before the study begins. Your random assignment is no more successful in making your groups similar than it was when you had only two participants. Consequently, to get random assignment to equalize your groups, you need to assign each participant **independently:** individually, without regard to how previous participants were assigned.

Your concern with independence does not stop at assignment. After you have assigned participants to condition, you want each of your participants to remain independent. To maintain independence, do *not* test the control subjects in one group session and the experimental subjects in a separate group session. There are at least two reasons why having one testing session for the control group and a second session for the experimental group hurts independence.

First, when participants are tested in groups, they may become group members rather than independent individuals. That is, they may influence each other's responses. For example, instead of giving their own individual, independent responses, participants might respond as a conforming mob.

As a concrete example of the perils of letting subjects interact, imagine that you are doing an extrasensory perception (ESP) experiment. In the experimental group, all 60 subjects correctly guessed that the coin would turn up heads. In the control group, all 60 participants incorrectly guessed that the coin would turn up tails. If each participant had made his or her decision independently, the results would certainly defy chance. However, if all the experimental group members talked to one another and made a group decision, they were not acting as 60 individual participants, but as one. In that case, the results would not be so impressive: Since all 60 experimental participants acted as one, the odds of them correctly guessing the coin flip were the same as the odds of one person correctly guessing a coin flip: 50-50.

Although the above example shows what can happen if participants are tested in groups and allowed to interact freely, interaction can disturb independence even when group discussion is prohibited. Participants may influence one another through inadvertent outcries (laughs, exclamations like, "Oh no!") or through subtle nonverbal cues. In our happiness experiment, one participant who is crying uncontrollably might cause the entire experimental group to be unhappy. In such a case, testing all the experimental subjects as a single group would cause us to falsely conclude that the treatment caused unhappiness. If, on the other hand, we tested participants individually, the unhappy participant's behavior would not affect anyone else's responses.

The second reason for not testing all the experimental subjects in one session and all the control subjects in another is that such group testing turns the inevitable, random differences between testing sessions into systematic effects. For example, suppose that when the experimental group was tested, there was a distraction in the hall, but there was no such distraction while the control group was tested. Like the treatment, this distraction was presented to all the experimental group subjects, but to none of the control group subjects. Thus, if the distraction did have an effect, its effect might be mistaken for a treatment effect. If, on the other hand, participants were tested individually, it's very unlikely that only the experimental subjects would be exposed to distractions. Instead, distractions would have a chance to even out so that participants in both groups would be almost equally affected by distractions.

But what if you are sure you won't have distractions? Even then, the sessions will differ in ways unrelated to the treatment. If you manage to test the participants at the same time, you'll have to use different experimenters and different testing rooms. If you manage to use the same experimenter and testing room, you'll have to test the groups at different times. Consequently, if you find a significant difference between your two groups, you have a problem in interpreting your results. Specifically, you have to ask, "Is the significant difference due to the groups getting different levels of the treatment or to the groups being tested under different conditions (having different experimenters, being tested at different times of day, etc.)?"

To avoid these problems in interpreting your results, make sure that the treatment is the only factor that systematically varies. In other words, use independent random assignment and then test your participants individually (or in small groups) so that random differences between testing sessions can even out. If you must run participants in large groups, do not run groups made up exclusively of experimental participants or exclusively of control participants. Instead, run groups made up of both control and experimental participants.

## THE VALUE OF ASSIGNMENT

We have focused on the importance of independence to independent random *assignment.* But assignment is also a very important aspect of independent random assignment.

Assignment is critical because we need to start the experiment with two "groups" of participants that are essentially equivalent. Random assignment lets us start the experiment with two equivalent groups by giving us two groups that are random samples of the same population—the subjects who participated in the experiment. For example, in our lighting experiment, we used random assignment to divide the participants who participated in our study into two equivalent groups. These two groups, because they were both random samples of the same parent population (all the subjects who participated in the experiment), were similar to each other.

After the experiment begins, the groups should differ in only one systematic way: the treatment. That is, one random sample of participants (the experimental group) should be *assigned* to receive a higher level of the independent variable and the other random sample of participants (the control group) should be *assigned* to receive a lower level of the independent variable. If, at the end of the study, the groups differed by more than would be expected by chance, we could say that the difference was due to the only non-chance difference between them: the treatment.

If you *cannot randomly assign* participants to your different treatments, then you *cannot do a simple experiment.* Because you cannot randomly assign participants to have certain personal characteristics, simple experiments cannot be used to study the effects of subject characteristics such as sex, race, personality, and intelligence.[3] For example, it makes no sense to assign a male to be a "female," a 7'2" person to be "short," or a shy person to be "outgoing."

Admittedly, we could get two groups that differ in terms of their personal characteristics by randomly **sampling** from two distinct populations. For example, we could get a random sample of smokers and a random sample of nonsmokers. Or, to go back to our lighting experiment, we could get a random sample of people who use light therapy and compare them to a random sample of people who do not use light therapy. What would be wrong with that?

The problem is that you are selecting two groups of people who you know are different in at least one way and then you are assuming that they don't differ in any other respect. That assumption is probably wrong. We know that people who use light therapy probably differ from those who don't in many ways. To list just a few of these differences: light users feel more depressed, they live in different climates, are more receptive to new ideas, are richer, etc. Because the groups differ in many ways other than in terms of the "treatment," it would be foolish to say that the "treatment"—rather than one of these many other differences between the groups—is what caused the groups to score differently on our happiness measure. For example, if the random sample of light users is more depressed than our sample of non-users, we could not conclude that the lighting caused their depression. The lighting might be a partial cure—rather than a cause—of their depression. But what if the random sample of lighting users is less depressed? Even then, we could not conclude that the lighting is causing the light users to be less depressed. They may be less depressed because they are richer, have more spare time, or differ in some other way from those who don't use lights. Thus, if you use random sampling instead of random assignment, you cannot conclude anything about the effects of a treatment.

If, on the other hand, you start with one group of subjects and then randomly assign half to full-spectrum lighting and half to no lighting, interpreting differences between the groups would be much simpler. That is, since the groups probably were equivalent before the treatment was introduced, large group differences in happiness are probably due to the only systematic difference between them—the lighting.

---

[3] You can, however, investigate how participants react to people who vary in terms of these characteristics. For example, you can have an experiment where participants read the same story except that one group is told that the story was written by a man, whereas the other group is told that the story was written by a woman. Similarly, you can randomly determine, for each participant, whether the participant interacts with a male or female experimenter or whether the participant interacts with an attractive or unattractive "stooge" (confederate).

## Collecting the Dependent Variable

Before you can determine whether the lighting caused the experimental group to be happier than the control group, you must measure each participant's happiness. You know that each person's happiness will *vary depending* on the individual's personality and you hope that their happiness will also *depend* on the lighting. Therefore, happiness is your **dependent variable.** Since the dependent variable is what the participant does that you *measure,* the dependent variable is often called the **dependent measure.**

## The Statistical Significance Decision

After measuring the dependent variable, you will want to compare the experimental group's happiness scores to the control group's. One way to make this comparison is to subtract the average of the happiness scores for the control (comparison) group from the average of the experimental group's happiness scores.

### STATISTICALLY SIGNIFICANT RESULTS

Unfortunately, knowing how much the groups differ doesn't tell you how much of an effect the treatment had. After all, even if the treatment had no effect, the groups may differ due to random sampling error.

How can you determine that the difference between groups is due to something more than random error? To determine the probability that the difference is not exclusively due to chance, you need to use **inferential statistics:** the science of chance.

If, by using statistics, you find that the difference between your groups is greater than could be expected if only chance were at work, then your results are **statistically significant.** The term means that you are sure, beyond a reasonable doubt, that the results were not a fluke. In the case of the simple experiment, it means that you are sure, beyond a reasonable doubt, that the treatment has caused your two groups to differ.

What is a reasonable doubt? Usually, researchers want to be at least 95% sure that the treatment is responsible for the difference. In other words, they want less than a 5% probability ($p < .05$) that the results could be solely due to random error. Thus, in journal articles, you will often see authors writing, "the results were statistically significant ($p < .05$)."

If you do a simple experiment and find that the difference between the groups is so large that it would occur less than 5% of the time by chance alone ($p < .05$), you would conclude that the independent variable caused a change in the scores on the dependent variable. That is, since it's unlikely that the difference between your groups is due to chance alone, you would conclude that some of the difference was due to the treatment. Thus, with statistically significant results, you would be relatively confident that if you repeated the study, you would get the same pattern of results.

**TABLE 6–1**
**Limits of Statistical Significance**

Statistically significant differences are:

    **1.** *probably* not due to chance;

    **2.** not necessarily large;

    **3.** not necessarily important.

Statistical significance does not mean that the results are significant in the sense of being large. Even a very small difference may be statistically reliable. For example, if you flipped a coin 5,000 times and it came up heads 51% of the time, this 1% difference from what would be expected by chance (50% heads) would be statistically significant.

Nor does statistical significance mean that the results are significant in the sense of being important. If you have a meaningless hypothesis, you may have results that are statistically significant, but meaningless (see Table 6-1).

**NULL RESULTS**

You now know how to interpret statistically significant results. But what if your results are not statistically significant? That is, what if you cannot reject the hypothesis that the difference between your groups could be due to chance? Then, you have failed to reject the null hypothesis. Therefore, your results would be described as "not significant."

The phrase "not significant" accurately describes the *inconclusiveness* of these findings. With nonsignificant results, you do not know whether the treatment has an effect that you *failed* to find or whether the treatment really has no effect (see Figure 6-1).

Nonsignificant results are analogous to a "not guilty" verdict: Is the defendant innocent or did the prosecutor present a poor case? Often, defendants get off, not because of overwhelming proof of their innocence, but because of lack of conclusive proof of their guilt.

You have seen that nonsignificant results (also called **null results**) neither confirm nor deny that the treatment had an effect. However, you will see people acting like null results provide conclusive evidence that the treatment has an effect—and others acting like null results prove that the treatment has no effect (see Table 6-2).

Surprisingly often, people act like nonsignificant results are really significant. For example, they may say, "The difference between my groups shows that the treatment had an effect, even though the difference is not significant." Re-read this statement because you're sure to hear it again: It's the most commonly stated contradiction in psychology. People making this statement are really saying, "The difference is due to the treatment, even though I've found no evidence that the difference isn't simply due to chance."

**FIGURE 6–1**

### The Meaning of Statistical Significance

If the results are statistically significant, we can conclude that the difference between the groups is not due to chance. Since it's not due to chance, it must be due to treatment. However, if the results are not statistically significant, then the results could be due to chance or they could be due to treatment. Put another way, we don't know any more than we did before we subjected the results to statistical analysis.

| | |
|---|---|
| Before doing a statistical analysis we know that the difference between groups could be due to *either:* | Treatment OR Chance |
| After doing a statistical analysis that reveals a significant difference, we know that the difference between the groups is *probably* due to: | Treatment ~~OR Chance~~ |
| If the statistical test fails to reach significance, then the difference could be due to *either:* | Treatment OR Chance |

As we have just discussed, some people act like nonsignificant results prove the experimental hypothesis. On the other hand, some people make the opposite mistake, believing that nonsignificant results disprove the experimental hypothesis. In other words, some people falsely conclude that null results definitely establish that the treatment had *no* effect. Some people make this mistake because they think the term "null results" implies that the results prove the null hypothesis. However, those people would be better off thinking of null results as "no results" than to think that null results support the null hypothesis.

Thinking that nonsignificant results support the null hypothesis is a mistake because it overlooks the difficulty of conclusively proving that a treatment has an effect. People should realize that not finding something is not the same as proving that the thing does not exist. After all, people often fail to find things that clearly exist: They fail to find books that are in the library, items that are in the grocery store, and keys that are on the table in front of them. Even in highly systematic investigations, failing to find something doesn't mean the thing does not exist. For example, in 70% of all fingerprint investigations, investigators do not find a single identifiable print at the murder scene—not even the victim's. Thus, the failure to find the suspect's fingerprints at the scene is hardly proof that the suspect is innocent. For essentially the same reasons, the failure to find an effect is not proof that there is no effect.

## Summary of the "Ideal" Simple Experiment

Thus far, we have said that the simple experiment gives you an easy way to determine whether a factor causes an effect. If you can randomly assign

**TABLE 6–2**
**Common Errors in Discussing Null Results**

| STATEMENT | FLAW |
|---|---|
| "The results were not significant. Therefore, the independent variable had no effect." | Failing to prove beyond a reasonable doubt that a treatment had an effect is not the same as proving that the treatment had no effect. An experiment using more participants, more powerful manipulations of the independent variable, and more sensitive measures may have found an effect. In short, saying "not that I know of" is not the same as proving "there isn't any." |
| "The treatment had an effect, even though the results are not significant." | "Not significant" means that you failed to find an effect. You cannot say, "I didn't find an effect for the treatment, but I really did." |

participants to either a treatment or no-treatment group, all you have to do is find out whether your results are statistically significant. If your results are statistically significant, then your treatment probably had an effect. No method allows you to account for the effects of nontreatment variables with as little effort as random assignment.

# ERRORS IN DETERMINING WHETHER RESULTS ARE STATISTICALLY SIGNIFICANT

Unfortunately, however, there is one drawback to random assignment: Differences between groups may be due to chance rather than to the treatment. Admittedly, statistics—by allowing you to predict the extent to which chance may cause the groups to differ—minimizes this drawback. However, although statistics will allow you to predict the effects of chance much of the time, you cannot predict chance all of the time. Thus, you can err by either underestimating or overestimating the extent to which chance is causing your groups to differ (see Table 6-3).

## Type 1 Errors

If you underestimate the role of chance, you may make a **Type 1 error:** mistaking a chance difference for a real difference. In the simple experiment, you would make a Type 1 error if you mistook a chance difference between your experimental and control groups for a treatment effect. More specifically, you would make a Type 1 error if you found a statistically significant difference between your groups, but the treatment really didn't have an effect. In nonpsychology settings, examples of Type 1 errors would include convicting an innocent person (mistaking a series of coincidences as evidence of guilt), a radar detector going off when there is no speed trap, or making a "false positive" medical diagnosis, such as telling someone she is pregnant when she isn't.

**TABLE 6–3**

**Possible Outcomes Of Statistical Significance Decision**

| | **REAL STATE OF AFFAIRS** | |
| --- | --- | --- |
| **STATISTICAL SIGNIFICANCE DECISION** | Treatment has an effect | Treatment does not have an effect |
| Significant: Reject the null hypothesis | Correct decision | Type I error |
| Not significant: Do not reject null hypothesis | Type II error | Correct decision |

### PREVENTING TYPE 1 ERRORS

What can you do about Type 1 errors? You can decide what risk of a Type 1 error you are willing to take. Usually, experimenters decide that they are going to take a 5% risk of making a Type 1 error. That is, they are comfortable with the odds of their making a Type 1 error being less than 5 in 100. But why take even that risk? Why not take less than a 1% risk?

To understand why not, imagine you are betting with someone who is flipping a coin. She always calls "heads," you always pick tails. She is winning most of the flips because she is cheating.

Let's suppose that you will continue betting until you have statistical proof that she is cheating. You do not want to make the Type 1 error of attributing her results to cheating when they are really due to luck. At what point would you stop betting?

If you wanted to be absolutely 100% sure, you would never stop betting because any kind of lucky streak is possible. If you wanted to be 99.9% sure, you would bet for quite a while. But if you only wanted to be 95% sure, you wouldn't have to bet very long.

As you may be able to infer from this example, you essentially determine your risk of making a Type 1 error by determining how much the groups must differ before you will declare that difference "statistically significant." The larger that difference, the less likely it is that the "statistically significant difference" will be due to chance. Thus, the larger that difference, the less likely it is that you will make a Type 1 error. To take an extreme example of this principle, if you would not even declare the biggest possible difference between your groups "statistically significant," then you would not be taking any risk of making a Type 1 error.

## Type 2 Errors

As you can see from these examples, in trying to be very, very sure that an effect is due to treatment and not to chance, you may make a **Type 2 error:** overlooking a genuine treatment effect because you think the differences between conditions might be due to chance. Examples of Type 2 errors in nonpsychological situations would include a jury letting a criminal go free (because they wanted to be sure beyond *any* doubt and they realized that it was possible that the evidence against the defendant was due to numerous, unlikely coincidences), a radar detector failing to detect a speed trap, and a physician making a "false negative" medical diagnosis, such as failing to detect that a woman was pregnant.

## Tradeoffs between Type 1 and Type 2 Errors

Clearly, you do not want to make a Type 2 error. That is, you do not want to fail to find the treatment's effect. But how do you avoid the error of overlooking a treatment's effect? One possibility is to take a larger risk of making a Type 1 error. To take an extreme example, if juries always convicted defendants, they would never make Type 2 errors—but they would run a much higher risk of Type 1 errors. Similarly, if you had a radar detector that was constantly beeping, it would never make a Type 2 error—but it would make Type 1 errors.

The tradeoffs between making a Type 1 error and making a Type 2 error may be easier to visualize if you think of Type 1 errors as "false alarms" and Type 2 errors as failures of the alarm to go off. If you buy a very sensitive burglar alarm system, it will not make many Type 2 errors. That is, it will not fail to go off when a burglar tries to enter your house. However, the sensitive detector may give you many false alarms, for example, going off when a dog runs close to your house or when there's a strong wind. To decrease the number of false alarms, you may try to reduce the sensitivity of the motion detectors. Or, you may disconnect the whole system. These steps will reduce your false alarm rate, but may prevent the alarm from going off when you do have a prowler.

As you have seen, we can reduce Type 2 errors by increasing our risk of making a Type 1 error. Conversely, we can reduce Type 1 errors by increasing our risk of making a Type 2 error. However, making tradeoffs between Type 1 and Type 2 errors is undesirable because you don't want to make either error.

On the one hand, you don't want to make the Type 1 error of "crying wolf." In other words, you want to be careful not to say that two groups differed because of the treatment when they really differed only by chance. (Just as you wouldn't want to be so reckless as to accuse someone of cheating merely because 6 of 10 coin flips came up heads.)

On the other hand, you do not want to make the Type 2 error of being silent when there is a wolf. You do not want to be so cautious that you fail to detect real treatment differences. That is, you want your study to have **power:** the ability to find statistically significant differences or, put another way, the ability to avoid making Type 2 errors.[4]

---

[4] More precisely, power = 1 − probability of making a Type 2 error. Thus, as the probability of making a Type 2 error decreases, power goes up. Power can range from 0 (no chance of finding a statistically significant result) to 1.00 (guaranteed of finding the difference significant).

# How to Prevent Type 2 Errors

Fortunately, you can have power without increasing your risk of making a Type 1 error. Unfortunately, many people don't do what it takes to have power. Indeed, most undergraduate research projects are so powerless that they are doomed from the start. The students carrying out these powerless experiments would not dream of looking for a cell's nucleus with anything other than a clean, high-powered microscope. Yet, like someone using a dirty magnifying glass to look for changes in the structure of a cell's nucleus, these students use an under-powered experiment that will be unable to find the treatment effect they are looking for. In other words, even if their treatment has an effect, statistical tests on their data will fail to find that effect statistically significant.

One reason students fail to design powerful experiments is they simply do not think about power—a "sin" that many professional researchers also commit (Cohen, 1991). But even when students do think about power, they often think that "power is a statistical concept and has nothing to do with design of experiments. There is nothing I can do about statistics."

Admittedly, power is a statistical concept. However, statistical concepts should influence the design of research. For example, if you take power into account when designing your study, your study will have enough power to find the differences that you are looking for.

To have enough power, *you must reduce the likelihood that chance differences will hide the treatment effect* (see Figure 6–2). Two ways of doing that are: (1) to reduce the effects of random error, and (2) to increase the size of the treatment effect.

## REDUCING RANDOM ERROR

One of the most obvious ways to reduce the effects of random error is to reduce the potential sources of random error. The major sources of random variability are differences between testing situations, unreliable dependent measures, differences between participants, and sloppy coding of data.

***Standardize procedures and use reliable measures.***   Since a major source of random variability is variation in the testing situation, you can reduce random error by standardizing your experiment: keeping the testing environment and the experimental procedures as constant as possible. Therefore, to improve power, you might want the noise level, illumination level, temperature, room, and time of day to be the same for each subject. Furthermore, you would want to treat all your experimental group subjects identically and all your control group subjects identically. Finally, you would also like to use a reliable and sensitive dependent measure.

The desire for both reliable measures and strict standardization makes some psychologists love both instruments and the laboratory. Under the lab's carefully regulated conditions, experimenters can create powerful and sensitive experiments.

FIGURE 6–2

Other experimenters, however, reject the laboratory setting in favor of real-world settings. The price they pay for leaving the laboratory is that they are no longer able to keep many nontreatment variables (temperature, distractions, noise level, etc.) constant. These variables, free to vary wildly, create a jungle of random error that may hide the treatment's effect.

Because of the large variability in real-world settings and the difficulties of using sensitive measures in the field, even diehard field experimenters may first look for a treatment's effect in the lab. Only after they have found that the treatment has an effect in the lab will they try to detect the treatment's effect in the field.

***Use a homogeneous group of subjects.***   Like differences between testing sessions, differences between subjects can hide treatment effects. Even if the treatment effect is large, you may overlook it, mistakenly ascribing the difference between your groups to the fact that your subjects are years apart in age and worlds apart in terms of their experiences.

To prevent between-subject differences from masking treatment effects, choose subjects who are similar to one another. For instance, select subjects who are the same sex, same age, and have the same IQ. Or, use rats as subjects. With rats, you can select subjects that have grown up in the same environment, have similar genes, and even have the same birthday. By studying homogeneous subjects under standardized situations, rat researchers can detect very subtle treatment effects.

***Code data carefully.***   Obviously, sloppy coding of the data can sabotage the most sensitively designed study. So, why do we mention this obvious fact? There are two reasons.

First, many undergraduates are guilty of sloppy coding. Although sloppiness does not necessarily bias the results, it will probably introduce random error that will rob you of power. Therefore, check and recheck the coding of your data.

Second, careful coding is a cheap way to increase power. If you increase power by using animal subjects, you may lose the ability to generalize to humans. If you increase power by using a lab experiment, you may lose the ability to generalize to real-world settings. But careful coding costs you nothing—except for a little time.

## LET RANDOM ERROR BALANCE OUT

Thus far, we have talked about the most obvious way to reduce the effects of random error—reduce the sources of random error. But there is another way. You can reduce the effects of random error by giving random error more chances to balance out. As you know, random error balances out in the long run. In the short run, you might get 5 tails in 6 coin flips, but in the long run, you'll end up with almost as many heads as tails.

To take advantage of the fact that random error balances out in the long run, use more subjects. If you use five subjects in each group, your groups probably won't be very equivalent before the experiment begins. Therefore, even if you found large differences between the groups at the end of the study, you might have to say that the difference could very well be due to chance. However, if you use 60 subjects in each group, your groups should be fairly equivalent before the study begins. Consequently, a treatment effect that would be undetected if you used five subjects per group might be statistically significant if you used 60 subjects per group.

## CREATE LARGER EFFECTS

Until now, we have talked about increasing power by making our experiment more sensitive to small differences. Specifically, we have talked about two ways of preventing random error from obscuring our treatment effect: (1) reducing the amount of random error, and (2) giving random error a chance to balance out. However, we have left out the most obvious way to increase our experiment's power: Increase the size of the effect. Bigger effects are easier to find.

Your best bet for increasing the size of the effect is to give the control group subjects a very low level of the independent variable while giving the experimental group a very high level of the independent variable. The assumption behind this advice is that if the treatment has an effect, the more treatment, the more effect. Consequently, the more the groups differ in terms of the treatment, the more the groups should differ in terms of behavior. Hence, to have adequate power in the lighting experiment, rather than giving the control group one hour of full spectrum light and the experimental group two hours, you might give the control group no full spectrum light and the experimental group 14 hours of full spectrum light.

To better understand the value of giving your experimental and control groups widely different levels of treatment, let's consider an experiment by Wilson and Schooler (1991). Wilson and Schooler wanted to determine whether thinking about the advantages and disadvantages of a choice could hurt one's ability to make the right choice. In one experiment, they had participants rate their preference for the taste of several fruit-flavored jams. Half the subjects rated their preferences after completing a "filler" questionnaire asking them to list reasons why they chose their major. The other half rated their preferences after completing a questionnaire asking them to "analyze why you feel the way you do about each jam in order to prepare yourself for your evaluations." As Wilson and Schooler predicted, the participants who thought about why they liked the jam made lower quality ratings than those who did not reflect on their ratings.

Although the finding that one can think too much about a choice is intriguing, we want to emphasize another aspect of Wilson and Schooler's study: the difference between the amount of time experimental subjects reflected on jams versus the amount of time that control subjects reflected on jams. Specifically,

**TABLE 6–4**
**Implications of Statistics for the Simple Experiment**

| STATISTICAL CONCERN/REQUIREMENT | IMPLICATIONS FOR DESIGNING THE SIMPLE EXPERIMENT |
| --- | --- |
| Observations must be independent. | You must use independent random assignment and you cannot allow one participant to influence another participant's response. |
| Groups must differ for only two reasons—random differences and the independent variable. | You must randomly assign participants to groups. |
| It is impossible to accept the null hypothesis. | You cannot use the experiment to prove that independent variable has no effect or to prove that two treatments have the same effect. |
| You need enough power to find a significant effect. | You should: 1. standardize procedures; 2. use sensitive, reliable dependent variables; 3. carefully code data; 4. use homogeneous participants; 5. use many participants; 6. use extreme levels of the independent variable. |

note that the researchers did not ask the control group to do any reflection whatsoever about the jams. To reiterate, Wilson and Schooler did not have the control group do a moderate amount of reflection and the experimental group do slightly more reflection. If they had, Wilson and Schooler might have failed to find a statistically significant effect.

## How Designing a Simple Experiment Is Affected by Statistical Considerations: A Summary

You have seen that statistical considerations either dictate or influence virtually every aspect of the design process (see Table 6-4). For example, statistical considerations dictate what kind of hypothesis you can test. Because you cannot accept the null hypothesis, the only hypotheses that you can hope to support are hypotheses that the groups will differ. Therefore, you cannot do a simple experiment to prove that two treatments have the same effect or that a group getting the treatment will do the same as a group getting no treatment.

Not only do statistical considerations dictate what types of hypotheses you can have, but they also mandate how you should assign your subjects. Specifically, if you do not assign your subjects to groups using independent random assignment, you do not have a valid experiment. Furthermore, statistical considerations also dictate how you should treat your subjects. That is, you will not have a valid experiment if you let subjects influence one another's responses or if you do anything else that would violate the statistical requirement that individual subjects' responses must be independent.

Even when statistics are not dictating what you must do, they are suggesting what you should do. To avoid making Type 2 errors, you should:

1. Standardize your procedures
2. Use sensitive and reliable dependent measures
3. Carefully code your data
4. Use homogeneous participants
5. Use many participants
6. Use extreme levels of the independent variable.

## NONSTATISTICAL CONSIDERATIONS

Yet statistical issues are not the only things that you should consider when designing a simple experiment. For example, if you only considered statistical power, you could harm your subjects, as well as your experiment's external and construct validity. Therefore, in addition to statistical issues such as power, you must also consider external validity, construct validity, and ethical issues.

### External Validity versus Power

Many of the things you can do to improve your study's power may hurt your study's external validity. By using a lab experiment to stop unwanted variables from varying, you may have more power to find an effect. However, by preventing unwanted variables from varying , you may hurt your ability to generalize your results to real life—where these unwanted variables do vary.

By using a homogeneous set of subjects (18-year-old, Caucasian males with IQs between 120 and 125), you reduce between-subject differences, thereby enhancing your ability to find treatment effects. However, because you used such a restricted sample, you may not be as able to generalize your results to the average American as a researcher who used a more heterogeneous sample. Finally, although using extreme levels of the independent variable might help you detect a treatment effect, using extreme levels may prevent you from determining the effect of realistic, naturally occurring levels of the treatment variable.

### Construct Validity versus Power

Not only may your efforts to improve power hurt external validity, but they may also hurt your experiment's construct validity. For example, suppose you had two choices for your measure. The first is a 100-point rating scale that is sensitive and reliable. However, the measure is vulnerable to subject bias: If participants guess your hypothesis, they can easily circle the rating they think you want them to. The second is a measure that is not very reliable or sensitive, but it is a measure that participants couldn't easily fake. If power was your only concern, you would pick the first measure. With it, you are more likely to find a statistically significant effect. However, many researchers would suggest that you pick the second measure—especially if participants could figure out your hypothesis.

If you sought only statistical power, you might also compromise the validity of your independent variable manipulation. For instance, to maximize your chances of getting a significant effect for full-spectrum lighting, you would give the experimental group full-spectrum lighting and make the control group an **empty control group:** a group that doesn't get any kind of treatment. Unfortunately, if you found an effect in such a study, you couldn't say that it was due to the effects of the full-spectrum lighting. It could be due to some other incidental effect of the manipulation: the treatment group getting a gift (the lights) from the experimenter; getting more interaction with and attention from the experimenter (as the experimenter checks subjects to make sure they are using the lights); adopting more of a routine than the controls (using the lights every morning from 6:00 a.m. to 8:00 a.m.); and having higher expectations of getting better (because they have more of a sense of being helped) than the controls.

To minimize these side effects of the treatment manipulation, you might give your control group a **placebo:** a substance or treatment that has no effect. Thus, rather than using a no-light condition, you might expose the control group to yellow light. You would further reduce the chances of bias if you made both the experimenters and subjects "blind": unaware of which kind of treatment the subject was getting. By making experimenters blind, you make it less likely that they will bias the results in favor of the experimental hypothesis. Similarly, by making participants blind, you make it less likely that participants will bias the results in favor of the hypothesis.

In short, the use of placebos, the use of **single blinds** (where either the subject or the experimenter is blind, and the use of **double blinds** (where both the subject and the experimenter are blind) all may reduce the chances that you will obtain a significant effect. However, if you use these procedures and you still find a significant effect, you can be relatively confident that the treatment itself, not some side effect of the treatment manipulation, is causing the effect.

You may be wondering what tradeoffs experimenters make between power and construct validity. Do experimenters use empty control groups to get significant effects? Or, do they avoid empty control groups to improve their construct validity? Do they avoid blind procedures to improve power? Or, do they use blind procedures to improve construct validity?

Often, experimenters decide to sacrifice power for construct validity. For example, in their jam experiment, Wilson and Schooler (1991) did not have an empty control group. That is, their control group did not simply sit around doing nothing while the experimental group filled out the questionnaire analyzing reasons for liking a jam. Instead, the control group also completed a questionnaire. The questionnaire was a "filler questionnaire" about their reasons for choosing a major. If Wilson and Schooler had used an empty control group, critics could have argued that it was the act of filling out a questionnaire—not the act of reflection—that caused the treatment group to make less accurate ratings than the controls. For example, critics could have argued that the controls' memory for the jams was fresher because they were not distracted by the task of filling out a questionnaire.

To prevent critics from arguing that the experimenters influenced subjects' ratings, Wilson and Schooler made the experimenters blind. To implement the blind technique, Wilson and Schooler employed two experimenters. The first experimenter supervised the tasting of the jams and the filling out of the "reasons" and the "filler" questionnaires. After introducing the subjects to Experimenter 2, Experimenter 1 left the room. Then, Experimenter 2—who was unaware of (blind to) whether the participants had filled out the reasons or filler questionnaire—had participants rate the quality of the jams.

## Ethics versus Power

As you have seen, increasing a study's power may conflict with both external and construct validity. In addition, increasing power may also conflict with ethical considerations. For example, suppose you want to use extreme levels of the independent variable (food deprivation) to insure large differences in the motivation of your animals. In that case, you need to weigh the benefits of having a powerful manipulation against ethical concerns (for more about ethical concerns, see Chapter 1 and Appendix A).

Not only do you have to be concerned about your experimental group, but also your control group. That is, not only might it be unethical to administer a potentially stressful stimulus to your experimental subjects, but it might also be unethical to completely withhold a potentially beneficial treatment from your control subjects. For instance, it might be ethically questionable to completely withhold a possible cure for schizophrenia from your controls. Therefore, rather than maximizing power by completely depriving the control group of a treatment, ethical concerns may dictate that you give the control group a moderate dose of the treatment. (For a summary of the conflicts between power and other goals, see Table 6-5.)

## ANALYZING DATA FROM THE SIMPLE EXPERIMENT: THE t-TEST

To understand how you are going to analyze your data, remember why you did the simple experiment. You did it to find out whether the treatment would have an effect on a unique population—all the subjects who participated in your experiment. More specifically, you wanted to know the answer to the hypothetical question: "If I had put all my subjects in the experimental condition,

**TABLE 6–5**

**Conflicts between Power and Other Research Goals**

| ACTION TO HELP POWER | HOW ACTION MIGHT HURT OTHER GOALS |
|---|---|
| Use a homogeneous group of participants to reduce random error due to participants. | May hurt your ability to generalize to other groups of participants. |
| Test participants under controlled laboratory conditions to reduce the effects of extraneous variables. | 1. May hurt your ability to generalize to real life situations where extraneous variables are present.<br>2. Artificiality *may* hurt construct validity. If the setting is so artificial that participants are constantly aware that what they are doing is not real and just an experiment, they may *act* to please the experimenter rather than expressing their "true" reaction to the treatment. |
| Use artificially high and low levels of the independent variable to get big differences between groups. | 1. You may be unable to generalize to realistic levels of the independent variable.<br>2. May be unethical. |
| Use an empty control group to maximize the chance of getting a significant difference between the groups. | Construct validity is threatened because the significant difference may be due to participants' expectations rather than to the treatment. |
| Use many participants to balance out the effects of random error. | May be too expensive or time-consuming. |

would they have scored differently than if I had put all of them in the control condition?" To answer this question, you need to know the averages of two **populations:**

Average of Population #1: what the average score on the dependent measure would have been if *all* your subjects had been in the control group

Average of Population #2: what the average score on the dependent measure would have been if *all* your subjects had been in the experimental group.

Unfortunately, you cannot measure both of these populations. If you put all your subjects in the control condition, then you won't know how they would have scored in the experimental condition. If, on the other hand, you put all your subjects in the experimental condition, you won't know how they would have scored in the control condition.

## Estimating What You Want to Know

Since you cannot directly get the population averages you want, you do the next best thing—you estimate them. You can estimate them because, thanks to independent random assignment, you divided all your subjects (your population of subjects) into two random samples. That is, you started the experiment

**FIGURE 6–3**

### The Control Group and the Experimental Group Are Two Samples Drawn from the Same Population

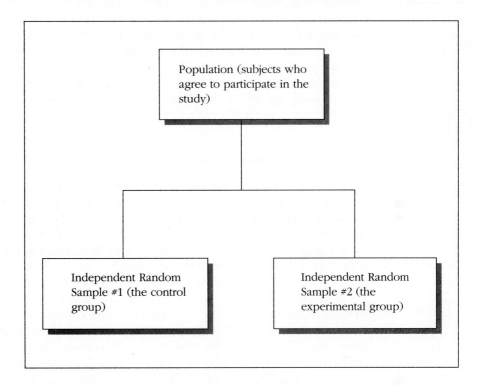

*Problem*: If the average score for experimental group is different than the average score for the control group, is this difference due to
a. the two groups receiving different treatments
*or*
b. random error related to sampling? (Two random samples from the same population may differ.)

with two random samples from your original population of subjects. Those two samples were the control group and the experimental group (see Figure 6-3).

The average score of the random sample of your subjects who received the treatment (the experimental group) is an estimate of what the average score would have been if all your subjects received the treatment. The average score of the random sample of subjects who received no treatment (the control group) is an estimate of what the average score would have been if all of your subjects had been in the control condition.

## CALCULATING SAMPLE MEANS

Even though only half your subjects were in the experimental group, you will assume that the experimental group is a fair sample of your entire population of subjects. Thus, the experimental group's average score should be a reasonably good estimate of what the average score would have been if all your subjects had been in the experimental group. Similarly, you will assume that the control group's average score is a fairly good estimate of what the average score would have been if all your subjects had been in the control group. Therefore, the first step in analyzing your data will be to calculate the average score for each group. Usually, the average you will calculate is the **mean:** the result of adding up all the scores and then dividing by the number of scores.

## COMPARING SAMPLE MEANS

Once you have your two sample means, you can compare them. Before talking about how to compare them, let's understand why we are comparing the means. We are comparing the sample means because we know that, before the treatment was administered, both groups represented a random sample of the population consisting of every subject who participated in the study. Thus, at the end of the experiment, if the treatment had no effect, the control and experimental group would both *still* be random samples from that population.

As you know, two random samples from the same population will be similar to each other. For example, two random samples of the entire population of New York City should be similar to each other, two random samples from the entire population of students at your school should be similar to each other, and two random samples from the entire group of subjects who participated in your study should be similar to each other. Thus, if the treatment has no effect, at the end of the experiment, the experimental and control groups should be similar to each other.

Because random samples of the same population should be similar, you might think all we need to do is subtract the control group mean from the experimental group mean to find the effect. But such is not the case: Even if the treatment has no effect, the means for the control group and experimental group will rarely be identical. To illustrate, suppose that Dr. N. Ept made a serious mistake while trying to do a double-blind study. Specifically, Dr. N. Ept succeeded in not letting his assistants know whether the subjects were getting the real treatment or a placebo, but failed in that all the subjects got the placebo. In other words, both groups ended up being random samples of the same population—subjects who did not get the treatment. Even in such a case, the two groups may have very different means.

Dr. N. Ept's study illustrates an important point: Even if groups are random samples of the same population, they may still differ because of *random sampling error.* You are aware of random sampling error from reading about public opinion polls that admit to a certain degree of sampling error or from reading about two polls of the same population that produced slightly different results.

If you want to see the effects of random sampling error for yourself, play around with Box 6-1. Specifically, pretend that you have 10 subjects and give each subject a name and a score between 0 and 100. Next, randomly assign each subject to either experimental or control group. Then, get an average for each group. Repeat this process several times. If you do this, you will simulate what happens when you do an experiment and the treatment has no effect.

As doing this simulation will reveal, which subjects end up in which group varies greatly depending on where on the random numbers table you happen to start—and there are many different places you could start. Not all of these possible ways of splitting subjects into control and experimental groups are going to produce identical groups. Indeed, you may even find that random assignment sometimes results in having all males in the experimental group and all females in the control group. In any event, you should find that the average scores for your groups differ considerably.

In summary, some random samples will *not* be representative of their parent population. Because of the possibility that a sample may be strongly affected by random sampling error, your sample means may differ even if the real, parent population means do not.

## Inferential Statistics: Judging the Accuracy of Your Estimates

We have told you that random error can throw off your estimates of population means. Because of random error, the treatment group mean is an imperfect estimate of what would have happened if all the subjects had received the treatment. Because of random error, the control group mean is an imperfect estimate of what would have happened if none of the subjects had received the treatment. Thus, the difference between your experimental and control group means could be due to random error. In other words, finding a difference between your experimental and control group means doesn't prove that you have a treatment effect.

If the difference between your group means could be due to random error, how can you determine whether a difference between the sample means is due to the treatment? You need to know how much of a difference random error could make. If the actual difference between your group means was much bigger than the difference that chance could make, then you could conclude that the treatment had an effect.

### ESTIMATING THE ACCURACY OF INDIVIDUAL SAMPLE MEANS

How can you determine whether the difference between your sample means is too large to be due to random error? Knowing the accuracy of each of your individual sample means should help. For example, suppose you knew the control group mean was within one point of its true population mean. Furthermore, suppose you knew that the experimental group mean was also within one point of its real population mean. In other words, you knew that the estimate for what the mean would be if everybody had been in the control group was not off by more than one point and that the estimate for what the mean would be if everyone had been in the experimental group was also not off by more than one point.

If you knew all that, and if your control group mean differed from your experimental group mean by 20 points, then you would know that your two sample means represent different population means. In other words, you could assume that if all your subjects had been given the treatment, then they would have scored differently than if they had all been deprived of the treatment.

If, on the other hand, the two group means had differed by less than one point, the difference between the groups could easily be due to random error. In that case, you would not be able to conclude that the treatment had an effect.

### *Consider Population Variability: The Value of the Standard Deviation.*

You have seen that a key to determining whether your treatment had an effect is to determine how accurately your two sample means reflect their population means. But how can you determine how closely each of your sample means are to their population means? One factor that affects how well a mean based on a random sample of the population reflects the population mean is the amount of variability in the population. If there is no variability in the population, then all scores in the population will be the same as the mean. Consequently, there would be no sampling error. For example, if everyone in the population scored a 5, the population mean would be 5, and the mean of every random sample would also be 5. Thus, since all Roman Catholic cardinals hold very similar positions on the morality of abortion, almost any sample of Roman Catholic cardinals you took would accurately reflect the views of Roman Catholic cardinals on that issue.

If, on the other hand, scores in a population vary considerably (for example, ranging anywhere from 0 to 1,000), then independent random samples from that population could be extremely inaccurate. For instance, even if the population mean was 500, you might get sample means ranging from 0 to 1,000. Thus, two sample means from such a heterogeneous population could be very different.

To recap, you have seen that the variability of scores in a population affects how accurately individual samples will reflect that population. Since the extent of the variability of scores in the population influences the extent to which we have random sampling error, it would be nice to have an index of the variability of scores within a population.

The ideal index of the population's variability is the population's **standard deviation:** a measure of the extent to which individual scores deviate from the population mean. Unfortunately, to get that index, you have to know the population mean (for the control condition, the average of the scores if all the subjects had been in the control condition; for the experimental condition, the average of the scores if all the subjects had been in the experimental condition). Obviously, you don't know the population mean for either the control or experimental condition—that's what you are trying to find out!

## BOX 6–2
## HOW TO COMPUTE A STANDARD DEVIATION

Assume we have four scores (108, 104, 104, 104) from a population. We could estimate the population's standard deviation by going through the following steps.

| STEP 1: Calculate the *mean (M)* | STEP 2: Subtract scores from mean [105] to get the *differences* | STEP 3: Square the *differences* |
|---|---|---|
| 108 | $-105 = +3$ | $(+3)^2 = +9$ |
| 104 | $-105 = -1$ | $(-1)^2 = +1$ |
| 104 | $-105 = -1$ | $(-1)^2 = +1$ |
| 104 | $-105 = -1$ | $(-1)^2 = +1$ |
| **Mean =** 420/4 = **105** | | **SS = 12** |

STEP 4: Add (sum) the squared differences obtained in step 3 to get sum of squared differences, otherwise known as sum of squares. Sum of Squares is often abbreviated as (SS). SUM OF SQUARES (SS) = **12**

STEP 5: Get variance by dividing SS (which was 12) by one less than the number of scores (4 − 1 = 3). This division yields a variance of 4 (since 12/3 = 4).

STEP 6: Get the standard deviation by taking the square root of variance. Since the variance is 4, the standard deviation is 2 (because the square root of 4 is 2).

For those preferring formulas:
$s^2 = \Sigma(X - M)^2/N-1$ where X stands for the individual scores, M is the sample mean, s is the estimate of the population's standard deviation, and N is the number of scores.

Although you cannot calculate the population standard deviation, you can estimate it by looking at the variability of scores within your samples. In fact, by following Box 6-2, you can estimate what the standard deviation would have been if everyone had been in the control group (by looking at variability within the control group) and what the standard deviation would have been if all your subjects had been in the experimental group (by looking at variability within the experimental group).

One reason the standard deviation is a particularly valuable index of variability is that many populations can be completely described simply by knowing the standard deviation and the mean. You probably already know that the mean is valuable for describing many populations. You know that, for many populations, most scores will be near the mean and that as many scores will be above the mean as will be below the mean.

What you may not know is that, for many populations, you can specify precisely what percentage of scores will be within a certain number of standard deviations of the mean. For instance, you can say that 68% of the scores will be within 1 standard deviation of the mean, 95% will be within 2 standard deviations of the mean, and 99% of the scores will be within 3 standard deviations of the mean. If a population's scores are spread out (distributed) in this manner, the population is said to be **normally distributed.**

As the term "*normally* distributed" suggests, many populations are normally distributed: from test scores to the heights of American women. Because normally distributed populations are common, graphing the distribution of scores in a population will often produce a **normal curve:** a bell-shaped, symmetrical curve that has its center at the mean (See Figure 6–4).

It's convenient to summarize an entire distribution of scores with just two numbers: the mean, which gives you the center of a normal distribution, and the standard deviation, which gives you an index of the width of the distribution. It's comforting to know that 68% of the scores will be within 1 standard deviation of the mean, that 95% of the scores will be within 2 standard deviations of the mean, and that virtually all the scores will be within 3 standard deviations of the mean.

But the standard deviation has more uses than merely describing a population. You could use the standard deviation to make inferences about the population mean. For example, suppose you don't know the population's mean, but you know that the distribution is normally distributed and that its standard deviation is 3. Then, you don't need much data to make certain inferences about that population. Specifically, you know that if you randomly selected a single score from that population, there would be a 68% chance that the population mean would be within 3 points (1 standard deviation) of that score, and a 95% chance that the population mean would be within 6 points (2 standard deviations) of that score.

***Consider Sample Size: The Role of the Standard Error.***    Of course, to estimate your control group's population mean, you would use more than one score. Instead, you would use the control group mean. Intuitively, you realize that using a sample mean based on several scores will give you a better estimate of the population mean than using a single score.

You also realize that using a sample mean based on many scores is better than using a sample means based on a few scores. In other words, the bigger your independent random sample, the better your random sample will tend to reflect the population. Consequently, the bigger your sample, the closer its mean should be to the population mean.

To reiterate, the accuracy of your sample mean depends on how many scores you use to calculate that mean. However, the standard deviation does not take into account how many scores the sample mean is based on. The

**FIGURE 6–4**

## The Normal Curve

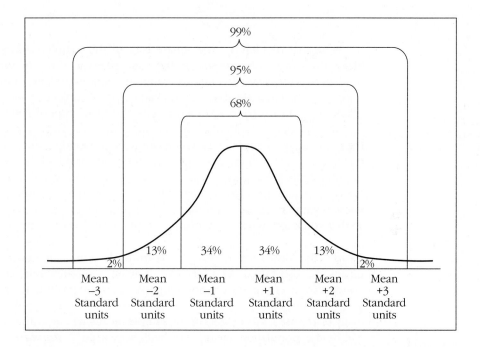

standard deviation will be the same whether the sample mean is based on 2 scores or 2,000. Because the standard deviation does not take into account sample size, the standard deviation is not a good index of your sample mean's accuracy.

A good index of the degree to which a sample mean may differ from its population mean must include both factors that influence the accuracy of a sample mean, namely:

**(1)** population variability (the less population variability, the more accurate the sample mean will tend to be) and

**(2)** sample size (the larger the sample, the more accurate the sample mean will tend to be).

Not surprisingly, both of these factors are included in the formula for the **standard error of the estimate of the population mean:** an index of the degree to which random error may cause a sample mean to be an inaccurate estimate of its population mean (see Table 6-6).

The *standard error* (of the estimate of the population mean) equals the:

standard deviation (a measure of population variability)

———————————————————————————————————————

the square root of the number of subjects (an index of sample size)

Thus, if the standard deviation were 40 and you had 4 people in your sample, the standard error would be:

$$\frac{40}{\sqrt{4}} \quad = \quad \frac{40}{2} \quad = \quad 20$$

Note that dividing by the square root of the sample size means that the bigger the sample size, the smaller the standard error. Thus, the formula reflects the fact that you have less random sampling error with larger samples. Consequently, in the example above, if you had used 100 subjects, your standard error would have shrunk from 20 to 4 (because 40/square root of 100 = 40/10 = 4).

What does the standard error tell you? Clearly, the larger the standard error, the more likely a sample mean will misrepresent the population mean. But does this random error contaminate all samples equally or does it heavily infest some samples while leaving others untouched? Ideally, you would like to know precisely how random error is distributed across various samples. You want to know what percentage of samples will be substantially tainted by random error so that you know what chance your sample mean has of being accurate.

***Using the Standard Error.***    Fortunately, you can know how sample means are distributed. As a result of drawing numerous independent random samples from a normally distributed population and plotting the means of each sample, statisticians have shown that the distribution of sample means is normally distributed. Most (68%) of the sample means will be within 1 *standard error* of the population mean, 95% will be within 2 *standard errors* of the population mean, and 99% will be within 3 *standard errors* of the population mean. Therefore, if your standard error is 1.0, you know that there's a 68% chance that the true population mean is within 1.0 points of your sample mean, a 95% chance that the population mean is within 2.0 points of your sample mean, and a 99% chance that the population mean is within 3.0 points of your sample mean.

When you can assume that the population is normally distributed, you can estimate how close your sample mean is to the true population mean. You do this by taking advantage of the fact that sample means from normally distributed populations will follow a very well-defined distribution: the normal distribution. But what if the underlying population isn't normally distributed?

Even then, as the **central limit theorem** states, the distribution of sample means will be normally distributed—*if your samples are large enough* (30 or more subjects). To understand why the central limit theorem works, realize that if you take numerous large random samples from the same population, your sample means will differ from one another for only one reason—random error. Since random error is normally distributed, your distribution of sample means will be normally distributed—regardless of the shape of the underlying population. Consequently, if you take a large random sample from any population, you can use the normal curve to estimate how closely your sample mean reflects the population mean.

**TABLE 6–6**
**How Close Will a Sample Mean Be to Its Population Mean?**

| FACTORS INCREASING THE CHANCES OF HAVING A SAMPLE MEAN THAT IS *CLOSE* TO THE ACTUAL POPULATION MEAN | FACTORS INCREASING THE CHANCES OF HAVING A SAMPLE MEAN THAT IS *FAR* AWAY FROM THE ACTUAL POPULATION MEAN |
| --- | --- |
| The sample mean is based on a population that has a *small standard deviation* (most of the scores are close to the population mean). | The sample mean is based on a population that has a *large standard deviation* (few of the scores are close to the population mean). |
| The sample mean is based on a *large sample* (big random samples tend to be good samples). | The sample mean is based on a *small sample.* |

## ESTIMATING ACCURACY OF YOUR ESTIMATE OF THE DIFFERENCE BETWEEN POPULATION MEANS

Because you know that sample means are normally distributed, you can determine how likely it is that a sample mean is within a certain distance of its population mean. But in the simple experiment, you are not trying to find a certain population mean. Instead, you are trying to find out whether two population means differ. As we mentioned earlier, you want to know whether there was a difference between two hypothetical population means: (1) what the mean score would have been if all your participants had been in the control group, and (2) what the mean score would have been if all your participants had been in the experimental group. Put another way, you are asking the question: "If all the subjects had received the treatment, would they have scored differently than if they had all been in the control group?"

Because you want to know whether the treatment made a difference, your focus is not on the individual sample means, but on the *difference* between the two means. Therefore, you would like to know how differences between sample means (drawn from the same population) are distributed.

***How the differences between means are distributed: The large sample case.*** Fortunately, statisticians know how differences between sample means drawn from the same population are distributed. Statisticians have repeated the following steps thousands of times:

1. take two random samples from the same population,
2. calculate the means of the two samples (group 1 and group 2),
3. subtract the group 1 mean from the group 2 mean to get the *difference* between group 1 and group 2.

From this work, statisticians have established three basic facts about the distribution of differences between sample means drawn from the same population.

First, if you subtracted the group 1 mean from the group 2 mean an infinite number of times, the average of all these differences would equal zero. This is because, in the long run, random error averages out to zero. Because random error averages out to zero, the mean of all the group 1 means would be the true population mean—as would the mean of all the group 2 means. Since the group 1 means and the group 2 means both average out to the same number, the average difference between them would be zero.

Second, the distribution of differences would be normally distributed. This makes sense because: (a) the only way random samples from the same population can differ is because of random error, and (b) random error is normally distributed.

Third, the standard unit of variability for the distribution of differences between means is not the standard deviation nor the standard error. Instead, it is the **standard error of the difference between means.**

The standard error of the difference between means is larger than the standard error of the mean. This fact shouldn't surprise you. After all, the difference between sample means is influenced by the random error that affects the control group mean *and* by the random error that affects the experimental group mean. In other words, sample means from the same population could differ because the first sample mean was inaccurate, because the second sample mean was inaccurate, or because both were inaccurate.

The formula for the standard error of the difference between means reflects the fact that this standard error is the result of measuring *two* unstable estimates. Specifically, the formula is:

$$\sqrt{\frac{s_1^2}{N1} + \frac{s_2^2}{N2}}$$

Where "$s_1$" is the estimate of the population standard deviation for group 1 and "$s_2$" is the estimate of the population standard deviation for group 2; "N1" is the number of subjects in group 1 and "N2" is the number of subjects in group 2.

We know that with large enough samples, the distribution of differences between means would be normally distributed. Thus, if the standard error of the difference was 1.0, we would know that 68% of the time, the true difference would be within 1 point of the difference we observed; that 95% of the time, the true difference would be within 2 points of the difference we observed; and that 99% of the time, the true difference would be within 3 points of the difference we observed. Therefore, if our two sample means (the control group mean and the experimental group mean) differed by more than 3 points, we would be confident that the treatment had an effect. In other words, we would be confident that the groups were samples from populations that had different means: If all the participants had received the treatment, their mean score would be different than if they had all been in the control condition.

If, however, we observed a difference of 1.0, we realize that such a difference might well reflect random error, rather than the groups coming from different populations. That is, with a difference of 1.0 and a standard error of the

**Figure 6–5**

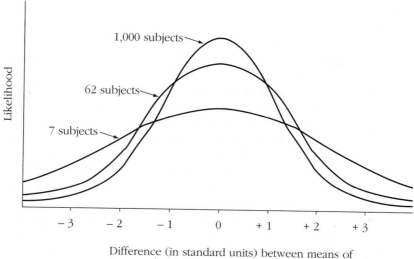

**With Larger Samples, t-distributions Approximate the Normal Curve**

Difference (in standard units) between means of
two random samples from the same population

difference of 1.0, we could not disprove the null hypothesis. In other words, we would not be able to conclude that the treatment had an effect.

***How differences are distributed: The small sample case.***     Although the distribution of differences would be normally distributed if you used large enough samples, your particular experiment probably will not use enough subjects. Therefore, you must rely on a more conservative distribution, especially designed for small samples: the *t-distribution.*

Actually, the t-distribution is a family of distributions. The member of the t-distribution family that you use depends on the sample size. That is, with a sample size of 10, you will use a different t-distribution than with a sample size of 11.

The larger your sample size, the more the t-distribution will be shaped like the normal distribution. The smaller your sample size, the more spread out your t-distribution will be (see Figure 6–5). Thus, with small samples, a difference between means of more than two standard errors of the difference might not be statistically significant (whereas such a difference would be significant with a large sample).

Although the particular t-distribution you use depends on sample size, you do not determine which particular t-distribution to use by counting how many subjects you have. Instead, you determine how many **degrees of freedom (df)** you have.

To calculate your degrees of freedom, simply subtract 2 from the number of subjects in your experiment. For example, if you had 32 subjects, your df would be 30 (because $32 - 2 = 30$).

## Executing the t-Test

You now understand that the difference between your experimental and control group means could be due to random error. You also realize that to estimate the chances that a difference between means could be due to random error, you need to do two things.

First, you need to compare the difference between the means to the standard error of the difference. In other words, you need to find out how far apart—in terms of standard errors of the difference—the two group means are.

Second, you need to use a t-distribution to figure out how likely it is that two means could differ by that many standard errors of the difference. The particular t-distribution you will use depends on your degrees of freedom.

Now that you understand the basic logic behind the t-test, you're ready to do one. Start by subtracting the means of your two groups. Then, divide this difference by the standard error of the difference (see Box 6–3). The number you will get is called a t-ratio. Thus, t = Difference between means/standard error of the difference. Less technically, the t-ratio is simply the difference between your sample means divided by an index of random error.

Once you have your t-ratio and your degrees of freedom, refer to a t-table to see whether your t-ratio is significant. Thus, if you used 32 subjects, you would look at the t-table in Appendix E under the row labeled 30 df.

When comparing the t-ratio you calculated to the value in the table, act like your t-ratio is positive. That is, even if you have a negative t-ratio, treat it as if it is a positive t-ratio. In other words, take the absolute value of your t-ratio.

If the absolute value of your t-ratio is not bigger than the number in the table, then your results are not statistically significant at the .05 level. If, on the other hand, the absolute value of your t-ratio is bigger than the number in the table, then your results are statistically significant at the .05 level.

If your results are statistically significant at the .05 level, there's less than a 5% chance that the difference between your groups is solely due to chance. Consequently, you can be reasonably sure that your treatment had an effect. You might report your results as follows: "As predicted, the experimental group's mean recall (8.12) was significantly higher than the control group's (4.66), $t(30) = 3.10$, $p < .05$."

### ASSUMPTIONS OF THE T-TEST

As with any statistical test, the t-test requires that you make certain assumptions. First, because the t-test compares the two sample means, the t-test requires you to have data that allow you to compute meaningful means. Consequently, you cannot do a t-test on ranked data because you cannot meaningfully

## Box 6–3
## Calculating the Between Subjects t-Test for Equal Sized Groups

$$t = \frac{\text{Group 1 Mean} - \text{Group 2 Mean}}{\text{Standard Error of the Difference}}$$

And where the standard error of the difference can be calculated in either of the following 2 ways:

1. $\sqrt{\dfrac{S_1^2}{N_1} + \dfrac{S_2^2}{N_2}}$

Where $S_1$ = standard deviation of group 1 (see Box 6-2), $S_2$ = standard deviation of group 2, $N_1$ equals number of participants in group 1, and $N_2$ equals number of participants in group 2.

2. $\sqrt{\dfrac{\text{SS group 1} + \text{SS group 2}}{N - 2}} \times (1/N_1 + 1/N_2)$

Where SS equals the sum of squares (see Box 6-2), $N_1$ equals the number of subjects in group 1, $N_2$ equals the number of subjects in group 2, and N equals the total number of subjects.

compute means based on ranked data. For example, although averaging the ranks of 2nd and 3rd finishers in a race would result in the same average rank (2.5) as averaging the ranks of the 1st and 4th place finishers, the average times of the two groups might vary greatly. The average times of the 1st and 4th place finishers could be much faster or much slower than the average of the times of the 2nd and 3rd place finishers. Similarly, you cannot do a t-test on qualitative data because you cannot compute meaningful means on qualitative data. (Try averaging scores when 1 = nodded head, 2 = gazed intently and 3 = blinked eyes—what does an average of 1.8 indicate?) In short, to perform the t-test, you must be able to assume that you have either interval scale or ratio scale data.

Second, since the t-test is based on estimating random error, the t-test requires that you independently and randomly assigned each participant to either the experimental or the control group. If this requirement is violated, the results of the t-test are worthless.

To reiterate, to do a meaningful t-test, your data must meet two key assumptions. You must have at least interval scale data and you must have used independent random assignment. In addition to these two pivotal assumptions, the t-test makes two less vital assumptions (see Table 6–7).

First, the t-test assumes that the population from which your sample means was drawn is normally distributed. The reason for this assumption is that if the populations are normally distributed, then the distribution of sample means will tend to be normally distributed. This assumption is usually nothing to worry about because most distributions are normally distributed. But what if the population isn't normally distributed? Even then, your sample means will probably be normally distributed because, as the central limit theorem states, with large enough samples, the distribution of sample means will be normally distributed.

The second assumption is that the standard deviation of your experimental group will be the same as the standard deviation of your control group. To be more precise, the assumption is that scores in both conditions will have the same variance (if you square the standard deviation, you get the variance). This is not a very strict assumption. If you have unequal variances, it won't seriously affect the results of your t-test, as long as one variance isn't more than $2\frac{1}{2}$ times larger than the other.

## Questions Raised by Results

Obviously, if you violate key assumptions of the t-test, people should question your results. But even if you don't violate any of the t-test's assumptions, your results will raise questions—and this is true whether or not your results are statistically significant.

### QUESTIONS RAISED BY NONSIGNIFICANT RESULTS

Nonsignificant results raise questions because the null hypothesis cannot be proven. Therefore, null results inspire questions about the experiment's power, questions such as:

1. Did you have enough participants?
2. Were the participants homogeneous enough?
3. Was the experiment sufficiently standardized?
4. Were the data coded carefully?
5. Was the dependent variable reliable enough?
6. Would you have found an effect, if you had chosen two different levels of the independent variable?

### QUESTIONS RAISED BY SIGNIFICANT RESULTS

If your results are statistically significant, it means you found an effect for your treatment. Since you found an effect for your independent variable, you don't

**TABLE 6–7**
**Effects of Violating the t-Test's Assumptions**

| ASSUMPTION | CONSEQUENCES OF VIOLATING ASSUMPTION |
| --- | --- |
| Random assignment | Serious violation, nothing can be done to salvage your study. |
| Observations are independent (random assignment is used and participants do not influence one another's responses). | Serious violation, probably nothing can be done to save study. |
| Data are interval or ratio scale (numbers do *not* represent ranks [1st, 2nd, 3rd, etc.] and they do represent different amounts of a quality). | Do not use a t-test. However, there are other statistical tests you can use. |
| The population from which your sample means was drawn is normally distributed. | If the study used more than 30 participants per group, this is not a serious problem. If, however, few participants were used, you may decide to use a different statistical test. |
| Scores in both conditions have the same variances. | Usually not a serious problem, especially if the study used a large number of participants. |

have to ask any questions about your study's power. But that doesn't mean your results don't raise any questions. On the contrary, a significant effect often raises many questions.

Sometimes, questions are raised because the experimenter sacrificed construct or external validity to obtain adequate power. For example, if you used an empty control group, you have questionable construct validity. Consequently, one question would be: "Does your significant treatment effect represent an effect for the construct you tried to manipulate or is it merely a placebo effect?" Or, if you used an extremely homogeneous group of participants, the external validity of your study might be questioned. For example, skeptics might ask: "Do your results apply to other kinds of participants?"

At other times, questions are raised because of a serious limitation of the simple experiment: it can only study two levels of a single variable. Therefore, there are two questions you can ask of any simple experiment:

1. To what extent do the results apply to levels of the independent variable that were not tested?
2. To what extent could the presence of other variables modify the treatment's effect?

## CONCLUDING REMARKS

Clearly, the results of a simple experiment always raise questions. Although results from any research study raise questions, many of the questions raised by the results of the simple experiment are due to the fact that the simple experiment is limited to studying only two levels of a single variable. If the logic of the simple experiment could be expanded to designs that would study several levels of several independent variables at the same time, these designs could answer the questions raised by the simple experiment. Fortunately, as you will see in the next two chapters, the logic of the simple experiment can be extended to produce experimental designs that will allow you to answer several research questions with a single experiment.

## SUMMARY

1. Psychologists want to know the causes of behavior so that they can understand people and help people change. Only experimental methods allow us to isolate the causes of an effect.

2. The simple experiment is the easiest way to establish that a treatment causes an effect.

3. The prediction that the treatment will cause an effect is called the experimental hypothesis.

4. The null hypothesis, on the other hand, states that the treatment will *not* cause an observable effect.

5. With the null hypothesis, you only have two options: You can reject it or you can *fail* to reject it. You can never accept the null hypothesis.

6. In the simple experiment, you administer a low level of the independent (treatment) variable to some of your participants (the comparison or control group) and a higher level of the independent variable to the rest of your participants (the experimental group). Near the end of the experimental session, you observe how each participant scores on the dependent variable: a measure of the participant's behavior.

7. To establish causality with a simple experiment, participants' responses must be independent. Because of the need for independence, your experimental and control groups are not really groups.

8. Independent random assignment is the cornerstone of the simple experiment. Without independent random assignment, you do not have a simple experiment.

9. Independent random assignment is necessary because it is the only way to make sure that the only differences between your groups are either due to chance or to the treatment.

10. Independent random assignment makes it likely that your control group is a fair comparison group. That is, the control and experimental group should be fairly equivalent before the treatment is introduced.

11. Random sampling is not random assignment. Random sampling from two different groups gives you two groups that differ systematically in at least one way, and probably differ in thousands of other ways.

12. Your goal in using independent random assignment is to create two samples that accurately represent your entire population of partici-

pants. You use the mean of the control group as an estimate of what would have happened if all your participants had been in the control group. You use the experimental group mean as an estimate of what the mean would have been if all your participants had been in the experimental group.

13. Does the treatment have an effect? In other words, would participants have scored differently had they all been in the experimental group than if they had all been in the control group? This is the question that statistical significance tests ask.

14. If the results are statistically significant, the difference between your groups is greater than would be expected by chance (random error) alone. Therefore, you reject the null hypothesis and conclude that your treatment has an effect. Note, however, that statistical significance does not tell you that your results are big, important, or of any practical significance.

15. There are two kinds of errors you might make when attempting to decide whether a result is statistically significant.

16. Type 1 errors occur when you mistake a chance difference for a treatment effect. You can determine your risk of making a Type 1 error. Most researchers decide to take a 5% risk.

17. Type 2 errors occur when you fail to realize that the difference between your groups is *not* solely due to chance. In a sense, you overlook a genuine treatment effect.

18. By reducing your risk of making a Type 1 error, you increase your risk of making a Type 2 error.

19. Because Type 2 errors can easily occur, nonsignificant results are inconclusive results.

20. To prevent Type 2 errors: (a) reduce random error; (b) use many participants to balance out the effects of random error; and (c) try to increase the size of your treatment effect.

21. If your experiment minimizes the risk of making Type 2 errors, your experiment has power. In the simple experiment, power refers to the ability to obtain statistically significant results when your independent variable really does have an effect.

22. Improving power may hurt your study's external and construct validity.

23. Using placebo treatments, single blinds, and double blinds can improve your study's construct validity.

24. Ethical concerns may temper your search for power, or even cause you to decide not to conduct your experiment.

25. Many distributions can be approximated by the normal curve.

26. The normal curve is a symmetrical, bell-shaped curve that can be described by two numbers: the mean and the standard deviation. The center of the normal distribution is the mean. Half the scores will be below the mean and half will be above. In addition, 68% of the scores

will be within 1 standard deviation of the mean and 95% will be within 2 standard deviations of the mean.

27. The standard deviation is an index of the variability of participants' individual scores.

28. The standard error is an index of the variability of sample means. It can be used to give you an idea of how much error has affected your estimate of the population mean.

29. The standard error is based on the two factors that will affect the accuracy of the sample mean: (a) the amount of variability in the population, and (b) the number of observations on which the sample mean is based.

30. Because of random error, you cannot determine whether your treatment had an effect simply by subtracting your experimental group mean from your control group mean. Instead, you must determine whether the difference between your group means could be due to random error.

31. To determine whether the difference between your group means could be due to random error, you need to compute an index of the degree to which your group means could differ by chance alone. This index is called the standard error of the difference between means.

32. The t-test involves dividing the difference between means by an estimate of the degree to which the groups would differ when the treatment had no effect. More specifically, the formula for the t-test is:

Mean 1 − Mean 2/standard error of the difference.

33. The degrees of freedom for a *two*-group between subjects t-test are *two* less than the total number of participants.

34. The t-test is the most common way to analyze data from a simple experiment.

35. Statistical analysis of the simple experiment will only give you correct results if the data meet the assumptions of the analysis.

## KEY TERMS

**placebo treatment:** a fake treatment that we know has no effect, except through the power of suggestion. For example, in medical experiments, a participant may be given a pill that does not have a drug in it. By using placebo treatments, you may be able to make people "blind" to whether a participant is getting the real treatment. (p. 180)

**single blind:** when either the participant or the experimenter is unaware of whether the participant is getting the real treatment or a placebo treatment. Making the participant "blind" prevents the participant from biasing the results of the study; making the experimenter blind prevents the experimenter from biasing the results of the study. (p. 180)

**double blind:** where neither the participant nor the experimenter know what type of treatment (placebo treatment or real treatment) the participant is getting. By making both the participant and the experimenter "blind," you reduce subject and experimenter bias. (p. 180)

**experimental group:** the treatment group. More specifically, the participants who are randomly assigned to get the treatment. (p. 164)

**control group:** the participants who are randomly assigned *not* to receive the treatment. The scores of these participants are compared to the scores of the experimental group to see if the treatment had an effect. (p. 164)

**empty control group:** a control group that does not receive any kind of treatment, not even a placebo treatment. The problem with an empty control group is that if the treatment group does better, we don't know if the difference is due to the treatment itself or whether the difference is due to a placebo effect. To maximize construct validity, most researchers avoid using an empty control group. (p. 180)

**independent variable:** the treatment variable; the variable manipulated by the experimenter. The experimental group gets more of the independent variable than the control group. Note: Don't confuse *independent variable* with *dependent variable.* (p. 163)

**levels of an independent variable:** the treatment variable is often given in different amounts. These different amounts are called levels. (p. 163)

**dependent variable (dependent measure):** participants' scores—the response that the researcher is measuring. In the simple experiment, the experimenter hopes that the dependent variable will be affected by the independent variable. (p. 168)

**independence:** a key assumption of almost any statistical test. In the simple experiment, observations must be independent. That is, what one participant does should have no influence on what another participant does and what happens to one participant should not influence what happens to another participant. Individually assigning participants to treatment or no-treatment condition and individually testing each participant are ways to achieve independence. (p. 165)

**independent random assignment:** randomly determining, for each individual participant, and without regard to what group the previous participant was assigned to, whether that participant gets the treatment. For example, you might flip a coin for each participant to determine group assignment. (p. 158)

**experimental hypothesis:** a prediction that the treatment will *cause* an effect. In other words, a prediction that the independent variable will have an effect on the dependent variable. (p. 162)

**null hypothesis:** the hypothesis that there is *no* treatment effect. Basically, this hypothesis states that any difference between the treatment and no-treatment groups is due to chance. This hypothesis can be disproven, but it cannot be proven. Often, disproving the null hypothesis lends support to the experimental hypothesis. (p. 162)

**simple experiment:** participants are independently and randomly assigned to one of two groups, usually to either a treatment group or to a no-treatment group. The simple experiment is the easiest way to establish that a treatment causes an effect. (p. 156)

**internal validity:** a study has internal validity if it can accurately determine whether an independent variable causes an effect. Only experimental designs have internal validity. (p. 156)

**randomly assign to:** in random assignment, you divide your group of participants into equivalent subgroups. Each subgroup starts off as a random sample of the same larger group. Because all the subgroups come from the same parent population, all the subgroups are similar to each other at the start of the study. However, because the subgroups are assigned to different treatments, the subgroups may differ from each other by the end of the experiment. Random assignment to experimental condition is the cornerstone of the simple experiment. (p. 166)

**randomly sample from:** in random sampling, you randomly select a few members from a population. If you randomly select enough participants, those participants will usually be fairly representative of the entire population. That is, your random sample will reflect its population. Often, random sampling is used to maximize a study's external validity. Note that random sampling—unlike random assignment—does not promote internal validity. (p. 167)

**inferential statistics:** see sampling statistics.

**sampling statistics** (also called **inferential statistics**): the science of inferring the characteristics of a population from a sample of that population. (p. 168)

**population:** the entire group that you are interested in. You can estimate the characteristics of a population by taking large random samples from that population. (p. 182)

**mean:** an average calculated by adding up all the scores and then dividing by the number of scores. (p. 184)

**normal curve:** a bell-shaped, symmetrical curve that has its center at the mean. (p. 188)

**normally distributed:** if the way the scores are distributed follows the normal curve, scores are said to be normally distributed. For example, a population is said to be normally distributed if 68% of the scores are within one standard deviation of the mean, 95% are within two standard deviations of the mean, and 99% of the scores are within 3 standard deviations of the mean. Many statistical tests, including the t-test, assume that sample means are normally distributed. (p. 188)

**central limit theorem:** the distribution of sample means will be normally distributed if your samples are large enough (30 or more participants). In other words, no matter how the individual scores that make up the sample means are distributed, the distribution of the sample means themselves will be normally distributed—if your samples are large enough. To guarantee that their sample means are normally distributed—a key assumption of the t-test—many researchers like to make sure that they have more than 30 participants in each group. (p. 190)

**sum of squared *differences:*** more commonly referred to as the **Sum of Squares.** Calculated in three steps:

1. Take the *difference* between each score and the mean
2. *Square* each of these differences.
3. Add (*sum*) these squared differences.

The sum of squares provides some indication of how closely scores stay to the mean. However, it is a sum total, not an average. Therefore, it does not tell us the average extent to which scores stray from the mean. To calculate the average degree to which scores deviate from the mean, the sum of squares is sometimes divided by the number of scores involved. More commonly, an index of the average extent to which scores deviate from the mean is calculated by dividing the sum of squares by the appropriate degrees of freedom (degrees of freedom are tied to the number of scores, but a group's degrees of freedom are usually one or two less than the total number of scores). This index is typically called the variance. (p. 187)

**variance:** a measure of variability based on the sum of squares. However, unlike the sum of squares, having more scores does not automatically make the variance bigger. Specifically, the variance corrects for having more scores by dividing the sum of squares by the number of scores (in the case of calculating the variance from the population) or by dividing the sum of squares by one less than the number of scores (in the case of estimating the population variance from a sample). When the population variance is estimated from a sample, this variance is abbreviated $s^2$. The square root of the variance is the standard deviation. (p. 187)

**standard deviation:** a measure of the extent to which individual scores deviate from the population mean. The more scores vary from each other, the larger the standard deviation will tend to be. If, on the other hand, all the scores were the same as the mean, the standard deviation would be zero. (p. 186)

**standard error (of the estimate of the population mean):** often called the standard error of the mean; sometimes just called the standard error. It is an index of the degree to which random error may cause the sample mean to be an inaccurate estimate of the population mean. The standard error of the mean is the standard deviation divided by an index of the number of scores making up the mean. So the standard error of the mean will always be smaller than the standard deviation. The standard error will be small when the standard deviation is small and the sample mean is based on many scores. (p. 189)

**standard error of the difference:** an index of the degree to which *two sample means,* randomly drawn from the same population, could be expected to *differ.* To be statistically significant, the difference between our experimental and control group means usually have to be at least twice as big as the standard error of the difference. To find out the exact ratio between our observed difference and the standard error of the difference, we conduct a t-test. (p. 192)

**t-test:** the most common way of analyzing data from a simple experiment. It involves computing a ratio between two things:

- the difference between your group means; and
- the standard error of the difference (an index of the degree to which group means could differ by chance alone).

If the difference you observe is more than three times bigger than the difference that could be expected by chance, then your results are probably statistically significant. We can only say "probably" because the exact ratio that you need for statistical significance depends on your level of significance and on how many participants you have. (p. 194)

**degrees of freedom (df):** an index of sample size. In the simple experiment, the df for your error term will always be two less than the number of participants. (p. 193)

**statistical significance:** when a statistical test says that the relationship we have observed is probably not due to chance alone, we say that the results are statistically significant. See also $p < .05.$ (p. 168)

$p < .05$: in the simple experiment, $p < .05$ indicates that if the treatment had no effect, a difference between the groups as big as what was discovered would happen fewer than 5 times in 100. Since the chances of such a difference occurring by chance alone is so small, experimenters usually conclude that such a difference must be due, at least in part, to the treatment. (p. 168)

**Type 1 error:** rejecting the null hypothesis when it is really true. In other words, declaring a difference statistically significant when the difference is really due to chance. If you set $p < .05$, there is less than a 5% chance that you will make a Type 1 error. (p. 171)

**Type 2 error:** failure to reject the null hypothesis when it is really false. In other words, failing to declare that a difference is statistically significant, even though the treatment had an effect. (p. 172)

**power:** the ability to find differences or, put another way, the ability to avoid making Type 2 errors. (p. 173)

**null results:** results that fail to disprove the null hypothesis. These results are inconclusive. Null results are often called nonsignificant results. Often, null results are due to a lack of power. In other words, many null results are Type 2 errors. (p. 169)

# EXERCISES

1. What two conditions must be met to establish that a factor causes an effect? How is the simple experiment able to establish these conditions?

2. Why isn't it necessary to do an experiment in a lab? What advantages are there to doing an experiment in a lab? What advantages are there to doing an experiment in a real-world setting? What are the disadvantages?

3. A professor has a class of 40 students. Half of the students chose to take a test after every chapter (chapter test condition). The chapter tests were taken outside of class. The other half of the students chose to take in-class "unit tests." Unit tests covered four chapters. The professor finds no statistically significant differences between the groups on their scores on a comprehensive final exam. The professor then concludes that type of testing does not affect performance.
   a. Is this an experiment?
   b. Is the professor's conclusion reasonable? Why or why not?

4. Participants are randomly assigned to meditation or no-meditation condition. The meditation group meditates three times a week. The meditation group reports being significantly more relaxed than the no-meditation group.
   a. Why might the results of this experiment be less clear-cut than they appear?
   b. How would you improve this experiment?

5. Can gender differences be studied in a simple experiment? Why or why not?

6. Theresa fails to find a significant difference between her control group and her experimental group $t(10) = 2.11$, not significant.
   a. Given that her results are not significant, what would you advise her to conclude?
   b. What would you advise her to do? (Hint: You know that her t-test, based on 10 degrees of freedom, was not significant. What does the fact that she has 10 degrees of freedom tell you?)

7. A training program significantly improves worker performance. What should you know before advising a company to invest in such a training program?

8. Jerry's control group is the football team; the experimental group is the baseball team. He assigned the groups to condition using random assignment. Is there a problem with Jerry's experiment? If so, what is it? Why is it a problem?

9. Leslie tests the experimental group at 10:00 a.m. and the control group at 11:00 p.m. Is this appropriate? Why or why not?

10. Students were randomly assigned to two different strategies of studying for an exam. One group used visual imagery, the other group was told to study the normal way.
   a. The visual imagery group scores 88% on the test as compared to 76% for the control group. This difference was not significant. What can the experimenter conclude?
   b. If the difference had been significant, what would you have concluded? What changes in the study would have made it easier to be sure of your conclusions?
   c. "To be sure that they are studying the way they should, why don't you have the imagery people form one study group and have the control group form another study group?" Is this good advice? Why or why not?
   d. "Just get a random sample of students who typically use imagery and compare them to a sample of students who don't use imagery. That will do the same thing as random assignment." Is this good advice? Why or why not?

11. Bob and Judy are doing basically the same study. However, Bob has decided to put his risk of a Type 1 error at .05 whereas Judy has put her risk of a Type 1 error at .01. That is, Bob is willing to take a 5 in 100 risk that the results declared statistically significant are really due to chance, whereas Judy is only willing to take a 1/100 risk of "significant results" being due to chance.
   a. If Judy has 22 participants in her study, what t-value would she need to get significant results?
   b. If Bob has 22 participants in his study, what t-value would he need to get significant results?
   c. Who is more likely to make a Type II error? Why?

12. Judy claims that the sample's standard deviation is 2 and the standard error is 4. Why must Judy be wrong?

13. Why don't participants in the control group all get the same score?

14. Complete the following chart:

| Action | Implication for Standard Deviation | Implication for Standard Error of the Mean |
| --- | --- | --- |
| Using a homogeneous group of participants | Decreases | Decreases |
| Using a highly reliable measure | | |
| Standardizing procedures | | |
| Using a large number of participants | | |

15. Why will the standard error of the difference tend to be larger than the standard error of the mean?

16. Your dependent measure is when people arrive to class. The distribution is not normally distributed. It tends to be "J" shaped. That is, whereas the average arrival time might be a minute before class, some people show up much earlier, but very few show up much later. Can you do a t-test on this data? Why or why not?

17. Gerald's dependent measure is the order in which people turned in their exam (1st, 2nd, 3rd, etc.). Can Gerald use a t-test on this data? Why or why not? What would you advise Gerald to do in future studies?

18. Are the results of experiment A or experiment B more likely to be significant? Why?

| EXPERIMENT A | | EXPERIMENT B | |
|---|---|---|---|
| CONTROL GROUP | EXPERIMENTAL GROUP | CONTROL GROUP | EXPERIMENTAL GROUP |
| 3 | 4 | 0 | 0 |
| 4 | 5 | 4 | 5 |
| 5 | 6 | 8 | 10 |

19. Are the results of experiment A or experiment B more likely to be significant? Why?

| EXPERIMENT A | | EXPERIMENT B | |
|---|---|---|---|
| CONTROL GROUP | EXPERIMENTAL GROUP | CONTROL GROUP | EXPERIMENTAL GROUP |
| 3 | 4 | 3 | 4 |
| 4 | 5 | 4 | 5 |
| 5 | 6 | 5 | 6 |
| | | 3 | 4 |
| | | 4 | 5 |
| | | 5 | 6 |
| | | 3 | 4 |
| | | 4 | 5 |
| | | 5 | 6 |

20. What would be the t-value for the following data?

| EXPERIMENT C | |
|---|---|
| CONTROL GROUP | EXPERIMENTAL GROUP |
| 3 | 2 |
| 4 | 4 |
| 5 | 6 |

21. Why do nonsignificant results raise more questions than they answer?

22. Under what circumstances should you *not* use a t-test?

# CHAPTER 7

———

# Expanding the Simple Experiment: The Multiple Group Experiment

*Overview*

*The Advantages of Using More than Two Values
of an Independent Variable*

COMPARING MORE THAN TWO KINDS OF TREATMENTS
COMPARING TWO KINDS OF TREATMENTS WITH NO TREATMENT
COMPARING MORE THAN TWO LEVELS (AMOUNTS) OF AN INDEPENDENT VARIABLE
TO INCREASE EXTERNAL VALIDITY
USING MULTIPLE LEVELS TO IMPROVE CONSTRUCT
VALIDITY OF EXPERIMENTS

*Analysis of Multiple Group Experiments*

ANALYZING THE MULTIPLE GROUP EXPERIMENT:
AN INTUITIVE OVERVIEW
A CLOSER LOOK AT THE ANALYSIS OF
A MULTIPLE GROUP EXPERIMENT

*Concluding Remarks*

*Summary*

*Key Terms*

*Exercises*

# *Chapter 7*

# EXPANDING THE SIMPLE EXPERIMENT: THE MULTIPLE GROUP EXPERIMENT

## OVERVIEW

In Chapter 6, you learned how to perform a simple experiment. You now know that the simple experiment is internally valid and easy to do. However, you are also aware that the simple experiment is limited: With it, you can only study two values of a single independent variable.

In this chapter, you will see why you might want to go beyond studying two values of a single variable. Then, you will see how the logic of the simple experiment (random assignment of participants to two groups) can be extended to experiments that study the effects of three or more values of a single independent variable.

## THE ADVANTAGES OF USING MORE THAN TWO VALUES OF AN INDEPENDENT VARIABLE

The simple experiment is ideal if an investigator wants to compare two different kinds of treatments. But investigators often want to compare three or more different kinds of treatments. For instance, Roediger (1980) wanted to compare five kinds of memory strategies (rote rehearsal, imagery, method of loci, the link method, and the peg system). Clearly, he could not compare all five treatments in one simple experiment.

### Comparing More than Two Kinds of Treatments

Therefore, instead of randomly assigning subjects to two different groups, Roediger randomly assigned his subjects to five different groups. To learn how to randomly assign subjects to more than two groups, see Box 7–1.

Admittedly, Roediger could have compared the five treatments by using a series of simple experiments. However, using a single multi-valued experiment has several advantages over using a series of simple experiments. We will only mention the two most obvious.

---

## BOX 7−1
## RANDOMLY ASSIGNING PARTICIPANTS
## TO MORE THAN TWO GROUPS

**STEP 1**  Across the top of a piece of paper write down your conditions. Under each condition draw a line for each participant you will need.

Group 1                    Group 2                    Group 3

_____        _____        _____

_____        _____        _____

_____        _____        _____

_____        _____        _____

**STEP 2**  Turn to a random numbers table. Roll a die to determine which column in the table you will use.

**STEP 3**  Assign the first number in the column to the first space under Group 1, the second number to the second space, etc. When you have filled the spaces for Group 1, put the next number under the first space under Group 2. Similarly, when you fill all the spaces under Group 2, place the next number in the first space under Group 3.

| Group 1 | Group 2 | Group 3 |
|---------|---------|---------|
| 12      | 20      | 63      |
| 39      | 2       | 64      |
| 53      | 37      | 95      |
| 29      | 1       | 18      |

**STEP 4**  Assign the first person who participates in your study to the condition with the lowest random number. The second participant will be in the condition with the second lowest random number, and so on. Thus, in this example, your first two participants would be in condition 2 and your third participant would be in condition 1.

---

First, by doing a single five-value experiment, Roediger greatly reduced the number of experiments he had to perform. To compare all five treatments with one another, Roediger would have had to do 10 simple experiments. Specifically, he would have had to do:

1. one experiment to compare rote rehearsal with imagery,
2. another experiment to compare rote rehearsal with the method of loci,
3. another to compare rote rehearsal with the link method,
4. another to compare rote rehearsal with a peg system,
5. another to compare imagery with the method of loci,

6. another to compare imagery with the link method,
7. another to compare imagery with a peg system,
8. another to compare method of loci with the link method,
9. another to compare method of loci with a peg system, and
10. another to compare the link method with a peg system.

Second, he reduced the number of subjects he had to test. If he had done 10 simple experiments, he would have needed 20 groups of subjects. To have any degree of power (the ability to find significant differences), he would need at least 15 subjects per group[1] or 300 (15 × 20) subjects. With the five-group experiment, he could have the same power with 75 (15 × 5) subjects.

## Comparing Two Kinds of Treatments with No Treatment

Even when you are only interested in comparing two types of treatments, you may be better off avoiding the simple experiment. To understand why, let's consider the following fact: For certain kinds of back problems, people going to a chiropractor end up better off than those going for back surgery. Although an interesting fact, it leaves many questions unanswered. For example, is either treatment better than nothing? It could be that chiropractic treatment is the lesser of two evils. On the other hand, both treatments could be substantially better than no treatment. We don't know because the researchers didn't compare either treatment to a no-treatment control condition.

In psychological research, we often compare two untested treatments. The simple experiment could tell us which is better than the other. However, we would not know whether the better one was the less harmful of two bad treatments or the more effective of two good treatments. Similarly, we would not know if the lesser of the two treatments was harmful, merely ineffective, or fairly helpful. However, by using a three-group experiment that had a no-treatment control group, we would be able to judge not only how effective the two treatments were relative to each other, but also their effectiveness to no treatment.

## Comparing More than Two Levels (Amounts) of an Independent Variable to Increase External Validity

In the simple experiment, you want to pick two levels of the independent variable that will allow you to find an effect. Intuitively, you realize that the greater the difference between how the two groups are treated, the greater the chances of finding a significant effect. Therefore, when choosing levels of the independent variable, you will usually try to choose levels that differ from each other as much as possible. Thus, if you were investigating the effects of exer-

---

[1] Many researchers would say that 30—not 15—should be the absolute minimum number of subjects per group. In that case, Roediger would have needed 600 subjects had he done several simple experiments versus 150 with a multiple-group experiment. In many cases, researchers should have at least 60 subjects per group (Cohen 1990).

cise on depression, half of your subjects would exercise very little, whereas the other half of your subjects would exercise a great deal. Your results might be as follows:

Group 1: Low amounts of aerobic exercise:    High levels of depression

Group 2: High amounts of aerobic exercise:    High levels of depression

## UNCOVERING RELATIONSHIPS

Based on these results, you would be tempted to conclude that there is no relationship between aerobic exercise and depression. However, this is a generalization: You have not tested other levels of the independent variable. Out of the many possible amounts of the independent variable you could have chosen, you have only sampled two. In this case, your generalization would be wrong if aerobic exercise had the following effects on depression:

Low amounts of aerobic exercise:    No effect on depression

Medium amounts of aerobic exercise:    Reduce depression

High amounts of aerobic exercise:    No effect on depression

The "u"-shaped relationship we have postulated between exercise and depression is fairly common. Psychologists often find "u"-shaped and upside-down "u"-shaped relationships. Perhaps the most famous case is the Yerkes-Dodson Law, which states, in part, that:

**1)**  with little motivation, performance is poor;

**2)**  with moderate levels of motivation, performance is good; and

**3)**  with too much motivation, performance is poor.

You can probably think of many examples where (to paraphrase the littlest of the three bears) too little of some factor can be bad, too much can be bad, but a medium amount is just right.

If the relationship between aerobic exercise and depression is "u"-shaped and you pick extreme levels of your independent variable, you will falsely conclude that the treatment has no effect. Therefore, you might be tempted to choose moderate levels of the treatment. However, if the relationship is not "u"-shaped and you use moderate levels, your levels may not be far enough apart to allow you to detect a treatment effect. Thus, as you can see, picking the right levels of your independent variable for a simple experiment is a risky business.

To avoid making hard choices about what two levels to use, avoid simple experiments. Instead of choosing two levels, do experiments that use several levels of the independent variable so that you can choose three or more levels. Thus, if you had used an experiment that examined three levels of aerobic exercise, you might have obtained the following pattern of results:

Group 1: Low aerobic exercise:    High levels of depression

Group 2: Medium aerobic exercise:    Low levels of depression

Group 3: High aerobic exercise:    High levels of depression

Based on these results, you would correctly conclude that aerobic exercise affects depression. However, what if you had only used two groups? If you had compared Groups 1 and 2, you would have concluded that exercise decreases depression. If you had compared Groups 2 and 3, you would have concluded that exercise increases depression. If you had compared Groups 1 and 3, you would have falsely concluded that exercise had no effect on depression (see Figure 7-1).

## DISCOVERING THE NATURE OF RELATIONSHIPS

You have seen that the researcher using the simple experiment may falsely conclude that a factor has no effect. Furthermore, even if the researcher using a simple experiment finds a significant effect, that effect may apply only to the two levels used in the experiment. Thus, researchers who rely on simple experiments have difficulty generalizing their results to unexplored levels of the independent variable.

To accurately generalize results to unexplored levels of an independent variable, the researcher must not only know that a relationship exists, but the researcher must also know the nature of that relationship. That is, the researcher must know the independent and dependent variables' **functional relationship:** the shape of the relationship. Simple experiments do not enable you to uncover the nature of a functional relationship.

To illustrate the weakness of the simple experiment in mapping the shape of a relationship, let's consider a simple experiment investigating the effects of aerobic exercise on happiness. Suppose that we obtained the following results:

| | | |
|---|---|---|
| Control group: | 0 minutes of exercise per day | 1.0 self-rating of happiness |
| Experimental group: | 100 minutes of exercise per day | 10.0 self-rating of happiness |

From this data, can you determine the functional relationship between aerobic exercise and happiness? Perhaps the functional relationship is linear (like a straight line), as in Figure 7-2.

However, the true relationship between exercise and happiness might not resemble a straight line. Instead, it might be a nonlinear function, such as one of the curved lines in Figure 7-3.

Because many different-shaped lines can be drawn between two points (your two group means), the simple experiment does not help you discover the functional relationship between the variables. Because you would not know the functional relationship, you could do little more than guess if we asked you about the effects of 70 minutes of aerobic exercise. You might *assume* that the relationship is linear and therefore say that exercising 70 minutes a day would be better than no exercise and would be less effective than exercising for 100 minutes a day. But if your assumption of a linear relationship is wrong—and it well could be—your guess would be inaccurate.

**FIGURE 7–1**

## How a Multiple Group Experiment Can Give You a More Accurate Picture of a Relationship than a Simple Experiment

### (a) A Multiple Group Experiment

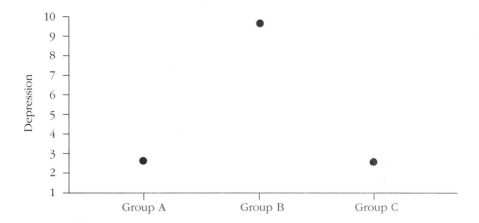

### (b) Simple Experiment 1 Finds that Exercise increases Depression

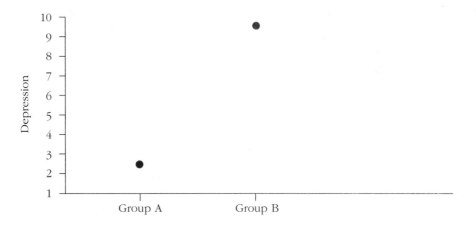

To get a line on the functional relationship between variables, you need to know more than two points. Therefore, suppose you expanded the simple experiment into a multi-level experiment by adding a group that gets 50 minutes of exercise a day. Then, you would have a much clearer idea of the functional relationship between exercise and happiness. As you can see in Figure 7-4,

**FIGURE 7–1 CONTINUED**

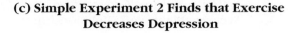

**(c) Simple Experiment 2 Finds that Exercise
Decreases Depression**

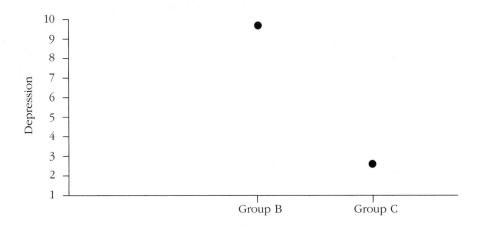

**(d) Simple Experiment 3 Fails to Find an Effect
of Exercise on Depression**

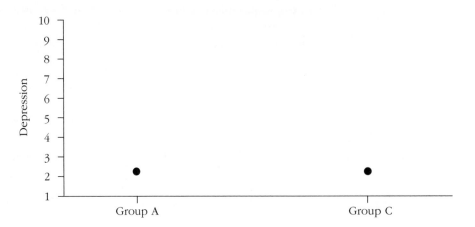

using three levels can give you a pretty good idea of the functional relationship among variables. If the relationship is linear, you should be able to draw a straight line through all three points. If the relationship is "u"-shaped, you will detect that too.

Because you can detect the nature of the functional relationship when you use three levels of the independent variable, you can make accurate predictions about unexplored levels of the independent variable. For example, if the

**FIGURE 7–2**

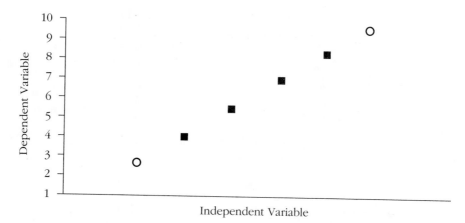

### Linear Relationship Between Two Points

*Note:* The circles represent known data points. The boxes in between the circles are what would happen at a given level of the independent variable if the relationship between the variables is linear. As you can see from the next figure (Figure 7-3), the functional relationship does not have to be linear.

functional relationship between aerobic exercise and happiness were linear, you would obtain the following pattern of results:

| Group 1: | 0 minutes of exercise per day | 1.0 self-rating of happiness |
| Group 2: | 50 minutes of exercise per day | 5.5 self-rating of happiness |
| Group 3: | 100 minutes of exercise per day | 10.0 self-rating of happiness |

In that case, you could confidently predict that 70 minutes of exercise would be less beneficial for increasing happiness than 100 minutes of exercise. If, on the other hand, the relationship was "s"-shaped (as in Figure 7-3), you would get the following pattern of results:

| Group 1: | 0 minutes of exercise per day | 1.0 self-rating of happiness |
| Group 2: | 50 minutes of exercise per day | 10.0 self-rating of happiness |
| Group 3: | 100 minutes of exercise per day | 10.0 self-rating of happiness |

In that case, you would predict that a person who exercised 70 minutes would do as well as someone exercising 100 minutes a day.

**FIGURE 7–3**

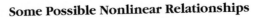

## Some Possible Nonlinear Relationships

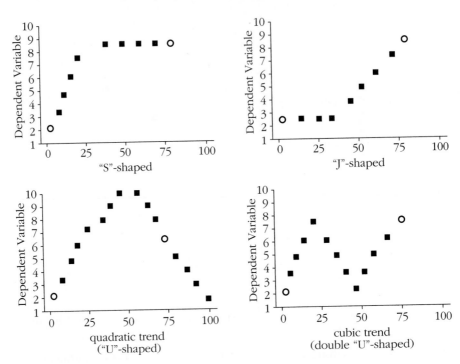

*Note:* The circles represent the known data points. The boxes in between the circles are what might happen at a given level of the independent variable depending on whether the relationship between the variables is characterized by (a) an "S" -shaped (negatively accelerated) trend, (b) a "J" -shaped (positively accelerated) trend, (c) a "U" -shaped (quadratic) trend, or (d) a double "U" -shaped (cubic) trend.

The more groups you use, the more accurately you can pin down the shape of the functional relationship. Yet, despite this fact, you do not have to use numerous levels of the independent variable. Why? Because nature prefers simple patterns. That is, most functional relationships are linear and few are more complex than "u"-shaped functions. Consequently, you will rarely need more than four levels of the independent variable to pin down a functional relationship. In fact, you will usually need no more than three carefully chosen levels to identify the functional relationship among variables.

## SUMMARY: MULTI-LEVEL EXPERIMENTS AND EXTERNAL VALIDITY

In summary, knowing the functional relationship between two variables is almost as important as knowing that a relationship exists. You want to be able to say more than: "If you exercise 100 minutes a day, you will be happier than someone who exercises 0 minutes a day." Who exercises exactly 100 minutes a

**FIGURE 7–4**

**Having Three Levels of the Independent Variable (Three Data Points) Aids Greatly in Determining the Shape of the Functional Relationship.**

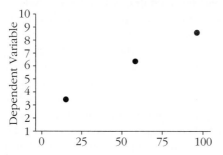 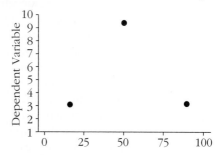

With these three points, we can be relatively confident that the relationship is linear. Most nonlinear relationships (see Figure 7-3) would not produce data that would fit these three data points.

If we got these three data points, we could be relatively confident that the relationship was curvilinear. Specifically, we would suspect we had a quadratic trend.

day? You want to be able to generalize your results so that you can tell people the effects of exercising 50 minutes, 56 minutes, 75 minutes, and so forth. Yet, you have no intention of testing the effects of every single possible amount of exercise a person might do. Instead, you want to test only a handful of exercise levels. If you chose these levels carefully, you would be able to accurately map the functional relationship between the variables. Knowing the functional relationship will allow you to make educated predictions about the effects of exercise levels that you have not directly tested.

## Using Multiple Levels to Improve Construct Validity of Experiments

You have seen that multi-level experiments have more external validity than simple experiments. In this section, you will learn that multi-level experiments can also have more construct validity than simple experiments.

### CONFOUNDING VARIABLES IN THE SIMPLE EXPERIMENT

In Chapter 6, you saw that simple experiments—thanks to random assignment—are able to rule out the effects of variables *unrelated to the treatment manipulation.* For example, because of random assignment, the effects of participant variables such as gender, race, and personality usually will *not* be confused for a treatment effect. In other words, a statistically significant difference between the control group and the experimental group will probably *not* be due to the groups being different before the treatment was introduced.

So, simple experiments effectively control for the effects of variables that have nothing to do with the treatment manipulation, such as individual differences among participants. But what if the treatment manipulation is manipulating more than one variable? For example, what if the "exercise" manipulation is also manipulating social support? Simple experiments are not always effective in ruling out the effects of variables that are manipulated along with the treatment.

In an ideal world, this limitation of the simple experiment would not be a problem. Ideally, your treatment would be a pure manipulation that creates one—and only one—difference between the experimental group and the control group. Unfortunately, it is rare to have a perfect manipulation. Instead, the treatment manipulation usually produces not one, but several, differences between how the experimental and control groups are treated. For example, suppose that we read that a simple experiment found that the "attractive" defendant was more likely to get a light sentence than the "unattractive" defendant. We would know that the "attractiveness" manipulation had an effect. However, it could be that, in addition to manipulating attractiveness, the researchers also manipulated perceived wealth. Thus, wealth, rather than attractiveness, might account for the manipulation's effect. For example, people may be less likely to give wealthy defendants long sentences.

Because of impurities in manipulations, the results of simple experiments are often difficult to interpret. That is, you often end up knowing that the treatment manipulation had an effect, but you may have trouble saying what it was about the treatment manipulation that produced the effect. In other words, you may worry that the treatment manipulated more than one variable. In short, simple experiments may lack construct validity because the independent variable manipulation is contaminated by **confounding variables:** variables that are unintentionally manipulated along with the treatment.

The following example[2] illustrates the general problem of confounding. Imagine being in a classroom that has five light switches. You want to know what the middle light switch does. Assume that in the "control" condition, all the light switches are off. In the "experimental" condition, you want to flick the middle switch. However, because it is dark, you accidentally flick on the middle three switches. As the lights come on, the janitor bursts into the room and your "experiment" is finished. What can you conclude? You can conclude that your manipulation of the light switches had an effect. That is, your study has internal validity. However, because you manipulated more than just the middle light switch, you can't say that you know what the middle light switch did. Put another way, if you were to call your manipulation a "manipulation of the middle switch," your manipulation would have little construct validity.

Because of confounding variables, it is often hard to know what it is about the treatment that caused the effect. In real life, variables are often confounded.

---

[2] We are indebted to an anonymous reviewer for this example and other advice about confounding variables.

For example, someone may know they got a hangover from drinking too much wine, but not know whether it was the alcohol in the wine, the preservatives in the wine, or something else about the wine that produced the awful sensations. A few years ago, a couple of our students joked that they could easily test the hypothesis that alcohol was responsible. All they needed us to do was donate enough money to buy mass quantities of a pure manipulation of alcohol—180 proof, totally devoid of impurities. These students understood how confounding variables can contaminate real-life manipulations, thus making it hard to know what it was about the manipulation that caused the effect.

To understand how confounding variables can contaminate a simple experiment, let's go back to the simple experiment on the effects of exercise that we proposed earlier in this chapter. You will recall that the experimental group got 100 minutes of exercise class per day, the control group got nothing. Clearly, the experimental group subjects are being treated very differently than the control group subjects. The groups didn't merely differ in terms of the independent variable (exercise). They also differed in terms of several other (confounding) variables: The exercise group received more attention and had more structured social activities than the control group.

## HYPOTHESIS-GUESSING IN SIMPLE EXPERIMENTS

Furthermore, subjects in the experimental group knew they were getting a treatment whereas subjects in the control group knew they were not receiving any special treatment. If experimental group subjects suspected that the exercise program should have an effect, the exercise program may *appear* to have an effect—even if exercise does not really improve mood. In other words, the construct validity of the study might be ruined because the experimental group subjects guessed the hypothesis.

Because of the impurities (confounding variables) of this manipulation, you cannot say that the difference between groups is due to exercise by itself. Although all manipulations have impurities, this study's most obvious—and avoidable—impurities stem from having an *empty control group:* a group that gets no treatment, not even a placebo. Thus, if you could get rid of—or replace—the empty control group, you could reduce the impact of confounding variables.

## HOW MULTI-LEVEL EXPERIMENTS CAN DETECT PROBLEMS
## WITH EMPTY CONTROL GROUPS

If you insist on using an empty control group, the multi-level experiment may alert you if there are problems with such a group. To illustrate, imagine that you have a three-level experiment where:

1. the first group gets no treatment,
2. the second group gets 20 minutes of aerobic exercise, and
3. the third group gets 40 minutes.

In this multi-level experiment, the two experimental groups are being treated almost identically. They only differ in terms of how much exercise they get. Consequently, any difference between the experimental groups is probably due to the amount of exercise, not to incidental, confounding variables (such as socializing with class members or setting goals).

The participants in the two experimental groups would also have a hard time figuring out the hypothesis and playing along with it. Probably, the only thing they might guess is that exercise is supposed to change their behavior. There is no way that they are going to figure out: (1) that there is an empty control group and two exercise groups, (2) that they are in the medium exercise group, and (3) that by acting a certain way, they will get scores that will be higher than the control group's and lower than the high exercise group's.

You have seen that participants in a multi-level experiment would have a hard time figuring out the hypothesis and even a harder time playing along with it. Even if participants guessed the hypothesis and tried to play along with it, they would only be partially successful. They would succeed in that the experimental groups would behave differently than the empty control groups. However, they would fail in that there would be no difference between the two experimental groups. That is, even though the two experimental groups got different levels of treatment, participants would not know that there were two experimental groups and thus would not be able to play along with that part of the hypothesis.

Consequently, you should be able to detect whether the results of a multi-level experiment are solely due to hypothesis-guessing. To see if you can, look at Table 7–1. The results from one of these experiments are invalid because of hypothesis-guessing. Do you think it is Experiment A or Experiment B? How do you know?

If you think Experiment B is the tainted experiment, you are correct! Why did you suspect Experiment B? You probably assumed that if exercise has an effect, a high level of exercise will have a greater effect than a medium level of exercise. It's important to recognize that this is an assumption—and this assumption could be wrong. However, it is remarkable how often nature conforms to this assumption.

## INCREASING VALIDITY THROUGH SEVERAL CONTROL GROUPS

You have seen that using a multiple group experiment allows you to do something you cannot do with a simple experiment—have a control group *and* have more than one treatment group. You have seen that using several treatment groups can sometimes allow you to detect a problem with your control group. In addition to allowing you to use multiple treatment groups, multiple-group experiments allow you to do something else you cannot do with a simple experiment—use multiple control groups.

**TABLE 7–1**
**A Comparison between Two Experiments**

| EXPERIMENT A | | EXPERIMENT B | |
| --- | --- | --- | --- |
| Condition | Mood | Condition | Mood |
| No exercise | 8.0 | No exercise | 8.0 |
| Medium exercise | 9.5 | Medium exercise | 11.5 |
| High exercise | 11.5 | High exercise | 11.5 |

*Note:* Numbers indicate ratings on a self-report scale of mood. Higher numbers indicate better mood.

Because you cannot use multiple control groups in a simple experiment, the person using a simple experiment is often forced to choose between control groups. The researcher may have to choose between using a placebo treatment group that gets a pseudo-treatment *or* an empty control group that gets no treatment whatsoever. Alternatively, the researcher may have to decide between one kind of placebo group and another kind of placebo group. With a multiple group experiment, on the other hand, you do not have to choose. You can have as many control groups as you need.

To see how hard it can be to choose between an empty control group and a placebo group, let's go back to the problem of examining the effects of aerobic exercise on mood. If you use an empty control group that has nothing done to them, interpreting your results may be difficult. For example, if the aerobic exercise group does better than this "left alone" group, the results could be due to hypothesis-guessing or to any number of confounding variables (such as socializing with other students in the class, being put into a structured routine, etc.).

If, on the other hand, you use a placebo-treatment group (for example, meditation classes), you would be able to control for many of these confounding variables. Still, your problems are not over.

Your problems are not over because you do not know what the effect of your placebo treatment will be. For example, suppose you find that the exercise group is more depressed than the meditation group. Would you conclude that exercise increases depression? No, because it might be that although exercise reduces depression, meditation reduces it more. Conversely, if you found that the exercise group is less depressed than the meditation group, you could not automatically conclude that exercise decreases depression. It may be that meditation increases depression greatly and exercise increases depression only moderately. That is, exercise may simply be the lesser of two evils. To find out whether exercise increases or decreases depression, you need to compare the exercise group to a no-treatment group. Thus, if you were interested in the effects of exercise on depression, you have two options: (1) Use a simple experiment and make the hard choice between an empty control group and a placebo group, or (2) Use a multiple group experiment so that you can include both an empty and a placebo control group.

Even if you are sure you do not want to use an empty control group, you may still need more than one control group because you will probably not have the perfect control group. Instead, you may have several groups, each of which controls for some confounding variables, but not for others. If you were to do a simple experiment, you may have to decide which of several placebo groups to use. Choosing one control group—when you realize you need more than one—is not fun. It would be better to be able to use as many as you need.

But how often do you really need more than one control group? More often than you might think. In fact, it is so easy to underestimate the need for control groups that even professional psychologists sometimes underestimate the need for control groups. Indeed, many professional researchers get their research articles rejected because a reviewer concluded that they failed to include enough good control groups (Fiske & Fogg, 1990).

To illustrate how even a good control group may still differ from the experimental group in several ways having nothing to do with the independent variable, consider the meditation control group. The meditation control group has several advantages over the empty control group. For example, if the exercise group was less depressed than a meditation control group, we could be confident that this difference was not due to hypothesis guessing, engaging in structured activities, or being distracted from worrisome thoughts for a while. Both groups received a "treatment," both engaged in structured activities, and both were distracted for the same length of time.

However, the groups may differ in that the exercise group did a more social type of activity, listened to louder and more upbeat music, and interacted with a more energetic and enthusiastic instructor. Therefore, the exercise group may be less depressed for several reasons having nothing to do with exercise: (1) liking their exercise partners; (2) feeling arousal and positive mood as a result of the music; and (3) being exposed to a very upbeat leader.

To rule out all these possibilities, you might use several control groups. For example, to control for the "social activity" and the "energetic model" explanations, you might add a group that went to a no-credit acting class taught by a very enthusiastic professor. To control for the music explanation, you might add a control group that listened to music or perhaps even watched aerobic dance videos. By using all of these control groups, you may be able to rule out the effects of confounding variables.

## ANALYSIS OF MULTIPLE GROUP EXPERIMENTS

You have seen that using multiple control groups and multiple experimental groups can improve construct validity. You have seen that multiple treatment groups may allow you to map the functional relationship between the independent variable and the dependent variable. You have also seen that the multiple group experiment allows you to compare several different treatments at one time. In short, you have seen that there are at least three good reasons to conduct a multiple group experiment.

To conduct a multiple group experiment, you must understand the logic behind analyzing the results of a multiple group experiment. Clearly, understanding that logic will help after you collect your data and want to analyze them. However, understanding that logic will also help you before you conduct your study. As you will see, the way that you must analyze your results has implications for what treatment groups you will use, how many participants you will have, and even what your hypothesis will be.

Even if you never conduct a multiple group experiment, you will read articles that report results of multiple group experiments. To understand those articles, you must understand the logic and vocabulary used in analyzing multiple group experiments. Therefore, in the next few sections, you will learn the logic behind analyzing the results of a multiple group experiment.

## Analyzing the Multiple Group Experiment: An Intuitive Overview

As a first step to understanding how multiple group experiments are analyzed, let's look at data from three experiments that compared the effects of no-treatment, meditation, and aerobic exercise on happiness. All of these experiments had 12 subjects rate their feelings of happiness on a 0 (not at all happy) to 100 (very happy) scale. Here are the results of Experiment A:

|  | No-treatment | Meditation | Exercise |
|---|---|---|---|
|  | 50 | 51 | 53 |
|  | 51 | 53 | 53 |
|  | 52 | 52 | 54 |
|  | 51 | 52 | 52 |
| Group Means | 51 | 52 | 53 |

Compare these results to the results of Experiment B:

|  | No-treatment | Meditation | Exercise |
|---|---|---|---|
|  | 40 | 60 | 78 |
|  | 42 | 60 | 82 |
|  | 38 | 58 | 80 |
|  | 40 | 62 | 80 |
| Group Means | 40 | 60 | 80 |

Are you more confident that Experiment A or Experiment B found a significant effect for the treatment variable? If you say "B," why do you give "B" as your answer? You answer "B" because the group means for Experiment B are farther apart than the group means for Experiment A.

Why does having the means farther apart—what statisticians call greater **variability between group means**—make you decide that Experiment B is more likely to be the study that obtained significant results? Intuitively, you realize that it is more likely that chance would cause small differences between group means than for chance to cause large differences.[3] In other words, the more variability there is between group means, the more likely that at least some of that variability is due to treatment.

Now, compare Experiment B with experiment C. The results of Experiment C are listed below.

| | No-treatment | Meditation | Exercise |
|---|---|---|---|
| | 10 | 10 | 100 |
| | 80 | 90 | 80 |
| | 60 | 60 | 60 |
| | 10 | 80 | 80 |
| Group Means | 40 | 60 | 80 |

Do you think the results from Experiment B or Experiment C are more likely to indicate a real treatment effect? Both experiments have the same amount of variability between group means. Therefore, you cannot choose one over the other simply because the group means differ more in Experiment B than in Experiment C. Yet, once again, you will pick Experiment B. Why?

You will pick Experiment B because you are concerned about one aspect of Experiment C: the extreme amount of variability *within* each group. You realize that the only reason that the scores within a group vary is because of random variability. (The scores cannot differ from each other due to the treatment because all those participants got the same treatment.) Thus, you see that Experiment C is more affected by random variability than Experiment B.

The large amount of random variability in Experiment C (as revealed by the **within groups variability**) disturbs you because you realize that this random variability might be the reason the groups differ from one another. That is, the same random variability that makes individual scores within a group differ from each other might also make the group means differ from each other.[4] In Exper-

---

[3] Similarly, if your favorite team lost by one point, you might blame luck. However, if your team lost by 30 points, you would be less likely to say that bad luck alone was responsible for the defeat.

---

[4] To get a sense of how random sampling error might cause the group means to differ, randomly sample two scores from the no-treatment group. Compute the mean of this group. If you do this several times, you will get different means. These different means cannot be due to a treatment effect because you are sampling from a group of participants who are *all* getting no treatment. The reason you are sampling the same group but getting different means is random sampling error. Fortunately, statistics can help us determine how likely it is that the differences among group means are entirely due to random error.

iment B, on the other hand, the small amount of within group variability indicates that there is virtually no random variability in the data. Therefore, in Experiment B, you feel fairly confident that random variability is *not* causing the group means to differ from one another. Instead, you believe that the means differ from one another because of the treatment.

Intuitively then, you understand the three most important principles behind analyzing the results of a multiple-group experiment. Specifically, you realize that:

1. Between group variability is not a pure measure of treatment effects. Admittedly, treatment effects should cause the groups to differ from one another. However, random variability will also cause the groups to differ from one another. That is, even if no treatment was administered, the group means would probably differ. In other words, between group variability is not a pure index of variability due to treatment (treatment effects) because it also is affected by random error.
2. Within group variability is not due to the treatment, but instead is due to random error.
3. If you compare between group variability (the effects of random error + any treatment effects) to within group variability (the effects of random error), you may be able to determine whether the treatment had an effect.

## A Closer Look at the Analysis of a Multiple Group Experiment

You now have a general idea of how to analyze data from a multiple-group study. To see how to perform an analysis, look at Box 7–2. To understand more fully the logic and vocabulary used in these analyses—a must if you are to understand an author's or a computer's report of such an analysis—read the next few sections.

### ASSESSING WITHIN GROUPS VARIABILITY

As you already know, within groups variability does not reflect the effects of treatment. Instead, it reflects the effects of random error. For example, since all the subjects in the meditation group are getting the same treatment (meditation), any differences among those participants' scores can't be due to the treatment. Instead of being due to treatment effects, the differences among scores of meditation group participants are due to such random factors as individual differences, unreliability of the measure, and lack of standardization. Similarly, differences among the scores of participants in the no-treatment group are not due to treatment, but to irrelevant random factors. The same is true for differences within the exercise group. Thus, calculating within groups variability will tell us the extent to which chance causes individual scores to differ from each other. If we know how much chance causes individual scores to differ from each other, we can estimate the extent to which chance causes group means to differ from each other.

# Box 7–2
## Analyzing Data from a
## Multiple Group Experiment

To analyze data from a multiple group experiment, most researchers use analysis of variance. To use analysis of variance, as was the case with the t-test,

1. your observations must be independent,
2. each of your groups should have approximately the same variance,
3. your scores should be normally distributed, and
4. you should be able to assume that your data are either interval or ratio.

In analysis of variance, you set up the **F-ratio:** a ratio of the between groups variance to the within groups variance. Or, to use proper terminology, you set up a ratio of Means Square between (MSB) to Mean Square within (MSW).

To calculate Mean Square within groups, you must first calculate the sum of squares for each group. You must subtract each score from its mean, square each of those differences, and then add up all those squared differences. If you had the following three groups, your first calculations would be as follows:

| | Group 1 | Group 2 | Group 3 |
|---|---|---|---|
| | 5 | 6 | 14 |
| | 4 | 5 | 12 |
| | 3 | 4 | 10 |
| **Group Mean** | **4** | **5** | **12** |

Sum of Squares within for Group 1:
$$(5 - 4)^2 + (4 - 4)^2 + (3 - 4)^2 =$$
$$(1)^2 \quad + \quad (0)^2 \quad + \quad (-1)^2 \quad =$$
$$1 \quad + \quad 0 \quad + \quad 1 \quad = \mathbf{2}$$

Sum of squares within for Group 2:
$$(6 - 5)^2 + (5 - 5)^2 + (5 - 6)^2 =$$
$$(1)^2 \quad + \quad (0)^2 \quad + \quad (-1)^2 \quad =$$
$$1 \quad + \quad 0 \quad + \quad 1 \quad = \mathbf{2}$$

Sum of squares within for Group 3:
$$(14 - 12)^2 + (12 - 12)^2 + (10 - 12)^2 =$$
$$(2)^2 \quad + \quad (0)^2 \quad + \quad (-2)^2 \quad =$$
$$4 \quad + \quad 0 \quad + \quad 4 \quad = \mathbf{8}$$

To get the sum of squares within groups, you add all of these sums of squares together ($2 + 2 + 8 = 12$).

To get the mean square within groups, you divide the sum of squares within groups by the within groups' degrees of freedom. In a multiple group experiment, the within groups' degrees of freedom equals the number of subjects − number of groups. Since you had 9 subjects and 3 groups, your within groups' degrees of freedom are 6 (because $9 - 3 = 6$). So, your mean square within is 2 (because $12/6 = 2$).[5]

To get the mean square between groups, subtract each of the group means from each other and square each difference.

$4 - 5 = -1$; $-1$ squared $= 1$
$4 - 12 = -8$; $-8$ squared $= 64$
$12 - 5 = 7$; 7 squared $= 49$

Add up all these squared differences:
$1 + 64 + 49 = 114$

---

[5] Note that you would have obtained the same mean square if you had calculated the variance for each of your groups ($1 + 1 + 4$) and averaged those variances ($\%$) = 2.

*continued*

*continued from previous page*

Thus, at this point, your ANOVA summary table would look like this:

| Source of Variance | Sum of squares | degrees of freedom | Mean Square | F-ratio |
|---|---|---|---|---|
| Treatment | 114 | ? | ? | ? |
| Error | 12 | 6 | 2 | |

To fill in the rest of the table, you need to know the degrees of freedom for the treatment. The degrees of freedom for the treatment is one less than the number of groups. Since you have three groups, df treatment = 2.

To get the mean squares treatment, simply divide the treatment sum of squares (114) by the df treatment (2). This gives you a mean square treatment of 57 (because 114/2 = 57).

Since your F-ratio is just the ratio of Mean Square Between (57) to Mean Square Within (2), your F-ratio is 57/2 or 28.5. Thus, your completed ANOVA summary table would look like this:

| Source of Variance | Sum of Squares | degrees of freedom | Mean Square | F-ratio |
|---|---|---|---|---|
| Treatment | 114 | 2 | 57 | 28.5 |
| Error | 12 | 6 | 2 | |

To determine whether the F of 28.5 is significant, you would look in the F table for the critical F value for 2 degrees of freedom in the numerator and 6 degrees of freedom in the denominator. If 28.5 is larger than that value, the results would be statistically significant.

To measure this within groups variability, we first calculate the variance of the scores within each group. If we have three groups, then this gives us three measures of within groups variability, or three estimates of random variability. Since we only need one estimate of variability due to random error, we average all these within group variances to come up with the best estimate of random variability—the within groups variance. Since the within groups variance gives us an index of the degree to which random error may cause your group means to differ, within groups variance is also referred to as *error variance.*

## ASSESSING BETWEEN GROUPS VARIABILITY

Once you have a measure of within groups variability, the next step is to get an index of the degree to which your groups vary from one another. It is at this step where it becomes obvious that you cannot use a t-test to analyze data from a multiple-group experiment. When using a t-test, you determine the degree to which the groups differ from one another in a very straightforward manner: You subtract the average score of Group 1 from the average score of Group 2. Subtraction works well when you want to compare two groups, but does not work well when you have more than two groups. You can only subtract two scores at a time. So, if you have three groups, which two groups do you compare? Group 1 with Group 2? Or, Group 2 with Group 3? Or, Group 1 with Group 3?

You might answer this question by saying "all of the above." Thus, with three groups, you would do three t-tests: one comparing Group 1 against Group 2, a second comparing Group 1 against Group 3, and a third comparing Group 2 against Group 3. However, that's not legal.

An analogy will help you understand why you cannot use multiple t-tests. Suppose a stranger comes up to you with a proposition: "Let's bet on coin flips. If I get a 'head,' you give me a dollar. If I don't, I give you a dollar." You accept the proposition. He then proceeds to flip three coins at once and then makes you pay up if even one of the coins comes up heads. Why is this unfair? This is unfair because he misled you: You thought he was only going to flip one coin at a time, so you thought he had only a 50% chance of winning. But since he's flipping three coins at a time, his chances of getting at least one head are much better than 50%.

When you do multiple t-tests, you are doing basically the same thing as the coin hustler. You start by telling people the odds that a single t-test will be significant due to chance alone. For example, if you use conventional significance levels, you would tell people that—if the treatment has no effect—the odds of getting a statistically significant result for a particular t-test are less than 5 in 100. In other words, you are claiming that your chance of making a Type 1 error is no more than 5%.

Then, just as the hustler gave himself more than a 50% chance of winning by flipping more than one coin, you give yourself a more than 5% chance of getting a statistically significant result by doing more than one t-test. The 5% odds you quoted would only hold if you had done a single t-test. If you are using t-tests to compare three groups, you will do three t-tests. If you do three t-tests, the odds of at least one turning out significant by chance alone is much more than 5%.

So far, we've talked about the problems of using a t-test when you have a three-group experiment. What happens if your experiment has more than three groups? Then, the t-test becomes more deceptive (just as you would be in even worse shape if the person you were betting against flipped more than three coins at a time). The more groups you use in your experiment, the greater the difference between the significance level you report and the actual odds of at least one t-test being significant by chance (Shultz, 1994). Just to give you an idea of how great the difference between your stated significance level and the actual odds can be, suppose you had six levels of the independent variable. To compare all six groups with one another, you would need to do 15 t-tests. If you did 15 t-tests and used a .05 significance level, the probability of getting at least one significant effect by chance alone would be more than 50%! That is, your risk of making a Type 1 error is 10 times greater than you are claiming it is.

As you have seen, the t-test is not useful for analyzing data from the multiple-group experiment because the t-test measures the degree to which groups differ by using subtraction—and you can only subtract two group averages at a time. To calculate the degree to which more than two group means differ, you need to calculate a variance between those means.

The variance you want to calculate should do more than indicate the extent to which the group means differ. When there is no treatment effect, you want this variance to be equivalent to the within groups variance. Furthermore, when there is a treatment effect, you want this between groups variance to be larger than the within groups variance. That is, the between group variance, like the within groups variance, should be an estimate of random error. But unlike the within groups variance, the between groups variance should also be an estimate of treatment effects. In other words, the between group variance should be the sum of two quantities: an estimate of random error plus an estimate of treatment effects. (To calculate the between groups variance, see Box 7-2.)

## COMPARING VARIANCES

Once you have the between groups variance (an estimate of random error plus any treatment effects) and the within groups variance (an estimate of random error), the next step is to compare the two variances. If the between groups variance is bigger than the within groups variance, then some of the between groups variance may be due to a treatment effect. Because you will determine whether the treatment had an effect by comparing (*analyzing*) the between groups variance to the within groups variance, this statistical technique is called **analysis of variance (ANOVA).**

But when doing an ANOVA, how do you compare your two variances? You might think that you would compare your two variances by subtracting them from one another. That is, you might hope to do something like this:

Between groups variance $-$ Within groups variance = Treatment effect
(random error + pos-        (random error)
sible treatment effects)

However, in analysis of variance (ANOVA), you compare your two variances by dividing rather than by subtracting. Specifically, you set up the following ratio:

$$\frac{\text{Between groups variance}}{\text{Within groups variance}}$$

In technical terminology, the index of between groups variance is referred to as the **Mean Square between** (abbreviated MS between). Since between groups variance (differences between groups) *may* be due to different groups getting different levels of treatment, MS between is also referred to as **Mean Square Treatment** (abbreviated MST).

The index of within groups variance is called the **Mean Square within** (MSW). Since within groups variance is also an estimate of the degree to which random error is affecting estimates of the treatment group means, Mean Square Within is also called **Mean Square Error** (MSE).

Finally, the ratio of two variances is called the **F-ratio.** Mathematically, the F-ratio reduces to:

$$\frac{MSB}{MSW} \quad \text{which is the same as} \quad \frac{MST}{MSE}$$

Thus, when reading articles, you may see tables resembling the one below:

| Source | Mean Square | F |
|---|---|---|
| Treatment | 10 | 2 |
| Error | 5 | |

Conceptually, the F-ratio can be portrayed as follows:

$$F = \frac{\text{Random Error} + \text{Possible Treatment Effect}}{\text{Random Error}}$$

By looking at the formula, you can see that the F-ratio will rarely be much less than 1. If there is no treatment effect, the formula reduces to random error/random error, and if you divide anything by itself (5/5, 8/8), you will usually get 1. Put another way, if the null hypothesis were true, the between groups variance and the within groups variance should be roughly equivalent because both are measuring the same thing—random error.

You now know that if the null hypothesis were true, the F-ratio would be approximately 1.00. That is,

$$F = \frac{\text{Random Error}}{\text{Random Error}} = 1.00[6]$$

But what would happen if the treatment had an effect? Again, Group 1's scores differ from one another only because of chance. The same is true of Group 2's scores differing from one another, and Group 3's scores differing from one another. In other words, within groups variance is still only due to random error.

But what would happen to the variance between the three group means if the treatment had an effect? Will they vary from each other merely because of chance? No, if the treatment has an effect, the groups will differ from each other because they received different levels of the treatment. Thus, the variance among group means would be not only due to random error, but also to

---

[6] If you get an F below 1.00, it indicates that you have found no evidence of a treatment effect. Indeed, in the literature, you will often find statements such as, "There were no other significant results, all F's < 1." If you get an F substantially below 1.00, you may want to check to be sure you did not make a calculation error.

the treatment causing real differences among groups. Therefore, the between groups variance would be larger than the within groups variance because in addition to estimating random error (the only thing within groups variance is doing), the between groups variance is also estimating the treatment effect. Consequently, you would expect the ratio of between groups variance to within groups variance to be greater than 1. That is:

$$F = \frac{\text{between groups variance}\ (\text{treatment} + \text{random error})}{\text{within groups variance}\ (\text{random error})} > 1 \quad \textit{when the treatment has an effect}$$

***Using an F-Table.***    However, not all Fs above 1.00 are statistically significant. To determine whether an F-ratio is large enough to indicate a difference between your groups, you need to consult an F-table, like the one in Appendix E. Just as the t-table told you how big a t-score had to be to reach significance, the F-table tells you how big an F-ratio has to be to reach significance. As was the case with the t-scores, how large a ratio has to be to reach significance depends on the degrees of freedom. The more degrees of freedom that the error term has, the smaller the F-ratio has to be to reach significance.

***Calculating Degrees of Freedom.***    To use the F-table, you need to know two degrees of freedom: one for the top of the F-ratio (between groups variance, MS treatment) and one for the bottom of the F-ratio (within subjects variance, MS error).

Calculating the degrees of freedom for the top of the F-ratio (between groups variance) is simple. It's just one less than the number of values of the independent variable. So, if you have three values of the independent variable (no-treatment, meditation, and exercise), you have two degrees of freedom. If you had four values of the independent variable (no-treatment, meditation, archery, aerobic exercise), then you would have three degrees of freedom. Thus, in experiments using one independent variable, the degrees of freedom for the between groups variance = Number of Groups − 1.

Computing the degrees of freedom for the error term in ANOVA is very similar to computing the degrees of freedom for the t-test. The formula for the degrees of freedom for the t-test is N(umber of subjects) − 2. Thus, if there are 20 subjects, the degrees of freedom = 18 (20 − 2 = 18). Since the t-test compares two groups, you could also use the formula N(umber of subjects) − G(roups).

As we have indicated, this N − G formula applies to ANOVA as well as to the t-test. Indeed, in a 2-group ANOVA with 20 subjects, the df for the error term = 18—just as it is for a two-group t-test involving 20 subjects.

Extending this logic to a multiple-group ANOVA, if we have 33 subjects and 3 groups, the df = 30 (because 33 − 3 = 30). If we have 30 subjects and 5 groups, the df = 25 (because 30 − 5 = 25). Thus, the simplest way of computing the error df for the experiments we discussed in this chapter is to use the formula $N - G$, where $N$ = total number of subjects and $G$ = total number of groups (see Table 7–2).

Once you know the degrees of freedom, you can simply find the column in the F-table that corresponds to those degrees of freedom. If your F-ratio is larger than the value listed, then the results are statistically significant at the .05 level.

## THE MEANING OF STATISTICAL SIGNIFICANCE

If your results are statistically significant, what does that mean? As you know, statistical significance means that you can reject the null hypothesis. In the multiple group experiment, the null hypothesis is that the differences among all your group means are due to chance. That is, all your groups are essentially the same. Rejecting this hypothesis means that, because of treatment effects, all your groups are not the same. In other words, you can conclude that at least two of your groups differ. But which ones? Even in a three-group experiment, there are numerous possibilities: Group 1 might differ from Group 2 and/or Group 2 might differ from Group 3 and/or Group 1 might differ from Group 3. A significant F does not tell you which groups differ. Therefore, once you have performed an F-test to determine that at least some of your groups differ, you need to do additional tests to determine which of your groups differ from one another.

## PINPOINTING A SIGNIFICANT EFFECT

You might think that all you would have to do to determine which groups differ is compare group means. However, some group means may differ from others solely as a result of chance. To determine which group differences are due to treatment effects, you need to do additional tests. These additional, more specific tests are called **post hoc t-tests.**

***Post Hoc t-Tests Among Group Means: Which Groups Differ?***   At this point, you may be saying that you wanted to do t-tests all along. Before you yell at us, please hear our two-pronged defense.

First, you can only go in and do post hoc tests after you get a significant F-test. That is why post hoc tests are called post hoc ("post hoc" means after the fact). To do post hoc tests without finding a significant F is considered statistical malpractice. Such behavior would be like a physician doing a specific test to find out which strain of hepatitis you had after doing a general test that established that you did *not* have hepatitis. At best, the test will not turn up anything and your only problem will be the expense and pain of an unnecessary test. At worst, the test results will be misleading because the test is being used under the wrong circumstances. Consequently, you may end up being treated for a hepatitis you do not have. Analogously, a good researcher does not ask which

**TABLE 7-2**
**Calculating Degrees of Freedom**

| SOURCE OF VARIANCE (SV) | CALCULATION OF DF |
|---|---|
| Treatment (between groups) | Levels of treatment $-1$ |
| Within subjects (error variance) | Number of participants minus levels of treatment |

groups differ from one another unless the more general, overall analysis of variance test has first established that at least some of the groups do indeed differ.[7]

Second, post hoc tests are not the same as conventional t-tests. Unlike conventional t-tests, post hoc t-tests are designed to correct for the fact that you are doing more than two comparisons. That is, as we mentioned earlier, doing more than one t-test at the $p < .05$ level is like flipping more than one coin at a time and saying the odds of a "heads" are only 50%. In both cases, the odds of getting the result you hope for are much greater than the odds you are stating. Thus, we cannot simply do an ordinary t-test. Instead, we must correct for the number of comparisons we are making. Post hoc t-tests take into consideration how many tests are being done and make the necessary corrections.

At this point, there is no reason for you to know how to do post hoc tests. You should simply be aware that if you choose to do a multiple group experiment, you should be prepared to do post hoc analyses. You should also be prepared to encounter post hoc tests if you read a journal article that reports a significant F for a multiple group experiment. If you read about a Bonferroni t-test (Dunn test), Tukey test, Scheffé test, Dunnett test, Newman-Keuls test, Duncan, or LSD test, do not panic. The author is merely reporting the results of a post hoc test to determine which means differ from one another. (If you want to know more about post hoc tests, see Appendix E.)

***Post Hoc Trend Analysis: What Is the Shape of the Relationship?*** If you are interested in generalizing your results to unexplored levels of the independent variable, you may not be extremely interested in determining which particular groups differ from one another. Instead, you may be more interested in determining the *shape* of the functional relationship between the independent and dependent variable. For example, as we mentioned earlier in the chapter, you might want to know the shape of the functional relationship to help you generalize to levels of the variable that were not tested. Or, you might

---

[7] However, Robert Rosenthal (1992) argues that if you have specific predictions about which groups differ, you can do normal t-tests to compare those group means. Those t-tests are called "planned comparisons" because you planned to make those comparisons *before* collecting your data rather than comparisons made after seeing which means are furthest apart. Rosenthal believes so strongly in planned comparisons that he doesn't believe that people should do the general, overall F-test.

---

**BOX 7–3**
**REQUIREMENTS FOR CONDUCTING A VALID**
**POST HOC TREND ANALYSIS**

1. Your independent variable must have a statistically significant effect.
2. Your independent variable must be quantitative and the levels used in the experiment should vary from one another by some constant proportion.

3. Your dependent variable must yield interval or ratio scale data so that your map of the functional relationship will be to scale.
4. The number of trends you can look for is one less than the number of levels of your independent variable.

---

be testing a theory that predicts a certain functional relationship. If you are interested in the functional relationship, instead of following up a significant main effect with post hoc tests between group means, follow up the significant effect with a post hoc trend analysis.

But why should you do a trend analysis to determine the shape of the functional relationship between your independent and dependent variable? Can't you see this relationship by simply graphing the group means? Yes and no. Yes, graphing your sample's means allows you to see the pattern in the data produced by your experiment. No, graphing does not tell you whether the pattern you observe is just due to random error or whether it reflects the actual relationship between the variables. Just as you needed statistics to tell you whether the difference between two groups was significant (even though you could easily see whether one mean was higher than the other), you need statistics to know whether the pattern you observe in your data (a straight line, a curved line, a combination of a curve and a straight line, etc.) would occur if you repeated the experiment. For example, if random error throws off even one of your sample means, the graph of your data could misrepresent the true functional relationship between your variables. Consequently, to determine whether the pattern in your data reflects the real functional relationship, you must do a post hoc trend analysis. If you want to do a post hoc trend analysis, refer to Appendix E and Box 7-3.

To plan an experiment, you do not need to know how to do a trend analysis. However, if you want to do a trend analysis on your data, there are three things you should know before you run your first participant.

First, to do a post hoc trend analysis, you must have selected levels of your independent variable that increase proportionally. For example, if you were using three levels of a drug, you would not use 5 mg., 6 mg., and 200 mg. Instead, you might use 10 mg., 20 mg., and 30 mg., or 10 mg., 100 mg., and 1000 mg.

Second, to do a trend analysis, you must have an interval scale measure of your dependent variable. That is, your map of the functional relationship can't be accurate unless your measure of the dependent variable is to scale.

Third, the more levels of the independent variable you have, the more trends you can look for. Specifically, the number of trends you can examine is one less than the number of levels you have. If you had only two levels, you can only test for straight lines (linear component). If you have three groups, you can test for straight lines (linear component), and for a "u"-shaped curve (quadratic component). With four levels, you can test for straight lines, "u"-shaped curves, and double-"u"-shaped lines (cubic component). Thus, if you are expecting a double-"u"-shaped curve, you must use at least four levels of the independent variable.

## CONCLUDING REMARKS

You have seen that you can expand a simple experiment by using more than two values of the independent variable. You have seen that expanding the simple experiment to include three or more values of the independent variable can pay off in two ways. First, using more control groups allows you more opportunities to rule out the effects of confounding variables. Second, using more treatment groups allows you to generalize your results more accurately to more values of the independent variable.

Yet, as valuable as expanding the simple experiment by adding more levels of the treatment can be, there is an even more powerful way to expand the simple experiment—by adding independent variables. As you will see in the next chapter, adding independent variables not only increases construct and external validity, but opens up a whole new arena of research questions.

## SUMMARY

1. The multiple group experiment is more sensitive to nonlinear relationships than the simple experiment. Consequently, the multiple group experiment is more likely to obtain significant treatment effects and to accurately map the functional relationship between your independent and dependent variables.
2. Knowing the functional relationship allows more accurate predictions about the effects of unexplored levels of independent variable.
3. To use the multiple group experiment to discover the functional relationship, you must carefully select your levels of the independent variable and your dependent variable must be measured on an interval scale.

4. Multiple group experiments may have more construct validity than a simple experiment because they can have multiple control groups and multiple treatment groups.

5. To analyze a multiple group experiment, you first have to conduct an analysis of variance (ANOVA). An ANOVA will produce an F-ratio.

6. An F-ratio is a ratio of between groups variance to within groups variance.

7. Different treatment groups will differ from each other due to random error. If the treatment has an effect, the treatment will also cause the groups to differ from each other. Therefore, between groups variance is due to random error and may also be due to treatment effects.

8. Scores within a treatment group differ due to random error. That is, the treatment cannot be responsible for variability within each treatment group. Therefore, within groups variance is an estimate of the degree to which random error affects the data.

9. The following table summarizes the mathematics of an F-table.

| Source of Variance (SV) | Sum of Squares (SS) | degrees of freedom (df) | Mean Square (MS) | F |
|---|---|---|---|---|
| Treatment (T) | SST | Levels of T $-1$ | $\dfrac{SST}{df\ T}$ | $\dfrac{MST}{MSE}$ |
| Error (E) also known as within groups variance | SSE | Participants $-$ Groups | $\dfrac{SSE}{df\ E}$ | |
| Total | SST $+$ SSE | Participants $-1$ | | |

10. If you get a significant F, you know that the groups are not all the same. To find out which groups are different, do not just look at the means to see which differences are biggest. Instead, do post hoc tests.

## KEY TERMS

**analysis of variance (ANOVA):** a statistical test that is especially useful when data are interval and there are more than two groups. For the experiments discussed in this chapter, ANOVA involves dividing between groups variance by within groups variance. (p. 231)

**between groups variance (Mean Square Treatment, Mean Square between):** at one level, between groups variance is just a measure of how much the group means differ from each other. Thus, if all the groups had the same mean, between groups variance would be zero. At another level, between groups variance is an estimate of the combined effects of the two factors that would make group means differ—treatment effects and random error. (p. 226, 231)

**within groups variance (Mean Square Error, Mean Square within):** at one level, within groups variance is just a measure of the degree to which scores within each group differ from each other. A small within groups variance means that participants within a group are all scoring similarly. At another level, within groups variance is an estimate of the effects of random error (because participants in the same treatment group score differently due to random error, not due to treatment). (p. 226, 231)

**F-ratio:**     $$\dfrac{\text{between groups variance (treatment} + \text{random error)}}{\text{within groups variance    (random error)}}$$

If the treatment has no effect, $F$ will tend to be close to 1.0, indicating that the difference between the groups could be due to random error. If the treatment had an effect, $F$ will tend to be above 1.0, indicating that the difference between the groups is bigger than would be expected if only random error were at work. (p. 228, 232)

**confounding variables:** variables, other than the independent variable, that may be responsible for the differences between your conditions. There are two types of confounding variables: ones that are manipulation-irrelevant and ones that are the result of the manipulation. Confounding variables that are irrelevant to the treatment manipulation threaten internal validity. For example, the difference between groups may be due to one group being older than the other, rather than to the treatment. Random assignment can control for the effects of those confounding variables. Confounding variables that are produced by the treatment manipulation hurt the construct validity of the study. They hurt the construct validity because even though we may know that the treatment manipulation had an effect, we don't know what it was about the treatment manipulation that had the effect. For example, we may know that an "exercise" manipulation increases happiness (internal validity), but not know whether the "exercise" manipulation worked because people exercised more, got more encouragement, had a more structured routine, practiced setting and achieving goals, or met new friends. In such a case, construct validity is harmed because we don't know what variable(s) are being manipulated by the "exercise" manipulation. (p. 220)

**hypothesis-guessing:** participants trying to figure out what the study is designed to prove. (p. 221)

**levels of the independent variable:** values of the independent variable. In the simple experiment, you only have two levels of the independent variable. In the multiple group experiment, you have more than two levels. Having more than two levels of the independent variable helps you determine the functional relationship between the independent and dependent variables. (p. 212)

**functional relationship:** the shape of the relationship between variables. For example, the functional relationship between the independent and dependent variable might be linear or curvilinear. (p. 214)

**linear trend:** a functional relationship between an independent and dependent variable that is graphically represented by a straight line. (p. 214)

**curvilinear relationship:** a functional relationship between an independent and dependent variable that is graphically represented by a curved line. (p. 214)

**trend analysis:** a type of post hoc test designed to determine whether a linear or curvilinear trend is statistically significant (reliable). (p. 235)

**post hoc test:** test used to follow up on significant results obtained from a more general test. Because a significant ANOVA says only that at least two of the groups differ from one another, post hoc tests are performed to find out which groups differ from one another. (p. 234)

## EXERCISES

1. A researcher randomly assigns a statistics class to two groups. In one group, each student is assigned a tutor. The tutor is available to meet with the student 20 minutes before each class. The other group is a control group not assigned a tutor.

   Suppose the researcher finds that the tutored group scores significantly better on exams.

   **a.** Can the researcher conclude that the experimental group students learned statistical information from tutoring sessions that enabled them to perform better on the exam? Why or why not?

   **b.** What changes would you recommend in the study?

2. Suppose people living in homes for the elderly were randomly assigned to two groups: a no-treatment group and a transcendental meditation (TM) group. Transcendental meditation involves more than sitting with eyes closed. The technique involves both a "mantra, or meaningless sound selected for its value in facilitating the transcending or settling down process and a specific procedure for using it mentally without effort again to facilitate transcending" (Alexander, Langer, Newman, Chandler, & Davies, 1989). Thus, the TM group was given instruction in how to perform the technique, then "they met with their instructors ½ hour each week to verify that they were meditating correctly and regularly. They were to practice their program 20 minutes twice daily (morning and afternoon) sitting comfortably in their own room with eyes closed and using a timepiece to ensure correct length of practice." (Alexander, Langer, Newman, Chandler, & Davies, 1989).

   Suppose that the TM group performed significantly better than other groups on a mental health measure.[8]

   **a.** Could the researcher conclude that it was the transcendental meditation that caused the effect?

---

[8] A modification of this study was actually done. The study included appropriate control groups.

    **b.** What besides the specific aspects of TM could cause the difference between the two groups?

    **c.** What control groups would you add?

    **d.** Suppose you added these control groups and then got a significant F for the treatment variable? What could you conclude? Why?

**3.** Assume you want to test the effectiveness of a new kind of therapy. This therapy involves screaming and hugging people in group sessions followed by individual meetings with a therapist. What control group(s) would you use? Why?

**4.** Assume a researcher is looking at the relationship between caffeine consumption and sense of humor.

    **a.** How many levels of caffeine should the researcher use? Why?

    **b.** What levels would you choose? Why?

    **c.** If a graph of the data suggests a curvilinear relationship, can the researcher assume that the functional relationship between the independent and dependent variable is curvilinear? Why or why not?

    **d.** Suppose the researcher *ranked* subjects based on their sense of humor. That is, the person who laughed least got a score of "1," the person who laughed second-least scored a "2," etc. Can the researcher use this data to do a trend analysis? Why or why not?

    **e.** Suppose the researcher used the following 4 levels of caffeine: 0 mg., 20 mg., 25 mg., 26 mg. Can the researcher do a trend analysis? Why or why not?

    **f.** If a researcher used four levels of caffeine, how many trends can the researcher look for? What are the treatment's degrees of freedom?

    **g.** If the researcher used three levels of caffeine and 30 subjects, what are the degrees of freedom for the treatment? The degrees of freedom for the error term?

    **h.** Suppose the F is 3.34. Referring to the degrees of freedom you obtained in your answer to "g" (above) and to Table E–3, are the results statistically significant? Can the researcher look for linear and quadratic trends?

**5.** A computer analysis reports that $F_{(6,23)} = 2.54$. The analysis is telling you that the F-ratio was 2.54, and the degrees of freedom for the top part of the F-ratio = 6 and the degrees of freedom for the bottom part = 23. Is this result statistically significant at the .05 level (refer to Table E–3)? How many groups did the researcher use? How many subjects were in the experiment?

**6.** How is the top part of the F-ratio like the top part of the t-ratio? How is the bottom part of the F-ratio like the bottom part of the t-ratio?

**7.** A friend gives you the following Fs and significance levels. On what basis would you want these Fs (or significance levels) re-checked?

    **a.** $F_{(2, 63)} = .10$, not significant

    **b.** $F_{(3, 85)} = -1.70$, not significant

    **c.** $F_{(1, 120)} = 52.8$, not significant

    **d.** $F_{(5, 70)} = 1.00$, significant

**8.** Complete the following table.

| Source of Variance (SV) | Sum of Squares (SS) | degrees of freedom (df) | Mean Square (MS) | F |
|---|---|---|---|---|
| Treatment (T) 3 levels of treatment | SST = 180 | _____ | _____ | _____ |
| Error (E) also known as within groups variance | SSE = 80 | 8 | _____ | |

**9.** Complete the following table.

| Source of Variance (SV) | Sum of Squares (SS) | degrees of freedom (df) | Mean Square (MS) | F |
|---|---|---|---|---|
| Treatment (T) | 50 | 5 | _____ | _____ |
| Error (E) also known as within groups variance | 100 | _____ | _____ | |
| Total | _____ | 30 | | |

**10.** A study compares the effect of having a snack, taking a 10 minute walk, or getting no treatment on energy levels. Sixty participants are randomly assigned to condition and then asked to rate their energy level of a 0 (not at all energetic) to 10 (very energetic) scale. The mean for the "do nothing" group is 6.0, for having a snack 7.0, and for walking 7.8. The F-ratio is 6.27.

    **a.** Graph the means.

    **b.** Are the results statistically significant?

        **1.** If so, what conclusions can you draw? Why?

        **2.** If not, what would you conclude?

    **c.** How would you extend this study?

# CHAPTER 8

---

# Expanding the Simple Experiment: Factorial Designs

*Overview*

*The 2 × 2 Factorial Design*

HOW ONE EXPERIMENT CAN DO AS MUCH AS TWO
HOW ONE EXPERIMENT CAN DO MORE THAN TWO
POTENTIAL RESULTS OF A 2 × 2 EXPERIMENT

*Analyzing the Results from a 2 × 2 Experiment*

INTERPRETING RESULTS OF AN ANOVA TABLE
INTERACTIONS

*Putting the 2 × 2 to Work*

ADDING A REPLICATION FACTOR TO INCREASE GENERALIZABILITY
USING AN INTERACTION TO FIND AN EXCEPTION TO THE RULE: LOOKING AT A POTENTIAL
MODERATING FACTOR
USING INTERACTIONS TO CREATE NEW RULES
STUDYING NON-EXPERIMENTAL VARIABLES

*Concluding Remarks*

*Summary*

*Key Terms*

*Exercises*

# *Chapter 8*

# EXPANDING THE SIMPLE EXPERIMENT: FACTORIAL DESIGNS

## OVERVIEW

In Chapter 6, you learned how the logic of the simple experiment enables it to be internally valid. However, you also learned that it was limited: With it, you could only study two levels of a single independent variable.

In Chapter 7, you learned that the basic logic behind the simple experiment could be extended to experiments that study three or more levels of a single independent variable. You saw that such multiple group experiments could possess impressive internal, external, and construct validity.

In this chapter, you will learn how to extend the basic logic of the simple experiment to study the effects of two or more independent variables in a single experiment. But beyond learning how to design and interpret the results of such experiments, you will learn why you should want to study the effects of two or more independent variables in a single experiment.

## THE 2 × 2 FACTORIAL DESIGN

To illustrate how you can study two independent variables in a single experiment, suppose you wanted to know the effect of two factors—caffeine and exercise—on appetite. You want to use two levels of caffeine (0 mg and 20 mg) and two levels of exercise (no exercise and 50 minutes of exercise). To study the effects of both these factors (caffeine and exercise) in a single experiment, you would randomly assign participants to four groups:

1. a no exercise, no caffeine group;
2. a no exercise, 20 mg caffeine group;
3. a 50 minutes of exercise, no caffeine group; and
4. a 50 minutes of exercise, 20 mg caffeine group.

In technical terminology, you would be using a **factorial experiment:** an experiment that examines the effects of two or more independent variables (*factors*). Specifically, since the exercise factor has two levels and since the caffeine factor has two levels, you have a 2 (no exercise/50 min. exercise) × 2 (no caffeine/20 mg caffeine) factorial experiment.[1]

## How One Experiment Can Do as Much as Two

If you wanted to study the effects of caffeine and exercise on appetite, you would not have to do a factorial experiment. Instead, you could do two simple experiments. One simple experiment would look at caffeine's effects on appetite. The other would look at exercise's effects on appetite. To visualize the difference between doing a single 2 × 2 factorial experiment versus doing two simple experiments, look at Table 8-1 at the top of page 246.

As you can see by looking at Table 8-1, the first three cells of the 2 × 2 experiment have every group that the two simple experiments have. That is, three cells of the 2 × 2 incorporate the two simple experiments.

If the two simple experiments have four groups, how can the 2 × 2 do the same work with three groups? A close look at Table 8-1 shows that although the two simple experiments have four groups, they only have three different groups. That is, two of those groups do the same thing—serve as a control group. By not duplicating the control group, three cells of the 2 × 2 can contain the three different groups that the two simple experiments have.

By getting double duty out of the control group, the three cells of the 2 × 2 incorporate the two simple experiments. Consequently, three cells of the 2 × 2 experiment can do everything that the two simple experiments do. Specifically, by comparing the two groups in the first row of the 2 × 2 (the control group and the caffeine group), you would get a **simple main effect** *for caffeine*—just as you would have gotten if you had done Simple Experiment #1. Similarly, by comparing the two groups in the first column of the 2 × 2 (the control group and the exercise group), you would get a **simple main effect** *for exercise*—just as you would if you had done Simple Experiment #2.

## How One Experiment Can Do More than Two

If the 2 × 2 can do everything two simple experiments can do with only three groups, why do we have the fourth group? We have the fourth group so we can discover things we could not have discovered had we used two simple experiments.

---

[1] If you had three levels of exercise, you would have a 3 (no exercise/50 minute exercise/100 minute exercise) × 2 (no caffeine/20 mg caffeine) factorial experiment. Within a 3 × 2 factorial, you would have 6 (3 × 2) groups of participants. If, instead of adding a level of exercise, you had decided to add the factor of temperature, you might have a 2 (no exercise/50 minute) × 2 (no caffeine/20 mg caffeine) × 2 (low temperature/high temperature) factorial design. In a 2 × 2 × 2 factorial, you would have 8 groups of participants.

**TABLE 8–1**

**How Three Cells of a 2 × 2 Experiment Contain the Information of Two Simple Experiments**

TWO SIMPLE EXPERIMENTS

Simple experiment #1

| Control group | Caffeine group |
|---|---|

Simple experiment #2

| Control group |
|---|
| Exercise group |

THREE OF THE FOUR CELLS OF A 2 × 2 EXPERIMENT

| Control group | Caffeine group |
|---|---|
| Exercise group | |

**TABLE 8–2**

**How the 2 × 2 Experiment Contains the Information of Four Simple Experiments**

|  | Simple experiment #1 (Effect of caffeine for subjects who don't exercise) | Simple experiment #2 (Effect of caffeine for subjects who do exercise) |
|---|---|---|
|  | Control group / Exercise group | Caffeine group / Caffeine + Exercise group |
| Simple experiment #3 (Effect of exercise when no caffeine is present) | Control group | Caffeine group |
| Simple experiment #4 (Effect of exercise when caffeine is present) | Exercise group | Caffeine + Exercise group |

A 2 × 2 EXPERIMENT

| (This row contains Simple Experiment #1) | Control group | Caffeine group |
|---|---|---|
| (This row contains Simple Experiment #2) | Exercise group | Caffeine + Exercise group |
|  | (This column contains Simple Experiment #3) | (This column contains Simple Experiment #4) |

## FOUR SIMPLE MAIN EFFECTS

As you can see from Table 8–2, because of the fourth group, the 2 × 2 incorporates four simple experiments. That is, if we use certain statistical techniques, we could use the 2 × 2 to find four simple main effects:

1. the simple main effect for caffeine in the no exercise conditions;
2. the simple main effect for caffeine in the exercise conditions;
3. the simple main effect for exercise in the no caffeine conditions; and
4. the simple main effect for exercise in the caffeine conditions.

However, we should stress that psychologists do *not* do 2 × 2 factorial experiments with the primary aim of detecting these four simple main effects. Indeed, psychologists often do not do any analysis that would help them isolate these individual simple main effects.

To reiterate, the main strength of the 2 × 2 is *not* that it could be used to test four separate simple main effects. If that were its only strength, researchers could just conduct four separate simple experiments. Instead, the strength of the 2 × 2 comes from the fact that it produces two *pairs* of simple main effects. That is, the researcher obtains a pair of main effects relating to the first independent variable and a pair of main effects relating to the second independent variable. These pairs of main effects can be combined and compared.

What are the advantages of being able to combine and compare pairs of main effects? As you'll see in the next section, there are two basic advantages.

## TWO OVERALL MAIN EFFECTS

First, researchers can average the pair of simple main effects relating to a treatment variable to find out what the average effect for that treatment variable is. Taking the *average* of a variable's two simple main effects yields the variable's **overall main effect**.

In the caffeine-exercise study, the researcher would average the two caffeine simple main effects to get an overall main effect for caffeine. Likewise, the researcher would average the two exercise main effects to get an overall main effect for exercise. If the overall exercise main effect was significant, it would mean that, on the average, participants getting exercise consumed a different number of calories than the no exercise participants.

One reason researchers emphasize overall main effects is convenience. It is easier to talk about one overall main effect than about two simple main effects. However, a much more important advantage of averaging the two simple main effects into an overall main effect is that it allows us to make more general statements about that variable's effects. For example, consider the advantage of averaging the two simple main effects of caffeine. Because we have combined two simple main effects, we are not confined to saying that caffeine has an effect if you exercise 50 minutes a day. Instead, we can say that, on the average, in a study that varied exercise levels, caffeine has an effect. The implication is that we can be more confident that the effect of caffeine generalizes across a variety of exercise levels.

## INTERACTIONS

But what if the effect of caffeine is different in the exercise condition than in the no exercise condition? Then, you should not make a general statement about the effects of caffeine without mentioning that the effect changes depending on how much exercise one does. That brings us to the second advantage of factorial experiments: You can see if combining variables has an effect that is different than the sum of their individual effects.

To determine if the effects of combining variables is different from the sum of their separate effects, you compare each factor's two simple main effects to see if they *differ*. If the simple main effects of caffeine differ *depending* on the level of exercise, there is an **interaction** between caffeine and exercise (see Table 8–3). If, on the other hand, they do not differ (caffeine has the same effect in the no exercise condition as it has in the exercise condition), then you do not have an interaction.

Interactions are a fact of life (see Table 8–4 on page 250). For example, milk is good for most people, but not for people who are lactose intolerant. In other words, there is a positive main effect for drinking milk, but milk-drinking interacts with type of person (lactose-tolerant versus intolerant).

In dealing with others, most people believe that interactions play a key role. That is, people think that the effect of an action depends on (interacts with) other factors.

Sometimes, those interfacing factors involve context. For example, telling someone "congratulations" will have a good effect if he has just been promoted, a bad effect if he has just been fired.

At other times, those interacting (*moderating*) factors are personal characteristics. That is, people often act as though the effectiveness of an approach depends on the type of person with whom they are dealing. For instance, people assume that one way of teaching will be best for some students, but that a different way will be best for other students (Shute, 1994). Similarly, the effect of college may be different for some types of students than for others (Astin, 1993).

Not surprisingly, research supports the popular notion that some treatments will have one effect on one group of participants, but a different effect on another group. For instance, if you have a group of participants who believe they have no control over the noise level in the room, increasing the noise level seriously harms performance. However, for participants who believe they can control the noise level, increasing the noise level does not harm performance. Thus, noise level interacts with perceived control (Glass and Singer, 1972).

Because of this interaction, you cannot simply say noise hurts performance. You have to say the effect of noise level on performance depends on perceived control. In other words, rather than stating a simple rule about the

**TABLE 8–3**
**Simple Main Effects, Overall Main Effects, and Interactions**

**Simple Main Effects**

*Definition:* The effects of one independent variable at a specific level of a second independent variable. The simple main effect could have been obtained merely by doing a simple experiment.

*How estimated:* By comparing the mean for one group with the mean for a second group (for instance, comparing the no caffeine, no exercise group mean to the caffeine, no exercise group mean).

*Question addressed:* What is the effect of the caffeine in the no exercise condition?

**Overall Main Effect**

*Definition:* The average effect of a treatment.

*How estimated:* By averaging a treatment's simple main effects. If the average of the two simple main effects is significantly different from zero, there is an overall main effect.

*Question addressed:* What is the average effect of caffeine in this study?

**Interaction**

*Definition:* The effect of a treatment is different, depending on the level of a second independent variable. That is, the effect of a variable is not consistent across conditions.

*How estimated:* By looking at the *differences* between a treatment's simple main effects. If the treatment's simple main effects are the same, there is no interaction. If, however, the treatment's two simple main effects differ significantly, there is an interaction.

*Question addressed:* Does caffeine have the same effect on appetite for those who exercise as it has on those who don't exercise?

effects of noise, you have to state a more complex rule. This complex rule puts qualifications on the statement that noise hurts performance. Specifically, the statement that noise hurts performance will be qualified by some word or phrase such as "depending on," "but only if," "however, that holds only under certain conditions."

Because the concept of interaction is so important, let's consider one more example. As a general rule, we can say that getting within one inch of another person will make that person uncomfortable. Thus, the main effect of getting physically closer to someone is to produce a negative mood. However, what if you are the other person's romantic partner? Then, getting closer may elicit positive feelings. Because the effect of interpersonal distance is moderated by initial liking of the target person, we can say that there is an interaction between distance and the participant's initial feelings toward the target person.

As psychology has progressed, psychologists have focused increasingly more attention on interactions. Part of the reason psychologists focus on interactions is because psychologists have already discovered the main effects of

**TABLE 8–4**

## Ways of Thinking about Interactions

| VIEWPOINT | HOW VIEWPOINT RELATES TO INTERACTIONS |
|---|---|
| Chemical Reactions | Lighting a match, in itself, is not dangerous. Having gasoline around is not, in itself, dangerous. However, the *combination* of lighting a match in the presence of gasoline is explosive. Since the explosive effects of combining gas and lighting a match are different from simply adding their separate, individual effects, gasoline and matches interact. |
| Personal Relationships | John likes most people.<br>Mary is liked by most people.<br>*But* John dislikes Mary.<br><br>Based only on their individual tendencies, we would expect John to like Mary. Apparently, however, like gasoline and matches, the combination of their personalities produces a negative outcome. |
| Sports | The whole is not the same as the sum of the parts. That is, a team is not the sum of its parts. The addition of a player may do more for the team than the player's abilities would suggest—or the addition may help the team much less than would be expected because the team "chemistry" is upset. In other words, the player's skills and personality may interact with those of the other players on the team or with the team's strategy. Sometimes, the result is that adding the player will help the team more than what would be expected by knowing only the team's characteristics and the player's characteristics. Sometimes, adding the player will help the team less than what would be expected if one only knew the team's characteristics and the player's characteristics. Knowing the interaction between the team and the player—how the two will mesh together—may be almost as important as knowing the player's abilities.<br><br>Good pitchers get batters out.<br>Poor hitters are easier to get out than good hitters.<br>*However,* sometimes a poor hitter may have a good pitcher's "number" because the pitcher's strengths match the hitter's strengths. Similarly, some "poor" pitchers are very effective against some of the league's best batters. Managers who can take advantage of these interactions can win more games than would be expected by knowing only the talents of the individual team members. |
| Prescription Drugs | Drug A may be a good, useful drug.<br>Drug B may also be a good, useful drug.<br>But, taking Drug A and B together may result in harm or death. Increasingly, doctors and pharmacists have to be aware of not only the effects of drugs in isolation, but their combined effects. Ignorance of these interactions can result in deaths and in malpractice suits. |
| Making General Statements | Interactions indicate that you cannot make a general, simple statement that one variable always has a specific effect. You cannot talk about the effects of one variable without mentioning that the effect of that variable depends on a second variable. Therefore, if you have an interaction, when discussing a factor's effect, you need to say "but," "except when," "depending on," "only under certain conditions." Indeed, you will often see results sections say that the main effect was "qualified by a ___ interaction" or "the effect of the ___ variable was different depending on the level of (the other) variable." |
| Visually | If you graph an interaction, the lines will not be parallel. That is, the lines either already cross or if they were extended, they would eventually cross. |
| Mathematically | If you have an interaction, the effect of combining the variables is *not* the same as adding their two effects together. Rather, the effect is better captured as the result of multiplying the two effects. That is, when you add 2 to a number, you know the number will increase by 2, regardless of what the number is. However, when you multiply a number by 2, the effect will depend on the other number. When doubling a number, the effect is quite different when the number to be doubled is 2 than when it is 1,000 or than when it is $-40$. To take another example of the effect of multiplication, consider the multiplicative effects of interest rates on your financial condition. If interest rates go up, that will have a big, positive effect on your financial situation if you have lots of money in the bank; a small, positive effect if you have little money in the bank; and a negative effect on your finances if you owe money to the bank (you will have to pay more interest on your debt). |

many variables. We know how many individual variables act in isolation. Now, it is time to go to the next step—addressing the question: "What is the effect of combining these variables?" Put another way, once we learn what the general effect of a variable is, we want to find out what specific conditions may modify (moderate) this general, overall effect.

Another reason psychologists focus on interactions is because we realize that: (1) individuals rarely are exposed to one and only one variable, and (2) interactions are common. Consequently, psychologists now frame general problems and issues in terms of interactions. That is, rather than saying, "What is the (main) effect of personality and what is the (main) effect of the situation?" psychologists are now asking, "How do personality and the situation interact?" Asking this question has led to research indicating that some people are more influenced by situational influences than others (Snyder, 1984).

Similarly, rather than looking exclusively at the main effects of heredity and the main effects of environment, many scientists are looking at the interaction between heredity and environment. In other words, rather than asking, "What is the effect of a certain environment," they are asking, "Are the effects of a certain environment different for some people than for others?"

Looking for these interactions sometimes produces remarkable findings. For example, psychologists have found that certain children may benefit from an environment that would be detrimental to children who had inherited a different genetic predisposition (Plomin, 1993). Eventually, such research may lead to new ways of educating parents. For instance, rather than telling parents the one right way to discipline children, parent education may involve teaching parents to identify their child's genetic predispositions and then alter their parenting strategies to fit that predisposition.

We do not mean to imply that the interest in interactions is an entirely new phenomenon. Anyone interested in external validity is interested in interactions. If you are concerned that a treatment won't work on a certain type of person (women, minorities, the elderly), you are concerned about a treatment by type of person interaction. If you are concerned that a treatment that worked in one setting (a hospital) won't have the same effect in a different setting (a school), you are concerned about a treatment × setting interaction. If you are concerned that a treatment won't have the same effect in another culture, you are concerned about a treatment × culture interaction. If you are concerned that the superiority of one treatment over another will diminish over time, you are concerned about a treatment × time interaction.

Understandably, applied psychologists have always been interested in interactions. One of the founders of applied psychology, Walter Dill Scott, was fascinated by the fact that some people will like an advertisement that others will hate. In other words, he wanted to investigate personality × type of ad interactions. Most applied psychologists after Scott have shared his interest in determining which treatments work on which type of people. For example, therapists know that a therapeutic approach (behavior therapy, drug therapy) that works well for some people (phobics) may not work as well for others. That is, they know that there are treatment × type of patient interactions.

## EXAMPLE OF QUESTIONS ANSWERED BY THE 2 × 2 FACTORIAL EXPERIMENT

Now that you have a general understanding of main effects and interactions, let's apply this knowledge to a specific experiment. If you were to do the caffeine and exercise experiment we describe earlier, you would look for three different kinds of effects:

1. the main (average) effect of caffeine;
2. the main (average) effect of exercise; and
3. the interaction between caffeine and exercise.

The main effect of caffeine would be calculated by averaging the simple caffeine main effects. Likewise, the main effect of exercise would be calculated by averaging the two exercise simple main effects.

The interaction, on the other hand, would be calculated by subtracting the two caffeine simple main effects from each other (or subtracting the two exercise main effects from each other). Consequently, if both pairs of caffeine main effects are the same, you do not have an interaction.

To review, a significant main effect for caffeine would mean that caffeine had an effect. A significant main effect for exercise would mean that exercise had an effect. Finally, a significant interaction would mean that the combination of exercise and caffeine produce an effect that is not simply the sum of their two separate effects (see Table 8-5).

As you can imagine, significant interactions force scientists to answer such questions as, "Does caffeine increase calorie consumption?" by saying, "Yes, but it depends on . . ." or "It's a little more complicated than that." Psychologists do not give these kinds of responses to make the world seem more complicated than it is.

On the contrary, psychologists would love to give simple answers. Like all scientists, they love parsimony (they prefer simple explanations to more complex explanations). Therefore, they would love to report main effects that are not qualified by interactions. They would like to say that exercise is always good, and drinking caffeine is always bad. However, if interactions occur, scientists have the obligation to report them—and in the real world, interactions abound. Only the person who says, "Give me a match, I want to see if my gas tank is empty," is unaware of the pervasiveness of interactions. Time and time again, you learn that when variables combine, the effects are different than you would expect from knowing only their independent effects.

Because we live in a world where we are exposed to a variety of variables and because these variables interact, you may be compelled to do experiments that capture some of this complexity. But how would you describe the results from such a study?

**TABLE 8–5**
**Questions Addressed by a 2 × 2 Experiment**

| EFFECT | QUESTION ADDRESSED |
|---|---|
| **Overall main effect for exercise** | On the average, does varying exercise levels have an effect? |
| **Overall main effect for caffeine** | On the average, does varying caffeine levels have an effect? |
| **Interaction between caffeine and exercise** | Does the effect of caffeine *differ depending on* how much exercise participants get? |
| | Put another way: |
| | Does the effect of exercise *differ depending on* how much caffeine participants get? |

**TABLE 8–6**
**Eight Potential Outcomes of a 2 × 2 Factorial Experiment**

| | | | |
|---|---|---|---|
| 1 | **A** Main effect for Variable 1 | **No** Main effect for Variable 2 | **No** Interaction |
| 2 | **No** Main effect for Variable 1 | **A** Main effect for Variable 2 | **No** Interaction |
| 3 | **A** Main effect for Variable 1 | **A** Main effect for Variable 2 | **No** Interaction |
| 4 | **A** Main effect for Variable 1 | **A** Main effect for Variable 2 | **An** Interaction |
| 5 | **No** Main effect for Variable 1 | **No** Main effect for Variable 2 | **An** Interaction |
| 6 | **A** Main effect for Variable 1 | **No** Main effect for Variable 2 | **An** Interaction |
| 7 | **No** Main effect for Variable 1 | **A** Main effect for Variable 2 | **An** Interaction |
| 8 | **No** Main effect for Variable 1 | **No** Main effect for Variable 2 | **No** Interaction |

Note that having (or not having) a main effect has no implications whatsoever for whether you will have an interaction.

## Potential Results of a 2 × 2 Experiment

There are eight basic patterns of results you could obtain from a 2 × 2 experiment. These patterns are listed in Table 8-6.

If you did a study, how would you know which of these patterns of results you obtained? The first step would be to calculate the mean response for each group and then make a table of those means.

### A MAIN EFFECT AND NO INTERACTION

Suppose you obtained the results displayed in Table 8-7. To understand your results, you might start looking at the experiment as though it were four separate simple experiments. Thus, if you look only at the first row, it is just like you

**TABLE 8–7**

**Main Effect for Caffeine, No Interaction**

|  | No Exercise | Exercise | Exercise simple main effects |
|---|---|---|---|
| No Caffeine | 2000 | 2000 | +0  (2000 − 2000 = 0) |
| Caffeine | 2200 | 2200 | +0  (2200 − 2200 = 0) |
| Caffeine simple main effects | +200 (2200 − 2000 = +200) | +200 (2200 − 2000 = +200) | |

**Averaging a treatment's simple main effects gives us its overall main effect:**

| | |
|---|---|
| Simple main effect of **Caffeine** in the no exercise condition | +200 |
| Simple main effect of **Caffeine** in the exercise condition | +200 |
| Average effect (overall main effect) of **Caffeine** | +400/2 = +200 |

| | |
|---|---|
| Simple main effect of **Exercise** in the no caffeine condition | +0 |
| Simple main effect of **Exercise** in the caffeine condition | +0 |
| Average effect (overall main effect) of **Exercise** | 0/2 = +0 |

**Comparing a treatment's simple main effects tells us whether there is an interaction:**

Since there are no differences between the two simple main effects for caffeine (both are +200), then there is no interaction. In other words, since the effect of caffeine is not affected by how much participants exercised, there is no interaction.

are looking at a simple experiment that manipulated exercise (while not giving any of the participants caffeine). Put another way, looking at the first row shows you what happened in the no caffeine groups.

As you can see, the no exercise group consumed just as many calories (2000) as the exercise group. That is, for the no caffeine groups, exercise had no effect.

To find out what happened with caffeine groups, look at the second row. Note that looking at the second row is just like looking at a simple experiment that varied exercise (while giving all the participants 20 mg of caffeine). As you can see by the fact that both the no exercise and the exercise groups consumed 2,200 calories, exercise had no effect in the caffeine conditions.

Averaging the effect of exercise over both the no caffeine and the caffeine conditions, you find that exercise's average (overall) effect was zero. Thus, there was no overall main effect for exercise.

Looking at the columns tells you about the effect of caffeine. For example, looking at the first column is like looking at a simple experiment that varied caffeine (while not having any participants exercise). Thus, looking at the first column (the no exercise conditions) shows you the effect of caffeine for the no

**TABLE 8–8**
**Main Effect for Exercise, No Interaction**

| | No Exercise | Exercise | Exercise simple main effects |
|---|---|---|---|
| **No Caffeine** | 2000 | <u>2500</u> | **+500** (<u>2500</u> − 2000 = **+500**) |
| **Caffeine** | 2000 | <u>2500</u> | **+500** (<u>2500</u> − 2000 = **+500**) |
| Caffeine simple main effects | **+0** (2000 − 2000 = **+0**) | **+0** (<u>2500</u> − <u>2500</u> = **+0**) | |

**Averaging a treatment's simple main effects gives us its overall main effect:**

| | |
|---|---|
| Simple main effect of **Caffeine** in the no exercise condition | **+0** |
| Simple main effect of **Caffeine** in the exercise condition | **+0** |
| Average effect (overall main effect) of **Caffeine** | **+0/2 = 0** |

| | |
|---|---|
| Simple main effect of **Exercise** in the no caffeine condition | **+500** |
| Simple main effect of **Exercise** in the caffeine condition | **+500** |
| Average effect (overall main effect) of **Exercise** | 1000/2 = **+500** |

**Comparing a treatment's simple main effects tells us whether there is an interaction:**

Since there are no differences between the two simple main effects for exercise (both are +500), then there is no interaction. In other words, since the effect of exercise is not affected by how much caffeine participants consumed, there is no interaction.

exercise groups. Specifically, for these no exercise groups, caffeine boosts calorie consumption by 200 calories.

Looking at the second column shows you the effect of caffeine for the exercise groups. That is, looking at the second column is like looking at a simple experiment that manipulated caffeine (while having all participants exercise).

As you can see, the caffeine group consumes 200 more calories than the no caffeine group. Thus, there is a simple main effect for caffeine in the exercise condition.

Since caffeine increases calorie consumption in both the no exercise and the exercise conditions, it appears that there is an overall main effect for caffeine. In other words, the average effect of caffeine is to increase calorie consumption.

Because the effect of caffeine does not depend on the level of exercise, there is no interaction. That is, the effect of caffeine is the same in the no exercise condition as it is in the exercise condition: In both cases, it boosts calorie consumption by 200.

Instead of having no interaction and a main effect for caffeine, you could have no interaction and a main effect for exercise. This pattern of results is shown in Table 8–8. From the top row, you can see that, when there was no caffeine, exercise increased calorie consumption by 500. Looking at the bottom row, you see that exercise also increased calorie consumption by 500 in the caffeine conditions. Averaging the effect of exercise over both the no caffeine and the caffeine conditions, you find that exercise's average (overall) effect, the overall main effect of exercise, was 500.

Looking at the columns tells you about the effect of caffeine. You see that, in the no exercise conditions, the participants getting caffeine consumed the same number of calories (2000) as participants in the no caffeine condition. Looking at the second column, you learn that, in the exercise condition, the caffeine group consumes the same number of calories (2500) as the no caffeine group. Thus, it appears that there is no main effect for caffeine.

You also know that there is no interaction because the effect of exercise is unaffected by the level of caffeine. As Table 8–8 demonstrates, exercise increases food consumption by 500 calories, regardless of the amount of caffeine that participants consumed.

Although making tables of means is a useful way to summarize data, perhaps the easiest way to interpret the results of an experiment is to graph your data. To see how useful graphing can be, get a sheet of notebook paper and a ruler.

Starting near the left edge of the sheet, draw a four-inch line straight down the page. This vertical line is called the y-axis. The y-axis corresponds to scores on the dependent measure. In this case, your dependent measure is calories consumed. So, label the y-axis "Calories Consumed."

Now that you have a yardstick (the y-axis) for recording calories consumed, your next step is to put marks on that yardstick. Having these marks will make it easier for you to plot the means accurately. Start marking the y-axis by putting a little horizontal tick mark on the very bottom of the y-axis. Label this mark "0." A half-inch above this mark, put another mark. Label the mark "500." Keep making marks until you get to "3000."

Your next step is to draw a horizontal line that goes from the bottom of the y-axis to the right side of the page. (If you are using lined paper, you may be able to trace over one of the lines that goes across the page.) The horizontal line is called the "x-axis." On the x-axis, you should put one of your independent variables. It doesn't really matter which independent variable you put on the x-axis. However, for the sake of this example, put caffeine on the x-axis. Specifically, put "caffeine (mg)" about an inch under the middle of the x-axis. Then, put a mark on the left-hand side of the x-axis and label this mark "No caffeine." Next, put a mark on the right side of the x-axis and label it "20 mg caffeine."

You are now ready to plot the means in the left column of Table 8–8. Once you have plotted those two means, draw a straight line between those two means. Label that line "no exercise." Next, plot the two means in the right column of Table 8–8. Then, draw a line between those two points. Label this

**FIGURE 8–1**

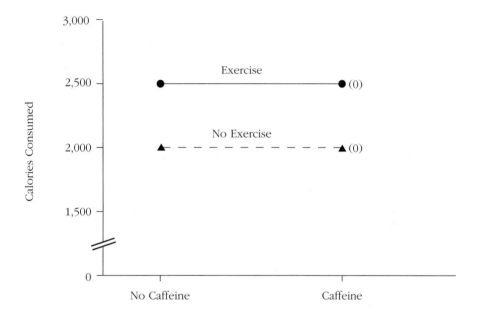

**Main Effect for Exercise, No Interaction**

Note: Numbers in parentheses represent the simple main effects of caffeine. Thus, the simple main effect of caffeine is zero in both the no exercise and the exercise conditions.

second line (which should be above your first line) "exercise." Your graph should look something like Figure 8-1.

The graph confirms what you saw in the table. Exercise increased calorie consumption, as shown by the exercise line being above the no exercise line. Caffeine did not increase calorie consumption as shown by the fact that both lines stay perfectly level as they go from no caffeine to 20 mg caffeine.

Finally, there is no interaction between exercise and caffeine on calorie consumption, as shown by the fact that the lines are parallel. The lines are parallel because exercise is having the same effect on the no caffeine group as it is on the caffeine group.

Thus, if you graph your data, you only need to look to see whether the lines are parallel to see whether you have an interaction. If your lines are parallel, you do not have an interaction. If, on the other hand, your lines have very different slopes, then you may have an interaction.

## TWO MAIN EFFECTS AND NO INTERACTION

Table 8-9 reflects another pattern of effects you might obtain. From the first row, you can see that, in the no caffeine groups, exercise increased calorie

**TABLE 8–9**

**Main Effects for Caffeine and Exercise, No Interaction**

|  | No Exercise | Exercise | Exercise simple main effects |
|---|---|---|---|
| **No Caffeine** | 2000 | <u>2500</u> | **+500** (<u>2500</u> − 2000 = **+500**) |
| **Caffeine** | 2200 | <u>2700</u> | **+500** (<u>2700</u> − **2200** = **+500**) |
| Caffeine simple main effects | **+200** (**2200** − 2000 = **+200**) | **+200** (<u>**2700**</u> − <u>2500</u> = **+200**) | |

**Averaging a treatment's simple main effects gives us its overall main effect:**

| | |
|---|---|
| Simple main effect of **Caffeine** in the no exercise condition | **+200** |
| Simple main effect of **Caffeine** in the exercise condition | **+200** |
| Average effect (overall main effect) of **Caffeine** | **+400/2 = +200** |

| | |
|---|---|
| Simple main effect of **Exercise** in the no caffeine condition | **+500** |
| Simple main effect of **Exercise** in the caffeine condition | **+500** |
| Average effect (overall main effect) of **Exercise** | 1000/2 = **+500** |

**Comparing a treatment's simple main effects tells us whether there is an interaction:**

Since there are no differences between the two simple main effects for exercise (both are +500), then there is no interaction. In other words, since the effect of exercise is not affected by how much caffeine participants consumed, there is no interaction. Put another way, since the simple main effect for caffeine is the same in both the no exercise and the exercise conditions (+200), there is no interaction.

consumption by 500 calories. Looking at the second row, you see that, in the caffeine groups, exercise also increased calorie consumption by 500. Averaging the effect of caffeine over all caffeine conditions, you find that the average effect of exercise (the overall main of exercise) was to increase calorie consumption by 500.

Looking at the columns tells you about the effect of caffeine. The first column tells you about what happens in the no exercise conditions. As you can see, in the no exercise conditions, the participants who get caffeine consume 200 more calories than those who don't get caffeine. Looking at the second column, you learn that, in the exercise condition, the caffeine group also consumes 200 more calories than the no caffeine group. Because caffeine increases calorie consumption in both the no exercise and the exercise groups, it appears that there is a caffeine main effect.

Finally, you also know that there is no interaction because the effect of caffeine is unaffected by the level of exercise. As Table 8-9 demonstrates, the effect of caffeine is independent of the amount of exercise. That is, caffeine

FIGURE 8–2

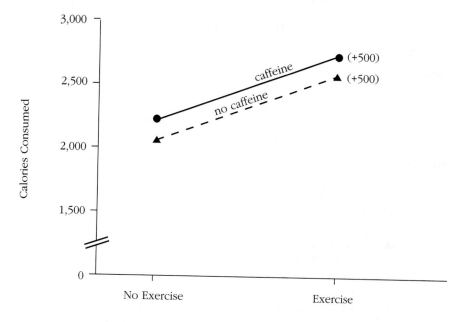

**Main Effects for Caffeine And Exercise, No Interaction**

Note: Numbers in parentheses represent the simple main effects of exercise. Thus, the simple main effect of exercise was +500 in the no caffeine condition and also in the caffeine condition.

increases food consumption by 200 calories in both the exercise and the no exercise conditions.

To look at this lack of interaction from a different angle, the effect of exercise is unaffected by the level of caffeine. Specifically, exercise increases food consumption by 500 calories for both the caffeine and no caffeine groups.

If you graph the means, as we did in Figure 8-2, you can see that the graph confirms what you saw in the table. Caffeine increased calorie consumption as shown by the caffeine line being above the no caffeine line. Similarly, exercise increased calorie consumption as shown by the fact that both lines slope upward as they go from no exercise to exercise. Finally, the graph tells you that there is no interaction between exercise and caffeine on calorie consumption because the lines are parallel.

## TWO MAIN EFFECTS AND AN INTERACTION

Now imagine that you got a very different set of results from your study. For example, suppose you found the results in Table 8-10.

**TABLE 8–10**

**Main Effects for Caffeine and Exercise with an Interaction**

|  | No Exercise | Exercise | Exercise simple main effects |
|---|---|---|---|
| **No Caffeine** | 2000 | 2200 | **+200** (2200 − 2000 = **+200**) |
| **Caffeine** | 2200 | 3000 | **+800** (3000 − 2200 = **+800**) |

| | | |
|---|---|---|
| Caffeine simple main effects | +**200** (**2200** − 2000 = +**200**) | +**800** (**3000** − **2200** = +**800**) |

**Averaging a treatment's simple main effects gives us its overall main effect:**

| | |
|---|---|
| Simple main effect of **Caffeine** in the no exercise condition | +200 |
| Simple main effect of **Caffeine** in the exercise condition | +800 |
| Average effect (overall main effect) of **Caffeine** | +1000/2 = **+500** |

| | |
|---|---|
| Simple main effect of **Exercise** in the no caffeine condition | +200 |
| Simple main effect of **Exercise** in the caffeine condition | +800 |
| Average effect (overall main effect) of **Exercise** | 1000/2 = **+500** |

**Comparing a treatment's simple main effects tells us whether there is an interaction:**

Since the simple main effect for caffeine in the no exercise condition (+200) is different than the simple main effect for caffeine in the exercise condition (+800), there is an interaction. In other words, since the effect of exercise is affected by how much caffeine participants consumed, there is an interaction.

As Table 8-10 shows, you have main effects for both exercise and caffeine. The average effect of caffeine is to increase calorie consumption by 500 and the average effect of exercise is to increase calorie consumption by 500 calories.

However, the effect of caffeine varies depending on how much exercise participants get. In the no exercise condition, caffeine increases calorie consumption by 200. In the exercise condition, on the other hand, caffeine increases consumption by 800 calories. Since the effect of caffeine varies depending on the amount of exercise, you have an interaction.

To see this interaction, look at Figure 8-3. As you can see, the lines are not parallel. They are not parallel because the slope of the caffeine line is much steeper than the slope of the no-caffeine line. That is, the lines are not parallel because the simple main effect of exercise is much stronger in the caffeine condition than in the no caffeine condition. In other words, the lines are not parallel because there is an exercise by caffeine interaction.

## INTERACTION WITHOUT MAIN EFFECTS

You have seen that you can have main effects with interactions, but can you have interactions without main effects? Consider the data in Table 8-11 and Figure 8-4.

**FIGURE 8–3**

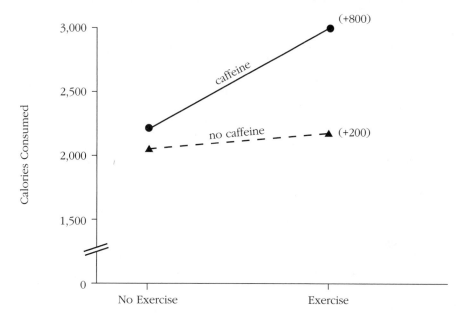

**Main Effects for Caffeine And Exercise, No Interaction**

Note: Numbers in parentheses represent the exercise simple main effects. Thus, the simple main effect of exercise was +200 in the no caffeine condition, but +800 in the caffeine condition.

From the graph (Figure 8–4), you can see that the lines are not parallel. Indeed, the lines actually cross, indicating that exercise has one kind of effect (increasing calorie consumption) in the no-caffeine condition, but an opposite effect (decreasing calorie consumption) in the caffeine condition. Therefore, you have an interaction.

Note, however, that you do not have a main effect for either caffeine or exercise. On the average, the no exercise groups consume as much as the exercise groups. Therefore, there isn't an exercise main effect. Similarly, the no caffeine groups consume as much as the caffeine groups (see Table 8-11). Thus, there is no main effect for either caffeine or exercise. Yet, you would not say that neither caffeine nor exercise have any effect on calories consumed. Instead, you would either say that:

1. caffeine has an effect, but its effect depends on the level of exercise; or,
2. exercise has an effect, but the kind of effect it has depends on the amount of caffeine consumed.

Note that no matter whether you emphasize the effect of caffeine (as in statement #1) or the effect of exercise (as in #2), you cannot talk about the effect of

**Figure 8-4**

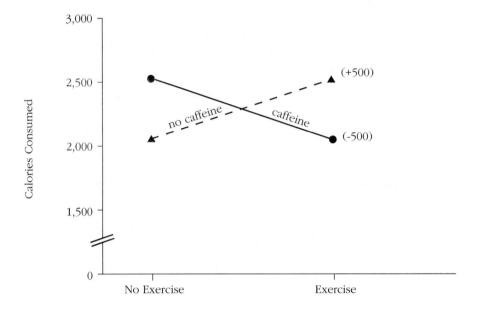

**No Main Effects for Caffeine or Exercise with an Interaction**

Note: Numbers in parentheses represent exercise simple main effects. Thus, the simple main effect of exercise was +500 in the no caffeine condition, but -500 in the caffeine condition.

one variable without talking about the other. That is, as with any interaction, the effect of one variable depends on the other.

## ONE MAIN EFFECT AND AN INTERACTION

You have seen that you can have no main effects and an interaction. You have also seen that you can have two main effects and an interaction. Can you also have one main effect and an interaction? Yes. Such a pattern of results is listed in Table 8-12 and graphed in Figure 8-5.

As Table 8-12 reveals, the average effect for caffeine is zero. The average effect for exercise, on the other hand, is to increase calorie consumption by 250 calories. Note, however, that exercise's effect is uneven. In the no caffeine condition, exercise increases consumption by 500 calories. But in the caffeine condition, exercise has no effect on calorie consumption. Thus, the effect of exercise is qualified by caffeine level.

Figure 8-5 (p. 265) tells the same story. By looking at that figure, you realize there may be an interaction because the lines are not parallel. They are not

**TABLE 8–11**

**No Overall Main Effects for Caffeine or Exercise with an Interaction**

|  | No Exercise | Exercise | Exercise simple main effects |
|---|---|---|---|
| No Caffeine | 2000 | <u>2500</u> | +**500** (<u>2500</u> − 2000 = +**500**) |
| Caffeine | 2500 | <u>2000</u> | −**500** (<u>2000</u> − 2500 = −**500**) |

| Caffeine simple main effects | +**500** (**2500** − 2000 = +**500**) | −**500** (**2000** − **2500** = −**500**) |
|---|---|---|

**Averaging a treatment's simple main effects gives us its overall main effect:**

| Simple main effect of **Caffeine** in the no exercise condition | +**500** |
|---|---|
| Simple main effect of **Caffeine** in the exercise condition | −**500** |
| Average effect (overall main effect) of **Caffeine** | 0/2 = +**0** |

| Simple main effect of **Exercise** in the no caffeine condition | +**500** |
|---|---|
| Simple main effect of **Exercise** in the caffeine condition | −**500** |
| Average effect (overall main effect) of **Exercise** | 0/2 = +**0** |

**Comparing a treatment's simple main effects tells us whether there is an interaction:**

Since there are very big differences between the two simple main effects for exercise, then there is an interaction. In other words, since the effect of exercise is affected by how much caffeine participants consumed, there is an interaction. Put another way, since the simple main effect for caffeine in the no exercise condition (+500) is different than the simple main effect for caffeine in the exercise condition (−500), there is an interaction.

parallel because the effect of exercise is fairly dramatic in the no caffeine condition, but nonexistent in the caffeine condition.

Determining the main effects requires a little more mental visualization. If there is a main effect for caffeine, one of the caffeine lines should, on the average, be higher than the other. When one line is above the other, it is easy to tell whether there seems to be a main effect. In this case, however, the lines cross. Thus, it is hard to tell whether one line is, on the average, above the other. However, if you study the graph carefully, you may see that the midpoint of both lines is at the same spot (2,250). Or, you may realize that the no caffeine line is below the caffeine line just as often and to just the same extent as it is above the caffeine line. In either case, you would conclude that there is no main effect for caffeine.

To determine whether there is a main effect for exercise, you could mentally combine the two lines. If you do that, you would "see" that this combined line slopes upward, indicating a main effect for exercise. Failing that, you could

**TABLE 8–12**

**Main Effect for Exercise with an Interaction**

|  | No Exercise | Exercise | Exercise simple main effects |
|---|---|---|---|
| **No Caffeine** | 2000 | <u>2500</u> | **+500**  (<u>2500</u> − 2000 = **+500**) |
| **Caffeine** | 2250 | <u>2250</u> | **+0**  (<u>2250</u> − 2250 = **+0**) |

| Caffeine simple main effects | +250 (2250 − 2000 = +250) | −250 (<u>2250</u> − <u>2500</u> = −250) |
|---|---|---|

**Averaging a treatment's simple main effects gives us its overall main effect:**

| Simple main effect of **Caffeine** in the no exercise condition | +250 |
|---|---|
| Simple main effect of **Caffeine** in the exercise condition | −250 |
| Average effect (overall main effect) of **Caffeine** | 0/2 = +0 |

| Simple main effect of **Exercise** in the no caffeine condition | +500 |
|---|---|
| Simple main effect of **Exercise** in the caffeine condition | +0 |
| Average effect (overall main effect) of **Exercise** | 500/2 = +250 |

**Comparing a treatment's simple main effects tells us whether there is an interaction:**

Since there are very big differences between the two simple main effects for exercise, there is an interaction. In other words, since the effect of exercise is affected by how much caffeine participants consumed, there is an interaction. To look at it another way, since the simple main effect for caffeine in the no exercise condition (+250) is very different than the simple main effect for caffeine in the exercise condition (−250), there is an interaction.

reason that since the no caffeine line slopes upward and the caffeine line stays straight, the average of the two lines would have to slope upward.

### NO MAIN EFFECTS AND NO INTERACTION

The last pattern of results you could obtain is to get no statistically significant results. That is, you could fail to find a caffeine effect, fail to find an exercise effect, and fail to obtain an interaction between caffeine and exercise. An example of such a dull and dreary set of findings is listed in Table 8–13 (p. 266).

## ANALYZING THE RESULTS FROM A 2 × 2 EXPERIMENT

You can now graph and describe the eight possible patterns of results from a 2 × 2 experiment. But how do you analyze your results? How do you know whether a main effect or an interaction is significant?

FIGURE 8–5

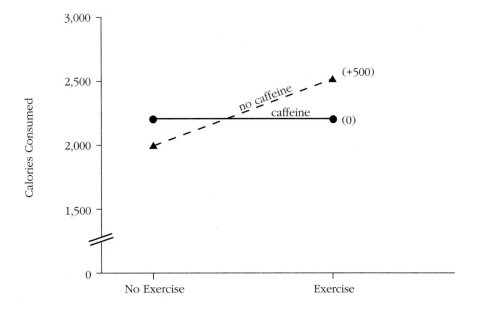

Note: Numbers in parentheses represent exercise simple main effects. Thus, the simple main effect of exercise was +500 in the no caffeine condition, but 0 in the caffeine condition.

As you did with the multiple group experiment, you would use analysis of variance to analyze your data. However, instead of testing for one main effect, you will be testing for two main effects and an interaction. Thus, your ANOVA summary table might look like this:

| Source of Variance | Sum of Squares | df | Mean Square | F |
|---|---|---|---|---|
| Exercise Main Effect (A) | 900 | 1 | 900 | 9.00 |
| Caffeine Main Effect (B) | 200 | 1 | 200 | 2.00 |
| Interaction (A × B) | 100 | 1 | 100 | 1.00 |
| Error Term (within groups) | 3600 | 36 | 100 | |
| Total | 4800 | 39 | | |

Despite the fact that this ANOVA table has two more sources of variance than an ANOVA for a multiple group experiment, most of the rules that apply to the multiple group ANOVA table apply to the table for a factorial design. In other words, the rules that you learned in Chapter 7 will serve you well. For example, the number of treatment levels is one more than the treatment's degrees of freedom. Since this ANOVA summary table tells us that the degrees of

**TABLE 8-13**
**No Main Effects and No Interaction**

|  | No Exercise | Exercise |
|---|---|---|
| **No Caffeine** | 2500 | <u>2500</u> |
| **Caffeine** | 2500 | **<u>2500</u>** |

freedom for exercise is 1, we know that the study used 2 levels of exercise. Likewise, since the degrees of freedom for caffeine is 1, we know the study used 2 levels of caffeine. In addition, as was the case with the multiple group experiment, the total of the degrees of freedom is 1 less than the number of participants. Therefore, the ANOVA table tells us that there were 40 participants in the experiment ($40 - 1 = 39$). For more advice about how to tap the information in an ANOVA summary table, consult Box 8-1.

The only new thing you need to figure out are the degrees of freedom for the interaction term. To calculate the interaction term's degrees of freedom, multiply the degrees of freedom for the main effects making up that interaction. For a $2 \times 2$ experiment, that would be 1 (df for first main effect) $\times$ 1 (df for second main effect) $= 1$. For a $2 \times 3$ experiment, the df for the first main effect would be 1 and the df for the second main effect would be 2. Therefore, the interaction term's degrees of freedom would be 2 (because $1 \times 2 = 2$).

## Interpreting the Results of an ANOVA Table

To determine whether an effect was significant, you compare the "F" for that effect to the value given in the "F" table under the appropriate number of degrees of freedom. If your obtained "F" is larger than the value in the table, the effect is significant.

Generally, you will want to start your inspection of the ANOVA results by seeing if any of your overall main effects are significant. Then, if you have a significant main effect, you will want to know whether this main effect was qualified by an interaction.

### MAIN EFFECTS WITHOUT INTERACTIONS

If the interaction was not significant, your conclusions are simple and straightforward. Having no interactions means there are no "ifs" or "buts" about your main effects. That is, you have not found anything that would lead you to say that the main effect occurs only under certain conditions. For instance, if you have a main effect for caffeine and no interactions, that means that caffeine had the same kind of effect throughout your experiment—no matter what the level

---

### Box 8-1
### The Mathematics of an ANOVA Summary
### Table for Between Subjects
### Factorial Designs

1. Degrees of freedom (df) for a main effect equals 1 less than the number of levels of that factor. If there are 3 levels of a factor (low, medium, high), that factor has 2 df.
2. Degrees of freedom for an interaction equals the product of the df of the factors making up that effect. If you have an interaction between a factor that has 1 df and a factor that has 2 df, that interaction has 2 df (because 1 × 2 = 2).
3. To get the df for the error term, add up the df for all the main effects and interactions. Then, subtract that total from the total number of participants. Finally, subtract 1 from that number.
4. To get the mean square for any effect, get the sum of squares for that effect, then divide by that effect's df. If an effect's sum of squares was 300, and its df was 3, its Mean Square would be 100.
5. To get the F for any effect, get its mean square and divide it by the mean square error. If an effect's mean square was 100 and the mean square error was 50, the F for that effect would be 2.

---

of exercise was. In other words, when you don't have interactions, you can just talk about the individual main effects.

## Interactions

If you find a significant interaction, your results are not as easy to interpret. Having an interaction means that a treatment factor has a different effect on one group of participants than on another. In this case, having an interaction means that caffeine has a different effect depending on the level of exercise the participant received. In other words, the simple main effect of caffeine in the no exercise condition is different from the simple main effect of caffeine in the exercise condition. Thus, to understand the main effect, you must understand the simple main effects that make up the overall main effect.

The easiest way to understand the pattern of the simple main effects—and thus understand the interaction—is to graph those simple effects.[2] Since

---

[2] Interactions suggest that the simple main effects making up the overall main effect differ from the overall main effect. Therefore, one way to understand the interaction is to do statistical analyses on the individual simple main effects. The computations for these tests are relatively simple. However, there are some relatively subtle issues involved in deciding which test to use.

you have a significant interaction, the lines representing these simple main effects will have different slopes, reflecting the fact that the treatment appears to have one effect in one condition, but a different effect in another condition. That is, since you have a significant interaction, the lines in your graph will not be parallel.

Closer inspection of these non-parallel lines will tell you what type of interaction you have. As you'll see, it's important to know whether you have an ordinal interaction or a cross-over (disordinal) interaction.

## ORDINAL INTERACTIONS

Suppose that your lines are not parallel. However, your lines are sloping in the same direction and do not actually cross. In that case, you have an **ordinal interaction**. Thus, in an ordinal interaction, you might find that both of the lines slope upward, but one of the lines has a steeper slope. Usually, ordinal interactions *suggest* that a treatment may have a more intense effect in one condition than another. For example, this type of interaction would occur if a treatment was more effective for one type of patient than for another. It would also occur if a teaching strategy helped both shy and outgoing children, but helped outgoing children more. In Figure 8–3, you can see another example of an ordinary interaction: Exercise boosted participants' calorie consumption by only 200 calories in the no caffeine condition, but it boosted calorie consumption by 800 calories in the caffeine condition.

As you have seen, ordinal interactions may reflect the fact that the effect of combining the two independent variables works particularly well—or particularly poorly. That is, an ordinal interaction reflects the fact that a factor *appears* to have more of an effect in one condition than in another condition.

We say appears to have more of an effect because it is not easy to determine whether a variable had more of a psychological effect in one condition than in another. For example, to state that the difference between 2200 calories and 2000 calories is less than the difference between 3000 calories and 2200 calories, you must have interval scale data.

Obviously, in this case, you have interval scale data—*if you are interested in number of calories consumed*. However, if you are using calories consumed as a measure of how hungry people felt, then your measure may not be interval. You may not have a one-to-one correspondence between number of calories consumed and degree of hunger. It may take the same increase in *perceived hunger* to make a person who normally eats 2000 calories consume an additional 200 calories as it does to get someone who would normally eat 2200 calories to eat an additional 800 calories. Consequently, the ordinal interaction may be an artifact of your hunger measure yielding ordinal rather than interval data.

To see how you might get an ordinal interaction even when the effect of combining two variables produces nothing more than the sum of their individual effects, consider Figure 8–6. In Figure 8–6a, the lines are not parallel and

**FIGURE 8-6**

**How an Ordinal Interaction May Not Be a True Interaction**

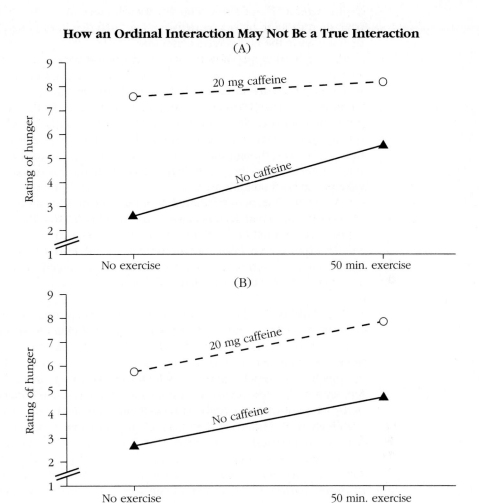

thus indicate an interaction. Now, look at Figure 8-6b, which is a graph of the same data. In Figure 8-6b, the lines are parallel, indicating no interaction.

Why does one graph yield an interaction whereas the other does not? The first graph yields an interaction because it, like most graphs you have seen, makes the distance between 3 and 4 equal to the distance between 7 and 8. However, by doing this, the author of the graph *assumes* that the data are interval. Thus, the difference in hunger between those participants who rate their hunger a "3" and those participants who rate their hunger a "4" is depicted as being the same as the difference in hunger between those who rate their hunger a "7" and those who rate their hunger an "8." If this assumption is true, then caffeine makes participants feel hungrier in the exercise condition than it does in the no exercise condition.

The second graph shows what can happen if we do not buy the assumption that the data are interval. Specifically, the graph shows what happens when the difference in feelings of hunger between rating a "7" and rating an "8" is greater than the difference in hunger between a "3" and "4." In that case, at the psychological level, caffeine's effect on the subjective state of "feeling hungry" is the same in the exercise condition as it is in the no-exercise condition. Thus, even though there is an interaction at the statistical level, there is not an interaction at the psychological level: Caffeine has the same psychological effect in both conditions.

As you have seen, ordinal interactions may be nothing more than an artifact of not having interval data. Because you can rarely be sure that you have interval data, you should be cautious when interpreting ordinal interactions. However, there are two basic situations that should lead you to be especially cautious in interpreting ordinal interactions: (1) when ceiling effects are likely, and (2) when floor effects are likely.

***Ceiling Effects.***     Both ceiling and floor effects are due to dependent measures that do not tap the full range of the variable being measured. In the case of ceiling effects, the measure does not allow participants who are extremely high on the variable to score as high as they should. For example, imagine an extremely easy knowledge test, in which half the class scores 100%. The problem with such a test is that we are unable to differentiate between those students who knew the material fairly well and students who knew the material extremely well. The test's "low ceiling" did not allow very knowledgable students to show that they knew more than somewhat knowledgable students.

To see how a ceiling effect can create an ordinal interaction, consider the following experiment. An investigator wants to know how information about a specific person affects the impressions people form of that person. The investigator uses a 2 (information about a stimulus person's traits [no information versus extremely positive information]) × 2 (information about a stimulus person's behavior [no information versus extremely positive information]) factorial experiment. For the dependent measure, participants rate the stimulus person's character on a 3-point scale (1 = below average, 2 = average, 3 = above average).

As you can see from Figure 8–7, the investigator obtains an ordinal interaction. The interaction suggests that getting information about a specific person's behavior has less of an impact if participants already have information about that person's traits. In fact, the interaction suggests that if participants already know about the stimulus person's traits, information about the person's behavior is worthless.

The problem in interpreting this interaction is that the results could be due to a ceiling effect. That is, even if getting additional favorable information about

FIGURE 8–7

## How a Ceiling Effect Can Create an Ordinal Interaction

### (a): An ordinal interaction caused by a ceiling effect

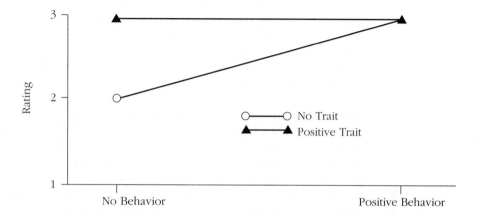

### (b): How the same subjects would have scored with a positive "higher ceiling"

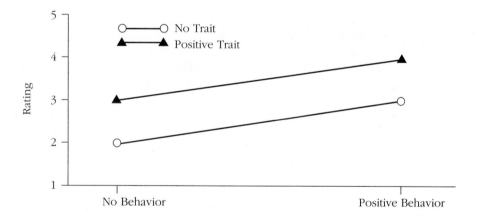

*Note:* With the higher ceiling, the lines are parallel and the "interaction" disappears.

the stimulus person raises participants' opinions of that person, participants cannot show this increased respect. That is, participants may feel that a person with a favorable trait is a "3" ("above average") and a person with both a favorable trait and a favorable behavior is a "4" ("well above average")—but they cannot rate the person a "4." The highest rating they can give a person is a "3." The highest rating ("above average") on this scale—the "ceiling" response—is not high enough.

By not allowing participants to rate the stimulus person as high as they wanted to, the investigator did not allow participants to rate the positive trait/positive behavior person higher than either the positive trait/no behavior person or the positive behavior/no trait person. Thus, the investigator's ordinal interaction was due to a **ceiling effect:** The effect of a treatment or combination of treatments is underestimated because the dependent measure is not sensitive to psychological states above a certain level. In other words, the interaction is due to the dependent measure placing an artificially low ceiling on how high a response can be. As you can see from Figure 8-7, "raising the ceiling" would eliminate some ordinal interactions.

*Floor Effects.*    Just as ceiling effects can account for ordinal interactions, so can their opposites—floor effects. For example, suppose the investigator uses the same 3-point rating scale as before (1 = below average, 2 = average, 3 = above average). However, instead of using no information and extremely positive information, the investigator uses no information and extremely *negative* information. The investigator might again obtain an ordinal interaction. Again, the interaction would indicate that adding behavioral information to trait information has little effect on participants' impressions. This time, however, the interaction could be due to the fact that participants could not rate the stimulus person lower than a 1. The bottom rating or "floor" is too high.

By not allowing participants to rate the person as low as they wanted to, the investigator did not allow participants to rate the negative trait/negative behavior stimulus person lower than the negative trait/no behavior person or the negative behavior/no trait person. Thus, this time, the investigator's ordinal interaction was due to a **floor effect:** The effects of the treatment or combination of treatments is underestimated because the dependent measure places too high a floor on what the lowest response can be. As you can see from Figure 8-8, "lowering the floor" can eliminate some ordinal interactions.

As floor and ceiling effects show, an ordinal interaction may reflect a measurement problem rather than a true interaction. So, be careful when interpreting ordinal interactions.

## CROSS-OVER (DISORDINAL) INTERACTIONS

You do not have to be so careful if you have a **cross-over interaction**. As the term "cross-over interaction" suggests, when you have a cross-over interaction, the lines in your graph actually cross.

Cross-over interactions often indicate that a factor has one kind of effect in one condition, and the opposite kind of effect in another condition. For example, you would have a cross-over interaction if a therapy that helps patients who have one kind of problem actually hurts patients who have a different kind of problem. In Figure 8-4, you can see another example of a cross-over interaction: In the no caffeine condition, exercise *increases* calorie consumption, but, in the caffeine condition, exercise *decreases* calorie consumption.

**FIGURE 8–8**

**How a Floor Effect Could Cause Us to Underesimate the Combined Effects of Knowing Both Negative Traits and Negative Behaviors on the Impressions We Form.**

**(a): An ordinal interaction caused by a floor effect**

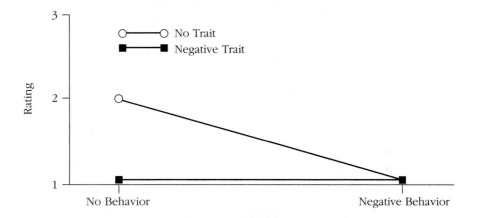

**(b): How the same subjects would have scored if there had been a"lower floor"**

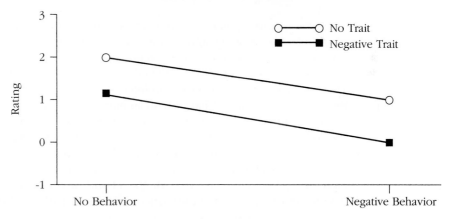

*Note:* In the second graph, the lines are parallel and the "interaction" disappears.

Cross-over interactions are also called **disordinal interactions**. They are called disordinal interactions because, unlike ordinal interactions, they can't be an artifact of having ordinal, rather than interval, data.

To understand why disordinal interactions can't be due to having ordinal data, let's imagine a factorial experiment designed to determine the effectiveness of watching exercise videos and monitoring what one eats on fitness. Specifically, middle-aged adult volunteers are assigned to one of four conditions: (1) no video/no diet monitoring, (2) no video/diet monitoring, (3) video/no diet monitoring, and (4) video/diet monitoring. After six weeks, fitness is assessed.

The experimenter assesses fitness by having the adults start one block east of 1st Street and seeing how many blocks the person can go in 10 minutes. Thus, if a person makes it to 1st Street, they have run one block, if they make it to 3rd Street, they get credit for running three blocks.

Unfortunately, the experimenter did not check to make sure that all the blocks are equal in length. Indeed, as it turns out, the blocks vary considerably in length.

Since some blocks are very short whereas others are fairly long, the measure provides only ordinal data. For example, we know someone who walked six blocks walked farther than someone who walked five blocks, but we don't know how much farther. Therefore, if Mary walks eight blocks to Mabel's six, and Sam walks four blocks to Steve's two blocks, we cannot say that Mary outwalked Mabel by the same distance as Sam outwalked Steve. Mary may have walked 100 feet more than Mabel, but Sam may have walked 10,000 feet more than Steve.

How will the use of an ordinal measure hurt the experimenter's ability to interpret the results? The answer to this question depends on the pattern of the results.

If the researcher gets the ordinal interaction depicted in Figure 8–9, there is a problem because the apparent interaction may only be an artifact of having ordinal data. For example, the interaction could be due to the distance between 7th and 8th Streets being longer than the distance between 3rd and 5th Streets. Thus, if the researcher had used an interval measure (number of feet walked), the researcher might not have found an interaction.

If, on the other hand, the researcher gets the disordinal interaction depicted in Figure 8–10, this interaction can't be due to having ordinal data. That is, even if the blocks are all of different lengths (not at all interval), the fact would remain that the interaction still would reflect the fact that the weight-monitoring was more effective for the people watching the exercise videos than for those not watching the videos. That is, regardless of the length of the blocks, we would know that the difference between being able to make it to 5th Street versus being able to make it to 7th Street is smaller than the difference between making it to 3rd Street versus making it to 8th Street. (We would know this because the distance between 3rd and 8th includes the distance between 5th and 7th.)

To reiterate, there are two possibilities for an ordinal interaction. One possibility is that the ordinal interaction can be taken at face value. That is, it really represents the fact that combining your two independent variables produces an

**FIGURE 8–9**

**An Ordinal Interaction between Diet and Exercise Videos**

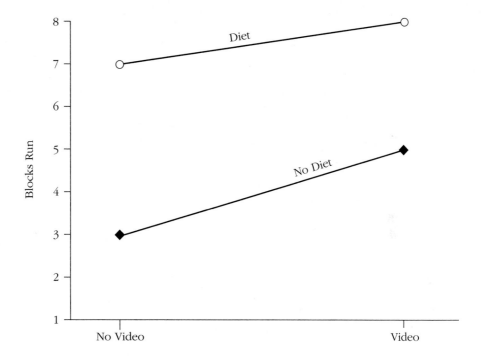

effect that is different from the sum of their individual effects. Specifically, combining the factors has either less of or more of an effect than the sum of their individual effects. The second possibility is that the apparent interaction is really an artifact of ordinal scale measurement (see Chapter 4 for a review of scales of measurement). If you had more accurately measured the construct, you would not have found an interaction. Therefore, if you want to say that an ordinal interaction represents a true interaction, you need to establish that you have interval data.

To illustrate the difficulty of interpreting an ordinal interaction, suppose you find that a treatment boosted scores from "15" to "19" in one condition, but from "5" to "8" in the other. At the level of scores, you have an interaction: the treatment increased scores more in one condition than in the other. But what about at the level of psychological reality? Can you say that going from a "15" to a "19" represents more psychological change than going from a "5" to an "8"? Only if you have interval or ratio scale data. In other words, with an ordinal interaction, you can only conclude that the variables really interact if you can say that a one point change in scores at one end of your scale is the same thing (psychologically) as a one point change at any other part of your scale.

**FIGURE 8–10**

### A Disordinal (Cross-Over) Interaction between Diet and Exercise Videos

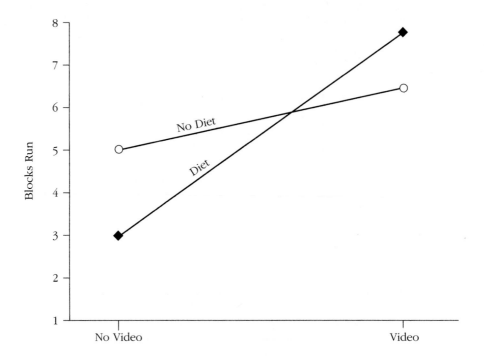

With cross-over (disordinal) interactions, on the other hand, you are not comparing differences between scores on one part of your scale with differences between scores on an entirely different part of your scale. Instead, you are making comparisons between scores that overlap. For example, with a cross-over interaction, you might only have to conclude that the psychological difference between "10" and "30" is bigger than a difference between "15" and "19." Since the difference between "10" and "30" includes 15–19, you can conclude that the difference between "10" and "30" is bigger—even if you only have ordinal data. Thus, when you have a cross-over (disordinal) interaction, you can conclude that your variables really do interact.

## PUTTING THE 2 × 2 TO WORK

You now understand the logic behind the 2 × 2 design. In the next sections, you will see how you can use the 2 × 2 to produce research that is more interesting, has greater construct validity, and has greater external validity than research produced by a simple experiment.

## Adding a Replication Factor to Increase Generalizability

The generalizability of results from a single simple experiment can always be questioned. Critics ask questions such as, "Would the results have been different if a different experimenter had performed the study?" and "Would the results have been different if a different manipulation had been used?" Often, the researcher's answer to these critics is to do a **systematic replication:** a study that varies from the original only in some minor aspect, such as using different experimenters or different stimulus materials.

For example, Morris (1986) found that students learned more from a lecture presented in a rock-video format than from a conventional lecture. However, Morris only used one lecture and one rock video. Obviously, we would have more confidence in his results if he had used more than one conventional lecture and one rock-video lecture.

Morris would have benefited from doing a 2 × 2 experiment. Since the 2 × 2 factorial design is like doing two simple experiments at once, he could have obtained his original findings and replicated them in a single 2 × 2 experiment. Specifically, in addition to manipulating the factor of presentation type, he could also have manipulated the replication factor of **stimulus sets:** the particular stimulus materials shown to two or more groups of participants. Thus, he could have done a 2 (presentation type [conventional lecture versus rock-video format]) × 2 (stimulus sets [material about Shakespeare versus material about economics]) study. Because psychologists often want to show that the manipulation's effect can occur with more than just one particular stimulus set, experimenters routinely include stimulus sets as a replication factor in their experiments.[3]

Similarly, it is not unusual to have more than one experimenter run a study and use experimenter as a factor in the design. Some investigators use experimenter as a factor to show the generality of their results. Specifically, they want to show that certain experimenter attributes (gender, attractiveness, status) do not affect the outcome of the experiment.

Other investigators use experimenter as a factor to establish that experimenters are not intentionally or unintentionally influencing the results. For example, Ranieri & Zeiss (1984) did an experiment in which participants rated their mood by filling out a self-rating form. Ranieri & Zeiss were worried that experimenters might unintentionally influence participants' responses. Therefore, they used three experimenters and randomly assigned participants to experimenter. If they had found that different experimenters achieved different patterns of results, they would suspect that the results might be due to experimenter effects rather than to the manipulation itself.

---

[3] Whether traditional, fixed effects, analysis of variance should be used to analyze such studies is a matter of debate (Clark, 1973; Cohen, 1976; Coleman, 1979; Kenny & Smith, 1980; Richter & Seay, 1987; Wickens & Keppel, 1983; Wike & Church, 1976).

## Using an Interaction to Find an Exception to the Rule: Looking at a Potential Moderating Factor

Thus far, we have discussed instances where the investigator's goal in using the factorial design was to increase the generalizability of the experimental results. Thus, in a study that uses stimulus set as a replication factor, researchers hope that the treatment $\times$ stimulus set interaction will not be significant. Similarly, most researchers that use experimenter as a factor hope that there will not be a treatment $\times$ experimenter interaction.

Often, however, you may read a research report and say to yourself, "But I bet that would not happen under ___ conditions." In that case, you should do a study in which you essentially repeat the original experiment, except that you add what you believe will be a moderating factor that will interact with the treatment.

To see how a moderating factor experiment would work, let's look at a study by Jackson and Williams (1985). Jackson and Williams were aware of the phenomenon of social loafing: Individuals don't work as hard on tasks when they work in groups than when they work alone. However, Jackson and Williams felt that social loafing would not occur on extremely difficult tasks. Therefore, they did a study, which, like most social loafing studies, manipulated whether or not participants worked alone or in groups. In addition, they added what they thought would be a moderating factor—whether the task was easy or difficult.

As expected, and as other studies had shown, social loafing occurred. However, social loafing only occurred when the task was easy. When the task was difficult, the reverse of social loafing occurred: Participants worked better in groups than alone. This interaction between task difficulty and number of workers confirmed their hypothesis that task difficulty moderated social loafing (see Figure 8–11).

## Using Interactions to Create New Rules

Although we have discussed looking for an interaction to find an exception to an existing rule, some interactions do more than complicate existing rules. Some interactions reveal new rules. Consider Barbara Tversky's (1973) 2 $\times$ 2 factorial experiment. She randomly assigned students to one of four conditions:

1. expected a multiple-choice test and received a multiple-choice test;
2. expected a multiple-choice test and received an essay test;
3. expected an essay test and received a multiple-choice test; and
4. expected an essay test and received an essay test.

She found an interaction between test expected and test received. Her interaction showed that participants did better when they got the same kind of test they expected. That is, they did better when the test *matched* their expectations (see Figure 8–12).

**FIGURE 8–11**

**Interaction between Task Difficulty and Number of Coworkers on Effort**

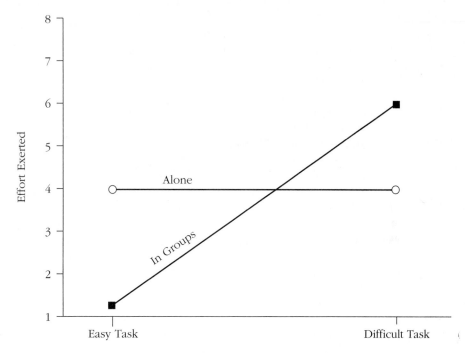

*Note:* Effort was scored on a 1-7 scale, with higher numbers indicating more effort.

Similarly, a researcher might find an interaction between mood (happy, sad) at the time of learning and mood (happy, sad) at the time of recall. The interaction might reveal that recall was best when participants were in the *same* mood at the time of learning as they were at the time of recall. As you can see, the 2 × 2 experiment may be useful for you if you are interested in assessing the effects of similarity.

## Studying Non-Experimental Variables

Rather than converting a simple experiment into a 2 × 2 experiment by adding a second experimental factor, you could convert a simple experiment into a 2 × 2 hybrid design by adding a non-experimental factor. The non-experimental factor could be any variable that you cannot randomly assign, such as age, sex, or personality type.

In such a hybrid 2 × 2 design, you could make causal statements about the effects of the experimental factor, but you could *not make any causal*

FIGURE 8–12

## The Effect of Expectations and Type of Test on Performance

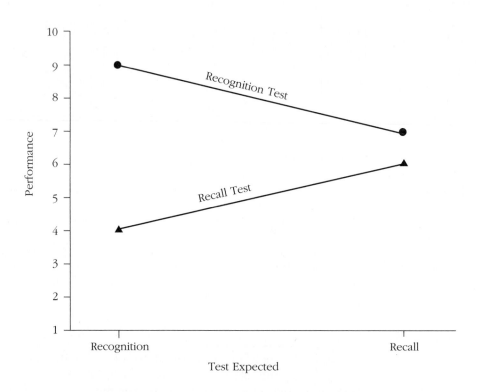

*statements regarding the non-experimental factor.* Thus, although the study described in Table 8-14 includes sex of participant as a variable, the study does not allow us to say anything about the effects of a participant's sex.

Why can't you make causal statements regarding the effects of the participant's sex? Because your two groups may differ in hundreds of ways besides their gender: college major, exercise habits, age, smoking habits, current stress levels, extent to which they cook their own food, etc. Any one of these differences might be responsible for the difference in behavior between the two groups. Therefore, you cannot legitimately say that sex differences—rather than any of these other differences—is the reason why your two groups behaved differently.

**TABLE 8–14**

**The Hybrid Design: A Cross between an Experiment and a Non-Experiment**

|  | Female | Male | **Differences between the group of women and the group of men participating in this study** | |
|---|---|---|---|---|
| **No Stress** | 2000 | 3000 | Simple main "effect" of gender in no stress condition = 1000 | Overall main "effect" of gender =1750 ([1000 + 2500]/2) |
| **Stress** | *1500* | *4000* | Simple main "effect" of gender in stress condition = 2500 | |

| Experimental effects: Effects caused by treatment | Simple main **effect** of stress for the female groups is −500 | Simple main **effect** of stress for the male groups is +1000 |
|---|---|---|
| | Overall main **effect** of stress is 250 | |
| | [(−500 + 1000)/2] | |

Note that the hybrid 2 × 2 design answers two questions that the simple experiment does not:

1. Do the male and female participants differ on the dependent variable? (Answered by the gender main effect.)

2. Is the effect of stress different in our sample of males than in our sample of females? (Answered by the gender by treatment interaction.)

If you cannot make causal statements about the non-experimental factor, why would you want to add a non-experimental variable to your simple experiment? The most obvious and exciting reason is that you are interested in that non-experimental variable.

To see how adding a non-experimental variable (age of participant, introvert-extrovert, etc.) can spice up a simple experiment, consider the following simple experiment: Participants are either angered or not angered in a problem-solving task by a confederate who poses as another participant. Later, participants get an opportunity to punish or reward the confederate. Obviously, we would expect participants to punish the confederate more when they had been angered. This simple experiment, in itself, would not be very interesting.

Holmes and Will (1985) added a non-experimental factor to this study—whether participants were Type A or Type B personalities. (People with Type A personalities are thought to be tense, hostile, and aggressive, whereas people with Type B personalities are thought to be more relaxed and less aggressive.) The results of this study were intriguing: If participants had not been angered, Type A participants were more likely to punish the confederate than Type B participants. However, if participants had been angered, Type A and Type B participants behaved similarly (see Figure 8–13).

Likewise, Hill (1991) could have done a relatively uninteresting simple experiment. He could have determined whether research participants are more likely to want to talk to a stranger if that stranger is supposed to be "warm" than if the stranger supposedly lacks warmth and empathy. The finding that people prefer to affiliate with people who are nice would not have been startling.

Fortunately, Hill conducted a more interesting study by adding another variable: need for affiliation. He found that participants who were high in need for affiliation were very likely to want to interact with an allegedly "warm" stranger, but very unlikely to want to interact with a stranger who allegedly lacked warmth. For low need for affiliation participants, on the other hand, the alleged warmth of the stranger made little difference.

As you have seen, adding a non-experimental factor can make a study more interesting. As you will see in the next sections, you can add a non-experimental variable to a simple experiment for most of the same reasons you would add an experimental variable: to increase the generalizability of the findings, to look for a similarity effect, and to look for a moderating factor.

## INCREASING GENERALIZABILITY

You could increase the generalizability of a simple experiment that used only males as participants by using both males and females as participants, and making sex of participant a factor in your design. This design would allow you to determine whether the effect held for both males and females.

## STUDYING EFFECTS OF SIMILARITY

If you were interested in similarity, you might include some participant characteristic (sex, status, etc.) as a factor in your design, while manipulating the comparable experimenter or confederate factor. For example, if you were studying helping behavior, you could use style of dress of the participant (dressed-up/casual) and style of dress of the confederate as factors in your design. You might find this interaction: Dressed-up participants were more likely to help confederates who were dressed-up, but casually dressed participants were more likely to help confederates who were dressed casually. This interaction would suggest that similarity of dress influences helping behavior.

## FINDING AN EXCEPTION TO THE RULE

If you thought that intelligence would be a moderating variable for the effectiveness of computerized instruction, you might use intelligence as a factor in your design. To do this, you would first give your participants an IQ test and then divide them into two groups (above-average intelligence and below-average intelligence). Next, you would randomly assign the high intelligence group

**FIGURE 8–13**

### The Effect of Being Angered on the Aggressiveness of Type A and Type B Personality Types

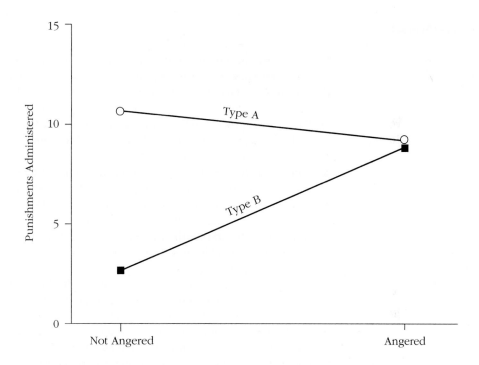

Data from: Holmes, D. S. & Will, M. J. (1985). Expression of interpersonal aggression by angered and nonangered persons with the Type A and Type B behavior patterns. *Journal of Personality and Social Psychology, 48*, 723-727.

to condition so that half of them were in computerized instruction and half were in group instruction. You would do the same for the low intelligence group.

This study might reveal some interesting findings. For instance, suppose you found that computerized instruction vastly improves learning for low IQ children, but slightly decreases learning for high IQ children. If you had only done a simple experiment, you might have found a significant positive effect for the new teaching technique. On that basis, you might have recommended using this technique with all schoolchildren. What a terrible mistake!

## CONCLUDING REMARKS

In this chapter, you have seen the benefits of using the $2 \times 2$ experiment. Your awareness of this design opens up new possibilities for research. Just as importantly, your understanding of this commonly used design increases your ability to read, understand, and evaluate the research of others. Therefore, you now have the ability to discover new paths for research that radiate from the research of others. In the next two chapters, you will refine this ability.

## SUMMARY

1. Factorial experiments allow you to look at the effects of more than one independent variable at a time.
2. The simplest factorial experiment is the $2 \times 2$ ("two by two") experiment.
3. The $2 \times 2$ allows you to study two independent variables in one experiment *and* it lets you see the effects of combining different levels of your two independent variables.
4. Whenever the effects of combining two independent variables is different from the sum of their individual effects, you have an interaction. In other words, an interaction occurs when an independent variable's effect *depends* on the presence of another (moderating) variable. For example, the independent variable may have one effect when the second factor is absent and a *different* effect when the second factor is present.
5. Interactions often indicate that a general rule does not always apply. For example, a treatment $\times$ gender interaction indicates that the rule does not apply equally to men and to women.
6. Interactions can most easily be observed by graphing your data. If your two lines aren't parallel, you may have an interaction.
7. If your lines cross, you probably have a cross-over (disordinal interaction). A cross-over interaction sometimes indicates that a treatment has one effect for one group and the *opposite* effect on another group. For example, a cross-over interaction may mean that a treatment helps one group, but harms the other.
8. If your lines are not parallel, but don't cross, you have an ordinal interaction. Ordinal interactions may be due to a treatment having more of an effect on one group than on another. However, ordinal interactions may be an artifact of ordinal data. That is, if you have ordinal data, you may have an ordinal interaction, even though the treatment has the same psychological effect in all conditions.
9. If you have an ordinal interaction, do not rush to conclude that a treatment has more of an effect in some conditions than in others. Instead, ask yourself whether the data were truly interval. For example,

ask yourself if ceiling or floor effects could be responsible for the interaction.

10. A significant interaction usually qualifies main effects. Thus, if you find a significant interaction, you can't talk about your main effects without referring to the interaction. If, on the other hand, you don't find a significant interaction, you can just talk about your individual main effects.

11. Sometimes the interaction in a 2 × 2 represents another variable. For instance, in a 2 × 2 with place of learning and place of testing as factors, an interaction may reveal that it is best to be tested in the *same* place you learned the information.

12. With the hybrid factorial design, you can look at an experimental factor and a factor that you do not manipulate (personality, gender, age) in the same study. However, because you did not manipulate the non-experimental factor, you cannot say that you know anything about the *effects* of your non-experimental factor.

13. Once you have an idea for a simple experiment, you can easily expand that idea into an idea for a factorial experiment. For example, you could add a replication factor or a personality variable to try to establish the generalizability of your treatment's effect. Thus, you would be hoping *not* to find a significant interaction. Alternatively, if you wanted to show that the treatment didn't have the same effect under all circumstances (or for all people), you could add a potential moderating variable. In that case, you would be hoping for a significant interaction between the treatment and the factor that you believe will moderate its effect.

## KEY TERMS

**factorial experiment:** an experiment that examines two or more independent variables (factors) at a time. (p. 244)

**simple main effect:** the effects of one independent variable at a specific level of a second independent variable. The simple effect could have been obtained merely by doing a simple experiment. (p. 245)

**main effect (overall main effect):** the average of a variable's simple main effects: the overall or average effect of an independent variable. (p. 247)

**interaction:** when the simple main effect of a variable is different in one condition than in another, you have an interaction. In other words, when you need to know how much of a certain variable participants have received to say what the effect of another variable is, you have an interaction between those two variables. If you graph the results from an experiment that has two or more independent variables, and the lines you draw between your points are not parallel, you may have an interaction. (p. 248)

**ordinal interaction:** reflects the fact that an independent variable *seems* to have more of an effect under one level of a second independent variable than under another level. If you graph an ordinal interaction, the lines will not be parallel, but they will not cross. It is called an ordinal interaction because the interaction, and the failure of the lines to be parallel, may be due to having ordinal data. Thus, in reality, the independent variable may have the same effect under all levels of the second independent variable. However, because equal psychological distances are not reflected by equal distances on your measuring scale (for example, the difference between a 1 and a 4 is the same, in terms of amount of a construct, as is the difference between a 6 and a 7), you may think the variables interact. Ordinal interactions may result from ceiling or floor effects. (p. 268)

**ceiling effect:** the effects of a treatment or combination of treatments is underestimated because the dependent measure cannot distinguish between participants who have somewhat high and those who have very high levels of the construct. The measure puts an artificially low ceiling on how high a participant may score and thus produces ordinal, rather than interval, data. Consequently, a ceiling effect may cause an ordinal interaction. (p. 272)

**floor effect:** the effects of a treatment or combination of treatments is underestimated because the dependent measure artificially restricts how low scores can be. The measure puts an artificially high floor on how low a participant may score and thus produces ordinal, rather than interval, data. Consequently, a floor effect may cause an ordinal interaction. (p. 272)

**cross-over (disordinal) interaction:** when an independent variable has one kind of effect in the presence of one level of a second independent variable, but a different kind of effect in the presence of a different level of the second independent variable. Examples: Getting closer to someone may increase their attraction to you if you have just complimented them, but may decrease their attraction to you if you have just insulted them. Called a cross-over interaction because the lines in a graph will cross. Called disordinal interaction because it cannot be explained as an artifact of having ordinal, rather than interval, data. (p. 272)

**replication factor:** a factor sometimes included in a factorial design to see whether an effect replicates (occurs again) under slightly different conditions. For example, suppose an investigator wants to see if a new memory strategy is superior to a conventional one. Instead of having all the participants memorize the same story, the researcher assigns different participants to get different stories. Type of story is the replication factor in the study. The researcher hopes that memory strategy manipulation will have the same effect regardless of which story is used. But, if story type matters (there is an interaction between memory strategy and story type), the researcher might do further research to understand why the strategy was less effective in helping participants remember certain types of stories. (p. 277)

**stimulus set:** the particular stimulus materials shown to two or more groups of participants. Researchers may use more than one stimulus set in a study so that they can see if the treatment effect replicates across different stimulus sets. (p. 277)

**systematic replication:** a study that varies from the original study only in some minor aspect, such as using different stimulus materials. Thus, if you include stimulus set as a factor in your design, your study, in a sense, contains a systematic replication. (p. 277)

## EXERCISES

1. Half the participants receive a placebo. The other half receive a drug that blocks the effect of endorphins (pain-relieving substances, similar to morphine, that are produced by the brain). Half the placebo group and half the drug group get acupuncture. Then, all participants are asked to rate the pain of various shocks on a 1 (not at all painful) to 10 (very painful) scale. The results are as follows: placebo, no acupuncture group, 7.2; placebo, acupuncture group, 3.3; drug, no acupuncture group, 7.2; drug and acupuncture group, 3.3.
   a. Graph the results.
   b. Describe the results in terms of main effects and interactions (making a table of the data may help).
   c. What conclusions would you draw?

2. Below is an ANOVA summary table of a study looking at the effects of similarity and attractiveness on liking.
   How many participants were used in the study?
   How many levels of similarity were used?
   How many levels of attractiveness were used?
   Complete the table.

| SV | SS | df | MS | F |
|----|----|----|----|----|
| Similarity (S) | 10 | 1 | ___ | ___ |
| Attractiveness (A) | ___ | 2 | 20 | ___ |
| S × A interaction | 400 | 2 | 200 | ___ |
| Error | 540 | 54 | ___ | |
| Total | 990 | 59 | | |

3. A professor does a simple experiment. In that experiment, the professor finds that students who are given lecture notes do better than those who are not given lecture notes. Replicate this study as a 2 × 2 factorial. What is your second variable? What predictions do you make? Do you predict an interaction? Why or why not?

4. A lab experiment on motivation yielded the following results:

| Group | Productivity |
|---|---|
| No financial bonus, no encouragement | 25% |
| No financial bonus, encouragement | 90% |
| Financial bonus, no encouragement | 90% |
| Financial bonus, encouragement | 90% |

   **a.** Graph these data.
   **b.** Describe the results in terms of main effects and interactions.
   **c.** What is your interpretation of the findings?

5. A memory researcher looks at the effects of processing time and rehearsal strategy on memory.

| Group | Percent correct |
|---|---|
| Short exposure, simple strategy | 20% |
| Short exposure, complex strategy | 15% |
| Long exposure, simple strategy | 25% |
| Long exposure, complex strategy | 80% |

   **a.** Graph these data.
   **b.** Describe the results in terms of main effects and interactions.
   **c.** What is your interpretation of the findings?

6. Suppose a researcher wanted to know whether lecturing was more effective than group discussion for teaching basic facts. Therefore, the researcher did a study and obtained the following results:

| Source of Variance | SS | df | MS | F |
|---|---|---|---|---|
| Teaching (T) | 10 | 1 | 10 | 5 |
| Introversion/Extroversion (I) | 20 | 1 | 20 | 10 |
| T $\times$ I interaction | 50 | 1 | 50 | 25 |
| Error | 100 | 50 | 2 | |

   **a.** What does the interaction seem to indicate?
   **b.** Even if there had been no interaction between teaching and extroversion, would there be any value in including the introversion-extroversion variable? Explain.
   **c.** What, if anything, can you conclude about the effects of introversion on learning?

# CHAPTER 9

---

# Within-Subjects Designs

*Overview*

*The Matched Pairs Design*

PROCEDURE
CONSIDERATIONS IN USING MATCHED PAIRS DESIGNS
ANALYSIS OF DATA
SUMMARY OF THE MATCHED PAIRS DESIGN

*Pure Within-Subjects Designs*

PROCEDURE
CONSIDERATIONS IN USING WITHIN-SUBJECTS DESIGNS
DEALING WITH THE ORDER PROBLEM
ANALYSIS OF DATA
SUMMARY OF PURE WITHIN-SUBJECTS DESIGNS

*Counterbalanced Within-Subjects Designs*

PROCEDURE
ADVANTAGES AND DISADVANTAGES OF COUNTERBALANCING
CONCLUSIONS ABOUT COUNTERBALANCED DESIGNS

*Choosing Designs*

CHOOSING DESIGNS: THE TWO CONDITIONS CASE
CHOOSING DESIGNS: WHEN YOU HAVE MORE THAN ONE INDEPENDENT VARIABLE

*Concluding Remarks*

*Summary*

*Key Terms*

*Exercises*

# *Chapter 9*

# WITHIN-SUBJECTS DESIGNS

## OVERVIEW

In Chapters 6, 7, and 8, you learned that you could perform an internally valid experiment by independently and randomly assigning participants to groups. Although you understand the logic of randomly assigning participants to groups, you may still have two basic reservations about between subjects designs.

First, you may believe that between subjects designs are wasteful in terms of the number of participants they require. For example, in the simple experiment, the participant is either in the control group *or* in the experimental group. Clearly, it would seem more efficient if each participant was in both the control group *and* in the experimental group. One participant would do the job of two.

Second, you may be concerned that between subject designs are not powerful enough. You may believe that if we use each participant as his or her own control, we could detect differences that would not be detected if we were comparing participants with one another. Your concern is based on the fact that between subject differences may hide the treatment's effect. For example, suppose you use a simple experiment to examine a treatment that produces a small effect. The treatment's small effect might be discounted as being due to random differences between the two groups. If, on the other hand, we use each participant as his or her own control, the difference that the treatment created between the two conditions could not be dismissed as being due to random differences between the two groups. Consequently, the treatment's effect might be detected and found to be statistically significant.

You are rightfully concerned about the twin weaknesses of between subjects experiments: They require many participants and have relatively little power. Therefore, in this chapter, you will learn some alternatives to pure between subjects designs. These alternatives require fewer participants and often have more power than between subjects experiments.

You will begin by learning about matched pairs designs. In matched pairs designs, you first reduce between subject differences by matching pairs of participants on a key characteristic. Then, you let random assignment and statistics take care of the effects of the remaining differences between subjects.

Next, you will learn about within-subjects designs. In these designs, you avoid the problem of between subject differences by using participants as their own controls. Then, you let randomization take care of the effects of the remaining uncontrolled variables. By limiting the variables that randomization has to account for, the pure within-subjects design—like the matched pairs design—often has impressive power.

After learning about pure within-subjects designs, you will learn about mixed designs. Mixed designs have aspects of both between and within-subjects designs. Specifically, mixed designs are factorial designs in which at least one factor is a between subjects factor and at least one factor is a within-subjects factor. In other words, different participants get different levels of the between subject factor(s), but all participants get all levels of the within-subjects factor(s).

Finally, you will learn how to weigh the tradeoffs involved in choosing among various experimental designs. Thus, by the end of this chapter, you will be better able to choose the best experimental design for your research problem.

# THE MATCHED PAIRS DESIGN

If you do not have enough participants to do a powerful simple experiment, you might use a design that requires fewer participants, such as a matched pairs design. As you will see, the matched pairs design combines the best aspects of matching and randomization: It uses matching to reduce the effects of irrelevant variables and it uses randomization to establish internal validity.

## Procedure

In the matched pairs design, you first measure your participants on a variable that correlates with the dependent measure. For example, if you were measuring memory, your matching variable could be education, IQ, or scores on a memory test. After measuring all your participants on the matching variable, you would form **matched pairs:** pairs of participants who have similar scores on this measure. Thus, if you were doing a memory experiment using a matched pairs design, you might first give all your participants a memory test. Next, you would rank their scores on this memory test from lowest to highest. Then, you would pair the two highest scorers, the next two highest scorers, and so on. This would give you pairs of participants with similar scores on the memory pretest. Finally, you would randomly assign one member of each pair to the control group and the other member to the experimental group.

**TABLE 9-1**

**Comparing the Matched Design with the Simple Experiment**

| MATCHED DESIGN | SIMPLE EXPERIMENT |
| --- | --- |
| First, *match* participants on key characteristics. | *No matching.* |
| Then, *randomly assign* each member of the pair to condition. | *Randomly assign* participants to condition. |

## Considerations in Using Matched Pairs Designs

You now have a general idea of how to conduct a matched pairs experiment. But should you use a matched pairs design? When considering a matched pairs design, you should consider four questions:

1. Can you find an effective matching variable?
2. How important is it that you have a powerful design?
3. Will matching harm extend validity?
4. Will matching harm construct validity?

### FINDING AN EFFECTIVE MATCHING VARIABLE

As we intimated earlier, you can only make effective use of the matched pairs design if you can match participants on a variable that correlates strongly with the dependent measure. Sometimes, you can match participants on the basis of earlier performance on the dependent measure task. Thus, in a memory experiment, participants could be matched based on scores on an earlier memory test; in a maze-running experiment, participants could be matched based on earlier maze-running performance.

If you cannot match on pretest scores, you may have to consult the research literature to find a matching variable (see Appendix B). Consulting the literature will not only tell you what matching variables other researchers have used, but also tell you what variables correlate with your dependent measure. Unfortunately, after doing your library research, you may find that (a) there are no variables that have a strong, documented relationship with performance on the dependent measure, or that (b) there are good matching variables, but for ethical or practical reasons you cannot use them.

### POWER

You want to find an appropriate matching variable so that your study will have adequate **power:** the ability to find differences between conditions. Indeed, the reason you may choose a matched pairs design is to avoid the problems that plague researchers using between subject designs. As you may recall from

Chapter 6, researchers using between subject designs lose power because individual differences between participants hide treatment effects. Thus, because participants differ from each other, researchers can't assume that the treatment group and the no-treatment group are identical before the start of the experiment. Consequently, if the groups differ at the end of the experiment, researchers may not know whether this difference is due to the treatment or to the groups being different before the experiment began. Thus, even a large difference between the groups could be due to random error rather than to treatment.

If matching makes your groups very similar to each other before the experiment begins, then random error due to individual differences is reduced. By reducing the amount of random error, the matched pairs design will give you more power than the simple experiment. Therefore, the same difference that would not be statistically significant with a simple experiment may be significant with a matched pairs design.

How is this possible? Because your t-value will be higher with the matched pairs design. Remember, the t-value is the difference between conditions divided by an estimate of random error (the standard error of the difference). With less random error, the t-value becomes larger. For example, if the standard error of the difference for a simple experiment is 6 seconds, then a difference of 6 seconds between conditions would yield a nonsignificant t-value of 1.0 (because 6/6 = 1.0). However, if a matched pairs design reduced random error so much that the standard error of the difference was only 1.0, then that same difference of six seconds would yield a significant t-value of 6.0 (because 6/1 = 6.0). In other words, if matching reduces the impact of individual differences, you may be able to find relatively small effects.

But what if matching fails to reduce random error? For example, suppose a researcher matched participants on shoe size. In that case, the matched pairs design may be less powerful than the simple experiment. Why? Because by using a matched pairs design instead of a simple experiment, you lose half your degrees of freedom.

You lose half your degrees of freedom because degrees of freedom for a simple experiment equals number of *participants* $-2$, but the degrees of freedom for a matched pairs study equals number of *pairs* $-1$. For instance, if you used 20 participants in a simple experiment, you would have 18 degrees of freedom (two fewer than the number of participants). But in a 20 participant, matched pairs design, you have only 9 degrees of freedom (one fewer than the number of pairs).

Losing degrees of freedom can cause you to lose power. As you can see by looking at the t-table in Appendix E, the fewer degrees of freedom you have, the larger your t-value must be to reach significance. For example, with 18 degrees of freedom (what you'd have if you tested 20 participants in a simple experiment), you would only need a t-value of 2.101 for your results to be statistically significant at the .05 level. On the other hand, with 9 degrees of freedom (what you'd have if you tested 20 participants [10 pairs of participants] in a matched pairs experiment), your t-value would have to be at least 2.262 to be statistically significant at the .05 level.

Thus, if you obtained the same t-value with the matched pairs design as you would have obtained with a simple experiment, then the matched pairs design cost you power. However, if your matching is any good, you should not get the same t-value with a matched pairs design as with a simple experiment. Instead, you will almost always get a larger t-value with a matched pairs design because you have reduced a factor that shrinks t-values—random error due to differences between participants. Usually, the increase in the size of the t-value will more than compensate for the degrees of freedom you will lose.

## EXTERNAL VALIDITY

Power is not the only consideration in deciding to use a matched pairs design. You may use—or avoid—matching for reasons of external validity.

For example, a matched pairs design may have more external validity than an equally powerful between subjects design. Why? Because the between subjects design may get you power by limiting what type of participant can be tested (male, albino rats between 180–185 days of age), whereas the matched pairs gets you power without limiting the kind of participant you can have. That is, to reduce random differences between treatment and no treatment groups, the between subjects experimenter may be forced to use participants who are *all* very similar. Thus, the between subjects researcher may only allow middle-class women with IQs between 115–120 to be in his experiment. However, with the matched pairs design, you can reduce random differences between the treatment and no treatment groups without choosing participants who are *all* alike. Because you can reduce random error by matching participants rather than limiting the kinds of participants you have, the matched pairs design may allow you to generalize your results to a broader population.

However, if participants drop out of the study between the time they are tested on the matching variable and the time they are to perform the experiment, matching will reduce the generalizability of your results. For instance, suppose you start off with 16 matched pairs, but end up with only 10 pairs. In that case, your experiment's external validity is compromised because your results may not apply to individuals resembling the participants who dropped out of your experiment.

Even if participants do not drop out, matching may still harm external validity. That is, you may find that your results only generalize to situations where individuals perform the matching task before getting the treatment.

To illustrate, imagine that an experimenter uses a matched pairs design to examine the effect of caffeine on anxiety. In that experiment, participants take an anxiety test, then either consume caffeine (the experimental group) or do not (the control group), and then take the anxiety test again. Suppose that the participants receiving caffeine become more anxious than those not receiving caffeine.

Can the investigator generalize her results to people who have not taken an anxiety test before consuming caffeine? No, it may be that caffeine only increases anxiety if it is consumed after taking an anxiety test. For example, taking the anxiety test may make participants so concerned about their level of anxiety that they interpret any increase in arousal as an increase in anxiety. Because of the anxiety test, the arousal produced by caffeine—which might ordinarily be interpreted as invigorating—is interpreted as anxiety.

### CONSTRUCT VALIDITY

In the caffeine study we just discussed, taking the anxiety test before and after the treatment might make participants aware that the experimenter is looking at the effects of a drug on anxiety. However, the fact that participants are guessing the hypothesis does not, by itself, ruin the experiment's construct validity.

For instance, if you used a treatment condition and a placebo condition, it does not matter if participants think that taking a pill is supposed to increase anxiety. Since both groups have the same hypothesis ("The pill I took will increase my anxiety"), knowing the hypothesis would not cause the treatment group to differ from the placebo group. Therefore, a significant difference between groups would have to be due to the drug.

If, on the other hand, your independent variable manipulation has poor construct validity (as would be the case if you had an empty control group), matching will make your manipulation's weaknesses more damaging. For instance, if, in the caffeine study, an empty control group was used (nothing was given to control subjects), matching might seriously threaten construct validity because the two groups might have different hypotheses. The experimental group subjects might hypothesize that the pill should increase their anxiety level. This expectation might cause them to be more anxious—or at least, to report being more nervous. The control group subjects, not having been given a pill, would not expect to become more nervous. Consequently, a significant difference between the groups might be due to the two groups acting on different hypotheses, rather than to any ingredient in the pill.

## Analysis of Data

We have talked about how matching can help you obtain a significant effect. We have also advised you to be cautious about interpreting such significant effects. But how do you know whether you have a significant effect? As we have already suggested, you cannot use a regular, between subjects t-test. That test compares the overall average score of the treatment group with the overall, average score of the no treatment group.

With a matched design, on the other hand, you need a test that will allow you to compare the score of one member of a matched pair with the score of the other member. You can do this by using the dependent groups t-test.[1]

Although you must go through several steps to compute the **dependent groups t-test,** the steps themselves are so simple that this is one of the easiest tests to perform. To learn how to do this simple statistical test, look at the example in Box 9–1.

## Summary of the Matched Pairs Design

In summary, the matched pairs design's weaknesses stem from matching. If matching alerts participants to the purpose of your experiment, matching can cost you the naiveté of your participants. If participants drop out of the experiment between the time they are measured on the matching variable and the time they are to be given the treatment, matching costs you the ability to generalize your results to the participants who dropped out. Furthermore, even if participants do not get suspicious and do not drop out, matching still costs you time and energy.

But although matching has its costs, matching offers one big advantage—power without restricting your subject population. Matching makes the matched pairs design very powerful, while random assignment makes the matched pairs design internally valid. Because of its power and internal validity, this design is hard to beat when you can only study a few participants.

## PURE WITHIN-SUBJECTS DESIGNS

The **within-subjects design** (also called the **repeated measures design**) is very similar to the matched pairs design. In fact, if you conduct both kinds of experiments, you will end up doing very similar things for the same reasons. Although the logic behind both designs is very similar, the two designs' similarities are most apparent when you look at the "nuts and bolts" of carrying out the two kinds of experiments.

## Procedure

The procedural differences between the two-condition, within-subjects experiment and matched pairs experiment stem from a single difference: In the within-subjects experiment, you get a pair of scores from a single participant, whereas in the matched pairs design, you get a pair of scores from a matched pair of participants. The matched pairs researcher randomly determines, for

---

[1] We are assuming that you have ratio or interval scale data. If you only have ordinal data, you should use the sign test.

# Box 9-1
## Calculating a Dependent Groups (Within-Subjects) t-Test in Seven Easy Steps

**STEP 1**—For each matched pair (in the matched pairs design) or for each participant (in the two-condition, within-subjects design), subtract the Condition 1 score from the Condition 2 score.

| Pair or Participant | Condition 1 Score | Condition 2 Score | Difference |
|---|---|---|---|
| 1 | 3 | 2 | 1 |
| 2 | 4 | 3 | 1 |
| 3 | 5 | 4 | 1 |
| 4 | 2 | 1 | 1 |
| 5 | 3 | 2 | 1 |
| 6 | 5 | 2 | 3 |
| 7 | 5 | 2 | 3 |
| 8 | 4 | 3 | 1 |
| 9 | 3 | 4 | −1 |
| 10 | 5 | 6 | −1 |

**STEP 2:** Sum up the differences between each pair of scores, then divide by the number of pairs of scores to get the average difference.

| Pair or Participant | Condition 1 Score | Condition 2 Score | Difference |
|---|---|---|---|
| 1 | 3 | 2 | 1 |
| 2 | 4 | 3 | 1 |
| 3 | 5 | 4 | 1 |
| 4 | 2 | 1 | 1 |
| 5 | 3 | 2 | 1 |
| 6 | 5 | 2 | 3 |
| 7 | 5 | 2 | 3 |
| 8 | 4 | 3 | 1 |
| 9 | 3 | 4 | −1 |
| 10 | 5 | 6 | −1 |

SUM OF DIFFERENCES = **10**
AVERAGE DIFFERENCE = **10**/10 = 1

**STEP 3:** Calculate the variance for the differences by subtracting each difference from the average difference. Square each of those differences, sum them up, and divide by one less than the number of pairs of scores.

| Pair or Participant | Average Difference (AD) | Observed Difference (D) | AD-D | AD-D Squared |
|---|---|---|---|---|
| 1 | 1 | 1 | 0 | 0 |
| 2 | 1 | 1 | 0 | 0 |
| 3 | 1 | 1 | 0 | 0 |
| 4 | 1 | 1 | 0 | 0 |
| 5 | 1 | 1 | 0 | 0 |
| 6 | 1 | 3 | −2 | 4 |
| 7 | 1 | 3 | −2 | 4 |
| 8 | 1 | 1 | 0 | 0 |
| 9 | 1 | −1 | 2 | 4 |
| 10 | 1 | −1 | 2 | 4 |

TOTAL SUM OF SQUARES = 16
VARIANCE OF DIFFERENCES = 16/9 = 1.77

**STEP 4:** Take the square root of the variance of the differences to get the standard deviation of the differences.

Standard deviation of the differences =
$$\sqrt{1.77} = 1.33$$

**STEP 5:** Get the standard *error* of the difference by dividing the standard deviation of the differences by the square root of the number of pairs of scores

$$\frac{1.33}{\sqrt{10}} = .42$$

*continued*

*continued from previous page*

**STEP 6:** Set up the t-ratio by dividing the average difference by the standard error of the difference.

$$t = \frac{1}{.42} = 2.38$$

**STEP 7:** Calculate the degrees of freedom by subtracting 1 from the number of pairs of scores. In this example, since we have 10 pairs of scores, we have 9 degrees of freedom. Then, compare your obtained t-value to the t-value needed to be statistically significant. That value is listed in Appendix E. In this case, the t-value needed to be significant at the .05 level with 9 degrees of freedom is 2.262. Since our value (2.380) is higher than that, our results are statistically significant at the .05 level.

each *pair,* who will get what treatment. In some pairs, the first member will get treatment "A"; in other pairs, the first member will get treatment "B."

The within-subjects researcher randomly determines, for each *individual,* the order in which participants will get each treatment. For some individuals, the first treatment will be treatment "A"; for other individuals, the first treatment will be treatment "B." Whereas the matched pairs experimenter randomly assigns members of pairs to different treatments, the within-subjects experimenter randomly assigns individual participants to different sequences of treatments. For example, Hilton and Fein (1989) had participants read information about college students. After reading the information, participants were to rate the assertiveness of each of these students on a 9-point scale ranging from very passive to very assertive. For 8 of the students, participants were given clearly irrelevant information ("Bob found 20 cents in a pay phone in the student union when he went to make a phone call"). For 8 of the students, the information was "pseudorelevant" (Bill has a 3.2 GPA and is thinking about majoring in psychology). The order of presenting the information was randomized. Hilton and Fein (1989) found that participants judged the students about which there was "pseudorelevant" information as more assertive than those about which there was "clearly irrelevant" information. Consequently, Hilton and Fein (1989) concluded that even irrelevant information may affect our judgments about people.

## Considerations in Using Within-Subjects Designs

Now that you have a general idea of how to conduct a within-subjects (repeated measures) experiment, you are in a position to decide whether you should conduct one. As you intuitively realize, a main advantage of within-subjects designs is their power. By comparing each participant with him or herself, even subtle treatment effects may be statistically significant. However, as

**TABLE 9–2**

**Advantages and Disadvantages of Matching**

| ADVANTAGES | DISADVANTAGES |
|---|---|
| More power because matching reduces the effects of differences between participants. | Matching makes more work for the researcher. |
| | Matching may alert participants to the experimental hypothesis. |
| Power is not bought at the cost of restricting the subject population. Thus, results may, in some cases, be generalized to a wide variety of participants. | Results cannot be generalized to participants who drop out after the matching task. |
| | The results may not apply to individuals who have not been exposed to the matching task prior to getting the treatment. |

**TABLE 9–3**

**Comparing Three Designs**

| | BETWEEN SUBJECTS | MATCHED PAIRS DESIGN | WITHIN-SUBJECTS |
|---|---|---|---|
| Role of random assignment | Randomly assign participants to treatment condition. | Randomly assign members of each pair to condition. | Randomly assign to sequence of treatment conditions. |
| Approach to dealing with the problem that differences between participants may cause differences between the treatment and no treatment conditions. | Allow random assignment and statistics to account for any differences between conditions that could be due to individual differences. | Use matching to reduce the extent to which differences between conditions could be due to individual differences. Then, use random assignment and statistics to deal with the effects of individual differences that were not eliminated by matching. | Avoid the problem of individual differences causing differences between conditions by comparing each participant's performance in one condition with his or her performance in the other condition(s). |

you may also intuitively realize, there are problems with comparing participants with themselves. Because participants change from day to day, from hour to hour, and even from minute to minute, a change in a participant may not be due to the treatment. Indeed, as we shall see, how a participant behaves after being exposed to a treatment sometimes depends on *when* the participant receives the treatment. That is, the sequence in which events unfold is very important. For example, the lecture that might have been scintillating had it been the first lecture you heard that day may only be tolerable if it is your fourth class of the day. Because order affects responses, if a participant reacts differently to the first treatment than to the last, we have a dilemma: Do we have an order effect or a treatment effect?

## POWER

Despite the problems with order effects, the within-subjects design is often used. Perhaps the major reason for the within-subjects design's popularity is power. The within-subjects design increases power in two ways.

The first way is similar to how the matched pairs design increases power—by reducing random error. As you may recall, the matched pairs experimenter tries to reduce random error by reducing individual differences. Therefore, the matched pairs experimenter compares similar participants with one another. Within-subjects experimenters are even more ambitious: They want to *eliminate* random error due to individual differences. Therefore, they do not compare one participant with another participant; instead, they compare each participant's score under one condition with that same participant's score under another condition. For example, Hilton and Fein did *not* compare how one group of participants rated students about which there is "pseudorelevant" information with how another group of participants rated students about which there is "clearly irrelevant" information. Hilton and Fein (1989) did not want to risk the possibility that individual differences in how participants rate (some people tend to give high ratings, whereas others give low ratings) might have hidden the effect. Therefore, Hilton and Fein (1989) compared each participant's ratings of the students described by "pseudorelevant" information with that same participant's ratings of students described by "clearly irrelevant" information.

The second way the within-subjects design increases power is by increasing the number of observations. As you know, the more observations you have, the more random error will tend to balance out, and the more power you will have. With the designs we have discussed up to now, the only way to get more observations was to get more participants (because with those designs, you can only get one score per participant). But in a within-subjects experiment, you get at least two scores out of each participant. In the simplest case, your participants serve double duty by being in both the control and experimental conditions. In more complex within-subjects experiments, your participants might do triple, quadruple, or even octuple duty. Thus, Hilton and Fein (1989) also increased their power by getting at least two scores from each research participant—an average rating of students described by "pseudorelevant" information and an average rating of students described by "clearly irrelevant" information.

## THE ORDER PROBLEM

Although getting more observations per participant improves power, this tactic has drawbacks. To get a general sense of these drawbacks, imagine being a participant in a within-subjects experiment where you take a drug, play a video game, take a second drug, and play the video game again.

If you perform differently on the video game the second time around, can the experimenter say that the second drug has a different effect than the first drug? No, because the conditions did not differ simply in that in one case, you took drug 1 and in the other case, you took drug 2 (see Table 9-4, page 302). In the first case, before you played the game, you took drug 1. However, in the second case, before you played the game, you (1) took drug 1, (2) played the video game, and then (3) took drug 2. Put another way, the only treatment you got before you played the video game the first time was drug 1. But before you played the video game the second time, you were exposed to three "treatments": the first drug, playing the video game, and the second drug.

In the next few sections, you will see how being exposed to "treatments" other than the second drug can hurt the study's internal validity. That is, you will see that getting the second drug is not the only reason your video game performance may be different than it was when you got the first drug. We will start by looking at an obvious reason why you may perform differently on the task after the second treatment—you are performing the task for the second time. Clearly, the second time you play the game you may score differently than you did the first time. Next, we will look at another reason you may score differently after the second treatment—you could be experiencing some lingering effects of the first drug. Then, we will look at a final reason you may score differently after getting the second treatment—learning the experimental hypothesis. Thus, by the end of the next few sections, you will understand how the **order** in which you get a treatment may affect the results. Specifically, you will know why treatment "A" may *appear* to have one kind of effect when it comes first, but may *appear* to have a different kind of effect when it comes second.

***Practice and Fatigue Effects.***     If you perform better after the second treatment than you did after the first treatment, your improvement may simply reflect the effects of **practice** on the video game. Participants often perform better as they warm up to the experimental environment and get used to the experimental task.

Even if your performance is not affected by practice, it may be affected by **fatigue.**[2] You may do worse on later trials merely because you are getting tired or less enthusiastic as the experiment goes on. Unfortunately, a researcher might interpret your fatigue as a treatment effect.

***Treatment Carryover Effects.***     Practice and fatigue effects have nothing to do with any of the treatments participants receive. Often, these effects are simply due to getting more exposure to the dependent measure task. Thus, in the video game example, performance may improve as you learn the game or worsen as you get bored with the game. However, exposure to the dependent measure is not the only thing that can affect performance in later trials. The

---

[2] Fatigue effect could be viewed as cases in which performance is hurt by practice whereas practice effects could be viewed as cases in which performance is improved by practice.

**TABLE 9–4**

**In a Within-Subjects Design, the Treatment May Not Be the Only Factor Being Manipulated**

| | Events That Occur Before Being Tested | |
|---|---|---|
| | Drug 1 Condition | Drug 2 Condition |
| Between Subjects Experiment | Get Drug 1 | Get Drug 2 |
| Within-Subjects Design | Get Drug 1 | Get Drug 1 |
| | | Play Video Game |
| | | Get Drug 2 |

effects of a treatment received before the first trial may affect responses in later trials. The effects of an earlier treatment on responses in later trials are called **treatment carryover effects.** To illustrate treatment carryover effects, suppose that on trial 1, the researcher gave you marijuana. Then, the researcher measured your video game performance. On trial 2, the researcher gave you alcohol and measured your video game performance. On trial 3, the researcher gave you a placebo and measured your video game performance. If your performance was worst in the placebo (no drug) condition, the researcher might think that your better performance on earlier trials was due to the drugs improving your performance. However, the researcher could be wrong. Your poor performance in the placebo condition may be due to carryover effects from the previous treatments. That is, during the placebo trial, you may just be starting to feel certain effects of the drugs that you consumed during the earlier trials. Indeed, depending on the time between the trials, you may be feeling either "high" or hungover.

*Sensitization.*    In addition to practice, fatigue, and treatment carryover effects, a fourth factor that might cause you to perform differently after the second treatment is **sensitization.** Sensitization occurs if, after getting several different treatments and performing the dependent variable task several times, participants realize (become sensitive to) what the independent and dependent variables are. Consequently, during the later parts of the experiment, you might guess the experimental hypothesis and play along with it. For example, by the third trial of the video game experiment, you should realize that the experiment had something to do with the effects of drugs on video game performance.

Note that sensitization has two effects. First, it threatens construct validity because participants figure out what the hypothesis is. Second, it threatens internal validity because it makes participants behave differently during the last trial than they did during the first trial.

# Dealing with the Order Problem

You have seen that because of fatigue, practice, carryover, and sensitization, the sequence in which participants get the treatments could affect the results. For example, suppose participants all received the sequence: Treatment A first, Treatment B second, and Treatment C last. Even if none of the treatments had an effect, the effect of order (first vs. second vs. last) might make it look like the treatments had different effects. Practice effects might cause a participant to do better on the last trial, even though none of the treatments had an effect. Alternatively, fatigue effects might cause a participant to do worst on the last treatment condition, even though none of the treatments had an effect. If carryover occurs, a participant could *appear* to be affected by one treatment when, in reality, the participant is being affected by a previous treatment.

Finally, you have seen how sensitization could cause an **order effect.** The participant is most naive about the experimental hypothesis when receiving the first treatment, least naive when receiving the last treatment. Thus, the ability of the participant to play along with the hypothesis increases as the study goes on. Changes in the ability to play along with the hypothesis may create order effects that could masquerade as treatment effects.

## MINIMIZING EACH INDIVIDUAL THREAT

You have seen that order effects threaten the internal validity of a within-subjects design and you have seen that there are four sources of order effects. Thus, there are four threats to the internal validity of a within-subjects design: practice, fatigue, carryover, and sensitization. Fortunately, there are steps you can take to minimize these threats.

To minimize the effects of practice, you can give participants extensive practice before the experiment begins. For example, if you are studying maze running and you have the rats run the maze 100 times before you start administering treatments, they've probably learned as much from practice as they can. Therefore, it's unlikely that the rats will benefit greatly from the limited practice they get during the experiment.

You can reduce fatigue effects by making the experiment interesting. In addition, try to make the experiment brief and not too taxing.

You can reduce carryover effects by lengthening the time between treatments. Allowing adequate time between treatments makes it more likely that the effect of earlier treatments will completely wear off before the participant receives the next treatment. Thus, there will be no treatment carryover. For instance, if you were looking at the effects of drugs on how well rats run a maze, you might space your treatments a week apart (for example, marijuana, wait a week, alcohol, wait a week, placebo).

You can reduce sensitization by preventing participants from noticing that you are varying anything (Greenwald, 1974). For example, suppose you were studying the effects of different levels of full-spectrum light on typing performance. There are three ways you could reduce sensitization problems. First, you could use very similar levels of the treatment in all your conditions. By using slightly different amounts of full-spectrum light, participants may not realize that you are actually varying amount of light. Second, you could change the level of the treatment so gradually that participants do not notice. Thus, while participants are between trials (in this case, while participants are handing in their typing sample from the previous trial), you could change the lighting level watt by watt until it reaches the desired level. Third, you might be able to reduce sensitization effects by using good placebo treatments. That is, rather than using darkness as the control condition, you use light from a normal bulb as the control condition.

You can also reduce order effects by reducing the number of experimental conditions—the fewer conditions, the fewer opportunities for practice, fatigue, carryover, or sensitization. To illustrate this fact, compare a within-subjects experiment that has 11 conditions with one that has only two conditions. In the 11-condition experiment, participants have 10 opportunities to practice on the dependent measure task before they get the last treatment; in the two-condition experiment, participants only have one opportunity for practice. The 11-condition participants have 11 conditions to tire them out; two-condition participants only have two. In the 11-condition experiment, there are 10 treatments that could carry over to the last trial; in the two-condition experiment there is only one. Finally, in the 11-condition experiment, participants have 11 chances to figure out the hypothesis; in the two-condition experiment, they only have two chances (see Table 9–5).

## RANDOMIZATION

Although you can take steps to reduce the impact of order, you can never be sure that you have eliminated its impact. Therefore, if a participant scores differently after receiving the second treatment than he did after receiving the first treatment, you will never know whether this difference is a treatment effect or an order (trials) effect.

Similarly, if you gave each participant the treatments in the sequence Treatment A first and Treatment B second, a difference between conditions could be due to order (trials) effects rather than to a treatment effect. Therefore, you should not give each participant the treatments in the same sequence. Instead, some participants should get the treatment sequence: Treatment A first, Treatment B second; whereas others should get the treatment sequence: Treatment B first and then Treatment A. You can do this by randomly determining, for each participant, which treatment they get first, which treatment they get second, and so on. Randomization should ensure that participants get the treatments in different sequences.

Unfortunately, randomization does not always balance out the effects of order. Thus, if you randomly assign each of 24 participants to a different

**TABLE 9–5**
**Order Effects and How to Minimize Their Impact**

| EFFECT | EXAMPLE | WAYS TO REDUCE IMPACT |
|---|---|---|
| Practice Effects | Getting better on the task due to being more familiar with the task or the research situation. | Give extensive practice and warm-up prior to introducing treatment. |
| Fatigue Effects | Getting tired as the study wears on. | Keep study brief, interesting. Use few levels of treatment. |
| Carryover Effects | Effects of one treatment lasting long enough to affect responses on other trials. | Allow sufficient time between treatments for treatment effect to wear off. |
| Sensitization | As a result of getting many different levels of the independent variable, the participant—during the latter part of the study—becomes acutely aware of what the treatment is and what the hypothesis is. | Use subtly different levels of treatment. Gradually change treatment levels. Use few treatment levels. |

sequence, you probably will not find that exactly 12 participants got treatment A first and that exactly 12 participants got treatment B first. For example, you may find that 16 of the 24 got treatment A first.

## Analysis of Data

Fortunately, you know that there is one reason why you may not end up with half of your participants getting the sequence A then B—random error. This is fortunate because you can use statistics to account for this random error—as well as for random error due to participants randomly doing better on one trial than on another.

What statistical test would you use to determine whether the difference between your conditions was due to more than random error? To analyze data from the two-condition within-subjects design, you can use the same dependent groups t-test (see Box 9–1) that you used to analyze matched pairs designs.[3] The only difference is that instead of comparing one member of a pair against the other, you compare each participant with him or herself. Specifically, instead of comparing, for each pair, the member who got one treatment with the member who got the other treatment, you compare, for each participant, the participant when he or she got one treatment with the same participant when he or she got the other treatment.

---

[3] For more complex within-subjects designs, you would use within-subjects analysis of variance (ANOVA) or multivariate analysis of variance (MANOVA).

## Summary of Pure Within-Subjects Designs

As you might expect from two designs that can be analyzed with the same technique, the within-subjects design and the matched pairs design are very similar. In terms of procedures, the only real difference is that the matched pairs experimenter randomly assigns members of pairs to treatments, whereas the within-subjects experimenter randomly assigns individual participants to sequences of treatments.

The two designs share some common strengths. Both designs have impressive power because they reduce the effects of differences between participants. Because of the power of these two designs, both should be seriously considered if participants are scarce.

The within-subjects design, however, has some unique strengths and weaknesses. These strengths and weaknesses stem from the fact that the within-subjects design collects more than one observation per participant (see Table 9–6). Because it uses individual participants (rather than matched pairs) as their own controls, the within-subjects design is the more powerful of the two designs. Because it uses participants as their own controls, the within-subjects design is also more useful if you want to generalize your results to real-life situations in which individuals get more than one "treatment." Thus, if you were studying persuasion, you might use a within-subjects design because a person is likely to be exposed to many types of persuasive messages (Greenwald, 1976).

Although there are benefits to collecting more than one observation per participant, there is one big drawback: You have to contend with order effects. To deal with order effects, you can try to minimize the effects of practice, fatigue, carryover, and sensitization. In addition, you can hope that randomization will make it so that each condition comes first about the same number of times as it comes last. That is, you hope that randomization will balance out the sequence of your treatments so that half your participants get one sequence (treatment A first, treatment B second) and half get the other sequence (treatment B first, treatment A second).

## COUNTERBALANCED WITHIN-SUBJECTS DESIGNS

Instead of hoping that chance might balance out the sequence of your treatments, why not make sure? That is, why not use a **counterbalanced design?** In a counterbalanced design, like the within-subjects design, each participant gets more than one treatment. However, unlike the within-subjects design, participants are randomly assigned to systematically varying sequences of conditions in a way that ensures that *routine* order effects are balanced out. Thus, if you were studying two levels of a factor, the counterbalanced design would ensure that half your participants got treatment A first and that half got treatment B first. Now that you understand the main objective of counterbalancing, let's look at an example to see how counterbalancing achieves this goal.

**TABLE 9–6**

**Comparing the Matched Pairs Design with the Within-Subjects Design**

| MATCHED PAIRS DESIGN | WITHIN-SUBJECTS DESIGN |
| --- | --- |
| Powerful. | More powerful. |
| Order effects are *not* a problem. | Order effects are a serious problem. |
| Uses random assignment to balance out differences between participants. | Uses randomization to balance out order effects. |
| Useful for assessing variables that vary between subjects in real life. | Useful for assessing variables that vary within-subjects in real life. |

## Procedure

If you were to use a counterbalanced design to study a two-level factor, you would randomly assign half your participants to receive treatment A first and treatment B second, while the other half would receive treatment B first and treatment A second. By randomly assigning your participants to these counterbalanced sequences, most order effects will be neutralized. For example, if participants tend to do better on the second trial, this will *not* help treatment A more than treatment B because both occur in the second position equally often.

## Advantages and Disadvantages of Counterbalancing

By using a counterbalanced design, you have not merely balanced out routine order effects. You have also added another factor to your design—the between subjects factor of counterbalancing. Adding this counterbalancing factor has two disadvantages and several advantages.

A minor disadvantage is that your statistical analysis is now more complex. Rather than using the dependent t-test, you now have to use a mixed analysis of variance. This would be a major disadvantage if you had to compute statistics by hand. However, since computers can do these analyses for you, this disadvantage really is minor.

The major disadvantage of adding the two-level between subjects factor of counterbalancing is that you now need more participants than you did when you were planning to use a pure within-subjects design. You need two groups of participants to determine if the two-level between subjects factor of counterbalanced sequence has an effect; you only needed one group when you were using a pure within-subjects design. In effect, by going from a within-subjects design to a counterbalanced design, you are going from having zero levels of a between subjects factor to having two levels of a between subjects factor. As you may recall from our discussion of multiple group experiments (Chapter 7), the more levels of a between subjects factor you have, the more participants you need.

The disadvantage of needing more participants is sometimes offset by being able to discover more effects. With the two-condition experiment, you only obtain a single main effect (the treatment main effect). Thus, you can only find out whether the treatment had an effect. By adding the two-level factor of counterbalancing, you converted the two-condition experiment into a 2 (the within-subjects factor of treatment) × 2 (the between subjects factor of counterbalancing sequence) experiment.

This 2 × 2 experiment gives you more information than the simple two-condition experiment. Specifically, rather than only looking for a single main effect (the within-subjects factor of treatment), you can look for three effects: two main effects and an interaction (see Table 9-7). As a result, you find out three things.

First, by looking at the treatment main effect, you find out whether the treatment had an effect. Thus, in the experiment described in Table 9-7, you can find out whether forming images of words is a more effective memory strategy than making sentences out of the words.

Second, by looking at the counterbalancing main effect, you find out whether participants getting the treatments in one sequence did better than the participants getting the other sequence. In the experiment described in Table 9-7, the question is "Did Group 1 (who formed images first and then formed sentences) recall more words than Group 2 (who formed sentences first and then formed images)?"

Third, by looking at the treatment × counterbalancing interaction, you find out whether participants score higher on the first trial or on the second. That is, looking at the treatment × counterbalancing interaction allows you to detect what some people call a "trials effect" and what others call an "order effect."

But how can looking at an interaction tell you that participants score differently on the first trial than the second? After all, significant interactions usually indicate exceptions to general rules rather than indicating a general rule such as, "participants do better on the first trial." To understand why the treatment by counterbalancing interaction tells us about the effects of order, let's take a closer look at what such an interaction would mean. It would mean that participants who get the treatments in one counterbalanced sequence score higher after getting one treatment, but that participants who get the treatments in the other counterbalanced sequence score higher after getting the other treatment. For example, it may be that participants who get treatment A first score highest after receiving treatment A, but participants who get treatment B first score highest after receiving treatment B. As you can see, the cause of this interaction is an order effect: Participants score highest on the first trial.

To get a clearer idea of what the treatment by counterbalancing interaction reveals, let's look at data from the memory experiment we discussed earlier. In that experiment, participants learned lists of words using two different rehearsal strategies. In one condition, they made a sentence out of the list; in the other, they formed mental images. Participants were randomly assigned to one of two different, counterbalanced sequences. Half the participants formed

**TABLE 9–7**

**A 2 × 2 Counterbalanced Design**

The first group gets a list of words, is asked to form images of these words, and is asked to recall these words. Then, they get a second list of words, are asked to form a sentence with these words, and are asked to recall the words.

The second group gets a list of words, is asked to form a sentence with these words, and is asked to recall these words. Then, they get a second list of words, are asked to form images of those words, and are asked to recall those words.

Group 1

| **First Task** | **Second Task** |
|---|---|
| Form Images | Form Sentences |

Group 2

| **First Task** | **Second Task** |
|---|---|
| Form Sentences | Form Images |

Questions this study can address:

1. Do people recall more when asked to form sentences than when asked to form images?

2. Do Group 1 participants recall more words than Group 2 participants? In other words, is one sequence of learning the two different memory strategies better than the other?

3. Do people do better on the first list of words they see than on the second? That is, does practice help or hurt?

---

sentences for the first list, then formed images to recall the second list. The other half formed images to recall the first list, then formed sentences to recall the second list. The means for that study are listed in Table 9–8 and the results of the analysis of variance are summarized in Table 9–9.

By looking at Table 9–9, we see that the main effect for the between subjects factor of counterbalancing sequence is not significant. As Table 9–8 shows, both groups recalled an average of 14 words. Next, we see that the within-subjects factor of memory strategy factor was also not significant. Because participants recalled the same number of words in the imagery condition (7) as they did in the sentence condition (7), we have no evidence that one strategy is superior to the other. Finally, we have a significant interaction of memory strategy and group sequence. By looking at Table 9–8, we see that this interaction is caused by the fact that Group 1 (which gets images first) recalls more words in the imagery condition whereas Group 2 (which gets sentences first) recalls more words in the sentences condition. In other words, participants do better on the first list than on the second.

What does this order effect mean? If the researchers were not careful in their selection of lists, the order effect could merely reflect the first list being

**TABLE 9–8**

**Table of Means for a Counterbalanced Memory Experiment**

|  | Memory Strategy | | |
| --- | --- | --- | --- |
| Group's Sequence | Images | Sentences | Images-Sentences Difference |
| **Group 1** (images lst, sentences 2nd) | <u>8</u> | <u>6</u> | +2 |
| **Group 2** (sentences 1st, images 2nd) | 6 | 8 | −2 |
|  | 14/2 = 7 | 14/2 = 7 | Strategy Main Effect = 0 |

**Counterbalancing Main Effect** = 0

> On the average, participants in both groups remembered a total of 14 words (8 in one condition, 6 in another)

**Strategy Effect** = 0

> Average recalled in image condition was 7 ([<u>8</u> + 6]/2),
>
> Average recalled in sentence condition was 7 ([<u>6</u> + 8]/2).

**Order Effect** = +2

> Participants remember the first list best.
>
> They averaged 8 words on the first list, 6 on the second.
>
> The order (first vs. second) effect is revealed by an *interaction* involving counterbalancing *group* and rehearsal *strategy*.
>
> That is, Group 1 did better in the image condition (**8 to <u>6</u>**), but Group 2 did better in the sentence condition (**8 to 6**).

made up of words that were easier to recall than the second list. However, we would hope that the researcher would counterbalance lists so that across participants, each list occurred equally often under each instructional condition. Therefore, if the experiment were properly conducted, the order effect must reflect either the effects of practice, fatigue, treatment carryover, or sensitization. In this case, it probably reflects the fact that recalling the second list is hurt by the practice participants got on the first list. This negative practice effect is not considered a nuisance by psychologists. On the contrary, this negative practice effect is one of the most important and most widely investigated facts of memory—proactive interference.

Now that you understand the three effects (two main effects and the treatment × counterbalancing interaction) that you can find with a 2 × 2 counterbalanced design, let's look at an experiment where the researcher is interested in all three effects. Suppose that Mary Jones, a politician, produces two

**TABLE 9–9**

**ANOVA Summary Table for a Counterbalanced Design**

Analysis of Variance Table

| SOURCE | SS | df | MS | F | p |
|---|---|---|---|---|---|
| Group Sequence (counterbalancing) | 0 | 1 | 0 | *0* | *n.s.** |
| Error Term for Between Subjects Factor | 44 | 22 | 2 | | |
| Memory Strategy | 0 | 1 | 0 | **0** | *n.s.* |
| Interaction between Memory Strategy and Group Sequence (effect of order— 1st versus 2nd list) | 10 | 1 | 10 | **10** | *p < .01* |
| Within-Subjects Error Term | 23 | 23 | **1.0** | | |

* n.s. is abbreviation for not statistically significant

*Note:* "*p*" values in an ANOVA summary table indicate the probability that the researchers could get differences between their conditions that were this big even if the variables were not related. That is, the "*p*" values tell you the probability that the difference between the groups could occur due to chance alone. Thus, the smaller the *p*-value, the less likely the results are due only to chance—and the more likely that the variables really are related.

commercials: an emotional commercial and a rational commercial. She hires a psychologist to find out which commercial is most effective so she'll know which one to give more airtime. The researcher uses a counterbalanced design to address the question.

By looking at the treatment main effect, the researcher is able to answer the original question: "Which ad is more effective?" By looking at the counterbalancing sequence main effect, the researcher is able to find out whether one sequence of showing the ads is better than another. He is able to answer the question: "Should we show the emotional ad first and then the rational ad or should we show the ads in the opposite sequence?" Finally, by looking at the ad by counterbalancing interaction, the researcher is able to determine whether there is an order effect. He is able to answer the question: "Are participants more favorable toward the candidate after they've seen the second ad?" Obviously, he would expect that voters would rate the candidate higher after seeing the second ad than they did after seeing the first ad.

But what if he does not find an order effect? Then, since there is no obvious benefit of showing both ads, he might suggest that the candidate only show the more effective ad. Or, what if he got an order effect such that people always rated the candidate worse after the second ad? In that event, he would take a

**TABLE 9–10**

**Effects Revealed by a 2 × 2 Counterbalanced Design**

GROUP 1

| FIRST AD | SECOND AD |
|---|---|
| EMOTIONAL AD | RATIONAL AD |

GROUP 2

| FIRST AD | SECOND AD |
|---|---|
| RATIONAL AD | EMOTIONAL AD |

**Questions Addressed by the Design:**

1. Is the rational ad more effective than the emotional ad? (Main effect of the within-subjects factor of type of ad)

2. Is it better to show the emotional ad and then the rational ad or the rational ad and then the emotional ad? (Main effect of the between subjects factor of counterbalancing sequence)

3. Are attitudes more favorable to the candidate after seeing the second ad than after seeing the first? (Ad by counterbalancing interaction)

long, hard look at the ads. It may be that both ads are making people dislike the candidate or it may be that the combination of these two ads does not work. Seeing both ads may reduce liking for the candidate by making her seem inconsistent. For example, one ad may suggest that she is for increased military spending while the other may suggest that she is against increased military spending.

## Conclusions about Counterbalanced Designs

As you can see from this last example, the counterbalanced design does more than balance out routine order effects. It also tells you about the impact of both order and sequence. Thus, you should use counterbalanced designs when you want to make sure that routine order effects are balanced out. In addition, you should also use counterbalanced designs when:

1. You are interested in sequence effects; or
2. You are interested in order effects.

You will often be interested in **sequence effects** because real life is often a sequence of treatments (Greenwald, 1974). That is, most of us are not assigned to receive either praise or criticism, to see either ads for a candidate or against a candidate, to experience only success or failure, pleasure or pain, etc. Instead, we receive both praise and criticism, see ads for and against a candidate, experience success and failure and both pleasure and pain. Counterbalanced designs allow us to understand the effects of different sequences of receiving these "treatments."

You will probably be most interested in sequence effects when you can control the sequence in which a series of events will occur. There are probably many situations in which you may ask yourself, "If I do these tasks in one sequence, will that lead to better outcomes than if I do these tasks in a different sequence?" For instance, would it be better to eat and then exercise—or to exercise and then eat? Would it be better to meditate and then study—or to study and then meditate? Or, if you are going to compliment and criticize a friend, would you be better off to criticize, then praise—or to praise, then criticize? To find out about these sequence effects, you would use a counterbalanced design and then look at the main effect for the between subjects factor of counterbalancing sequence.

Order (trials) effects, on the other hand, will probably interest you if you can control whether a particular event will be first or last in a series of events. Thus, you might be interested in using a counterbalanced design to find out whether it's best to be the first or the last person interviewed for a job. Or, if you want to do well in one particular course (research design, of course), you might like to know whether you'd do better in that particular course if it were the first subject you studied or whether you'd do better if it were the last course for which you studied. To find out about these order effects, you'd use a counterbalanced design and look at the treatment $\times$ counterbalancing interaction.

## CHOOSING DESIGNS

If you want to compare two levels of an independent variable, you have several designs you can use: matched pairs, within-subjects designs, counterbalanced designs, and the simple between subjects design. To help you choose among these designs, we will briefly summarize the ideal situation for using each design.

### Choosing Designs: The Two Conditions Case

The matched groups design is ideal when:

1. you can readily obtain each participant's score on the matching variable without arousing their suspicions about the purpose of the experiment;
2. the matching variable correlates highly with the dependent measure; and
3. participants are scarce.

The pure within-subjects design is ideal when:

1. sensitization, practice, fatigue, or carryover are not problems;

2. you want a powerful design;
3. participants are hard to get; and
4. you want to generalize your results to real-life situations, and in real life, individuals tend to be exposed to both levels of the treatment.

The 2 × 2 counterbalanced design is ideal when:

1. you want to balance out the effects of order or you are interested in learning the nature of any order or sequence effects;
2. you have enough participants to meet the requirement of a counterbalanced design; and
3. you are not concerned that being exposed to both treatment levels will alert participants to the purpose of the experiment.

The simple experiment is ideal when:

1. you think fatigue, practice, sensitization, or carryover could affect the results;
2. you have access to a relatively large number of participants;
3. you want to generalize your results to real-life situations, and in real life, individuals tend to receive either one treatment *or* the other, but not both.

## Choosing Designs: When You Have More than One Independent Variable

Thus far, we have discussed the case where you were studying the effects of a single variable. Often, however, you may want to investigate the effects of two or more variables.

In that case, you would appear to have three choices: a between subjects factorial design, a within-subjects factorial design, and a counterbalanced design. However, counterbalancing becomes less attractive—especially for the beginning researcher—as the design becomes more complicated. Thus, as a general rule, beginning researchers who plan on manipulating two independent variables usually are choosing between a two-factor within-subjects design and a two-factor between subjects design.

You should use a pure within-subjects design if:

1. you can handle the statistics (you will have to use within-subjects analysis of variance or multivariate analysis of variance);
2. sensitization, practice, fatigue, and carryover are not problems;
3. you are concerned about power; and
4. in real-life situations, people are exposed to all your different combinations of treatments.

**TABLE 9–11**
**Ideal Situations for Different Designs**

| SIMPLE EXPERIMENT | MATCHED GROUPS | WITHIN-SUBJECTS | COUNTERBALANCED DESIGN |
|---|---|---|---|
| Participants are plentiful | Participants are very scarce. | Participants are very scarce. | Participants are somewhat scarce. |
| Order effects could be a problem. | Order effects could be a problem. | Order effects are not a problem | Want to assess order effects<br>or<br>order effects can be balanced out. |
| Power isn't vital. | Power is vital. | Power is vital. | Power is vital. |
| In real life, people usually only get one or the other treatment. Rarely get both. | In real life, people usually only get one or the other treatment. Rarely get both. | In real life, people usually get both treatments. Rarely get only one or the other. | In real life, people usually get both treatments. Rarely get only one or the other. |
| Multiple exposure to dependent measure will tip participants off about hypothesis. | Exposure to matching variable will *not* tip participants off about hypothesis. | Multiple exposure to dependent measure will *not* tip participants off about hypothesis. | Multiple exposure to dependent measure will *not* tip participants off about hypothesis. |
| Exposure to different levels of the independent variable will tip participants off about hypothesis. | Exposure to different levels of the independent variable will tip participants off about hypothesis. | Exposure to different levels of the independent variable will *not* tip participants off about hypothesis. | Exposure to different levels of the independent variable will *not* tip participants off about hypothesis. |
|  | Matching variable is easy to collect and correlates highly with the dependent measure. |  |  |

On the other hand, you should use a between subjects design if:

1. you are worried about the statistics of a complex within-subjects design;
2. you are worried that order effects would destroy the internal validity of a within-subjects design;
3. you are not worried about power; and
4. in real-life situations, people are exposed to either one combination of treatments *or* another.

Sometimes, however, you will find it difficult to choose between a completely within-subjects design and a completely between subjects design. For example, consider the following two cases.

Case #1: You are studying the effects of brain lesions and practice on how well rats run mazes. On the one hand, you do not want to use a completely

**TABLE 9–12**

**Ideal Situations for Making a Factor Between or Within**

**Should a Factor Be a Between Subjects Factor or a Within-Subjects Factor?**

| MAKE FACTOR BETWEEN SUBJECTS | MAKE FACTOR WITHIN-SUBJECTS |
|---|---|
| Order effects pose problems. | Order effects are not a problem. |
| Lack of power is *not* a concern. | Lack of power is a serious concern. |
| You want to generalize the results to situations where participants receive either one treatment or another. | You want to generalize the results to situations where participants receive all levels of the treatment. |

within-subjects design because you consider brain damage to occur "between subjects" in real life. On the other hand, you do not want to use a completely between subjects design because you think that practice occurs "within-subjects" in real life.

Case #2: You are studying the effects of subliminal messages and marijuana on creativity. You expect that if subliminal messages have any effect, it will be so small that only a within-subjects design could detect it. However, you feel that oral ingestion of marijuana should not be studied in a within-subjects design because of huge carryover effects.

Fortunately, in these cases, you are not forced to choose between a totally within-subjects factorial and a totally between subjects factorial. As you know from our discussion of counterbalanced designs, you can do a study in which one variable is between and one is within. Such designs are called **mixed designs** and are analyzed using a mixed analysis of variance.

In the two cases we just discussed, the mixed design is an ideal solution. For example, in Case #1, we could make brain lesion a between subjects variable by randomly assigning half the participants to get lesions and half not. That way we do not have to worry about carryover effects. We could make practice a within-subjects variable by having each participant run the maze three times. Consequently, we have the power to detect subtle differences due to practice (see Table 9–13 and Figure 9–1)

Note that in this lesion experiment, the interesting statistical effects might have little to do with the two main effects. That is, we would not be terribly surprised to find a main effect for lesion, telling us that the brain-lesioned rats performed worse. Nor would we be surprised to find a main effect for practice, telling us that participants improve with practice. However, we would be interested in knowing about the practice $\times$ lesion interaction. A significant practice by lesion interaction would tell us that one group of rats was benefiting from practice more than the other. In this case, as you can see from Figure 9–1, it is the non-lesion group that is benefiting most from practice.

Similarly, we could investigate the hypotheses in Case 2 using a mixed design. We would randomly assign participants so that half ingested marijuana

**FIGURE 9–1**

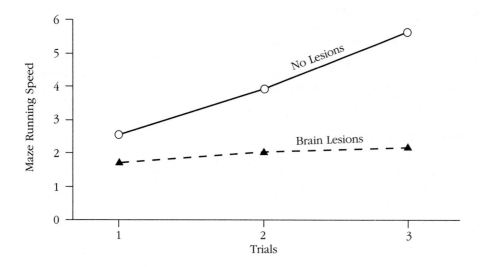

## An Interaction in a Mixed Design

**TABLE 9–13**
**Analysis of Variance Summary Table for a Mixed Design**

| Source of Variance | df | SS | MS | F | p |
|---|---|---|---|---|---|
| Brain Lesion | 1 | 51.0 | *51.0* | *10.0* | .0068 |
| Between Subjects Error | 14 | 72.4 | _5.1_ | | |
| | | | | | |
| Trials | 2 | 26.6 | **13.3** | **11.1** | .0003 |
| Lesions × Trials | 2 | 13.7 | **6.8** | **5.7** | .0083 |
| Within-Subjects Error | 28 | 33.6 | _1.2_ | | |

Note: The mean square error for the within-subjects term is much smaller than the between subjects error term (1.2 to 5.1), giving the design tremendous power for detecting within-subjects effects. This table corresponds to the graph in Figure 9.1.

and half did not. This random assignment would allow us to avoid carryover effects. Then, we would expose all participants to a variety of subliminal messages. Some of these would be designed to encourage creativity, some of these messages would be neutral. By comparing the average overall creativity scores from the marijuana group to that of the no marijuana group, we could assess the effect of marijuana. By comparing participants' scores following the "creative" subliminal messages to their scores following "neutral" subliminal messages, we could detect even rather subtle effects of subliminal messages.

Finally, by looking at the interaction between marijuana and messages, we could determine whether the marijuana group was more influenced by the subliminal messages.

In both Case 1 and in Case 2, the mixed design is the ideal solution for two reasons. First, the mixed design allows you to examine the effects of two independent variables and their interaction. Second, instead of trading off the needs of one variable for the needs of another variable, you are able to give both variables the design they need. Because of its versatility, the mixed design is one of the most popular experimental designs.

## CONCLUDING REMARKS

You are now familiar with most of the basic experimental designs. You know what they are, how to perform them, how to analyze them, and how to choose among them. Therefore, your comfort level while reading research should be improving. In the next chapter, you will further refine your ability to read and interpret research.

## SUMMARY

1. The matched pairs design uses matching to reduce the effects of random differences between participants and uses random assignment and statistics to account for the remaining effects of random error. Because of random assignment, the matched pairs design has internal validity. Because of matching, the matched pairs design has power.

2. Because the matched pairs design gives you power without limiting the kind of participant you can use, you may be able to generalize your results to a broader population than if you had used a simple experiment.

3. The matched pairs design's weaknesses stem from matching: Matching may sensitize participants to your hypothesis and participants may drop out of the study between the time of the matching and the time the experiment is performed.

4. The two-condition, within-subjects design gives you two scores per participant.

5. The within-subjects design increases power by eliminating random error due to individual differences, and by increasing the number of observations that you obtain from each participant.

6. Both the matched pairs design and the two-condition, pure within-subjects design can be analyzed by the dependent groups t-test. Complex within-subjects designs require more complex analyses. Specifically, they should be analyzed by within-subjects analysis of variance (ANOVA) or by multivariate analysis of variance (MANOVA).

7. Because of practice effects, fatigue effects, carryover effects, and sensitization, the order in which a participant gets the treatments may affect the results.

8. To reduce the effects of order, you should randomly determine the sequence in which each participant will get the treatments.

9. In the counterbalanced design, participants are randomly assigned to systematically varying sequences of conditions to ensure that routine order effects are balanced out.

10. Order effects are different from sequence effects.

11. Order effects refer to whether participants respond differently on one trial (e.g., the first) than on some other trial (e.g., the last).

12. Sequence effects refer to whether participants respond differently to getting a series of treatments in one sequence than getting the treatments in a different sequence. For example, participants who get the treatments arranged in the sequence Treatment A, then Treatment B may have higher overall average scores than participants who get the treatments arranged in the sequence Treatment B, then Treatment A.

13. A counterbalanced design allows you to assess both the effect of order (whether participants respond differently on the first trial than on the last) and the effects of receiving different counterbalanced sequences of treatments.

14. Because you must include the between subjects factor of counterbalancing in your analyses, counterbalanced designs require more participants than pure within-subjects designs.

15. In counterbalanced designs, participants will be exposed to several treatments. Consequently, participants may be sensitized to the hypothesis.

16. If you want to compare two levels of an independent variable, you can use matched pairs, within-subjects designs, counterbalanced designs, and simple between subjects designs.

17. Mixed designs have both a within and a between subjects factor. Counterbalanced designs are one form of a mixed design.

18. Mixed designs should be analyzed by using a mixed analysis of variance.

## KEY TERMS

**matched pairs design:** an experimental design in which the participants are paired off by matching them on some variable assumed to be correlated with the dependent variable. Then, for each matched pair, one member is randomly assigned to one treatment condition, whereas the other is assigned to the other treatment condition (or to a control condition). This design usually has more power than a simple between groups experiment. (p. 291)

**dependent groups t-test** (also called **within-subjects t-test**): a statistical test for analyzing matched pairs designs or within-subjects designs that only use two levels of the treatment. (p. 296)

**repeated measures design:** see within-subjects design

**within-subjects design:** an experimental design in which each participant is tested under more than one level of the independent variable. Because each participant is measured more than once (for example, after receiving treatment A, then after receiving treatment B), this design is also called a *repeated measures design.* In a within-subjects (repeated measures) design, a participant may receive treatment A first, treatment B second, and so on. To make sure that not every participant receives treatment A first and treatment B second, within-subjects researchers may randomly determine which treatment comes first, which comes second, etc. In other words, participants all get the same treatments, but they receive different sequences of treatments. (p. 296)

**order:** the position in a sequence (first, second, third, etc.) in which a treatment occurs. (p. 301)

**order effects** (do not confuse with **sequence effects**): a big problem with within-subjects designs. The order in which the participant receives a treatment (first, second, etc.) will affect how participants behave. Order effects may be due to practice effects, fatigue effects, carryover effects, or sensitization. (p. 303)

**practice effects:** after doing the dependent measure task several times, a participant's performance may improve. In a within-subjects design, this improvement might be incorrectly attributed to receiving a treatment. (p. 301)

**fatigue effects:** decreased performance on the dependent measure due to being tired or less enthusiastic as the experiment continues. In a within-subjects design, this decrease in performance might be incorrectly attributed to a treatment. Fatigue effects could be considered negative practice effect. (p. 301)

**carryover effects** (also called **treatment carryover**): the effects of a treatment administered earlier in the experiment persist so long that they are present even while participants are receiving additional treatments. Carryover effects create problems for within-subjects designs because you may believe that the participant's behavior is due to the treatment just administered when, in reality, the behavior is due to the lingering effects of a treatment administered some time ago. (p. 302)

**sensitization:** after getting several different treatments and performing the dependent variable task several times, participants in a within-subjects design may realize (become sensitive to) what the hypothesis is. Consequently, a participant in a within-subjects design may behave very differently during the last trial of the experiment (now that the participant knows what the experiment is about) than the participant did in the early trials (when the participant was naive). (p. 302) counterbalancing: giving participants the treatments in different sequences in an attempt to balance out order effects. (p. 306)

sequence effects (do not confuse with order effects): participants who receive one sequence of treatments score differently than those participants who receive the treatments in a different sequence. (p. 312)

mixed designs: a design that has at least one within-subjects factor and one between subjects factor. Counterbalanced designs are a type of mixed design. (p. 316)

power: the ability to find statistically significant results when variables are related. Within-subjects designs are popular because of their power. (p. 292)

## EXERCISES

1. A researcher uses a simple between subjects experiment involving 10 participants to examine the effects of memory strategy (repetition versus imagery) on memory. Do you think the researcher will find a significant effect? Why or why not? What design would you recommend?

2. If the researcher had used a matched pairs study involving 10 participants, would the study have more power? Why? How many degrees of freedom would the researcher have? What type of matching task would you suggest? Why?

3. An investigator wants to find out whether hearing jokes will allow a person to persevere longer on a frustrating task. The researcher matches participants based on their reaction to a frustrating task. Of the 30 original participants, five quit the study after going through the "frustration pretest." Beyond the ethical problems, what problems are there in using a matched pairs design in this situation?

4. What problems would there be in using a within-subjects design to study the "humor-perseverance" study (discussed in question 3)? Would a counterbalanced design solve these problems? Why or why not?

5. Why are within-subjects designs more powerful than matched pairs designs?

6. Two researchers hypothesize that spatial problems will be solved more quickly when the problems are presented to participants' left visual fields than when stimuli are presented to participants' right visual fields (because messages seen in the left visual field go directly to the right brain, which is often assumed to be better at processing spatial information). Conversely, they believe verbal tasks will be performed more quickly when stimuli are presented to participants' right visual fields than when the tasks are presented to participants' left visual fields. What design would you recommend? Why?

7. A student hypothesizes that alcohol level will affect sense of humor. Specifically, the student has two hypotheses. First, the more people drink, the more they will laugh at slapstick humor. Second, the more people drink, the less they will laugh at other forms of humor. What design would you recommend the student use? Why?

8. In a study using a mixed design, one Mean Square Error is 12, the other Mean Square Error is 4. Which Mean Square Error is probably the Between Subjects error term? Why?

9. You want to determine whether caffeine, a snack, or a brief walk has a more beneficial effect on mood. What design would you use? Why?

# CHAPTER 10

---

# Reading and Evaluating Research

*Overview*

*Reading for Understanding*

CHOOSING AN ARTICLE
READING THE ABSTRACT
READING THE INTRODUCTION
READING THE METHOD SECTION
READING THE RESULTS SECTION
READING THE DISCUSSION

*Developing Research Ideas from Existing Research*

THE DIRECT REPLICATION
THE SYSTEMATIC REPLICATION
THE CONCEPTUAL REPLICATION
THE VALUE OF REPLICATIONS
EXTENDING RESEARCH

*Concluding Remarks*

*Summary*

*Key Terms*

*Exercises*

# Chapter 10

## Reading and Evaluating Research

### Overview

In this chapter, you will learn how to benefit from reading other people's research. You will start by learning how to make sense of a research article. Then, you will learn how to spot flaws and limitations in research. Finally, you will learn how you can get research ideas by reading research. Thus, the aim of this chapter is to make you an intelligent consumer *and* producer of research.

## Reading for Understanding

You wouldn't find a "how to" manual about how to fix a Volkswagen very useful unless you were reading it while you were fixing a Volkswagen. Similarly, you will find this "how to read an article" chapter little more than a review of what you already know, unless you read it while you are reading an article. Therefore, before you go on to the next section, get an article.

### Choosing an Article

But do not get just any article. To repeat, don't just read the first article you come across! Since critically evaluating means *actively* applying what you have learned about research design, get an article that will motivate you to apply what you know about research design. That is, choose an article that uses a design with which you are familiar and that deals with an area that you find interesting.

To start your quest for such an article, you could:

1. Look at sections of texts that you find particularly interesting and look up the articles they reference (for example, you might want to look up a study referenced in this text, such as the study by Wilson and Schooler on when thinking about why we like something hurts our ability to know how much we like it).
2. Consult Appendix B: Library Research.
3. Skim the table of contents of current journals.

Your first clue to whether an article is interesting is its title. Usually, the title identifies the key variables in the study. For example, in articles describing an experiment, the independent variable(s) and the dependent variable may be in the title. In some cases, the title may hint at what the hypothesis was or even what the main findings were.

Once you find an article that has an interesting title, the next step is to read a brief, one-paragraph summary of that article. This one-paragraph summary of the research's purpose, methodology, and results is called the **abstract.**

Even if you don't have the original article, you can read its abstract—provided you have access to either *Psychological Abstracts* or *PsycLit* (see Appendix B). If you have the original article, the only problem in finding the abstract is that it is usually not labeled. To find the abstract, turn to the article's first page. Right under the title, you will see a paragraph that stands apart from the rest of the article. Although unlabeled, this one-paragraph summary of the study is called the abstract.[1]

## Reading the Abstract

By reading the abstract, you should get a general sense of what the researchers' hypotheses were, how they tried to test those hypotheses, and whether the results supported those hypotheses. But most importantly, you will get an idea about whether you want to read the article.

Because reading the abstract can be so informative, you may want to start your literature search by skimming the *Psychological Abstracts*. The *Psychological Abstracts* contains abstracts from a wide variety of journals and can be searched by year of publication, topic of article, or author (see Appendix B for more information on how to use the *Psychological Abstracts*).

## Reading the Introduction

Once you find an article that has an interesting title and abstract, you are ready to start reading the rest of the article. For the beginning student, the best place to start reading an article is at the beginning. Although unlabeled, the beginning of the article is called the **introduction**. The introduction is the most difficult, most time consuming, and the most important part of the article to understand. You must understand the introduction because it is where the authors tell you:

1. How they came up with the hypothesis, including reasons why they think the hypothesis will be supported;
2. Reasons why the hypothesis might not be correct;
3. Why the hypothesis is important; and
4. Why the authors' way of testing the hypothesis is the best way to test the hypothesis (see Figure 10–1).

---

[1] Some older articles do not have an abstract but do contain a summary placed at the end of the article.

**FIGURE 10–1**

## General Flow Chart of an Introduction

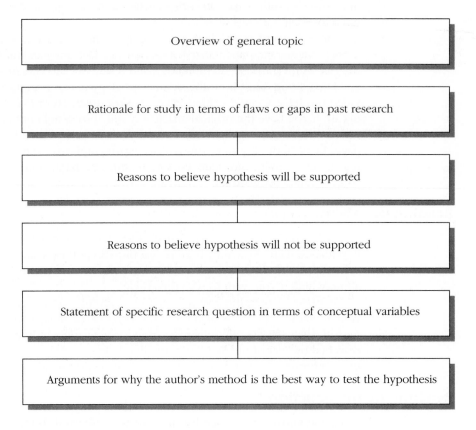

One way of thinking of the introduction is as a commercial for the article. The authors try to sell you on the importance of their research. They may try to sell you on their study by claiming that, relative to previous research ("our competitor's brands"), their methodology is "clearly superior."

Sometimes, they argue that their methodology is superior because their study has better construct validity. For example, they may argue that they use a more valid measure, a more valid manipulation, or a better way of preventing participants and experimenters from biasing the results. Sometimes, they argue that their study has more internal validity because they have used random assignment to make sure that their results are not due to non-treatment factors. Sometimes, they argue that their study has more external validity because they are using random sampling, a broader range of participants, or more naturalistic settings. Sometimes, they argue that their study has more power because they are using a more sensitive design, more reliable measures, or more participants.

If they don't try to sell you on the methodological superiority of their study, they may try to sell you on their study by telling you that, relative to previous hypotheses, their hypothesis is "new and improved." In other words, they will try to say that their study has a special ingredient that other studies don't have. Thus, they will try to get you to say, "It's incredible that people have done all this other, related research, but not tested this hypothesis! Why didn't anyone else think of this?" Generally, they are trying to excite you about a study that extends existing research by:

1. Using a different sample than previous research (women versus men);
2. Looking at a different behavior (gait instead of facial expression, gambling rather than bar-pressing);
3. Looking at a variable that might moderate or alter a previously discovered relationship;
4. Looking at cognitive or physiological variables that may mediate a previously discovered relationship;
5. Testing a competing explanation for a treatment's effect; or
6. Attempting to reconcile the fact that studies have produced apparently conflicting results.

A second way of looking at the introduction is as a preview to the rest of the article. The authors start by giving you a general overview of the research area. Next, the authors give you the rationale for the study. Usually, the rationale is either that the research fills a gap in past research or that it fixes a flaw in past research. Then, the authors explicitly state the research question. Finally, the authors may explain why their method for testing the hypothesis is the best way (see Figure 10-1). For example, they may justify their choice of design, their choice of measures, and their choice of participants. Consequently, if you understand the introduction, you should be able to anticipate what will be said in the rest of the article.

Unfortunately, understanding the introduction is not always easy. The main reason the introduction may be hard for you to understand is that the authors are not writing it with you in mind. Instead, they are writing it to other experts in the field. Their belief that the reader is an expert has two important consequences for how they write up their research. First, because they assume that the reader is an expert in the field, they do not think that they have to give in-depth descriptions of the published articles they discuss. In fact, authors often assume that just by mentioning the authors and the year of work (for instance, Miller & Smudgekins, 1956) will make the reader instantly recall the essentials of that article. Second, because they assume that the reader is an expert, they do not think they have to define the field's concepts and theories.

Since you are not an expert in the field, the authors' failure to describe studies and define concepts may make it difficult to understand what they are trying to say. Fortunately, you can compensate for not having the background the authors think you have by doing two things. First, read the articles to which the authors refer. Second, look up unfamiliar terms or theories in a psychological dictionary, advanced textbook, or other sources listed in Table 10-1.

**TABLE 10–1**
**Deciphering Journal Articles**

Even experts may need to read a journal article several times to understand it fully. One way to help discipline yourself and to show that you are making progress is to photocopy the article. Next, highlight any terms or concepts that you do not understand. That shows you what you don't understand (if you highlight the entire article, maybe you should find another article). Once you identify the terms that you don't understand, decipher those terms by using one of the techniques listed below.

TO DECIPHER HIGHLIGHTED TERMS

Consult an introductory psychology text.

Consult an advanced psychology text.

Consult a psychological dictionary or encyclopedia.

Consult a professor.

Consult general sources such as *Psychological Science, Psychological Bulletin, Annual Review,* and *American Psychologist.*

Consult other articles that were referenced in the article.

To encourage yourself to look up all relevant terms and theories, make a photocopy of your article. On the photocopy, use a yellow Magic Marker to highlight any terms or concepts you do not understand (Brewer, 1990). Then, do some background reading and reread the introduction. This time through the article, highlight any terms or concepts you do not understand with a pink Magic Marker. Do some more background reading to get a better understanding of those terms. Then, reread the introduction using a green Magic Marker to highlight terms you still do not understand.

By the third time you go through the introduction, you should see much less green than yellow, visually demonstrating that you are making progress. However, even if you know all the individual terms, how do you know that you understand the introduction? One test is to try to describe the logic behind the hypothesis in your own words. A more rigorous test is to design a study to test the hypothesis, and then describe the impact of those results for current theory and further research.

To reiterate, do not simply skim the introduction and then move on to the method section. The first time through the introduction, ask yourself two questions:

**1.** What concepts do I need to look up?
**2.** What references do I need to read?

Then, after doing your background reading, reread the introduction. Do not move on to the method section until you can answer these six questions:

**1.** What variables are they interested in?
**2.** What is the hypothesis involving these variables? (What is being studied?)
**3.** Why does the prediction make sense?
**4.** Why is the authors' study a reasonable way to test this hypothesis?

**5.** Does the study correct a weakness in previous research? If so, what was that weakness? Where did others go wrong?

**6.** Does the study fill a gap in previous research? If so, what was that gap? What did others overlook?

## Reading the Method Section

After you are clear about what predictions are being made, why those predictions are being made, and why the study provides a good test of those predictions, read the method section. That is, once you know why the authors did their research, you are ready to find out what they did.

In the **method section,** the authors will tell you what was done in terms of:

**1.** Who the participants were and how they were selected;

**2.** What measures and equipment were used; and

**3.** What the researchers said and did to the participants.

Consequently, the method section is usually subdivided into at least three subsections: participants, apparatus, and procedure. Some method sections will also describe the research design. For example, researchers will often tell you whether the design was a between subjects design, a within-subjects design (often referred to as a *repeated measures* design), or a mixed design.

The method section should be easy to understand for two reasons. First, the only thing the method section is trying to do is to tell you what happened in the experiment—who the participants were, how many participants there were, and how they were treated. Like a good recipe, the method section should give you enough information so that you could repeat the study yourself.

Second, the method section should be easy to understand because the introduction should have foreshadowed how the author planned to test the hypothesis.[2] Therefore, the only trouble you may have in understanding a method section is if you are unfamiliar with some task (for example, a Stroop task) or piece of equipment (such as a tachistoscope) that the researchers used. If you run into unfamiliar apparatus, look up that apparatus in the index of either an advanced text or a laboratory equipment catalog. If that fails, ask your professor. If you run into an unfamiliar measure, find a source that describes the measure in detail. Such a source should be referenced in the original article's bibliography. If it is not, look up the measure in the index of one or more texts. If that fails, look up the concept the measure is claiming to assess in *Psychological Abstracts*. The *Abstracts* should lead you to an article that will describe the measure.

---

[2] We do not mean to say that all method sections are easy to read. We mean that authors *should* be able to write a clear, understandable method section. Unfortunately, authors sometimes do not write coherent method sections. So, if you do not understand a method section, it is probably not your fault. It is the fault of the author and editor. In such cases, we have found that professors are more than happy to help you translate a poorly written method section.

After reading the method section, take a few minutes to think about what it would have been like to be a participant in each of the study's conditions. Then, think about what it would have been like to be the researcher.

Do not go on to the results section until you understand what happened well enough that you could act out the roles of both researcher and participant. More specifically, do not go on to the results section until you can answer the following questions:

1. Who were the participants?
2. How were they obtained?
3. What was done to the participants?
4. What tasks or actions did the participants perform?
5. What was the design?

## Reading the Results Section

Now, turn to the **results section** to find out what happened. At the beginning of the results section (if they did not do so in the method section), the authors will briefly explain how they got the numbers they analyzed. That is, they will describe how they scored participants' responses. Often, these scores are fairly straightforward. For example, researchers may say, "The data were the number of correctly recalled words." Or, they may say, "The number of anagrams solved by each participant was divided by the total number of anagrams used in the study to obtain a percentage solved. These percentages were analyzed in a one-way ANOVA."

Occasionally, computing a score for each participant involves a little more work. For example, in one study, researchers were looking at whether participants believed a person to be normal or pathological (Hilton & von Hippel, 1990). To measure these beliefs, the researchers had participants answer two questions. First, participants answered either "yes" or "no" to a question about whether the person had a pathology. Then, researchers had participants rate, on a 1–9 scale, how confident participants were of their decision. How did the researchers turn these two responses into a single score? To quote the authors,

> In creating this scale, a value of $-1$ was assigned to "no" responses and a value of $+1$ was assigned to "yes" responses. The confidence ratings were then multiplied by these numbers. All ratings were then converted to a positive scale by adding 10 to the product. This transformation led to a scale in which 1 indicates a high degree of confidence that the person is normal and 19 represents a high degree of confidence that the person is pathological.

Do not merely glance at the brief section describing the scores to be used. Before leaving that section, be sure you know what a low score indicates and what a high score indicates. If you do not understand what the numbers being analyzed represent, you will not be able to understand the results of analyses based on those numbers.

After explaining how they got the scores for each participant, the authors may explain how those scores were analyzed. For example, they may say "these data were subjected to a 2 (attractiveness) $\times$ 2 (type of crime) analysis of variance (ANOVA)."

Both the kind and the number of analyses will depend on the study. Depending on the study, the authors will usually report anywhere from one to four kinds of results.

## BASIC DESCRIPTIVE STATISTICS

The first kind of result that may be reported—but often is not—are basic, descriptive statistics. That is, the authors may summarize the sample's scores on one or more measures. Typically, they will describe the average score using the mean (which they will abbreviate as $M$), the range of scores (or the standard deviation, abbreviated $SD$), and the degree to which the scores were normally distributed. For instance, they may report that: "Overall, recall was fairly good ($M = 12.89$, $SD = 2.68$) and recall scores were normally distributed."

Knowing that the data are normally distributed is useful because many statistical tests, such as the t-test and ANOVA, assume that data are normally distributed. If the data are not normally distributed, the researcher may choose not to use those tests. Alternatively, the researcher may perform some mathematical operation on the scores to get a more normal distribution (see Figure 10–2). Occasionally, this transformation is relatively simple. For instance, rather than analyze how much *time* it took participants to scan a word, a researcher may analyze the scanning *speed*. The time to speed transformation involves inverting the time scores. Thus, a scanning time of **1/2** a second per word may become a speed of 2 words per second (**2/1.**)

If a new measure is used, the authors may report evidence of the measure's reliability or internal consistency. For example, if a scale was internally consistent, they might report that the scale had a "coefficient alpha of .91." Similarly, they may report that: "Interobserver reliability computed for overall stopwatch readings was .98" or that "Inter-rater reliability was extremely high ($r = .98$)."

## RESULTS OF THE MANIPULATION CHECKS

The next type of results that may be reported would be in a section that describes the results of the manipulation check. Usually, these results will be statistically significant and unsurprising. For example, if a study manipulates attractiveness of defendant, the researchers might report that: "Participants rated the attractive defendant ($M = 6.2$ on a 1–7 scale) as significantly more attractive than the unattractive defendant ($M = 1.8$), $F(1,44) = 11.56$, $p < .01$." Once they've shown you that they manipulated the factor they said they manipulated, they are ready to discuss the effects of that factor.

FIGURE 10-2

## How Transforming Scores Can Cause Scores to
## Become Normally Distributed

Many statistical tests assume that your data are normally distributed. If the assumption of normality is violated, the conclusions from the statistical test may be misleading. However, your data might not be normally distributed. For example, you might get data like the reaction time scores below.

(a) Before transformation

**Distribution of Time It Took Participants To React**

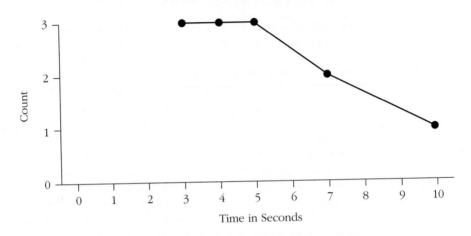

Fortunately, such "non-normally" distributed data can often be transformed into data that are normally distributed. For example, the graph below represents the same data as the graph above. The only difference is that the data above are reaction times, whereas the data below are reaction speeds.

(b) After transformation

**Speed at which Participants Reacted**

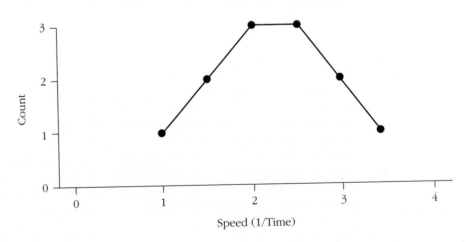

## RESULTS RELATING TO HYPOTHESES

The next findings the authors would discuss are the findings that every author discusses—those that relate to the hypotheses. The authors try to connect the results to the hypotheses so that the reader can easily tell how the hypotheses fared. For example, if a hypothesis was that attractive, defendants would receive lighter sentences than unattractive defendants, the author would report what the data said about this hypothesis: "The hypothesis that attractive defendants would receive lighter sentences was not supported. Attractive defendants received an average sentence of 6.1 years whereas the average sentence for the unattractive defendants was 6.2 years. This difference was not significant, $F(1,32) = 1.00$, *ns*."

## OTHER SIGNIFICANT RESULTS

After reporting results relating to the hypotheses (whether or not the results are statistically significant), authors will dutifully report any other statistically significant results. Even if the results are unwanted and make no sense to the investigator, significant results must be reported. Therefore, you may read things like: "There was an unanticipated interaction between attractiveness and type of crime. Unattractive defendants received heavier sentences for violent crimes whereas attractive defendants received heavier sentences for nonviolent crimes, $F(1,32) = 18.62$, $p < .05$." Or, you may read: "There was also a significant four-way interaction between attractiveness of defendant, age of defendant, sex of defendant, and type of crime. This interaction was uninterpretable." Typically, these results will be presented last: Although the author is obligated to report these unexpected and unwelcomed findings, the author is not obligated to emphasize them.

In conclusion, depending on the statistics involved, reading the results section may be difficult. The first time through the results section, you may not understand everything. However, before moving on to the discussion section, you should be able to answer the following questions:

1. What are the scores they are putting into the analysis?
2. What are the average scores for the different groups? Which types of participants score higher? Lower?
3. Do I understand all the tables and figures that contain descriptive statistics, such as tables of means, percentages, correlations, etc.?
4. Do the results appear to support the authors' hypotheses? Why or why not?
5. What type of statistical analysis did the authors use?

# Reading the Discussion

Finally, read the **discussion.** The discussion should hold few surprises. In fact, before reading the discussion, you could probably write a reasonable outline of it. All you would have to do is to

1. Jot down the main findings;
2. Relate these findings to the introduction; and
3. Speculate about the reasons for any surprising results.

Because many discussion sections follow this three-step formula, the discussion is mostly a reiteration of the highlights of the introduction and results sections—if the authors get the results they expect. If, on the other hand, the results are unexpected, the discussion section is usually an attempt to reconcile the introduction and results sections. Thus, by the time you finish the discussion section, you should be able to answer these five questions:

1. How well do the authors think the results matched their predictions?
2. How do they explain any discrepancies between their results and their predictions?
3. Do the authors admit that their study was flawed or limited in any way? If so, how?
4. What additional studies, if any, do the authors recommend?
5. What are the authors' main conclusions?

## DEVELOPING RESEARCH IDEAS FROM EXISTING RESEARCH

Once you understand the article, you can take advantage of what you have learned in previous chapters to question the article's conclusions. For example, you can question the study's power as well as its internal, external, and construct validity.

As you can see from Box 10-1, there are many questions you can ask of any study. But what good is this questioning? Questioning a study pays off in at least two ways.

First, because you become aware of the study's limitations, you avoid the mistake of believing that something has been proven to be true when it has not. Consequently, you are less likely to act on the basis of misinformation. Acting on the basis of bad information will often be bad for you—as a consumer, you may buy the wrong product; as a citizen, you may support the wrong policies. As you assume more power and responsibility, acting on the basis of misinformation may often harm others. Thus, the executive acting on wrong information may bankrupt the company. Similarly, a therapist using an ineffective or harmful treatment may harm many people.

Second, because you are aware that no single study answers every question, you realize that additional studies should be done. In other words, a common result of asking questions about research is that you end up designing additional studies that will either document, destroy, or build on the previous research. Thus, familiarity with research breeds more research.

## BOX 10–1
## QUESTIONS TO ASK OF A STUDY

### Questions about Construct Validity

1. Was the manipulation valid?
   a. Is the manipulation consistent with definitions of the construct that is allegedly being manipulated?
   b. Did the researchers use a manipulation check to see how participants interpreted the manipulation?
   c. Are more or better control conditions needed? The control condition(s) and the experimental condition(s) should be identical except for those aspects directly related to the construct being manipulated.
2. Was the measure valid?
   a. Was it reliable?
   b. Was it objectively scored?
   c. Did research show that it correlated with other measures of that same construct?
   d. Did research show that it was uncorrelated with measures of unrelated constructs?
   e. Was the measure consistent with accepted definitions of the construct?
3. Could the researchers have biased the study's results?
   a. Were researchers "blind"?
   b. Did the lack of standardization make it easy for researchers to bias the results?
4. Could participants have figured out the hypothesis?
   a. Could participants have learned about the study from former participants?
   b. Were participants experienced enough to figure out the hypothesis (for instance, senior psychology majors who had participated in several studies)?
   c. Was the hypothesis a fairly easy one to figure out?
   d. Was an empty control group used?
   e. Did the researcher fail to make the study a double-blind study?
   f. Were any procedures used that might sensitize participants to the hypothesis (matching on dependent variable, a within-subjects design, etc.)?
   g. Was it obvious to participants what was being measured? (For example, did participants fill out a self-report scale?)
   h. Did the study lack *research realism:* the ability to psychologically involve participants in the task so that they would not merely be playing the role of cooperative participant?
   i. Did the researchers fail to have an effective "cover story" that disguised the true purpose of the study?

### Questions about External Validity

1. Would results apply to the average person?
   a. Were participants human?
   b. Are participants distinct in any way?
   c. Are the participants too homogeneous? That is, were there certain types of individuals (women,

*continued*

*continued from previous page*

minorities) who were not included in the study?

  **d.** Was the drop-out rate high—or high among certain groups (for example, the elderly)? If so, the results only apply to those who would stay in the study.

  **e.** Is there any specific reason to suspect that the results would not apply to a different group of participants?

2. Would the results generalize to different settings? Can you pinpoint a difference between the research setting and a real-life setting *and* give a specific reason why this difference would prevent the results from applying to real life?

3. Would the results generalize to different levels of the treatment variable?

  **a.** What levels of the treatment variable were included?

  **b.** What levels of the treatment variable were not used?

  **c.** How many levels of the treatment variable were used?

### Questions about Internal Validity

1. Was an experimental design used?

  **a.** Was the treatment manipulated? (Otherwise, the alleged effect may have occurred before the alleged cause.)

  **b.** Was the influence of non-treatment factors dealt with in at least one of the following three ways:

   **1.** those factors were kept constant;

   **2.** randomization was used to allow the researcher to statistically account for those variables;

   **3.** counterbalancing was used to balance out the effects of those variables?

2. If an experimental design was used, there should not be any problems with the study's internal validity unless:

  **a.** Independence was not established or maintained.

  **b.** More participants dropped out of the treatment group than the control group.

  **c.** A within-subjects design was used, even though order effects posed a serious threat.

3. If an experimental design was not used, the study probably does not have internal validity.

### Questions about Power

1. If null results were obtained, ask:

  **a.** Were measures sensitive enough?

  **b.** Was the study sufficiently standardized? That is, did lack of standardization and lack of control over the testing environment create so much error variance that the treatment effect was overlooked?

  **c.** Were enough participants used?

  **d.** Did conditions differ enough on treatment/predictor variable?

  **e.** Were participants homogeneous enough—or did between subject differences hide the treatment effect?

  **f.** Was the design sensitive enough? For example, perhaps the researchers should have used a within-subjects design instead of a between subjects design.

*continued*

*continued from previous page*

**g.** Could the null results be due to a floor or ceiling effect?

### Questions about Statistical Analyses

1. Do the data meet the assumptions of the statistical test?
   a. If they did an independent groups t-test, did they have independent observations, random assignment, and at least interval scale data?
   b. If they used a matched pairs design and had interval scale data, did they use the dependent groups t-test?
2. Are they running a high risk of making a Type 1 error?
   a. Are they doing multiple statistical tests without correcting for the fact that their reported significance level is only valid if they are doing a single test? For example, if they use a .05 (5%) significance level, but do 100 tests, 5 tests could turn out significant by chance alone.
   b. Are they using fairly liberal significance levels? For example, are they using a .13 or .25 level rather than a .05 level?
3. Were the appropriate follow-up tests done so that the right conditions are being compared?
   a. In a multiple-condition experiment, did they claim that particular groups differed from each other without doing a post hoc test (or planned comparison) to determine which groups were significantly different from each other?
   b. In a multiple-condition experiment, did they claim to know that the relationship between variables was linear, cubic, or quadratic without doing a trend analysis to verify whether that particular linear, cubic, or quadratic trend was statistically significant?
4. Did they accurately interpret the results of their statistical analyses?
   a. Did they fail to realize that an ordinal interaction may merely be the result of a floor or ceiling effect?
   b. Did they represent differences between means as real, even though the results were not statistically significant?

## The Direct Replication

Whenever you read a study, one obvious research idea always comes to mind—repeat the study. That is, do a **direct replication.**

Clearly, one reason to do a direct replication is for educational purposes. Many professors—in chemistry, biology, physics, as well as in psychology—have their students repeat studies to help students develop research skills.

But, from a research standpoint, isn't repeating a study fruitless? Isn't it inevitable that you will get the same results the author reported? Not necessarily—especially if there was an error in the original study. Unfortunately, there are at least three reasons why the relationships reported in the original study may never have existed: fraud, Type 1 errors, and Type 2 errors.

## SUSPICION OF FRAUD

Although fraud is very unusual, it does occur. Researchers may cheat for personal fame or simply because they believe their ideas are right even though their results fail to reach the .05 level of significance.

Since thousands of researchers want to be published and since many are under great pressure to publish, why is cheating so uncommon? Because if other scientists cannot replicate your results, you are in trouble. Thus, the threat of direct replication keeps would-be cheats in line. However, some scientists are beginning to worry that science's fraud detectors are not as effective as they once were because people are not doing replications as often as they once did (Broad & Wade, 1982).

## SUSPICION OF TYPE 1 ERRORS

Although fraud is one reason that some findings in the literature are probably inaccurate (Broad & Wade, 1982), perhaps more common sources of non-replicable findings are Type 1 and Type 2 errors. Partly because of psychologists' concerns about Type 1 and Type 2 errors, some journals solicit and accept studies that replicate—or fail to replicate—previously published research.

To understand how the original study's results may have been significant because of a Type 1 error, imagine that you are a crusty journal editor who only allows simple experiments that are significant at the .05 level to be published in your journal. If you accept an article, the chances are less than 5 in 100 that the article will contain a Type 1 error. Thus, you are appropriately cautious. But what happens once you publish 100 articles? Then, you may have published five articles that have Type 1 errors.

In fact, you may have many more Type 1 errors than that. How? Because people do not send you nonsignificant results. They may have done the same experiment eight different times, but it only came out significant the eighth time. Thus, they only send you the results of the eighth replication. Or, let's say 20 teams of investigators do the same experiment, only the team that gets significant results (the team with the Type 1 error) will submit their study to your journal. For example, while serving as editor for the *Journal of Personality and Social Psychology,* Dr. Anthony Greenwald received an article that found a significant effect for ESP. Since Dr. Greenwald was aware that many other researchers had done ESP experiments that had not obtained significant results, he asked for a replication. The authors could not replicate their results.

## SUSPICION OF TYPE 2 ERRORS

Just as studies that find significant effects may be victimized by Type 1 errors, studies that fail to find significant effects may be victimized by Type 2 errors (see chapter 6 for a discussion of Type 1 and Type 2 errors). Indeed, there are reasons to expect that Type 2 errors may be even more common than Type 1 errors. Realize that, in a typical study, the chance of a Type 1 error is usually about 5%. However, in most studies, the chance of a Type 2 error is much higher. Dr. Cohen, a person who has championed planning studies with adequate power, suggests setting the chance of a Type 2 error at about 20%. However, few researchers conduct studies that come close to having that much power. For example, Cohen (1990) reports that, even in some highly esteemed journals, the studies published are ones that ran more than a 50% chance of making a Type 2 error. Similarly, when reviewing the literature on the link between attributions and depression, Robins (1988) found that only 8 of 87 published analyses had the level of power that Cohen recommends. No wonder some studies found relationships between attributions and depression whereas others did not! Thus, when a study fails to find a significant effect, do not assume that a direct replication would also fail to find a significant effect. The study may bear repeating.

## The Systematic Replication

However, rather than merely repeating the study, you could do a **systematic replication:** a study that varies in some systematic way from the original study. Generally, systematic replications fall into two categories.

First, the systematic replication refines the design or methodology of the previous study. For example, the systematic replication may use more participants, more standardized procedures, or more objective methods of coding behavior than the original research.

Second, the person doing the systematic replication may make different tradeoffs than the original researcher. That is, whereas the original researcher traded construct validity for power, the replicator may trade power for construct validity. Because you can always make different tradeoffs than the original researcher and because most studies can be improved, you can almost always do a useful systematic replication.

In conclusion, there are two basic advantages of doing a systematic replication. First, because the systematic replication is similar to the original study, the systematic replication, like the direct replication, can help verify that the results reported by the original author are not due to a Type 1 error, a Type 2 error, or to fraud. Second, because the systematic replication changes the original study in some way, the systematic replication may have more power, more external validity, or more construct validity than the original.

### IMPROVING POWER BY TIGHTENING-UP THE DESIGN

As we suggested earlier, if a study obtains null results, you may want to repeat the study, but add a few minor refinements to increase power (see Table 10-2). You might improve power by increasing standardization. For example, you might have researchers follow a very detailed script, or have a computer present the stimuli. You might improve power by using more participants than the original study and choosing participants who were more homogeneous than those used in the original study. Alternatively, you might increase power by using a more sensitive measure or by using more extreme levels of the

**TABLE 10–2**

**How to Devise a Systematic Replication That Will Have More Power than the Original Study**

1. Improve standardization of procedures.
2. Use more participants.
3. Use more homogeneous participants.
4. Use more extreme levels of treatment or predictor variables.
5. Use a more sensitive dependent measure.
6. Use a more powerful design (within or matched pairs design) rather than simple between groups design.

treatment variable. Finally, you might replicate the experiment using a more sensitive design. For instance, if the authors used a simple experiment and found no effect for a mnemonic strategy on recall, you might replicate the experiment with a matched pairs design (matching participants on IQ), or with a repeated measures (within-subjects) design.

## IMPROVING EXTERNAL VALIDITY

If the study has adequate power, this power may come at the expense of other valued characteristics (see Table 10–3), such as external validity. Note that many of the things you were doing to improve power reduce the generalizability of the results. If the researcher uses a homogeneous group of participants to increase power, the researcher may decrease the extent to which the results can be generalized to other kinds of participants. What applies to this particular group of participants (for example, white, middle-class, first-year college students) may not apply to other groups of people (for instance, poor, uneducated, elderly).

If a study was done in a laboratory to reduce error variance, you do not know that the results would generalize outside of this artificial environment. If the researcher measured the dependent variable immediately after the participant gets the treatment to maximize your chances of obtaining a significant effect, you do not know whether the treatment's effects will last.

To increase a study's generalizability, there are at least four things you can do (see Table 10–4). To help you visualize these four possibilities, suppose that some students performed a lab experiment at their college to examine the effects of defendant attractiveness. First, you can systematically vary the kinds of participants used. If the study used all male participants, you might use all female participants. Second, you can change a lab experiment into a field experiment. For example, suppose that the defendant study used college students as participants. By moving the defendant study to the field, you might be able to use real jurors as participants rather than college students. Third, you

**TABLE 10–3**
**Tradeoffs Involving Power**

| | STEPS THAT INCREASE POWER |
|---|---|
| POWER versus CONSTRUCT VALIDITY | Using empty control group, not controlling for placebo effects. |
| | Using sensitive measure, despite its vulnerability to self-report biases. |
| | Using a within-subjects design despite serious sensitization problems. |
| | Using a matched pairs design despite the fact that matching alerts participants to the hypothesis. |
| POWER versus EXTERNAL VALIDITY | Using a restricted sample of participants to reduce random error due to subject differences. |
| | Using a simple, controlled environment to reduce random error due to uncontrolled situational variables. |
| | Using a within-subjects design even though—in real life—individuals rarely receive more than one level of the treatment. |
| | Maximizing the number of participants per group by decreasing the number of groups. That is, you may choose to do a simple experiment rather than multi-level or factorial experiment. Consequently, the degree to which the results generalize to various levels of treatment or across different factors is hard to assess. |
| POWER versus INTERNAL VALIDITY | Using a within-subjects design even when carryover, fatigue, and practice effects are likely. |
| | Increasing risk of Type 1 error to increase power. |

can wait a while before collecting the dependent measure to see whether the effect lasts. Fourth, you can use different levels of the independent variable to see whether the effects would generalize to different levels of the independent variable. In the defendant study, researchers may have only compared attractive versus unattractive defendants. Therefore, you might replicate the study to see whether extremely attractive defendants have an advantage over moderately attractive defendants.

## IMPROVING CONSTRUCT VALIDITY

Finally, you might do a systematic replication to improve a study's construct validity. Often, you can make some minor changes that will reduce the threat of hypothesis-guessing (see Table 10–5).

To illustrate, imagine a two-group experiment where one group gets caffeine (in a cola), whereas the other group gets nothing. You might want to

**TABLE 10–4**

**How to Devise a Systematic Replication That Will Have More External Validity than the Original Study**

1. Use more heterogeneous group of participants or use a participant group (for instance, females) that was not represented in the original study.
2. Repeat as a field study.
3. Delay measurement of the dependent variable to see whether treatment effect persists over time.
4. Use more levels of the independent or predictor variable.

**TABLE 10–5**

**How to Devise a Systematic Replication That Will Have More Construct Validity than the Original Study**

1. Replace an empty control group with a placebo treatment group.
2. Use more than two levels of the independent variable.
3. Alter the study so that it is a double-blind study.
4. Add a cover story or improve the existing cover story.
5. Replicate it as a field study.

replace this empty control group with a placebo treatment (a caffeine-free cola). Or, you might keep the empty control group, but add a treatment condition in which participants get a very small amount of caffeine. This will give you three levels of the treatment variable. If both treatment conditions differ from the control group, but do not differ from one another, you might suspect that participant and experimenter expectancies were responsible for the treatment effect. Because of the advantages of using three levels of the treatment variable, you may wish to replicate a $2 \times 2$ study as a $3 \times 2$ or even as a $3 \times 3$.

Besides adding levels of the independent variable, there are three other minor alterations you can do to make it harder for participants to figure out the hypothesis. First, you could replicate the study, making it a double-blind experiment. Second, you could mislead the participants regarding the purposes of the study by giving them a clever cover story. Third, you could do the study in the field: If participants do not know they are in a study, they probably will not guess the hypothesis.

## The Conceptual Replication

Suppose you think there were problems with the original study's construct validity. However, you believe that these problems cannot be solved by making minor procedural changes. Then, you should perform a **conceptual replication:** a study that is based on the original study, but uses different methods to better assess the true relationships between the variables. In a conceptual replication, you might use a different manipulation or a different measure.

Because there is no such thing as a perfect measure or manipulation, virtually every study's construct validity can be questioned. Since the validity of a finding is increased when the same basic result is found using other measures or manipulations, virtually any study can benefit from conceptual replication. Therefore, you should have little trouble finding a study you wish to conceptually replicate.

There are many ways to go about a conceptual replication (see Table 10–6). For example, you could use a different way of manipulating the treatment variable. The more manipulations of a construct that find the same effect, the more confident we can be that the construct actually has that effect. Indeed, you might use two or three manipulations of your treatment variable and use the type of manipulation as a factor in your design. For instance, suppose a study used photos of a particular woman dressed in either a "masculine" or "feminine" manner to manipulate the variable "masculine versus feminine style." You might use the original experiment's photos for one set of conditions, but also add two other conditions that use your own photos. Then, your statistical analysis would tell you whether your manipulation had a different impact than the original study's manipulation.

Of course, you are not limited to using the same type of manipulation as the original study. Thus, instead of manipulating "masculine" versus "feminine" by dress, you might manipulate "masculine" versus "feminine" by voice (masculine versus feminine-sounding voice).

Although varying the treatment variable for variety's sake is worthwhile, changing the manipulation to make it better is even more worthwhile. One way of improving a treatment manipulation is to make it more consistent with the definition of the construct. Thus, in our previous example, you might feel that the original picture manipulated "fashion sense" rather than "masculine/feminine style." Therefore, your manipulation might involve two photos: one photo of a woman who was fashionably dressed in a feminine way, one of a woman who was fashionably dressed in a masculine manner. You might also want a manipulation check to get more evidence as to the validity of the manipulation. Thus, you might ask participants to rate the masculine and feminine photos in terms of attractiveness, fashion sense, and masculinity-femininity.

Because no manipulation is perfect, replicating a study using a different treatment manipulation is valuable. Similarly, because no measure is perfect, replicating a study using a different measure is valuable. Often, you can increase the construct validity of a study by replicating it with a measure that is more behavioral or less obtrusive than the measure used in the original study. Such manipulations may be less vulnerable to demand characteristics and self-report biases.

## The Value of Replications

Replications are important to advancing psychology as a science. Direct replications are essential for guaranteeing that the science of psychology is rooted in solid, documented fact. Systematic replications are essential for making

**TABLE 10–6**

**How to Devise a Conceptual Replication That Will Have More Construct Validity than the Original Study**

1. Use a different manipulation of the treatment variable and add a manipulation check.
2. Use a different dependent measure, one that is:
   a. More behavioral, therefore less vulnerable to demand characteristics, as well as self-report and social desirability biases, and
   b. Less obtrusive and thus less vulnerable to subject biases.

---

psychology a science that applies to all people. Conceptual replications are necessary for psychology to go beyond knowing about the effects of specific operations on specific measures to knowing about broad, universal constructs.

In addition to replicating previous research, systematic and conceptual replications extend previous research. Consider, for a moment, the conceptual replication that uses a better measure of the dependent variable or the systematic replication that shows the finding occurs in real-world settings. Such conceptual and systematic replications can transcend the original research.

## Extending Research

In addition to systematic and conceptual replications, there are two easy ways to extend published research. First, you could both replicate and extend research by repeating the original study while adding a variable that you think might moderate the observed effect. For instance, if you think that being attractive would hurt a defendant if the defendant had already been convicted of another crime, you might add the factor of whether or not the defendant had been previously convicted of a crime. Second, you could extend the research by doing the follow-up studies that the authors suggest in their discussion section. For a more extensive list of ways to extend research, see Table 10–7.

In short, much of the work done by scientists is a reaction to reading other scientists' work. Sometimes, the reaction is excitement: The researcher thinks the authors are on to something special and so the researcher follows up on that work. Sometimes, the reaction is anger: The researcher thinks that the authors are wrong and so the researcher designs a study to prove them wrong. Regardless, the outcome is the same: The publication of an article not only communicates information, but it also creates new questions. As a result of scientists reacting to each others' work, science progresses. Because this exchange is so vital, some professionals skim the reference section before reading an article. If they find that the author has not cited the relevant work in the field, they conclude that they should not waste their time reading the article. Therefore, if you want your research to be meaningful and to be read, critically read the relevant research before conducting your study and thoroughly cite that research when writing it up.

**TABLE 10-7**
**Extending Research**

1. Replicate the research, but add a factor (subject or situational variable) that may moderate the effect. That is, pin down under what situations and for whom the effect is most powerful.

2. Conduct studies suggested by authors in their discussion section.

3. Look for variables that may mediate the relationship. That is, look for cognitive or physiological factors that may be the underlying causes of the effect.

4. Look for related treatments that might have similar effects. For example, if additional time to rehearse is assumed to improve memory by promoting the use of more effective rehearsal strategies, consider other variables that should promote the use of more effective rehearsal strategies, such as training in the use of effective rehearsal strategies.

5. See if the effects last. For example, many persuasion and memory studies only look at short-term effects.

6. Instead of using a measure of a general construct, use a measure that will tap a specific aspect of that construct. This focused measure will allow you to pinpoint exactly what the treatment's effect is. For example, if the original study used a general measure of memory, replicating the study with a measure that could pinpoint what aspect of memory (encoding, storage, or retrieval) was being affected would allow a more precise understanding of what happened.

7. If the study involves basic (non-applied) research, see if the finding can be applied to a practical situation. For example, can a memory effect demonstrated in the lab be used to help students on academic probation?

8. If the study describes a correlational relationship between two variables, do an experiment to determine if one variable causes the other. For example, if you find that teams wearing black are more likely to be penalized, do an experiment to find out if wearing black causes one to be more violent.

9. Do a study to test competing explanation for the study's results. For example, if the researchers argue that people wearing black are more likely to be violent, you might argue that there is an alternative explanation: People wearing black are more likely to be perceived as violent.

## CONCLUDING REMARKS

You not only know how to criticize research, but also how to improve it. Thus, every time you read an article, you should get at least one research idea.

## SUMMARY

1. In the introduction, the authors tell you what the hypothesis is, why it is important, and justify their method of testing it.

2. To understand the introduction, you need to refer to theory and previous research.

3. The method section tells you who the participants were, how many participants there were, and how they were treated.

4. In the results section, authors should report any results relating to their hypotheses and any statistically significant results.

5. The discussion section either reiterates the introduction and results sections or tries to reconcile the introduction and results sections.

6. When you critique the introduction, question whether: testing the hypothesis is vital; the hypothesis follows logically from theory or past research; and the authors have found the best way to test the hypothesis.

7. When you critique the method section, question the construct validity of the measures and manipulations and determine whether participants may have played along with the hypothesis.

8. When you look at the results section, question any null results.

9. In the discussion section, question the authors' interpretation of the results, try to explain results that the authors have failed to explain, find a way to test your hypothesis, and note any weaknesses that the authors concede.

10. The possibility of Type 1 error, Type 2 error, or fraud may justify doing a direct replication.

11. You can do a systematic replication to improve power, external validity, or construct validity.

12. Conceptual replications are mandated when problems with a study's construct validity cannot be ameliorated through minor changes.

13. Replications are vital for the advancement of psychology as a science.

14. Reading research should stimulate research ideas.

## KEY TERMS

*Psychological Abstracts:* a useful resource that contains abstracts from a wide variety of journals. The *Abstracts* can be searched by year of publication, topic of article, or author. (p. 325)

**abstract:** a short, one-page summary of a research proposal or article. The abstract should not be more than 120 words long. It comes before the introduction. (p. 325)

**introduction:** the part of the article that occurs right after the abstract. In the introduction, the authors tell you what their hypothesis is, why their hypothesis makes sense, how their study fits in with previous research, and why their study is worth doing. (p. 325)

**method section:** the part of the article immediately following the introduction. Whereas the introduction explains why the study was done, the method section describes what was done. For example, it will tell you what design was used, what the researchers said to the participants, what measures and equipment were used, how many participants were studied, and how they were selected. The method section could also be viewed as a "how we did it" section. The method section is often subdivided into three subsections: participants, apparatus, and procedure. (p. 329)

**results section:** the part of the article, immediately following the method section, that reports statistical results and relates those results to the hypotheses. From reading this section, you should know whether the results supported the hypothesis. (p. 330)

**discussion:** the part of the article, immediately following the results section, that interprets the results. For example, the discussion section may explain the importance of the findings and suggest research projects that could be done to follow up on the study. (p. 333)

**direct replication:** a later copy of the original study. Direct replications are useful for establishing that the findings of the original study are reliable. (p. 337)

**systematic replication:** a study that varies from the original study only in some minor aspect. For example, a systematic replication may use more participants, more standardized procedures, more levels of the independent variable, or a more realistic setting than the original study. (p. 339)

**conceptual replication:** a study that is based on the original study, but uses different methods to better assess the true relationships between the treatment and dependent variables. In a conceptual replication, you might use a different manipulation or a different measure. The conceptual replication is the most sophisticated kind of replication. (p. 342)

## EXERCISES

1. Find an article to critique. If you are having trouble finding an article, consult Appendix B (Using Library Resources) or use the article in Appendix F. Using Box 10–1, critique the article you selected.
2. What are the major weaknesses of the article?
3. Design a direct replication of the study you critiqued. Do you think your replication would yield the same results as the original? Why or why not?
4. Design a systematic replication based on the study you critiqued. Describe your study. Why is your systematic replication an improvement over the original study?
5. Design a conceptual replication based on the study you critiqued. Describe your study. Why is your conceptual replication an improvement over the original study?

# CHAPTER 11

———

# Single-n Experiments and Quasi-Experiments

*Overview*

*Inferring Causality in Randomized Experiments*

ESTABLISHING COVARIATION
ESTABLISHING TEMPORAL PRECEDENCE
CONTROLLING FOR IRRELEVANT FACTORS WITHOUT KEEPING EVERYTHING CONSTANT

*Single-n Experiments*

KEEPING NONTREATMENT FACTORS CONSTANT: THE A—B DESIGN
VARIATIONS ON THE A—B DESIGN
EVALUATION OF SINGLE-N EXPERIMENTS
CONCLUSIONS ABOUT SINGLE-N EXPERIMENTS

*Quasi-Experiments*

THE PROBLEM: ACCOUNTING FOR NONTREATMENT FACTORS
THE PRETEST—POSTTEST DESIGN
TIME SERIES DESIGNS
THE NON-EQUIVALENT CONTROL GROUP DESIGN
CONCLUSIONS ABOUT QUASI-EXPERIMENTAL DESIGNS

*Concluding Remarks*

*Summary*

*Key Terms*

*Exercises*

# Chapter 11

## SINGLE-N EXPERIMENTS AND QUASI-EXPERIMENTS

### OVERVIEW

To this point, we have shown you only one way to infer causality—by using random assignment. In this chapter, you will learn how to infer causality without the benefit of random assignment.

We will begin by reviewing how randomized experiments meet the requirements for establishing causality. Then, you will examine two types of designs that attempt to meet these requirements without random assignment: single-n experiments and quasi-experiments.

In short, after reading this chapter, you should be well prepared to design a study to determine if a treatment causes an effect. Specifically, you will know a variety of designs that can be used to establish causality, as well as the advantages and disadvantages of these designs.

## INFERRING CAUSALITY IN RANDOMIZED EXPERIMENTS

Whether you use a randomized experiment or any other design, you must satisfy three criteria if you are to infer that one variable (smiling at others) causes a change in another variable (others helping you). Specifically, you must establish covariation, temporal precedence, and control of irrelevant factors.

### Establishing Covariation

Before you can show that the treatment causes a change in behavior, you must first establish **covariation:** that changes in the treatment are accompanied by changes in the behavior. Therefore, to show that smiling causes people to help you, you must prove that people are more helpful to you when you smile than when you do not.

In the randomized experiment, you would establish covariation by seeing if the amount of help you received when you smiled was greater than when you did not smile. If the mean amount of helping was the same in both groups, then you would not have covariation. Because varying the independent variable would not be accompanied by variations (changes) in the dependent variable, you would conclude that the independent variable did not have an effect. If, on the other hand, you received more help in the smiling condition than in the no smile condition, then you would have covariation.

## Establishing Temporal Precedence

Establishing covariation, by itself, does not establish causality. You must also establish **temporal precedence:** that the treatment comes before the change in behavior. In other words, you must show that you smile at others *before* they help out. Otherwise, it may be that you react with a smile after people help you. Thus, without temporal precedence, you can't determine which variable is the cause and which is the effect.

In a randomized experiment, you automatically establish that the cause comes before the change in behavior (temporal precedence) by manipulating the independent variable. You always present the independent variable (smiling) *before* you present the dependent measure task (giving participants an opportunity to help).

## Controlling for Irrelevant Factors without Keeping Everything Constant

In addition to establishing temporal precedence, you must show that the covariation you observed could only be due to the treatment. Ideally, you would do this by showing that the treatment is the only thing that varies, that everything else is constant. Therefore, to show that your smiling causes others to help you, you must show that everything—except for your smiling—is the same during the times that you smile and the times that you do not smile.

It's difficult to prove that the *only* difference between the times when you get help and times when you don't is your smile. But without such proof, you can't say that your smiling causes people to be more helpful. Why not? Because you might be smiling more when the weather is nicer or when you are with your friends. These same conditions (being with friends, nice weather) may be the reason you are getting help—your smile may have nothing to do with it. If you cannot be sure that everything else was the same, then the relationship between smiling and helpfulness may be **spurious:** due to other variables.

In the randomized experiment, you do not keep everything, except for the treatment variable, constant. Instead, you use random assignment so that the effects of uncontrolled variables (such as individual differences) are converted into random error and then you use statistical tests to subtract out the effects of random error.

To be more specific, random assignment ensures that uncontrolled variables do not vary systematically. Your conditions will be equivalent except for the effects of the independent variable and the chance impact of random variables. Therefore, as a result of randomization, only random variables stand in the way of keeping irrelevant variables constant.

If you could remove those random variables, you would be able to keep everything constant. Unfortunately, you cannot remove them. However, you can use statistics to estimate their effects: If the difference between groups is much greater than the estimated effects of random error, the results are declared "statistically significant."

If you find a statistically significant effect for your treatment variable, you can argue that your treatment variable causes a change in scores on the dependent measure. However, you may be wrong. You may have underestimated the amount of random error and falsely identified a chance difference as a treatment effect. That is, you may have made a Type 1 error. Fortunately, before you do the study, you establish what your chances are of making a Type 1 error. Usually, most investigators make the chances of committing a Type 1 error fairly remote. Specifically, most investigators set the probability of mistaking chance variation as a genuine treatment effect at less than 5 in 100 ($p < .05$).

## SINGLE-N EXPERIMENTS

Because all experimental designs must establish causality, all experimental designs are similar. Thus, all experimental designs establish that the cause comes before the effect by manipulating the treatment variable (smiling) before presenting the dependent measure task (helping). All experimental designs establish covariation by comparing the different treatment conditions (comparing the amount of help received in the smiling versus no-smiling conditions). However, not all experimental designs rely on randomization and statistical tests to rule out the effects of nontreatment factors.

The single-n experiment, for example, strives to control, rather than to estimate, nontreatment factors. Instead of letting nontreatment variables vary and then statistically accounting for the effects of those variables, single-n experimenters stop nontreatment factors from varying (see Table 11–1).

### Keeping Nontreatment Factors Constant: The A–B Design

To understand how single-n experimenters keep nontreatment factors constant, let's examine the simplest **single-n design,** the A–B design. In the **A–B design,** as in all single-n designs, the experimenter studies a single participant. The experimenter makes sure that the participant's behavior on the dependent measure task (pecking) occurs at a consistent rate. This is called establishing a **stable baseline.** This first step is designated as "A." Next, the experimenter introduces the treatment. The experimenter then compares post-treatment behavior (B) with baseline (A).

The A–B design strives to keep nontreatment variables constant by eliminating the effects of two basic sources of nontreatment variables: between subject variability and within subject variability.

**TABLE 11–1**

**How Different Experimental Designs Establish Causality**

| REQUIREMENT | RANDOMIZED EXPERIMENTS | A–B SINGLE-N DESIGN |
| --- | --- | --- |
| TEMPORAL PRECEDENCE (Treatment came before changes in scores) | Introduce treatment *before* there is a change in the dependent variable. | Introduce treatment *before* there is a change in the dependent variable. |
| COVARIATION (Different treatment conditions score differently on measure) | Observing difference between treatment and control conditions. | Observing difference between conditions A (baseline) and B (post-treatment behavior). |
| ACCOUNTING FOR IRRELEVANT VARIABLES (Determining that the change in behavior is not due to nontreatment factors) | 1. Independent random assignment to make sure all irrelevant factors vary randomly rather than systematically. 2. Then, use statistics to account for effects of these random factors. If the difference between groups is greater than would be expected as a result of these random factors, the difference is assumed to be the effect of the one non-random, systematically varied factor: the treatment. | 1. Eliminate between subject variables by using only one participant. 2. Control relevant environmental factors. Demonstrate that those factors have been controlled by establishing stable baseline. Then, introduce treatment. If change occurs, that change is assumed to be due to the treatment. |

Between subject variability is not a problem for the single-n design. Differences between individuals cannot account for differences between conditions because the same participant is in all conditions.

Within subject variability, however, is a problem. With or without treatment, a participant's behavior may vary. How does the single-n experimenter know that the treatment is responsible for the change in the participant's behavior?

The single-n experimenter is confident that the difference between no-treatment and treatment conditions is not due to random within subject variability because she has established a stable baseline. The baseline shows that the subject's behavior is not varying.

But how does a single-n experimenter obtain a stable baseline? After all, behavior is variable. To obtain a stable baseline, the single-n experimenter must control all relevant environmental variables. That is, the single-n experimenter strives to hold constant all those variables that might affect the participant's responses.

If the experimenter does not know what the relevant variables are, the experimenter tries to keep the participant's environment as constant as possible. For example, the researcher might perform the experiment under highly controlled conditions in a soundproof laboratory. If the experimenter knows what the relevant variables are, then the experimenter only needs to control those variables. Thus, if an experimenter knew that parental praise was the only relevant variable in increasing studying behavior, the experimenter would only need to control that one variable. However, the experimenter usually does not know which variables can be safely ignored. Psychology has not advanced to the state where we can catalog what variables affect and don't affect every possible response.

After attempting to control variables, the experimenter checks to see whether she has succeeded by looking at the baseline. If the baseline is not stable, the experimenter continues to control variables until the behavior becomes stable.

But what if a researcher cannot achieve a stable baseline? Then, the researcher planning to use an A–B design has a problem: Changes in behavior that occur after the treatment are introduced may be due to something other than the treatment. In other words, the researcher probably wouldn't know whether the change in behavior is due to normal fluctuations in the participant's behavior or whether the change is due to treatment.

As you will soon see, some single-n researchers are often able to determine whether the behavioral change is due to normal fluctuations by using single-n designs that are more sophisticated than the simple A–B design. In addition, as you can see from Figure 11–1, A–B researchers can make a convincing case that the results are *not* due to normal baseline fluctuations if the participants' behavior changes dramatically after the treatment is introduced.

Although it is difficult to achieve a stable baseline, we should point out that single-n experimenters often do achieve a stable baseline. They are especially successful when they have a simple organism (pigeon, rat, planarium, neuron) perform a rather simple behavior (pecking) in a simple environment, such as in a Skinner Box.

Thus far, we have seen how the single-n experimenter using an A–B design can hold individual difference variables and relevant environmental variables constant. But how does the experimenter know that the difference between conditions is not due to **maturation:** natural biological changes in the organism, such as those due to development or fatigue?

The single-n experimenter may limit maturation by choosing an organism that she knows won't mature substantially during the course of the study. Thus, she might use a pigeon or a rat because the extent of their maturation as it relates to certain tasks (bar pressing and pecking) is well-documented.

Or, as you will soon see, the experimenter may use a design that will allow her to account for maturation. But before looking at a design that accounts for maturation, let's look at an example of the A–B design, the simplest of single-n designs.

In an early study of the effects of psychoactive drugs, Howard Blough (1957) wanted to study the impact of LSD on a pigeon's visual perception. His first step was to place the pigeon in a highly controlled environment, a Skinner Box, equipped with a light that illuminated a spot on the stimulus panel.

FIGURE 11–1

## A Behavior Modification Program Appears to
## Reduce a Client's Cigarette Smoking

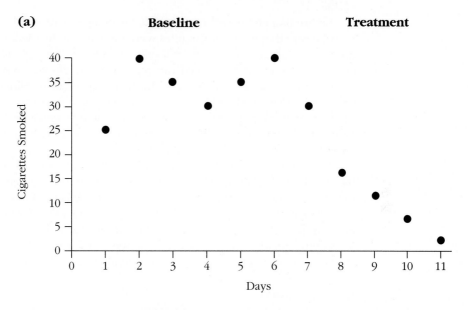

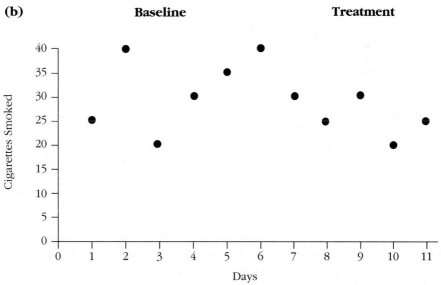

*Note:* The data from the participant in Figure 11a strongly suggests that the treatment (begun on day 7) had an effect. The data from the participant in Figure 11b, on the other hand, might be due to normal fluctuations in the participant's behavior rather than to the treatment.

By varying the intensity of the light, Blough could make the spot easier—or more difficult—to see. On the wall of the Skinner Box were two disks—"1" and "2." As an index of visual threshold, the pigeon was conditioned to peck at disk "1" when the spot was visible, and to peck at disk "2" when the spot was not visible.

Before Blough began to manipulate his independent variable (LSD), he had to make sure that no other variables were influencing the pigeon's behavior. To do this, he had to keep all the relevant variables in the pigeon's environment constant. Therefore, he placed the pigeon in the Skinner Box and carefully observed the pigeon's behavior. If he had succeeded in eliminating all non-treatment variables, the pigeon's behavior would be relatively stable—the relationship between pecking and illumination would be constant. If he had failed, he would observe fluctuations in the pigeon's behavior (for example, erratic increases and decreases in pecking).

Once the pigeon's behavior was stable, Blough was ready to introduce the independent variable, LSD. After administering the LSD, Blough compared the pigeon's behavior after the treatment (B), to its behavior before the treatment (A). Blough found that after taking the LSD, the pigeon's visual ability decreased. Specifically, the pigeons pecked at disk "2" (cannot see spot) under a level of illumination that—prior to treatment—always led to a peck at disk "1." Because Blough had insured that nontreatment variables were not influencing the pigeon's behavior, he concluded that the LSD was the sole cause of the decrease in visual ability.

Howard Blough's study was exceptional because he knew that the pigeon's behavior on this task normally wouldn't change much over time. However, in studies with other kinds of participants or tasks, the researcher would not know whether participants would change, develop, or learn over a period of time. Therefore, most experimenters are not so confident that they have controlled all the important variables. They know that two potentially important non-treatment variables have changed from measurement at baseline (A) to measurement after administering the treatment (B).

First, because the posttest occurs after the pretest, participants have had more practice on the task when performing the posttest than they had when performing the pretest. Thus, their performance may have improved as a result of **testing:** the effects of doing the dependent measure task on subsequent performance on that task. For example, the *practice* a participant gets doing the task during the "A" phase may help the participant do better during the "B" phase.

Second, because the posttest occurs after the pretest, time has passed from pretest to posttest. Consequently, changes from pretest to posttest may be due to **maturation.** For example, the participant's behavior may have changed over time as a result of fatigue, boredom, or development.

## Variations on the A–B Design

Because psychologists want to know that their results are due to the treatment rather than to testing or maturation, single-n experimenters rarely use the A–B design. Instead, they use variations on the A-B design, such as the reversal design, psychophysical designs, and the multiple baseline design.

## THE REVERSAL DESIGN

In the **reversal design,** also known as the **A–B–A design,** the experimenter measures behavior (A), then administers the treatment and measures behavior (B), then withdraws the treatment and measures behavior (A).

To see why the A-B-A design is superior to the A-B design, consider one in a series of classic single-n experiments that first demonstrated that behavior modification was an effective therapy for mental patients (Ayllon & Azrin, 1968). Specifically, Ted Ayllon and Nathan Azrin worked with a group of psychotics in a mental hospital to see if a token economy was an effective way of increasing socially desirable behavior. In a typical experiment, Ayllon and Azrin first identified a desirable behavior (for instance, feeding oneself). Next, the experimenters collected baseline behavior for a patient (A). They then attempted to reinforce this behavior with a "token." Like money, the token could be exchanged for desirable outcomes such as candy, movies, social interaction, or privacy. Thus, they gave the patient tokens for each instance of the socially desirable behavior and measured the behavior (B). They found that the patient performed more socially desirable behaviors once the tokens were introduced. Great! A token economy increases socially desirable behavior. Right?

If Ayllon and Azrin's study had ended here, you could not be confident about that conclusion. Remember, with an A-B design, you don't know whether the increase in socially desirable behavior is due to maturation, testing, or the treatment.

Fortunately, Ayllon and Azrin expanded the A-B design to an A-B-A design by stopping the treatment while continuing to observe their patient's behavior. After removing the treatment, the incidence of socially desirable behavior decreased. Consequently, Ayllon and Azrin were able to determine that the treatment (tokens) increased socially desirable behavior.

If, after withdrawing the treatment, socially desirable behavior had continued to increase, they would *not* have concluded that the increase in socially desirable behavior was due to the treatment. Instead, they would have concluded that the increase could be due to maturation or testing.

We should point out that the results were not quite as neat as we described. Admittedly, they found that socially desirable behavior increased when they introduced the tokens and decreased when they stopped giving out tokens. However, removing the tokens did not cause the behavior to fall back all the way to baseline levels. Instead, the behavior fell back to near-baseline levels.

If tokens caused the effect, shouldn't their withdrawal cause the behavior to fall to baseline rather than near baseline? Ideally, you would like to see the dependent measure (socially desirable behavior) fall back to baseline level. However, most behaviors won't return to baseline after you withdraw the treatment because of:

1. maturation effects;
2. testing effects; and
3. **carryover effects:** the treatment's effects persisting even after the treatment has been removed.

Because of these effects, you can infer causality as long as there is a substantially higher (or lower) level of the dependent variable during treatment phase (B) than during both the pre-treatment (A) and post-treatment (A) conditions (see Figure 11-2).

Certainly, you would be justified in inferring causality if treatment behavior is substantially different from both pre-treatment and post-treatment behavior. Unfortunately, justified or not, your inference of causality could be wrong.

How could you be wrong? You could be wrong if the effects of practice and/or maturation are cyclical. For instance, suppose performance was affected by menstrual cycles. Thus, performance might be good during the pre-treatment phase (before menstruation), poor during the treatment phase (during menstruation), and good during the post-treatment phase (after menstruation). Although such an unsteady effect of maturation or testing would be unlikely, it's possible.

To rule out the possibility that apparent treatment effects are due to some simple cyclical pattern involving either maturation or practice, you might extend the A–B–A design. For example, you might make it an A–B–A–B design. Ayllon and Azrin did this, and found that reintroduction of the token rewards led to an increase in the socially desirable behavior.

By adding even more measurements, you could use an A–B–A–B–A–B–A design to rule out the possibility of an even more complicated maturational or practice cycle. Obviously, the more measurements you collect, the less likely it is that maturation or practice would increase performance every time the treatment is introduced, but never increase performance when the control condition occurs. Thus, it would be very hard to describe a cycle of maturation and practice effects that could mimic treatment effects in an A–B–A–B–A–B–A–B–A–B–A–B–A–B design.

## PSYCHOPHYSICAL DESIGNS

Psychophysical experiments extend the A–B–A–B–A design. In psychophysical experiments, participants are asked to judge stimuli. For example, they may be asked to rate whether one light is brighter than another, one weight is heavier than another, or one picture is more attractive than another. The idea is to see how variations in the stimulus relate to variations in judgments. Since the dependent variable is *psycho*logical judgment and the independent variable is often some variation of a stimulus's *physi*cal characteristic (loudness, intensity, etc.), the name psychophysics is appropriate.

Since a participant can make psychophysical judgments quickly, participants can—and are—asked to make many judgments. Indeed, in a few exceptional cases, participants have been asked to make 67,000 judgments!

**FIGURE 11–2**

### Results from A-B-A Design: Number of Violent Acts Performed by Jim During the No Punishment and "Time-out" Punishment Phases

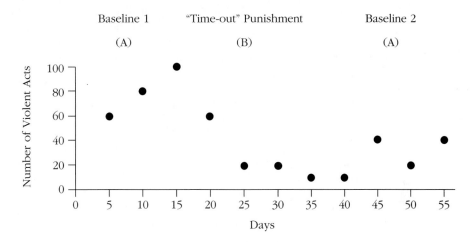

*Note:* Even though post-treatment violence did not revert back to pre-treatment levels, a strong case can still be made that the time-out punishment reduced the violent behavior.

With so many judgments, you might worry about maturation effects. For example, participants might get tired as the experimental session goes on—and on.

In addition, you might be concerned about treatment carryover effects. Specifically, you might worry that earlier stimuli may affect ratings of later stimuli. For instance, suppose you were rating how heavy a 50-pound weight was. If the last 10 weights you had judged were all about 100 pounds, you might tend to rate 50 pounds as light. However, if the last 10 weights had all been around 10 pounds, you might tend to rate 50 pounds as heavy. Similarly, if you were judging how wealthy a person making $50,000 was, your rating would be affected by whether the previous people you had judged had been multimillionaires or poverty-stricken (Parducci, 1989).

To deal with these order effects, researchers may use three techniques, all of which were suggested by one of the earliest pioneers in psychophysics—Gustav Fechner. First, researchers usually have participants rate each stimulus more than once. If the same stimulus receives different ratings when it is presented at different times, then they know there are order effects. Second, they average the ratings that the stimulus receives. The idea is that whereas one rating may be inflated (or deflated) because of order effects, the average of several ratings won't be. However, to say that the stimulus's average rating is not due to order effects, we have to be confident that the stimulus isn't preceded by the same stimuli each time it is presented, which brings us to Fechner's third set of tips. Fechner recommended that researchers either randomize the order in which stimuli are presented or they counterbalance the order in which they present the stimuli. Randomization makes it unlikely that Stimulus A will always come before Stimulus B; counterbalancing guarantees that Stimulus A will not always come before Stimulus B. Specifically, in counterbalancing, researchers present Stimulus A before Stimulus B half the time; the other half of the time Stimulus B comes before Stimulus A. By using these three techniques (multiple ratings, averaging, randomizing or counterbalancing), maturation, testing, and carryover should not be problems.

### THE MULTIPLE BASELINE DESIGN

Another single-n experimental design that rules out the effects of maturation, testing, and carryover is the **multiple baseline design.** In a typical multiple baseline design, you would collect baselines for several behaviors. For example, you might collect baselines for a child making her bed, putting her toys away, washing her hands, and vacuuming her room. Then, you would reinforce one of the behaviors. If the behavior being reinforced increases (putting her toys away), you would suspect that reinforcement is causing the behavior to increase.

But the effects might be due to the child becoming more mature or to some other nontreatment effect. To see whether the child's improvement in behavior is due to maturation or some other nontreatment factor, you would look at her performance on the other tasks. If those tasks are still being performed at baseline level, then nontreatment factors such as maturation and testing are not improving performance on those tasks. Since maturation and testing have no effect on the other behaviors, maturation and testing probably are not increasing the particular behavior you decided to reinforce. Therefore, you would be relatively confident that the improvement in putting toys away was due to reinforcement.

To be even more confident that the reinforcement is causing the change in behavior, you would reinforce a second behavior (washing hands) and compare it against the other non-reinforced behaviors. You would continue the process until you had reinforced all the behaviors. You would hope to find that when you reinforced hand-washing, hand-washing increased—but that no other behavior increased. Similarly, when you reinforced tooth-brushing, you would hope tooth-brushing—and only tooth-brushing—increased. If increases in behavior coincided perfectly with reinforcement, you would be very confident that reinforcement was responsible for the increases in behavior (see Figure 11–3).

## Evaluation of Single-n Experiments

You have now examined some of the more popular single-n designs. Before leaving these designs, let's see how they stand up on three important criteria: internal, external, and construct validity.

## INTERNAL VALIDITY

The single-n experimenter uses a variety of strategies to achieve internal validity. Like the physicist, the single-n experimenter keeps many relevant variables constant. That is, the single-n experimenter holds individual difference variables constant by studying a single participant and may hold environmental variables constant by placing that participant in a highly controlled environment. For example, the single-n experimenter may study a single rat that is inside a soundproof Skinner Box.

Like the within-subjects experimenter (see Chapter 9), the single-n experimenter must worry that the changes in the participant's behavior could be due to the participant changing or maturing over time or to changing as a result of gaining practice and experience on the task (testing). Thus, within-subjects and single-n experimenters may adapt similar strategies to deal with the threats of maturation and testing.

Both within-subjects and single-n experimenters may try to rule out maturation by keeping their study so short that there is not enough time for maturation to occur. Both may try to reduce the effects of testing by giving participants extensive practice on the task prior to beginning the study. By giving extensive pre-experimental practice on the task, they reduce the likelihood that participants will benefit from any additional practice they get during the experiment. Single-n experimenters, in particular, like to make sure that the participant's response rate is stable before the treatment is introduced.

We do not mean to say that within-subjects and single-n experimenters always use the same methods to eliminate threats to validity. Indeed, their primary methods of dealing with these threats are fundamentally different. That is, whereas the within-subjects design experimenter relies primarily on randomization to rule out practice and fatigue effects, the single-n experimenter relies on introducing and removing the treatment in a systematic order.

Both the single-n and the within-subjects experimenter must also be concerned about carryover effects. Because of carryover, investigators using an A–B–A design frequently find that participants do not return to the original baseline. These carryover problems multiply when you use more levels of the independent variable and/or when you use more than one independent variable. Because carryover effects are a serious concern, most single-n experimenters minimize carryover's complications by doing experiments that use only two levels of a single independent variable. That is, rather than use an A–B–C–D–E–F–G–G–F–D–C–B–A design, most single-n researchers only use A–B–A–B designs.

## CONSTRUCT VALIDITY

The single-subject researcher and the within-subjects experimenter have even more in common when they attack threats to construct validity (see Table 11–2). For both researchers, sensitization (participants figuring out the hypothesis because they have been exposed to several levels of the treatment) poses a

**FIGURE 11–3**

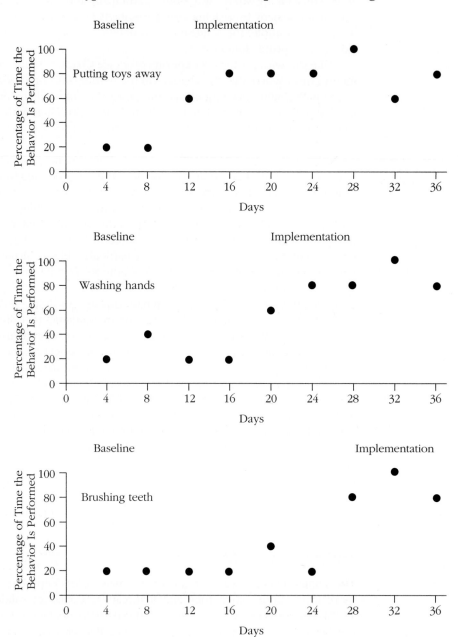

**Hypothetical Data from a Multiple-Baseline Design**

**TABLE 11–2**

**Similarities between Within-Subjects Experiments and Single-N Experiments**

| PROBLEM | SINGLE-N EXPERIMENT | WITHIN-SUBJECTS DESIGN |
|---|---|---|
| Practice effects may harm internal validity | Give extensive practice before introducing treatment. | Give extensive practice before introducing treatment. |
| Fatigue or maturation may harm internal validity | Keep study brief. | Keep study brief. |
| Assorted order effects may harm validity | Counterbalance sequence. | Counterbalance sequence, and randomly assign participants to different sequences. |
| Carryover effects may harm internal validity | Use few levels and few variables. Wait a long time between treatments. | Use few levels and few variables. Wait a long time between treatments. |
| Participants may learn what study is about (sensitization), thus harming construct validity | 1. Placebo treatments 2. Few levels of treatment 3. Gradually increase or decrease intensity of treatment or use very similar levels. | 1. Placebo treatments 2. Few levels of treatment 3. Gradually increase or decrease intensity of treatment or use very similar levels. |

serious problem and both researchers use the same solution. Specifically, both try to reduce the effects of sensitization by:

1. making the difference between the treatment conditions so subtle that participants don't even realize that anything has changed (such as gradually varying the loudness of a stimulus),
2. using placebo treatments, and
3. using very few levels of treatment.

Researchers' concerns about sensitization may account for the popularity of the A–B–A design over more complicated single-subject designs. That is, the A–B–A design is more popular than the A–B–A–B–A–B–A–B–A–B or A–B–C–D–D–C–B–A designs.

## EXTERNAL VALIDITY

At first glance, the single-n experiment seems to have less external validity than other designs. How can the results from one participant be generalized to others? Furthermore, how can the results from an experiment conducted in such a highly controlled setting be generalized to other settings? Although it seems that other designs must have more external validity than the single-n experiment, things are not always as they seem.

Whether you use one participant or 1,000 participants, you can only *infer* that your results will apply to individuals who weren't in your study. In other words, you are assuming that no other individual difference variables interact with your treatment to reverse or negate its effects. There are at least two main reasons why single-n researchers can frequently justify this assumption.

First, single-n researchers often replicate their studies. That is, they examine the effects of their treatment on several individuals. By demonstrating that the treatment has the same effect on each individual, they provide some evidence that the effect generalizes across individuals.

Second, single-n researchers often investigate fundamental processes that are well understood and known to occur in all organisms. The results of such experiments can be generalized to other members of the same species. Thus, the results of psychophysical and operant conditioning experiments performed on a single member of a species can often be generalized to other members of that species.[1]

Similarly, the results of an experiment conducted under highly controlled conditions can be generalized to other settings, especially when the single-n experiment investigates universal phenomena that are relatively unaffected by setting (such as sensation). Even when single-n investigators cannot generalize their results to all settings, their detailed knowledge of the phenomena may allow them to be specific about the extent to which their results can be generalized to different settings.

## Conclusions about Single-n Experiments

Not coincidentally, the single-n experiment bears a close resemblance to the traditional chemistry experiment. As is the case with experiments in the physical sciences, the single-n experiment is most easily interpreted when the potential causal variables have been identified and controlled. Furthermore, just as universal physical laws (such as gas laws) allow the results of chemistry experiments done on a few hydrogen molecules to be generalized to all hydrogen molecules, universal laws (for instance, psychophysical laws, laws of operant conditioning) may allow experiments done on a single member of a species to be generalized to most members of that species. Finally, like the physics or chemistry experiment, when much is known about the variables that affect a given phenomenon, scientists can accurately predict the extent to which the results of a highly controlled study can be applied to other settings.

Thus far, we have acted like researchers who use the single-n design are always trying to achieve the same goal as those who use a randomized experiment—to see if, on the average, a treatment has an effect. However, such is not always the case. At times, researchers may only be interested in a treatment's effect on a single individual. For example, suppose you were trying to change your own behavior or the behavior of a family pet. Or, suppose a therapist is

---

[1] For a dissenting view, see Brewer (1974) who argues that there is no convincing evidence for operant conditioning in humans.

treating a patient and wants to see if the treatment is having a measurable effect on that particular patient. In all these cases, the single-n design would be the best way to evaluate the effect of the treatment.

In summary, there are two main reasons why the single-n design is a popular alternative to the randomized experiment. First, the single-n is a good design to use when you are interested in the causes of one individual's behavior. Thus, therapists frequently use the single-n design to help them determine whether a treatment is working for a particular client. Second, the single-n design is a good choice when you want to make statements about fundamental, universal processes. It is wasteful to examine numerous participants if the treatment has the same effect on everyone. Because all people tend to respond similarly to reinforcements, the single-n design is commonly used in behavior modification research. Because everyone seems to respond similarly to psychophysical manipulations, the single-n design is also a popular alternative to the randomized experiment in psychophysical research.

# QUASI-EXPERIMENTS

Another popular alternative to the randomized experiment is the quasi-experiment. According to Cook and Campbell (1979), quasi-experiments are, "experiments that have treatments, outcome measures, and experimental units, but *do not use random assignment* to create the comparisons from which treatment-caused change is inferred" (p. 6).

Quasi-experiments are useful when researchers want to establish a causal relationship, but random assignment is impossible or impractical. For example, when it comes to letting one group of individuals have a certain type of therapy, drug, training, social program, or technology, organizations want to be the ones who decide who gets what treatment. Government agencies, businesses, and individuals are often quite resistant to the idea of using random assignment to determine who gets the treatment. Consequently, often the only way to determine the effect of a treatment is to use a **quasi-experimental design.**

Because quasi-experimental designs are so useful for assessing the effects of real-life treatments, we will devote the rest of this chapter to these designs. We will begin by discussing the general logic behind quasi-experimental designs. Then, we will take a more detailed look at some of the more popular quasi-experimental designs.

## The Problem: Accounting for Nontreatment Factors

Like experiments, quasi-experiments establish temporal precedence because the treatment comes before the change in behavior. Like experiments, quasi-experiments assess covariation by comparing treatment versus non-treatment conditions. However, unlike experiments, quasi-experiments are unable to automatically control for or account for all relevant nontreatment factors. Unlike randomized experiments, quasi-experiments cannot randomize the effects of nontreatment factors and then statistically control for those random effects. Unlike single-n experiments, quasi-experiments are unable to control for nontreatment factors by keeping those factors constant.

## IDENTIFYING NONTREATMENT FACTORS: THE VALUE OF CAMPBELL AND STANLEY'S SPURIOUS EIGHT

Thus, the challenge in quasi-experiments is to rule out the effects of nontreatment variables without either the aid of random assignment or the ability to control nontreatment variables. The first step to meeting this challenge is to identify all the variables other than your treatment that might account for the change in participants' scores. Once you have identified those nontreatment factors, you will try to demonstrate that those nontreatment factors did *not* account for the change in participants' scores. After you have ruled out all those nontreatment factors, you can argue that your treatment did cause the effect.

To identify all the nontreatment factors that might account for the relationship between the treatment and the change in scores is a tall order. Fortunately, however, Campbell and Stanley (1963) discovered that all possible nontreatment factors fall into eight categories. More specifically, as we discussed in Chapter 5, Campbell and Stanley (1963) discovered that there are eight threats to internal validity:

1. **maturation:** apparent treatment effects that are due to natural biological changes—from changes due to growing and developing to changes due to becoming more tired or more hungry.
2. **testing:** apparent treatment effects that are due to participants having learned from the pretest. For example, practice on the pretest may improve performance on the posttest.
3. **history:** apparent treatment effects that are due to events in the outside world that are unrelated to the treatment.
4. **instrumentation:** apparent treatment effects that are due to changes in the measuring instrument. For example, the researcher may use a revised version of the measure on the retest.
5. **statistical regression:** apparent treatment effects that are due to regression to the mean (the tendency for participants who receive extreme scores on the pretest to receive less extreme scores on the posttest).
6. **mortality:** apparent treatment effects that are due to participants dropping out of the study. For instance, suppose that participants who would score poorly drop out of the treatment condition, but not out of the no treatment condition. In that case, the treatment group would score higher than the no treatment group, even if the treatment had no effect.
7. **selection:** differences between groups that are not due to the treatment, but to the groups being different from each other to start with (comparing apples and oranges).

8. **selection-maturation interaction:** differences between two groups who scored similarly on the pretest that are due to the groups naturally growing apart. In other words, just because two groups scored similarly at the beginning of the study, you cannot assume that they would have scored identically at the end of the study.

As you will soon see, the eight threats to validity fall into three general categories. First, there are those environmental and physiological events—other than the treatment—that cause individuals to change. Second, there are errors in measurement that cause changes in participants' scores. Third, there are problems related to the fact that treatment and no treatment groups—because different individuals are in the two groups—may differ from each other even when the treatment has no effect.

The first three threats to validity—maturation, testing, and history—include all the nontreatment factors that can change individual participants. The first two—maturation and testing—are threats we talked about in terms of the single-n design. That is, we were concerned that changes in an A–B design might be due to *testing:* the participant learning from doing the dependent measure task several times. We were also concerned about *maturation:* any changes in the participant's internal, physiological environment. However, because we could keep the outside environment constant, we did not concern ourselves with *history:* any nontreatment changes in the external environment.

The next two threats, instrumentation and statistical regression, are reasons why participants in the treatment conditions may have different *scores,* even though the participants themselves have not changed. With *instrumentation,* participants are tested with one measuring instrument in one condition and a different measuring instrument in another condition. No wonder their scores are different.

*Statistical regression* is more subtle. To understand statistical regression (also called *regression*), remember that most scores contain some random error. Usually, this is not a problem because random error tends to balance out to zero. That is, random error pushes some scores upward, others downward, but the net effect on the overall average score is zero. However, what if we measure a bunch of people, but only select those participants whose scores have been pushed up by random error? When we retest them, their scores will go down. This might fool us into thinking they had really changed. In fact, all that has happened is that random error isn't going to push all these scores up again (just as lightning is unlikely to strike the same place twice). Instead, it will push some up, but some down.

You might wonder how we would select scores that have been pushed up by random error. One way is to select extreme scores. For example, if we select only those people who got 100% on an exam, we know that random error did not act to decrease their score. However, random error (lucky guesses, scorer failing to see a question that was missed) could have increased those scores. Thus, if we give these people a test again, their scores will go down. This tendency for extreme scorers to score less extreme when they are retested is called *regression to the mean.*

Regression to the mean is a powerful effect. Whether watching a baseball player on a hitting (or non-hitting) streak, watching the economy, or observing a patient, you will find that extreme events tend to revert back to more normal levels.

To this point, we have talked about factors that could change an individual's scores. We explained that a participant in the treatment condition may change for reasons having nothing to do with the treatment (maturation, testing, history). We have also talked about how an individual's score can change, even though the individual doesn't really change (instrumentation, regression). As you have seen, these changes in individual participants' scores could cause a treatment group to score differently from a no treatment group. However, even when the individual scores are accurate and are unaffected by treatment-irrelevant influences, the treatment group may differ from the no treatment group for reasons having nothing to do with the treatment. That is, the treatment and no treatment groups may differ because the participants in the treatment group have different characteristics than those in the no treatment group. Basically, there are three, treatment-irrelevant reasons why participants in the treatment condition may systematically differ from participants in the no treatment condition: mortality, selection, and selection-maturation.

With *mortality,* for example, your poor performers may have dropped out of the treatment condition. As a result, your treatment condition scores are higher than your no treatment condition scores. However, that doesn't mean that the treatment had an effect.

With *selection,* you are comparing groups that were different before the study began. As the saying goes, "that's not fair—you're comparing apples and oranges." Since your treatment group started out being very different from your no treatment group, the differences between your group's scores at the end of the experiment may not be due to the treatment. Therefore, you shouldn't conclude that the difference in scores between your two groups is due to the treatment.

Unfortunately, even if you selected two groups who scored similarly on your measure before you introduced the treatment, you can't conclude that they would have scored similarly at the end of the study. Why not? Because of *selection-maturation interactions:* Groups that scored similarly in the pretest may naturally mature at different rates.

## USING LOGIC TO COMBAT THE SPURIOUS EIGHT

Once you have identified the threats to internal validity, you must determine which threats are ruled out by the design and which threats you can eliminate through logic (see Table 11–3). Whereas experimental designs rule out the eight threats to internal validity automatically, quasi-experimental designs vary in their ability to automatically rule out these threats. Some rule out most of

TABLE 11–3
**Steps Quasi-Experimenters May Take to Minimize Threats to Internal Validity**

| THREATS | PRECAUTIONS |
|---|---|
| History | Isolate participants from external events during the course of the study. |
| Maturation | Conduct the study in a short period of time to minimize the opportunities for maturation.<br>Use participants who are maturing at slow rates. |
| Testing | Only test participants once.<br>Give participants extensive practice on task prior to collecting data so that they won't benefit substantially from practice they obtain during the study.<br>Know what testing effects are (from past data) and subtract out those effects.<br><br>Use different versions of same test to decrease the testing effect. |
| Instrumentation | Administer same measure, same way, every time. |
| Mortality | Use rewards, innocuous treatments, and brief treatments to keep participants from dropping out of the study.<br>Use placebo treatments or subtly different levels of the treatment so that participants won't be more likely to drop out of the treatment condition.<br><br>Make sure participants understand instructions so that participants aren't thrown out for failing to follow directions. |
| Regression | Don't choose participants on basis of extreme scores.<br><br>Use reliable measures. |
| Selection | Match on all relevant variables.<br>Don't use designs that involve comparing one group of participants with another. |
| Selection Interactions | Match on all relevant variables, not just on pretest scores. In addition, use tips from earlier in this table to reduce the effects of variables—such as history and maturation—that might interact with selection. In other words, reducing the role of maturation will also tend to reduce selection by maturation interactions. |

these threats, some rule out only a few. Yet, even with a quasi-experimental design that automatically rules out only a few of these threats, you may occasionally be able to infer causality.

## The Pretest–Posttest Design

To illustrate the potential usefulness of quasi-experimental designs, we will start by looking at a design that most people would not even consider to be in the same class as a quasi-experimental design: the **pretest–posttest design.** The pretest–posttest design is very similar to the single-n A-B design. As the name suggests, you test one group of participants, administer a treatment, and then retest them.

This design does not rule out many threats automatically; hence, its low status as a design. However, since you are testing individuals against themselves, you don't have to worry about selection or selection-maturation interactions.

Although you do have to worry about mortality, instrumentation, regression, maturation, history, and testing, you may be able to rule out these threats on the grounds that they are extremely improbable. If nobody dropped out of your study, mortality is not a problem. Similarly, if you were careful enough to use the same measure and administer it in the same way, instrumentation is not a problem. If there were only a few minutes between the pretest and posttest, then history is unlikely.

Similarly, if there is a very short time between pretest and posttest, maturation is unlikely. About the only maturation that could occur in a short period of time would be boredom or fatigue. Obviously, you could rule out boredom and fatigue, and thus maturation, if performance was better on the posttest than on the pretest.

You might be able to rule out regression by arguing that pretest scores were not pushed upward or downward by random error. To do this, you could argue that your measure was so reliable that random error would have little impact on scores. You could also argue that people were not in the study because their pretest scores were extreme.

Thus far, in this particular study, you have been able to rule out every threat except testing. And, you might even be able to rule out testing. For instance, if your measure was an unobtrusive one, testing might not be a problem because participants wouldn't know they had been observed. Or, if you used a standardized test, you might know how much people tend to improve when they take the test the second time. If your participants improved substantially more than people typically improve upon retesting, you could rule out the testing effect as the explanation for your results.

As you have seen, the pretest–posttest design eliminates very few threats to internal validity. However, by using your wits, you may be able to rule out the remaining threats and thereby infer causality (see Table 11–4 for a review). Furthermore, as you will soon see, by extending the pretest–posttest design, you can create a quasi-experimental design that does eliminate most threats to internal validity—the time series design.

## Time Series Designs

Just as the complex single-n design is an extension of the basic A–B design, the time series design is an extension of the basic pretest–posttest design. Like the pretest–posttest design, the time series design tests and retests the same participants. Thus, it is not threatened by selection biases. However, unlike the pretest–posttest design, the time series design does not use a single pretest and a single posttest. Instead, the time series design uses several pretests and posttests. Thus, you could call time series designs "pre-pre-pre-pre-post-post-post-post" designs.

To illustrate the differences between the pretest–posttest design and the time series design, suppose you are interested in seeing if disclosing a profes-

**TABLE 11–4**

**How to Deal with the Threats to Internal Validity If You Must Use a Pretest–Posttest Design**

| THREAT | HOW DEALT WITH |
|---|---|
| Selection | Automatically eliminated since participants are tested against themselves. |
| Selection by Maturation | Automatically eliminated since participants are tested against themselves. |
| Mortality | Not a problem if participants don't drop out. Conduct study over short period of time and use an undemanding treatment. |
| Instrumentation | Standardize the way you administer the measure. |
| Regression | Do not select participants based on extreme scores. Use a reliable measure. |
| Maturation | Minimize the time between pretest and posttest. |
| History | Minimize the time between pretest and posttest. |
| Testing | Use an unobtrusive measure.<br>Have data from previous studies about how much participants' scores tend to change from test to retest. |

sor's marital troubles affects how students evaluate her. With a pretest–posttest design, you would have a class evaluate the professor before she tells them about her marital problems, then have them rate her after she discloses her problems. If you observed a difference between pretest and posttest ratings, you would be tempted to say that the difference was due to the disclosure. However, the change in ratings might really be due to history, maturation, testing, mortality, instrumentation, or regression. Since you have no idea of how much of an effect history, maturation, testing, mortality, and instrumentation may have had, you cannot tell whether you had a treatment effect.

## ESTIMATING THE EFFECTS OF THREATS OF VALIDITY WITH A TIME SERIES DESIGN

But what if you extended the pretest–posttest design? That is, what if you had students rate the professor after every lecture for the entire term, even though the professor would not disclose her marital problems until the fifth week? Then, you would have a **time series design.**

What do you gain by all these pretests? From plotting the average ratings for each lecture, you know how much of an effect maturation, testing, instrumentation, and mortality tend to have (see Table 11–5). In other words, when you observe changes from pretest to pretest, you know those changes are not due to the treatment. Instead, those differences must be due to maturation, testing, history, instrumentation, or mortality. For example, suppose ratings steadily improve at a rate of .2 points per week during the five-week, pre-disclosure period. If you then found an increase of .2 points from week 5 (when the professor made the marital disclosure) to 6, you would not attribute

**TABLE 11–5**

**How Pretest–Posttest Designs and Time Series Designs Stack up in Terms of Dealing with Campbell and Stanley's Threats to Internal Validity**

| | TYPE OF DESIGN | |
|---|---|---|
| **THREAT TO VALIDITY** | **PRETEST–POSTTEST DESIGN** | **TIME SERIES DESIGN** |
| Selection | Automatically eliminated | Automatically eliminated |
| Selection X Maturation Interactions | Automatically eliminated | Automatically eliminated |
| Mortality | Through logic and careful planning, this threat can be eliminated. | Through logic and careful planning, this threat can be eliminated. |
| Instrumentation | Through logic and careful planning, this threat can be eliminated. | Through logic and careful planning, this threat can be eliminated. |
| Maturation | Problem! | Often, you will be able to estimate the extent to which differences between your groups could be due to maturation. |
| History | Problem! | Often, you will be able to estimate the extent to which differences between conditions could be due to history. |
| Regression | Problem! | You should be able to determine whether regression is a plausible explanation for the difference between conditions. |

that increase to the disclosures. Instead, you would view such a difference as being due to the effects of history, maturation, mortality, testing, or instrumentation. If, on the other hand, you found a much greater increase in ratings from week 5 to week 6 than you found between any other two consecutive weeks, you would conclude that the professor's disclosures about her marital problems improved her student evaluations (see Figure 11–4).

***Problems in Estimating Effects of Nontreatment Factors.*** Unfortunately, that conclusion could be wrong. That is, your conclusion is valid only if you can correctly estimate the effects of history, maturation, mortality, testing, and instrumentation during the time that the treatment was administered. On the surface, it seems safe to assume that you can estimate the effects of those variables. After all, for the pretest period, you know what the effects of those variables were. Thus, you may feel safe assuming that the effects of those variables were the same during the treatment period as they were during the pretest period. However, this assumption is only correct if the effects of history, maturation, mortality, instrumentation, and testing are relatively consistent over time. In other words, your conclusions about the treatment's effect could

FIGURE 11–4

### Two Very Different Patterns of Results in a Time Series Design in which the Treatment Was Introduced after the Fifth Week

**(a): Little evidence of a treatment effect**

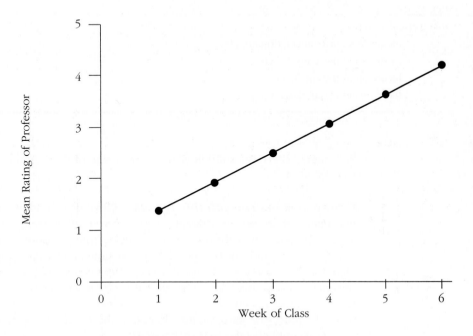

**(b): Evidence of a treatment effect**

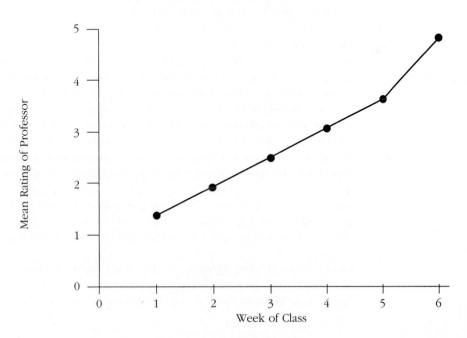

**TABLE 11–6**
**Threats to Time Series Designs**

History!

Regression

Inconsistent effects

>    Inconsistent instrumentation effects

>    Inconsistent mortality effects

>    Inconsistent testing effects

>    Inconsistent maturation effects

be wrong if there is a sudden change in any one of these nontreatment factors (see Table 11-6).

***Inconsistent Instrumentation Effects.***    Obviously, sudden changes in these nontreatment factors are possible. Suppose you administered the same rating scale in the same way for the first five weeks. Your measurements from weeks 1 through 5 would not be affected by instrumentation. As a result, your estimate for the amount of change to expect between week 5 and week 6 would not include any effect for instrumentation. However, what if you ended up handing out a refined version of your rating scale during week 6—the same week the professor started telling her class about her marital problems? In that case, you could mistake an instrumentation effect for a treatment effect.

***Inconsistent Mortality Effects.***    Likewise, if mortality does not follow a consistent pattern, you might mistake mortality's effects for treatment effects. For example, suppose that the last week to drop the course was the same week that the professor started to tell the class about her problems. In that case, a disproportionate number of students who did not like the professor might drop out during that week. Consequently, the professor's ratings might improve because of mortality, rather than because of her disclosures.

Note that if the students who didn't like the professor dropped the class at a consistent rate, the time series design would allow us to discount the mortality effect. In other words, if mortality was gradually causing an increase in ratings during weeks one through five and this trend continued into week six, you would not mistake a mortality effect for a treatment effect. However, if there is a sudden rash of mortality during week 6 (as unhappy students drop the class right before the deadline), then mortality will have more of an effect than the data from weeks 1 through 5 would lead you to expect. Consequently, you could mistake this inconsistent mortality effect for a treatment effect.

***Inconsistent Testing Effects.***    In the study we've been discussing, the effect of testing should be gradual and consistent. However, the effect of testing will not be consistent in every study. For example, in some studies, participants might develop insight into the task. As a result of discovering the rule behind the task, their performance may increase dramatically. Even when participants are not aware of having insight, practice does not always lead to steady improvement. As you know from experience, after weeks of practice or study with little to show for it, you may suddenly improve greatly.

***Inconsistent Maturation Effects.*** Similarly, maturation's effect may sometimes be discontinuous. For instance, suppose you measure young children every three months on a motor abilities test. Then, you expose them to an enriched environment and measure them again. Certainly, you will see a dramatic change. But is this change due to the treatment? Or, is it due to the children jumping to a more advanced developmental stage (for example, learning to walk)?

Unfortunately, you cannot escape sudden, sporadic maturation by studying adults. Even in our teacher evaluation study, participants might mature at an inconsistent rate. That is, first-year students might mature rapidly after getting their first exams back, or students might suddenly develop insight into the professor's lecturing style. If this sudden development occurred the same week the professor started to disclose her marital problems, maturation could masquerade as a treatment effect.

***History.*** Although you can often reasonably assume that the effects of testing, instrumentation, mortality, and maturation are consistent across time, history is less predictable. There are many specific events that could affect performance on the posttest. For instance, ratings of the professor might change as a result of students getting the mid-term back, the professor getting ill, the professor reading a book on teaching, etc. Unlike the single-n design, the time series design does not control all these history effects. Indeed, you could argue that the time series design's lack of control over history, and thus its vulnerability to history, prevent it from reaching experimental design status.

Although history is the one threat to which the time series is vulnerable, you can try to reduce its effects. One strategy is to have a very short interval between testing sessions. With an extremely short interval, you give history fewer opportunities to have an effect.

In addition to reducing the effects of history, you can also try to do a better job of estimating its effects. Since intimately knowing the past should enhance your ability to predict the future, you might collect an extensive baseline. Ideally, you would collect baseline data for several years. This baseline will help you identify any historical events or patterns that tend to repeat themselves regularly. For instance, your baseline would alert you to cyclical patterns in student evaluations, such as students being very positive toward the professor during the first two weeks of the term, more negative toward the professor after the mid-term examination, then becoming more favorable during the last week of the term. Thus, your baseline would prevent you from mistaking these cyclical fluctuations for a treatment effect.

***The Threat of Regression.***    To this point, we have discussed threats to validity that might be expected to change steadily from week to week. But what about regression? Since regression is due to chance measurement error, regression will not change steadily from week to week. Therefore, you cannot use a time series design to measure regression's effect. However, you can use time series designs to determine whether regression is a likely explanation for your results. Specifically, you should suspect regression if:

1. the ratings immediately before the treatment are extremely high or extremely low relative to the previous ratings, and
2. the post-treatment ratings, although very different from the most immediate pre-treatment level, are not substantially different from earlier pre-treatment ratings.

## ELIMINATING, RATHER THAN ESTIMATING, THREATS TO VALIDITY

You have seen that the time series design can rule out certain threats to validity by estimating the effects of those threats (see Table 11–7). When using a time series design, however, do not focus so much on estimating the impact of the threats to validity that you don't try to eliminate those threats. For example, try to eliminate the threat of instrumentation by using the same measuring instrument each time and administering it the same way. For our student evaluation study, we would give students the same rating scales and the same instructions each time.

Likewise, try to eliminate mortality, whenever possible. Thus, if you had students sign their rating sheets, you could eliminate mortality by only analyzing data from students who had perfect attendance. If the ratings were anonymous, you could eliminate mortality by only analyzing ratings from days when attendance was perfect.

Furthermore, try to reduce the effects of maturation and history by keeping the interval between pretest and posttest short. Finally, minimize the likelihood of regression occurring by choosing the time that you will administer the treatment well in advance—don't administer the treatment as an immediate reaction to extremely low ratings.

## TYPES OF TIME SERIES DESIGNS

Now that you are familiar with the basic logic behind the time series design, you are ready to see how it can be extended. One simple way of extending a time series design is to increase the number of pretest and posttest measurements you take. The more measurements you take, the more able you will be to estimate the combined effects of maturation, history, mortality, testing, and instrumentation.

In addition, the more measurements you have, the less likely that an unusual history, maturation, mortality, testing, or instrumentation effect would influence only the measurement taken after you administered the treatment.

**TABLE 11–7**

**How the Time Series Design Deals with Threats to Internal Validity**

| THREAT | APPROACH |
|---|---|
| Selection | Automatically eliminated because testing and retesting same participants. |
| Selection by Maturation | Automatically eliminated because testing and retesting same participants. |
| Instrumentation | If effects are constant, effects can be estimated. In addition, try to give same instrument in the same way every time. |
| Mortality | If effects are constant, effects can be estimated. In addition, if no participants drop out, mortality is not a problem. |
| Testing | If effects are constant, effects can be estimated. |
| Maturation | If effects are constant, effects can be estimated. In addition, study slowly maturing participants or make sure that time between last pretest and the posttest is very brief. |
| Regression | Regression unlikely if ratings prior to introducing the treatment were not extreme and did not differ greatly from previous ratings. Use a reliable measure. |
| History | Try to collect extensive pretest data to predict history's effects. In addition, you *may* try to make sure that: |
| | 1. Time between last pretest and the posttest is brief, and |
| | 2. Participants are isolated from outside events. |

For example, suppose you only measure student evaluations on the fifth, sixth, and seventh weeks. You administer the treatment between the sixth and seventh weeks. Would it be an unusual coincidence if history, maturation, mortality, testing, or maturation had more of an effect between the sixth and seventh weeks than between the fifth and sixth weeks? No—consequently, a threat to validity might easily imitate a treatment effect. However, what if you had students evaluate the teacher from week 1 to week 12? Then, it would be quite a coincidence for a threat to have an extraordinarily large effect between the sixth (the same week you gave the treatment) and seventh week, but not have such an effect between any of the other weeks.

***Reversal Time Series Designs.***    In addition to taking more measurements, you can extend your time series design by administering *and* withdrawing the treatment. That is, you can imitate the single-n experimenter's reversal design. For example, you might pretest, administer the treatment, posttest, withdraw the treatment, and test again. You might even withdraw and introduce the treatment several times.

To see the beauty of this "reversal" design, imagine that you were able to get increases each time the professor tells her class about her marital problems, then decreases when she stops talking about her problems, followed by increases when the professor again tells her class about her marital woes. With that pattern of results, you would be very confident that the disclosures made a difference.

Despite the elegance of this "reversal" design, there are cases when you shouldn't use it. In some situations, you cannot ethically withdraw the treatment after you have administered it (for example, psychotherapy, reinforcement for wearing seatbelts).

In other situations, withdrawing and re-administering the treatment may alert participants to your hypothesis. However, you may be able to prevent participants from guessing the hypothesis or becoming resentful when you withdraw the treatment by using placebo treatments or multiple levels of the treatment. Thus, if you were to use this design for your student evaluations study, you might have a placebo condition in which the professor discloses innocuous facts about her marriage. Alternatively, you might use several levels of disclosure ranging from innocuous to intimate.

***Two-Group Time Series Design.***   A final way of extending the time series design is to collect time series data on two groups. One group, the control group, would not get the treatment. The advantage of using a control group is that it allows you to rule out certain history effects. In your disclosure study, the control group might be another section of the same professor's class. If, after the treatment was administered, the ratings went down only in the treatment group, you could rule out general history effects (mid-term blues, spring fever) as an explanation of the results.

However, you can't rule out every history effect because the two classes may have different histories. For example, the professor may have gotten mad at one class and not the other. To better understand the problems and strengths of incorporating a control group into a time series design, let's look at the parent of this design: the nonequivalent control group design.

## The Non-Equivalent Control Group Design

The **non-equivalent control group design** is the simple experiment without randomization. Because of the non-equivalent control group design's similarity to the simple experiment, it has many of the simple experiment's strengths.

For example, because every participant is only tested once, the non-equivalent control group design, like the simple experiment, is not bothered by maturation, testing, or instrumentation. Furthermore, because of the control group, the non-equivalent group design, like the simple experiment, can usually deal with the effects of history, maturation, and mortality.

But because this design does not use random assignment, the control and treatment groups are not equivalent. Since the control and treatment groups are not equivalent, comparing them may be like comparing apples and oranges. Thus, with the non-equivalent control group design, the threat of selection is serious.

**TABLE 11–8**

**How Two Non-Equivalent Control Group Designs Stack Up in Terms of Dealing with Threats to Internal Validity**

| | TYPE OF NON-EQUIVALENT CONTROL GROUP | |
| --- | --- | --- |
| THREAT TO VALIDITY | UNMATCHED | MATCHED |
| Selection | Big problem! | Problem. |
| Selection × Maturation | Problem. | Problem. |
| Regression | Not a problem. | Big problem! |
| Mortality | Should not be a problem. | Should not be a problem. |
| Instrumentation | Should not be a problem. | Should not be a problem. |
| Maturation | Automatically eliminated by the design. | Automatically eliminated by the design. |
| Testing | Automatically eliminated by the design. | Automatically eliminated by the design. |
| History | Automatically eliminated by the design. | Automatically eliminated by the design. |

## WHY MATCHING DOESN'T MAKE GROUPS EQUAL

To address the selection threat, some investigators match participants. That is, they try to make sure that each participant in one treatment group is identical in several key respects to a participant in the other group. Sometimes, participants are matched on a few background variables (age, gender, IQ) that are expected to correlate with task performance. Sometimes, participants are matched on actual task performance (pretest scores). Although matching seems effective, realize two important points about matched participants:

1. matched participants are *only* matched on a *few* variables rather than on every variable;
2. matched participants are not matched on characteristics directly, but on imperfect measures of those characteristics.

***You Can't Match on Everything.***    Just because two groups are matched on a few variables, you shouldn't think that they are matched on all variables. They aren't. The unmatched variables may cause the two groups to score differently on the dependent measure (see Table 11-8). For instance, suppose you decide to use a non-equivalent group design to test your hypothesis about the effect of marital disclosure. To make the two classes similar, you match the classes on IQ scores, grade point average, proportion of psychology majors, proportion of females and males, and proportion of sophomores, juniors, and seniors. However, you have not matched them in terms of interest in going on to graduate school, number of times they had taken classes from this professor before, and a few hundred other variables that might affect their ratings of the professor. Unfortunately, these unmatched variables, rather than the treatment, may be responsible for the difference between your treatment and control groups.

Since investigators realize that they cannot match participants on every single factor that may influence task performance, some investigators try to match participants on task performance (pretest scores). Yet, even when groups are matched on pretest scores, unmatched variables can cause the groups to score differently on the posttest. That is, just because two groups of students start out with the same enthusiasm for a course, you cannot be sure that they will end the term with the same enthusiasm for the course. For example, one group may end the term with more enthusiasm because that group began the course with a clearer understanding of what the course would be like, what the tests would be like, and how much work was involved. Consequently, although both groups might rate the professor the same at first, the groups may differ after they get the first exam back. For instance, because the naive group had misconceptions about what the professor's exams would be like, they may rate the professor more harshly than the experienced group. Although this change in student attitudes toward the professor might appear to be a treatment effect, it is not. Instead, the difference between the two groups is due to the fact that participants changed over time in different ways because of variables on which they were not matched. Technically, there was a selection by maturation interaction. Because of interactions between selection and other variables, even matching on pretest scores does not free you from selection problems.

What can be done about interactions between selection and other variables? One approach is to *assume* that nature prefers simple, direct main effects to complex interactions. Thus, if an effect could be due to either a treatment main effect or an interaction between selection and maturation, assume that the effect is a simple treatment main effect. Be aware, of course, that your assumption could be wrong.

If you want to go beyond merely assuming that selection interactions are unlikely, you can make them less likely. One way to make selection interactions less likely is to make the groups similar on as many selection variables as possible. That is, not only can you match the groups on pretest scores, but also on other variables. Since there would be fewer variables on which the groups differed, there would be fewer selection variables to interact with maturation. Hence, you would reduce the chance of these interactions occurring.

You have seen one way to reduce interactions between selection variables and maturation—reduce differences between groups that might contribute to selection. The other way to reduce interactions between selection and maturation is to reduce opportunities for maturation. After all, if neither group can mature, then you won't have a selection-maturation interaction. Therefore, to reduce the potential for a selection by maturation interaction, you may decide to present the posttest as soon after the pretest as possible.

***You Match on Measures of Variables—Not on Variables.***     Another problem with matching is that participants must be matched on *observed* scores, rather than on true scores. Unfortunately, observed scores are not the same as true scores. Observed scores are merely imperfect reflections of true scores because observed scores are contaminated by measurement error. As a result of this measurement error, two groups might appear to be similar on certain variables, although they are actually very different on these same variables.

To illustrate this point, suppose a researcher wanted to examine the effect of a drug on treating clinical depression. The practitioner/researcher has received approval and patients' permissions to give the drug to the 10 clinically depressed patients at her small psychiatric facility. However, she realizes that if the participants improve after getting the drug, it proves nothing. Maybe the patients would get better anyway. She wants to have a comparison group that does not get the drug. After getting a phone call asking her to give a guest lecture at a nearby college, she gets an idea. She could use some college students as her comparison group. After testing hundreds of students, she obtains a group of 10 college students who *score* the same on the depression scale as her group of 10 mental patients. But are the two groups equal in terms of depression?

Probably not. The college students' scores are extremely depressed relative to the average college student. This is important because extreme scores tend to have an extreme amount of random error. Thus, when the students are tested again, their scores will be less extreme because their scores will not be as dramatically swayed by random error. That is, on the posttest, the college student participants will score more like average college students—less depressed. Thus, because of the regression effect, it may appear that the drug hurts recovery from depression.

How can you stop from mistaking such a regression effect for a treatment effect? The obvious approach is to reduce regression. Since regression takes advantage of random measurement error, you can reduce regression by using a measure that is relatively free of random measurement error: a reliable measure. In addition, since extreme scores tend to have more random error than less extreme scores, don't select participants who have extreme pretest scores.

A trickier approach to combat regression is to obtain results that regression cannot account for. In our depression example, regression would tend to make it look like the college students had improved in mood more than the mental patients. Thus, if you found that college students improved more than mental patients, your results might be due to regression. However, if you found the opposite results—mental patients improving in mood more than college students—regression would not be an explanation for your results. So, the key is to get results exactly opposite from what regression would predict.

Unfortunately, there is no way to guarantee that your effect will be in exactly the opposite direction of the way regression is pushing the scores. Furthermore, even if the effect is in the opposite direction of what would be expected by regression, regression may overwhelm the effect. That is, even though your treatment had a positive effect, the treatment group's scores—because of regression—may still decline. When regression and selection by maturation are both pushing scores in the opposite direction of the treatment, the effect of even a moderately effective treatment may be hidden.

To illustrate how regression and selection by maturation can hide a treatment's effect, consider research attempting to determine the effects of social programs. Sometimes, researchers try to find the effect of a social program by matching a group of individuals who participate in the program with individuals who are not eligible. For example, researchers compared children who participated in "Head Start" with an upper-income group of children who had the same test scores. Unfortunately, this often meant selecting a group of upper-income children whose test scores were extremely low compared to their upper-income peers. Consequently, on retesting, these scores regressed back up toward the mean of upper-income children. Because of this regression toward the mean effect, scores in the "no treatment" group increased more than scores in the "Head Start" group.

Not only was regression a problem, but there was also the potential for a selection by maturation interaction—especially for studies that looked for long-term effects of "Head Start." That is, even if the groups started out the same, the upper-income group, because of superior health, nutrition, and schools, might mature academically at a faster rate than the disadvantaged group. Thus, not surprisingly, some early studies of "Head Start" that failed to take regression and selection by maturation into account make it look like "Head Start" harmed, rather than helped, children. Thus, as you can see, matching is far from the perfect solution that it first appears to be (see Table 11-9).

## Conclusions about Quasi-Experimental Designs

Quasi-experimenters ensure temporal precedence and assess covariation. However, quasi-experimenters do not automatically rule out the effects of nontreatment factors.

Quasi-experimenters use a variety of tactics to compensate for the limitations of their designs. They may combine two quasi-experimental designs, using one design to cover for another's weaknesses. For example, they may use a time series design to rule out selection biases and then use a non-equivalent control group design to rule out history effects. They may identify a specific threat to their study's internal validity and then take steps to minimize that threat (see Table 11-3). For instance, they may eliminate instrumentation biases by administering the same measure, the same way, every time. Finally, they may eliminate some threats by arguing that the particular threat is not a likely explanation for the effect. That is, they may argue that mortality was low and therefore not a threat or that pretest scores were not extreme and so regression is not a problem.

When arguing that nontreatment factors are unlikely explanations for their results, quasi-experimenters often invoke the law of parsimony. The law of

**TABLE 11−9**

**Problems with Trying to Make Groups Equivalent by Matching**

| PROBLEM | IMPLICATION |
| --- | --- |
| You cannot match on all variables. | Selection by maturation interactions are possible. |
| You cannot match on true scores. Instead, you have to match on observed scores, which are not totally accurate. | Regression effects are possible. |

parsimony is the assumption that the simplest explanation is the most likely. Thus, the time series researcher argues that the simplest assumption to make is that the effects of maturation, instrumentation, testing, and mortality are consistent over time. Therefore, a dramatic change after introducing the treatment should not be viewed as a complex, unexpected maturation effect, but as a simple, straightforward treatment effect.

Clearly, the quasi-experimenter's job is a difficult one, requiring much creativity and effort. But there are rewards. Quasi-experimenters can often study the effects of treatments that couldn't be studied with conventional experimental designs. For example, quasi-experimenters can study treatments that could not—or should not—be randomly assigned. Thus, quasi-experimenters can study the effects of disasters, new laws, new technology, and new social-programs. Furthermore, because quasi-experimenters often study real-world treatments, their studies sometimes have more external validity than traditional experimental designs.

## CONCLUDING REMARKS

If you want to infer causality, the methods described in the last few chapters are extremely useful. But what if you don't want to infer causality? What if you want to describe or predict behavior? Then, you will want to use one of the methods discussed in the next two chapters.

## SUMMARY

1. To infer that a treatment causes an effect, you must show that changing the amount of the treatment is accompanied by changes in participants' behavior (covariation), that changes in the treatment come before changes in the behavior (temporal precedence), and that no other variables are responsible for the change in behavior.

2. By comparing treatment and nontreatment conditions, you can see whether the cause and the effect covary.

3. When you manipulate the treatment, you make sure that the treatment comes before the change in behavior, thereby establishing temporal precedence.

4. Randomization is an effective way of ruling out the likelihood that nontreatment effects may be responsible for the effect.

5. Like randomized experiments, single-n experiments manipulate the treatment to ensure temporal precedence and compare conditions to assess covariation.

6. Single-n experimenters try to identify the important, nontreatment variables. Once identified, they try to keep those variables constant.

7. Single-n experimenters keep relevant individual difference variables constant by using a single participant.

8. Single-n experimenters often keep relevant environmental variables constant by keeping the participant in a highly controlled environment.

9. The A–B–A or reversal design and the multiple baseline design are used by single-n experimenters to rule out the effects of maturation and testing.

10. When it comes to construct validity, the single-n experimenter and the within-subjects experimenter are very similar. To prevent participants from figuring out the hypothesis, both experimenters may use: (1) few levels of the independent variable, (2) placebo treatments, and (3) gradual variations in the levels of the independent variable.

11. Unlike single-n experimenters, quasi-experimenters do not know all the relevant variables that impact the key behavior or construct and/or cannot exercise control over those variables.

12. Quasi-experimenters must explicitly rule out the eight threats to validity: history, maturation, testing, instrumentation, mortality, regression, selection, and selection by maturation interactions.

13. Instrumentation can be ruled out simply by using the same measure, the same way, every time.

**14.** Mortality can be eliminated merely by keeping participants in your study.

**15.** You can rule out regression if participants were not chosen on the basis of their extreme scores or if your measuring instrument is extremely reliable.

**16.** The time series design is very similar to the single-n design. The main difference is that the time series design doesn't isolate participants from history the way the single-n experiment does. As a result, the time series' Achilles' heel is history.

**17.** The non-equivalent control group design resembles the simple experiment. However, because participants are not randomly assigned to groups, selection is a serious problem in the non-equivalent control group design.

**18.** Although quasi-experimental designs are not as good as experimental designs for inferring causality, they are more versatile.

## KEY TERMS

**temporal precedence:** the treatment factor was introduced before the effect occurred. Because causes come before effects, researchers trying to establish causality must establish temporal precedence. Experimental designs establish temporal precedence by manipulating the treatment variable. (p. 351)

**covariation:** changes in the treatment are accompanied by changes in the behavior. To establish causality, you must establish covariation. (p. 350)

**spurious:** when the covariation observed between two variables is not due to the variables influencing each other, but because both are being influenced by some third variable. For example, the relationship between ice cream sales and assaults in New York is spurious—not because it does not exist (it does!)—but because ice cream does not cause assaults and assaults do not cause ice cream sales. Instead, high temperatures probably cause both increased assaults and ice cream sales. Beware of spuriousness whenever you look at research that does not use an experimental design. (p. 351)

**single-n designs:** designs that try to establish causality by studying a single participant and arguing that the covariation between treatment and changes in behavior could not be due to anything other than the treatment. A key to this approach is preventing factors other than the treatment from varying. (p. 352)

**baseline:** the participant's behavior on the task prior to receiving the treatment. (p. 352)

**stable baseline:** when the participant's behavior, prior to receiving the treatment, is consistent. To establish a stable baseline, the researcher may have to keep many factors constant. If the researcher establishes a stable baseline and then is able to change the behavior after administering the treatment, the researcher can make the case that the treatment caused the effect. (p. 352)

**A–B design:** the simplest single-n design, consisting of measuring the participant's behavior at baseline (A) and then measuring the participant after the participant has received the treatment (B). (p. 352)

**A–B–A reversal design:** a single-n design in which baseline measurements are made of the target behavior (A), then a treatment is administered and the participant's behavior is recorded (B), and then the treatment is removed and the target behavior is measured again (A). The A–B–A design makes a more convincing case for the treatment's effect than the A–B design. (p. 357)

**carryover effects:** the effects of a treatment condition persist into later conditions. Because of carryover, investigators using an A–B–A design frequently find that the participant's behavior does not return to the original baseline. The possibilities for carryover effects increase dramatically when you use more levels of the independent variable and/or when you use more than one independent variable. Because carryover effects are a serious concern, many single-n experimenters minimize carryover's complications by doing experiments that use only two levels of a single independent variable. (p. 358)

**multiple baseline design:** a single-n design in which the researcher studies several behaviors at a time. The researcher collects a baseline on these different behaviors. The researcher then introduces a treatment to try to modify one of the behaviors. The researcher hopes that the treatment will change the selected behavior, but that the other behaviors will stay at baseline. Next, the researcher tries to modify the second behavior and so on. For example, a manager might collect baseline data on employee absenteeism, tardiness, and cleanliness. Then, the manager would reward cleanliness while continuing to collect data on all three variables. Then, the manager would reward punctuality, etc. (p. 360)

**history:** events in the environment—other than the treatment—that have changed. Differences between conditions that are believed to be due to treatment may sometimes be due to history. (p. 366)

**instrumentation:** the way participants were measured changed from pretest to posttest. In instrumentation, the actual measuring instrument changes or the way it is administered changes. (p. 366)

**testing:** participants score differently on the posttest as a result of what they learned from taking the pretest. Practice effects could be considered a type of testing effect. (pp. 356, 366)

**maturation:** changes in the participant that naturally occur over time. Physiological changes such as fatigue, growth, and development are common sources of maturation. (pp. 354, 356, 366)

**mortality:** differences between conditions are due to participants dropping out of the study. (p. 366)

**selection:** treatment and no treatment groups were different at the end of the study because the groups differed before the treatment was administered. (p. 366)

**selection by maturation interaction:** treatment and no treatment groups, although similar at one point, would have grown apart (developed differently) even if no treatment had been administered. (p. 367)

**regression** (also known as **statistical regression**): one reason we don't know an individual's true score on a variable is that measurements are affected by random error. Averaged over all scores, random error has no net effect. That is, although random error pushes some individuals' scores up higher than their true scores, it pushes other individuals' scores down. However, if we only select participants with extremely high scores, we are selecting—for the most part—only those pretest scores that random error increased (if it had decreased them, those scores wouldn't be so high). If we retest these individuals, their retest scores will be lower because random error will probably not push all of their scores up two times in a row. Consequently, these participants' retest scores will be less extreme. In other words, their retest scores will regress toward the mean. Likewise, if you select participants based on their having extremely low pretest scores, you will find that the scores of those participants will be less low on the posttest. (p. 366)

**quasi-experiment:** a study that resembles an experiment except that random assignment played no role in determining which participants got which level of treatment. Usually, quasi-experiments have less internal validity than experiments. The time-series design and the non-equivalent control group design are considered quasi-experimental designs. (p. 365)

**pretest–posttest design:** a before-after design in which each participant is given the pretest, administered the treatment, then given the posttest. The pretest–posttest design is not vulnerable to selection and selection by maturation interactions. It is, however, extremely vulnerable to history, maturation, and testing effects. (p. 369)

**time series design:** a quasi-experimental design in which a series of observations is taken from a group of participants over time before and after they receive treatment. Because it uses many times of measurement, it is an improvement over the pretest–posttest design. However, it is still extremely vulnerable to history effects. (p. 371)

**non-equivalent control group design:** a quasi-experimental design that, like a simple experiment, has a treatment group and a no treatment comparison group. However, unlike the simple experiment, random assignment does not determine which subjects get the treatment and which do not. Having a comparison group is better than not having one, but if the comparison group was not really equivalent to the treatment group at the start of the study, you may be comparing apples with oranges. Thus, you may mistakenly believe that the treatment had an effect when it did not. In other words, selection is a serious threat to the validity of the non-equivalent control group design. (p. 378)

## EXERCISES

1. Compare and contrast how single-n experiments and randomized experiments account for nontreatment factors.
2. What arguments can you make for generalizing results from the single-n experiment?
3. How do single-n subjects and time series designs differ?
4. Design a quasi-experiment that looks at the effects of presidential assassinations on the stock market. What kind of design would you use? Why?
5. An ad depicts a student who has improved his grade point average from 2.0 to 3.2 after a stint in the military. Consider Campbell & Stanley's "spurious eight." Is the military the only possible explanation for the improvement?
6. According to one study, holding students back a grade harmed students. The evidence: Students who had been held back a grade did much worse in school than students who had not been held back.
   a. Does this evidence prove that holding students back harms their performance? Why or why not?
   b. If you were a researcher hired by the Department of Education to test the assertion that holding students back harms them, what design would you use? Why?

# CHAPTER 12

## Introduction to Descriptive Methods

*Overview*

*Uses for Descriptive Methods*

DESCRIPTIVE RESEARCH AND CAUSALITY
DESCRIPTION FOR DESCRIPTION'S SAKE
DESCRIPTION FOR PREDICTION'S SAKE
WHY DO WE NEED SCIENCE TO DESCRIBE BEHAVIOR?
CONCLUSIONS ABOUT THE NEED FOR DESCRIPTIVE RESEARCH

*Sources of Data*

EX POST FACTO RESEARCH
ARCHIVAL DATA
OBSERVATION
TESTS

*Describing Your Data*

GRAPHING YOUR DATA
CORRELATION COEFFICIENTS: WHEN A NUMBER MAY BE WORTH
A THOUSAND POINTS
SUMMARY OF DESCRIBING CORRELATIONAL DATA

*Making Inferences from Data*

ANALYSES BASED ON CORRELATION COEFFICIENTS
ANALYSES NOT INVOLVING CORRELATION COEFFICIENTS
INTERPRETING SIGNIFICANT RESULTS
INTERPRETING NULL RESULTS

*A Look Ahead*

*Summary*

*Key Terms*

*Exercises*

# *Chapter 12*

# INTRODUCTION TO DESCRIPTIVE METHODS

*"The invalid assumption that correlation implies cause is probably among the two or three most serious and common errors of human reasoning."*

—Stephen Jay Gould, THE MISMEASURE OF MAN (1981), p. 242.

## OVERVIEW

In this chapter, you will be introduced to descriptive research. Descriptive research is relatively straightforward because to describe behavior, all you need to do is measure variables.

In fact, at the most primitive level of describing behavior, you only have to measure a single variable, such as counting how many times something happens. Thus, the earliest research on "date rape" involved finding out how frequently women were raped by their dates.

At a more sophisticated level of description, you would measure your original variable and several other variables to see if they are related. Thus, research on date rape evolved from testing hypotheses about the number of date rapes to testing hypotheses about variables that might be associated with being a date rapist or victim. For example, researchers studied whether date rapists exhibited aggressive tendencies prior to raping their victim and whether certain situations were more likely to lead to a date rape (like blind dates).

As you can see, descriptive research quickly progresses from describing a single variable to describing relationships among variables. Almost as soon as researchers had estimated the number of date rapes, they were finding factors that related to date rape. Because descriptive research almost always involves determining how variables *co*-vary, or how variables *relate* to one another, descriptive research methods are also called *correlational* methods.

# USES FOR DESCRIPTIVE METHODS

When you use descriptive methods, you gain the ability to test hypotheses about virtually any variable in virtually any situation. For example, you can use descriptive methods even when you can't manipulate variables. You can use descriptive methods even when you can neither control irrelevant variables nor account for their effects. In short, if your hypothesis is that two or more variables are related, descriptive methods give you the flexibility to test that hypothesis.

## Descriptive Research and Causality

But this flexibility comes at a cost. Without being able to manipulate variables and account for the effects of irrelevant variables, you cannot legitimately make cause-effect statements. As a result, you cannot determine the reason for the relationships you find. Thus, if you find a relationship between low self-esteem and people who have been raped, you cannot say *why* low self-esteem and rape are related. Certainly, you cannot say that low self-esteem causes one to be raped.

Why not? First, because you do not know that rape victims had low self-esteem *before* they were raped. It may be that prior to being raped, rape victims had high self-esteem but that rape lowered self-esteem. Instead of low self-esteem being the cause of rape, it may be an effect of rape.

Second, you haven't controlled for or accounted for other variables that might be responsible for the relationship between self-esteem and rape. Many factors might lead both to having low self-esteem and to being raped. For example, being short may lead to low self-esteem as well as decreasing one's ability to fight off an attacker. Or, having a low income may lead to low self-esteem and also make one more vulnerable to rape—if low income people live in more dangerous neighborhoods (see Figure 12–1).

To repeat a very important point, correlational methods do not establish causality. When you use a correlational method to find a relationship between two variables, you do not know whether the relationship is due to:

**1.** changes in the first variable causing changes in the second variable;
**2.** changes in the second variable causing changes in the first variable; or
**3.** a third variable causing the changes in both variables.

### STIMULATING CAUSAL HYPOTHESES

Although correlational methods do not allow you to infer causality, they may stimulate causal hypotheses. As you can see from Table 12–1, there are two ways that correlational methods may stimulate causal hypotheses.

First, if you find a relationship between two variables, you may want to do an experiment to determine whether the relationship is a causal relationship.

FIGURE 12.1

## Three Basic Possibilities for an Observed Relationship

1. The "first" factor causes a change in the "second" factor.

2. The "second" factor causes a change in the "first" factor.

3. Some "third" factor could cause a change in both the "first" and "second" factors.[1]

3 a.

3 b.

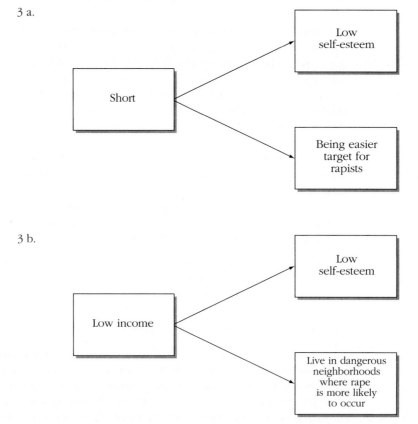

[1] Note that there are many "third" factors that might account for the relationship. We have listed only two (height and income).

**TABLE 12–1**

**Generating Causal Hypotheses from Correlational Data**

For each correlational finding listed below, develop an experimental hypothesis.

1. Listeners to country music tend to be more depressed than people who listen to other types of music.

2. There is a correlation between attendance and good grades.

3. Attractive people earn higher salaries than less attractive people.

4. In restaurants, large groups tend to leave lower tips (percentage-wise) than individuals.

5. Teams that wear black uniforms are more often penalized than other teams.

6. People report being more often persuaded by newspaper editorials than by television editorials.

7. Students report that they would be less likely to cheat if professors walked around the class more during exams.

8. Students who take notes in outline form get better grades than those who don't.

For instance, knowing that there was a correlation between smoking and lung cancer led to experiments that tested whether smoking caused lung cancer.

Second, even if you know that the two factors do not directly influence each other, you may try to find out what causes them to be statistically related. That is, you may try to find out what third factor accounts for their relationship. For example, suppose you find that students who study more have lower grade point averages. Because this finding is puzzling, you may decide to try to figure out why this relationship exists. Consequently, you might try to determine if this relationship is due to poor students using study strategies that are both time-consuming and ineffective. This idea may lead you to do experiments to test whether some study strategies are more effective than others. Alternatively, if you think the relationship is due to poorer students being slower and poorer readers, you might design an experiment to see whether training in reading skills improves grades.

In summary, descriptive research does not allow you to infer causality (see Table 12-2). However, descriptive research may stimulate research that will allow you to infer causality: Once you use a descriptive design to find out what happens, you can use an experimental design to try to find out why it happens.

## Description for Description's Sake

By hinting at possible causal relationships, descriptive research can indirectly help psychologists achieve two goals of psychology—explaining behavior and controlling behavior. But the main purpose of descriptive research is to achieve another important goal of psychology—describing behavior.

But is description really an important scientific goal? Yes, in fact, description is a major goal of every science. What is chemistry's famed periodic table, but a description of the elements? What is biology's system of classifying plants

**TABLE 12–2**

**Questions That Must Be Answered to Establish That Two Variables Are Causally Related**

**Is there a relationship between the two variables in the sample?**

Did the researchers accurately measure the two variables?

Did the researchers accurately record the two variables?

Did the researchers accurately perceive the degree to which the variables were related?

**If the variables are related in the sample, are the variables related in the population?**

Is the sample a random sample of the population?

Even if the sample is a random sample of the population, is the sample big enough—and the relationship strong enough—that we can be confident that the relationship really occurs in the population?

**If the variables are related, did the predictor variable cause changes in the criterion?**

Is it possible that the "criterion" variable caused changes in the predictor variable? In other words, is our "cause" really the effect?

Do we know which variable came first?

Do we have data that suggest to us which came first? For example, high school records might provide information about self-esteem before being victimized. If there is no difference between victims' and non-victims' self-esteem before the attack, we would be more confident that the attacks came before the lowered self-esteem.

Can we logically rule out the possibility that one variable preceded the other? For example, if height and being a victim were correlated, we can make a good case that the person's height was established before he or she was attacked. (Posture might be affected, but we would rely on accurate measurement to correct for this.)

Is it possible that a third variable could be responsible for the relationship? That is, neither variable may directly influence (cause) the other. Instead, the two variables might be statistically related because they are both effects of some other variable. For example, increases in assaults and ice cream consumption may both be consequences of heat.

Were all other variables kept constant or randomized? (This only happens in experimental designs.)

Does the researcher know what the potential third variables are? If so, the researcher may be able to statistically control for those variables. However, it is virtually impossible to know and measure every potential third variable.

---

and animals into Kingdom, Phylum, Genus, and Species, but a way of describing living organisms? What is astronomy's mapping of the stars, but a description of outer space? What is science, but systematic observation and measurement? Thus, one reason psychologists value descriptive methods is because description is the cornerstone of science. Besides, psychologists, like everyone else, want to be able to describe what people think, feel, and do.

## Description for Prediction's Sake

Psychologists also like descriptive methods because knowing what is happening helps us predict what will happen. In the case of suicide, for example,

**FIGURE 12–2**

### Steps Involved in Determining That There Really is a Relationship Between Two Variables

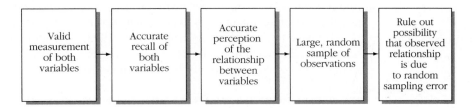

*Note:* People who draw conclusions based on their own personal experience could be making mistakes at every single one of these stages.

Do you know anyone who executes all 5 steps correctly?
Probably not. Indeed, even some scientific studies fail to execute all 5 steps correctly.

psychologists discovered that certain signals (giving away precious posses- sions, abrupt changes in personality) were associated with suicide. Conse- quently, psychologists now realize that people sending out those signals are more likely to attempt suicide than people not behaving that way.

## Why Do We Need Science to Describe Behavior?

Certainly, describing behavior is an important goal of psychology. But do we need to use scientific methods to describe what's all around us? Yes! Intuition alone cannot objectively measure variables, keep track of these measurements, determine the degree to which variables are related, and then accurately in- fer that the observed pattern of results reflects what typically happens (see Fig- ure 12–2).

### WE NEED SCIENTIFIC MEASUREMENT

We need scientific methods to accurately measure the variables we want to measure. As you saw in Chapter 3, reliable and valid measurement of psycho- logical variables is not automatic. If you are to observe psychological variables in a systematic, objective, and unbiased way, you must use scientific methods. Imagine using intuition to measure a person's level of motivation, intelligence, or some other psychological variable!

### WE NEED SYSTEMATIC, SCIENTIFIC RECORD-KEEPING

Even if you could intuitively get *accurate* measurements of psychological variables, you could not rely on your memory to keep track of your observations. Your memory can fool you, especially when it comes to estimating how often things occur. For example, our memories may fool us into believing that more people die from plane crashes than actually do and that more words start with "r" than have "r" as their third letter (Myers, 1992). Therefore, if you are to describe behavior accurately, you need to record your observations systematically so that your conclusions are not biased by memory's selectivity.

### WE NEED OBJECTIVE WAYS TO DETERMINE WHETHER VARIABLES ARE RELATED

Obviously, if you're poor at keeping track of observations of one variable, you are going to be even worse at keeping track of two variables—plus the relationship between them. Therefore, you cannot rely on your judgment to determine whether two things are related.

People seem so anxious to see relationships that they see variables as being related, even when the variables are not related. In several experiments on **illusory correlation** (Chapman & Chapman, 1967; Ward & Jenkins, 1965), researchers showed participants some data that did not follow any pattern and that did not indicate any relationship among variables. However, participants usually "found" patterns in this data and "found" relationships (illusory correlations) between variables. Out of the lab, we know that people "see" systematic patterns in the stock market, even though the stock market behaves in an essentially random fashion (Shefrin & Statman, 1986). Similarly, many people believe that the interview is an invaluable selection device, even though research shows that interviews have virtually no validity (Schultz & Schultz, 1990; Dawes, 1994).

Even when there is a relationship between two variables, the relationship people "see" between two variables may be exactly opposite of the relationship that exists. For example, basketball players and coaches swear (both literally and figuratively) that if a player makes a shot, that player will be more likely to make the next shot. However, as Kahneman and Tversky (1985) have discovered, a shooter is *less* likely to make the next shot if he has made the previous shot. Similarly, many people are aware of the famed "*Sports Illustrated* Jinx"—the "fact" that a team or person on the cover of *Sports Illustrated* will perform worse from then on. The belief in the "jinx" is so strong that many fans hate to see their favorite team on the magazine's cover. But fans needn't fear—the truth is that players and teams do better after appearing on the cover of *Sports Illustrated.*

Of course, sports fans are not the only ones to misperceive relationships. Many Americans think that terrorism has increased since the late 1970s; in fact, terrorism has declined fairly steadily since the late 1970s. Many bosses and parents swear that rewarding people doesn't work while punishing them does, even though research shows that rewards are more effective than punishments. And many students swear that cramming for exams is more effective than studying consistently, even though research contradicts this claim.

### WE NEED SCIENTIFIC METHODS TO GENERALIZE FROM EXPERIENCE

But even if you accurately describe your own experience, how can you generalize the results of that experience? After all, your experience is based on a limited and small sample of behavior.

One problem with small samples is that they may cause you to overlook a real relationship. Thus, it's not surprising that one man wrote to "Dear Abby" to inform her that lung cancer and smoking were not related: He knew many smokers and none had lung cancer.

Another problem with small samples is that the relationship that exists in the sample may not reflect what typically happens in the population. Thus, our experiences may represent the exception rather than the rule. That is, the relationship you observe may simply be due to a coincidence. For example, if we go by some people's experiences, playing the lottery is a financially profitable thing to do.

But how can you intuitively determine the likelihood that a pattern of results is due to a coincidence? To discount the role of coincidence, you need to do two things. First, you need to have a reasonably large and random sample of behavior. Second, you need to use probability theory to determine the likelihood that your results are due to random error. Thus, even if you were an intuitive statistician, you would still face one big question: What's to say that your experience is a large, random sample of behavior? Your experience may be a small and biased sample of behavior. Results from such biased samples are apt to be wrong. For example, several years ago, George Bush beat Michael Dukakis by one of the biggest margins in the history of United States presidential elections. However, right up to election eve, some ardent Dukakis supporters thought that Dukakis would beat George Bush. Why? Because everybody they knew was voting for Dukakis.

## Conclusions about the Need for Descriptive Research

As you can see, we need descriptive research if we are to accurately describe and predict what people think, feel, or do. Fortunately, descriptive research is relatively easy to do. To describe how two variables are related, you need to get a representative sample of behavior; accurately measure both variables; and then objectively assess the association between those variables. Thus, the bottom line in doing descriptive research is getting accurate measurements from a representative sample.

The key to getting a representative sample is to get a large and random sample. But how can you get accurate measurements from a large and random sample?

In the next few sections, we'll look at several ways to get measurements. We'll start by examining ways of making use of data that have already been collected, then we'll move to collecting our own data.

# SOURCES OF DATA

One possible source of data for descriptive research is data that you have already collected. For example, you may have done an experiment looking at the effects of time pressure on performance on a verbal task. At the time you did the study, you may not have cared about the age, gender, personality type, or other personal characteristics of your participants. For testing your experimental hypothesis (that the treatment had an effect), these individual difference variables were irrelevant. However, like saving money for a rainy day, you collected this information anyway.

## Ex Post Facto Research: Data You Have Already Collected

After the experiment is over, you might want to go back and look for relationships between these "nuisance variables" and task performance. This kind of research is called **ex post facto research:** research done after the fact.

### EXTERNAL VALIDITY

Suppose your ex post facto research revealed that women did better than men on the verbal task. Although this finding is interesting, you should be careful about generalizing your results. Unless the males and females in your study are a random sample drawn from the entire population of males and females, you cannot say that females do better at this verbal task than males do. Your effect may simply be due to sampling males of average intelligence and females of above average intelligence. This sampling bias could easily occur, especially if your school was one that had higher admissions standards for women than for men. (Some schools did this when they switched from being all-women colleges to co-educational institutions.)

You could have a bit more confidence that your results were not due to sampling error if you had also included a mathematical task and found that although the women did better than the men on the verbal task, men did better on the mathematical task. If, in this case, your results are due to sampling error, they aren't due to simply having sampled women who are above average in intelligence. Instead, your sampling error would have to be due to something rather strange such as sampling women who were better than the average woman in verbal ability *and* who were worse than the average woman in mathematical ability. Although such a sampling bias is possible, it is not as likely as having merely sampled women who are above average in intelligence. Therefore, with this pattern of results, you would be a little more confident that your results were not due to sampling error.

## CONSTRUCT VALIDITY

Even if you could show that your results are not due to sampling error, you could not automatically conclude that women had greater verbal ability than men. To make this claim, you would have to show that your measure was a valid measure of verbal ability *and* that the measure was just as valid for men as it was for women. That is, you would have to show that your measure wasn't biased against men (for example, using vocabulary terms relating primarily to different colors, women's fashions, and ballet).

## INTERNAL VALIDITY

Through careful random sampling and choice of measures, you might be able to determine that women had better verbal ability than men. However, you could not say *why* women had superior verbal ability. As you'll recall, correlational methods are *not* useful for inferring causality. Therefore, you could not say whether the difference in men's and women's verbal ability was due to inborn differences between men and women or due to differences in how men and women are socialized.

## CONCLUSIONS ABOUT EX POST FACTO RESEARCH

In summary, ex post facto research takes advantage of data you have already collected. Therefore, the quantity and quality of ex post facto research depends on the quantity and quality of data you collect during the original study. The more information you collect about your participants' personal characteristics, the more ex post facto hypotheses you can examine. The more valid your measures, the more valid your conclusions. The more representative your sample of participants, the more external validity your results will have. Therefore, if you are doing a study, and there's any possibility that you will do ex post facto research, you should prepare for that possibility by using a random sample of participants and/or collecting a lot of data about each participant's personal characteristics.

# Archival Data

Rather than use data that you have collected, you can use **archival data:** data that someone else has already collected. Basically, there are two kinds of archival data—coded data and uncoded data.

## COLLECTED AND CODED DATA

Coded data are data that have been collected and tabulated by others. Market researchers, news organizations, behavioral scientists, and government researchers are all collecting and tabulating data. How much data? To give you some idea, more than 5,000 Americans are surveyed every day—and surveys are just one way that these researchers collect data.

If you can get access to archival research, you can often look at data that you could never have collected yourself. Unfortunately, much of these data you never would have wanted to collect because they were collected and coded in a way that is inappropriate for your research problem.

### COLLECTED BUT UNCODED DATA

If you want to code data yourself, but you do not want to collect your own data, you can use the second kind of archival data—data that have been recorded, but are uncoded. Records of behavior range from letters to the editor, to transcripts of congressional hearings, to videotapes of "The People's Court," to baseball statistics, to ads in the personal columns for a dating partner.

The primary advantage of using records of data is that the basic data have already been collected for you. All you have to do is code them. And you can code them as best suits your needs.

The disadvantage of this kind of data is that you have to code them. That is, you have to convert these videotapes or transcripts into a form that you can meaningfully and objectively analyze. To succeed at this task, use **content analysis.** Content analysis has been used to categorize a wide range of free responses—from determining whether a threatening letter is really from a terrorist to determining whether someone's response to an ambiguous picture shows that they have a high need for achievement.

In content analysis, you code behavior according to whether it belongs to a certain category (aggressive, sexist, superstitious, etc.). To use content analysis, you must first carefully define your coding categories. To define these categories, you should do a review of the research to find out how others have coded those categories. If you can't borrow or adopt one of their coding schemes, you might decide to do a mini-study just to get an idea of the types of behavior you will be coding. After you have defined your categories, you should provide examples of behavior that would fit into each of your categories. Finally, train your raters to use these categories.

The primary aim in content analysis is to define your categories as objectively as possible. Some researchers define their categories so objectively that all the coder has to do is count the number of times certain words come up. For example, to get an indication of America's mood, a researcher might count the number of times words like "war," "fight," and so on appear in *The New York Times.* These word-counting schemes are so easy to use that even a computer can do them. In fact, researchers have invented a computer program that can tell genuine suicide notes from fake ones (Stone, Dunphy, Smith, & Ogilvie, 1966).

Unfortunately, objective criteria are not always so valid. To get totally objective criteria, you often have to ignore the context—yet the meaning of behavior often depends on the context. For example, you might use the number of times the word "war" appears in the paper as a measure of how eager we are for war. This method would be objective, but what if the newspaper was merely reporting wars in other countries? Or, what if the newspaper was full of editorials urging us to "avoid war," no matter what the cost? In that case, our measure would be objective, but invalid.

Indeed, context is so important that completely objective scoring criteria of certain variables is virtually impossible. For example, whether a remark is sarcastic, humorous, or sexist may depend more on when, where, and how the statement is made than on what is said. Nevertheless, researchers have developed highly objective ways of coding archival data.

To get a clearer picture of both the advantages and disadvantages of archival research, suppose that you wanted to know whether people were more superstitious when they were worried about the economy. As your measure of concern about the economy, you use government statistics on unemployment. As your measure of how superstitious people are, you have the computer count the number of key words such as "magic," "superstition," and "voodoo" that appear in local newspapers and then divide this number by the total number of words in the newspaper. This would give you the percentage of superstitious words in local newspapers.

## INTERNAL VALIDITY

Once you had your measures of both economic concern and of superstitiousness, you would correlate the two. Suppose you found that the more unemployment, the more superstitious words were used in the newspaper. Since you have done a correlational study, you cannot say why the two variables are related. That is, you do not know whether:

1. The economy caused people to become superstitious;
2. Superstitious beliefs caused the downfall of the economy; or
3. Some other factor (a bad freeze or drought ruining crops) is responsible for both an increase in superstitious beliefs and a decline in the economy.

## CONSTRUCT VALIDITY

In addition to the normal problems associated with correlational data, you have several problems specific to archival data. You are using measures of a construct, not because they're the best, but because they are the only measures that someone else bothered to collect. Although you are using unemployment records as an index of how insecure people felt about the economy, you would have rather asked people about how they felt about the economy. To the degree that the relationship between how many people were unemployed and how people felt about the economy is questionable, your measure's construct validity is questionable.

Even if there is a strong relationship between unemployment and concerns about the economy, your measure may lack construct validity because it may not accurately assess unemployment. It may have poor construct validity because of **instrumentation bias:** the criteria for who is considered unemployed changing over time. Sometimes this change in criteria is planned and is formally announced. For example, the government may change the definition from "being unemployed" to "being unemployed and showing documentation that he or she looks for three jobs every week." Other times, the change may not be announced. For instance, computerization and unemployment compensation make current unemployment statistics more complete than they were in the early 1900s. Or, since the people who would collect unemployment statistics—social workers and other government workers—are sometimes laid off during hard economic times, unemployment statistics might be less complete during periods of high unemployment. Or, more sinisterly, politicians may distort unemployment data to make things seem better than they are.

Of course, the construct validity of your measure of superstition is also questionable. Is the number of times superstitious terms are mentioned in newspapers a good index of superstition? Perhaps these articles sell papers and major newspapers only stoop to using these articles when sales are very low. About the only advantage of this measure over having results of some nationwide survey that questioned people directly about their superstitious beliefs is that your measure is **nonreactive:** your collecting it does not change participants' behavior.

### EXTERNAL VALIDITY

Because you can collect so much data so easily, your results should have good external validity. In some cases, your results may apply to millions of people because you have data from millions of people. For example, you can easily get unemployment statistics for the entire U.S. Furthermore, because you can collect data for a period of years rather than for just the immediate present, you should be able to generalize your results across time.

### THE LIMITS OF AGGREGATE DATA

Gaining access to group data (for instance, the unemployment rate for the entire U.S. for 1931) is convenient and may aid external validity. However, as psychologists, we are interested in what individuals do. Therefore, we want individual data. Consequently, even if we find that there is a correlation between unemployment for the nation as a whole and superstition for the nation as a whole, we are still troubled. We do not care about knowing about the nation as a whole, we care about individual behavior. Are the people who are unemployed the ones who are superstitious? Or, are the superstitious ones the people whose friends have been laid off? Or, do the rich become superstitious? With aggregate data, we cannot say.

### CONCLUSIONS ABOUT ARCHIVAL RESEARCH

By using archival data, you can gain access to a great deal of data that you did not have to collect. Having access to these data may allow you to test hypotheses you would otherwise be unable or unwilling to test. Furthermore, because these data often summarize the behavior of thousands of people, your results may have impressive external validity.

Unfortunately, relying on others to collect data has its costs. You may find that data were not collected as carefully and as consistently as you would have collected them. You may find that others used measures that have less construct validity than the measures you would have used. You may find that you have data about groups, but no data about individuals. You will almost always find that the data were collected by people who were not asking the question you want to answer. As a result of these problems with archival data, you may decide that the best way to get data that will answer your questions is to collect your own data.

## Observation

One way to collect your own data is through observation. As the name implies, observation involves simply watching behavior. As such, observation is often incorporated into many research methods. For example, an experimenter, rather than collecting the dependent measure by having a participant fill out a questionnaire or having a machine record responses, may observe and categorize each participant's behavior.

Observation is also of interest for its own sake. Describing behavior is a vital concern of every field of psychology. Developmental psychologists use observation to describe child-parent interactions, social psychologists to describe cults, clinical psychologists to describe abnormal behavior, counseling psychologists to describe human sexual behavior, and comparative psychologists to describe animal behavior.

### TYPES OF OBSERVATIONAL RESEARCH

Basically, there are two kinds of observation: naturalistic observation and participant observation. In **naturalistic observation,** you try to observe the participant unobtrusively. Often, naturalistic observation involves keeping your distance—both physically and psychologically. In **participant observation,** on the other hand, you actively interact with your participants. In a sense, you become "one of them."

Both types of observation can lead to ethical problems. Naturalistic observation may involve spying on your participants. Often, it involves collecting data without participants' informed consent. Participant observation, on the other hand, may involve infiltrating a group and collecting data without the participants' informed consent. Because the participant observer has more effect on participants, most people consider participant observation to present more ethical problems than naturalistic observation.

But which method provides more valid data? Not everyone agrees on the answer to this question. Advocates of participant observation claim that you get more "inside" information by using participant observation.

Advocates of naturalistic observation counter that the information you get through participant observation may be tainted. As a participant, you are in a position to influence (bias) what your participants do. Furthermore, as an active participant, you may be unable to sit back and record behavior as it occurs. Instead, you may have to rely on your (faulty) memory of what happened.

## PROBLEMS WITH OBSERVATION

Whether you use participant or naturalistic observation, you face two major problems. First, if participants know they are being watched, they may not behave in their normal, characteristic way. Second, even if participants act "natural," you may not be objective as you observe and record their behavior. That is, your personality and motives may affect what things you ignore and how you interpret what you do pay attention to.

***Effects of the Observer on the Observed.*** There are two basic strategies you can use to minimize the degree to which you change behavior by observing it. First, you can observe participants unobtrusively. For example, you might want to observe participants through a one-way mirror.

If you cannot be unobtrusive, you may try the second strategy—become less noticeable. There are two basic strategies for becoming less noticeable. First, you can observe participants from a distance, hoping that they will ignore you. Second, you can let participants become familiar with you, hoping that they will eventually habituate to you. Once participants are used to you, they may forget that you are there and revert back to normal behavior.

***Difficulties in Objectively Coding Behavior.*** While you are observing behavior, you will also be recording it. As was the case with archival data, one problem with observation is that different coders may code data differently. As was the case with archival data, the solution is to develop a content analysis scheme. You need to:

1. Define your categories in terms of specific target behaviors;
2. Develop a check sheet to mark off each time a target behavior is exhibited;
3. Train and motivate raters to use your check sheet.

There are two reasons why training and motivating your raters is even more important in observational research than in archival research. First, in observational research, the rater not only codes the data, but also collects the data. Second, in observational research, there usually are no permanent records of data. Because there are no permanent records, unmotivated or disorganized raters do not get a second chance to rate a behavior they missed: There is no instant replay. Furthermore, because there are no permanent records, you cannot check or correct a rater's work.

Training should involve at least three steps. First, you should spell out what each category means, giving both a definition of each category and some examples of behaviors that belong and do not belong in each category. Second, you should have raters judge several videotapes, then you should tell them why their ratings are right or wrong. Third, you should continue the training until each rater is at least 90% accurate.

# Tests

If you do not want to rely on observers, you may decide to use tests. Tests are especially useful if you want to measure ability, knowledge, or personality variables. For instance, you might correlate scores on an ability to delay gratification test with scores on an intelligence test or with scores on a social adjustment test.

## EXTERNAL VALIDITY

As was the case with ex post facto research, the external validity of your findings depends on the representativeness of your sample. You cannot generalize your results to a population unless you have a random sample of that population. Therefore, you cannot say that women are more extroverted than men unless you have a random sample of all men and women. Similarly, you cannot say that extroverts are happier than introverts unless you have a random sample of all introverts and extroverts.

## INTERNAL VALIDITY

As is the case with all correlational research, if you find a relationship, it is not necessarily a causal relationship. For example, if extroverts are happier than introverts, we don't know whether extroversion causes happiness, happiness causes extroversion, or some other factor (supportive parents, social skills, etc.) causes both extroversion and happiness. This is important to keep in mind because many researchers try to show a genetic basis for some characteristic (career preferences, schizophrenia, introversion, etc.) by showing a correlation between identical twins on that trait. However, identical twins could be similar on the trait because they share a similar environment or because they have influenced one another.

## CONCLUSIONS ABOUT TESTING

By using tests, you can take advantage of measures that other people have spent years developing. As a result, construct validity is usually less of a problem than if you had devised your own measures. Furthermore, tests are often easier to use than other measures. Because of these advantages, tests are often used in experimental as well as nonexperimental research. However, when tests are used in nonexperimental research, this research has the same weaknesses as other correlational research: It doesn't allow you to establish causality and the generalizability of your results will only be as good as the representativeness of your sample (to compare different descriptive designs, see Table 12–3).

## DESCRIBING YOUR DATA

Once you have coded your data, you want to compile and summarize them. You want to know what the data "look like."

You may start by describing participants' scores on key variables. Often, describing those scores will involve calculating the average score and an index of the degree of the variability of the scores. For example, you might report that the mean score on the personality test was 78 and the range was 50. Or, instead of reporting the range (the highest score minus the lowest score), you might report the standard deviation (an index of the extent to which individual scores differ from the mean). Thus, you might say that the mean was 78 and the standard deviation was 10.

Usually, however, you will want to do more than describe how participants scored on individual measures. Instead, you will want to know how participants' scores on one measure relate to their scores on some other measure. To describe these relationships between variables, you should graph your data and compute correlation coefficients.

### Graphing Your Data

Usually, one of the first things you should do after collecting your scores is to graph them. Start by labeling the x-axis (the horizontal axis) with the name of your predictor variable. More specifically, go a few spaces below the bottom of the graph and then write the name of your predictor variable. Next, label the other axis, the y-axis (the vertical axis), with the name of your criterion/ dependent variable. Then, plot each observation.

For example, suppose we were looking at the relationship between self-esteem and grade point average (GPA). Figure 12–3 shows the beginning of such a graph. As you can see, we have plotted the score of our first participant, a student who has a score of 4 on the self-esteem scale and a 2.0 GPA. For reasons that will be obvious after we plot all our data, this graph is called a **scatterplot.** There are four basic relationships that the scatterplot could reveal.

First, the scatterplot could reveal a pattern like the one shown in Figure 12–4. The figure indicates that the higher one's self-esteem, the higher one's grade point average is likely to be. Put another way, the lower one's self-esteem, the lower one's grade point average. This kind of relationship indicates a **positive correlation** between the variables. One common example of a positive

**TABLE 12–3**

**Comparing Different Correlational Methods**

| VALIDITY | EX POST FACTO | ARCHIVAL | OBSERVATION | TESTS |
|---|---|---|---|---|
| Internal validity | Poor | Poor | Poor | Poor |
| Construct validity | Fair | Fair to poor | Fair to poor | Fair to good |
| Objective— Avoids observer bias | Good | May be good | May be poor | Good |
| Non-reactive— Avoids subject bias | Often a problem | Often good | Can be poor | Reactive—But steps taken to control for subject biases |
| Operational definition fits definition of construct | Fair to good | Often poor | Fair | Good |
| External validity | | | | |
| Ease of getting a large, representative sample | Depends on original study | May be easy | Difficult | May be easy |

**FIGURE 12–3**

## The Beginning of a Scatterplot

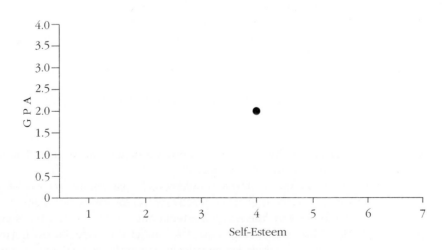

**FIGURE 12–4**

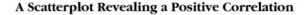

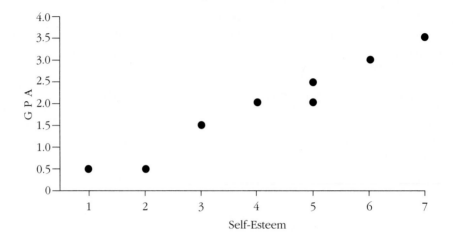

## A Scatterplot Revealing a Positive Correlation

**FIGURE 12–5**

## A Scatterplot Revealing a Negative Correlation

correlation is the relationship between height and weight: The taller you are, the more you are likely to weigh.

Second, the scatterplot could reveal a pattern like the one shown in Figure 12-5, where the higher one's self-esteem, the lower one's grade point average. Put another way, the less self-esteem one has, the higher one's grade point average. This relationship indicates a **negative correlation** between the variables. Many variables are negatively (inversely) related. One common example

FIGURE 12–6

**A Scatterplot Revealing a Zero Correlation**

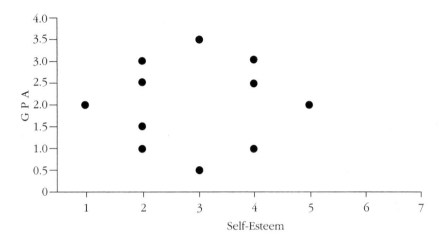

of a negative correlation is the relationship between exercise and weight: The more you exercise, the less you tend to weigh.

Third, the scatterplot might reveal that there is no relationship between self-esteem and grade point average. This pattern, indicating that the two variables are uncorrelated, is depicted in Figure 12–6.

Fourth, you could have a nonlinear relationship between self-esteem and grade point average (GPA). As you can see from Figure 12–7, in a complex, nonlinear relationship, the relationship between self-esteem and GPA may vary, depending on the level of the variables. Thus, in the low ranges of self-esteem, self-esteem may be positively correlated with GPA, but in the high ranges, self-esteem may be negatively correlated with GPA. Such a pattern could emerge in any situation in which a low amount of a variable could be too little, a medium amount of a variable could be just right, and a high level of the variable could be too much. For example, with too little motivation, performance may be poor; with a moderate amount of motivation, performance could be good; and with too much motivation, performance might be poor.

## Correlation Coefficients: When a Number May Be Worth a Thousand Points

Although a graph gives a good picture of your data, you may want to summarize your data with a single number: a **correlation coefficient.** The kind of correlation coefficient you use will depend on the nature of your data (see Table 12–4). However, the most commonly used correlation coefficient is the Pearson $r$.

The Pearson $r$, like all correlation coefficients, summarizes the relationship described in your scatterplot with a single number. In addition, the Pearson $r$, like most correlation coefficients, ranges from $-1$ to $+1$.

FIGURE 12–7

## A Scatterplot Revealing a Nonlinear Relationship

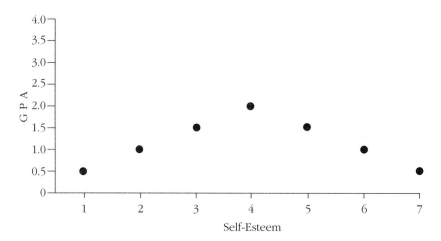

Most importantly, the Pearson $r$ should be consistent with the data in your scatterplot. If your scatterplot indicates a positive correlation between the two variables, your correlation coefficient should also be positive. If the scatterplot indicates that your variables are not related, then your correlation coefficient should be near zero. Finally, if your variables are negatively correlated (inversely related), then the correlation coefficient should be negative.

### THE LOGIC BEHIND THE PEARSON $r$

If you want to compute a Pearson $r$, you can use a computer, a calculator, or the formula described in Box 12-1. However, at this point, we do not want you to focus on how to compute the Pearson $r$. Instead, we want you to focus on understanding the logic behind the Pearson $r$. Basically, there are two ways to think about that logic: in terms of the definition of correlation and in terms of a scatterplot of the data.

As you know, the correlation coefficient is a number that describes the relationship between two variables. If the variables are positively correlated, then, when one variable is above average, the other is usually above average. In addition, when one variable is below average, the other tends to be below average. If the variables are negatively correlated, the reverse happens: When one is above average, the other is usually below average.

To see how the Pearson $r$ mathematically matches that description, suppose that we have the scores of several students on two variables—how well they learned definitions of certain words and how well they pick up on nonverbal cues.[1] To see if student learning is correlated with sensitivity to

---

[1] For a published example of a Pearson $r$ calculated on these two variables see Bernieri, F. J. (1991). Interpersonal sensitivity in teaching interactions. *Personality and Social Psychology Bulletin, 17,* 98–103.

**TABLE 12–4**
## Different Kinds of Correlation Coefficients

In reading the literature, you may come across correlation coefficients other than the Pearson $r$. In addition, you may be called on to compute correlations other than the Pearson $r$. This table should help you understand the distinctions among these different coefficients.

| NAME OF COEFFICIENT | LEVEL OF MEASURE-MENT REQUIRED | EXAMPLE | DATA ENTERED |
|---|---|---|---|
| Pearson $r$ | Both variables must be at least Interval | Height with weight | Actual scores |
| Point bi-serial | One variable is interval, the other nominal | Weight with gender | Actual scores for the interval variable, 0 or 1 for the nominal variable. |
| Spearman's rho | Ordinal data | High school rank with military rank | Ranks |
| Phi coefficient | Nominal data | Race with learning style | 0's and 1's. Zero if the participant is not a member of a category, 1 if the participant is a member of that category. |

Although this table focuses on the differences between these correlation coefficients, these coefficients share commonalities. For example, all of them yield coefficient between $-1$ (a perfect negative correlation) and $+1$ (a perfect positive correlation). Furthermore, as Cohen and Cohen (1983, pp. 38–39) point out, the Pearson $r$, the point biserial, the phi coefficient, and Spearman's rho can all be computed using the same formula. That formula is the formula for the Pearson $r$ (see Box 12-1). The difference between them comes in what data are entered into that formula (see the right-hand column of the table). Thus, for calculating Spearman's rho, you would not use participants' actual scores. Instead, you would convert those scores to ranks and then enter those ranks into the formula.

nonverbal cues, we convert those scores in the following way. If a student scores below the average in terms of recalling the definitions, the student gets a negative score on learning (a score of $-1$). If the student recalls more than the average student in the study, then the participant gets a positive score (a score of $+1$). We do the same thing for the students' scores on reading nonverbal cues: A score of "$-1$" indicates the participant is below average, a score of "$+1$" indicates the participant is above average.

Next, we multiply each participant's learning score times their sensitivity score. For example, if someone is above average in both learning and sensitivity to nonverbal cues, we multiply $+1 \times +1$. If someone is below average in both definitions learned and nonverbal sensitivity, we multiply $-1 \times -1$. Thus, in both cases, the product of the multiplication will be $+1$. However, if someone is below average in definitions learned ($-1$) and above average in nonverbal sensitivity ($+1$), the product for that person would be $-1$. Note that we could consider each of these products as an association score: When, for a given individual, definitions learned and nonverbal sensitivity are positively associated, the product is $+1$; when, for a given individual, definitions learned and nonverbal sensitivity are negatively associated, the product is $-1$. By adding up the results of all these multiplications (these association scores) and then dividing this total by the number of research participants, we will end up with a number between $-1$ and $+1$.

This number will be positive if there is a positive correlation between amount learned and nonverbal sensitivity. That is, people who are high in both amount learned and nonverbal sensitivity will contribute $+1$'s (because $+1 \times +1 = +1$), as will people who are low in both amount learned and nonverbal sensitivity (because $-1 \times -1 = +1$). Therefore, if the variables are positively correlated for most people, most of these products (their association scores) will be $+1$'s. Consequently, the total of everyone's association scores will be positive. Furthermore, the greater the percentage of people who are either high on both variables or low on both variables, the closer the average of all these scores will be to $+1$.

Conversely, if participants who are above average on one variable ($+1$) are usually below average on the other variable ($-1$), we will end up with a negative correlation. Indeed, if everyone who is high on one variable is low on the other, our average score will be $-1$ (because $+1 \times -1 = -1$).

Finally, consider the case in which there is no relationship between the variables. In at case, half the participants who are above the average in nonverbal sensitivity are also above average in amount learned. However, half of the participants who are above average in nonverbal sensitivity are below average on amount learned. In other words, half those participants are contributing a $+1$ (because $+1 \times +1 = +1$), whereas half are contributing a $-1$ (because $+1 \times -1 = -1$). The $+1$'s and the $-1$'s cancel each other out, summing to 0. Similarly, half the participants who are below average on nonverbal sensitivity are below average on amount learned. They contribute $+1$'s. However, half the participants who are below the average on nonverbal sensitivity are above average on amount learned. They contribute $-1$'s. In other words, half of those participants who are below average in nonverbal sensitivity are contributing a $+1$ (because $-1 \times -1 = +1$), whereas half are contributing a $-1$ (because $-1 \times +1 = -1$). The $+1$'s and the $-1$'s cancel each other out, summing to 0. Consequently, our coefficient will end up being 0.

Mathematically, the Pearson $r$ is a little more complex than this. However, this is the basic the logic behind it.

We have discussed how the Pearson $r$ produces a number that is consistent with a verbal description of the data. Now, we will show how the Pearson $r$ produces a number that is consistent with a graph of the data.

Pearson $r$ could be calculated by drawing a straight line through the points in your scatterplot. If the line slopes upward, the correlation is positive. If the line slopes upward and every single point in your scatterplot fits on that line, you have a perfect correlation of $+1.00$. Usually, however, there are points that are not on the line. For each point that is not on the line, the correlation coefficient is made closer to zero by subtracting a value from the coefficient.

# Box 12–1
## Calculating the Pearson *r*

The formula for the Pearson *r* is:

$$\frac{\Sigma XY - ((\Sigma X * \Sigma Y)/N)}{N * sd\ x * sd\ y}$$

where N = number of participants, sd x = standard deviation of the x scores (the first set of scores), and sd y = standard deviation of the y scores (the second set of scores).

This formula for the Pearson *r* makes sense once you realize three important facts:

1. The formula must produce an index of the degree to which two variables (which we will denote as "X" and "Y") vary together.
2. The formula must produce positive numbers when the variables are positively correlated, negative numbers when the variables are inversely related, and the number zero when the variables are unrelated.
3. The formula must produce numbers between −1 and +1. That is, the formula can't produce numbers above +1 (or below −1), no matter how many scores there are and no matter how large those scores may be.

Since the Pearson *r* is an index of the degree to which two variables vary *together*, each pair of scores is multiplied together. Specifically, the "X" member of each pair is multiplied by the "Y" member of the pair. We then add up all these X * Y products.

However, correlations may be negative. Indeed, if X and Y are inversely related, Pearson *r* should indicate that by being negative. But if X and Y are both always positive (height and salary), how can we obtain a negative number? If both variables are always positive, we would obviously never get a negative number if all we did was multiplied X times Y for each pair of scores and then added up those products. Thus, there must be more to the formula for correlation coefficients than just adding up all the XY products.

How can we obtain a negative number if X and Y are both always positive? To allow ourselves to get negative numbers when the variables are negatively (inversely) related, we subtract a number from the sum of the XY products. That number is an estimate of what the sum of all the XY products would have been if the two sets of scores were completely unrelated. Thus, if the variables are positively related, subtracting this estimate will still leave us with a positive number. If the variables are not related, subtracting this estimate will leave us with zero. Finally, if the variables are inversely related, subtracting this estimate from the actual product of X*Y will result in a negative number.

To this point, we have a formula that can produce positive and negative numbers. However, it cannot meet our final criterion for the correlation coefficient: that it must always be between −1 and +1. The numbers produced by our incomplete version of the correlation

*continued*

*continued from previous page*

formula might be far outside of the −1 to +1 range, especially if:

1. we have many pairs of scores, and
2. the scores are extremely spread out.

Thus, the more XY pairs there are, the more scores there will be to add up, and the larger the total will tend to be. Similarly, the more spread out the scores, the more extreme the products of the scores can be. For example, if scores range from 1 to 5 on both variables, the individual XY products cannot be greater than 25 (because 5 * 5 = 25). However, if the scores on both variables can range from 1 to 10, the XY products can be as large as 100 (10 * 10).

You have seen that our incomplete formula would produce "correlation coefficients" that would be far outside the −1 to +1 boundaries of conventional correlation coefficients. More importantly, the "correlation coefficients" would be influenced by two factors that have nothing to do with the extent to which two variables are related to each other: the number of pairs and the variability (spread) of the distributions. Therefore, we need to add one more step to our formula. That is, we need to take the number we have obtained so far and divide it by an index composed of (1) the number of XY pairs, (2) a measure of the variability of the X scores (the first set of scores), and (3) a measure of the variability of the Y scores (the second set of scores).

By dividing by this index, the correlation coefficient will range between −1 and +1, regardless of whether you compute a correlation based on 5 pairs or 5,000 and regardless of whether participants' raw scores range from 1.5 to 1.6 or from 200 to 200,000.

Thus, one formula for the Pearson *r* is:

$$\frac{\Sigma XY - ((\Sigma X * \Sigma Y)/N)}{N * \text{sd } x * \text{sd } y}$$

where N = number of participants, sd x = standard deviation of the x scores (the first set of scores), and sd y = standard deviation of the y scores (the second set of scores).

To see this formula in action, imagine that you collected data from five students at your school on self-esteem (X) and grade point average (Y). Furthermore, assume that self-esteem and grade point are interval scale variables. To see if the variables were related, you would use the following steps to compute a Pearson *r*.

**STEP 1:** List each pair of scores in the following manner:

|  | SCORE FOR X | SCORE FOR Y | X TIMES Y |
|---|---|---|---|
| 1st pair of scores | 1 | 1 | 1 |
| 2nd pair of scores | 2 | 2 | 4 |
| 3rd pair of scores | 3 | 2 | 6 |
| 4th pair of scores | 4 | 4 | 16 |
| 5th pair of scores | 5 | 3 | 15 |
| **STEP 2:** Sum the scores in each column. | **15** | **12** | **42** |
| **STEP 3:** Calculate the means for variables X and Y | **15/5 = 3** (Mean of X) | **12/5 = 2.4** (Mean of Y) | |

*continued*

*continued from previous page*

**STEP 4:** Calculate the Sum of Squares (SS) for variables X and Y.

| $(X - \bar{X})^2$ | $(Y - \bar{Y})^2$ |
|---|---|
| $(1 - 3)^2$ | $(1 - 2.4)^2$ |
| $(2 - 3)^2$ | $(2 - 2.4)^2$ |
| $(3 - 3)^2$ | $(2 - 2.4)^2$ |
| $(4 - 3)^2$ | $(4 - 2.4)^2$ |
| $(5 - 3)^2$ | $(3 - 2.4)^2$ |
| **10** | **5.2** |

**STEP 5:** Calculate the variance for X and Y (Variance = SS/N)

$$10/5 = 2.0 \qquad 5.2/5 = 1.04$$

**STEP 6:** Calculate the standard deviations for X and Y (sd = square root of the variance)

$$\sqrt{2.0} = 1.41 \qquad \sqrt{1.04} = 1.02$$

**STEP 7:** Multiply the sum of X by the sum of Y. Then, divide by the number of pairs.

$$(15 * 12)/5 = 180/5 = \mathbf{36}$$

**STEP 8:** Subtract the result that we calculated in Step 7 (**36**) from the sum of X * Y that we calculated in Step 1 (**42**)

$$42 - 36 = 6$$

**STEP 9:** Divide the result (6) by the number of pairs times the standard deviation of X times the standard deviation of Y.

$$6/(5 * 1.41 * 1.02) = \mathbf{.83}$$

The farther the point is from the line, the larger the value that is subtracted. Once all the misfit points are accounted for, you end up with the correlation coefficient.

If the line that fits the points slopes downward, the correlation is negative. If every single point fits on that line, you have a perfect negative relationship, thus your correlation coefficient equals $-1.00$. However, perfect negative relationships are rare. Therefore, many points probably are not on that line. For each point that is not on the line, the correlation coefficient is made closer to zero by adding a value to the coefficient. The farther the point is from the line, the larger the value that is added. After all the misfit points are accounted for, you end up with the correlation coefficient.

As you can see, the correlation coefficient describes the nature of the linear relationship between your variables. However, it ignores nonlinear relationships, such as the one depicted in Figure 12-7.

The fact that the correlation coefficient examines only the degree to which variables are linearly related is not as severe a drawback as you may think. Why? First, because totally non-linear relationships among variables are rare. Second, even if you encounter a non-linear relationship, you would know that you had such a relationship by looking at your scatterplot. That is, you would notice that the points on your scatterplot fit a nonlinear pattern, such as a "u"-shaped curve.

## THE COEFFICIENT OF DETERMINATION

The sign of the correlation coefficient tells you the kind of relationship you have (positive or negative). However, you may want to know not only what kind of relationship you have, but how strong this relationship is.

The strength of the relationship is revealed by how far the correlation coefficient is from zero. The farther the correlation coefficient is from zero, the stronger the relationship. Thus, *the strength of the relationship has nothing to do with the sign of the correlation coefficient.* To emphasize this point, realize that to find out how closely two variables are associated, many scientists square the correlation coefficient. Thus, if they had a +.8 correlation, they would get +.64—just as they would if they had a correlation of −.8. Squaring the correlation coefficient not only gets rid of the sign, but yields the **coefficient of determination.**

The coefficient of determination, as the name suggests, tells the degree to which knowing one variable helps you know (*determine*) the other. The coefficient of determination can range from 0 (knowing participants' scores on one variable is absolutely no help in guessing what their scores on the other variable will be) to +1.00 (if you know participants' scores on one variable, you will know exactly what their scores are on the other variable).

So, if you have a correlation of +1, you have a coefficient of determination of 1.00 (because +1 × +1 = 1.00). This means that if you know one variable, you can predict the other one with 100% accuracy. The same would be true if you had a correlation coefficient of −1 (because −1 × −1 = 1.00).

Essentially, the coefficient of determination tells you the amount of scatter in your scatterplot. If the coefficient of determination is near 1, there is little scatter in your scatterplot. If you draw a line through your scatterplot, most of the points would be on or near that line. If, on the other hand, the coefficient of determination is near zero, there is a lot of scatter in your scatterplot. If you draw a line through the scatterplot of that data, very few of the points will be close to your straight line.[2]

### Summary of Describing Correlational Data

You now have two ways to summarize data from a correlational study. First, you can visually summarize your data with a scatterplot. Second, you can use two numbers that summarize the essence of your scatterplot: the correlation coefficient and the coefficient of determination.

## MAKING INFERENCES FROM DATA

Once in a while, a person may only want to describe what happened in a particular sample. For example, a professor may be interested in the average self-esteem of students in one of her courses. If she is only concerned about the

---

[2] The exception to this rule would occur if: (1) the line you drew went straight up or straight across, and (2) there was no variability in scores for one of the variables (for example, you were correlating attractiveness and attitudes toward helping others and everyone scored a "5" on your attitude measure).

average self-esteem of those students, then all she needs to do is compute a mean. Thus, she might find that the average self-esteem of those students was 3.2 on a 1–7 self-esteem scale.

If, however, she wants to make inferences about the mean level of self-esteem of all the students on campus, she would have to do more. She would have to test a random sample of students, calculate a mean, and then calculate a standard error of the mean.

Having the standard error would allow her to estimate the accuracy of her sample mean. For example, 95% of the time, the true mean will be within 2 standard errors of the sample mean. Thus, if her sample mean is 3.2 and the standard error of the mean is 0.1, she can say that it is highly likely that the campus mean is between 3.0 and 3.4.

Similarly, suppose you find that, in one of your classes, there is a relationship between self-esteem and GPA. If you only want to describe the relationship between those two variables in that particular class during that particular term, scatterplots and correlation coefficients are all you need.

Most of the time, however, you are interested in generalizing the results obtained in a limited sample to a larger population. You know what happened in this sample, but you want to know what would happen in other samples.

To generalize your results to a larger population, you first need a random sample of that population. If you want to generalize results based on observing a few students in your class to all the students in your class, then the participants you examine should be a random sample of class members. If you want to generalize the results based on measuring a few people to all Americans, you must have measured a random sample of Americans. If you want to generalize results based on observing two rats for an hour a day to all the times that the rats are awake, then the times you observe the rats must be a random sample from the rats' waking hours.[3]

Of course, random samples are not perfect samples. Even with a random sample, you are going to have sampling error. Thus, if you studied a random sample of sophomores at your school and you found a correlation of −.30 between grade point average and self-esteem, you cannot say that if you had studied all sophomores at your school, you would have obtained a negative correlation coefficient.

To convince yourself that what happens in a sample does not necessarily mirror what happens in the population, you could conduct the following

---

[3] Many researchers do not randomly sample from a population, but they still generalize their results. How? They argue that their sample could be considered a random sample of an unknown population. Then, they use statistics to determine whether the results are due to sampling error or whether the results hold in the larger population. If their results are statistically significant, they argue the results hold in this unspecified population. (The "unspecified population" might be "participants I would study at my institution.") Although you might see some problems with generalizing to an unspecified population, researchers argue that significant results indicate that if they repeated the study, they would probably obtain the same pattern of results.

study. Find two people. Have each person flip a coin. Record each person's height and the number of "heads" the person flipped. Do this for 10 different "samples" and graph each sample individually. Some of your graphs will reveal a positive correlation, others will reveal a negative correlation. The true relationship between a person's height and how many "heads" they obtain, of course, is no relationship.

## Analyses Based on Correlation Coefficients

As you have seen, even if the two variables are not related, they will appear to be related in some samples. That is, a relationship that exists in a particular sample may not exist in the population. Consequently, if you observe a relationship, you will want to know if you have observed a real pattern that is characteristic of the population—or whether the relationship you observe is just a mirage caused by random sampling error.

Fortunately, there is a way to determine whether what is true of your sample is true of the population: use inferential statistics. Inferential statistics will allow you to determine how likely it is that the relationship you saw in your sample could be due to random error. Specifically, inferential statistics allow you to ask the question: "If there is no relationship between these variables in the population, how likely is it that I would get this large a correlation coefficient in this particular random sample?" If the answer to this question is "not very likely," then you can be relatively confident that the correlation coefficient in the population is not zero. To use proper terminology, you would say that your correlation coefficient is significantly different from zero (see Figure 12–8).

How you determine whether a correlation coefficient is statistically different from zero depends on what kind of correlation coefficient you have. If you have a Pearson $r$, a point biserial, or a Spearman's rho, you can use the formula described in Box 12–2. Traditionally, if you have nominal (qualitative) data, you should use a Chi-Square test (see Box 12–3). Regardless of what test you use, the test will rely on two principles.

First, the farther the sample's correlation coefficient is from zero, the less likely the population coefficient is zero. Thus, a correlation coefficient of .8 is more likely to be significantly different from zero than a correlation coefficient of .2.

Second, the larger the sample, the closer its correlation coefficient will be to zero—if the variables are not related in the population. Put another way, the larger the sample, the more likely that a large correlation coefficient means that the variables really are related in the population. Thus, a correlation coefficient of .30 is more likely to be significantly different from zero if it comes from a sample of 100 observations than if it comes from a sample of 10 observations.

Thus far, we have discussed the most popular statistical test involving correlation coefficients: Determining whether the coefficient is significantly different from zero. Significant results allow the researcher to conclude that the two

**FIGURE 12–8**

**Necessary Conditions for Producing Generalizable Results**

variables are related. However, you are not limited to asking if the correlation between your variables is different from zero. That is, by using other types of statistical tests, you could ask the following questions:

**1.** Is the correlation between self-esteem and GPA higher among women than among men?

**2.** Is the correlation between self-esteem and GPA greater than the correlation between impulsivity and GPA?

**3.** In the population, is the correlation between self-esteem and GPA fairly strong? For example, rather than asking whether the correlation is different from zero, you might ask if it is greater than .60.

If you wish to ask these kinds of questions, consult Cohen & Cohen's (1983) book on correlational analysis.

## Analyses Not Involving Correlation Coefficients

You do not have to use correlations to analyze data from correlational research. That is, if you are trying to see whether there is a relationship between gender and scores on a self-esteem test, you do not have to calculate the correlation between gender and self-esteem scores. Instead, you could compute the mean self-esteem score for men and the mean score for women. You could then compare the differences between means, using a t-test or an analysis of variance (ANOVA).

Doing a t-test to see whether the differences between the group means is greater than zero is very similar to seeing whether the correlation between the variables is greater than zero (see Box 12–4). In both cases, a significant result would indicate that, for the population that you randomly sampled from, gender and self-esteem are related.

To do a t-test, you need two groups. But what if you don't have two groups? For example, what if you have a bunch of people's self-esteem scores and their grade point averages? In that case, you could create two groups by dividing your participants into high scorers or low scorers depending on their test score. Then, you would compare the average grade point average of "high" scorers (participants with above average self-esteem) with the average grade

## BOX 12–2
## HOW TO DETERMINE THE SIGNIFICANCE
### OF A PEARSON $r$

If your data on self-esteem and grade point average were collected from a random sample of students at your school, you could use that data to determine whether there is a relationship between impulsivity and grade point average for the entire school. All you would have to do would be to determine whether the observed Pearson $r$ is significantly different from zero by following the steps listed below. In this case let's suppose that $r = +.58$ and there were 5 participants.

**STEP 1:** Compute a $t$-value, using the formula:

$$t = \frac{r \cdot \sqrt{(N - 2)}}{\sqrt{([1 - (r \cdot r)]}}$$

$r$ = the Pearson $r$ and n = number of participants

Note that, all other things being equal, the bigger n is, the bigger $t$ will be. Also, note that the bigger $r$ is, the bigger $t$ will tend to be. Not only does a larger $r$ increase the size of the numerator, but it shrinks the size of the denominator. In other words, the larger the relationship and the more participants you have, the greater the chance of finding a statistically significant result.

$$t = \frac{.58 \cdot \sqrt{(5 - 2)}}{\sqrt{1 - (.58 \cdot .58)}}$$

$$t = \frac{.58 \cdot 1.73}{\sqrt{1 - .34}}$$

$$t = \frac{1.00}{.81} = 1.23$$

**STEP 2:** After computing the $t$-value, look the value up in the $t$-table under 3 degrees of freedom (n − 2) for the .05 level of significance. That value is 3.182. Since 1.23 does not reach that value, you would conclude that the correlation coefficient was not significantly greater than zero.

point average for "low" scorers (participants with below average self-esteem). The procedure of dividing participants into two groups depending on whether they scored above or below the **median** (the middle score) is called a **median split.**

Doing a median split and then conducting a t-test is a common way of analyzing correlational data. You will frequently encounter such analyses in published articles. However, rather than doing a median split and then computing a t-test, you should simply determine whether the correlation is statistically significant (see Table 12–5). Why? Because using a t-test based on median splits reduces your ability to find relationships (Cohen, 1983). You are less able to find relationships because you have less information with which to work. Put

## Box 12-3
## Computing a 2 × 2 Chi Square and the Phi Coefficient

Suppose you asked men and women whether they believed homosexuals deserved the same employment opportunities as heterosexuals. If you wanted to know whether there was a gender difference in their responses, you could find out by calculating a Chi Square using the following steps.

**STEP 1:** Set up a table like the one below.

|  | Female | Male | Total |
|-----|--------|------|-------|
| YES | A | B | |
| NO | C | D | |

(**N**) = Total number of participants

**STEP 2:**

Replace the letter "A" with the number of women who said "yes."

Replace the letter "B" with the number of men who said "yes."

Replace the letter "C" with the number of women who said "no."

Replace the letter "D" with the number of men who said "no."

Replace "N" with the total number of participants.

By the end of this process, your table might look like the one below:

|  | Female | Male | Total |
|--------|--------|------|-------|
| YES | 20 | 15 | 35 |
| NO | 55 | 10 | 65 |
| TOTALS | 75 | 25 | (**N**) 100 |

**STEP 3:** Multiply the number in the "B" square by the number in the "C" square. Then, multiply the number in the "A" square by the number in the "D" square.

For the data above, that would be:

$$B * C = 15 * 55 = 825$$
$$A * D = 20 * 10 = 200$$

**STEP 4:** Plug in the appropriate numbers in the following formula:

$$X^2 = \frac{N(B \cdot C - A \cdot D)^2}{(A + B) \cdot (C + D) \cdot (A + C) \cdot (B + D)}$$

$$X^2 = \frac{100(825 - 200)^2}{35 * 65 * 75 * 25}$$

$$X^2 = \frac{100 * 390625}{4265625} = \frac{39062500}{4265625} = 9.16$$

**STEP 5:** Turn to the Chi Square table in Appendix E and find the row corresponding to 1 degrees of freedom. (For a 2 × 2, your degrees of freedom will always be 1 because df equals the number of rows minus one, times the number of columns minus one).

**STEP 6:** Determine whether your Chi Square is one-tailed or two-tailed. If you predicted only that the groups would differ, then you have a two-tailed test. For example, if you just predicted that there would be a difference between the genders in views towards homosexuals' employment rights, you have a two-tailed test. If, on the other hand, you predicted which group would score higher than the other, then you have a one-tailed test. Thus, if you predicted that men were less likely to think homosexuals should have equal employment opportunities, then you have a one-tailed test.

*continued*

*continued from previous page*

**STEP 7:** If you have a two-tailed test with a value of 3.84 or more, your test is significant at the .05 level. Our value of 7.937 exceeds that value, so our test would be significant at the .05 level.

To compute the phi coefficient, simply use the following formula:

$$\frac{BC - AD}{\sqrt{(A + B) \cdot (C + D) \cdot (A + C) \cdot (B + D)}}$$

In this case,

$$\frac{825 - 200}{\sqrt{4265625}} = .30$$

another way, you have less ability to find differences because you are re-coding data in a way that hides differences. That is, instead of using participants' specific scores, you are using the median split to lump together all the participants who scored above average. Thus, a participant who scores one point above average gets the same score—as far as the analysis is concerned—as a participant who scores 50 points above average. Similarly, you are lumping together everyone who scored below average, despite the differences in their scores. In a sense, you are deliberately throwing away information about participants' actual scores.

Not surprisingly, some researchers object to this waste. For example, Cohen (1990) argues that researchers should not lose power and information by "mutilating" variables. Instead of "throwing away" the information regarding a participant's specific score by doing a median split, Cohen believes that researchers should do correlational analyses that use participants' actual scores.

Rather than breaking your participants down into two groups (top half, bottom half), you might decide to break your participants into three or more groups. You could then compare the different groups by doing an analysis of variance (ANOVA).

With a multiple-group ANOVA, your analysis includes more detail about participants' scores than if you just did a t-test. For instance, rather than coding that a participant scored in the top half, you might code that the participant scored in the top fourth. Because you have more information about participants' scores, you may have more power (see Table 12–6). But if you want more information about participants' scores, why not simply use a correlation analysis that will allow you to use everyone's precise score?

**TABLE 12–5**

**Advantages and Disadvantages of Using a t-Test Based on a Median Split to Analyze Results of Correlational Research**

| ADVANTAGES | DISADVANTAGES |
|---|---|
| The t-test is a convenient way to analyze data. | Before you can do a t-test, you may have to recode scores based on median split. |
| | "Convenience" of the t-test may cost you power. You have less power than correlational analysis because you are not using actual scores. Instead, you are using much less detailed information. That is, instead of using a participant's actual score, you are recording only whether the score is in the top half or bottom half of distribution. |
| Familiar, conventional way to analyze data. | Because it is a conventional way to analyze *experimental* data, some may *falsely* conclude that significant results indicate that one variable causes the other. |

The reason you might choose ANOVA is so that you can do one of two types of analyses.[4] First, you might use an ANOVA to determine whether the relationship is non-linear. For example, an ANOVA might find that the group with moderately high self-esteem got better grades than the groups with very high or very low self-esteem. Second, you could use ANOVA to examine the relationships among three or more variables. That is, with an ANOVA, you could look at the relationship among self-esteem, gender, and grade point average. Specifically, an ANOVA would allow you to compare the grade point averages of: (1) women with low self-esteem, (2) women with high self-esteem, (3) men with low self-esteem, and (4) men with high self-esteem. By doing this analysis, you might find that high self-esteem is related to high grade point averages for women, but that high self-esteem is related to low grade point averages for men. (See Table 12–7 for a summary of the advantages and disadvantages of using ANOVA to analyze the results of correlational research.)

## Interpreting Significant Results

No matter what statistical tests you use, remember what a statistically significant result means (see Table 12–8). It means that the relationship you observed is probably not due to random error. Instead, the relationship you observed in the sample probably also exists in the population from which you randomly sampled.

---

[4] These analyses can be done using sophisticated correlational analyses. However, most researchers are more familiar with how to do these analyses using ANOVA.

Keep in mind that statistical significance does *not* mean that the variables are causally related. As we said earlier in the chapter, to infer causality, you must do much more than establish that your variables are statistically related. For example, to infer that self-esteem caused low grade point averages, you would have to show not only that self-esteem and grade point average are related, but also that:

1. no other differences between your high and low self-esteem individuals could account for this relationship (there were no differences between groups in terms of parental encouragement, IQ, ability to delay gratification, etc.); and
2. the low self-esteem students had low self-esteem *before* they got low grades, whereas the high self-esteem students had high self-esteem before they got high grades.

As we've seen, significant results in correlational research do not mean that changes in one variable caused a change in the other. At best, significant results only mean that both variables are correlated. However, all too often significant results don't even prove that two variables are correlated.

---

## Box 12–4
## The Similarities Between a t-Test, an F-Test, and a Test to Determine Whether a Correlation Coefficient Is Significantly above Zero

When you only have two groups, doing a t-test, an F-test, and an analysis of correlation is the same. Thus, in the simple experiment, the three procedures are quite similar. In all three cases, you are seeing if there is a relationship between the treatment and the dependent variable. That is, in all three cases you would be looking to see if the treatment and the dependent variable covary.

The only difference is in what you use as your measure of covariation. In the t-test, you use the difference between means of the two groups as your measure of covariation; in the F-test, you use the squared difference between means of the two groups as the measure of covariation; and in testing the significance of a correlation, you use the correlation between the treatment and the dependent variable as the measure of covariation. Consequently, regardless of which technique you use to analyze the results of a simple experiment, significant results will allow you to make causal statements. Furthermore, regardless of which technique you use to analyze the results of a correlational study, significant results will *not* allow you to make causal statements.

To show you that the three analyses are the same, we have done these three analyses of the same data. The results of these analyses are:

*continued*

To understand why they don't, suppose that a researcher is trying to determine whether two variables are correlated. The researcher uses the conventional $p<.05$ significance level. Suppose further that, in reality, the variables aren't correlated. What are the chances that the researcher will obtain significant results? You might be tempted to say "about 5%." You would be correct—if the researcher had only conducted one statistical test. However, because correlational data are often easy to obtain, some researchers correlate hundreds of variables with hundreds of other variables. If they do hundreds of statistical tests, many of these tests will be significant by chance alone. Put another way, if the researcher uses a $p<.05$ level of significance and does 100 tests, the researcher might obtain 5 Type 1 errors.

---

*continued from previous page*

### T-TEST ANALYSIS

| Group: | N | Mean: | Standard error of the difference $=.565$ |
|---|---|---|---|
| Group 1 | 59 | 9.429 | |
| Group 2 | 58 | 8.938 | |

$$t = \frac{9.429 - 8.938}{.565} = \frac{.491}{.565} = .87$$

| df: | | | | *t*-value | Probability* |
|---|---|---|---|---|---|
| 115 | | | | .87 | .3859 |

### ANALYSIS OF VARIANCE

| Source: | df: | Sum of Squares | MS | F-value** | Probability |
|---|---|---|---|---|---|
| Treatment | 1 | 4.155 | 4.155 | .758 | .3859 |
| Error | 115 | 630.768 | 5.485 | | |

### CORRELATIONAL ANALYSIS

| Count: | R: |
|---|---|
| 117 | .081 |

Using the formula from Box 12–2, we find that:

$$t = \frac{r \sqrt{(N-2)}}{\sqrt{[1 - (r \cdot r)]}} = \frac{.081 \cdot \sqrt{115}}{\sqrt{.993}} = \frac{.868}{.996} = 0.87, \quad \text{Probability} \atop .3859$$

---

\* Probability (often abbreviated as "$p$") refers to the chances of finding a relationship in your sample that is as large as the one you found if the two variables are really unrelated in the population. Thus, the smaller $p$ is, the less likely it is that the relationship observed in your sample is just a fluke. In other words, the smaller $p$ is, the more likely it is that the variables really are related in the population. Note that the $p$ value is exactly the same (in this case, .3859) whether we do a t-test, F-test, or a correlational analysis.

\*\* Note that if you square the t-value (.87), you get the F-value (.758). Thus, if you want to check your work, you can do a t-test and an F-test on the same data. If the square root of the F-test is different than the t-value, then you have made a mistake. An even easier way to check your work is to see whether the $p$ values produced by the two analyses are the same.

**TABLE 12–6**
**Tests That Use More Information Have More Power**

The more detailed the information we put into an analysis, the more information we get out. Put another way, the finer the distinctions made between participants in the data plugged into the analysis, the finer the distinctions that will be pulled out. Thus, the t-test that only looks to see if the participant is above or below the median has very little power. An F-test that divides scores into low, medium, or high would have more power. An F-test that divided scores into very low, low, medium, high, and very high would have even more power. However, the analysis that would have the most power is the one that would use each individual's actual score—the test to see if the correlation coefficient is above zero.

| STATISTICAL TEST | AMOUNT OF INFORMATION OBTAINED FROM INDIVIDUAL SCORES | POWER OF THE TEST |
|---|---|---|
| Two-group t-test | Very little—only look to see whether the score is above or below the median | Very Low |
| Three-level ANOVA | Little—look to see whether the score was low, medium, or high | Low |
| Test for significance of the correlation | Much—use actual scores | High |

Therefore, we urge you to resist temptation. Don't go wild and compute every possible correlation coefficient. Decide what hypotheses you have and test those correlations.

If you are doing more than one statistical test, make your significance level more conservative than .05. Use a .01 or even a .001 level. Or, repeat your study with another random sample of participants to see if the correlations that were significant the first time are still significant the second time around.

## Interpreting Null Results

If your results are not statistically significant, it means that you failed to show that your results were not due to sampling error. It does not mean your variables are not related—it only means that you have failed to establish that they were related. There are several reasons why you may get null results, even though a relationship exists between your variables.

First, you may not have had enough observations. Even if you observed a fairly strong relationship in your sample, it's hard to say that your observed relationship is not a fluke unless you have enough observations.

Second, your measures might be so insensitive that they did a poor job of distinguishing between participants. For example, if your measures were unreliable, the true relationship between your variables is obscured by measurement error.

**TABLE 12–7**

**Advantages and Disadvantages of Using ANOVA to Analyze the Results from a Correlational Study**

| ADVANTAGES | DISADVANTAGES |
|---|---|
| Allows you to perform a variety of analyses fairly easily. | You have less power than testing the statistical significance of a correlation coefficient because ANOVA doesn't use actual scores. Instead, it uses much less detailed information. For example, if you use a two level ANOVA, you are only recording whether the score is in the top half or the bottom half of the distribution. |
| 1. You can do more than look at the simple relationships between two variables. Instead, you can look at the relationship among three or more variables at once. | |
| 2. You could determine whether the relationship between variables is non-linear. | |
| You can minimize the problem of losing detail by dividing scores into more groups. That is, you are not limited to just comparing the top half versus the bottom half. Instead, you could compare the top fifth, vs. the 2nd fifth, vs. the 3rd fifth, vs. the 4th fifth, vs. the bottom fifth. Because you would be entering more detailed information into your analysis, you would have reasonable power. | However, you still do not have as much detail and power as if you had used participants' actual scores. |
| Convenient way to analyze data. | It may not be so convenient if you have an unequal number of participants in each group. In that case, you would have what is called an unbalanced ANOVA. Many computer programs can't accurately compute statistics for an unbalanced ANOVA. |
| Familiar way to analyze data. | Because it is a conventional way to analyze experimental data, people may *falsely* conclude that significant results mean that one variable *causes* changes in the other. |

Third, your variables may be related in a nonlinear way. This would be a problem because your statistical tests are most sensitive to straight line (linear) relationships. You could tell if this is the problem by looking at a scatterplot of your data. Thus, if a graph of your data revealed a nonlinear relationship, such as a definite "U" shaped curve, you would know that a conventional correlation coefficient would greatly underestimate the strength of the relationship between the variables.

Fourth, you may have failed to find a significant relationship because of **restriction of range:** you sampled from a population in which everyone scores similarly on one of the variables. Restriction of range is a problem because, to say that variables vary together, you need both variables to vary. If both variables don't vary, you end up with correlations of zero. For example, suppose you were looking at the relationship between IQ and grade point average, but everyone in your sample scored between 125 and 130 on the IQ test. In this case, the correlation between IQ and grade point average would be pretty

**TABLE 12-8**

**The Different Meanings of Statistical Significance**

| QUESTION ASKED ABOUT A STATISTICALLY SIGNIFICANT RESULT | CORRELATIONAL STUDY | EXPERIMENT |
|---|---|---|
| Are the variables related? | Yes | Yes |
| Do we know whether the predictor variable caused changes in the criterion variable? | No. We do not know which variable changed first. (Our "cause" may really be an effect.) In addition, changes in both the predictor variable and the criterion variable could be due to some third factor. | Yes. The experimental design guaranteed that the treatment came before the change in the dependent variable. |
| | | The experimental design also guaranteed that the treatment was the only systematic difference between treatment conditions. Thus, the relationship between the variables could not be due to some third factor. |

small. Consequently, the correlation might not be significant. However, if your participants' IQs had ranged from 85 to 185, you would probably have a sizable and statistically significant correlation between IQ and GPA.

## A LOOK AHEAD

In this chapter, you have been introduced to the logic of descriptive research. However, you have not learned about the most common method of doing descriptive research: asking questions. Therefore, the next chapter is devoted to showing you how to conduct surveys.

## SUMMARY

1. Descriptive research allows you to describe behavior accurately. The key to descriptive research is to measure and record your variables precisely using a representative sample.
2. Although descriptive research cannot tell you whether one variable causes another, it may stimulate causal hypotheses.
3. Description is an important goal of science. Description also paves the way for prediction.
4. Ex post facto research uses data that you collected before you came up with your hypothesis.
5. Archival research uses data collected and sometimes coded by someone else.
6. With both ex post facto and archival research, data may not have been measured, collected, or coded in a way appropriate for testing your hypothesis.

7. Observational methods are used in both correlational and experimental research.

8. In both naturalistic observation and participant observation, the researcher must be careful that the observer does not affect the observed and that coding is objective.

9. Using pre-existing, validated tests in your correlational research may increase the construct validity of your study. As with all research, external validity is dependent on the representativeness of your sample.

10. Using a scatterplot to graph your correlational data will tell you the direction of the relationship (positive or negative) and give you an idea of the strength of the relationship.

11. Correlational coefficients give you one number that represents the direction of the relationship (positive or negative). These numbers range from $-1.00$ to $+1.00$.

12. A positive correlation between two variables indicates that if a participant scores high on one of the variables, the participant will probably score high on the other.

13. A negative correlation between two variables indicates that if a participant scores high on one of the variables, the participant will probably score low on the other variable.

14. The further a correlation coefficient is away from zero, the stronger the relationship. Thus, a $-.4$ correlation is stronger than a $+.3$.

15. By squaring the correlation coefficient, you get the coefficient of determination, which tells you the strength of the relationship. The coefficient of determination can range from 0 to 1.

16. If your results are based on a random sample, you may want to use inferential statistics to analyze your data.

17. Remember, statistical significance only means that your results can be generalized to the population from which you randomly sampled. Statistical significance does not mean that you have found a causal relationship.

18. You may obtain null results even though your variables are related. Common culprits are: insufficient number of observations, insensitive measures, nonlinear relationships, and restriction of range.

19. Beware of doing too many tests of significance. Remember, if you do 100 tests and use a .05 level of significance, 5 of those tests might be significant by chance alone.

## KEY TERMS

**ex post facto research:** when a researcher goes back, after the research has been completed, looking to test hypotheses that were not formulated prior to the beginning of the study. The researcher is trying to take advantage of hindsight. Often, an attempt to salvage something out of a study that did not turn out as planned. (p. 400)

**archival data:** data from existing records and public archives. (p. 401)

**instrumentation bias:** apparent changes in participants that are really due to changes in the measuring instrument. A real problem in archival research because the way records are kept may change over time. For example, unemployment statistics are difficult to interpret because the government has changed its definition of unemployment. (p. 404)

**content analysis:** a way to categorize a wide range of open-ended (unrestricted) responses. Content analysis schemes have been used to code the frequency of violence on certain television shows and are often used to code archival data. (p. 402)

**nonreactive:** measurements that are taken without changing the participant's behavior. Researchers in both participant and naturalistic observation try to be nonreactive, but both often fail. (p. 404)

**participant observation:** an observation procedure in which the observer participates with those being observed. The observer becomes "one of them." Some worry that, in participant observation, the observer may change the behavior of the people being observed. (p. 405)

**naturalistic observation:** a technique of observing events as they occur in their natural setting. Advocates believe that naturalistic observation has more external validity than lab observation. In addition, they hope that naturalistic observation will be less reactive than lab observation. (p. 405)

**scatterplot:** a graph made by plotting the scores of individuals on two variables (for instance, plotting each participant's height and weight). By looking at this graph, you should get an idea of what kind of correlation (positive, negative, zero) exists between the two variables. (p. 408)

**correlation coefficient:** a number that can vary from $-1.00$ to $+1.00$ and indicates the kind of relationship that exists between two variables (positive or negative as indicated by the sign of the correlation coefficient) and the strength of the relationship (indicated by the extent to which the coefficient differs from 0). (p. 411)

**negative correlation:** an inverse relationship between two variables (such as number of suicide attempts and happiness). (p. 410)

**positive correlation:** a relationship between two variables in which the two variables tend to change in the same direction—when one increases, the other tends to increase. (For example, height and weight: The taller one is, the more one tends to weigh; the shorter one is, the less one tends to weigh.) (p. 408)

**zero correlation:** when there doesn't appear to be a relationship between two variables. For practical purposes, any correlation between $-.10$ and $+.10$ may be considered so small as to be nonexistent. (p. 411)

**illusory correlation:** when there is really no relationship (a zero correlation) between two variables, but people perceive that the variables are related. (p. 398)

**coefficient of determination:** the square of the correlation coefficient; tells the degree to which knowing one variable helps to know another. Can range from 0 (knowing a participant's score on one variable tells you absolutely nothing about the participant's score on the second variable) to 1.00 (knowing a participant's score on one variable tells you exactly what the participant's score on the second variable was). Note that the sign of the correlation coefficient (whether it is positive or negative) has absolutely no effect on the coefficient of determination. (p. 418)

**restriction of range:** to observe a sizable correlation between two variables, both must be allowed to vary widely (if one variable does not vary, the variables cannot vary together). Occasionally, investigators fail to find a relationship between variables because they study one or both variables only over a highly restricted range. Example: Saying that weight has nothing to do with playing offensive line in the NFL on the basis of your finding that great offensive tackles do not weigh much more than poor offensive tackles. Problem: You only compared people who ranged in weight from 285 to 300. (p. 429)

**median:** if you arrange all the scores from lowest to highest, the middle score will be the median. (p. 422)

**median split:** the procedure of dividing participants into two groups ("highs" and "lows") based on whether they score above or below the median. (p. 422)

# EXERCISES

1. Steinberg and Dornbusch (1991) find that there is a positive correlation between class-cutting and hours of week adolescents work. In addition, they find a negative correlation between grade point average and number of hours worked.
   a. Describe, in your own words, what the relationship is between class-cutting and hours of week that adolescents work.
   b. Describe, in your own words, what the relationship is between grade point average and hours of week that adolescents work.
   c. What conclusions can you draw about the effects of work? Why?
   d. If you had been analyzing their data, what analysis would you use? Why?
2. Steinberg and Dornbusch (1991) also reported that the correlation between hours of employment and interest in school was statistically significant. Specifically, they reported that $r(3,989) = -.06$, $p < .001$. [Note that the $r(3,989)$ means that they had 3,989 participants in their study.] Interpret this finding.
3. Brown (1991) found that a measure of aerobic fitness correlated $+.28$ with a self-report measure of how much people exercised. He also found that the measure of aerobic fitness correlated $-.41$ with resting

heart rate. Is resting heart rate or self-report of exercise more closely related to the aerobic fitness measure?

4. In the same study, sex was coded as 1 = male, 2 = female. The correlation between sex and aerobic fitness was −.58, which was statistically significant at the *p*<.01 level.

   **a.** In this study, were men or women more fit?

   **b.** What would the correlation have been if sex had been coded as 1 = female and 2 = male?

   **c.** From the information we have given you, can you conclude that one gender tends to be more aerobically fit than the other? Why or why not?

5. Suppose you wanted to see whether the magazine *Psychology Today* became more psychological after the American Psychological Association took it over in 1984. Your strategy might be to count the number of articles that dealt with psychology. But to determine whether an article was psychological or not, you would want to set up a content analysis system. How would you operationalize "psychological"? How would you sample the articles?

6. A physician looked at 26 instances of crib death in a certain town. The physician found that some of these deaths were due to parents suffocating their children. As a result, the physician concluded that most crib deaths in this country are not due to problems in brain development, but to parental abuse and neglect. What problems do you have with the physician's conclusions?

7. A study began by looking at how a sample of 5-year-olds were treated by their parents. Then, 36 years later, when the participants were 41-year-olds, the study looked the degree to which these individuals were socially accomplished. The investigators then looked at the relationship between childrearing practices when the child was 5 and how socially accomplished the person was at 41 (Franz, McClelland, & Weinberger, 1991). They concluded that having a warm and affectionate father or mother was significantly associated with "adult social accomplishment."

   **a.** What advantages does this prospective study have over a study that asks 41-year-olds to reflect back on their childhood?

   **b.** How would you measure "adult social accomplishment?"

   **c.** How would you measure "parental warmth?" Why?

   **d.** Assume, for the moment, that the study clearly established a relationship between parenting practices and adult social accomplishment. Could we then conclude that parenting practices account for (cause) adult social accomplishment? Why or why not?

   **e.** Imagine that they had failed to find a significant relationship between the variables of "adult social accomplishment" and parental warmth. What might have caused their results to fail to reach significance?

# CHAPTER 13

---

# Survey Research

*Overview*

*Determining Whether to Do Survey Research*

APPLICATIONS
CONSIDERATIONS

*The Advantages and Disadvantages
of Different Survey Instruments*

QUESTIONNAIRES
PSYCHOLOGICAL TESTS
INTERVIEWS

*Planning a Survey*

WHAT IS YOUR HYPOTHESIS?
FORMAT OF QUESTIONS
FORMAT OF SURVEY
THE ART OF ASKING GOOD QUESTIONS

*Sampling*

RANDOM SAMPLING
STRATIFIED RANDOM SAMPLING
CONVENIENCE SAMPLING
QUOTA SAMPLING
CONCLUSIONS ABOUT SAMPLING TECHNIQUES

*Administering the Survey*

*Analyzing Survey Data*

SUMMARIZING DATA
SUMMARIZING INTERVAL DATA
SUMMARIZING ORDINAL AND NOMINAL DATA
USING INFERENTIAL STATISTICS
USING INFERENTIAL STATISTICS WITH NOMINAL DATA

*Concluding Remarks*

*Summary*

*Key Terms*

*Exercises*

# Chapter 13

## SURVEY RESEARCH

### OVERVIEW

If you want to know *why* people do what they do or think what they think, you should use an *experimental* design. If, on the other hand, you want to know *what* people are thinking, feeling, or doing, you should use a *nonexperimental design*, such as a **survey research design**.

There are two main aspects of the survey design. First, your questionnaire, test, or interview must accurately measure the thoughts, feelings, or behaviors in which you are interested. Second, your results should apply to a certain, specific group. Depending on your purposes, this group, called a **population**, could be anything from all U.S. citizens to all employees at a local company. To be able to generalize your results to an entire population, you must question either the entire population or a representative sample of that population.

Because there are two main aspects to survey research, there are two main ways that survey research can go wrong. First, survey research may be flawed because the questionnaire, test, or interview measure has poor construct validity. For example:

- The questions may be unclear or confusing.
- The questions may demand knowledge that participants don't have.
- The questions may, by hinting at the answer the researcher wants to hear, invite participants to lie.
- Participants' answers may be inaccurate.
- The researcher may misinterpret or miscode participants' answers.

Second, the survey may have little external validity because the people who were questioned did not represent the target population.

As you can see, there is more to survey research than asking a bunch of people some questions that you jotted down. Instead, survey research, like all research, requires careful planning. You have to determine whether the survey design is appropriate for your research problem. Then, you have to decide what questions you are going to ask, why you are going to ask those questions, to whom you are going to ask those questions, how you are going to ask those questions, and how you are going to analyze the answers to those questions.

Unfortunately, few people engage in the careful planning necessary to conduct sound survey research. Consequently, even though the survey is by far the most commonly used research method, it is also the most commonly abused. By reading this chapter, you can become one of the relatively few people who conduct sound and ethical survey research.

# DETERMINING WHETHER TO DO SURVEY RESEARCH

The most obvious—but least asked—question in survey research is, "Should I use a survey?" To respond appropriately to this question, you must understand the strengths and weaknesses of survey research.

## Applications

The main strength of survey research is that you can gather information about what people are thinking from a large sample of people with less effort and expense than with most other data-gathering techniques. Primarily because of this strength, the survey method is generally a good method to use if you want to describe a group's beliefs, attitudes, intentions, or values.

### PREDICTION

Sometimes, you want to describe a group's attitudes because you want to predict their behavior. For example, the "Gallup Poll" surveys try to predict the results of elections. Similarly, market researchers ask people about products they plan to buy.

### DESCRIPTION

Sometimes, you want to describe a group's attitudes because you want to find out how many people have a certain characteristic or support a certain position. For example, a social worker may want to know what percentage of adolescents in the community have contemplated suicide or a politician may want to know what percentage of her constituents support a certain position.

Beyond telling us *how many* people have a certain characteristic, surveys can help us develop a detailed profile of those people. That is, we can use surveys to develop a list of differences between those who try to commit suicide and those who don't, those who support gun control and those who don't, or computer users versus non-users, etc.

## Considerations

Clearly, there are many situations in which you could use a survey. However, before doing a survey, you should ask five questions:

1. What is my hypothesis?
2. Will I know what to do with the data after the survey is finished?
3. Am I interested only in describing and predicting behavior, or do I want to infer causality?
4. Will respondents answer accurately?
5. Do my results apply only to those people who responded to the survey, or do the results apply to a larger group?

## KNOW YOUR HYPOTHESIS

The first question to ask is, "What is my hypothesis?" Since good research begins with a good hypothesis, you might think that everyone would ask this question. Unfortunately, many inexperienced researchers try to write their survey questions without clear research questions. What they haven't learned is that you can't ask pertinent questions if you don't know what you want to ask. Therefore, before you write your first survey question, make sure you have a clear hypothesis on which to base your questions.

## ASK PERTINENT QUESTIONS AND ASK FEW QUESTIONS

Having a hypothesis doesn't do you much good unless you are disciplined enough to focus your questions on that hypothesis. In other words, if you don't focus your questions on your hypothesis, you may end up with an overwhelming amount of data—and still not find out what you wanted to know. For example, the now-defunct United States Football League (USFL) spent millions of dollars on surveys to find out whether they should be a spring or fall league. Despite the fact that it took more than 20 books to summarize the survey results, the surveys did not answer their research question (*USA Today,* 1984). So, don't be seduced by how easy it is to ask a question. Instead, ask questions that address the purpose of your research.

We take two steps to make sure that we ask useful questions. First, we determine what analyses we plan to do *before* we administer the questionnaire. If we don't plan on doing any analyses involving responses to a specific question, we get rid of that question. Second, with the remaining questions, we imagine participants responding in a variety of ways. For example, we may graph the results we predict and results that are completely opposite of what we would predict. If we find that no pattern of answers to that question would give us useful information, we eliminate those questions. For example, we may find that, no matter how participants answer the question, it won't disprove any of our hypotheses. Or, if we are doing a survey for an organization, we may find that, no matter how participants answer a certain question, it wouldn't change how that organization runs its business.

## DON'T TRY TO ESTABLISH CAUSALITY

Usually, if your questions focus on the research hypothesis, your survey will be able to address your research question. However, there is one big exception to this rule—when you have a *causal* hypothesis. Like all nonexperimental designs, the survey design cannot establish causality.

To illustrate why you cannot make causal inferences from a survey design, let's imagine that you find that professors are more sympathetic toward students than administrators are. In that case, you cannot say that being an administrator causes people to have less sympathy for students. For example, it could be that professors who didn't like students became administrators. Or, it could be that some other factor (like being bossy), causes one to be an administrator and that factor is also associated with having less sympathy toward students.

## DON'T ACCEPT RESPONDENTS' ANSWERS AS GOSPEL

Even people who realize the weaknesses of nonexperimental methods want to use survey methods to establish causality. They argue that all they have to do to establish causality is ask people why they behaved in a certain manner. Admittedly, respondents can give reasons for their behavior, but these reasons may not be accurate. For example, Nisbett and Wilson (1975) demonstrated that if participants are shown a row of television sets, participants will prefer the TV farthest to the right. Yet, when asked why they preferred the TV on the right, nobody says, "I like it because it's on the right."

This example illustrates a general problem with questioning people: People's answers may not reflect the truth. There are numerous reasons why respondents' answers may be inaccurate. In the example we just mentioned, the participants did not know the truth. This is often the case. People do not know why they do everything they do or feel everything they feel. For example, we do not know why we call "heads" more often than "tails" or why we find some comedians funnier than others. People do not know everything that goes on in their heads. For instance, we do not know what goes through our mind that allows us to regain control of our car after it starts skidding on the ice or what causes us to think of a particular joke. The bottom line: Although asking people questions about why they behave the way they do is interesting, you can't accept their answers at face value.

As Nisbett and Wilson's (1975) study showed, when people do not know the real cause, they make up a reason—and they believe that reason. Similarly, even though people have forgotten certain facts, they may still think they remember. For example, obese people tend to underreport what they have eaten and students tend to overreport how much they study. Both groups are surprised when they actually record their behavior (Williams and Long, 1984). Because memory is fallible, you should be very careful when interpreting responses that place heavy demands on participants' memories. If you aren't skeptical about the meaning of those responses, be assured that your critics will be. Indeed, one of the most commonly heard criticisms of research is that "the results are questionable because they are based on **retrospective self-reports** (participants' statements about what they remembered)."

As bad as people are at remembering the past, they are even worse about predicting the future. Thus, asking people "What would you do in _____ situation?" may make for interesting conversation, but the answers will have little to do with what people would actually do if they were put in that situation (Sherman, 1982). For example, most people claim that, if they were in a conformity experiment, they would not conform. Thus, if we relied on what people told us they would do in a certain situation, virtually none of the participants in the classic conformity experiments would conform. In reality, however, 60–80% of participants conform. For example, nearly ⅔ of Milgram's participants went along with an experimenter's orders to give high intensity shocks to another person (Milgram, 1974).

To this point, we have discussed honest mistakes that respondents make. Sometimes, however, respondents deliberately distort the truth.

They may give you the answer that will impress you the most. For example, to impress you, they may exaggerate the amount of money they give to charity. In other words, the *social desirability bias* is a problem. Or, they may give you the answer you want to hear. Their behavior may be very similar to yours when, after having a lousy meal, the server asks you, "Was everything okay?" In such a case, rather than telling the server everything was lousy and ruining his day, you say what you think he wants to hear—"Yes, everything was okay." In technical terms, you have obeyed the *demand characteristics* of the situation.

In short, participants will lie. They may lie to impress you (social desirability bias) or to please you (obeying demand characteristics). Participants are most likely to lie if your questions are extremely personal (such as, "Have you cheated on your taxes?"). Therefore, don't ask personal questions unless they are crucial to your study.

## TO WHOM DO YOUR RESULTS APPLY?

Even if you have a good set of questions focused on your hypothesis and you can get accurate answers to those questions, your work is probably not done. Usually, you want to generalize your results beyond the people who responded to your survey. For example, you might survey a couple of classes at your university, not because you want to know what those particular classes think, but because you think those classes are a representative sample of your college as a whole. But are they? Unfortunately, they probably aren't. Instead, they probably are a biased sample.

Even if you start out with an unbiased sample, your sample may be biased by the end of the study. Why? People often fail to or refuse to respond to a questionnaire. In fact, if you do a mail survey, don't be surprised if only 10% of your sample returns the survey. Is this 10% typical of your population? Probably not. It's very likely that these participants feel more strongly about the issue than non-respondents. Consequently, **non-response bias** is one of the most serious threats to the survey design's external validity.

## SUMMARY

A survey can be a relatively inexpensive way to get information about people's attitudes, beliefs, and behaviors. With a survey, you can collect a lot of information on a large sample in a short period of time.

Although surveys can be valuable, realize their limitations. Realize that self-report can be inaccurate. Therefore, to get accurate answers to your questions, you will need to be careful about what you ask and how you ask it. Otherwise, your survey's results may not have construct validity. Furthermore, realize that most samples will be biased. Thus, unless you take the trouble to get a good, unbiased sample, your survey results will have limited external validity. Finally, realize that the survey method has no internal validity. Therefore, if you want to know what causes a certain effect, don't use a survey design.

# THE ADVANTAGES AND DISADVANTAGES OF DIFFERENT SURVEY INSTRUMENTS

After weighing the advantages and disadvantages of the survey method, you may decide that a survey is the best approach for your research question. In that case, you need to decide what type of survey instrument you are going to use. Basically, you have three types of survey instruments you can employ to collect your dependent variable: questionnaires, tests, and interviews.

## Questionnaires

If you are considering a **questionnaire,** you have essentially two options: self-administered and investigator-administered. In this section, we will discuss the advantages and disadvantages of both types of questionnaires.

### SELF-ADMINISTERED QUESTIONNAIRES

A **self-administered questionnaire,** as the name suggests, is filled out by participants in the absence of an investigator. Self-administered questionnaires are used by behavioral scientists, as well as manufacturers, businesspeople, special interest groups, and magazine publishers. You probably have seen some of these questionnaires in your mail, at restaurant tables, in newspapers or magazines, or attached to stereo warranties.

Self-administered questionnaires have two main advantages. First, self-administered questionnaires are easily distributed to a large number of people. Second, self-administered questionnaires often allow anonymity. Allowing respondents to be anonymous may be important if you want honest answers to highly personal questions.

Using a self-administered questionnaire can be a cheap and easy way to get valid data. However, there are at least two major drawbacks to this method.

First, surveys that rely on self-administered questionnaires usually have a low return rate. Since the few individuals who return the questionnaire may not be typical of the people you tried to survey, you may have a biased sample.

Second, because the researcher and the respondent are not interacting, problems with the questionnaire can't be corrected. Thus, if the survey contains an ambiguous question, the researcher can't help the respondent understand the question. For example, suppose we ask people to rate the degree to which they agree with the statement, "College students work hard." One respondent might think this question refers to a job a student might hold down in addition to school. Another respondent might interpret this to mean, "students work hard at their studies." Because respondent and researcher are not interacting, the researcher will have no idea that these two respondents are answering two different questions.

### INVESTIGATOR-ADMINISTERED QUESTIONNAIRE

The investigator-administered questionnaire is filled out in the presence of a researcher. Answers may be recorded by either the respondent or the investigator.

Investigator-administered questionnaires share many of the advantages of the self-administered questionnaire. With both types of measures, many respondents can be surveyed at the same time. With both types of measures, surveys can be conducted in a variety of locations, including: the lab, the street, in class, over the phone, and at respondents' homes.

A major advantage of having an investigator present is that the investigator can clarify questions for the respondent. In addition, the investigator's presence encourages participants to respond. As a result, surveys that use investigator-administered questionnaires have a higher response rate than surveys using self-administered questionnaires.

Unfortunately, the investigator's presence may do more than just increase response rates. The investigator-administered questionnaire may reduce perceived anonymity. Because respondents feel their answers are less anonymous, respondents may be less open and honest.

## Psychological Tests

An extremely refined form of the investigator-administered questionnaire is the psychological test. Whereas questionnaires are often developed in a matter of days or hours, psychological tests are painstakingly developed over months, even decades. Nevertheless, the distinction between questionnaires and tests is sometimes blurred.

To see that this distinction is sometimes blurred, you only need to look at research involving questionnaires. You'll find that questionnaires often incorporate items from psychological tests. For example, in a study of people's concern about body weight, Patricia Pliner (1990) and her colleagues incorporated two psychological tests in their questionnaire: The Eating Attitudes Test (EAT; Garner & Garfinkel, 1979), and the Feeling of Social Inadequacy Scale ( Janis & Field, 1959).

Even if you do not include a test as part of your questionnaire, your questionnaire should try to emulate the characteristics of good tests. That is, in developing your questionnaire, you should use as many principles from Chapter 3 as you can. Specifically, you should consider doing as much of the following as possible:

- Pretest your questionnaire.
- Standardize the way you administer the questionnaire.
- Score answers as objectively as possible. For example, use "objective" items (such as multiple-choice questions) that do not require the person scoring the test to interpret the participant's response. In addition, develop a detailed scoring key for those responses that do require the scorer to interpret responses. Finally, don't let scorers know the identity of the respondent. For example, if the hypothesis is that male respondents will be more aggressive, do not let coders know whether the respondent is male or female.
- Balance out the effects of response set biases, such as "yea" saying (always agreeing) and "nay" saying (always disagreeing) by re-asking the same question in a variety of ways. For example, you might ask, "How much do you like the President?" as well as, "How much do you dislike the President?"
- Make a case for your measure's reliability. For example, re-survey respondents a month later to see if they score similarly both times. Finding a strong positive correlation between the two times of measurement will suggest that you are measuring some stable characteristic—and that you are not merely assessing random error.
- Make a case for your measure's validity by correlating it with measures that do not depend on self-report. For example, Steinberg and Dornbusch (1991) justified using self-reported grade point average (GPA) rather than actual grade point average by establishing that previous research had shown that school-reported and self-reported GPA were highly correlated.

## Interviews

At one level, there is very little difference between the questionnaire and the interview. In both cases, the investigator is interested in participants' responses to questions. However, in an **interview,** rather than having respondents read the questions and write down their responses, the interviewer *orally* asks respondents a series of questions and also *records* responses. As subtle as these differences seem to be, they have important consequences.

One important consequence is that interviews are more time-consuming than questionnaires. Interviews are more time-consuming because you should not interview more than one person at a time. If you did interview more than one person at a time, each individual's response would not be independent. Instead, what one participant said might depend on what other participants had already said. In other words, participants might go along with the group rather than disclosing their true opinions. Because interviews are more time-consuming than questionnaires, they are also more expensive than questionnaires.

What does the added expense of the interview buy you? Basically, the expense buys you more interaction with the participant. Because of this interaction, you can clarify questions the respondents don't understand. You can follow up on ambiguous or interesting responses—a tremendous asset in exploratory studies in which you have not yet identified all the important variables. Finally, this personal touch may increase your response rate.

Unfortunately, the personal nature of the interview creates two major problems. First, there is the problem of **interviewer bias:** The interviewer may influence respondents' responses by verbally or nonverbally encouraging and rewarding "correct" answers. Second, because participants are interviewed by the investigator, they may be more apt to give socially desirable responses than if they were merely writing their answers on an anonymous questionnaire.

## TELEPHONE INTERVIEWS

Psychologists have found that the telephone interview is less affected by social desirability bias and interviewer bias than the personal interview. Furthermore, the telephone interview generates such a high response rate that it is often less vulnerable to sampling bias than any other survey method.

Since the telephone-interviewer can't see the respondents, the interviewer cannot bias respondents' responses via subtle visual cues. Furthermore, by monitoring and tape-recording all the interviews, you can discourage interviewers from saying anything that might bias respondents' responses. For example, you could prevent interviewers from changing the wording or order of questions, or from giving more favorable verbal feedback for expected answers.

The telephone survey also appears to reduce the effects of subject biases such as the social desirability bias and obeying demand characteristics by giving participants a greater feeling of anonymity (Groves and Kahn, 1979). This feeling of anonymity is also partly responsible for the fact that telephone surveys sometimes have a higher response rate than personal interviews. Thus, thanks to anonymity, the telephone survey may be less vulnerable to both nonresponse bias and subject biases than other survey methods.

***How to Conduct a Telephone Interview.***    Soon, we'll discuss the general issues you should consider when planning any survey—whether it's a telephone survey, a mail survey, or another type. But, at this point, we'd like to give you a few words of advice that apply only to conducting a telephone survey.

Your first step is to determine what population you wish to sample and figure out a way of getting all of their phone numbers. Often, your population is conveniently represented in a telephone book, membership directory, or campus directory. Once you obtain the telephone numbers, you are ready to draw a random sample from your population. (Later in this chapter, you will learn how to draw a random sample.)

When you draw your sample, pull more names than you actually plan to survey. You won't be able to reach everyone that you attempt to phone so you'll need some alternate names. Usually, we draw 25% more names than we actually plan on interviewing.

Then, follow the advice in the next section, "Planning a Survey." Next, refine your survey by conducting practice surveys. For example, interview a friend on the phone. In addition, have someone read the survey to you. Often, you'll need to improve your questions to make them *sound* more understandable. Remember there are differences between the spoken word and the written word. Make your questions short and concise, and keep your voice clear and slow. Be careful not to bias your interview through inflection. Tape yourself reading the questions and play it back. Is your voice hinting at the answer you want participants to give? If not, you're ready to begin calling participants.

If you get a busy signal or a phone isn't answered, try again later. As a general rule, you should phone a person 3-4 times at different times of the day before replacing them with an alternate name or number.

When you do reach a person, identify yourself and ask for the person on the list. As with any study, informed consent is a necessary ingredient. Therefore, after you identify yourself, give a brief description of what the survey is about and ask the person if she or he is willing to participate.

Then, ask the questions slowly and clearly. Be prepared to repeat and clarify questions.

Once the survey is completed, thank your respondent. Then, volunteer to answer any questions they have. Often, you may give participants the option of being mailed a summary of the survey results.

***Conclusions about Telephone Interviews.***   You have seen that the telephone survey is superior to the personal interview for reducing subject biases, interviewer biases, and nonresponse biases. However, the main reason for the popularity of the telephone interview is practicality: The telephone survey is more convenient, less time-consuming, and cheaper than the personal interview.

Although there are many advantages to using the telephone interview, you should be aware of its limitations. First, as with any survey method, there is the possibility of a biased sample. Even if you followed proper random sampling techniques, telephone interviews are limited to those households with phones. Although this may not seem serious, you should be aware that not everyone has a telephone. Furthermore, some people will not be available to answer their phones or will choose to screen their calls through an answering machine or through "Caller ID." For example, one study reported that 25% of men between the ages of 25 and 34 screen all their calls (*Marketing News,* 1990).

Even when a person does answer the phone, he or she may refuse to answer your questions. In fact, some people get very angry when they receive a phone call regarding a telephone survey. The authors have been yelled at on more than one occasion by people who believe that telephone interviews are a violation of their privacy.

With telephone surveys, you are limited to asking very simple and short questions. Often, participants' attention spans are very short. Realize that, rather than answering your questions, their interest may be focused on the television show they are watching, the ice cream that is melting, or the baby who is crying.

Finally, by using the telephone survey, you limit yourself to only learning what participants tell you. You can't see anything for yourself. Thus, if you want to know what race the respondent is, you must ask. You don't see the respondent or the respondent's environment, and the respondents know you don't. Therefore, a 70-year-old bachelor living in a shack could tell you he's a 35-year-old millionaire with a wife and five kids. He knows you have no easy way of verifying his fable.

## PLANNING A SURVEY

All research requires careful planning. The survey is no exception. In this section, we will show you the necessary steps in developing and executing your survey.

### What Is Your Hypothesis?

As with all psychological research, the first step in designing a survey is to have a clear research question. You need a hypothesis to guide you if you are to develop a cohesive and useful set of survey questions. Writing a survey without a hypothesis to unify it is like writing a story without a plot: In the end, all you have is a set of disjointed facts that tell you nothing.

Not only do you want a clear research question, you want an important one. Therefore, before you write your first survey item, justify why your research question is important. That is, you should be able to answer at least one of these questions:

1. What useful information about human behavior will the survey provide?
2. What would be the practical implications of the survey results?

### Format of Questions

You've decided that your research question is appropriate. In addition, you've decided what kind of survey instrument (questionnaire, test, or interview) will give you the best information. Now, you are ready to decide what types of questions to use.

## FIXED ALTERNATIVE

In a fixed alternative question, you give participants the question and a choice of several answers. Their job is to pick the appropriate alternative.

Actually, there are a variety of fixed alternative formats. For example, true/false and multiple-choice questions are fixed alternative items, as are items that require people to choose a number on a rating scale.

***Nominal-dichotomous.***    Sometimes, fixed alternative questions ask respondents to tell the researcher whether they belong to a certain category. That is, participants may be asked to classify themselves according to gender, race, or religion. These types of questions, which essentially ask people whether they have a certain quality, yield nominal data.

Dichotomous questions—questions that allow only two responses (usually yes or no)—give you *qualitative* data. That is, they ask whether a person has a given *quality*. Often, respondents are asked whether they are a member or non-member of a category (for instance, "Are you employed?" or "Are you married?").

Sometimes, several dichotomous questions are asked at once. For example, "Are you African-American, Hispanic, Asian, or Caucasian (non-Hispanic)?" Note, however, that this question can be re-phrased as several dichotomous questions: "Are you African-American?" (yes or no), "Are you Hispanic?" (yes or no), etc. Thus, the information is still dichotomous—either participants claim to belong to a category or they don't. Consequently, the information you get from these questions is still categorical, qualitative information. That is, if you code African-American as a "1," Hispanic as "2," and so on, there is no logical order to your numbers. Higher numbers would not stand for having more of a quality. In other words, different numbers stand for different types (different *qualities*), rather than for different amounts (quantities).

There are several advantages to nominal-dichotomous items. Well-constructed **nominal items** can be easier to answer and score than other types of questions. Specifically, it's a lot easier for respondents to decide between two alternatives (such as, "Are you for or against animal research?"), than between 13 (for example, "Rate how favorably you feel toward animal research on a 13-point scale."). Furthermore, because there are only two—usually very different—options, there is a greater chance respondents and investigators will have similar interpretations of the items. Therefore, a well-constructed dichotomous item can be a highly reliable and valid measure.

Although there are many advantages to nominal-dichotomous items, there are some disadvantages. The main disadvantage is that some respondents will think that their viewpoint is not represented by the two alternatives given. To illustrate this point, consider the following question:

"Do you think abortion should continue to be legal in the U.S.?"
Yes/No

How would people who are ambivalent toward abortion respond? How would people who are fervently opposed to legalized abortion feel about not being allowed to express the depth of their feelings?

If you have artificially limited your respondents to two alternatives, your respondents may not be the only ones irritated by the fact that your alternatives prevent them from accurately expressing their opinions. You too should be annoyed—because by depriving yourself of information about subtle differences among respondents, you deprive yourself of *power:* the ability to find relationships among variables.

***Likert-type and Interval Items.***   One way to give yourself power is to use a Likert-type scale. With a Likert-type scale, participants typically respond to a statement by checking "strongly agree" (scored a "5"), "agree" (scored a "4"), "undecided" ("3"), "disagree" ("2"), or "strongly disagree" ("1").

Traditionally, most psychologists have assumed that a participant who "strongly agrees" (a "5") and a participant who merely "agrees" (a "4") differ by as much, *in terms of how they feel*, as a participant who is "undecided" (a "3") differs from someone who "disagrees" (a "2") because, in both cases, participants differed by 1 point. In other words, Likert-type scales are assumed to yield interval data. With interval data, differences between ratings correspond perfectly to differences in mental feelings. Questions 9 through 14 in Box 13–1 are examples of Likert-type, interval scale items.

**Likert-type items** are extremely useful in questionnaire construction. Whereas dichotomous items allow respondents to only agree or disagree, Likert-type items give respondents the freedom to: strongly agree, agree, be neutral, disagree, or strongly disagree. Thus, Likert-type items yield more information than nominal-dichotomous items. Furthermore, because Likert-type items yield interval data, responses to Likert-type items can be analyzed by more powerful statistical tests than nominal-dichotomous items.

The major disadvantage of Likert-type items is that respondents may resist the fixed-alternative nature of the question. One approach to this problem is to have a "Don't Know" option. That way, respondents won't feel forced into an answer that doesn't reflect their true position. In an interview, you can often get around the problem by reading the question as if it were an **open-ended question.** Then, you would simply record the answer under the appropriate alternative. As you can see, all the questions in Box 13–1 can be read like open-ended items.

***Summated Scores.***   If you have several Likert-type items that are designed to measure the same variable (like student sympathy), you can sum each respondent's answers to these questions. For example, the possible answers for questions 9–14, in Box 13–1, are based on the same five-point interval scale, in which "strongly agree" could be a 5, "agree" a 4, "undecided" a neutral 3,

# Box 13-1
## Sample Telephone Survey

Hello my name is ____. I am conducting a survey for my Research Design Class at Bromo Tech. Your name was drawn as a part of a random sample of university faculty. I would greatly appreciate it if you would answer a few questions about your job and your use of computers. The survey should take only five minutes. Will you help me?

### Demographics

1. **Gender** (Don't ask)
   ___ Male
   ___ Female
2. **What is your position at Bromo Tech?**[1]
   ___ Instructor
   ___ Assistant Professor
   ___ Associate Professor
   ___ Professor
   ___ Other (If other, terminate interview)
3. **How long have you been teaching college?**
   ___ 0-4 years
   ___ 5-9 years
   ___ 10-14 years
   ___ 15-19 years
   ___ 20 or more years
4. **What department do you teach in?**
   ___ Anthropology
   ___ Art
   ___ Biology
   ___ Business
   ___ Chemistry
   ___ English
   ___ History
   ___ Math
   ___ Physical Education
   ___ Physics
   ___ Political Science
   ___ Psychology
   ___ Sociology
5. **What is the highest academic degree you have earned?**
   ___ B.A./B.S.
   ___ M.A./M.D.
   ___ Ph.D./Ed.D.
6. **How old are you?**
   ___ ≤25
   ___ 26-34
   ___ 35-44
   ___ 45-54
   ___ 55-64
   ___ ≥65

### End of Demographics

7. **Do you use computers?**
   ___ Yes
   ___ No (skip to 9)
8. **How many hours a week do you estimate you use computers?**
   ___ ≤1 hour
   ___ 2-4 hours
   ___ 5-9 hours
   ___ 10-14 hours
   ___ 15-19 hours
   ___ ≥20 hours

Please indicate how much you agree or disagree with the following statements. State whether you strongly agree, agree, disagree, strongly disagree, or are undecided.

9. **I like college students.**

   SA        A        U        D        SD

10. **College is stressful for students.**

    SA        A        U        D        SD

*continued*

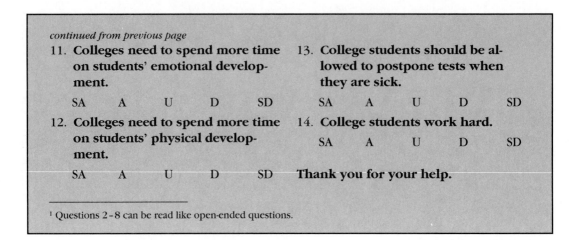

*continued from previous page*

11. **Colleges need to spend more time on students' emotional development.**

    SA      A      U      D      SD

12. **Colleges need to spend more time on students' physical development.**

    SA      A      U      D      SD

13. **College students should be allowed to postpone tests when they are sick.**

    SA      A      U      D      SD

14. **College students work hard.**

    SA      A      U      D      SD

    **Thank you for your help.**

[1] Questions 2–8 can be read like open-ended questions.

"disagree" a 2, and "strongly disagree" a 1. Once each response has been transformed into a number that ranges from 1 to 5, the answers for questions 9–14 can be added (summed) to produce a **summated score.** Thus, suppose we obtained the following pattern of responses:

> question  #9 =     "1"
>
> question #10 =     "2"
>
> question #11 =     "1"
>
> question #12 =     "3"
>
> question #13 =     "1"
>
> question #14 =     "2"

Then, the summated score (total score for liking students) would be 10 (because $1 + 2 + 1 + 3 + 1 + 2 = 10$).

There are two statistical advantages to using summated scores. First, just as a 50-question multiple-choice test is more reliable than a one-question test, a score based on several questions is more reliable than a score based on a single question. Second, analyses are often simpler for summated scores. If we summed the responses for the six Likert-type items in Box 13-1, we could compare computer users and non-computer users on "student sympathy" by doing one t-test. Without a summated score, you would have to perform six separate t-tests, and then correct the t-test for the effects of having done multiple analyses.[1]

***Conclusions about Fixed Interval Items.***    Fixed alternative questions can be used to ask the respondent how much of a quality they have. For ex-

---

[1] Or, you could use more complex analysis, such as multivariate analysis of variance (MANOVA).

ample, a question might ask, "How much do you agree or disagree with the following statement?" (the fixed alternatives would be strongly agree, agree, disagree, strongly disagree). Or, the question might ask how much of a certain behavior the person did. For instance, "How many days a week do you study (a. 0, b. 1, c. 2, d. 3, e. 4, f. 5, g. 6, h. 7)?" If asked the right way, these "how many ___," "how much ___," and "how high ___" questions can yield interval data.

Unfortunately, many of these "how much ___," "how many ___," and "how high ___" questions are not asked the right way. Consequently, they do not yield interval data. For example, when asking respondents about their grade point averages, some researchers make 1 = 0.00–0.99, 2 = 1.0–1.69, 3 = 1.7–2.29, 4 = 2.3–2.7, 5 = 2.8–4.0. Note that the response options do not cover equal intervals. The interval covered by option "4" is .4, whereas the range of GPAs covered by option "5" is 1.2. Because there aren't equal intervals between response options, averaging respondents' responses is meaningless. A better choice of options would be 1 = 0.00–0.99, 2 = 1.00–1.99, 3 = 2.00–2.99, and 4 = 3.00–4.00.[2]

## OPEN-ENDED QUESTIONS

Whereas fixed response items resemble multiple-choice items, open-ended questions resemble short answer or essay questions. That is, rather than having respondents choose among several researcher-determined response options, participants are free to respond in their own words. This format gives respondents more freedom about how they answer questions than fixed-alternative and scaled items. This flexibility makes open-ended questions a useful exploratory device because it allows unexpected, but important, responses.

Open-ended questions also enable you to find out how much participants know about the survey topic. Consequently, you may find out whether your respondents really have the information you are seeking. In addition, you may find out the opinions and beliefs that underlie their ratings. For example, one professor may respond to question 9 in Box 13–1, "I like college students," with an "undecided" because he is new to the college and doesn't know. Another professor may give the same rating because she has mixed feelings about students. Asking open-ended questions would allow you to see that these two respondents have different reasons for giving the same response.

Although there are numerous advantages to open-ended questions, these are tempered by some potentially serious disadvantages. First, open-ended questions take more time to record and score than other question formats. This not only places greater demands on you, it also requires more from your respondents. Because of the difficulty of generating their own responses, participants will often skip open-ended questions.

---

[2] Probably the best thing to do would be simply to ask subjects for their grade point average. However, some investigators are so eager to get their data on multiple choice forms that can be computer scored that they insist that every question be answered as a, b, c, d, or e.

It will also take some skill to accurately record responses to open-ended interview questions. If you don't take shorthand, you might consider video-recording or tape-recording the interview.

But perhaps the biggest disadvantage of open-ended questions, whether in an interview or questionnaire, is that they are difficult to score. Answers may be so varied that you won't see an obvious way to code them. Often the coding strategy you finally adopt will be arbitrary. To help you come up with a logical and systematic method of coding open-ended questions, try to come up with a content analysis scheme (see Chapters 3 and 12) *before* you start collecting data.

Once you have done a content analysis, you may convert the information from your open-ended questions into nominal or interval data where appropriate. For example, if you ask people how old they are, you would analyze these quantitative data as interval data. If you ask participants what religion they are, you would analyze these qualitative, categorical data as nominal data.

## Format of Survey

The format of your questions will largely determine your **survey** format. In this section, we will discuss the three survey formats: structured, semi-structured, and unstructured.

### STRUCTURED

The **structured survey** is the kind most often used in psychological research. In a structured survey, all respondents are asked a standard list of questions in a standard order. In many structured surveys, all respondents are asked a standard list of **fixed alternative items** in a standard order.

The structured format will ensure that each participant is asked the same questions. By using a standard list of questions, you reduce the risk of interviewer bias. By using a standard list of fixed alternative questions, you can obtain easily interpretable responses.

### SEMI-STRUCTURED

A **semi-structured survey** is constructed around a core of standard questions. However, unlike the structured survey, the interviewer may expand on any question in order to explore a given response in greater depth. Like the structured questionnaire, the semi-structured questionnaire can yield accurate and comprehensive data. In addition, the semi-structured interview allows the investigator to ask additional questions to follow up on any interesting or unexpected answers to the standard questions.

Unfortunately, these advantages are often outweighed by two major disadvantages. First, data from a semi-structured survey may be hard to interpret. It is difficult to compare participants' responses when different participants are asked different follow-up questions. Second, in giving the interviewer more freedom to follow up answers, you may be giving the interviewer more freedom to bias the results. That is, by deciding which answers to probe and how to probe them, the interviewer may affect what participants say.

The semi-structured questionnaire is best when you are examining uncharted waters. It provides enough standard information so that you can make meaningful interpretations. In addition, it provides you with new information that may be useful for future studies.

### UNSTRUCTURED

**Unstructured surveys** are very popular in the media, in the analyst's office, and with inexperienced researchers. In the unstructured survey, interviewers have objectives that they believe can be best met without an imposed structure. Therefore, there isn't a set of standard questions. The interviewer is free to ask what she wants, how she wants to, and the respondent is free to answer how he pleases. Without standardization, the information is extremely vulnerable to interviewer bias and is usually too disorganized for analysis.

Because of these problems, the unstructured interview is best used as an exploratory device. As a research tool for reaping meaningful and accurate information, the unstructured survey is limited. As a tool for a beginning researcher like yourself, the unstructured interview is virtually worthless.

## The Art of Asking Good Questions

Although it's important to decide how participants should respond to questions (open-ended, Likert-type, dichotomous), it's more important to ask good questions. Although asking questions is a part of everyday life, asking good survey questions is not. In this section, you will learn the criteria for good questionnaire construction. By adhering to these criteria, you will get the most out of your surveys.

### FRAMING QUESTIONS

Accurate communication is the major goal in questionnaire construction. To communicate accurately, your questions must adhere to several criteria.

*Use Words a Third-grader Would Understand.*    Your task is not to impress respondents with your command of vocabulary and technical jargon. Instead, your task is to make sure respondents understand you. Therefore, use simple words and avoid jargon.

*Use Words and Terms That Won't Be Misinterpreted.*    There are several steps you can take to make sure that participants know *exactly* what you are talking about.

First, avoid slang terms. Slang terms often have different meanings to different groups. Thus, if you want to know people's attitudes toward marijuana, use the word "marijuana" rather than a slang term like "dope." "Dope" may be interpreted as meaning marijuana, heroin, or all drugs.

Second, be specific. If you want to know whether your respondents like college students, don't ask, "How do you feel about students?" Instead, ask, "Do you like college students?"

Finally, you can avoid misinterpretations through extensive pretesting. Often, the only way to find out that a question or term will be misinterpreted is by asking people what they think the question means. For example, through extensive pretesting, you might find that a seemingly straightforward question such as, "Should Pittsburgh increase coke production?" may be interpreted in at least five different ways:

**a.** Should Pittsburgh increase cocaine production?
**b.** Should Pittsburgh increase coal production?
**c.** Should Pittsburgh increase steel production?
**d.** Should Pittsburgh increase soft drink production?
**e.** Should Pittsburgh increase Coca-Cola production?

***Avoid Personal Questions Unless You Really Need the Information.*** Personal questions tend to arouse suspicion and resistance.

***Make Sure that Your Sample Has the Information You Seek.*** Obviously, respondents can't give you accurate answers if they don't know the answer. Therefore, you should avoid asking questions like, "How much marijuana do your children smoke a month?" If you suspect that some participants won't know the answer to a certain question, allow participants to say that they don't know the answer. Such a question might read, "I spent ___ percentage of my office hours advising students on personal matters last year: less than 20; between 20–40; between 40–60; between 60–80; between 80–100; don't know."

***Avoid Leading Questions.*** Remember, your aim is to get accurate information, not to get conformity. Therefore, don't ask **leading questions** that clearly point participants to your desired response. For example, don't ask the question: "You disapprove of the horrible way television presents violence, don't you?" Instead ask, "How much do you approve or disapprove of television's presentation of violence?"

***Avoid Questions That Are Loaded with Social Desirability.*** Don't ask questions that have a socially correct answer, like, "Do you donate money to student causes?" Generally, the answers to such questions cannot be trusted because participants will respond with the socially desirable answer. Furthermore, such questions may contaminate participants' responses to subsequent questions because such questions may arouse respondents' suspicions. For instance, the respondent may think, "They said there were no right or wrong answers. They said they just wanted my opinion. But obviously, there are right and wrong answers to this survey." Or, the respondent may think, "They know I would give that answer. Anyone would give that answer. This survey is starting to feel like one of those 'surveys' used by people who try to sell you something. What are they trying to sell?"

***Avoid Double-barreled Questions.***    You wouldn't think of asking a respondent more than one question at the same time. But that's exactly what happens when you ask a **double-barreled question:** more than one question packed into a single question (like, "How much do you agree with the following statement: 'Colleges need to spend more time on students' emotional *and* physical development'?"). The responses to this question are uninterpretable because you don't know whether participants were responding to the first statement, "Colleges need to spend more time on students' emotional development," the second statement, "Colleges need to spend more time on students' physical development," or both statements.

As you can see, the conjunction "and" allowed this question to be double-barreled. Almost all double-barreled questions are joined by "and" or some other conjunction. So when looking over your questions, look suspiciously at all "and's," "or's," "nor's," and "but's."

***Keep Questions Short and Concise.***    Being brief will help you avoid ambiguity, confusion, and double-barreled questions. Remember, short questions are easier to understand. A useful guideline is to keep most of your questions under 10 words (one line) and all your questions under 20 words.

***Choose Response Options Carefully.***    From your experiences with multiple-choice tests, you are keenly aware that the response options are part of the question. Not only should you carefully consider the wording of each option, but you should also carefully consider how many options you will include.

As a general rule, the more options, the greater your ability to detect subtle differences between participants. According to this rule, if you use a 1–3 scale, you may fail to find differences that you would have found if you had used a 1–7 scale.

However, like most rules, this one has exceptions. If you give participants too many options, participants may be overwhelmed. Likewise, if the options are too similar, participants may be confused. The easiest way to determine how many options are appropriate is to pretest your questions.

***Avoid Negations.***    The appearance of a negation, such as "no" or "not," in a questionnaire item increases the possibility of misinterpretation. Furthermore, it takes more time to process and interpret a negation than a positively stated item. To illustrate, compare the next two statements: "Don't you not like it when students don't study?" versus "Do you like it when students study?"

***Avoid Irrelevant Questions.***    Be sensitive to the relevancy of a question-naire item for your population and your research question. For example, "Do you eat fondue?" is irrelevant to the research question, "Are professors who use computers more sympathetic to students?"

Although there are many obvious reasons for not including irrelevant questions, the most important reason is that irrelevant questions annoy respondents. If you ask an irrelevant question, many respondents will conclude that you are either incompetent or disrespectful. Since they have lost respect for you, they will be less likely to give accurate answers to the rest of your questions. In fact, they may even refuse to continue with the survey.

***Pretest the Questionnaire.***    Even if you carefully evaluate and edit each question, there are some problems that you can only discover by having people try to answer your questions. Therefore, pretesting questions is one of the most important steps in developing questions.

## SEQUENCING QUESTIONS

Once you have developed a good set of questionnaire items, you need to decide in what order to ask them. Ordering questions is important because the sequence of questions can influence results (Krosnick & Schuman, 1988). To appropriately sequence questions, follow these four general rules.

***Put Innocuous Questions First, Personal Questions Last.***    Participants are often tense or anxious at the beginning of a survey. They don't know what to expect. They don't know whether they should continue the survey. The questions you ask at the beginning of the survey set the tone for the rest of the survey. Thus, if the first question is extremely personal, participants may decide to withdraw from the survey. Even if they don't withdraw, they will be very defensive throughout the survey. If, on the other hand, your initial questions are innocuous, participants may relax and feel comfortable enough to respond frankly to personal questions.[3]

Putting the most sensitive questions at the end of your survey will not only increase the number of candid responses, it will also yield more data. To illustrate, suppose that you have a 20-item survey in which all but one of the questions are relatively innocuous. If you put the sensitive item first, respondents may quit the survey immediately. Since this item was the first question you asked, you have gathered no information whatsoever. If, on the other hand, you

---

[3] Not everyone agrees with this rule. For example, Dillman (1978) suggests that surveys should start with questions that hook the respondent's interest. If you are having trouble getting people to participate in your survey, you might consider Dillman's advice. However, we have found that, by carefully explaining the purpose of the survey before administering it (in accordance with the principle of informed consent), participants will conscientiously answer questions.

put the sensitive item last, respondents may still quit. But, even though they've quit, you still have their responses to 19 of the 20 questions.

*Qualify Early.*     If people must meet certain qualifications to be asked certain questions, find out if your participant has those qualifications before asking her those questions. In other words, don't ask people questions that don't apply to them. There is no need to waste their time, and yours, by collecting useless information. Participants don't like saying, "no, doesn't apply" repeatedly.

Box 13-1 has two qualifying questions. The first is question 2, "What is your position at Bromo Tech?" This question establishes the presence of two qualifications for the survey: (1) that the person is a professor; and (2) the person teaches at Bromo Tech. If people don't meet these qualifications, the survey is terminated at the start of the interview, not at the end. This saves time and energy. Can you identify the second qualifying question?

*Be Aware of Response Sets.*     If all your questions have the same response options, people sometimes get locked into one answer. For example, if each question has the alternatives, "Strongly Agree, Agree, Neutral, Disagree, Strongly Disagree," respondents may answer each question with the same alternative, for example, "undecided." By always checking the neutral option, they can get the questionnaire over with as soon as possible. To avoid the neutral response set, you may want to eliminate the neutral option. Unfortunately, the neutral response set isn't the only response bias. As you learned earlier in this chapter, there are a variety of **response sets,** including the "yea-saying" (always agreeing) and the "nay-saying" (always disagreeing) biases.

One of the most common ways of dealing with response sets is to alternate the way you phrase the questions. That is, you might ask respondents to strongly agree, agree, disagree, or strongly disagree to the statement, "Students are hard-working." Then, later in the questionnaire, you could ask them to strongly agree, agree, disagree, or strongly disagree with the statement, "Students are lazy."

*Keep Similar Questions Together.*     There are three reasons why you get more accurate responses when you keep related questions together.

First, your participants will perceive the survey to be organized and professional. Therefore, they will take the survey seriously.

Second, participants will be less likely to misunderstand your questions. You minimize the problem of participants thinking that you are asking about one thing when you are really asking about another topic.

Third, by asking all the related questions together, participants are already thinking about the topic before you ask the question. Since they are already thinking about the topic, they can respond quickly and accurately. If respondents aren't thinking about the topic before you ask the question, it may take some respondents awhile to think of the answer to the question. At best, this makes for some long pauses. At worst, respondents will avoid long pauses by saying they don't know or by making up an answer.

## ADD DEMOGRAPHIC QUESTIONS

In addition to writing items that directly address your research question, you should ask some questions that will reveal your sample's **demographics:** characteristics, such as age, gender, and education level. Thus, in our survey of college professors (see Box 13-1), we asked six demographic questions.

By comparing our sample's responses to these demographic questions with the population's demographics, we can see how representative our sample is. For example, we can look in the college catalog or go to the personnel office to find out what percentage of the population is male. Then, we can compare our sample demographics to these population demographics. If we found that 75% of the faculty was male, but that only 25% of our sample was male, we would know that our sample wasn't representative of the faculty.

Note that we put the demographic questions first (questions 1-6). Why? We put our demographic questions first because they were relatively innocuous. Thus, these questions would put our respondents at ease before we asked more personal questions.

## PUTTING THE FINAL TOUCHES ON YOUR QUESTIONNAIRE

You've written your questions, carefully sequenced them, and pretested them. Now, you should carefully proof and pretest your questionnaire to make sure that it is accurate, easy to read, and easy to score.

Obviously, participants are more likely to take your research seriously if your questionnaire looks professional. Therefore, your final copy of the questionnaire should be free of smudges and spelling errors. The spaces between questions should be uniform.

Even though the questionnaire is neatly typed, certain key words may have been scrambled and omitted. At best, these scrambled or missing words could cause embarrassment. At worst, they would cause you to lose data. Therefore, not only should you proof the questionnaire to ensure that the form of the questionnaire looks professional, you should also pretest the questionnaire to ensure that the content is professional.

Once you have thoroughly checked and rechecked both the form and the content of the questionnaire, you should fill out the questionnaire and then code your own responses. After coding your responses, you should consider ways of making coding easier. Basically, there are three strategies you can use to facilitate coding:

1. Put the answer blocks in the left margin. This will allow you to score each page quickly because you can go straight down the page without shifting your gaze from left to right and without having to filter out extraneous information (see Box 13-1).

2. Have respondents put their answers on an answer sheet. With an answer sheet, you don't have to look through and around questions to find the answers. The answer sheet is an especially good idea when your questionnaire is more than one page long because the answer sheet saves you the trouble of turning pages.

3. Have participants put their responses on a coding sheet that can be scored by computer. Computer scoring is more accurate than hand scoring. Besides, since computers like dull, time-consuming tasks, why not let them code responses?

## SAMPLING

Once you have decided what questions you will ask and how you will ask them, you need to decide *whom* you will ask. To decide whom you will ask, you first have to decide *exactly* what population you want to study. If your population is extremely small (all art history teachers at your school), you may decide to survey every member of your population. Usually, however, your population is so large that you can't survey everyone. Therefore, instead of surveying the entire population, you will survey a *sample* of people from that population. Whether you acquire your sample by random sampling, stratified random sampling, convenience sampling, or quota sampling, your goal is to get a sample that is representative of your population.

## Random Sampling

In **random sampling,** each member of the population has an equal probability of being selected. Furthermore, the selection of respondents is independent. In other words, the selection of a given person has no influence on the selection or exclusion of other members of the population from the sample.

To select a random sample for a survey, you would first identify every member of your population. Next, you would go to a random numbers table and use that table to assign each member of the population a random number. Then, you would rank each member from lowest to highest based on the size of his or her random number. Thus, if a person were assigned the random number 00000, that person would be the first person on the list, whereas a person assigned the number 99999 would be the last person on the list. You would select your sample by selecting names from the beginning of this list until you got the sample size you needed. Thus, if you needed 100 respondents, you would select the first 100 names on the list.

As you can imagine, random sampling can be very time-consuming. First, you have to identify every member of the population. That can be a chore, depending on your population. If you are interested in a student sample, then a trip to the Registrar's Office might yield a list of all currently enrolled students. In fact, some schools can generate a computerized random sample of students for you. If you are interested in sampling a community, the local telephone company is a good place to start. Or, if you are willing to spend the money, you can buy census tapes from the government or from marketing research firms.

After you've identified the population, you have to assign random numbers to your respondents. Just the first step—assigning random numbers to all members of a population—can be cumbersome and time-consuming. Imagine assigning 1,000,000 random numbers to names! But after that's done, you still have to order the names based on these random numbers to determine whom you will sample. Fortunately, computers can eliminate many of the headaches of random sampling—especially if you can find a computer file or database that has the names of everybody in your population.

Despite the hassles involved with random sampling, people are willing to put up with it because random sampling allows you to generalize the results of your study to a larger population. As you'll recall, you can use inferential statistics to infer the characteristics of a population from a random sample of that population.

### DETERMINING SAMPLE SIZE FOR RANDOM SAMPLES

As you know, your random sample may differ from the population by chance. That is, although your population may have 51% females, your random sample may have 49% females. You also know that you can reduce random sampling error by increasing your sample size. In other words, a sample of 10,000 will tend to reflect the population more accurately than a sample of 10. However, surveying 10,000 people may cost more time and energy than the added accuracy it buys. To figure out how many people you will need to randomly sample, consult Table 13-1.

## Stratified Random Sampling

With pure random sampling, you leave everything to chance. You count on using a large sample size so that the effects of chance will be small. With **stratified random sampling,** on the other hand, you don't leave everything to chance. Instead, you make sure that the sample is similar to the population in certain respects. For example, if you know that the population is 75% male and 25% female, you make sure your sample is 75% male and 25% female. You would accomplish this goal by dividing your population (stratum) into two subpopulations, or substrata. One substratum would consist of male members of the population, the other substratum would consist of female members. Next, you would decide on how many respondents you would sample from each substratum (for example, 75 from the male stratum, 25 from the female stratum). Finally, you would draw random samples from each substratum, following the same basic procedures you used in random sampling. The only difference is that you are collecting two samples from two substrata, rather than one sample from the main population.

**TABLE 13–1**

**Required Sample Size as a Function of Population Size and Desired Accuracy (within 5%, 3%, or 1%) at the 95% Confidence Level**

| SIZE OF THE POPULATION | SAMPLING ERROR | | |
| --- | --- | --- | --- |
| | 5% | 3% | 1% |
| 50 | 44 | 48 | 50 |
| 100 | 79 | 92 | 99 |
| 200 | 132 | 169 | 196 |
| 500 | 217 | 343 | 476 |
| 1,000 | 278 | 521 | 907 |
| 2,000 | 322 | 705 | 1661 |
| 5,000 | 357 | 894 | 3311 |
| 10,000 | 370 | 982 | 4950 |
| 20,000 | 377 | 1033 | 6578 |
| 50,000 | 381 | 1066 | 8195 |
| 100,000 | 383 | 1077 | 8926 |
| 1,000,000 | 384 | 1088 | 9706 |
| 100,000,000 | 384 | 1089 | 9800 |

**Example of how this table works:** If you are sampling from a population that consists of 50 people and you want to be 95% confident that your results will be within 5% of the true percentage in the population, you need to randomly sample 44 people.

**Note:** Table provided by David Van Amburg of MarketSource, Inc.

By using stratified random sampling, you have all the advantages of random sampling, but you don't need to sample nearly as many people. As a result, the Gallup Poll can predict the outcome of presidential elections based on samples of only 300 people. Furthermore, a stratified random sample ensures that your sample matches the population on certain key variables.

## Convenience Sampling

In **convenience sampling,** you simply sample people who are easy to survey. Convenience surveys are very common. Newspapers ask people to mail their responses to a survey question, and radio stations ask people to call in their reactions to a question. Even television stations have gotten into the act, asking people to call one number if they are in favor of a position on an issue, another number if they are opposed to that position.

To see how you would get a convenience sample, suppose that you were given one week to get 1,000 responses to a questionnaire. What would you do? You might go to areas where you would expect to find lots of people, such as a shopping mall. Or, you might ask your professors if you could do a survey in their classes. Or, you might put an ad in the newspaper, offering people money if they would respond to a questionnaire.

In conclusion, you can use convenience sampling techniques to get a relatively large sample quickly. Unfortunately, you do not know whether the sample represents your population. Your best bet is that it doesn't. In fact, if your respondents are actively volunteering to be in your survey, you can bet that your sample is extremely biased. People who call in to radio shows, write letters in response to questions in the newspaper, or respond to ads asking for people to be in a survey do *not* represent a significant portion of the population: those without the time or desire to respond to such surveys.

## Quota Sampling

**Quota sampling** is designed to make your convenience sample more representative of the population. Like stratified random sampling, quota sampling is designed to guarantee that your sample matched the population on certain characteristics. For instance, you might make sure that 25% of your sample was female, or that 20% of your sample was Hispanic.

Unlike stratified random sampling, however, quota sampling doesn't involve random sampling. Consequently, even though you met your quotas, your sample may not reflect the population at all. For example, you may meet your 20% quota of Hispanics by hanging around a hotel where there is a convention of high school Spanish teachers. Obviously, the Hispanics in your survey are not representative of the Hispanics in your community.

## Conclusions about Sampling Techniques

To get samples that represent your population, we recommend that you use either random sampling or stratified random sampling. However, no sampling technique is totally free of sampling bias because, ultimately, respondents choose the sample. That is, you can try to question participants, but they may choose not to answer you. As a result, your sample will not represent members of the population who choose not to respond.

There are two things you can do about the bias caused by non-response. First, you can get your response rate so high that non-response is not a problem. For example, by using brief, telephone surveys, some investigators obtain response rates of 97% or better.

Second, keep detailed records on the people who refused. If possible, unobtrusively record their gender, race, and estimated age. By knowing who is dropping out of your sample, you may know to whom your results don't apply.

## ADMINISTERING THE SURVEY

You have your survey questions. You've carefully sequenced your questions, and you've determined your sampling technique. You have had your study approved by your professor and any appropriate ethical review committees. Now it's time for you to actually administer your survey. Basically, you are going to follow the same advice you received for administering experiments, quasi-experiments, and other correlational studies. That is, you must follow APA's ethical guidelines (APA, 1992) and you must conduct yourself professionally during every step of the survey (see Appendixes A and C).

For example, participants should always be greeted. If participants can't be greeted in person (as with a mail questionnaire) then the questionnaire should always be accompanied by a cover letter—a written greeting. In this written greeting, you should introduce yourself, explain the nature of your study, and request the participant's help—just as you would if you were greeting the participant in person.

Participants should always be given clear instructions. As with any other study, an important part of these instructions is making it clear that participation is entirely voluntary. In an interview, the instructions are oral. In a questionnaire, they are written. However, if an investigator is administering the questionnaire, any written instructions can be backed up with oral ones.

After participants complete the survey, they should be debriefed about the purpose of the survey and thanked. Thus, at the end of a mail questionnaire, you should write a debriefing, thank your participants, and give them any additional instructions. For example, "Please mail your questionnaire in the enclosed envelope. To find out more about the survey, put a check mark in the upper left-hand corner of the questionnaire and we will send you a summary of the results once the survey is completed."

Finally, as in all studies, you should be careful to ensure your participants' confidentiality. This means that you should not only be careful when collecting data (for example, by using a cover page and spreading participants out so that they do not see each other's responses), but also when storing and disposing of data (see Appendixes A and C).

## ANALYZING SURVEY DATA

Once you have collected your survey data, you need to analyze them. In this section, we will show you how to summarize and make inferences from your data.

### Summarizing Data

The first step in analyzing survey data is to determine what data are relevant to your hypotheses. Once you know what data you want, you need to summarize that data. How you summarize your data will depend on what kind of data you have.

The type of data you have will depend on the type of questions you ask. When you ask rating scale questions or when you ask people to quantify their behavior ("How *many* hours a week do you use a computer?"), then you probably can assume that your data are interval scale data. If you ask questions that people have to answer either "yes" or "no" ("Do you use a computer?" "Do you like students?"), or questions that call on people to classify themselves ("Are you male or female?"), then you have nominal data.

## Summarizing Interval Data

If you simply want to know the typical response to an interval-scale question, ("On the average, how many hours do people in the sample use computers?"), then you only need to calculate the mean for that question. More often, however, you will be interested in the relationship between the answer to one question with the answers to other questions. That is, you probably will be interested in the relationship between two or more variables. If you are interested in such a relationship, you will usually want to construct tables of means that reflect that relationship.

In our survey example, we expect that there would be a relationship between computer use and sympathy for students. Therefore, we compared computer users' average sympathy for students with non-computer users' average sympathy for students (see Table 13–2). In addition, as you can tell from Table 13–2, we were also interested in seeing whether male or female professors were more sympathetic to students. To supplement your tables of means, you may want to compute a correlation coefficient (the Pearson $r$) to get an idea of the strength of the relationship between your two variables.

### LOOKING AT COMPLEX RELATIONSHIPS

Thus far, you have seen how to compare the relationship between pairs of variables (for example, computer use and sympathy; gender and sympathy; gender and computer use). Sometimes, however, you may want to see how three or more variables are related. The easiest way to compare three or more variables is to construct a table of means, as we have done at the bottom of Table 13–2. As you can see, this $2 \times 2$ table of means allows us to look at how both computer use and gender are related to sympathy.

## Summarizing Ordinal and Nominal Data

If your data are not interval scale data, don't summarize your data by computing means. For example, if you code 1 = male, 2 = female, do not say that "the mean sex in my study was 1.41."

Similarly, if you are having participants rank several choices, do not say that the mean rank for option "B" was 2.2. To understand why not, imagine that five persons were ranking three options. All five people ranked option A as second best (the rankings were "2-2-2-2-2") whereas two ranked option B best and three ranked option B third best (the rankings were "1-1-3-3-3"). The mean rank for option A is 2.0, the mean rank for option B is 2.2 (Semon, 1990). Thus,

**TABLE 13–2**
**Table of Means and Interactions**

TABLE OF MEANS FOR COMPUTER USAGE ON QUESTION 9:

"I LIKE COLLEGE STUDENTS"

Computer Usage

| Yes | No |
|-----|-----|
| 4.0 | 3.0 |

Average score on a 1 (strongly
disagree) to 5 (strongly agree)
scale.

TABLE OF MEANS FOR GENDER ON QUESTION 9:

"I LIKE COLLEGE STUDENTS"

Gender

| MALE | FEMALE |
|------|--------|
| 3.25 | 3.75 |

Average score on a 1 (strongly
disagree) to 5 (strongly agree)
scale.

INTERACTION FOR GENDER BY COMPUTER USAGE ON QUESTION 9:

"I LIKE COLLEGE STUDENTS"

Computer Usage

| Gender | Yes | No |
|--------|-----|-----|
| MALE | 3.5 | 3.0 |
| FEMALE | 4.5 | 3.0 |

Average score on a 1 (strongly
disagree) to 5 (strongly agree)
scale.

according to the mean, A is assumed to be better-liked (because it is closest to
the average rank of 1.0, which would mean 1st choice).

The mean, however, is misleading. The mean gives the edge to A because
the mean assumes that the difference between being a second choice and being
a third choice is the same as the difference between being a first choice and being a second choice. As you know, this is not the case. There is usually a considerable drop-off between a person's favorite and their second choice, but not
such a great difference between their second and third choices (Semon, 1990).
For example, you may find an enormous drop-off between your liking of your
favorite opposite sex friend and your second best opposite sex friend or between your favorite football team and your second favorite football team.

To go back to our example of options A and B, recall that A's average rank
was better than B's. However, because two people ranked B best and nobody

ranked A first, we could argue that option B was more liked (Semon, 1990). The moral of this example: If you do not have interval data, do not use means to summarize your data. Instead, use frequencies or percentages.

To look at relationships among nominal variables, use tables of either percentages or frequencies to compare different groups' responses. As you can see from Table 13-3, these tables can help you visualize similarities and differences between groups.

If you want to compute a measure to quantify how closely two variables are related, you can calculate a correlational coefficient called the *phi coefficient* (see Box 12-3). Like most correlation coefficients, phi ranges from $-1$ (strong negative correlation) to $+1$ (strong positive correlation).

### LOOKING AT COMPLEX RELATIONSHIPS

If you want to look at how three or more variables are related, do not use the phi coefficient. Instead, construct tables of frequencies, as we have done in Table 13-3. These two $2 \times 2$ tables of frequencies do for our ordinal data what the $2 \times 2$ table of means did for our interval data—allow us to look at three variables at once.

## Using Inferential Statistics

In addition to using descriptive statistics to describe the characteristics of your sample, you may wish to use inferential statistics. Inferential statistics may allow you to generalize the results of your sample to the population it represents. There are two reasons why you might want to use inferential statistics.

First, you might want to use inferential statistics to estimate certain **parameters**, such as the population mean for certain characteristics. Thus, if you wanted to estimate the average amount of time students spend using computers, you might want to use inferential statistics. This use of inferential statistics is called **parameter estimation**.

Second, you might want to determine whether the relationship you found between two or more variables would hold in the population. For example, you might want to determine whether using computers and grade point average are related in the population. Because you are deciding whether to reject the null hypothesis (that the variables are not related in the population), this use of inferential statistics is called **hypothesis-testing**.

### PARAMETER ESTIMATION WITH INTERVAL DATA

As we just mentioned, one reason for using inferential statistics would be to estimate population parameters. For example, from our survey of computer usage and student sympathy, we might want to estimate one parameter: the amount of sympathy the average professor at our school has for students.

**TABLE 13–3**
**Tables of Nominal Data**

**COMPUTER USE BY GENDER**

Gender

Use computers?

|  | Male | Female |
|---|---|---|
| Yes | **(A)** 20 | **(B)** 15 |
| No | **(C)** 55 | **(D)** 10 |

The Relationships Among Computer Use, Gender, and Academic Department

| Use Computers | **Gender** | | | Use Computers | **Gender** | |
|---|---|---|---|---|---|---|
|  | Male | Female | |  | Male | Female |
| Yes | 10 | 10 | | Yes | 20 | 20 |
| No | 80 | 0 | | No | 40 | 20 |
| | **Physical Science Professors** | | | | **Social Sciences Professors** | |

Our best guess of the amount of sympathy the average professor at our school has for students is the average amount of sympathy the average professor in our sample has for students. However, the average for our sample may differ from the average in the population. Therefore, it is often useful to establish a range in which the population mean is likely to fall. For example, you may want to establish a *95% confidence interval:* a range in which you can be 95% sure that the population mean falls.

You can establish 95% confidence intervals for any population mean from the sample mean, if you know the **standard error of the mean.** (If you don't have a computer or calculator that will compute the standard error of the mean for you, see Chapter 6.) You establish the lower limit of your confidence interval by subtracting two standard errors from the sample mean. Then, you establish the upper limit of your confidence interval by adding two standard errors to the sample mean. Thus, if the average sympathy rating for all the professors in our sample was 4.0 and the standard error was .5, we could be 95% confident that the true population mean is somewhere between 3.0 and 5.0.

**HYPOTHESIS TESTING WITH INTERVAL DATA**

You can also use statistics to see if there are significant differences between groups. For example, we might want to know if the differences we observe in our sample also apply to the population at large. Through a t-test, we could test whether the differences in sympathy we observed between computer users and non-computer users was too large to be due to sampling error and thus probably represented a true difference.

The t-test between means is not the only way to determine whether there is a relationship between computer usage and student sympathy. We could also determine whether a relationship exists between computer usage and student sympathy by determining whether the correlation coefficient between those two variables was significant. (To do this test, consult Box 12-2.)

If you were comparing more than one pair of variables, you could do several t-tests or test the significance of several correlations. In either case, you should correct for doing more than a single statistical test by using a more stringent significance level than the conventional .05 level. For example, if you looked at five comparisons, you might use the .01 level; if you looked at 50 comparisons, you might use the .001 level.

***Relationships Among More than Two Variables.*** If you wanted to look at more than two variables at once (relationship between computer usage, gender, and sympathy, Table 13-2), you might use analysis of variance (ANOVA). If you perform multiple ANOVAs, you should correct your significance level for the number of ANOVAs you computed, just as you would if you use multiple t-tests.

***More Complicated Procedures.*** You should be aware that we have just scratched the surface of how interval data from a survey can be analyzed. Factor analysis, multivariate analysis of variance, and multiple regression are all techniques that could be used to analyze survey research data. However, these statistical techniques are beyond the scope of this book.

## Using Inferential Statistics with Nominal Data

Just as statistical tests can be performed on interval data, they can be performed on nominal data. The difference is that tests based on nominal data tend to be less powerful than those using interval scale data.

***Estimating Overall Percentages in Population.*** If you chose your sample size according to the first column of Table 13-1, you can be 95% confident that your sample percentages are within 5% of the population's percentages. Thus, if you found that 35% of your participants were female, you would be 95% confident that 30-40% of your population was female.

### HYPOTHESIS-TESTING WITH NOMINAL DATA

With nominal data, you can use significance tests to determine whether differences between sample percentages reflect differences in population percentages. For example, in your sample, you may find that more men than women use computers. Is that a relationship that holds in your population—or is that pattern due to random sampling error? To find out, you would use a statistical test. But instead of using a t-test, as you would with interval data, you would use the **chi-square** test (see Box 12–3).

If you are performing more than one Chi-square test, you should correct for the number of analyses performed. Just as with the t-test, you should raise your significance level to compensate for doing multiple analyses. Thus, if you are comparing five chi-squares, you should use a .01 significance level rather than a .05 significance level.

## CONCLUDING REMARKS

In this chapter, you learned the essence of good survey research. Early in the chapter, you were introduced to the applications and limitations of survey research. You saw the advantages and disadvantages of different survey formats, as well as the strengths and weaknesses of different kinds of questions. After learning how to write a survey, you learned how to administer, score, and analyze survey data. Thus, if you apply what you have learned in this chapter, you can become a skilled survey researcher.

## SUMMARY

1. Surveys can help you describe what people are thinking, feeling, or doing.
2. Surveys allow you to gather information from a large sample with less effort and expense than most other data-gathering techniques.
3. In a survey, it is important to ask only pertinent questions.
4. Don't accept respondents' answers as gospel. People don't always tell the truth or know what the "truth" is.
5. Know to whom you want to generalize your results before you start your study.
6. Remember, surveys yield only correlational data. You cannot determine causality with the survey method.
7. There are several drawbacks to self-administered questionnaires: They have a low return rate; respondents may misinterpret questions; and participants may object to question format.
8. Investigator-administered questionnaires have a higher response rate than self-administered questionnaires.
9. Interviews are especially useful for exploratory studies. However, interviews are expensive and the interviewer may bias participants' responses.
10. Telephone surveys have higher response rates, are easier to administer, and offer greater anonymity than personal interviews.
11. Your first step in survey research is to have a hypothesis.

12. There are three basic question formats: nominal-dichotomous, Likert-type, and open-ended.
13. Structured surveys are generally more useful than unstructured.
14. Asking good questions and having a representative sample are the keys to good survey research.
15. Be sure to edit and pretest your survey questions.
16. Careful attention should be placed on sequencing questions. Keep similar questions together and put personal questions last.
17. Be aware of response biases, such as a tendency of participants to agree with statements or the tendency to answer questions in a way that puts the participant in a positive light.
18. Spending a little time deciding how to code your questionnaire before you administer it can save a great deal of time later on.
19. Random and stratified random sampling allow you to make statistical inferences from your data.
20. Participants in survey research should be treated with the same respect as human participants in any other kind of study.

## KEY TERMS

**survey research design:** a non-experimental design useful for describing how people think, feel, or behave. The key is to design a valid questionnaire, test, or interview and administer it to a representative sample of the group in which you are interested. (p. 436)

**population:** everyone to whom you want to generalize your results. Depending on your goals, a population could be everyone who votes in the presidential election, everyone at your school, or everyone who spends more than $100 a year on videos. Since you don't have the time to survey everyone in your population, you will usually survey a sample of those individuals. (p. 436)

**convenience sampling:** choosing to include people in your sample simply because they are convenient to survey. It is hard to generalize the results accurately from a study that used convenience sampling. (p. 461)

**quota sampling:** making sure you get the desired number of (meet your quotas for) certain types of people (certain age groups, minorities, etc.). This method does not involve random sampling and usually gives you a less representative sample than random sampling would. It may, however, be an improvement over convenience sampling. (p. 462)

**random sampling:** a sample that has been randomly selected from a population. If you want to generalize your results, random sampling is better than both quota sampling and convenience sampling. (p. 459)

**stratified random sampling:** like quota sampling, a strategy for ensuring that the proportion of certain subgroups (e.g., men and women) is the same in the sample as it is in the population. However, goes beyond quota sampling because it involves randomly sampling. For example, if the population of interest was 75% women and 25% men, you might obtain a list of all the women and randomly sample 75 from that list. Then, you would obtain a list of all the men in that population and randomly sample 25 from that list. Has all the advantages of random sampling with even greater accuracy. Thus, a relatively small stratified random sample may more accurately represent the population than a larger, non-stratified random sample. (p. 460)

**non-response bias:** the problem caused by people who were in your sample refusing to participate in your study. Non-response bias is one of the most serious threats to a survey design's external validity. (p. 440)

**double-barreled question:** a statement that contains more than one question. Responses to a double-barreled question are difficult to interpret. For example, if someone responds, "NO," to the question, "Are you hungry and thirsty?" we do not know whether they are hungry, but not thirsty; not hungry, but thirsty; or neither hungry nor thirsty. (p. 455)

**leading question:** questions structured to lead respondents to the answer the researcher wants (such as, "You like this book, don't you?"). (p. 454)

**response set:** pattern of responding to questions that is independent of the particular question's content (for instance, a participant might always check "agree" no matter what the statement is). (p. 457)

**retrospective self-report:** participants telling you what they said, did, or believed in the past. In addition to problems with ordinary self-report (response sets, giving the answer that a leading question suggests, etc.), retrospective self-report is vulnerable to memory biases. Thus, retrospective self-reports should *not* be accepted at face value. (p. 439)

**fixed alternative items:** items on a test or questionnaire in which a person must choose an answer from among a few specified alternatives. Multiple-choice, true-false, and rating scale questions are all fixed alternative items. (p. 452)

**open-ended items:** questions that do not provide fixed response alternatives. Essay and fill-in-the-blank questions are open-ended. (p. 448)

**nominal items:** items that lead to concluding that the participant belongs to a certain category or has a certain quality. Data from qualitative items cannot be scored in terms of saying that one participant has more of a certain quality than another. Questions asking about gender and group membership are nominal items. Data from nominal items are analyzed differently than data from Likert-type items. (p. 447)

**Likert-type items:** items that typically ask participants whether they strongly agree, agree, are neutral, disagree, or strongly disagree with a certain statement. These items are assumed to yield interval data. (p. 448)

**summated scores:** when you have several Likert-type questions that all tap the same dimension (such as attitude toward democracy), you could add up (sum) each participant's responses from the different questions to get an overall (summated) score. (p. 450)

**standard error of the mean:** an index of the degree to which random error may cause the sample mean to be an inaccurate estimate of the population mean. The more participants you sample, the smaller the standard error will be. (p. 467)

**parameters:** characteristics of populations—not samples. Thus, the mean of a sample is not a parameter, but the mean of the entire population is a parameter. (p. 466)

**parameter estimation:** using measurements obtained from a sample to estimate the true characteristics of the entire population. (p. 466)

**hypothesis-testing:** the use of inferential statistics to determine if the relationship found between two or more variables in a particular sample holds true in the population. (p. 466)

**chi-square:** a statistical test used to do hypothesis testing on nominal data (data from nominal items). (p. 469)

**questionnaire:** a survey that respondents read. (p. 441)

**self-administered questionnaire:** a questionnaire filled out in the absence of an investigator. (p. 441)

**interview:** a survey in which the researcher orally asks questions. (p. 443)

**interviewer bias:** when the interviewer influences participant's responses. For example, the interviewer might verbally or nonverbally reward the participant for giving responses that support the hypothesis. Or, the interviewer might adopt a more enthusiastic tone of voice when reading the desired response than when reading the less desired response. (p. 444)

**unstructured survey:** when the interviewer has no standard set of questions that he or she asks each participant. Virtually worthless approach if the goal is to collect scientifically valid data. (p. 453)

**semi-structured survey:** a survey constructed around a core of standard questions; however, the interviewer may expand on any question in order to explore a given response in greater depth. (p. 452)

**structured survey:** a survey in which all respondents are asked a standard list of questions in a standard order. For collecting valid data, the structured survey is superior to the semi-structured and unstructured survey. (p. 452)

**demographics:** characteristics of a group, such as sex, age, social class. (p. 458)

## EXERCISES

1. Develop a hypothesis that can be tested by administering a survey.

2. Is a survey the best way to test your hypothesis? Why?

3. Is an interview or a questionnaire the best way to test your hypothesis? Why?

4. For the three basic question formats list their advantages and disadvantages in the grid below.

| Question Format | Advantages | Disadvantages |
|---|---|---|
| Nominal-dichotomous | | |
| Likert-type | | |
| Open-ended | | |

5. Write three nominal-dichotomous questions that might help you test your hypothesis.

6. Write three Likert-type questions that might help you test your hypothesis.

7. Write three open-ended questions that might help you test your hypothesis.

8. Edit your questions using the points presented in this chapter.

9. Why can you make statistical inferences from data obtained from a random sample?

# CHAPTER 14

## Putting It All Together: Writing Research Proposals and Reports

*Overview*

*Aids to Developing Your Idea*

THE RESEARCH JOURNAL
THE PROPOSAL

*Writing the Introduction to Your Research Proposal*

THE ELEMENTS OF AN INTRODUCTION
JUSTIFYING SPECIFIC TYPES OF STUDIES

*Writing the Method Section*

PARTICIPANTS
DESIGN
APPARATUS AND MATERIALS
PROCEDURE

*Writing the Results Section*

*Writing the Discussion Section*

*Putting On the Front and Back*

TITLE AND TITLE PAGE
ABSTRACT
REFERENCES

*Writing the Final Report*

WHAT STAYS THE SAME OR CHANGES VERY LITTLE
WRITING THE RESULTS SECTION
WRITING THE DISCUSSION SECTION

*Concluding Remarks*

*Summary*

*Key Terms*

# Chapter 14

-----

# PUTTING IT ALL TOGETHER: WRITING RESEARCH PROPOSALS AND REPORTS

*"Don't know what I want, but I know how to get it."*
— "ANARCHY IN THE UK"

## OVERVIEW

Your research should be carefully planned before you run your first participant. Without such planning, you may fail to have a clear hypothesis or you may fail to test your hypothesis properly. In short, poor planning leads to poor execution.

Poor execution can lead to unethical research. At best, it wastes participants' time; at worst, it harms participants. Therefore, the purpose of this chapter is to help you avoid unethical research by showing you how to plan and report the results of your study. If you follow our advice, your research should be humane, valid, and meaningful.

## AIDS TO DEVELOPING YOUR IDEA

In this section, you will learn about two major research tools—the research journal and the research proposal. Many scientists regard the research journal and the research proposal as essential to the development and implementation of sound, ethical research.

### The Research Journal

We recommend that you keep a *research journal:* a diary of your research ideas and your research experiences. Keeping a journal will help you in at least three ways. First, you won't have to rely on memory to explain why and how you did what you did. Second, writing to yourself helps you think through design decisions. Third, the research journal can help you in preparing a research proposal.

Since the journal is for your eyes only, your journal does not have to be neatly typed and free of spelling and grammatical errors. What's in the journal is much more important than how it is written.

What should you put in your journal? Every idea you have about your research project. So, at the beginning of the research process, when you're trying to develop a research hypothesis, use your research journal for brainstorming. For example, write down any research ideas that you think of and indicate what stimulated each idea. When you decide on a given idea, explain why you decided on that particular research idea. When reading related research, summarize and critique it in your journal. Remember to write down the authors, year, title, and publisher for each source. This information will come in very handy when you write your research proposal. In short, whenever you have an insight, find a relevant piece of information, or make a design decision, record it in your journal.

To use the information in your journal, you will have to organize it. One key to effective organization is to write down only one idea per page. Another key is to rewrite or rearrange your entries every couple of days. The idea in rearranging your entries is to put them in an order that makes sense to you. For example, your first section may deal with potential hypotheses, your second section may deal with ideas related to the introduction section of your paper, and your third section may deal with methods and procedures.

## The Proposal

Like the research journal, the purpose of the research proposal is to help you think through each step of your research project. In addition, the research proposal will also let others (such as friends and professors) think through your research plan so that they can give advice that will improve your study. Thus, by writing the proposal, you will have the opportunity to try out ideas and explore alternatives without harming a single participant. In other words, the process of writing the proposal will help you make intelligent and ethical research decisions.

Although the research proposal builds on the research journal, the research proposal is much more formal than the journal. In writing the proposal, you will have to go through several drafts. The result of this writing and re-writing will be a proposal that is not only clear, but also conforms in content, style, and organization to the guidelines given in the American Psychological Association's *Publication Manual* (1994).

We want to emphasize that it is not enough to have good ideas. You must present them in a way that people will receive them. History is full of examples of people who had ideas but got little credit because they expressed them poorly. Conversely, some people have become famous more for how well they expressed their ideas than for the originality of their ideas.

If you fail to write a research proposal or article that conforms to APA (American Psychological Association) format, some people will judge the content of your proposal very harshly. They will feel that if you cannot follow that format, you are incapable of doing good research. Thus, to reiterate, following APA format is important. Indeed, one of the best-known professors of research design, Dr. Charles Brewer, cites learning APA format as one of the most important things students learn from his design class (Brewer, 1990). Think of APA format as a kind of language that makes it easier for professionals in the psychology field to communicate with one another.

However, before you worry about how to communicate your content clearly, you need to have content: Style without substance is worthless. The substance of your proposal will be your statements regarding:

1. why your general topic is important;
2. what your hypothesis is;
3. how your hypothesis is consistent with theory or past research;
4. how your study fits in with existing research;
5. how you define and operationalize your variables;
6. who your participants will be;
7. what procedures you will follow;
8. how you will analyze your data;
9. what implications you hope your results will have for theory, future research, or real life.

Thus, the introduction and the method sections you write for your research proposal should be highly polished drafts of the introduction and method sections of your final report. Furthermore, parts of the research proposal will serve as rough drafts of your abstract, results, and discussion sections. In short, writing the research proposal lays the groundwork for both the study and the final report.

## WRITING THE INTRODUCTION TO YOUR RESEARCH PROPOSAL

Now that you know what a research proposal is, it's time for you to begin writing one. We will first show you how to write the introduction.

### The Elements of an Introduction

The purpose of the **introduction** is to demonstrate to your readers that you have read the relevant research and thoroughly understand your research question. Once you have articulated the reasoning behind your hypothesis, you will explain your general strategy for testing the hypothesis. After reading the introduction, your reader should know:

1. why your research area is important;
2. why your predictions make sense;

**3.** what your hypothesis is; and

**4.** why your study is the best way to test the hypothesis.

## ESTABLISHING THE IMPORTANCE OF YOUR STUDY

To persuade people that your study is important and interesting, you must first let them know exactly what you are studying. You must define your concepts. Once you've explained what your concepts are, then you can explain why the concepts are important. In this section, we will discuss three common strategies for establishing the importance of concepts:

**1.** presenting statistical or other evidence of the concept's prevalence;

**2.** presenting a case study or other arguments to illustrate the concept's relevance; and

**3.** demonstrating historical precedence.

***Demonstrate the Concept's Prevalence.***    One strategy for showing that your concept is important is to show that it is a common or frequent part of real life. You might document the prevalence of the concept by presenting *statistical evidence*. Thus, if you are studying widowhood, you might present statistics on the percentage of people who are widowed. In the absence of statistics, you could use quotations from influential people or organizations (for example, the American Psychological Association) to stress the prevalence of your concept. Occasionally, the frequency of an event is so obvious (such as the prevalence of stress) that you may be able to assert simply that your concept is of great interest.

***Demonstrate the Concept's Relevance to Real Life.***    Rather than emphasizing the concept's prevalence, you might emphasize its relevance. For example, you might stress the practical problems that might be solved by understanding the concept. Alternatively, you might demonstrate the problem's relevance by presenting a real-life example of your concept in action. Giving an example of the concept is a very good way to define the concept and provide a vivid picture of its importance simultaneously.

***Demonstrate Historical Precedence.***    Finally, you might show that there is a *historical precedence* for your study. You could emphasize the great minds that have pondered the concept you will study, the number of people through the ages who have tried to understand the behavior, or the length of time that people have pondered the concept. Generally, you will also want to show that the research topic has—or should have—been important to both researchers and theorists.

## THE LITERATURE REVIEW

One way of establishing historical precedence is to summarize research done on the topic. In addition to helping the reader understand your research question, citing research shows the reader that the field considers your general research area important. That is, if the field did not consider these concepts important, investigators would not be researching these areas and their findings would not be published. Thus, it is not uncommon for introductions to include statements such as, "The focus of research for years . . ." or "Research emphasized . . ."

However, even if you do not use the literature review to establish the importance of the general concepts, you will still want to write a literature review. To reiterate, *all introductions should contain a literature review.*

The literature review shows how your particular research study fits in with existing work. In other words, whereas there are several ways to show that the general concepts are important, there is only one way to show that your particular research study is important—the literature review. Without a thorough literature review, the reader will not be convinced that your study hasn't been done before or that you understand the important issues.

***Goals of the Literature Review.***    Because the literature review is designed to "sell" your particular study, you need to do more than merely summarize previous work. You must also use the summary to set the stage for your study. You will set the stage for your study by either:

1. showing that your study corrects a weakness in previous research; or
2. showing that your work builds on and extends work of previous researchers.

As you can see, you have to set the stage for your research by showing that existing research is in some way deficient or not extensive enough. That is, you need to make the reader feel that there is a *need* for more research.

***Deciding Which Research to Summarize.***    We have addressed the goals of the literature review. You know why you should review the literature. Now, let's talk about what you will review. When citing research, review several older, classic works as well as recent research (see Appendix B about how to find articles to review). Critiquing—rather than merely summarizing—these articles will show that you have thought about what you have read. By critiquing a number of articles, you will establish that you have done your homework.

Although critiquing these journal articles may establish you as a scholar, realize that your goal is not simply to establish your credibility. Instead, your primary goal is to show how your study follows from existing research.

You may find that these two goals conflict. On the one hand, you want to establish that you know what you are talking about. Therefore, you may feel that you should cite all research ever done in the field. On the other hand, you want to use the literature review to set up your research study. Consequently, you want to cite and analyze only those studies that bear directly on your study. There are two things you can do to address the apparent conflict between these two goals.

First, realize that your main goal is to set up your study. Thus, you will be offering in-depth critiques of only those studies that directly apply to your study.

Second, realize that introductions begin by talking about the general area and then start to focus on the specific research question. Thus, classic research and basic, established findings that establish the importance of your general topic, but relate only indirectly to your work, should probably be cited only in the first paragraph or two.

Before you start writing, group together the studies that seem to have something in common. Thus, if you have summaries of all your studies on large index cards, you might put all the ones that obtained one kind of finding in one pile and all those that obtained the opposite finding in another pile. Then, for each pile, write a sentence summarizing what all the cards have in common. Each pile's sentence could be the topic sentence, with the rest of the pile providing evidence and citations for the statements made in that sentence (Kuehn, 1989). Alternatively, you may find that one pile will deal with ways of measuring your construct, another may deal with methodological flaws of previous studies, and another pile may deal with reasons why your prediction will be supported.

Once you have finished a draft of your literature review, re-read it. This literature review should do more than evaluate other people's work. It should also set the stage for your study. For example, the measure you praise will be in your study; the manipulation you attack will not. Furthermore, just from reading your literature review, a very astute reader could guess what your hypothesis is and how you plan to test it.

However, you won't make people guess the rationale for your hypothesis and for your study. After summarizing the relevant research, spell out the reasoning that led to your hypothesis. Spell out your reasoning so carefully and explicitly that your readers will know what your hypothesis is before you actually state it.

## STATING YOUR HYPOTHESIS

Even though your readers may have guessed your hypothesis, leave nothing to chance: *State your hypothesis!* To emphasize a point that can't be emphasized enough, state your hypothesis boldly and clearly so that readers can't miss it. Let them know what your study is about by writing, "The hypothesis is . . ."

When you state your hypothesis, be sensitive to whether you'll be testing it with an experiment or a correlational study. Only with an experiment may you use the word "cause." ("A sedentary life-style causes depression.") If you don't plan on directly manipulating your predictor variable, you have a correlational study—you can test only whether two or more variables are related. ("A sedentary life-style is related to depression.")

Once you've stated your hypothesis, you need to convince people that your study is the best way to test your hypothesis. Thus, you must describe what you are going to do and why you are going to do it.

## JUSTIFYING YOUR MANIPULATIONS AND MEASURES

You should justify your method of testing your hypothesis with the same care you took in justifying the hypothesis itself. Early in the introduction, when you are reviewing the literature, plant the idea in the reader's head that certain procedures are better than others. You will plant the idea that your procedures are best by explaining why researchers who are using your procedures decided to use them (high reliability, etc.) and why research using other procedures may be flawed (demand characteristics, etc.). Near the end of the introduction, build on what you already said, spelling out your reasons for choosing your methods and procedures.

For example, suppose your justification for using a set of procedures, manipulations, or measures is that these procedures are commonly used and accepted. Then, when you summarize the relevant research, let your readers know about these procedures and about how well accepted they are.

But what if you are using novel procedures or measures? In that case, when you review the relevant research, let your readers know that you are dissatisfied with existing measures. Point out problems with existing measures or emphasize that there are no existing measures. Later in the proposal, when you justify your procedures, you will draw on your earlier criticisms to show why your methods are best. For instance, if you are using a new measure, you will refer back to the definition of the concept you gave earlier and point out how your measure captures the essence of this definition. Then, you will remind your readers of the weaknesses you spotted in other measures and point out that your measure avoids these weaknesses.

## OVERVIEW OF THE INTRODUCTION

We have given you some general advice about how to write an introduction. You have seen the importance of clearly defining your concepts, critically summarizing research, carefully explaining the reasoning behind your hypothesis, explicitly stating your hypothesis, and justifying your way of testing the hypothesis.

# Justifying Specific Types of Studies

Thus far, you have been given only general advice because the specific way you will justify your study will depend on the kind of study you are doing. In the next section, you will learn how to justify six common types of studies:

1. exploratory;
2. direct replication;
3. systematic replication;
4. conceptual replication;
5. replication and extension;
6. theory-testing study.

## THE EXPLORATORY STUDY

In introducing an **exploratory study**—a study investigating a new area of research—you must take special care to justify your study, your hypothesis, and your procedures. You must compensate for the fact that your reader will not have any background knowledge about this new research area.

***New Is Not Enough.***    You can't use a strategy that is very common in introductions, that of stating that your research area is important because it has inspired a lot of research. It hasn't—that's why your study is an exploratory study. To justify an exploratory study, don't merely state that your research question has been ignored. Convince your readers that your research question deserves top priority. After all, it is a tragedy that your research question has been overlooked. This wrong must be righted to help psychology advance as a science.

One approach you can use to justify your exploratory study is to discuss hypothetical or real-life cases that could be solved or understood by answering your research question. For example, consider how Latané and Darley (1966) opened their pioneering work on helping behavior. They did say that helping behavior had not been extensively investigated. However, they did not stop there. Instead, they referred to the case of murder victim Kitty Genovese. Ms. Genovese was brutally attacked for more than half an hour in the presence of more than 30 witnesses—none of whom intervened. Thus, Latané and Darley effectively convinced readers that understanding why people fail to help is an important research area.

To reiterate, your first step in justifying an exploratory study is to show that the area is important. Once you have convinced your readers that the research area is important, you can further excite them by emphasizing that you are exploring new frontiers, going where no investigators have gone before.

***Spell Out Your Reasoning.***    In an exploratory study, as in all studies, you must spell out the rationale for your hypothesis. Since you are studying an unexplored dimension, you must give your readers the background to understand your predictions. Therefore, be extremely thorough in explaining the logic behind your predictions—even if you think your predictions are just common sense. Not everyone will share your common sense.

How do you explain the logic behind "common sense" predictions? Even common sense predictions can often be justified by theory or research on related variables. For example, suppose you are interested in seeing how low-sensation seekers and high-sensation seekers differ in their reactions to stress. You might argue that differences would be expected based on the arousal optimization theory—the theory that we all have an ideal level of arousal. Thus, you might argue that high-sensation seekers like stress because it raises their arousal up to the optimal level, whereas low-sensation seekers hate stress because it raises their arousal beyond the optimal level.

In addition to—or instead of—using theory to support your hypothesis, you could use research on related concepts. Thus, in our example, you might start by arguing that introversion-extroversion and sensation-seeking are related concepts. Then, you might argue that since introversion and sensation-seeking are related, and since stress has different effects on introverts and extroverts, stress should also have different effects on low-sensation seekers versus high-sensation seekers.

***Defend Your Procedures.*** In addition to explaining your predictions, you may have to take special care in explaining your procedures. That is, you may be studying variables that have never been studied before. In that case, you can't tell the reader that you are using well-accepted measures and manipulations with which the reader is familiar. Instead, you may have to invent your own measures and manipulations. Therefore, you will need to explain, either here or in the method section, why your manipulations and measures are valid.

## THE DIRECT REPLICATION

When doing a **direct replication** (a repetition of an original study), you must be very clear about why you are repeating the study. If you are not careful, the reader may think you performed the study before you realized that someone else had done your study. Even if you do spell out why you repeated the study, some journal reviewers will find the fact that you did a direct replication a legitimate reason to reject the paper for publication (Fiske & Fogg, 1990). However, there is a two-pronged strategy you can use to persuade people that your study is worth doing.

***Document the Original Study's Importance.*** First, to justify a direct replication, you should show that the original study was important. To establish the study's importance, discuss its impact on psychology. To get some objective statistics that support your opinion, note the number of times the study has been cited using the Social Science Citation Index described in Appendix B.

***Explain Why the Results Might Not Replicate.*** Then, after establishing the study's importance, try to convince your readers that the study's results might not replicate. That is, argue that the findings wouldn't occur today, that the findings contradict other published work, or that a Type 1 or Type 2 error occurred.

For instance, if the results from the original study were barely significant or if similar studies failed to find significant effects, you could justify a direct replication by arguing that a Type 1 error may have occurred. On the other hand, if the original study reported null results, you could argue that random error or poor execution of the study may have hidden real differences. If the original study's findings seem to conflict with several other published papers that did find a significant relationship between those variables, you have a compelling rationale for replicating the study.

Finally, you can justify a direct replication if you think the study would not come out the same today. For example, you might want to replicate a conformity study because you feel that people are no longer as conforming as they were when the original study was conducted. Regardless of what approach you take, you must present a compelling rationale for any study that is merely a re-run of another study.

## THE SYSTEMATIC REPLICATION

As you may recall from Chapter 10, the **systematic replication** involves making a minor modification in the original study. As such, the systematic replication accomplishes everything the direct replication does and more. Therefore, every reason for doing a direct replication is also a reason for doing a systematic replication. In addition, you can justify a systematic replication by showing that modifying the procedures would improve the original study's power, construct validity, or external validity.

*Improved Power.*    If you thought the original study's null results were due to Type 2 error, you might make a minor change in procedure to improve power. For example, you might use more participants, more extreme levels of the predictor/independent variable, or a more accurate way of measuring participants' responses (for instance, a more accurate stopwatch) than the original study used.

*Improved Construct Validity.*    You might also want to modify the original study if you thought that the original study's results were biased by demand characteristics. Thus, you might repeat the study using a double-blind procedure to reduce subject and researcher bias.

*Improved External Validity.*    If you are systematically replicating a study to improve external validity, you should explain why you suspect that the results may not generalize to different stimulus materials, levels of the treatment variable, or participants. Even if it seems obvious to you why a study done on rats might not apply to humans; why a study done on college students might not apply to factory workers; why a study done on men might not apply to women; or why the results wouldn't hold if different levels of the treatment were used—*spell out your reasons* for suspecting that the results wouldn't generalize.

## THE CONCEPTUAL REPLICATION

Most of the reasons for conducting a systematic or direct replication are also relevant for introducing and justifying a **conceptual replication:** a study that is based on the original, but uses different methods to better assess the true relationships between the variables being studied. In addition, the conceptual replication has several other unique selling points, depending on how you changed the original study.

***Using a Different Measure.***    Your conceptual replication might differ because you used a way of measuring the dependent variable that differed from what the original authors did. In that case, you should show that your measure is more reliable, sensitive, or valid than the original measure. To make the case for your measure, you may want to cite other studies that used your measure. As in the legal arena, precedent carries weight in psychology. If someone else published a study using a given measure, the measure automatically gains some credibility.

***Using a Different Manipulation.***    Instead of trying to use a different measure of a construct, you might want to use a different manipulation of a construct. For example, if one researcher induced stress in participants by suggesting that they would get painful electric shocks, you might decide to replicate the study, but induce stress by giving participants a very short period of time to do certain mathematical problems. If you use a different treatment manipulation, you should start by defining the variable you are trying to manipulate. Next, you should discuss weaknesses of previous manipulations. Then, show why your manipulation avoids these weaknesses. Conclude by showing that your manipulation is consistent with definitions of the concept you are trying to manipulate.

***Using a Different Design.***    If you are changing the original study's design, explain why. If you are replicating a between-subjects design using a within-subjects (repeated measures) design to improve power, tell your readers. If you are converting a within-subjects design to a between-subjects design because you feel participants will be less likely to guess the hypothesis in a between-subjects design, tell your readers. Your readers will *not* instantaneously realize the advantages of using a different design.

## THE REPLICATION AND EXTENSION

Your study may go beyond a conceptual replication to looking at additional factors or measures. In that event, your introduction would not only contain everything a conceptual replication would, but also a rationale for the additional factors or measures.

***Rationale for Additional Factors.***    For example, suppose the original author found that people loaf in groups. You might think of a situation (for example, a group in which all members were good friends) where social loafing wouldn't occur. Thus, you might include friendship as a factor in your design. Be sure to justify your reasoning for including the factor, defend your manipulation of that factor, and state your predictions regarding the factor.

***Rationale for Additional Dependent Measures.***     Instead of adding a predictor/independent variable to a study, you might add a criterion/dependent measure. Your purpose would be to discover *how* the treatment produces the effect. In other words, you are trying to figure out what mental or physiological reactions are triggered by the treatment and then see if you can show that one of these reactions is the mechanism by which the treatment has its effect.

How would you go about finding out the invisible processes underlying an observable effect? In a social loafing experiment, you might collect measures of participants' perceptions of others to find out the cognitive processes responsible for social loafing (such as perceptions that their efforts are not being noticed). Or, you might record their interactions with others to find out the behavior responsible for social loafing (such as working is punished, but socializing is rewarded). Or, you might monitor arousal levels in an attempt to discover the physiological reasons for social loafing (for example, lower physiological arousal in a group setting).

The tricky part about writing an introduction to a "process" study is to persuade your readers that you really are measuring the underlying causes of a phenomenon. You must do more than merely show that these "processes" occur before the phenomenon. These "processes" could be incidental side effects of the treatment. For instance, a fever may seem to appear before you get ill and may intensify as you get ill, but a fever doesn't cause you to be ill. It's just a side effect of your illness. In the same way, a mental or physiological event may accompany a change in behavior, but not be the cause of that behavioral change.

### THE THEORY-TESTING STUDY

If you are testing a prediction from a theory, there's good news and bad news. The good news is that you won't have to spend much effort justifying your study's importance. Almost everyone assumes that testing a theory is important.

The bad news is that not everyone will agree that your predictions follow from the theory. To protect yourself, you must clearly spell out how your predictions follow from theory. By being clear, everyone will follow your logic, and some may even agree with it.

## WRITING THE METHOD SECTION

You have reviewed the literature, developed a hypothesis, decided how to measure your variables, and stated your reasons for testing your hypothesis.

However, your preliminary work is still not done. You must now decide exactly what specific actions you will take. In other words, although you probably have decided on the general design (for example, a simple experiment), your plan is not complete until each detail of your study has been thought through and written down.

In your journal, specify *exactly* what procedures you will follow. For example, what instructions will participants be given? Who will administer the treatment? Where? Will participants be run in groups or individually? How should the researcher interact with participants? Although your answers must be accountable to issues of validity, your paramount concern must always be ethics. You do not have the right to harm another.

Once you have thoroughly thought out each step of your study, you are ready to write the method section of your proposal. This is the *how* section—here you will explain exactly how you plan to conduct your study. However, keep in mind that, just like the introduction, the method section is written on two levels. As you will recall, at one level, the introduction summarizes existing research. But, at another level, the introduction sells the need for your study by pointing out deficiencies in existing research. Similarly, on one level, the **method section** tells the reader what you are going to do. However, at another level, it sells the reader on the idea that what you plan to do is the correct thing to do.

Although the introduction may have already set this section up by pointing out which participants should be studied, which measures should be used, and what variables should be controlled for, do not hesitate to remind your reader again. Thus, in the method section, you may mention that your measure is valid, that your manipulation is widely accepted, or that you are doing something a certain way to reduce demand characteristics, researcher biases, random error, or some other problem.

In short, selling the value of a research strategy is a never-ending job. If possible, you should sell your strategy in each of the method section's subsections: participants, design, apparatus and materials, and procedure.

## Participants

In the participants section, you will describe the general characteristics of your participants. State how many participants you plan to have, how many will be male, how many will be female, their ages, how you plan to obtain or recruit them. In addition, include any other relevant information (like what strain of rat). You should also indicate whether they will be tested individually or in groups. If they will be tested in groups, you should state the size of the groups. If you plan to exclude data from some participants, state the precise criteria for exclusion (such as scores above 16 on a depression inventory) and your reasons for choosing those criteria.

The participants section is written in a straightforward and somewhat mechanical fashion. In fact, it is so mechanical that you can often use the following as a guideline.[1]

*Participants*

The participants will be 80 introductory psychology students (52 men and 28 women) from Clarion University who will either be paid $5 or given course credit for their participation. Participants will be run individually and will be randomly assigned to experimental condition.

## Design

The design section is also easy to write. Merely describe the design of your study. For an experiment, state the number of levels for each independent variable, and state whether the independent variable is a between-subjects variable or a within-subjects variable. Then, state the dependent variable. For example, you might write that "The design is a 2 (Source Expertise: expert/nonexpert) × 2 (Information Type: important/unimportant) between-subjects design. The dependent measure is memory for the presented information."

## Apparatus and Materials

In the apparatus and materials section, describe the equipment and materials you plan to use. This includes laboratory equipment, tests, computers, etc.

If you plan to use equipment made by a company, list the brand name and the make of the product. If you designed your equipment, briefly describe it. You need to give enough detail so that readers will have a general idea of what it looks like. In the appendix, include a photo or diagram of your apparatus.

If you used a test or questionnaire, reference the source of the test, and give at least one example of a typical item. This gives readers a feel for what the participants will see. In the appendix, include a copy of your test or questionnaire.

## Procedure

As the name suggests, your procedure section will be a summary of what you actually are going to do. The $64,000 question is: "How much detail should I include?" To help you answer this question, we offer four suggestions.

---

[1] Do not copy this word-for-word. You should create an original participants subsection that best describes how participants were recruited and assigned in your study. Also note that, at times, you will find sections of articles that say what you want to say. If you quote from these articles, use quotation marks. Even if you don't quote directly from an article, cite that article. To do otherwise, is to commit plagiarism—using someone else's words, thoughts, or work without giving proper credit. Plagiarism is considered a serious act of academic dishonesty. Indeed, at some institutions, students convicted of plagiarism are expelled.

First, be sure to include enough information so that the reader will understand how you operationalized your independent and dependent variables. To help the reader understand your independent variable, don't forget to include key elements of instructions to participants, especially instructions that are different for the experimental group than they are for the control group. To help the reader understand your dependent variable, you may decide to say "The dependent variable was . . ."

Second, include any methodological wrinkles that you feel are critical to the study's internal, external, or construct validity. For example, if you used a placebo treatment or double-blind procedures, tell the reader that you did so.

Third, read the procedure sections of several related studies and mimic their style. Reading these sections will help you understand how much detail to include.

Finally, don't worry if your procedure section seems too brief. You can include your complete protocol in the appendix of your proposal.

## WRITING THE RESULTS SECTION

In the proposal's **results section,** you should state how you plan to analyze your data. As was the case with the method section, your goal is not only to tell the reader what you are going to do, but also to sell the reader on the idea that you are doing the right thing. Thus, it is important to be clear about not only what analysis you are going to do, but why. Ideally, your proposal should answer four questions:

1. What data will be analyzed? That is, how will a participant's behavior be converted into a score?
2. What statistical test will be used on those scores?
3. Why can that statistical test be used? Thus, you might show that the data meet the assumptions of the statistical test or you might cite a text or article that supports the use of the test under these conditions.
4. Why should the analysis be done? Usually, you will remind the reader of the hypothesis you want to test. To emphasize the value of the analysis, you may want to describe what results of that analysis would support your hypothesis and what outcomes would not. You might even plug in imaginary outcomes of your study to give the reader a concrete example of how your analyses correspond to your hypotheses.

To illustrate how a results section might accomplish these goals, consult the following sample results section:

Results

I will sum participants' responses to the two altruism items to come up with an altruism score for each participant that will range from 2 (very low) to 10 (very high). Such scores are assumed to be interval (Winer, 1972).

Consequently, those scores will then be subjected to a 2 × 2 between subjects analysis of variance.

I hypothesize that mood will affect altrusim. If the results turn out as I predict, positive mood participants will score significantly higher on my altruism scale than negative mood participants. This significant main effect would indicate support for the hypothesis that mood influences altrusim.

## WRITING THE DISCUSSION SECTION

Once you have decided how you will analyze your data, you are ready to discuss how you will interpret them. If your hypothesis is supported, how will this information relate to the literature and arguments you covered in the introduction? How will you interpret results that don't support your hypothesis?

In addition to addressing these questions, the **discussion** is the place to present the limitations of your study, to speculate about what research should be done to follow up on your study, and to discuss the practical implications of your study.

Writing the discussion section of the proposal is difficult because you do not know how the study will turn out. Probably the easiest thing to do is to imagine that your study turned out as you expected. In that case, your discussion can be primarily a rehash of the introduction. To be more specific, your discussion should probably devote a paragraph to each of the following six points:

1. relating the predicted results to the hypothesis ("Consistent with our predictions, . . .");
2. relating the predicted results to previous research and theory discussed in the introduction ("This study joins others in showing . . ." or "The findings are consistent with ___ theory.");
3. discussing the limitations of the study ("However, the current research is only correlational so we cannot say whether our variables are causally related" or "The results may not generalize to non-college students.");
4. discussing future research that would build on the present study ("Future research might consider testing the generality of this effect.");
5. discussing practical implications of the research findings;
6. stressing the importance of remembering or building on the study's major findings

    ("To summarize, we found that the effectiveness of rewards depended on the participant's personality. This finding suggests that teachers should not use salient rewards on intrinsically motivated students. Furthermore, in light of these findings, learned industriousness theory must be revised. In short, this research takes an enormous step toward understanding creativity.").

## PUTTING ON THE FRONT AND BACK

You've written the introduction, method, results, and discussion sections. Now it's time to return to the beginning of your proposal. Specifically, it's time to type the title page and the abstract.

### Title and Title Page

The title is the first thing readers will see. Your title should be simple, direct, honest, and informative. Ideally, your title should be a brief statement about the relationship between your predictor/independent and criterion/dependent variables.

Avoid being too cute or obscure. If there is some catchy saying or title that you must include, use a colon to add this extra title to the simpler title. Such a title might be, "The effect of eating sugar on anxiety: A bittersweet dilemma."

The title should appear centered on a separate piece of paper. Two lines below the title, center your name. For more information about the title page, see Table 14–1.

The title should also appear, centered, at the top of the first page of your introduction. Thus, in the introduction, the title takes the place of the heading "Introduction."

### Abstract

Once they've read your title, readers will continue to the next section—the **abstract.** In your abstract, you will give them a short, one-page summary of your research proposal.

Jolley, Murray, & Keller (1993) describe six basic sentences that are included in most abstracts. The first sentence describes the general research topic (for example, "Love is a common topic in popular music"). The order of the next five sentences often varies. However, there should be a sentence that gives the number of participants and their treatment (Sixteen participants will listen to love ballads for one hour, while 16 control participants will sit in a quiet room for one hour). In another sentence, you should explain how you plan to collect the dependent measure (such as, "Participants will fill out the Reuben Love-Like Scale 10 minutes after treatment"). You should have a sentence that spells out the hypothesis (for instance, "It is hypothesized that listening to love ballads will raise scores on the Love-Like Scale"). The last sentence will not be in your proposal, but will be in your final research report. In that sentence, you'll describe the main results—the results that relate to your hypothesis.

In addition to these six sentences, you should end your abstract with a sentence or two about the implications of your results. This miniature version of your discussion section might read something like, "The implications for ___ theory are discussed," or "The results are discussed in light of previous studies."

# References

Now that you have the title and abstract written, it's time to write your reference list. To help you organize your references, we suggest you write each reference on an index card and alphabetize the cards. If you have more than one reference for an author, put the cards for that author in chronological order (from oldest to most recent). By writing references on cards before you type them up, you reduce the chances of making two common errors: (1) not including all your references, and (2) not typing all your references in alphabetical order.

You should use the reference style given in the American Psychological Association's *Style Manual* (1994). This style is also consistent with the Modern Language Association's style manual (MLA). For examples of proper referencing, see the sample paper in Appendix F.

# WRITING THE FINAL REPORT

Much of the work on your research report already has been done. Essentially, your research proposal was the first draft of your research report. To complete your research report, follow the advice in this section.

## What Stays the Same or Changes Very Little

The title page, introduction, and references from your proposal can be transferred to your research report without any changes. You will, however, need to make three changes in the method section.

First, you will need to change the method section to reflect any changes you made in how you conducted the study. Generally, the procedures you initially proposed are not the ones you end up following. Sometimes, after reading your proposal, your professor will ask you to make some modifications. Sometimes, an ethics committee may mandate some changes. Often, after testing out your procedures on a few participants, you will make some changes so that the actual study will run more smoothly.

Second, you probably will have to make some minor changes in the participants section. Prior to running the study, you can rarely anticipate who your participants will be and how many you will have to exclude.

Third, you need to rewrite the method section in the *past tense*. In the proposal, you told people what you were going to do; in the report, you tell them what you did.

Like your method section, your abstract needs only minor modifications. Specifically, you need to add a sentence to describe the main results.

In contrast to the other sections, the results and discussion sections cannot always be transferred to the final report. Instead, you often will have to revise these sections extensively before you can put them in your final report.

Because these sections change the most from proposal to final report, the rest of this chapter will be devoted to these two sections.

# Writing the Results Section

There are two main purposes of the results section: (1) to show the reader that you competently analyzed the data, and (2) to tell the reader what you found. To accomplish these goals, you will report anywhere from one to five kinds of results:

1. results describing the distribution of participants' scores;
2. results supporting the validity of your measure;
3. results of the manipulation check;
4. results relating to your hypothesis; and
5. other statistically significant results.

### RESULTS DESCRIBING THE DISTRIBUTION OF SCORES

At the beginning of your results section, you might include a section that describes the distribution of scores on your dependent variable. Thus, you might give the mean and the standard deviation (or range) of scores.[2] For example, you might report that, "The scores on the measure were normally distributed ($\underline{M} = 75$, range $= 50 - 100$)."

This section is often omitted. If you do include this section, it probably will be for one of the following reasons:

1. to make a case that the sample is representative of some population by showing either that the scores are very similar to the population's distribution of scores or that the scores were not unusually extreme;
2. to argue that the data meet the assumptions of the statistical tests by showing that the scores were normally distributed or that the different groups had the same variances;
3. to show that the data had to be transformed or that the data could not be analyzed by a certain statistical test because the data were not normally distributed;
4. to argue that there should be no problems due to ceiling effects, floor effects, or restriction of range because there was a wide range of scores and those scores were normally distributed; or
5. because the distribution of scores is of interest in its own right, as would be the case if reporting percentage of sample who had attempted suicide.

### RESULTS SUPPORTING THE MEASURE'S VALIDITY

Like the section describing the distribution of scores, the section supporting the measure's validity often is omitted. If you are using an accepted, validated

---

[2] If the data are not normally distributed, you may want to provide a graph of the raw scores.

measure, you probably will omit this section. If you choose to include this section, you probably will stress the results that emphasize the measure's:

1. test-retest or alternate forms reliability, indicating that the measure is not unduly influenced by random error as shown by the fact that participants get the same score from one day to the next;
2. inter-observer reliability, indicating that the measure is objectively scored because different observers give the participants the same scores;
3. internal consistency, indicating that the items of a test or sub-scale are all measuring the same thing because the items correlate with each other (people who get a high score on one item will tend to get a high score on the other test items).

## RESULTS OF THE MANIPULATION CHECK

If you used a manipulation check, you should put these findings near the beginning of the results section. Although these results usually will be statistically significant and unsurprising, it is important to demonstrate that you manipulated what you said you would manipulate. Thus, reporting the outcome of your manipulation check is a good lead into discussing results relating to your hypothesis. That is, once you have shown the reader that you manipulated the variable you planned to manipulate, the reader is ready to know whether that variable produced the effects you expected.

## RESULTS RELATING TO YOUR HYPOTHESIS

As you introduce the results relating to your hypothesis, clearly connect the results to the hypothesis. Make it very easy for your readers to tell how the hypothesis fared. For example, if a hypothesis was that people who own cats are less likely to hit their children, report what the data said about this hypothesis: "The hypothesis that people who own cats are less likely to hit their children was supported. Cat owners hit their children on the average 2.3 times a month per child, whereas people who did not own cats hit their children on the average 4.6 times, $F(1,64) = 18.2, p < .05$."

## OTHER SIGNIFICANT RESULTS

After reporting results relating to your hypothesis (whether or not the results were significant), you should report any other statistically significant results. Even if the results are unwanted and make no sense to you, significant results must be reported. Therefore you might report: "There was an unanticipated relationship between gender of the child and cat ownership. Girls were more likely to own cats, $F(1,64) = 20.1, p < .05$."

## TIPS ON WRITING THE RESULTS SECTIONS

Now that you are familiar with the general parts of the results section, it's time to start writing the results section. One thing always to keep in mind is that the results section is where you tell readers what you found out. It is here that they find out whether your hypothesis was supported or refuted.

You may find it useful to think of this section as an "analysis of results" section. That is, instead of just giving the reader your raw data, you are reporting your analysis of that data. Thus, just as you would not simply include every participant's score, you would not merely stick the reader with the computer print-out of all the statistical tests. If you did that, the reader would be completely lost. You do not want to lose the reader. Instead, you want to guide the reader through this section. You should give a clear picture of:

1. How a participant's behavior was converted into a score.
2. Why these scores are being analyzed. Usually, this question can be answered by explaining what hypothesis is being tested.
3. What happened? That is, was the hypothesis supported?
4. What statistical test was used to find this out?
5. What were the results of that test? (value of the statistic and the probability value)
6. What were the participants' actual scores? That is, include summary statistics (means, percentages, etc.) to help readers see for themselves whether the pattern of your results supports the hypothesis. The means (or other summary statistics, such as medians or percentages) help readers understand the nature of the relationship. You may choose to use tables or graphs to show these means, especially if many numbers are involved.

In short, you should try to make your results section as clear and understandable as possible. Your general approach to making the results section clear is to do two things.

First, start off by discussing simple or general findings and then move to more specific tests. For example, report main effects before interactions, and report the results of the overall F test before talking about the results of more specific follow-up tests.

Second, ask yourself if the reader will understand your results section. Specifically, will the reader leave the results section knowing whether the results supported your hypothesis? Focusing on this question will cause you to do many of the things we mentioned above: be clear about what scores are being analyzed, explain why those scores are being analyzed, explain how the results of the statistical test support—or fail to support—the hypothesis, and show that the pattern of means seems to support—or fail to support—the hypothesis. If you focus your results section on your hypothesis and have empathy for your reader, you should be able to write an understandable and useful results section.

## Writing the Discussion Section

If the results matched your predictions, the discussion section you wrote for your proposal might work as the discussion section for the final report. However, there are two reasons why the discussion section you wrote for your proposal probably will have to be substantially modified. First, it is unlikely that you will get exactly the results you expected. Second, during the course of conducting the research or writing the paper, you probably will think of problems or implications that you did not think of when you wrote your proposal.

In the discussion section, you should:

1. briefly review the research question or hypothesis;
2. briefly summarize the results, relating them to the hypothesis;
3. interpret the results in light of the arguments made in your introduction;
4. acknowledge alternative explanations for your results, trying to dismiss these alternatives, if possible;
5. discuss unexpected findings and speculate on possible reasons for them;
6. discuss, in general terms, future research. What would you do if you were to follow up on this research (assume an unlimited budget)? Follow-up research might focus on improving the methodology of your study, exploring unexpected findings, trying to rule out alternative theoretical explanations for your findings, testing the generality of your findings, looking for practical implications of the findings, looking for variables that might have similar effects, or looking for mental or physiological factors that mediate the observed relationship; and
7. discuss the practical or theoretical implications of your findings.

Once you have written your discussion section, you are nearly finished. However, as with most papers, you will need to write several drafts before you have a polished paper. To help you edit your paper so that it conforms to APA format, check your "next-to-final draft" against the checklist in Table 14–1. In addition, you should see if your paper matches the style of the model paper in Appendix F.

## CONCLUDING REMARKS

Well, you've done it! If you carefully followed the advice in this book, you should have just completed a carefully planned, meaningful, and ethical research project. Congratulations and best wishes for your continued success as a researcher!

**TABLE 14–1**
**Format Checklist**

## TITLE PAGE

**1.** Is there a separate title page?

**2.** On the top right-hand corner do you have:

    **a.** a short, two- or three-word "mini-title" of your paper? This "mini-title" is simply the first two or three words of your title.

    **b.** To the right of the mini-title, do you have the number "1," indicating that this is page 1? The "1" should be flush right and five spaces to the right of the mini-title. Or, you can put the page number flush right and one double-spaced line below the mini-title.

**3.** One double-spaced line below the short title and the page number, do you have a line that:

    **a.** starts at the left margin (about an inch from the left edge of the page); and

    **b.** begins with the words "Running head:" followed by a short (two-to-six word) phrase that describes your paper's topic? Note: The running head is *not* the same as the mini-title.

**4.** Is the four- to six-word running head in all capital letters?

**5.** Is title centered? Is it one double-spaced line below the running head?

**6.** Is the title simple and to the point? Does it include the names of the relevant variables (in an experiment, the independent and dependent variables; in a correlational study, the predictor and criterion variables)?

**7.** Is your name (first name, middle initial, and last name):

    **a.** one double-spaced line below the title?

    **b.** centered?

**8.** Is your institution's affiliation:

    **a.** one double-spaced line below your name?

    **b.** centered?

## ABSTRACT

**1.** Is it on its own separate page?

**2.** Is the heading "Abstract" centered at the top of the page?

**3.** Is the text one double-spaced line below the heading?

**4.** Is it fewer than 120 words long?

**5.** Is it a single paragraph?

**6.** Is the beginning of the abstract *not* indented? That is, the entire abstract (other than the title "Abstract") should look like a single block, with all lines beginning at the left margin.

**7.** Is it numbered page "2"?

## INTRODUCTION

**1.** Does it begin on a separate page (page "3")?

**2.** Is the title of the article centered at the top of the first page of the introduction?

**3.** Remember, you do *not* label the introduction with the label "introduction."

**4.** When citing people, did you avoid footnotes? Citations should be in parentheses. If you mention the authors in the sentence, simply put the date in parentheses. For example, "Jolley and Mitchell (1996) argued that . . ." If the authors' names are not part of the sentence, put their names and the date in parentheses. Separate the names from the dates with a comma. For example, "Some have argued that . . . (Jolley & Mitchell, 1996)."

5. If you are citing several articles within one set of parentheses, are the articles listed in alphabetical order? Did you separate the articles with a semi-colon? For example, (Brickner, 1980; Jolley, 1994; Mitchell, 1982; Ostrom, 1965; Pusateri, 1995; Williams, 1992).

6. If you are discussing a paper with three or more authors, mention all the authors the first time you cite that paper. Only after you have referred to all the authors can you—in subsequent citations—use the first author's last name, followed immediately (with no comma) by et al. (for example, Glick et al., 1996).

7. Did you cite all your sources? Even when you don't quote them, you must still cite them. To reiterate, if you summarize or paraphrase a work, it must be cited!

## METHOD SECTION

1. Is it written in the past tense?
2. Is the heading "Method" centered and one double-spaced line below the last line of the introduction?
3. Is the word "Participants" one double-spaced line below "Method"?
4. Is the label "Participants" on the left margin and underlined?
5. Does the text for the participants section begin on the line below the "Participants" heading?
6. If you started a sentence with a number (such as, "Twenty undergraduates served as participants,") did you write out the number? Note: You can say: "Participants were 20 undergraduates," but you cannot say "20 undergraduates were participants." Instead, you must say "Twenty undergraduates were participants."
7. Is the word "Procedure" on the left margin and underlined?
8. Is it one double-spaced line below the last line of the previous section?
9. Does the text for the procedure section start on the line below the "Procedure" heading?
10. If you used standard laboratory equipment, did you identify the manufacturer and model number?

## RESULTS SECTION

1. Does it immediately follow the method section? (Don't skip to a new page.)
2. Is the title "Results" centered? Is it one double-spaced line below the last line of the method section?
3. Is it written in the past tense?
4. Are all statistics and probability values underlined?

   Right:        . . . $t = 9.08$, $p < .05$.

   Wrong:      . . . t = 9.08, p < .05.

5. When you report the result of a statistical test, did you give the statistic, the degrees of freedom for the test, the value of the statistic, and the level of significance (the p value)? The format, *except for the spacing,* should follow that shown below:

| Statistic | df | numerical value of the test | probability |
|---|---|---|---|
| $F$ | $(2,46) =$ | 3.85, | $p < .05$ |
| $t$ | $(24) =$ | 3.0, | $p < .001$ |
| $r$ | $=$ | .71, | $p < .01$ |
| $\chi^2$ | $(6, N = 80) =$ | 11.48, | $p < .05$ |

Note that you need to underline the statistic ($F, t, r,$ etc.) and the "$p$." Also note that with chi-square ($\chi^2$), you need to report degrees of freedom and sample size (N). Also note that, in your report, you won't leave the spaces that are included in the table. Thus, in text, you would write $F(2,46) = 3.85$, $p < .05$.

6. If you have tables, do you refer to those tables in the text of your paper (such as, "As Table 1 indicates . . .")? Are tables numbered sequentially as they appear in the text of your paper?

7. Are all tables and graphs at the very end of your report—after the references? Is each one on a separate page?

8. Have you referred to all graphs as figures (figure 1, not graph 1)? Did you label both the "x" and "y" axes? Did you give each graph an informative heading?

9. Is everything in each table double-spaced?

10. Do the tables adhere to the format illustrated below?

Table 1

Pearson Product Moment Correlation for Self-Esteem

| | Body Concept | |
|---|---|---|
| Group | Attractiveness | Fitness |
| Female | .65*** | .50** |
| Male | .35* | .70*** |

$*p < .05, **p < .01, ***p < .001$

Table 2

Analysis of Variance: Exercise and Self-Esteem

| Source | SS | df | MS | F |
|---|---|---|---|---|
| Between (Treatment) | 499.41 | 2 | 249.71 | 9.75 |
| Within (Error) | 145.76 | 57 | 2.56 | |

## DISCUSSION

1. Does it immediately follow the results section?

2. Is the title "Discussion" centered? Is it one double-spaced line below the last line of the results section?

3. Did you use the same rules for citing people as you did in the introduction (see points 4–7 of the introduction checklist)?

4. Did you avoid footnotes?

5. Did you cite any source from which you got ideas—even if you did not directly quote that source? If you have any doubt about whether you should cite a source, then cite it!

## REFERENCES

1. Do they start on a separate page?

2. Is the word "References" on the top of the page, centered?

3. Is everything double-spaced?

4. Are they in alphabetical order (according to the last name of the first author)?

5. Is the first line of every reference indented five spaces?

6. If a reference takes up more than one line, are the additional lines of that reference *not indented*?

7. Does each individual reference start with the authors' last names and initials, followed by the year of publication (in parentheses) and then a period?

8. Are the titles of all books underlined?

9. Are the titles of all journals underlined?

10. Are the volume numbers of every journal underlined?

11. Did you avoid underlining the titles of journal articles?

12. When citing journal articles, did you avoid the word "pages" and the abbreviation "pp."?

13. Does every individual reference end with a period?

14. Are all the references in this section also cited in your paper? Your reference section should include only those references you actually cited. All works cited in the reference section must also be cited in the body of the paper.

15. Are all the references cited in your paper also listed in this section? All works cited in your paper should also be listed in your reference section. It's considered sloppy to fail to reference a paper that you cited.

## GENERAL FORMAT

1. Is everything double-spaced? Nothing should be single-spaced!

2. Are the first two or three words of the title and the page number on the top, right-hand corner of every page?

3. Did you start every paragraph by indenting 5 spaces? (One exception: Don't indent the abstract.)

4. Have you avoided sexist and racist language?

5. Have you avoided passive sentences as much as possible?

6. Is the paper's appearance professional (no typos, neatly typed, etc.)?

7. Do not hyphenate words at the end of a line.

8. Do not have narrow margins. You should be able to take a ruler and find that there is nothing but white space within 1 inch from any edge of any page.

9. Are all main headings (Abstract, Method, Results, Discussion, References, etc.) centered, but not underlined? Are only the first letters of words in these headings capitalized?

10. Are all subheadings (Participants, Procedure, etc.) flush left (not indented) and underlined? Are only the first letters of words in these subheadings capitalized?

11. Be sure that you have not included anyone's first name or affiliation in your paper (except for the title page).

## SUMMARY

1. The research journal and proposal will help you do the planning necessary for conducting ethical and valid research.

2. The research proposal is more formal than the journal and should conform to the *Publication Manual* (1994) of the American Psychological Association.

3. In the introduction of your proposal, you need to summarize and critique relevant research. This critique should set up the reasons you think that your hypothesis: (a) will be supported, (b) should be tested, and (c) should be tested the way you are going to test it.

4. In the introduction, state your hypothesis, explain why your predictions make sense, and explain why your study will provide a valid test of your hypothesis.

5. Before writing the method section, you should carefully plan out each step of your study.

6. Once you have planned out every detail of your study, you should formalize your plan in the method, results, and discussion sections in your proposal.

7. The method section is the "how" section, in which you explain how you plan to conduct your study and why you are going to do it that way.

8. In the results section, you will plan your statistical analyses.

9. In the discussion section, you will explore the implications of your anticipated research findings for theory, future research, or real life.

10. Once you finish the body of the proposal, write the abstract (a brief summary of the proposal), the title page, and the reference section.

11. Much of your final report will be based on your proposal—provided you wrote a good proposal.

12. The title page, introduction, and reference sections of your proposal can be transferred directly to your final report. After you change the method section to the past tense, it may also be transferred (with only minor modifications) to the final report.

13. Try to make the results section as understandable as possible. Tell the reader what you are trying to find out by doing the analysis, and then tell the reader what you actually did find out from doing the analysis.

14. In the results section, be sure to stress whether the results supported or failed to support your hypothesis.

15. In the discussion section, summarize the main findings of your study and relate these to the points you made in the introduction.

16. Writing involves a great deal of re-writing.

# KEY TERMS

**abstract:** a short, one-page summary of a research proposal or article. The abstract must be no longer than 120 words. It comes before the introduction. (p. 492)

**introduction:** after the abstract, comes the introduction to the study. In the introduction, the authors tell you what their hypothesis is, why their hypothesis makes sense, how their study fits in with previous research, and why their study is worth doing. (p. 478)

**method section:** the part of the article immediately following the introduction. Whereas the introduction explains why the study was done, the method section describes what was done. For example, it will tell you what design was used, what the researchers said to the participants, what measures and equipment were used, how many participants were studied and how they were selected. The method section could also be viewed as a "how we did it" section. The method section is usually subdivided into at least three subsections: participants, apparatus, and procedure. (p. 488)

**results section:** the part of the article, immediately following the method section, that reports statistical results and relates those results to the hypotheses. From reading this section, you should know whether the results supported the hypothesis. (p. 490)

**discussion:** the part of the article, immediately following the results section, that discusses the research findings and the study in a broader context and suggests research projects that could be done to follow up on the study. (p. 491)

**exploratory study:** a study investigating an entirely new area of research. Unlike replications, an exploratory study does not follow directly from an existing study. (p. 483)

**direct replication:** a copy of the original study. Direct replications are useful for establishing that the findings of the original study are reliable. (p. 484)

**systematic replication:** a study that varies from the original study only in some minor aspect. For example, a systematic replication may use more participants, more standardized procedures, more levels of the independent variable, or a more realistic setting than the original study. (p. 485)

**conceptual replication:** a study that is based on the original study, but uses different methods to better assess the true relationships between the treatment and dependent variables. In a conceptual replication, you might use a different manipulation or a different measure. The conceptual replication is the most sophisticated kind of replication. (p. 485)

# *Appendix A*

# ETHICS

Throughout this text, we have mentioned the importance of conducting research in an ethical manner. Therefore, you may wonder why we have an appendix on ethics. The main reason is so that you can have quick access to APA's ethical guidelines governing research.

## HUMAN RESEARCH

Although we have included APA's guidelines on human research in this appendix, we will first highlight the main principles. The first thing a researcher should do is to try to foresee the risks to the people who would participate in the study. Knowing the risks can help in devising safeguards, in deciding whether the study should be conducted, and in letting participants decide whether to participate.

If there seems to be any risks to participants, the researcher should seek out the advice of others to determine whether the study should be done. (As a student researcher, you should do this even if you think the study involves virtually no risk.) That is, the researcher should ask other researchers. In addition, researchers are often required by federal law or by their institution to submit their research to their department's ethics committee or the institution's Internal Review Board. (Your professor will tell you which committee[s] you have to deal with.) In consulting other people, the researcher may end up filling out a form like the one in Box A–1.

The point of consulting others is twofold. First, consulting others will help you look at alternatives. That is, others will ask the question. "Are there ways of answering the research question that would put participants at less risk?" Second, consulting with others may help you decide whether to do the study at all. Other people may see risks you did not see or they may be more objective than you when it comes to weighing the risks to the participants against the potential gain. As a result of seeing and weighing the risks, your professor or an ethics committee may demand that the study not be done.

Even if the research is approved by a review board, the bottom line is that the investigator is still the one person who is responsible for any harm done to

## Box A–1
## Sample Ethical Review Form

Title

Researcher:

1. Main hypothesis to be tested or brief statement of the problem to be investigated:

2. Will extra credit be given to students who participate in the project?

    Yes          No

3. Will participants include anyone other than students from our school?

    Yes          No

4. Will participants include children under 18, adults who are not legally competent, mentally handicapped, physically handicapped, prisoners, or pregnant women?

    Yes          No

    If yes, circle group or groups.

5. Will participants be video/audio taped?

    Yes          No

6. Will anyone other than the researchers be able to find out how an individual participant responded (are participants' responses coded in such a way that others could identify a particular participant's responses)?

    Yes          No

7. Does the research deal with sensitive aspects of participants' behavior, such as illegal conduct, drug use (including alcohol), or sexual behavior?

    Yes          No

8. Are participants free to withdraw at any time without penalty?

    Yes          No

9. Are there any deceptive elements to the study?

    Yes          No

10. Will participants be exposed to any psychological stress, such as fatigue, assault on values, or threats to self-esteem?

    Yes          No

11. Will participants be exposed to physical stress (electric shock, cold temperatures, etc.)?

    Yes          No

Attach the following:

1. Draft of the method section: Describe, in detail, the methodology of your study (essentially, how will the study be conducted from start to finish, as far as human participants are concerned?). Be specific about any manipulations used and any measurement instruments involved.

2. Copies of questionnaires, surveys, tests, or other paper-and-pencil measures to be used in the study.

3. Informed consent form.

the participants. To help minimize this harm, the researcher should have participants sign an informed consent form (see Box A–2) prior to participating in the study. The form should stress:

1. any foreseeable risks or discomforts that might cause the participant to decide not to participate;

2. that the participant's participation is totally voluntary;
3. that the participant can quit the study at any time. Participants do not have to explain why they want to leave and there is no penalty for leaving; and
4. that their responses will be confidential (if responses won't be confidential, this should be explained).

In regard to the last point (maintaining confidentiality), there are two steps you can take. First, do not use names. Second, if you must use names, use code names or numbers. Store the data with the code name in one place, store the names and the code names or code numbers in a different place.

After the participant has filled out the consent form and participated in your study, you should debrief the participant. During this *debriefing,* you should:

1. correct any misconceptions that were planted by the researchers;
2. try to detect and remove any harm that may have been produced by the study;
3. give a summary of the study in non-technical terms (many departments believe this summary should be both written and oral, the written part being about one full page typed, describing the hypotheses, why the procedures were used, and why the study was important);
4. provide participants an opportunity to ask whatever questions they may have (some departments want you to provide a number for participants to call so research participants can ask follow-up questions);
5. thank the participant for participating; and
6. explain why deception was necessary (if deception was used).

Debriefing is a good time to assess the degree to which you and your co-investigators are conducting the study in an ethical manner. To do so, ask participants to complete an anonymous questionnaire that assesses their perceptions of the study. Such a questionnaire might include the following questions:

1. Could you quit the study at any time?
2. Were you given enough information to decide whether you wanted to participate? If not, what should you have been told before you took part in the study?
3. What was the purpose of this research?
4. Were you treated with respect?
5. Was the researcher polite?
6. Did you have all your questions answered?
7. Were you deceived in any way? If so, did the researcher provide justification for the deception? Are you satisfied with that justification? Why or why not?
8. Did you experience more discomfort than you would in your day-to-day activities?

## BOX A–2
## SAMPLE INFORMED CONSENT FORM

I have been informed that the study in which I have been asked to participate is investigating personnel decision-making. I have also been informed that I will be asked to read personnel files of two job applicants and then asked to decide which of the two individuals I would be more likely to hire. I also understand that I will be asked to justify my decision. Furthermore, I understand that the study will take about 30 minutes of my time.

I understand that the responses I give will be kept confidential. Although the researchers may write up the results of this study, my name will never be used.

I understand that I can withdraw from the study at any time without any problems. That is, if I choose to withdraw, I will receive full credit for participating. Furthermore, I understand that if participating becomes too stressful, I should withdraw from the study.

I understand that, after I have finished the study, the researcher will gladly answer any questions I might have. If I have any questions after that, I should feel free to call

Dr. _____ at _____.

Name (printed) _____.

I have read this statement and have had all my questions answered. Therefore, I give my written consent to participate in this investigation.

Signature _____ Date _____

Signature of person obtaining consent

_____ Date: _____

---

If so, did the researcher provide sufficient justification for discomfort? What caused this discomfort?

9. Do you think your responses will be kept confidential?

As you can see, the ideal study would not involve stress or deception. Participants would choose whether to participate only after reading an accurate description of the study. After the study was done, all data would be kept entirely confidential and participants would be completely debriefed.

The ethical principles, however, recognize that studies may be ethical even though the studies may involve unpleasantness of some kind, may involve deception, may have participants participate without the benefit of informed consent, or may be done without completely debriefing participants. However, when such guidelines as informed consent and complete debriefing are violated, it can be for only one of two reasons.

First, the potential benefits of the study must justify such a violation—and an outside committee, rather than the researcher, should make the judgment.

However, even if an impartial committee agrees that the benefits outweigh the costs, alternatives to the study must be considered.

Second, the guidelines may be violated if upholding one guideline means harming the participant. For example, suppose that a participant's response was bizarre and unusual. Telling a participant that their behavior was bizarre might meet the guideline of giving a complete debriefing. However, such a disclosure might upset the participant. For a closer look at ethical guidelines for human research, see Box A-3.

# ANIMAL RESEARCH

Conducting animal research in an ethical manner is vital. Unethical treatment of animals is inhumane and, in many cases, illegal. However, we have not spent much time on ethics in animal research for two basic reasons.

First, the basic concepts that govern human research also govern animal research. For example, in animal research, as in human research, pain and discomfort should be minimized. Likewise, in both human and animal research any study that inflicts stress must be justifiable on the basis that: (1) the study is likely to produce some benefit that outweighs the risks, and that (2) there is no other way to get that potential benefit.

Second, because humane treatment of animals is so important, APA has taken the following three steps to almost guarantee that you cannot do animal research without knowing APA's ethical standards:

1. If you conduct research with animal participants, you must be trained in the humane care, handling, and maintenance of animals.
2. As a student, you cannot conduct research with animals unless you are supervised by someone who is well-trained in both animal research and in how to handle, care for, and maintain animals.
3. A copy of the ethical guidelines relating to animal research must be posted in the animal lab.

Because you will be shown how to take care of the animals, because you will be supervised, and because the guidelines will be right in the lab, you probably will not violate ethical principles out of ignorance. However, since violating ethical procedures in animal research may violate federal law, you should be very careful.

If you are conducting research with animals, you should consult APA's ethical guidelines for animal research at the end of this appendix (see Box A-4). In addition, you should work closely with your research supervisor. Finally, figure out some strategy so that you do not forget to take care of your animal. Unless you have a routine or a system, it is easy to forget to check on your animal during the weekend. However, animals need food, water, gentle handling, and a clean living environment *every single day*.

---

### Box A–3
### THE AMERICAN PSYCHOLOGICAL ASSOCIATION'S PRINCIPLES COVERING THE TREATMENT OF HUMAN PARTICIPANTS

#### 1.14 Avoiding Harm

Psychologists take reasonable steps to avoid harming their patients or clients, research participants, students, and others with whom they work, and to minimize harm where it is foreseeable and unavoidable.

#### 6.06 Planning Research

(a) Psychologists design, conduct, and report research in accordance with recognized standards of scientific competence and ethical research.

(b) Psychologists plan their research so as to minimize the possibility that results will be misleading.

(c) In planning research, psychologists consider its ethical acceptability under the Ethics Code. If an ethical issue is unclear, psychologists seek to resolve the issue through consultation with institutional review boards, animal care and use committees, peer consultations, or other proper mechanisms.

(d) Psychologists take reasonable steps to implement appropriate protections for the rights and welfare of human participants, other persons affected by the research, and the welfare of animal subjects.

#### 6.07 Responsibility

(a) Psychologists conduct research competently and with due concern for the dignity and welfare of the participants.

(b) Psychologists are responsible for the ethical conduct of research conducted by them or by others under their supervision or control.

(c) Researchers and assistants are permitted to perform only those tasks for which they are appropriately trained and prepared.

(d) As part of the process of development and implementation of research projects, psychologists consult those with expertise concerning any special population under investigation or most likely to be affected.

#### 6.08 Compliance with Law and Standards

Psychologists plan and conduct research in a manner consistent with federal and state law and regulations, as well as professional standards governing the conduct of research, and particularly those standards governing research with human participants and animal subjects.

#### 6.09 Institutional Approval

Psychologists obtain from host institutions or organizations appropriate approval prior to conducting research, and they provide accurate information about their research

*(continued)*

*(continued from previous page)*

proposals. They conduct the research in accordance with the approved research protocol.

### 6.10 Research Responsibilities

Prior to conducting research (except research involving only anonymous surveys, naturalistic observations, or similar research), psychologists enter into an agreement with participants that clarifies the nature of the research and the responsibilities of each party.

### 6.11 Informed Consent to Research

(a) Psychologists use language that is reasonably understandable to research participants in obtaining their appropriate informed consent (except as provided in Standard 6.12, Dispensing with Informed Consent). Such informed consent is appropriately documented.

(b) Using language that is reasonably understandable to participants, psychologists inform participants of the nature of the research; they inform participants that they are free to participate or to decline to participate or to withdraw from the research; they explain the foreseeable consequences of declining or withdrawing; they inform participants of significant factors that may be expected to influence their willingness to participate (such as risks, discomfort, adverse effects, or limitations on confidentiality, except as provided in Standard 6.15, Deception in Research); and they explain other aspects about which the prospective participants inquire.

(c) When psychologists conduct research with individuals such as students or subordinates, psychologists take special care to protect the prospective participants from adverse consequences of declining or withdrawing from participation.

(d) When research participation is a course requirement or opportunity for extra credit, the prospective participant is given the choice of equitable alternative activities.

(e) For persons who are legally incapable of giving informed consent, psychologists nevertheless (1) provide an appropriate explanation, (2) obtain the participant's assent, and (3) obtain appropriate permission from a legally authorized person, if such substitute consent is permitted by law.

### 6.12 Dispensing with Informed Consent

Before determining that planned research (such as research involving only anonymous questionnaires, naturalistic observations, or certain kinds of archival research) does not require the informed consent of research participants, psychologists consider applicable regulations and institutional review board requirements, and they consult with colleagues as appropriate.

### 6.13 Informed Consent in Research Filming or Recording

Psychologists obtain informed consent from research participants prior to filming or recording them in any form, unless the research involves simply naturalistic observa-

*(continued)*

*(continued from previous page)*

tions in public places and it is not anticipated that the recording will be used in a manner that could cause personal identification or harm.

### 6.14  Offering Inducements for Research Participants

(a) In offering professional services as an inducement to obtain research participants, psychologists make clear the nature of the services, as well as the risks, obligations, and limitations. (See also Standard 1.18, Barter [with Patients or Clients].)

(b) Psychologists do not offer excessive or inappropriate financial or other inducements to obtain research participants, particularly when it might tend to coerce participation.

### 6.15  Deception in Research

(a) Psychologists do not conduct a study involving deception unless they have determined that the use of deceptive techniques is justified by the study's prospective scientific, educational, or applied value and that equally effective alternative procedures that do not use deception are not feasible.

(b) Psychologists never deceive research participants about significant aspects that would affect their willingness to participate, such as physical risks, discomfort, or unpleasant emotional experiences.

(c) Any other deception that is an integral feature of the design and conduct of an experiment must be explained to participants as early as is feasible, preferably at the conclusion of their participation, but no later than at the conclusion of the research. (See also Standard 6.18, Providing Participants with Information about the Study.)

### 6.16  Sharing and Utilizing Data

Psychologists inform research participants of their anticipated sharing or further use of personally identifiable research data and of the possibility of unanticipated future uses.

### 6.17  Minimizing Invasiveness

In conducting research, psychologists interfere with the participants or milieu from which data are collected only in a manner that is warranted by an appropriate research design and that is consistent with psychologists' roles as scientific investigators.

### 6.18  Providing Participants with Information about the Study

(a) Psychologists provide a prompt opportunity for participants to obtain appropriate information about the nature, results, and conclusions of the research, and psychologists attempt to correct any misconceptions that participants may have.

(b) If scientific or humane values justify delaying or withholding this information, psychologists take reasonable measures to reduce the risk of harm.

*(continued)*

*(continued from previous page)*

### 6.19  Honoring Commitments

Psychologists take reasonable measures to honor all commitments they have made to research participants.

### 5.02  Maintaining Confidentiality

Psychologists have a primary obligation and take reasonable precautions to respect the confidentiality rights of those with whom they work or consult, recognizing that confidentiality may be established by law, institutional rules, or professional or scientific relationships. (See also Standard 6.26, Professional Reviewers.)

### 5.03  Minimizing Intrusions on Privacy

(a) In order to minimize intrusions on privacy, psychologists include in written and oral reports, consultations, and the like, only information germane to the purpose for which the communication is made.

(b) Psychologists discuss confidential information obtained in clinical or consulting relationships, or evaluate data concerning patients, individual or organizational clients, students, research participants, supervisees, and employees, only for appropriate scientific or professional purposes and only with persons clearly concerned with such matters.

### 5.04  Maintenance of Records

Psychologists maintain appropriate confidentiality in creating, storing, accessing, transferring, and disposing of records under their control, whether these are written, automated, or in any other medium. Psychologists maintain and dispose of records in accordance with law and in a manner that permits compliance with the requirements of this Ethics Code.

### 6.21  Reporting of Results

(a) Psychologists do not fabricate data or falsify results in their publications.

(b) If psychologists discover significant errors in their published data, they take reasonable steps to correct such errors in a correlation, retraction, erratum, or other appropriate publication means.

### 6.22  Plagiarism

Psychologists do not present substantial portions or elements of another's work or data as their own, even if the other work or data source is cited occasionally.

From: Ethical Principles of Psychologists and Code of Conduct (1992). *American Psychologist, 47,* 1597–1611. Reprinted with the kind permission of the American Psychological Association.

## Box A–4
## Guidelines for Ethical Conduct in the Care and Use of Animals

### I. Justification of the Research

**A.** Research should be undertaken with a clear scientific purpose. There should be a reasonable expectation that the research will a) increase knowledge of the processes underlying the evolution, development, maintenance, alteration, control, or biological significance of behavior; b) increase understanding of the species under study; or c) provide results that benefit the health or welfare of humans or other animals.

**B.** The scientific purpose of the research should be of sufficient potential significance to justify the use of animals. Psychologists should act on the assumption that procedures that would produce pain in humans will also do so in other animals.

**C.** The species chosen for study should be best suited to answer the question(s) posed. The psychologist should always consider the possibility of using other species, nonanimal alternatives, or procedures that minimize the number of animals in research, and should be familiar with the appropriate literature.

**D.** Research on animals may not be conducted until the protocol has been reviewed by the institutional animal care and use committee (IACUC) to ensure that the procedures are appropriate and humane.

**E.** The psychologist should monitor the research and the animals' welfare throughout the course of an investigation to ensure continued justification for the research.

### II. Personnel

**A.** Psychologists should ensure that personnel involved in their research with animals be familiar with these guidelines.

**B.** Animal use procedures must conform with federal regulations regarding personnel, supervision, record keeping, and veterinary care.

**C.** Behavior is both the focus of study of many experiments as well as a primary source of information about an animal's health and well-being. It is therefore necessary that psychologists and their assistants be informed about the behavioral characteristics of their animal subjects, so as to be aware of normal, species-specific behaviors and unusual behaviors that could forewarn of health problems.

**D.** Psychologists should ensure that all individuals who use animals under their supervision receive explicit instruction in experimental methods and in the care, maintenance, and handling of the species being studied. Responsibilities and activities of all individuals dealing with animals should be consistent with their respective competencies, training, and experience in either the laboratory or the field setting.

*(continued)*

*(continued from previous page)*

### III. Care and Housing of Animals

The concept of "psychological well- being" of animals is of current concern and debate and is included in Federal Regulations (United States Department of Agriculture [USDA], 1991). As a scientific and professional organization, APA recognizes the complexities of defining psychological well-being. Procedures appropriate for a particular species may well be inappropriate for others. Hence, APA does not presently stipulate specific guidelines regarding the maintenance of psychological well-being of research animals. Psychologists familiar with the species should be best qualified professionally to judge measures such as enrichment to maintain or improve psychological well-being of those species.

**A.** The facilities housing animals should meet or exceed current regulations and guidelines (USDA, 1990, 1991) and are required to be inspected twice a year (USDA, 1989).

**B.** All procedures carried out on animals are to be reviewed by a local IACUC to ensure that the procedures are appropriate and humane. The committee should have representation from within the institution and from the local community. In the event that it is not possible to constitute an appropriate local IACUC, psychologists are encouraged to seek advice from a corresponding committee of a cooperative institution.

**C.** Responsibilities for the conditions under which animals are kept, both within and outside of the context of active experimentation or teaching, rests with the psychologist under the supervision of the IACUC (where required by federal regulations) and with individuals appointed by the institution to oversee animal care. Animals are to be provided with humane care and healthful conditions during their stay in the facility. In addition to the federal requirements to provide for the psychological well-being of nonhuman primates used in research, psychologists are encouraged to consider enriching the environments of their laboratory animals and should keep abreast of literature on well-being and enrichment for the species with which they work.

### IV. Acquisition of Animals

**A.** Animals not bred in the psychologist's facility are to be acquired lawfully. The USDA and local ordinances should be consulted for information regarding regulations and approved suppliers.

**B.** Psychologists should make every effort to ensure that those responsible for transporting the animals to the facility provide adequate food, water, ventilation, space, and impose no unnecessary stress on the animals.

**C.** Animals taken from the wild should be trapped in a humane manner and in accordance with applicable federal, state, and local regulations.

**D.** Endangered species or taxa should be used only with full attention to required permits and ethical concerns. Information and permit applications can be obtained from

*(continued)*

*(continued from previous page)*

the Fish and Wildlife Service, Office of Management Authority, U.S. Dept. of the Interior, 4401 N. Fairfax Dr., Rm. 432, Arlington, VA 22043, 703-358-2104. Similar caution should be used in work with threatened species or taxa.

## V. Experimental Procedures

Humane consideration for the well-being of the animal should be incorporated into the design and conduct of all procedures involving animals, while keeping in mind the primary goal of experimental procedures—the acquisition of sound, replicable data. The conduct of all procedures is governed by Guideline I.

**A.** Behavioral studies that involve no aversive stimulation or overt sign of distress to the animal are acceptable. This includes observational and other noninvasive forms of data collection.

**B.** When alternative behavioral procedures are available, those that minimize discomfort to the animal should be used. When using aversive conditions, psychologists should adjust the parameters of stimulation to levels that appear minimal, though compatible with the aims of the research. Psychologists are encouraged to test painful stimuli on themselves, whenever reasonable. Whenever consistent with the goals of the research, consideration should be given to providing the animals with control of the potentially aversive stimulation.

**C.** Procedures in which the animal is anesthetized and insensitive to pain throughout the procedure and is euthanized before regaining consciousness are generally acceptable.

**D.** Procedures involving more than momentary or slight aversive stimulation, which are not relieved by medication or other acceptable methods, should be undertaken only when the objectives of the research cannot be achieved by other methods.

**E.** Experimental procedures that require prolonged aversive conditions or produce tissue damage or metabolic disturbances require greater justification and surveillance. This includes prolonged exposure to extreme environmental conditions, experimentally induced prey killing, or infliction of physical trauma or tissue damage. An animal observed to be in a state of severe distress or chronic pain that cannot be alleviated and is not essential to the purposes of the research should be euthanized immediately.

**F.** Procedures that use restraint must conform to federal regulations and guidelines.

**G.** Procedures involving the use of paralytic agents without reduction in pain sensation require particular prudence and humane concern. Use of muscle relaxants or paralytics alone during surgery, without general anesthesia, is unacceptable and shall not be used.

**H.** Surgical procedures, because of their invasive nature, require close supervision and attention to humane considerations by the psychologist. Aseptic (methods that

*(continued)*

*(continued from previous page)*

minimize risks of infection) techniques must be used on laboratory animals whenever possible.

**1.** All surgical procedures and anesthetization should be conducted under the direct supervision of a person who is competent in the use of the procedures.

**2.** If the surgical procedure is likely to cause greater discomfort than that attending anesthetization, and unless there is specific justification for acting otherwise, animals should be maintained under anesthesia until the procedure is ended.

**3.** Sound postoperative monitoring and care, which may include the use of analgesics and antibiotics, should be provided to minimize discomfort and to prevent infection and other untoward consequences of the procedure.

**4.** Animals can not be subjected to successive surgical procedures unless these are required by the nature of the research, the nature of the surgery, or for the well-being of the animal. Multiple surgeries on the same animal must receive special approval from the IACUC.

**I.** When the use of an animal is no longer required by an experimental protocol or procedure, in order to minimize the number of animals used in research, alternatives to euthanasia should be considered. Such uses should be compatible with the goals of research and the welfare of the animal. Care should be taken that such an action does not expose the animal to multiple surgeries.

**J.** The return of wild-caught animals to the field can carry substantial risks, both to the formerly captive animals and to the ecosystem. Animals reared in the laboratory should not be released because, in most cases, they cannot survive or they may survive by disrupting the natural ecology.

**K.** When euthanasia appears to be the appropriate alternative, either as a requirement of the research or because it constitutes the most humane form of disposition of an animal at the conclusion of the research:

**1.** Euthanasia shall be accomplished in a humane manner, appropriate for the species, and in such a way as to ensure immediate death, and in accordance with procedures outlined in the latest version of the "American Veterinary Medical Association (AVMA) Panel on Euthanasia."

**2.** Disposal of euthanized animals should be accomplished in a manner that is in accord with all relevant legislation, consistent with health, environmental, and aesthetic concerns, and approved by the IACUC. No animal shall be discarded until its death is verified.

## VI. Field Research

Field research, because of its potential to damage sensitive ecosystems and ethologies, should be subject to IACUC approval. Field research, if strictly observational, may not require IACUC approval (USDA, 1989, pg. 36126).

*(continued)*

*(continued from previous page)*

**A.** Psychologists conducting field research should disturb their populations as little as possible—consistent with the goals of the research. Every effort should be made to minimize potential harmful effects of the study on the population and on other plant and animal species in the area.

**B.** Research conducted in populated areas should be done with respect for the property and privacy of the inhabitants of the area.

**C.** Particular justification is required for the study of endangered species. Such research on endangered species should not be conducted unless IACUC approval has been obtained and all requisite permits are obtained (see above, III D).

From *Guidelines for Ethical Conduct in the Care and Use of Animals* (1993). Reprinted with the kind permission of the American Psychological Association.

# *Appendix B*

# LIBRARY RESOURCES

Library research is a necessary and useful component of any research project. Library research can help you come up with your basic research question, refine that question into a hypothesis, and inform you about research and theories that relate to your hypothesis.

Once you have refined and justified your hypothesis, a literature review can help you design your study. Specifically, a thorough search through your library's resources can save you from wasting time and effort in at least two ways. First, searches can help by directing your attention to measures and manipulations that other researchers have found fruitful. Second, searches can help you by directing your attention away from measures and manipulations that other researchers have found fruitless.

To conduct a literature review, there are nine basic steps you can take. Specifically, you could:

1. Consult general sources
   a. Introductory psychology texts
   b. Specialized texts (texts on your general topic [such as memory]. These texts may target juniors, seniors, or even graduate students).
2. Consult books or chapters written for experts in the field. You may be able to find these texts by:
   a. Looking in *Books In Print*
   b. Looking at *PsycBooks: Books & Chapters in Psychology,* a set of volumes especially designed to help psychologists locate recent books and chapters that are relevant to their specific interest area.
   c. Looking at the *Annual Review of Psychology*
   d. Consulting the Card Catalog or browsing through the "BF" section of your library.
3. Track down articles referenced in those books. Note: Older, bound issues of journals may be in different parts of the library than newer issues.
4. Read those articles and their reference sections. Then, track down the research cited in those articles.

5. To see if the authors have done more recent research, look them up in the author index of *Psychological Abstracts* or in the *Social Science Index* (both are located in the reference section of your library).

6. Look up your topic in the subject index of *Psychological Abstracts*.

7. See what recent articles have referenced your key articles by consulting the *Social Science Citation Index* (located in the reference section of your library).

8. Scan current issues of journals that are general in scope (*Psychological Bulletin, American Psychologist, Psychological Science, Psych Scans, Current Contents*).

9. Identify key terms (often, with the assistance of a reference librarian and the *Psychological Thesaurus*) that will allow you to use the library's computer system to search the literature.

The first four steps of the literature search (looking at books and the articles they cite) are fairly straightforward. The remaining steps are not. Therefore, the rest of this appendix is devoted to making those steps more manageable.

## Psychological Abstracts

Many people start their literature search with the *Psychological Abstracts.* The *Psychological Abstracts* include brief (fewer than 120 words) summaries of a wide range of work in psychology and related fields. To get a sense of what a rich resource the *Abstracts* are, consider that they summarize articles from hundreds of journals, as well as summarizing books and doctoral dissertations.

The inclusiveness of the *Abstracts* means that they probably include any relevant article you might want. However, the inclusiveness also poses a problem: How do you find the articles you want from among the thousands of articles summarized in the *Abstracts*? Reading the *Abstracts* from cover to cover is not a practical option. Fortunately, because the *Abstracts* are well organized, it is fairly easy to get all the information you need.

## Searching by Subject

Since the *Abstracts* are organized and indexed by topic, the first step is to decide what topics you want to look up. At the very least, you will want to look up your dependent measure and the general topic you are investigating.

### USING THE THESAURUS

At best, looking under these topics will probably cause you to miss some important references. At worst, looking under these topics might give you no references. Why? Because psychologists may have used other names for the topics and concepts you wish to research. To find out about those other terms, look at the *Psychological Thesaurus*. The thesaurus will tell you other terms under which your criterion variable might be listed. For example, "self" is also called identity, personality, and ego. Because the *Psychological Thesaurus* is so useful for searching the *Abstracts,* it usually will be located with the *Abstracts.*

Once you have consulted the thesaurus (and perhaps also talked to a reference librarian), you should be armed with key terms that will guide a productive search. At that point, you are ready to tackle the *Abstracts.*

## Current Issues of *Psychological Abstracts*

If you are trying to find current references, locate the *Abstracts* issues over the past year. The abstracts published during the year will be found in several softbound issues that share the same volume number. For example, all of the issues published in 1996 are classified as Volume 83.

Once you have rounded up all the issues for the year, the rest of your job is simple. Look up your terms in the subject index in the back of each issue. The index will give you the *numbers* of the abstracts relating to that term. For example, if next to your term you saw "1029," that would tell you that the abstract is number 1029, the 1,029th abstract of that volume. (Each abstract has a number. Like page numbers, abstract numbers go in order. Thus, 1,000 is right after *Abstract* number 999 and right before number 1,001. At first, you might think it would be better to give page numbers rather than abstract numbers. However, abstract numbers are more useful because there could be 20 abstracts on a single page. Thus, the numbers tell you exactly where to look. Consequently, after using the abstracts for just a few minutes, you will appreciate the value of using the abstract's specific number.)

After reading the numbers of all the potentially important abstracts from the index, go back through the issue locating those abstracts. The only hassle is that since each monthly index covers only that issue, you will have to look up your terms several times. That is, you have to look up "self" in the January issue index as well as in the March issue.

### HARDBOUND ISSUES

To help people avoid the hassle of looking up the same term again and again, most libraries bind together the previous years' issues. Specifically, they bind all the issues of the *Abstracts* that bear the same volume number. For example, all of the issues published in 1996 are probably bound together with a hardbound cover and labeled Volume 83. However, they do not bind the indexes with the *Abstracts.* Instead, the subject and author indexes are bound separately. Thus, there are three "books" for each year: a subject index, an author index, and a volume containing the actual abstracts. In other words, for each of the hardbound volumes there is a hardbound subject index and a hardbound author index. The indexes will have the same volume number as the *Abstracts* to which they refer. Consequently, the 1996 Abstracts, the 1996 subject index, and the 1996 author index are all labeled Volume 83.

In short, if you want to locate references for previous years, find the hardbound indexes that correspond to the years in which you are interested. Look up your terms in the subject indexes. When you find a listing for one of your terms, write down both the volume number of the index and the abstract numbers. Then, go to that volume of the *Abstracts.*

***Looking up References by Author.***    If you know the names of investigators who have done research relating to your study, you may want to see whether they have done more recent work. In that case, look up their names in a recent volume's author index.

***Browsing through the Abstracts.***    In a given volume, all abstracts that are on the same topic are located together. Thus, once you find an abstract that addresses your topic, look at the surrounding abstracts.

***Finding the Original Resource.***    After reading an abstract of the study, you will have a good idea whether you want to read the original source. If so, you will find a reference for the original publication with the abstract. Go to your library's catalog files to locate the original source. If your library doesn't own it, ask the library if you can get it through inter-library loan.

## Social Sciences Index

A source that is like the *Abstracts,* but even more inclusive, is the *Social Sciences Index.* This index is a comprehensive source for journal references in all the social sciences. In addition to psychology, such fields as anthropology, sociology, social work, and geography are included. Since psychologists are not the only people who conduct behavioral research, *Social Science Index* can help you locate useful references published in non-psychological journals.

Like *Psychological Abstracts,* several issues are published each year. Like the *Abstracts,* the issues for a particular year are identified by the same volume number and bound together in hardback. Finally, like the *Abstracts,* the most recent indexes will probably be in several softbound issues, each bearing the same volume number.

Unlike the *Abstracts,* the *Social Sciences Index* does not summarize the studies it cites. Thus, it is more like the indexes to the *Abstracts* than the *Abstracts* themselves. Indeed, if you combined the subject and author indexes of the *Abstracts*—and kept everything in alphabetical order—this combined index would resemble the *Social Sciences Index.*

In short, there are five points to keep in mind about the *Social Sciences Index.*

**1.** You can search it by author and topic.

**2.** If you search it by topic, consult the *Psychological Thesaurus* to be sure that you are using the appropriate term(s) for your topic.

**3.** It contains citations to work in psychology and to fields other than psychology.

**4.** It does not provide summaries of the articles it references.

**5.** It is simpler to use than *Psychological Abstracts*.

## Social Science Citation Index

Unlike the Social Sciences Index, the *Social Science Citation Index* (SSCI) gives you three different ways to locate references. You can find references by topic, by who wrote it, and by who referenced (cited) it. The *Social Science Citation Index* is able to do this because it consists of three separate but related indexes: a subject index, author index, and citation index. Each index covers the same journal articles. They all index more than 70,000 articles that appear in more than 2,000 journals. The difference is in how they index those articles.

The fact that they all cover the same articles has two important implications. First, you can start your search using any of the indexes. Where you start will probably depend on what you already know. If you only know the topic, you will use the subject index. If you know a researcher who does work in this area, you may start with the author index. If you know of a classic study in your area, you may want to find articles that cite that study. Therefore, you would start your search in the citation index.

Second, you may get information in one index that will give you leads that you can follow up in another index. For instance, in searching the subject index, you may repeatedly find the name of a certain author. Therefore, you may choose to look up that author in the author index.

***The Permuterm Subject Index.***    The *Social Science Citation Index* refers to its subject index as the *"Permuterm Subject Index"* (PSI). In the PSI, every major word or phrase from the title of an article is paired with every other major word in that title. The goal is to develop word pairs that indicate what the study is about. For example, if an article were titled "Sex differences in the effect of television viewing on aggression" the article would be indexed under Sex Differences and Aggression; Sex Differences and Television Viewing; and Television Viewing and Aggression. These permuted (arranged in all possible ways) pairs are alphabetically listed as two-level indexing entries and linked to the names of the authors who used them in the titles of their articles. For example, an entry in the *PSI* might look like this:

AGGRESSION
    SEX DIFFERENCES            ERON M
    TELEVISION VIEWING      BUNKER A
SEX DIFFERENCES
    AGGRESSION                ERON M
    TELEVISION VIEWING      MUTIN SS

TELEVISION VIEWING
    AGGRESSION                         BUNKER A
    SEX DIFFERENCES                    MUTIN SS

Thus, the *PSI* tells you that during the period indexed, the authors Bunker and Mutin used the words shown opposite their name ("Television Viewing and Aggression" and "Television Viewing and Sex Differences," respectively).

To use PSI, simply think of words and word pairs that are likely to appear in the titles of articles related to your study. By looking up these words, you will discover the names of authors who have used the words in the titles of their articles. Once you find the names of authors, look them up in the *Source Index.*

***The Source Index.***    The "Source Index" is a straightforward author index for the articles covered each year. For each article indexed, you are given the language it is written in (if it isn't English), its title, authors, journal, volume number, page numbers, year, the number of references cited in the article, and the journal issue number. In addition, beginning with the May–August 1974 issue, the references contained in each indexed article are listed. To facilitate reprint requests and other correspondence, a mailing address is often provided for each first author. Below is a sample entry:

BUNKER, A
    THE RELATIONSHIP OF AGGRESSION AND TV VIEWING
        J APPL PSY    25 09 87 20R N3
        CTR FOR REHABILITATIVE CHANGE, CENTER AVENUE
        NEW MEXICO, MEXICO

As the entry's third line reveals, the entry comes from an article published in the *Journal of Applied Psychology,* volume 25. It begins on page 9, was published in 1987, has 20 references, and is in issue number 3.

***The Citation Index.***    The final index included in the *Social Science Citation Index* is the "Citation Index." This index looks at what references authors cite in their paper. The Citation Index is based on two related assumptions. First, if a paper cites an article, then the paper is on the same topic as the older (cited) reference. Second, papers that refer to (cite) the same article, usually address the same topic. For example, many of the papers that cite an article on the effects of chlorpromazine on the sexual behavior of rats probably investigate the effects of drugs on the sexual behavior of rats.

To start a search in the *Citation Index,* look up the name of an author who published material relevant to your topic. If anything the author has written was cited during the indexing period, the names of the publications that cited it will be listed. This feature is useful in at least two ways. First, if you are not completely familiar with the author's work, you may find out about other interesting articles by that author. Second, if nobody cited the paper in which you are interested, you will know instantly because the article will not appear.

If the article you are interested in was cited, the *Citation Index* will include the name of that article. Next to the article name will be the names of the authors who cited the publication. Now that you know who referenced the publication, you need to find out in which journal and in which article they referenced it. To do this, look up their names in the *Source Index.*

In summary, the *Social Sciences Citation Index* allows you to do at least three basic types of searches. If you know of a classic study in your area of research, you can do a citation search. If you do not know of an earlier, relevant paper, you can do a search by looking up the variables you are studying: a Permuterm (subject) search. Finally, when you know the name of a researcher who has recently published on your topic (or learn of such a person as a result of a Permuterm or Citation search), do an Author search.

## Current Contents

In contrast to the sources we described earlier, *Current Contents* is very easy to use. *Current Contents* simply lists the table of contents for several journals. Since you can often figure out whether an article is relevant to your topic from its title, this reference can be very useful. Thus, by looking at titles you can determine which articles you want to find and read. Although you might prefer that the articles were organized by topic rather than by journal, you will soon find that most journals cover only certain topics. That is, if you are looking for a measure of aggression, you would not look at the contents for *"The Journal of Memory and Cognition."* To get a better idea of what journals you should scan, see Table B–1.

## Computer Searches

The quickest way to locate references is to do a computer search. Whereas it might take you hours to search through all the resources we discussed in this appendix to find the references you need, computer searches can condense that time into minutes. For example, you can use either PsycINFO or PsycLit to quickly search most journals in psychology and you can use the ERIC database to search a wide range of research relating to educational psychology.

One way that computer searches save you time is by allowing you to do searches for groups of terms rather than merely searching for individual terms. For example, if your topic is aggression in food-deprived monkeys, the computer can find only those references that concern "aggression" in "food deprived" "monkeys." If you were using a non-computerized abstract or index, you could look up only one (two at the most) of these variables at a time. Thus, if you looked up aggression, you would have to read through all the references concerning aggression in humans, rats, birds, and lions to find ones that dealt with monkeys. You would then have to sort through all the scattered monkey listings to find "food-deprived" monkeys.

**TABLE B-1**

## A Look at Selected Journals

| JOURNAL | RELEVANCE TO YOU |
| --- | --- |
| Psychological Bulletin | Publishes articles that review existing work on either a research area or on a research/statistical technique. |
| Psychological Review | Publishes work that compares and criticizes existing theories. |
| American Psychologist | Publishes theoretical articles, review articles, and empirical articles. Although articles are often written by distinguished scholars, they are written to a broad audience and are thus relatively easy to understand. |
| Psychological Science | Publishes theoretical articles, review articles, and empirical articles. Although articles are often written by distinguished scholars, they are written to a fairly broad audience and are thus relatively easy to understand. You may find the articles slightly harder to understand than those in the *American Psychologist.* |
| Contemporary Psychology | Review of recent books. Easy to read. Covers a wide range of topics. |
| Psychological Abstracts | Presents brief summaries of most published articles in psychology. Good browsing or reference tool. The abstracts are indexed by both author and topic. |
| Psych/Scan | Like *Psychological Abstracts,* contains summaries of recent articles. There are six different *PsychScans* for six different content areas: (1) developmental, (2) clinical, (3) learning disorders and mental retardation, (4) applied psychology, (5) applied experimental and engineering, and (6) psychoanalysis. |
| American Journal of Psychology | Primarily original research in basic psychological science. |
| Journals of Experimental Psychology (JEP) | Usually original experimental studies concerning basic mechanisms of perception, learning, motivation, and performance. Four different journals: |
| | JEP: General |
| | JEP: Animal behavior processes |
| | JEP: Learning, memory, and cognition |
| | JEP: Human perception and performance |
| Behavioral Neuroscience | Emphasizes biological basis of behavior. Because of the interdisciplinary nature of the journal, you may find some of the articles hard to understand if you do not have a background in chemistry and endocrinology. |
| Journal of Comparative Psychology | Articles may include both laboratory and field observation of species. Emphasis is on relating findings to the theory of evolution. |
| Bulletin of the Psychonomic Society | Articles cover any area of general experimental psychology. Good source of short articles describing relatively simple studies. |
| Memory and Cognition | A good source of articles in human experimental psychology. See also *Cognitive Science, Cognitive Psychology*, and *Journal of Experimental Psychology: Learning, Memory, and Cognition.* |
| Journal of Applied Behavior Analysis | Articles reporting a sizable effect on an important behavior, usually employing a single-n design. |
| Psychological Record | Articles discussing theory or reporting experiments. Average article is relatively brief. |

| | |
|---|---|
| Psychological Reports | Articles in general psychology. Good source of brief articles. |
| Journal of Consulting and Clinical Psychology | Wide range of articles and brief reports dealing with theory and research in counseling. Some use of the case study method. |
| Psychological Assessment: A Journal of Consulting and Clinical Psychology | Studies assessing the validity of a variety of tests and measures. |
| Journal of Counseling Psychology | Publishes research articles evaluating the effectiveness of counseling, studies on the effectiveness of selecting and training counselors, theoretical articles, and other articles relating to counseling. |
| Journal of Abnormal Psychology | Occasionally reports experimental studies on humans or animals related to emotion or pathology, some studies that test hypotheses derived from psychological theories. |
| Psychology and Aging | Research reporting on physiological and behavioral aspects of aging during older adulthood. Fairly easy to read. |
| Developmental Psychology | Primarily research relating to development. See also, *Child Development, Merrill Palmer Quarterly, Psychology and Aging.* In addition, can track down related work by consulting *Psych Scan/Developmental.* |
| Journal of Educational Psychology | Research and theoretical articles relating to teaching and learning. Fairly easy to read. |
| American Education Research Journal | Research in education. Single study papers are accepted. |
| Journal of Applied Psychology | Reports research relating to industry, government, health, education, consumer affairs, and other applied areas. |
| Journal of Personality and Social Psychology | Contains three sections: (1) attitudes and social cognition, (2) interpersonal relations and group processes, and (3) personality and individual differences. |
| | Primarily reports articles involving several studies or fairly complex designs. Discussions may suggest follow-up studies that could be performed. |
| Journal of Experimental Social Psychology | Almost all articles report the result of experiments. |
| Journal of Social Psychology | Source of fairly simple studies. |
| Personality and Social Psychology Bulletin | Contains short articles that are often easy to understand. |

Although computer searches can save time, you will save time only if you have some knowledge about how to conduct a computer search. To help you plan your search, APA publishes two workbooks called *Search PsycINFO* intended to provide this training. One workbook is for students, the other for instructors. Both can be published from APA's Order Department. Additional help may be obtained from your reference librarian or from Table B–2.

**TABLE B–2**

**Using the Computer to Find References: Tips for Using "PsycLit," "PsychINFO," "ERIC" and Related Tools**

| PROBLEM | POSSIBLE SOLUTION |
|---|---|
| Not finding enough references | 1. Find other names for your key concept. For example, brainstorm, use the thesaurus (or hit key labeled F9), or consult with a reference librarian. |
| | 2. Use the term "or" to look for articles that have any of the terms you are looking for. |
| | 3. Use the stem of the term you are interested in followed by an asterisk (*). This will give you all articles that have this root word as a stem. Thus, doing teen* will get you articles that mention "teen," "teens," "teenage," and "teenagers." |
| | 4. If you are using an author search, check the index (F5) to make sure that: (1) you have the author's name spelled correctly, and (2) that the author doesn't use more than one way of presenting his or her name (with or without middle initial, etc.). |
| Finding too many references | 1. Use the "and" command to make sure that the reference has to satisfy several criteria before it is captured by your search. For example, you might search "death and English in la" to get only articles that are both on death and in English. Often, you will want "and" between the predictor and criterion variables you are searching for. |
| | 2. If you find that you are getting articles that have your keyword in the abstract, but don't have anything to do with your concepts, narrow your search by making sure that you get only articles that someone else has described as pertaining to your topic. To do this, add "in de" (this means in a reviewer's description) to your key word. Thus, instead of searching for "recall," you might search for "recall in de." |
| | 3. If you find that many of the "wrong references" you get are calling up a certain term, you could add "and not ___ (that irrelevant term)" to your search. Or, if the search keeps giving you articles from a journal (e.g., *Child Development*) that your library doesn't have, you could add "and not child-development in jn"). Or, if you didn't want any animal research references, you could add "and not animal in po." |
| | 4. You could limit your search to only the most recent year ("and 1996 in py"). |
| | 5. If you only want literature reviews, include "and literature-review in de." If you want to exclude literature reviews, include "and not literature-review in de." |

# *Appendix C*

# CONDUCTING A STUDY

## PLANNING YOUR PROCEDURES

You have reviewed the literature, developed a hypothesis, operationalized your variables, and given sound reasons for testing your hypothesis. However, your preliminary work is still not done. You must now decide exactly what specific actions you will take. In other words, although you probably have decided on the general design (such as a simple experiment or a 2 × 2), your plan is not complete until each detail has been thought through and written down.

You should write down *exactly* what procedures you will follow. For example, what instructions, word-for-word, will participants be given? Who will administer the treatment? Where? Will participants be run in groups or individually? In answering these questions, you must take into account issues of validity. However, your paramount concern must always be ethics. You do not have the right to harm another.

## Ethical Considerations: Human Research

Ethics should be the foundation of your research plan. Therefore, you should read Appendix A (ethics) before conducting a study.

In addition to reading Appendix A, you must be extremely careful not to harm your participants. Ideally, your participants should feel just as well when they leave the study as they did when they began the study. Unfortunately, even in the most innocuous studies, protecting your participants from discomfort is much easier said than done.

### WEIGHING THE RISKS

Realize that any experience may be traumatic to some participants. Trauma can occur from things you would never think of as being traumatic. Because any study has risks and because you won't know all of the risks, *don't run a single participant without your professor's permission.*

To begin to sensitize yourself to the risks involved in your proposed study, list the 10 worst things that could possibly happen to participants. If you are using human participants, be aware that not all participants will react in the same way. Some may experience trauma because the study triggers some painful memory. Some participants may feel bad because they think they did poorly. Other participants may feel bad because they think their behavior ruined your study. Realize that some of your participants may be mentally unbalanced and any attack on their self-esteem might lead to disastrous consequences. Since participants are often fragile, you should list some serious consequences in your worst-case scenario.

## REDUCING RISKS

Since any study has the potential for harm, the possibility of severe consequences doesn't mean that your professor won't allow you to do the study. However, you and your professor should think about ways to minimize the risks.

***Screening Participants.***    One method of minimizing risks is to screen out "vulnerable participants." For instance, if there is any reason to believe that your study may increase heart rate or blood pressure, you may want to make sure that only people in good health participate in your study. If your study might harm people with low self-esteem, you may want to use only well-adjusted participants who have high levels of self-esteem. Therefore, you might give a measure of self-esteem to potential participants to eliminate those with low self-esteem.

***Informed Consent.***    Not only should you screen participants, but you should also let participants screen themselves. That is, participants should be volunteers who give their *informed consent:* They should know what the study is about before volunteering for it.

How informed is informed consent? Very informed, when it comes to telling participants about any unpleasant aspect of the study. If participants are going to get shocked, exposed to loud noises or extreme cold, they should be informed of this before they volunteer. Consequently, if your study does involve unpleasantness, you may have difficulty getting participants to volunteer.

Informed consent is considerably less informed when it comes to more innocuous aspects of the study. After all, the study would be ruined if participants knew everything that would happen (and why it happened) before it happened. So, although participants are usually told the truth, they are not always told the whole truth. For example, a memory experiment's description would mention that participants have to memorize words, but might omit the fact that the researcher is looking at the order in which facts are recalled or that there is a surprise recall of all the lists at the end of the study.

Because participants are not fully informed about your study, there may be some things about it that they dislike. For example, suppose a participant finds the task too difficult or finds it upsetting to try the surprise recall task. What can you do?

One protection against these unexpected problems is to make sure participants understand that they can quit the study at any time. So, before the participants begin your study, tell them that if they find any aspect of the study uncomfortable, they can and *should* escape this discomfort by quitting the study. Assure them that it is their duty to quit if they experience discomfort and that they will still get full credit.

## MODIFYING THE STUDY

You have seen that you can minimize ethical problems by letting participants know what they are in for and by letting participants gracefully withdraw from the study. You should also minimize harm by making your study as humane as possible. You can make your study more ethical by reducing the strength of your treatment manipulation, carefully selecting stimulus materials, and by being a conscientious researcher.

***Reducing the Treatment Strength.***    Although using extreme levels of your predictor variable may help you get a significant change in the criterion variable, extreme levels may harm your participants. For example, 24 hours of food deprivation is more likely to cause hunger than 12 hours. However, 24 hours of deprivation is more stressful to the participant. If you plan an unpleasant manipulation, remember your participants' welfare and minimize the unpleasant consequences as much as possible. Consider using levels of the predictor variable that are less severe than you originally intended.

***Modifying Stimulus Materials.***    By modifying your stimulus materials, you may be able to prevent them from triggering unpleasant memories. For instance, if you were interested in the effects of caffeine on memory for prose, you wouldn't want the prose passage to cover some topic like death, divorce, alcoholic parents, or rape. Instead, you would want to use a passage covering a less traumatic topic, such as sports. If the sports article referred to someone's death or hospitalization, you might want to delete that section of the article.

## THE CONSCIENTIOUS RESEARCHER

Often, it's not the study that's unethical, it's the researcher's arrogance. For example, an arrogant researcher may rush through research sessions providing only superficial explanations and little or no time for questions and feedback. Although we know of a few participants who were hurt as a direct result of a research manipulation, we know of many more who were hurt because the researcher treated them like dirt. To ensure that you are sensitive, courteous, and respectful to all of your human participants, you should do two things.

First, when scheduling your research sessions, make sure you leave a 10-minute gap between the end of one session and the beginning of the next session. Some investigators feel that, like a physician, they should efficiently schedule people one after another. Their "efficiency" results in participants having to wait for the investigator, the investigator having to rush through the formalities of greeting participants, or—even worse—the investigator rushing through debriefing. Thus, the "efficient" investigator, like the efficient physician, is seen as unconcerned. Although this conduct does not become physicians, it's intolerable for psychological researchers! After a research participant has given an hour of his or her time, you should be more than willing to answer any questions the participant has. Furthermore, if you rush through greeting or debriefing each participant, the participants will see you as uncaring. Consequently, they will be less likely to tell you about any psychological discomfort they felt and less likely to accept any aid you might offer. Thus, the first step is to walk, rather than to run, participants through your study.

Second, give the participants power. That is, allow participants to rate your study on a scale such as the one in Table C-1. Give each participant's rating sheet to your instructor. Following this simple procedure helps you to be a conscientious and courteous researcher.

### DEBRIEFING

Although you should try to anticipate and prevent every possible bad reaction a participant may have to being in your study, you won't be successful. Inevitably, your procedures will still cause some unpleasantness. After the study is over, you should try to remove this unpleasantness by informing participants about the study, reassuring them that their reactions were normal, and expressing your appreciation for their participation.

You should also listen to participants and be sensitive to any unexpected, unpleasant reactions to your study. By being a good listener, you should be able to undo any damage you have unwittingly done. This process of informing your participants about the study and removing any harm done is called *debriefing*. Occasionally, ordinary debriefing will not undo the harm caused to the research participant. In those cases, there are several steps you may take to alleviate distress. For participants who are upset with their responses, you should ask them whether they want you to destroy their data. For participants that you cannot calm down, you should take them to talk to a professor, counselor, or friend—even if this means canceling a research session you had scheduled.

In summary, you should be very concerned about ethics. Since ethics involve weighing the costs of the study against the potential benefits, you should do everything you can to minimize the risk of participants becoming uncomfortable. If, despite your efforts, a participant experiences discomfort, you should try to reduce that discomfort during debriefing.

## Ethical Considerations: Animal Research

With animal participants, you incur the same responsibilities that you did with human participants—you must protect animal participants from undue stress

**TABLE C–1**
**Sample Debriefing Rating Scale** [1]

Being a participant in psychology studies should provide you with a firsthand look at research. On the scale below, please indicate how valuable or worthless you found being in today's study by circling a number from +3 to −3.

**WORTHLESS:**    −3    −2    −1    +1    +2    +3    **:VALUABLE**

If you wish to explain your rating or to make comments on this study, either positive or negative, please do so below.

NOTE: This scale is a slightly modified version of a scale that has been used at The Ohio State University.

and discomfort. In many ways, you have even more responsibility to animal participants because they are dependent on you for their mere existence. You must keep them fed, clean, warm, and comfortable—24 hours a day. To fulfill your responsibility to animal participants, you must follow APA's guidelines for proper housing, food and water, and handling (see Appendix A).

Furthermore, because your animal participants do not have the power to give their informed consent, nor the power to quit the study, you must carefully question the value of your study. Ask yourself and your professor this question: "Is the potential knowledge gained from the study worth the cost to the animals?" Finally, if you must euthanize (kill) your animal participants at the end of your study, follow APA's guidelines to ensure that this is done in the most humane way.

## Maximize the Benefits: The Other Side of the Ethics Coin

We have discussed ways of minimizing harm to participants. However, minimizing harm is not enough to ensure that your study is ethical. For your study to be ethical, the potential benefits must be greater than the potential harm. Thus, an extremely harmless study can be unethical if the study has no potential benefits. So, just as you owe it to your participants to reduce potential harm, you owe it to your participants to maximize the potential benefits of your study. You maximize that potential by making sure your study provides accurate information. To provide accurate information, your study needs to have power and validity.

### POWER IS KNOWLEDGE

One of the most serious obstacles to obtaining accurate information is lack of power. Remember, null results don't prove the null hypothesis. They only

---

[1] For more detailed information on debriefing scales and procedures, please see Appendix A.

make people wonder about the study's power. There is no point in doing a study that is so powerless that it will lead to inconclusive, null results.

To have power, you should use a strong manipulation, a sensitive dependent measure, well-standardized procedures, a sensitive design, and enough participants.

***Sample Size: There's Power in Numbers.***    Perhaps your most important obstacle to finding a significant effect is a lack of participants. As a general rule, you should have at least 16 participants in each group.[2] However, the number of participants you need in each group will be affected by the sensitivity of your design, the heterogeneity of your participants, the number of observations you get from each participant, the size of the difference you expect to find between conditions, and the sensitivity of your dependent measure.

If you have a within-subjects design, a reliable and sensitive dependent variable, and expect a rather large difference between your conditions, you may be able to use fewer than 16 participants per group.

If, on the other hand, you are using a simple, between-subjects design, heterogeneous participants, a manipulation that may have little effect, and a relatively insensitive dependent measure, you may want at least 100 participants per condition.

## HUNTING FOR PARTICIPATION

How are you going to get all the volunteer participants you need to conduct a powerful study? The threat of death is not ethical.

***The Draft.***    Some researchers rely on "captive" samples. For example, many colleges "volunteer" students in introductory psychology courses for the research draft. In fact, most of the research strength of modern psychology has been built using this research draft. If your school has such a draft, count yourself among the blessed. All you have to do is ask your professor how to become a recruiter.

***Enlisting Volunteers.***    If your school does not have a draft, an effective way of getting participants is to ask professors to request volunteers from their classes. Many professors will gladly do this. Some will even give volunteers extra credit as an incentive for participating in your study.

***Non-College Samples.***    But what if you don't want to use college students in your study? For example, suppose you want to study children or retirees? Or,

---

[2] The more subjects, the more power. Indeed, some (Cohen, 1990) would consider 64 subjects per group to be a reasonable minimum. In some cases, however, a researcher might use a design that is so powerful that even the smallest of effects, no matter how practically and theoretically insignificant, would be statistically significant. Having a design that is too powerful is rarely a problem for novice researchers.

suppose you agree with the skeptics who claim that results from studies done on college students cannot be applied to "normal people." Then, you would look beyond college classrooms for participants. A note of caution: You may find that getting "real world" participants takes as much work and creativity as planning your study.

***Children.***     If you want to study children, you may be able to take advantage of the "captive" audience approach. After all, most children have to go to school. However, obtaining access to those children may turn into a nightmare of red tape. You will have to obtain permission from all or many of the following: the school board, the superintendent, principal, teacher, parent, child, your professor, and university. If you are going to get these permissions in time for your study, you'll need to plan ahead—and be very lucky.

***Adults.***     Finding adult participants can be even more challenging than finding children. For example, one of your text's authors wanted an adult population for her doctoral dissertation. Her first thought was to contact a major company and gain access to its employees. This tactic failed. Next, she tried to run a newspaper ad asking for volunteers. One newspaper refused to print it. Another would only run it in the "Personal" section. Thus, her appeal for participants appeared with ads for astrological advice, massage services, and people wanting dates. Although a few "volunteers" called, most wanted either a date or an obscene conversation. We do not recommend newspaper ads—especially if your goal is to get a representative sample of the adult population.

***Older Adults.***     The authors have had greater success recruiting elderly participants. Nutrition centers, retirement communities, friendship networks, and nursing homes have been fruitful sources of participants. In addition, we recommend the "grandmother connection": having an older relative or friend introduce you to other prospective participants.

Obviously, finding human participants will take planning, perseverance, and luck. Once you contact prospective participants, you should explain your study to them and have them sign a permission form. The permission form will protect both you and your participants. Basically, it states that you have explained the study to the volunteers and that they agree to participate (see Table C-2). If minors are participating in your study, you need to have separate forms for both the participants and their parents.

***Animal Participants.***     Our experiences with recruiting human participants might have increased your enthusiasm for animal research. In many ways, animals are better participants than humans. You don't have to worry about permission slips, extra credit, or obscene phone calls. Consult with your instructor about obtaining animals for your research. Often, schools have rat colonies or purchase animals for student research.

**TABLE C–2**
**Sample Informed Consent Form**

Students taking PSY 455, Research Design, are investigating the effects of noise and sleep deprivation on anxiety.

If you participate in this study, you will be deprived of sleep for two nights and exposed to common city noise for one hour. During that hour, you will be asked to fill out two questionnaires, and your pulse and blood pressure will be measured several times.

You will be asked to spend two nights in a special dorm room so that your sleep can be monitored. In addition, it will take 90 minutes for the noise treatment and measures to be completed.

You will receive $20 for participating in the study.

Physical injury, psychological injury, or deception are not part of this study. In addition, all your responses and answers will be held confidential. No one other than the investigators will see information about your particular responses.

Any questions you have regarding this project should be addressed to the investigators or to Dr. _____, faculty supervisor.

If you agree to participate in this study, please sign the following statement.

- - - - - - - - - - - - - - - - - - - - - - - - - - - - - - - - - - - - - - - - - - - - - - - - - - - - -

I have read the above Consent Form and understand the proposed project. I consent to participate in this study. I understand that I can quit the study at any time. Finally, I will be paid $20 whether or not I complete the study.

_____
Signature                    Date

## REDUCING THREATS TO CONSTRUCT VALIDITY

After ensuring that your study has adequate power, we would like to be able to tell you that you can take it easy and relax. Unfortunately, however, you can't relax. Power is not your only concern when conducting psychological research. You must also ensure that the construct validity of your results is not destroyed by:

1. Researchers failing to conduct your study in an objective, standardized way, or
2. Participants reacting to how they think you want them to react to the treatment, rather than reacting to the treatment itself.

***Researcher Effects.***     If you use more than one investigator, you may be able to detect researcher effects by including the researcher as a factor in your design. In other words, randomly assign participants to both a condition and to a researcher. If you have two treatment conditions (A and B) and two researchers (1 and 2), you would have four conditions: (1) A1, (2) B1 (conditions run by researcher 1), and (3) A2 and (4) B2 (conditions run by researcher 2).

Then, do an analysis of variance (ANOVA) using researcher as a factor to see whether different researchers got different results.[3]

However, using ANOVA to detect researcher effects is not the solution to reducing researcher effects for two reasons. First, this statistical approach will only tell you whether one researcher is getting different results than other researchers. If all your researchers are biased, you may not get a significant researcher effect. (Besides, if you are the only researcher, you can't use researcher as a factor in an ANOVA.) Second, and more importantly, detecting researcher effects is not the same as preventing researcher effects.

To prevent researcher effects, you must address the three major causes of researchers failing to conduct studies in an objective and standardized manner. What are these causes? First, researchers may not know how to behave because the procedures for how the researchers should conduct the study have not been spelled out. Second, researchers may not follow those procedures. Third, the researchers may strongly expect or hope for participants to behave in certain ways.

### Loose Protocol Effect: The Importance of Developing a Protocol.

Often, the researchers aren't behaving in an objective and standardized way because of the *loose protocol effect:* The instructions aren't detailed enough. Fortunately, the loose protocol effect can avoided.

Before you start your study, carefully plan everything out. As a first step, you should write out a set of instructions that chronicles the exact procedure for each participant. These procedures should be so specific that by reading and following your instructions, another person could run your participants the same way you do.

To make your instructions specific, you might want to write a computer program based on these instructions. Since computers don't assume anything, writing such a program forces you to spell out everything down to the last detail. If you can't program, just write the script as if a robot were to administer the study. Write out each step, including the actual words that researchers will say to the participants. The use of such a script will help standardize your procedures, thus reducing threats to validity.

Once you have a detailed draft of your protocol, give it a test run. For example, to ensure that you are as specific as you think you are, pretend to be a participant and have several different people run you through the study using *only* your instructions. See how the different individuals behave. This may give you clues as to how to tighten up your procedures. In addition, you should run several practice participants. Notice whether you change procedures in some

---

[3] You may want to consult with your professor as to the type of ANOVA you should use. There is some debate as to whether conventional ANOVA should be performed or whether a "random effects" model should be used.

subtle way across participants. If so, adjust your instructions to get rid of this variability.

At the end of your test runs, you should have a detailed set of instructions that you and any co-investigator can follow to the letter. To double-check your protocol, see Table C–3.

***Inspiring the Troops to Avoid Researcher Effects.*** Unfortunately, even if you write out your *protocol* (procedures) in detail, you or your co-investigators may still fail to follow that protocol. To avoid the *researcher failure to follow protocol effect,* you need to make sure that: (1) all investigators know the procedures, and (2) that everyone is motivated to follow the procedures.

To make sure investigators learn the procedures, you should hold training sessions. Supervise investigators while they practice the procedures on each other and on practice participants.

Once researchers know the right way to run the study, the key is to make sure that they are motivated to run the study the same way every time. To increase researchers' motivation to be consistent, you might have them work in pairs. While one researcher runs the participants, the other will listen in through an intercom or watch through a one-way mirror. You may even wish to record research sessions.

If your researchers still have trouble following procedures, you may need to automate your study. For instance, you might use a computer to present instructions, administer the treatment, or collect the dependent measure. Computers have the reputation for following instructions to the letter, so using a computer may help standardize your procedures. Of course, computers aren't the only machines that can help you. Some of the machines that could help you give instructions and present stimuli include automated slide projectors, tape recorders, and videotape players. Countless other devices can be used to record your data accurately, from electronic timers and counters to noise-level meters.

***Researcher Expectancy Effect.*** The final source of researcher bias is the *researcher expectancy effect:* Researchers' expectations are affecting the results. You can take three steps to prevent the researcher expectancy effect:

1. Be very specific about how investigators are to conduct themselves. Remember, researcher expectancies probably affect the results by changing the investigator's behavior rather than by causing the investigator to send a telepathic message to the participants.
2. Don't let the investigators know the hypothesis.
3. Don't let investigators know what condition the participant is in—making the investigator "*blind.*" Although making investigators blind is easiest in drug experiments where participants take either a placebo or the real drug, you can make investigators blind in non-drug experiments.

**TABLE C–3**
**Protocol Checklist**

How will you manipulate your treatment variables?

How will you measure your dependent (criterion) variables?

How many participants will you need?

Do you have your professor's permission to conduct the study?

Do you have a suitable place to run your participants?

How will you get your participants?

If you are using animals, how will they be cared for?

What will you do with your animals after the study?

If you are using human participants, how will you make your sign-up sheets available to potential participants?

Have you included a description of the study (including how long it takes) on the sign-up sheet?

Will participants be rewarded for volunteering to be in your study (such as money or extra credit)?

If you are conducting an experiment, how will you assign participants to condition?

Have you written out a detailed research protocol?

If you are using human participants, have you developed a consent form?

If you are using human participants, have you written out the oral instructions you will give your participants?

If you are using human participants, have you written out what you will say during debriefing?

If volunteers are college students seeking extra credit, how will you notify professors about which students participated?

Will you inform participants about the outcome of your study? How?

For example, if you present stimuli in booklets, you can design your booklets so that booklets for different conditions look very similar. In that way, an investigator running a group of participants might not know what condition each participant is in. For some studies, you may be able to use a second investigator who does nothing except collect the dependent measure. This second investigator could easily be kept in the dark as to what condition the participant was in.

***Review of Researcher Effects.***    Whether you are the only investigator or one of a team of investigators, researcher effects may bias your results. Therefore, you should always try to prevent the loose protocol effect, the failure to follow protocol effect, and the researcher expectancy effect.

## PARTICIPANT EFFECTS

Unfortunately, in psychological research, you must be aware not only of researcher effects, but also of *participant effects:* Participants may see through the study and try to play along with what the investigator wants. Fortunately, there are various ways of preventing participants' expectancies from biasing your results.

***Preventing Participants' Expectancies.***    For starters, you might make your researcher blind to reduce the chance that the participant will get any ideas from the researcher. In experimental investigations, you might use a be-tween-subject design rather than a within-subject design because participants who are exposed to only one treatment condition are less likely to guess the hy-pothesis than participants who are exposed to all treatment conditions.

***Placebo Treatments.***    A related tactic is to prevent participants from knowing whether they are in the comparison or treatment condition. There-fore, if you have comparison condition(s), use placebo treatment(s) rather than "no treatment" condition(s). That way, all groups think they are receiving the treatment. Thus, any treatment effect you find will not be due to participants changing their behavior because they expect the treatment to have an effect.

***Unobtrusive Recording.***    Participants are less likely to know the hypothe-sis if they don't know what you are measuring. Obviously, if they don't even know they are being observed—as in some field studies—they won't know what you are measuring. Thus, if your hypothesis is an obvious one, you might try to do a field study.

Although field studies lend themselves to unobtrusive recording, unobtru-sive recording can even occur in a laboratory study. That is, participants will as-sume that if you are not in the room with them, you are not observing them. However, thanks to one-way mirrors and intercoms, you can monitor partici-pants' behavior from the next room.

***Unobtrusive Measures.***    Even if the participant knows you are watching, the participant doesn't have to know *what* you are watching. That is, you can use unobtrusive measures. For example, you might put the participant in front of a computer and ask the participant to type an essay. Although the participant thinks you are measuring the essay's quality, you could have the computer pro-grammed to monitor speed of typing, time in between paragraphs, number of errors made, and times a section was rewritten. In addition, you might also have tape-recorded and videotaped the participant, monitoring his or her facial expressions, number of vocalizations, and loudness of vocalizations.

***Research Realism.***    Rather than trying to obscure or confuse participants as to the purpose of the study, you might try to prevent participants from think-ing about the purpose of the study. How? By designing a study that has a high degree of *research realism:* a study that involves participants in the task. Re-search realism means that participants aren't constantly saying to themselves: "What does the researcher really want me to do?" or "If I were a typical person, how would I behave in this situation?" Note that research realism doesn't mean the study is like real life; it means that participants are engrossed in the task. In this age of video games, even a fairly artificial task can be very high in research realism.

## Ethics Summary

Before now, you might have been surprised to see research realism and other strategies for reducing participant effects in a section on ethics. However, you now know that planning an ethical study involves taking into account many factors. Not only must you ensure the safety of your participants, but you must also demonstrate the validity of your methods. To avoid overlooking an important ethical consideration, consult Table C–4, Appendix A, and your professor.

# BEYOND THE PROPOSAL: THE PILOT STUDY

Even after you have carefully designed your study, modified it based on comments from your instructor, and been given your professor's go-ahead to run it, you may still want to run several participants (friends, family members, other members of the class) just for practice. By running practice participants, you'll get some of the "bugs" out of your study. Specifically, by running and debriefing practice participants, you will discover:

1. whether participants perceived your manipulation the way you intended;
2. whether you can perform the study the same way every time or whether you need to spell out your procedures in more detail;
3. whether you are providing the right amount of time for each of the research tasks and whether you are allowing enough time in between tasks;
4. whether your instructions were clear;
5. whether your cover story was believable;
6. whether you need to revise your stimulus materials;
7. how participants like the study;
8. how long it takes you to run and debrief a participant.

In short, running practice participants helps you to fine-tune your study. Because running practice participants is so useful, many professional investigators run enough practice participants to constitute a small study—what researchers call a *pilot study*.

# CONDUCTING THE ACTUAL STUDY

The dress rehearsal is over. Final changes in your proposal have been made. Now you are ready for the real thing—you are ready to "run" your study! This section will show you how.

**TABLE C-4**
**Research with Human Participants: An Ethics Checklist**

Is a physically unpleasant stimulus going to be used in your study? If so:

**1.** Is this fact clearly stated

    **a.** on the sign-up sheet?

    **b.** on the consent form?

**2.** Have you considered alternatives that would be less unpleasant?

**3.** Have you limited the intensity of this stimulus?

**4.** Have you taken steps to reduce potential harm to your participants caused by a physically unpleasant stimulus?

Are you going to use stress of some sort (such as sense of insecurity or failure, assault upon values, fatigue, or sleep deprivation) in your study? If so:

**1.** Is this fact clearly stated

    **a.** on the sign-up sheet?

    **b.** on the consent form?

**2.** Have you considered alternatives that would be less stressful?

**3.** Have you limited the intensity of this stimulus?

**4.** Have you taken steps to reduce potential harm to your participants caused by a psychologically unpleasant stimulus?

What will you do if participants exhibit signs of harm (for instance, crying, disoriented behavior)?

Are you prepared to describe the purpose and nature of your study to your participants during debriefing?

Will you use deception in your study? If so, what will you tell participants during debriefing?

Are you aware that participants can quit your study at any time? If a participant does drop out, will you give your participants credit for participating? Is this fact stated on the informed consent form? Is this fact part of your instructions to the participants?

What educational gain do you think participants will obtain from participating in your study?

How will you ensure the confidentiality of each participant's data?

## Establishing Rapport

As you may imagine, some of your prospective participants may be apprehensive about the study. Participants often aren't sure whether they are in the right place, or even whether the researcher is a Dr. Frankenstein.

To put your participants at ease, let them know they are in the right place and be courteous. You should be both friendly and businesslike. The expert investigator greets the participant warmly, pays close attention to the participant, and seems concerned that the participant know what will happen in the study. The expert investigator is obviously concerned that each participant is treated humanely and that the study is done professionally.

Being professional doesn't hurt how participants view you. Why? First, most participants like knowing that they are involved in something important.

Second, some will view your efficiency as a way of showing that you value their time—which you should.

So, how can you exude a professional manner? Some novice investigators think that they appear professional when they act aloof and unconcerned. Nothing could be less professional. Participants are very turned off by a disinterested attitude. They feel that you don't care about the study and that you don't care about them.

To appear professional, you should be neatly dressed, enthusiastic, well-organized, and prompt. "Prompt" may be an understatement. You should be ready and waiting for your participants at least 10 minutes before the study is scheduled to begin. Once your participants arrive, concentrate exclusively on the job at hand. Never ask a participant to wait a few minutes while you socialize with friends.

What do you lose by being a "professional" investigator? Problem participants. If you seem enthusiastic and professional, your participants will also become involved in doing your study—even if the tasks are relatively boring. Thus, if you are professional in your manner and attitude, you will probably not even have to ask the participants to refrain from chatting throughout the study. Similarly, if you are professional, participants will stop asking questions about the study if you say, "I'll explain the purpose at the end of the study."

After you have established rapport, you need to give your participants instructions. To get participants to follow instructions to the letter, you might:

1. be repetitive;
2. have participants read the instructions;
3. orally paraphrase those instructions;
4. run participants individually;
5. invite participants to ask questions;
6. have participants demonstrate that they understand the instructions by quizzing them or by giving them a practice trial before beginning the study.

Once the study has begun, try to follow the procedure to the letter. Consistently following the same procedures improves power and reduces the possibility of bias. Therefore, don't let participants change your behavior by reinforcing or punishing you. For instance, imagine you are investigating *long-term memory*. You want to expose participants to information and then see what they can write down. However, if you do this, participants may be writing down information that is in *short-term memory*. Thus, you would not be assessing long-term memory. Therefore, you add a counting backwards task that should virtually eliminate all of the information from short-term memory. Specifically, in your memory study, participants are exposed to information, are supposed to count backwards from a number like 781 by three's for 20 seconds, and then are asked to recall the information. Ideally, their recall will represent only what they have in long-term memory. Unfortunately, many participants will find the counting task unpleasant, embarrassing, or simply an unwanted nuisance. Consequently, some participants will thank you for telling them they can stop; others will plead nonverbally for you to stop. Clearly, you cannot let any of these strategies stop you from making them count backwards for the full 20 seconds. If you vary your procedures from participant to participant based on each participant's individual whims, your study will have questionable validity.

## Debriefing

Once the study is over, you should debrief your participants. In debriefing, you should first try to find out whether the participants suspected the hypothesis. Simply ask participants what they thought the study was about. Then, explain the purpose of your study.

If you deceived your participants, you need to make sure they are not upset about the deception. You also need to make sure that they understand why deception was necessary. Participants should leave the study appreciating the fact that there was one and only one reason you employed deception: It was the only way to get good information about an important issue.

Making sure participants accept your rationale for deception is crucial for three reasons. First, you don't want your participants to feel humiliated or angry. Second, if they get mad, they may not only be mad at you, but also at psychologists in general. Perhaps that anger or humiliation will stop them from visiting a psychologist when they need help. Third, the unhappy participant may spread the word about your deception, ruining your chances of deceiving other participants.

After explaining the purpose of the study, you should answer any questions the participants have. Although answering questions may sometimes seem like a waste of time, you owe it to your participants. They gave you their time, now it's your turn.

After participants' questions and doubts have been dealt with, give them an opportunity to rate how valuable they felt the study was. These ratings: (1) encourage you to be courteous to your participants; (2) let you know whether your study is more traumatic than you originally thought; and (3) make participants feel that you respect them because you value their opinions.

After the rating, you should assure participants that their responses during the study will be kept confidential. Tell them that no one but you will know their responses. Then, ask the participants not to talk about the study because it is still in progress. For example, you might ask them not to talk about the study until next week. Finally, you should thank your participants, escort them back to the waiting area, and say good-bye.

## PROTECTING DATA: CONFIDENTIALITY

You might think that once a participant leaves the study, your responsibilities to that participant end. Wrong! You are still responsible for guaranteeing the participant's privacy. Knowledge about a given participant is between you (the investigator) and the participant—*no one else*. Never violate this confidentiality. To ensure confidentiality, you should take the following precautions:

1. Assign each participant a number. When you refer to a given participant, always use the assigned number—never that participant's name.
2. Never store a participant's name and data in a computer—this could be a computer hacker's delight.
3. If you have participants write their names on booklets, tear off and destroy the cover of the booklet after you have analyzed the data.
4. Store a list of participants and their numbers in one place, and the data with the participants' numbers on it in another place.
5. Watch your mouth. There is rarely a reason to talk casually about a participant's behavior. Even if you don't mention any names, other people may guess or think they have guessed the identity of your participant. We realize that it is hard to keep a secret. But to talk freely about someone who participated in your study is to betray a trust. Furthermore, keeping secrets will, for many of you, be an important part of your professional role: Therapists, researchers, consultants, lawyers, and physicians all must keep their clients' behaviors confidential.

# *Appendix D*

# MARKETING YOUR RESEARCH SKILLS IN THE REAL WORLD

In this course, you have learned how to conduct and evaluate research. In the process, you have refined your ability to think critically, logically, and creatively. Furthermore, you have demonstrated the ability to plan and complete projects. In short, you now possess some highly marketable skills.

## ABILITY TO ASK QUESTIONS

One of the skills you have refined is the ability to ask concise and cogent questions. Not only have you formulated your own research questions, but you have also learned how to question research findings.

Your mastery of the art of question asking—often called critical thinking—will be respected by researchers and non-researchers alike. On a superficial level, this skill will help you because people frequently will judge you based on the kinds of questions you ask. From your questions, people will decide how educated, informed, and intelligent you are. The key to impressing interviewers is often not what you know, nor who you know, but what you ask.

On a deeper level (and the reason job interviewers like applicants who ask good questions), the ability to question is vital to job success. When people make disastrous decisions, it's usually because they failed to ask the right questions. Because critical thinking is so vital to success, entrance exams for medical, law, business, and graduate schools incorporate tests of critical thinking.

### Ability to Ask Questions of Data

Although most intelligent people can ask intelligent questions, not all intelligent people can ask intelligent questions of data. To most people, data are data. But you know that not all data are created equal. That is, you know that how data are collected affects their validity. Before accepting data at face value, you try to determine what kind of design was used and whether that design was used properly. Thus, in looking at data from an "experiment," you ask how participants were assigned, how independence was achieved, how participant and experimenter bias were reduced, etc. In looking at results from an observational design, you would question anyone who would conclude that cause-effect statements could be made. In addition, you might ask if the results might be due to observer bias. The ability to question and interpret data will become increasingly important in the future: Computers can collect and store data, but they are not experts at interpreting it (Toffler, 1990).

In addition to questioning how data were collected, you also question how the data were analyzed. Your eyes no longer glaze over when you hear terms like "interaction," and "statistically significant." In fact, you are so familiar with data that you may be able to suggest alternative ways of presenting, interpreting, or analyzing existing information. In short, you are aware of what the analyses say—and what they don't.

## Ability to Get Answers

Although your finesse at scrutinizing, interpreting, and using existing data is very marketable, your most marketable asset may be your ability to create new data. That is, not only do you know how to ask questions, you know how to ask questions to get answers. In short, your experience in turning abstract questions into specific testable hypotheses will be very useful.

In a related way, your experience in generating operational definitions will also be useful. By operationalizing variables, you can turn unanswerable questions into answerable ones. Thus, the question: "Will a diet plan be a financial success?" becomes the question: "Will a diet plan with these features, marketed in this way, get X number of sales at Z price?"

You might be surprised at how rare and how valued the skill of operationalizing variables is. Even very intelligent people are mystified by individuals who can find answers to hard questions. For example, a lawyer was defending a cartoonist in a libel suit. The other side was suing over an allegedly insulting and defamatory cartoon, claiming that everyone knew who the devious cartoon character was supposed to be. The cartoonist's lawyer was so apprehensive about the case that he hired a psychologist to help him in selecting the jury. However, even with the right jury, the lawyer was concerned: How could he defend his client against such a subjective charge? The psychologist mentioned that one way to answer such a question would be to survey people in the community and ask them who, if anybody, they thought the cartoon looked like. The lawyer's response: "You mean you could do that?!" This true story shows that although you may tend to undervalue your ability to get answers, others won't.

## Making Logical Arguments

In this course, you have also refined your ability to think logically. You have had to be explicit about your logic and the assumptions you made. In writing introduction and discussion sections, you have practiced spelling out the rationale and assumptions behind your thinking.

## Making Logical Arguments Supported by Data

In writing introduction, results, and discussion sections, not only have you argued logically, but you have used data to support your arguments. You have used data to support the assumptions behind your arguments as well as to support your conclusions.

In addition to using data to support your conclusions, you can challenge questionable conclusions, even if those conclusions appear to be supported by data. For example, because you are aware of the limits of correlational data, you know that the statement, "Profits have increased since Jim took over. Therefore, Jim is a good manager" is not necessarily true. In short, you are well aware of the uses and abuses of data.

## Communicating Complex or Technical Information

In this course, you have not only learned to think creatively, critically, and logically, but you have also articulated your reasoning. You have spelled out the rationale behind: (1) your hypothesis, (2) the procedures you used, (3) the analyses you chose, and (4) the conclusions you made. In addition, you have summarized the results of other studies, some of which contained complex and technical information. Your ability to present complex information in an understandable manner should be an asset, no matter what profession you enter.

## Planning and Completing Projects

Thus far, we have mentioned that, by carrying out a research project, you demonstrated an ability to:

1. collect data,
2. think logically,
3. articulate both your logic and your assumptions,
4. ask questions, and
5. analyze and interpret data.

However, these are only some of the skills you used in carrying out your research project. As is the case in designing and implementing any kind of project, you had to take initiative, map out all your steps, anticipate potential flaws and problems, challenge your basic assumptions, choose from among several alternative courses of action, prepare a timeline, overcome inevitable obstacles to your progress, aggregate all the information, come to a conclusion, and compile the final report. We can't imagine a more strenuous test of your planning and problem-solving abilities.

## Selling Yourself

Clearly, you have much to offer a prospective employer. To get a good job, however, you must convince your employer that you have these skills. Your initial efforts to convince an employer of your value will involve sending a resume and cover letter. To help you, we have prepared a sample resume (please see Box D-1).

Prospective employers will want you to be able to back up your claims about your abilities. To convince employers that you have the skills you claim, use your skills at constructing operational definitions to describe yourself in objective and quantifiable terms. For example, don't say, "I am a good student"; instead, say "I have a 3.7 grade point average." To help convince employers of your abilities, you may want to send them copies of your final research report. The report demonstrates your ability to write reports and finish projects.

Once you have convinced your prospective employers of your skills, you will have to convince them that these skills will generalize to the job. That is, your prospective employer might say, "Sure, you're a good student and had a rigorous class, but how do I know you will do well at our company?" To show the value of your skills to their company, you should give specific examples of how your skills would apply to the job.

Although Table D-1 should give you a general idea of how research skills might apply to business, you will want your examples to be so specific and relevant that the interviewer could visualize you succeeding on the job. Of course, to generate these specific examples, you must learn as much about the job as possible before the interview. (As we've implied all along, everything boils down to having done your research.)

Despite your best efforts, some interviewers may not feel that your skills will generalize to their business. Some may say, "If you were a business major, I'd hire you without reservation. But you're not." At this point, it may be tempting to give up. After all, the interviewer is judging you on the basis of a superficial criterion—face validity. Although you may be sorely tempted to quit, don't.

Instead, try to see whether you can make a case for yourself on the basis of face validity. Mention any courses or internships you have had in business.

Because face validity has a big impact in the real world, you may want to acquire experiences that will improve the face validity of your candidacy. Fortunately, because face validity is superficial, it's often easy to acquire. For example, you can improve the face validity of your candidacy by:

1. picking up the jargon of business by subscribing to business-related publications such as the *Wall Street Journal;*
2. doing a survey for a company (even free of charge), so you can put it on your resume;
3. doing research in the area in which you want a job. For example, one of our students wanted a job in personnel, so she did a research project on productivity and sent it to a prospective employer. She got the job and is now a director of personnel.

## BOX D–1
## SAMPLE RESUME

RESUME
Ms. Ima Sharpe
100 Resource Drive
City of Industry, CA 76278
(426) 754-5533

*OBJECTIVE:* To be an asset to your company through the application of my skills in writing, logical thinking, organizing, research, communication, and leadership.

*EDUCATION:* B.A. The Wright University

Major: Psychology
Senior Thesis: Reducing errors on a motor task

*WRITING SKILLS:* The rigors of conducting good research have honed my competencies in research proposal and reporting writing.

—I received an "A" for my research proposal.
—My research report was handed out in class as an example of how a research report should be written.

*LOGICAL THINKING SKILLS:* Training in research methodology has finely tuned my inductive and deductive reasoning. These powers of critical thinking are vital for optimal problem solving in any business situation:

—independent thinking
—ability to recognize problems
—ability to ask the right questions
—ability to make the abstract concrete
—ability to generate possible solutions
—ability to recognize the flaws of each solution
—ability to determine the best solution through research and analysis of relevant variables

*ORGANIZATIONAL SKILLS:* In order to plan, execute, interpret, and apply research I have developed and demonstrated organizational skills:

—arranged for experimental facilities and equipment
—recruited participants
—supervised and conducted an experiment
—organized The Wright University's Annual Rat Olympics

*(continued)*

*(continued from previous page)*

*RESEARCH SKILLS:* As a consequence of my course in research design I know many research techniques:

—how to set up timetables for studies
—survey research
—experimental research
—library research
—how to use computer packages to analyze data
—how to interpret statistics

*ORAL PRESENTATION SKILLS:* To speak about research effectively I had to make the complex sound simple, the technical sound basic. To speak convincingly about research I had to be a good salesperson.

—I presented an experimental report at a regional psychology conference.
—I received an A+ for a verbal critique of technical research in class.

*LEADERSHIP:*

—President of Psi Chi
—Vice-president of the Student Experimental Psychology Club

Reference: My research methods professor.

In addition to marketing your general problem-solving skills, you may want to market your specific research skills. These skills might be especially attractive to a small firm. Small companies may find that your ability to do research will save them from paying large fees to outside research consulting firms.

There are many ways in which a small firm might be able to use your research skills. For example, you might conduct research relating to the company's workers. In this capacity, you might design surveys to assess workers' attitudes and opinions toward the company. Alternatively, you could assess the impact of training programs and/or policy changes on productivity.

You might also do some research to get feedback from customers. This could be as simple as designing questionnaires to find out who your customers are and what they like about your company or it could be more complex. For instance, you might do research that would pretest the effectiveness of the ads your company is designing. Or, you might evaluate the effectiveness of a new advertising campaign. You may end up saving the company a lot of money by telling them where not to spend their advertising dollars.

Another avenue would be to use consumer input to develop a new product or service. For example, you might question customers regarding features they

**TABLE D–1**

**Similarities between Executives and Researchers**

| Executive | Researcher |
|---|---|
| Identifies problem | Identifies problem |
| Collects background data on problem | Collects background data on problem |
| Makes proposals to collect other needed information | Makes proposals to collect other needed information |
| Establishes timeline | Establishes timeline |
| Attends to detail | Attends to detail |
| Analyzes data | Analyzes data |
| Reports findings | Reports findings |

desire in a product, the cost they are willing to tolerate, where they would buy such a product, etc. Such advance planning could save your company from creating another Edsel.

If you want a job in which you are constantly involved in research, there are several careers you should consider. If you enjoy the hands-on, interpersonal part of research, but don't like the writing, planning, and statistical aspects, you could become a field interviewer or a telephone interviewer for the government or for a survey research organization. Or you might be able to get a job at a mental hospital as a psychological test administrator.

If you desire a job that would fully immerse you in research, you should consider market research and research assistant jobs. Market research is one of the fastest growing fields in the country. Primarily, you would conduct and analyze consumer surveys, but you might be able to do some laboratory research. Market researchers are hired not only by market research firms, but also by advertising agencies and by large companies.

Research assistant jobs are not as common, but they can be found. Many of these jobs focus on *evaluation research*. The purpose of evaluation research is to determine whether a program (job training program) or treatment (wellness center) is working. Thus, large hospitals and the federal government do a substantial amount of evaluation research.

Other jobs involve analyzing data the government has collected. The federal government collects data about almost anything you can imagine—from people's attitudes toward life to how much meat they buy. The government needs research assistants to help analyze the data collected from the census and from numerous other surveys.

There are also jobs working for institutions who do research for the federal government. For example, universities and large research companies (Rand Company, Battelle) that receive government money to do research often have

**TABLE D–2**

**Specific Jobs That Would Be Available to a Good Research Design Student and Courses That Would Help in Obtaining That Job**

| JOB TITLE | SUPPLEMENTARY COURSE(S) |
|---|---|
| Business person | Accounting/Economics |
| Interviewer | Public Speaking/Theater |
| Laboratory Assistant | Neuropsychology w/lab |
| Marketing Researcher | Marketing |
| Newspaper Reporter | English/Journalism |
| Personnel Administrator | Personnel Psychology |
| Public Health Statistician | Biology |
| Public Opinion Researcher | Computer Science |
| Research Assistant—Company | Computer Science |
| Research Assistant—Government | Computer Science |
| Research Assistant—Hospital | Biology w/lab |
| Research Assistant—Mental Health | Psychological testing |
| Technical Writer | English/Journalism |
| Professional Psychologist | Graduate degree necessary. Advanced courses in statistics and research methods increase chances of acceptance into graduate school. |

research assistant jobs. In addition, some universities also have jobs for laboratory assistants. Usually, lab assistants maintain the university's animal laboratory.

## CONCLUSIONS

As you know, conducting research requires the ability to define problems clearly, propose solutions to those problems, and implement those solutions *on time.* In performing your projects, you demonstrated initiative in problem-solving, attention to detail, logical thought, and the ability to write clearly. In short, you are able to ask questions and get answers. Virtually all employers need people with your skills.

Certain employers (research firms) will immediately recognize that they need your skills. Other employers, equally desperate for your skills, may not recognize that they need you. You will need to convince them by using your persuasive ability and the strategies we suggested earlier. In addition, you may want to improve the appearance of your application by taking courses or taking on jobs that will improve its face validity (please see Table D–2). Good luck!

# *Appendix E*

# STATISTICS AND RANDOM NUMBERS TABLES

## INTRODUCTION TO STATISTICAL TABLES

To analyze statistical data correctly, you must choose the correct statistical test. Often, the type of test depends on what type of data you have. That is, you will do one kind of test if you have nominal data, another kind of test if you have interval data. This fact is summarized below:

| SCALE OF MEASUREMENT | EXAMPLE | SUMMARY STATISTIC (AVERAGE) | MEASURE OF CORRELATION | TYPICAL STATISTICAL ANALYSIS |
|---|---|---|---|---|
| Nominal | When numbers represent categories, such as 1 = Democrat, 2 = Republican, 3 = Independent | Mode (most common score) or simply describe the percentage of participants in each category | Phi coefficient | Chi-square |
| Ordinal | Ranks | Median (middle score) | Spearman's rho | Mann-Whitney "u" (if testing two groups), Kruskal-Wallis (testing more than 2 groups), Friedman test (within-subjects design) |
| Interval | Rating scales | Mean | Pearson $r$ | t-test, ANOVA |
| Ratio | Height, magnitude estimation | Mean | Pearson $r$ | t-test, ANOVA |

Another factor that determines whether you have chosen the right statistic is whether you are using a within-subjects design (comparing each participant with him- or herself) or a between-subjects design. For example, if you were using a within-subjects design, you would not use a between-subjects ANOVA or an independent groups t-test. Instead, you would use a dependent groups t-test or a within-subjects ANOVA.

Finally, you must also consider the number of conditions you are comparing. If you are only comparing two conditions, you can use a t-test. If you are comparing more than two conditions, you cannot use a t-test. Instead, you would use ANOVA (if you have interval or ratio data).

These facts are summarized below:

| TYPE OF DATA | NUMBER OF CONDITIONS | |
| --- | --- | --- |
| | Two | More than 2 |
| Nominal, between-subjects | Chi-square | Chi-square |
| Nominal, within-subjects or matched pairs | McNemar Test | Cochran Q Test |
| Ordinal, between-subjects | Mann-Whitney Test | Kruskal-Wallis Test |
| Ordinal, within-subjects or matched pairs | Wilcoxon Matched Pair | Friedman Test |
| Interval/Ratio, between-subjects | Independent groups t-test or between-subjects ANOVA | Between-subjects ANOVA |
| Interval/Ratio, within-subjects or matched subjects | Dependent t-test or within-subjects ANOVA | Within-subjects ANOVA |

# DIRECTIONS FOR USING TABLE E–1

Find the row that has the same number of degrees of freedom that your study had (for the simple experiment, that row will have a number that is two less than the number of participants you had). Then, unless you have a one-tailed test, read across until you find the column corresponding to your level of significance. The number in that cell will be the critical value of "t" for your study. To be statistically significant, the absolute value of "t" that you obtain from your study must be greater than the value you found in the table. For example, suppose df = 40 and $p < .05$ (two-tailed test). In that case, to be statistically significant, the absolute value of the "t" you calculated must be greater than 2.021.

**TABLE E–1**
**Critical Values of *t***

| | LEVEL OF SIGNIFICANCE FOR TWO-TAILED *T*-TEST | | | |
|---|---|---|---|---|
| *DF* | .1 | .05 | .02 | .01 |
| 1 | 6.314 | 12.706 | 31.821 | 63.657 |
| 2 | 2.920 | 4.303 | 6.965 | 9.925 |
| 3 | 2.353 | 3.182 | 4.541 | 5.841 |
| 4 | 2.132 | 2.776 | 3.747 | 4.604 |
| 5 | 2.015 | 2.571 | 3.365 | 4.032 |
| 6 | 1.943 | 2.447 | 3.143 | 3.707 |
| 7 | 1.895 | 2.365 | 2.998 | 3.499 |
| 8 | 1.860 | 2.306 | 2.896 | 3.355 |
| 9 | 1.833 | 2.262 | 2.821 | 3.250 |
| 10 | 1.812 | 2.228 | 2.764 | 3.169 |
| 11 | 1.796 | 2.201 | 2.718 | 3.106 |
| 12 | 1.782 | 2.179 | 2.681 | 3.055 |
| 13 | 1.771 | 2.160 | 2.650 | 3.012 |
| 14 | 1.761 | 2.145 | 2.624 | 2.977 |
| 15 | 1.753 | 2.131 | 2.602 | 2.947 |
| 16 | 1.746 | 2.120 | 2.583 | 2.921 |
| 17 | 1.740 | 2.110 | 2.567 | 2.898 |
| 18 | 1.734 | 2.101 | 2.552 | 2.878 |
| 19 | 1.729 | 2.093 | 2.539 | 2.861 |
| 20 | 1.725 | 2.086 | 2.528 | 2.845 |
| 21 | 1.721 | 2.080 | 2.518 | 2.831 |
| 22 | 1.717 | 2.074 | 2.508 | 2.819 |
| 23 | 1.714 | 2.069 | 2.500 | 2.807 |
| 24 | 1.711 | 2.064 | 2.492 | 2.797 |
| 25 | 1.708 | 2.060 | 2.485 | 2.787 |
| 26 | 1.706 | 2.056 | 2.479 | 2.779 |
| 27 | 1.703 | 2.052 | 2.473 | 2.771 |
| 28 | 1.701 | 2.048 | 2.467 | 2.763 |
| 29 | 1.699 | 2.045 | 2.462 | 2.756 |
| 30 | 1.697 | 2.042 | 2.457 | 2.750 |
| 40 | 1.684 | 2.021 | 2.423 | 2.704 |
| 60 | 1.671 | 2.000 | 2.390 | 2.660 |
| 120 | 1.658 | 1.980 | 2.358 | 2.617 |
| ∞ | 1.645 | 1.960 | 2.326 | 2.576 |

# DIRECTIONS FOR USING TABLE E-2

Find the row that has the same number of degrees of freedom that your study had (To calculate your df, subtract one from the number of columns in your chi-square, then subtract one from the number of rows, and then multiply those results together. Thus, with a 2 × 2 chi-square, you would have 1 df [because 1 × 1 = 1], and with a 3 × 2 chi-square, you would have 2 df [because 2 × 1 = 2]). Then, unless you have a one-tailed test, look across until you find the column corresponding to your level of significance. The number in that cell will be the critical value of "chi-square" for your study. To be statistically significant, your chi-square value must be greater than the value you found in the table. For example, if df = 1 and your significance level is $p < .05$, then your chi-square value must be greater than 3.84146.

**TABLE E–2**
**Critical Values for Chi-Square Tests**

| | LEVEL OF SIGNIFICANCE | | | |
|---|---|---|---|---|
| DF | .10 | .05 | .01 | .001 |
| 1 | 2.70554 | 3.84146 | 6.63490 | 10.828 |
| 2 | 4.60517 | 5.99147 | 9.21034 | 13.816 |
| 3 | 6.25139 | 7.81473 | 11.3449 | 16.266 |
| 4 | 7.77944 | 9.48773 | 13.2767 | 18.467 |
| 5 | 9.23635 | 11.0705 | 15.0863 | 20.515 |
| 6 | 10.6446 | 12.5916 | 18.5476 | |
| 7 | 12.0170 | 14.0671 | 18.4753 | 24.322 |
| 8 | 13.3616 | 15.5073 | 20.0902 | 26.125 |
| 9 | 14.6837 | 16.9190 | 21.6660 | 27.877 |
| 10 | 15.9871 | 18.3070 | 23.2093 | 29.588 |
| 11 | 17.2750 | 19.6751 | 24.7250 | 31.264 |
| 12 | 18.5494 | 21.0261 | 26.2170 | 32.909 |
| 13 | 19.8119 | 22.3621 | 27.6883 | 34.528 |
| 14 | 21.0642 | 23.6848 | 29.1413 | 36.123 |
| 15 | 22.3072 | 24.9958 | 30.5779 | 37.697 |
| 16 | 23.5418 | 26.2962 | 31.9999 | 39.252 |
| 17 | 24.7690 | 27.5871 | 33.4087 | 40.790 |
| 18 | 25.9894 | 28.8693 | 34.8053 | 42.312 |
| 19 | 27.2036 | 30.1435 | 36.1908 | 43.820 |
| 20 | 28.4120 | 31.4104 | 37.5662 | 45.315 |
| 21 | 29.6151 | 32.6705 | 38.9321 | 46.797 |
| 22 | 30.8133 | 33.9244 | 40.2894 | 48.268 |
| 23 | 32.0069 | 35.1725 | 41.6384 | 49.728 |
| 24 | 33.1963 | 36.4151 | 42.9798 | 51.179 |
| 25 | 34.3816 | 37.6525 | 44.3141 | 52.620 |
| 26 | 35.5631 | 38.8852 | 45.6417 | 54.052 |
| 27 | 36.7412 | 40.1133 | 46.9630 | 55.476 |
| 28 | 37.9159 | 41.3372 | 48.2782 | 56.892 |
| 29 | 39.0875 | 42.5569 | 49.5879 | 58.302 |
| 30 | 40.2560 | 43.7729 | 50.8922 | 59.703 |
| 40 | 51.8050 | 55.7585 | 63.6907 | 73.402 |
| 50 | 63.1671 | 67.5048 | 76.1539 | 86.661 |
| 60 | 74.3970 | 79.0819 | 88.3794 | 99.607 |
| 70 | 85.5271 | 90.5312 | 100.425 | 112.317 |
| 80 | 96.5782 | 101.879 | 112.329 | 124.839 |
| 90 | 107.565 | 113.145 | 124.116 | 137.208 |
| 100 | 118.498 | 124.342 | 135.807 | 149.449 |

SOURCE: This table is taken from Table 8 of the *Biometrika Tables for Statisticians* (Vol. 1, 3rd ed.) by E. S. Pearson and H. O. Hartley (Eds.), 1970, New York: Cambridge University Press. Used with the kind permission of the Biometrika trustees.

# DIRECTIONS FOR USING TABLE E–3

Look up the degrees of freedom for the effect (the first df) and the error term (the 2nd df). Thus, if you had 1 df for the effect and 25 for the error term, you would look for the effect under the column labeled "1" for the row labeled "25." There, you would find the critical value 4.24. To be statistically significant at the $p < .05$ level, your obtained F would have to be greater than 4.24.

**TABLE E-3**

**Critical Values of F for $p < .05$**

| 1ST DF / 2ND DF | 1 | 2 | 3 | 4 | 5 | 6 | 7 | 8 | 9 | 10 |
|---|---|---|---|---|---|---|---|---|---|---|
| 1 | 161.4 | 199.5 | 215.7 | 224.6 | 230.2 | 234.0 | 236.8 | 238.9 | 240.5 | 241.9 |
| 2 | 18.51 | 19.00 | 19.16 | 19.25 | 19.30 | 19.33 | 19.35 | 19.37 | 19.38 | 19.40 |
| 3 | 10.13 | 9.55 | 9.28 | 9.12 | 9.01 | 8.94 | 8.89 | 8.85 | 8.81 | 8.79 |
| 4 | 7.71 | 6.94 | 6.59 | 6.39 | 6.26 | 6.16 | 6.09 | 6.04 | 6.00 | 5.96 |
| 5 | 6.61 | 5.79 | 5.41 | 5.19 | 5.05 | 4.95 | 4.88 | 4.82 | 4.77 | 4.74 |
| 6 | 5.99 | 5.14 | 4.76 | 4.53 | 4.39 | 4.28 | 4.21 | 4.15 | 4.10 | 4.06 |
| 7 | 5.59 | 4.74 | 4.35 | 4.12 | 3.97 | 3.87 | 3.79 | 3.73 | 3.68 | 3.64 |
| 8 | 5.32 | 4.46 | 4.07 | 3.84 | 3.69 | 3.58 | 3.50 | 3.44 | 3.39 | 3.35 |
| 9 | 5.12 | 4.26 | 3.86 | 3.63 | 3.48 | 3.37 | 3.29 | 3.23 | 3.18 | 3.14 |
| 10 | 4.96 | 4.10 | 3.71 | 3.48 | 3.33 | 3.22 | 3.14 | 3.07 | 3.02 | 2.98 |
| 11 | 4.84 | 3.98 | 3.59 | 3.36 | 3.20 | 3.09 | 3.01 | 2.95 | 2.90 | 2.85 |
| 12 | 4.75 | 3.89 | 3.49 | 3.26 | 3.11 | 3.00 | 2.91 | 2.85 | 2.80 | 2.75 |
| 13 | 4.67 | 3.81 | 3.41 | 3.18 | 3.03 | 2.92 | 2.83 | 2.77 | 2.71 | 2.67 |
| 14 | 4.60 | 3.74 | 3.34 | 3.11 | 2.96 | 2.85 | 2.76 | 2.70 | 2.65 | 2.60 |
| 15 | 4.54 | 3.68 | 3.29 | 3.06 | 2.90 | 2.79 | 2.71 | 2.64 | 2.59 | 2.54 |
| 16 | 4.49 | 3.63 | 3.24 | 3.01 | 2.85 | 2.74 | 2.66 | 2.59 | 2.54 | 2.49 |
| 17 | 4.45 | 3.59 | 3.20 | 2.96 | 2.81 | 2.70 | 2.61 | 2.55 | 2.49 | 2.45 |
| 18 | 4.41 | 3.55 | 3.16 | 2.93 | 2.77 | 2.66 | 2.58 | 2.51 | 2.46 | 2.41 |
| 19 | 4.38 | 3.52 | 3.13 | 2.90 | 2.74 | 2.63 | 2.54 | 2.48 | 2.42 | 2.38 |
| 20 | 4.35 | 3.49 | 3.10 | 2.87 | 2.71 | 2.60 | 2.51 | 2.45 | 2.39 | 2.35 |
| 21 | 4.32 | 3.47 | 3.07 | 2.84 | 2.68 | 2.57 | 2.49 | 2.42 | 2.37 | 2.32 |
| 22 | 4.30 | 3.44 | 3.05 | 2.82 | 2.66 | 2.55 | 2.46 | 2.40 | 2.34 | 2.30 |
| 23 | 4.28 | 3.42 | 3.03 | 2.80 | 2.64 | 2.53 | 2.44 | 2.37 | 2.32 | 2.27 |
| 24 | 4.26 | 3.40 | 3.01 | 2.78 | 2.62 | 2.51 | 2.42 | 2.36 | 2.30 | 2.25 |
| 25 | 4.24 | 3.39 | 2.99 | 2.76 | 2.60 | 2.49 | 2.40 | 2.34 | 2.28 | 2.24 |
| 26 | 4.23 | 3.37 | 2.98 | 2.74 | 2.59 | 2.47 | 2.39 | 2.32 | 2.27 | 2.22 |
| 27 | 4.21 | 3.35 | 2.96 | 2.73 | 2.57 | 2.46 | 2.37 | 2.31 | 2.25 | 2.20 |
| 28 | 4.20 | 3.34 | 2.95 | 2.71 | 2.56 | 2.45 | 2.36 | 2.29 | 2.24 | 2.19 |
| 29 | 4.18 | 3.33 | 2.93 | 2.70 | 2.55 | 2.43 | 2.35 | 2.28 | 2.22 | 2.18 |
| 30 | 4.17 | 3.32 | 2.92 | 2.69 | 2.53 | 2.42 | 2.33 | 2.27 | 2.21 | 2.16 |
| 40 | 4.08 | 3.23 | 2.84 | 2.61 | 2.45 | 2.34 | 2.25 | 2.18 | 2.12 | 2.08 |
| 60 | 4.00 | 3.15 | 2.76 | 2.53 | 2.37 | 2.25 | 2.17 | 2.10 | 2.04 | 1.99 |
| 120 | 3.92 | 3.07 | 2.68 | 2.45 | 2.29 | 2.17 | 2.09 | 2.02 | 1.96 | 1.91 |
| ∞ | 3.84 | 3.00 | 2.60 | 2.37 | 2.21 | 2.10 | 2.01 | 1.94 | 1.88 | 1.83 |

## Using Table E–4 to Compute Trend Analyses

Suppose you had the following significant effect for sugar on aggression.

|  | df | SS | MS | F |
|---|---|---|---|---|
| Sugar Main Effect | 2 | 126.95 | 63.47 | 6.35 |
| Error Term | 21 | 210.00 | 10.00 |  |

How would you compute a trend analysis for this data? In other words, how would you calculate an F-ratio for the linear and quadratic effects so that you could complete the following ANOVA table?

|  | df | SS | MS | F |
|---|---|---|---|---|
| Sugar Main Effect | 2 | 126.95 | 63.47 | 6.35 |
| Linear Component | 1 |  |  |  |
| Quadratic Component | 1 |  |  |  |
| Error Term | 21 | 210.00 | 10.00 |  |

Before you generate an F-ratio, you must have a sum of squares. To compute the sum of squares for a trend, you must first get the sum of the scores for each condition. Simply add up all the scores for each condition or, if you prefer, multiply each condition's average by the number of scores making up each average. Thus, if one condition's mean was 10 and there were 8 scores making up that mean, the sum for that condition would be $8 \times 10$ or 80.

Next, arrange these totals, starting with the total for the lowest level of independent variable and ending with the total for the highest level of the independent variable. That is, place the sum for the condition with the lowest level of the independent variable first, the sum for the condition with the next highest level of the independent variable next, and so on. In our example, you would order your sums like so:

### Total Number of Violent Instances per Condition

| AMOUNT OF SUGAR | TOTAL NUMBER OF VIOLENT INSTANCES |
|---|---|
| 0 mg | 10.0 |
| 50 mg | 50.0 |
| 100 mg | 12.0 |

Now, you are ready to consult the tables of orthogonal polynomials in Table E–4. Because this example involves three conditions, you would look for the three-condition table. The table reads:

### Three-Condition Case

|  | TREND | |
|---|---|---|
|  | 1 (Linear) | 2 (Quadratic) |
| CONDITION 1 | −1 | 1 |
| CONDITION 2 | 0 | −2 |
| CONDITION 3 | 1 | 1 |
| WEIGHTING FACTOR | 2 | 6 |

To get the numerator for the sum of squares for the linear trend, multiply the sum for the lowest level of the independent variable by the first value in the Linear column of the table (−1), the second sum by the second value in the Linear column of the table (0), and the third sum by the third value in the Linear column of the table (+1). Next, get a sum by adding these three products together. Then, square that sum. So, for the sugar example we just described, you would do the following calculations:

$$[(-1 \times 10) + (0 \times 50) + (1 \times 12)]^2$$

or

$$(-10 + 0 + 12)^2$$

or

$$(2)^2$$

or

$$4$$

To get the denominator for the sum of squares, multiply the weighting factor for the linear trend (2) by the number of observations in each condition. Because there were eight observations in each condition, the denominator would be 16 (2 × 8). The sum of squares linear would be the numerator (4) divided by the denominator (16), which equals .25.

Once you have computed the sum of squares for the linear trend, the rest is easy. All you have to do is compute F-ratio by dividing the mean square linear by the mean square error and then see if that result is significant.

Calculating the mean square linear involves dividing the sum of squares linear by the degrees of freedom linear. Because the degrees of freedom for any trend is always 1.00, you could divide your sum of squares (.25) by 1.00 and get .25. Or, you could simply remember that a trend's mean square is always the same as its sum of squares.

Getting the mean square error is also easy: just find the mean square error in the printout that was used to test the overall main effect. In this example, that would be 10.0.

So, to get the F-value for this linear comparison, you would divide the mean square for the comparison (.25) by the mean square error used on the overall main effect (10.0). Thus, the $F$ would be .25/10, or .025. Because the $F$ is below 1.00, this result is obviously not significant.

But how large would the $F$ have had to be to be significant? That depends on how many trends you were analyzing. If you had decided to look only at the linear trend, the significant $F$ at the .05 level would have to exceed the value in the F-table for 1 degree of freedom (the $df$ for any trend) and 21 degrees of freedom, the $df$ for the error term. That value is 4.32.

However, if you are going to analyze more than one trend, you must correct for the number of $F$s you are going to compute. The correction is simple: you divide the significance level you want (say .05), by the number of trends you will test. In this example, you are computing two $F$s. Therefore, you should use the $F$ for .05/2 or .025. So, in this example, you would only declare a trend significant if the $F$ for that trend exceeds the critical value for $F(1,21)$ at the .025 level: 5.83.

Obviously, the $F$ for the linear component, $F(1,21) = .025$, falls far short of the critical value of 5.83. But what about the quadratic component? To determine whether the quadratic component is significant, you would follow the same steps as before. The only difference is that you would look at the Quadratic column of the table instead of the Linear column.

Thus, you would first multiply the treatment sums by the constants listed in the Quadratic column, add them together, and square that sum. In other words,

$$((1 \times 10) + (-2 \times 50) + (1 \times 12))^2$$

or

$$(10 + (-100) + 12)^2$$

or

$$(-78)^2$$

or

$$6084$$

Then, you would divide 6084 by 8 (the number of observations in each condition) × 6 (the weighting factor for the quadratic effect). So, $SS$ quadratic is 6084/(8 × 6) = 6084/48 = 126.7, as is the $MS$ quadratic ($SS$ (126.7)/$df$ (1) = $MS$ (126.7)).

To get the $F$, you would divide the $MS$ quadratic by $MS$ error. Therefore, the $F$ would be 126.7/10 = 12.67. As before, the critical value for the comparison is the F-value for the .025 significance level with 1 and 21 degrees of freedom: 5.83. Because our $F$ of 12.67 exceeds the critical value of 5.83, we have a statistically significant quadratic trend.

So, our complete ANOVA table, including the linear and quadratic components, would be as follows:

|  | df | SS | MS | F |
|---|---|---|---|---|
| Sugar Main Effect | 2 | 126.95 | 63.47 | 6.35* |
| Linear | 1 | 0.25 | 0.25 | 0.02 |
| Quadratic | 1 | 126.70 | 126.70 | 12.67* |
| Error Term | 21 | 210.00 | 10.00 |  |

*Significant at .05 level.

From looking at the table, you see that if you add up the degrees of freedom for all the trends involved in the sugar main effect (1 + 1), you get the total $df$ for the main effect (2). More importantly, note that if you add up the sum of squares for the components (126.70 + .25), you get the sum of squares for the overall effect (126.95). This fact gives you a way to check your work. Specifically, if the total of the sums of squares for all the components does not add up to the sum of squares for the overall effect, you have made a mistake.

**TABLE E-4**

## Coefficients of Orthogonal Polynomials

| CONDITION | 3-CONDITION CASE TREND | | 4-CONDITION CASE TREND | | | 5-CONDITION CASE TREND | | | |
|---|---|---|---|---|---|---|---|---|---|
|  | 1 (LIN) | 2 (QUAD) | 1 (LIN) | 2 (QUAD) | 3 (CUBIC) | 1 (LIN) | 2 (QUAD) | 3 (CUBIC) | 4 |
| 1 | −1 | 1 | −3 | 1 | −1 | −2 | 2 | −1 | 1 |
| 2 | 0 | −2 | −1 | −1 | 3 | −1 | −1 | 2 | −4 |
| 3 | 1 | 1 | 1 | −1 | −3 | 0 | −2 | 0 | 6 |
| 4 |  |  | 3 | 1 | 1 | 1 | −1 | −2 | −4 |
| 5 |  |  |  |  |  | 2 | 2 | 1 | 1 |
| Weighting Factor | 2 | 6 | 20 | 4 | 20 | 10 | 14 | 10 | 70 |

| CONDITION | 6-CONDITION CASE TREND | | | | | 7-CONDITION CASE TREND | | | | | |
|---|---|---|---|---|---|---|---|---|---|---|---|
|  | 1 (LIN) | 2 (QUAD) | 3 (CUBIC) | 4 | 5 | 1 (LIN) | 2 (QUAD) | 3 (CUBIC) | 4 | 5 | 6 |
| 1 | −5 | 5 | −5 | 1 | −1 | −3 | 5 | −1 | 3 | −1 | 1 |
| 2 | −3 | −1 | 7 | −3 | 5 | −2 | 0 | 1 | −7 | 4 | −6 |
| 3 | −1 | −4 | 4 | 2 | −10 | −1 | −3 | 1 | 1 | −5 | 15 |
| 4 | 1 | −4 | −4 | 2 | 10 | 0 | −4 | 0 | 6 | 0 | −20 |
| 5 | 3 | −1 | −7 | −3 | −5 | 1 | −3 | −1 | 1 | 5 | 15 |
| 6 | 5 | 5 | 5 | 1 | 1 | 2 | 0 | −1 | −7 | −4 | −6 |
| 7 |  |  |  |  |  | 3 | 5 | 1 | 3 | 1 | 1 |
| Weighting Factor | 70 | 84 | 180 | 28 | 252 | 28 | 84 | 6 | 154 | 84 | 924 |

SOURCE: This table is adapted from Table VII of *Statistics* (pp. 662–664) by W. L. Hays, 1981, New York: Holt, Rinehart & Winston. Copyright © 1982 by Holt, Rinehart & Winston, Inc. Adapted by permission.

## Using Table E–5 to Compute Post Hoc Tests

Post hoc tests, such as the Tukey test, can be used after finding a significant main effect for a multilevel factor. These tests help determine which conditions are significantly different from one another.

To see how you could use table E-5 to compute post hoc tests, suppose that an investigator uses twenty-four subjects (eight in each group) to examine the effect of color (blue, green, or yellow) on mood. As you can see from the following table, the investigator's ANOVA table reveals a significant effect of color.

| SOURCE | SUM OF SQUARES | DEGREES OF FREEDOM | MEAN SQUARE | F |
|--------|------|------|------|------|
| Color | 64 | 2 | 32.0 | 4.0* |
| Error | 168 | 21 | 8.0 | |

*Significant at .05 level.

The means for the three color conditions are

| Blue | Green | Yellow |
|------|-------|--------|
| 10.0 | 5.0 | 8.0 |

Now, the question is "Which conditions differ from one another?" Does yellow cause a different mood than green? Does blue cause a different mood than yellow? To find out, we need to do a post hoc test. For this example, we will do the Tukey test.

The formula for the Tukey test is

$$\frac{\text{Mean 1} - \text{Mean 2}}{\sqrt{(\text{MSE} \times 1/\text{number of observations per condition})}}$$

Because the mean square error is 8 (see original ANOVA table) and there are eight subjects in each group, the denominator in this example will always be:

$$\sqrt{(8 \times 1/8)}$$

or

$$\sqrt{8/8}$$

or

$$\sqrt{1}$$

or

$$1$$

The numerator will change, depending on what means you are comparing. Thus, if you are comparing blue and green, the numerator would be $10 - 5$ or 5. So, to see whether the blue and green conditions differ significantly, you would do the following calculations.

$$\frac{\underset{\text{(blue mean) (green mean)}}{10.0 - 5.0}}{\sqrt{(8 \times 1/8)}} = \frac{5.0}{\sqrt{1}} = \frac{5.0}{1.0} = 5.0$$

To find out whether 5.0 is significant, go to table E-5 and look at the column labeled 3 because you have three means you are comparing. Then, go down and look at the row numbered 21 because you have 21 degrees of freedom in your error term (as you can see by looking at the original ANOVA table). The value in that table is 3.57. This is the critical value that you will use in all your comparisons. If your Tukey statistic for a pair of means is larger than this critical value, there is a significant difference between conditions. Because 5.0 is greater than 3.57, your result is significant at the .05 level.

But, do blue and yellow differ? To find out, compute the Tukey statistic.

$$\frac{10.0 - 8.0}{\sqrt{(8 \times 1/8)}} = \frac{2.0}{\sqrt{1}} = \frac{2.0}{1.0} = 2.0$$

Because 2.0 is less than our critical value of 3.57, the difference between blue and yellow is not statistically significant at the .05 level.

Do yellow and green differ?

$$\frac{8.0 - 5.0}{\sqrt{(8 \times 1/8)}} = \frac{3.0}{\sqrt{1}} = \frac{3.0}{1.0} = 3.0$$

Because 3.0 is less than our critical value of 3.57, the difference between yellow and green is not statistically significant at the .05 level.

**TABLE E-5**
**Critical Values for the Tukey Test at the .05 Level of Significance**

| | | | | NUMBER OF MEANS | | | | |
|---|---|---|---|---|---|---|---|---|
| $df$ error | 2 | 3 | 4 | 5 | 6 | 7 | 8 | 9 |
| 10 | 3.15 | 3.88 | 4.33 | 4.65 | 4.91 | 5.12 | 5.30 | 5.46 |
| 11 | 3.11 | 3.82 | 4.26 | 4.57 | 4.82 | 5.03 | 5.20 | 5.35 |
| 12 | 3.08 | 3.77 | 4.20 | 4.51 | 4.75 | 4.95 | 5.12 | 5.27 |
| 13 | 3.06 | 3.73 | 4.15 | 4.45 | 4.69 | 4.88 | 5.05 | 5.19 |
| 14 | 3.03 | 3.70 | 4.11 | 4.41 | 4.64 | 4.83 | 4.99 | 5.13 |
| 15 | 3.01 | 3.67 | 4.08 | 4.37 | 4.59 | 4.78 | 4.94 | 5.08 |
| 16 | 3.00 | 3.65 | 4.05 | 4.33 | 4.56 | 4.74 | 4.90 | 5.03 |
| 17 | 2.98 | 3.63 | 4.02 | 4.30 | 4.52 | 4.70 | 4.86 | 4.99 |
| 18 | 2.97 | 3.61 | 4.00 | 4.28 | 4.49 | 4.67 | 4.82 | 4.96 |
| 19 | 2.96 | 3.59 | 3.98 | 4.25 | 4.47 | 4.65 | 4.79 | 4.92 |
| 20 | 2.95 | 3.58 | 3.96 | 4.23 | 4.45 | 4.62 | 4.77 | 4.90 |
| 21 | 2.95 | 3.57 | 3.95 | 4.22 | 4.43 | 4.60 | 4.75 | 4.88 |
| 30 | 2.89 | 3.49 | 3.85 | 4.10 | 4.30 | 4.46 | 4.60 | 4.72 |
| 40 | 2.86 | 3.44 | 3.79 | 4.04 | 4.23 | 4.39 | 4.52 | 4.63 |
| 60 | 2.83 | 3.40 | 3.74 | 3.98 | 4.16 | 4.31 | 4.44 | 4.55 |
| 120 | 2.80 | 3.36 | 3.68 | 3.92 | 4.10 | 4.24 | 4.36 | 4.47 |
| ∞ | 2.77 | 3.31 | 3.63 | 3.86 | 4.03 | 4.17 | 4.29 | 4.39 |

SOURCE: This table is abridged from Table 29 of the *Biometrika Tables for Statisticians* (Vol. 1, 3rd ed.) by E. S. Pearson and H. O. Hartley (Eds.), 1970, New York: Cambridge University Press. Used with the kind permission of the Biometrika Trustees.

TABLE E-6
**Table of Random Numbers**

| | | | | | | | | | | | | | | | | | | |
|---|---|---|---|---|---|---|---|---|---|---|---|---|---|---|---|---|---|---|
| 5 | 28 | 80 | 31 | 99 | 77 | 39 | 23 | 69 | 0 | 15 | 49 | 100 | 2 | 22 | 64 | 73 | 92 | 53 |
| 29 | 71 | 48 | 4 | 87 | 32 | 17 | 90 | 89 | 9 | 99 | 34 | 58 | 8 | 61 | 73 | 98 | 48 | 89 |
| 90 | 94 | 19 | 80 | 70 | 36 | 2 | 17 | 48 | 63 | 82 | 39 | 85 | 26 | 65 | 27 | 81 | 69 | 83 |
| 62 | 66 | 48 | 74 | 86 | 6 | 66 | 41 | 15 | 65 | 6 | 41 | 85 | 57 | 84 | 64 | 70 | 39 | 64 |
| 67 | 54 | 3 | 54 | 23 | 40 | 25 | 95 | 93 | 55 | 59 | 46 | 77 | 55 | 49 | 82 | 26 | 8 | 87 |
| 75 | 27 | 62 | 15 | 81 | 36 | 22 | 26 | 69 | 42 | 44 | 91 | 55 | 0 | 84 | 48 | 68 | 65 | 5 |
| 70 | 19 | 7 | 100 | 94 | 53 | 81 | 76 | 73 | 40 | 22 | 58 | 49 | 42 | 96 | 18 | 66 | 89 | 8 |
| 75 | 7 | 9 | 20 | 58 | 92 | 41 | 42 | 79 | 26 | 91 | 44 | 63 | 87 | 45 | 21 | 23 | 15 | 6 |
| 55 | 70 | 10 | 23 | 25 | 73 | 91 | 72 | 29 | 47 | 93 | 58 | 21 | 75 | 80 | 52 | 9 | 12 | 36 |
| 83 | 42 | 62 | 53 | 55 | 12 | 11 | 54 | 19 | 2 | 45 | 43 | 67 | 13 | 5 | 74 | 30 | 93 | 11 |
| 94 | 20 | 76 | 23 | 65 | 72 | 55 | 27 | 44 | 19 | 10 | 72 | 50 | 67 | 83 | 18 | 67 | 22 | 49 |
| 51 | 10 | 72 | 9 | 59 | 47 | 66 | 32 | 17 | 6 | 75 | 8 | 54 | 22 | 37 | 3 | 46 | 83 | 95 |
| 99 | 50 | 22 | 2 | 92 | 9 | 98 | 9 | 40 | 23 | 34 | 8 | 63 | 58 | 49 | 31 | 70 | 39 | 83 |
| 9 | 12 | 3 | 23 | 2 | 0 | 82 | 75 | 36 | 63 | 71 | 19 | 78 | 26 | 66 | 63 | 16 | 75 | 7 |
| 20 | 40 | 50 | 29 | 51 | 82 | 81 | 47 | 73 | 69 | 74 | 100 | 80 | 37 | 14 | 67 | 1 | 90 | 92 |
| 90 | 92 | 54 | 52 | 74 | 0 | 88 | 71 | 45 | 49 | 38 | 54 | 80 | 2 | 85 | 42 | 75 | 47 | 20 |
| 25 | 6 | 92 | 30 | 19 | 31 | 22 | 41 | 0 | 22 | 79 | 87 | 84 | 61 | 6 | 19 | 67 | 97 | 60 |
| 13 | 12 | 94 | 76 | 29 | 61 | 50 | 67 | 29 | 76 | 27 | 70 | 97 | 16 | 83 | 88 | 100 | 22 | 48 |
| 91 | 77 | 51 | 3 | 92 | 85 | 46 | 22 | 0 | 58 | 84 | 64 | 87 | 93 | 94 | 94 | 13 | 98 | 41 |
| 29 | 12 | 39 | 35 | 32 | 47 | 30 | 81 | 40 | 32 | 37 | 8 | 48 | 81 | 50 | 77 | 18 | 39 | 7 |
| 43 | 96 | 86 | 14 | 91 | 24 | 22 | 85 | 16 | 51 | 42 | 37 | 41 | 100 | 94 | 76 | 45 | 50 | 67 |
| 57 | 44 | 72 | 45 | 87 | 21 | 7 | 29 | 26 | 82 | 69 | 99 | 10 | 39 | 76 | 29 | 11 | 17 | 85 |
| 63 | 10 | 10 | 76 | 7 | 75 | 19 | 91 | 2 | 31 | 45 | 94 | 54 | 72 | 10 | 48 | 52 | 7 | 12 |
| 34 | 28 | 11 | 95 | 4 | 82 | 51 | 7 | 69 | 53 | 93 | 36 | 81 | 66 | 93 | 88 | 15 | 73 | 54 |

SOURCE: This table is taken from the Random numbers table in Appendix D of *Foundations of Behavioral Research,* 3rd ed. (pp. 642–643) by F. N. Kerlinger, 1986, New York: Holt, Rinehart & Winston. Copyright © 1986 by Holt, Rinehart & Winston. Reprinted by permission.

*Appendix F*
_____

# SAMPLE RESEARCH PAPER

Running head: BLACK UNIFORMS AND AGGRESSION

The Dark Side of Self Perception:

Black Uniforms and Aggression

Mark G. Frank and Thomas Gilovich

Cornell University

Abstract

Black is viewed as the color of evil and death in virtually all cultures. With this association in mind, we were interested in whether a cue as subtle as the color of a person's clothing might have a significant impact on the wearer's behavior. To test this possibility, we performed a laboratory experiment to determine whether wearing a black uniform can increase a person's inclination to engage in aggressive behavior. We found that participants who wore black uniforms showed a marked increase in intended aggression relative to those wearing white uniforms. Our discussion focuses on the theoretical implications of these data for an understanding of the variable, or "situated," nature of the self.

The Dark Side of Self Perception:

Black Uniforms and Aggression

A convenient feature of the traditional American Western film was the ease of which the viewer could distinguish the good guys from the bad guys: The bad guys wore the black hats. Of course, film directors did not invent this connection between black and evil, but built upon an existing association that extends deep into our culture and language. When a terrible thing happens on a given day, we refer to it as a "black day," as when the Depression was ushered in by the infamous "Black Thursday." We can hurt ourselves by "blackening" our reputation or be hurt by others by being "blacklisted," or "blackballed," or "blackmailed" (Williams, 1964). When the Chicago White Sox deliberately lost the 1919 World Series as part of a betting scheme, they became known as the Chicago Black Sox, and to this day the "dark" chapter in American sports history is known as the Black Sox Scandal. In a similar vein, Muhammed Ali has observed that we refer to white cake as "angel food cake" and dark cake as "devil's food cake."

These anecdotes concerning people's negative associations to the color black are reinforced by the research literature on color meanings. In one representative experiment, groups of college students and seventh graders who were asked to make semantic differential rating of colors were found to associate black with evil, death, and badness (Williams & McMurty, 1970). Moreover, this association between black and evil is not strictly an American or Western phenomenon, because college students in Germany, Denmark, Hong Kong, and India (Williams, Moreland, &

Underwood, 1970) and Ndembu tribesmen in Central Africa (Turner, 1967) all report that the color black connoted evil and death. Thus, Adams and Osgood (1973) concluded that black is seen, in virtually all cultures, as the color of evil and death.

The intriguing question is whether these associations influence people's behavior in important ways. For example, does wearing black clothing lead the wearer to actually act more aggressively?

This possibility is suggested by studies on anonymity and "deindividuation" which show that a person's clothing can affect the amount of aggression he or she expresses. In one study, female participants in a "learning" experiment were asked to deliver shocks to another participant whenever she made a mistake. Under the pretense of minimizing individual identities, one half of the participants wore nurses uniforms (a prosocial cue), and the other half wore outfits resembling Ku Klux Klan uniforms (an antisocial cue). As predicted, participants who wore nurses uniforms delivered less shock to the "learner" than did participants who wore the Ku Klux Klan uniforms, which demonstrates that the cues inherent in certain clothes can influence the wearer's aggressive behavior (Johnson & Downing, 1979).

Although such studies are suggestive, they involve rather contrived situations that raise troubling questions of experimental demand. Accordingly, we decided to seek parallel evidence for a link between clothing cues and aggressiveness by examining the effect of a much more subtle cue, the color of a person's uniform.

There are a couple of difficulties that confront any attempt to test whether wearing a black uniform tends to make a person more aggressive. First, any such test is fraught with the usual ethical problems involved in all research on human aggression. Second, since black is associated with violence, observers may be biased when judging the behavior of participants wearing black. The usual solution to these twin problems is to use some version of the bogus shock paradigm (Buss, 1961). However, we chose not to use this procedure because of the difficulty in finding participants who--given the publicity of Milgram's (1965, 1974) work--would not view the proceedings with extreme suspicion.

Our solution to these problems was to collect "behavioroid" data (Carlsmith, Ellsworth, & Aronson, 1976) in the form of the participants' intended aggressive behavior. Volunteers for an experiment on competition were led to believe that they would be vying against other participants in several competitive events. They were also led to believe that they could exercise some control over which events they were to participate in by selecting their 5 most preferred events from a list of 12. The 12 events varied in the amount of aggressiveness they called for, allowing us to use participants' choices as a measure of their reading to engage in aggressive action. By means of a suitable cover story, we elicited participants' choices twice: once individually when wearing their usual clothes, and later as a team of 3 wearing black or white jerseys. We hypothesized that wearing black jerseys would induce participants to view themselves as more mean and aggressive and thus would produce more of a "group shift" toward aggressive choices by participants wearing black jerseys than by those wearing white (Drabman & Thomas, 1977; Jaffe, Shapir, & Yinon, 1981; Jaffe & Yinnon, 1979).

Method

## Overview

Participants participated in groups of 3 in an experiment ostensibly on the "psychology of competition." Each group was told that they would be competing against another team of 3 on a series of five games of everyone's choosing. To find out their preferences, they were asked to individually rank order 5 activities from a group of 12. After making their choices, the participants were outfitted in either white or black uniforms in the guise of facilitating team identity. Then, while the experimenter was supposedly administering instructions to the other team, the 3 participants were told to discuss their individual choices and to decide as a group on the rank ordering of the five activities they would like to include in the competition. This second ranking allowed us to assess whether the participants would choose more aggressive games as a group after donning black uniforms than after putting on white uniforms. Finally, as an auxiliary measure of aggression, participants were administered a brief version of Murray's (1943) Thematic Apperception Test (TAT) to assess their level of aggressive ideation.

## Participants

The participants were 72 male students from Cornell University who were paid $3 for their participation. They were run

in groups of 3, with the members of each group unacquainted with
one another.

<u>Procedure</u>

As the participants reported for the experiment they were
brought together in one room and led to believe that another group
of participants was assembling in a different room. Participants
were told that:

> You will be competing, as a team, on a series of five games
> against another group of three participants who are waiting
> in the next room. I matched the two teams for size as you
> came in, so the contests should be fair. This study is
> designed to mimic real-life competition as closely as
> possible...[and so]...we want you to choose the games you
> want to play.

Participants were then given a list of descriptions of 12 games
and were asked to indicate, individually, which games they would
like to play. They were asked to choose 5 of the 12 games and to
rank order those 5. After reminding the participants not to
discuss their choices with one another, the experimenter left the
room, ostensibly to elicit the choices of the other team.

Upon his return, the experimenter collected the participants'
individual choices and stated that "now I would like you to make a
group decision as to which games you will play, because many times
people's preferences are so divergent that we need to use a group
choice to serve as a tie-breaker when deciding on which games to
play." The experimenter further explained that "to make the
experiment more like real-world competition and to build team

cohesion, I would like you to put these uniforms on over your
shirts. From now on you will be referred to as the black [white]
team." The participants were then given black or white uniforms
with silver duct-tape numerals (7,8, and 11) on the backs.

The experimenter once again left the room to allow the
participants to make their group choices and then returned after 5
minutes. He then explained,

> Now that I have everyone's individual and team selections, I
> will go and set up the five games that received the most
> votes. While I am doing this, I want you to complete a
> standard psychological task to get all of you in the same
> state of mind before we start.

Participants were asked to write a brief story about a scene
depicted in a TAT card (Card 18 BM from Murray's, 1943, original
series). Participants were given 4 minutes to write a story based
on the following questions: (a) what is happening in the picture?
(b) what is being thought by the characters in the picture? (c)
what has led up to this picture? and (d) what will happen to the
characters in the picture?

After 4 minutes the experimenter returned, collected the TAT
protocols, and thoroughly debriefed the participants. All
participants seemed surprised (and many disappointed) to learn
that the experiment was over. The debriefing interview also made
it clear that none of the participants had entertained the
possibility that the color of the uniforms might have been the
focus of the experiment.

Dependent Measures

The primary measure in this experiment was the level of aggressiveness involved in the games participants wanted to include in the competition. A group of 30 participants had earlier rated a set of descriptions of 20 games in terms of how much aggressiveness they involved. The 12 games that had received the most consistent ratings and that represented a wide spectrum of aggressiveness were then used as the stimulus set in this experiment. These 12 games were ranked in terms of these aggressiveness ratings and assigned point values consistent with their ranks, from the most aggressive (12, 11, and 10 points for "chicken fights," "dart gun duel," and "burnout," respectively) to the least aggressive (1, 2, and 3 points for "basket shooting," "block stacking," and "putting contest," respectively). Participants were asked to choose the five games that they wanted to include in the competition and to rank order their five choices in terms of preference. To get an overall measure of the aggressiveness of each participant's preferences, we multiplied the point value of his first choice by 5, his second choice by 4, and so forth, and then added these five products. When comparing the choices made by the participants individually (without uniforms), we compared the average individual choices of the 3 participants with their group choice.

The second dependent measure in this experiment was participants' responses to the TAT card. Participants' TAT stories were scored on a 5-point aggressiveness scale (Feshbach, 1955). Stories devoid of aggression received a score of 1, those with a little indirect aggression a score of 2, those with considerable indirect or a little direct aggression a 3, those with direct physical aggression a 4, and those with graphic violence a 5. These ratings were made by two judges who were unaware of the participants' condition. The judges' ratings were in perfect agreement on 47% of the stories and were within one point on another 48%.

## Results

The mean levels of aggressiveness in participants' individual and group choices are presented in Table 1. As expected, there was no difference in participants' individual choices across the two groups ($\underline{MS}$ = 113.4 vs. 113.5), because they were not wearing different-colored uniforms at the time these choices were made. However, the participants who donned black uniforms subsequently chose more aggressive games (mean change in aggressiveness = 16.8), whereas those who put on white uniforms showed no such shift (mean change = 2.4). A 2 X 2 mixed between/within ANOVA of participants' choices yielded a significant interaction between uniform color and individual/group choice $\underline{F}(1,22)$ = 6.14, $\underline{p}$<.05, indicating that the pattern of choices made by participants in black uniforms was different from that of those wearing white. Wearing black uniforms induced participants to seek out more aggressive activities, matched-pairs $\underline{t}(11)$ = 3.21, $\underline{p}$<.01; wearing white uniforms did not, matched-pairs $\underline{t}(11)$ = 1.00, $\underline{ns}$.

The participants who wore black uniforms also tended to express more aggressive ideation ($\underline{M}$ = 3.20) in their TAT stories than did participants wearing white uniforms ($M =$ 2.89), although this difference was not significant, $t < 1$.

## Discussion

The results of this experiment support the hypothesis that wearing a black uniform can increase a person's inclination to engage in aggressive behavior. Participants who wore black uniforms showed a marked increase in intended aggression relative to those wearing white uniforms.

It should be noted, however, that our demonstration involved only intended aggression. It did not involve actual aggression. It would have been interesting to have allowed our participants to compete against one another in their chosen activities and seen whether those in black jerseys performed more aggressively. We refrained from doing so because of ethical and methodological difficulties (i.e., the difficulty of objectively measuring aggression, especially given that observers tend to be biased toward viewing people wearing black uniforms as being more aggressive). Nevertheless, the results of this experiment make the important point that in a competitive setting at least, merely donning a black uniform can increase a person's willingness to seek out opportunities for aggression. If the wearing of a black uniform can have such an effect in the laboratory, there is every reason to believe that it would have even stronger effects on the playing field (or rink), where many forms of aggression are considered acceptable behavior.

One question raised by this research concerns the generality of the effect of uniform color on aggression. It is very unlikely that donning any black uniform in any situation would make a person more inclined to act aggressively. We do not believe, for example, that the black garments worn by Catholic clergymen or Hassidic Jews don't make them any more aggressive than their secular peers. Rather, it would seem to be the case that the semantic link between the color black and evil and aggressiveness would be particularly salient in domains that already possess overtones of competition, confrontation, and physical aggression.

With this in mind, any speculation about other domains in which analogous effects might be obtained should center on those areas that also possess inherent elements of force and confrontation. The actions of uniformed police officers and prison guards may be one such area. Is it the case, in other words, that the color of the uniforms worn by such individuals influences the amount of aggressiveness they exhibit in performing their duties? This intriguing possibility could readily be tested by examining archival indicators of aggression and violence involving police officers and prison guards, such as charges of police brutality and assaults on police officers (Mauro, 1984). These analyses could involve both cross-sectional comparisons of police departments (or prisons) with different-colored uniforms, as well as longitudinal comparisons within departments that have changed uniform colors. We should point out, however, that we strongly doubt whether there are any police departments or penal institutions in this country that issue black uniforms to their personnel, possibly out of implicit recognition of this article's central thesis. Nevertheless, the uniforms of police officers and prison guards do vary in color a great deal, from dark blue to light khaki. Thus, one might still expect to find an effect of uniform color on aggressiveness if the subsequent research alluded to above indicates that the uniform effect we have documented is indeed more than a simple dichotomous difference between black and nonblack uniforms.

Perhaps the most important question raised by this research concerns the exact mechanisms by which the color of a uniform might affect the behavior of the wearer. Our own explanation for this phenomenon centers upon the implicit demands on one's behavior generated by wearing a particular kind of uniform. To wear a certain uniform is to assume a particular identity, an identity that not only elicits a certain response from others but also compels a particular pattern of behavior from the wearer (Stone, 1962). Wearing an athletic uniform, for example, thrusts one into the role of athlete, and leads one to "try on" the image that such a role conveys. When the uniform is that of a football or hockey player, part of that image--and therefore part of what one "becomes"--involves toughness, aggressiveness, and "machismo." These elements are particularly salient when the color of one's uniform is black. Just as observers see those in black uniforms as tough, mean, and aggressive, so too does the person wearing that uniform (Bem, 1972). Having inferred such an identity, the person then remains true to the image by acting more aggressively in certain prescribed contexts.

More broadly construed, then, our results serve as a reminder of the flexible or "situated" nature of the self (Alexander & Knight, 1971; Goffman, 1959; Mead, 1934; Stone, 1962). Different situations, different roles, and even different uniforms can induce us to try on different identities. Around those who are socially subdued or shy, we become a vivacious extrovert; around true socialites, we may retreat into the more reserved role of resident intellectual. In the presence of family members, we play the role of learned scholar granted us by our advanced degrees; in the company of Nobel laureates, we think of ourselves less as scientists and more as amateur musicians, devoted fathers and mothers, or fun-loving globetrotters. Some of these identities that we try to adopt do not suit us, and they are abandoned. This sustains our belief that personalities are stable and reassures us that at our core lies a "true" self. To a surprising degree, however, the identities we are led to adopt do indeed fit, and we continue to play them out in the appropriate circumstances. Perhaps the best evidence for this claim is the existence of identity conflict, such as that experienced by college students who bring their roommates home to meet their parents. This is often a disconcerting experience for many students because they cannot figure out how they should behave or "who they should be"--with their parents they are one person and with their friends they are someone else entirely.

The present investigation demonstrates how a seemingly trivial environmental variable, the color of one's uniform, can induce such a shift in a person's identity. This is not to suggest, however, that in other contexts the direction of causality might not be reversed. The black uniforms worn by gangs like the Hell's Angels, for example, are no doubt deliberately chosen precisely because they convey the desired malevolent image. Thus, as in the world portrayed in the typical American Western, it may be that many inherently evil characters choose to wear black. However, the present investigation makes it clear that in certain contexts at least, some people become the bad guys because they wear black.

References

Adams, F. M., & Osgood, C. E. (1973). A cross-cultural study of the affective meanings of color. <u>Journal of Cross-Cultural Psychology, 4,</u> 135-156.

Alexander, C. N., & Knight, G. (1971). Situated identities and social psychological experimentation. <u>Sociometry, 34,</u> 65-82.

Bem, D. J. (1972). Self-perception theory. In L. Berkowitz (Ed.), <u>Advances in experimental social psychology</u> (Vol.6, pp.1-62). New York: Academic Press.

Carlsmith, J. M., Ellsworth, P. C., & Aronson, E. (1976). <u>Methods of research in social psychology.</u> Reading, MA: Addison-Wesley.

Drabman, R. S., & Thomas, M. H. (1977). Children's imitation of aggressive and prosocial behavior when viewing alone and in pairs. <u>Journal of Communication, 27,</u> 199-205.

Feshbach, S. (1955). The drive-reducing function of fantasy behavior. <u>Journal of Abnormal and Social Psychology, 50,</u> 3-11.

Goffman, E. (1959). <u>The presentation of self in everyday life.</u> New York:Doubleday.

Jaffe, Y., Shapir, N., & Yinon, Y. (1981). Aggression and its escalation. <u>Journal of Cross-Cultural Psychology, 12,</u> 21-36.

Johnson, R. D. & Downing, L. L. (1979). Deindividuation and valence of cues: Effects of prosocial and antisocial behavior. _Journal of Personality and Social Psychology, 37,_ 1532-1538.

Mauro, R. (1984). The constable's new clothes: Effects of uniforms on perceptions and problems of police officers. _Journal of Applied Social Psychology,14,_ 42-56.

Mead, G. H. (1934). _Mind, self, and society._ Chicago: University of Chicago Press.

Milgram, S. (1965). Some conditions of obedience and disobedience to authority. _Human Relations, 18,_ 57-76.

Milgram, S. (1974). _Obedience to authority._ New York: Harper.

Murray, H. A. (1943). _Thematic Apperception Test Manual._ Cambridge, MA: Harvard University Press.

Stone, G. P. (1962). Appearance and the self. In A. M. Rose (Ed.), _Human behavior and social process_ (pp.86-118). Boston: Houghton Mifflin.

Turner, V. (1967). _The forest of symbols: Aspects of Ndembu ritual._ Ithaca, NY: Cornell University Press.

Williams, J. E. (1964). Connotations of color names among Negroes and Caucasians. _Perceptual and Motor Skills, 18,_ 721-731.

Williams, J. E., & McMurty, C. A. (1970). Color connotations among Caucasian 7th graders and college students. _Perceptual and Motor Skills, 30,_ 701-713.

Williams, J. E., Moreland, J. K., & Underwood, W. I. (1970). Connotations of color names in the U.S., Europe, and Asia. Journal of Social Psychology, 82, 3-14.

Table 1

Mean Level of Aggressiveness Contained in Participants'

Chosen Activities as a Function of Uniform Condition

| Uniform color | Mean individual choice (without uniforms) | | Group choice (with uniforms) | | Change in aggression | |
|---|---|---|---|---|---|---|
| | M | SD | M | SD | M | SD |
| White | 113.4 | 23.9 | 115.8 | 25.4 | +2.4 | 8.5 |
| Black | 113.5 | 18.4 | 130.3 | 22.9 | +16.8 | 18.1 |

# *Appendix G*

# THE FIELD EXPERIMENT

## THE FIELD EXPERIMENT

What allows a randomized, laboratory experiment to establish causality? It is not a sterile lab filled with fancy equipment. Indeed, it is not the lab at all—it is random assignment.

You do not need a lab to randomly assign participants to groups. Therefore, if you do not want to do your experiment in a lab, you could conduct a *field experiment:* an experiment performed in a natural setting.

### Advantages of Doing the Field Experiment

Why would you want to leave the comfort of the lab to do a field experiment? There are four major reasons for leaving the lab:

1. the desire to generalize your results to different settings;
2. the desire to generalize your results to a different group of people;
3. the desire to ensure that participants are reacting to the treatment rather than feigning the reaction they think will please you; and
4. the desire for more power to detect a treatment's effect.

#### EXTERNAL VALIDITY

First, you might want to generalize your results beyond the laboratory setting. The controlled, isolated lab is a far cry from the chaotic, crowded world that we live in. Consequently, some people question whether an effect found in a lab would hold in a real-world setting. The field experiment lets you find out.

Second, you might want to generalize your results to people other than those who volunteer to be in psychology experiments. In most lab experiments, participants are students in introductory psychology courses. These students are probably not "typical" of the average person. In the field experiment, on the other hand, your participants can be anyone—even real people!

#### CONSTRUCT VALIDITY

Third, you might want to avoid lab experiments because volunteers for these experiments know they are in an experiment. Because they know the treatments aren't "real," their responses may be more of an act than an honest reaction to the treatment. Thus, rather than reacting to the treatment as they naturally would, they may act the way they think you want them to act. In other words, they may act to confirm your hypothesis.

To field experiment participants, on the other hand, the treatment is real. These participants aren't trying to confirm your hypothesis. In fact, they may not even know you're doing an experiment on them. Because of their naiveté, they are more likely to give natural responses.

### POWER

Fourth, you might leave the lab because you do not have enough volunteer participants. As you may remember from Chapter 6, the more participants you have, the more able you are to find significant effects. When confronted with having only a few people who might agree to come to the lab for your experiment, and a world of potential participants waiting for you outside the lab, you may decide to go where the participants are.

## Limitations of the Field Experiment

Although the field experiment *may* give you more power, more construct validity, and greater external validity, the field experiment is not an automatic cure-all. The field experiment may lack external, construct, and internal validity. Furthermore, field experiments may lack power, be unethical, and demand more time and energy than you would ever suspect.

### IS IT ETHICAL?

The first problem to consider is an ethical one. According to the American Psychological Association's Code of Ethics (1992), all participants for an experiment should be volunteers. Not only should participants be volunteers, but you should get their *informed consent* prior to their participation. That is, participants should have a good idea of what is going to happen to them and should give their written permission before the experiment begins. Furthermore, after the experiment, participants should be *debriefed:* informed about what they have just done and why.

These ethical guidelines may conflict with your research goals. You may not want to use volunteers because volunteers are atypical, but the guidelines suggest that you use volunteers. If you were forced to use volunteers, you might not want to tell them what the experiment was about so they wouldn't play along with your study. However, the guidelines recommend that human participants know what they are volunteering for. Finally, you may not want to debrief your participants for fear that your participants might tell other potential participants about the study. The ethical guidelines, on the other hand, recommend that you debrief participants so that participants get some benefit from their participation and so that you can remove any harm you may have inadvertently caused.

What's the solution to these thorny ethical issues? Unfortunately, there are no easy answers. Your desire for valid information must be weighed against participants' rights to privacy. Since you may not be able to weigh fairly participants' rights against your desires, you should consult informed individuals (such as, your research design professor) before doing a field experiment. In addition to consulting with your professor, you may also have to get your experiment approved by your institution's ethics committee.

Perhaps the easiest way to deal with ethical problems is to avoid violating the guidelines. For example, you might do a field experiment, but ask for volunteers, give informed consent, and debrief your participants. Under these conditions, you have lost some advantages of field experimentation, but you *may* still get participants that are more "typical" than laboratory participants and you *do* get to see whether your results generalize to a real-world setting.

A more controversial approach is to perform a field experiment on unsuspecting volunteers while they think they are waiting for an experiment to begin. For example, Latané (1968) had participants witness a theft while they were in a waiting room ostensibly waiting to start a laboratory experiment.

The "experiment in the waiting room" is a compromise between ethical principles and research goals. To meet the ethical guidelines requesting the use of volunteer participants, you lose the ability to get participants who are more like "real people" than volunteer participants and you lose the ability to overcome a shortage of volunteer participants.

To meet the research goal of seeing whether the effect would occur with naive participants, you violated the ethical guidelines for informed consent. Because participants signed up for one experiment, but ended up in another study, this kind of study raises serious ethical questions.


## EXTERNAL VALIDITY IS NOT GUARANTEED

If you think that by doing a field experiment you will get participants who represent the average person, you may be disappointed. In the "waiting room" study we just described, the participants are the same college sophomores who would participate in a lab study. Even doing an experiment in the field (like a shopping mall) won't insure that your participants will represent "the average person." In fact, in many field experiments, you may not know whom your participants represent. Sometimes, the only thing you can say is that participants "represented people who used the telephone booth at the Tarfield Mall between 2:00 P.M. and 4:00 P.M. during March 1996." Consequently, you may not be surprised by what Dipboye & Flanagan (1979) found when they examined published research in industrial psychology. They found that field research typically dealt with a rather narrow range of participants and generally had no more external validity than the lab studies.

## CONSTRUCT VALIDITY IS NOT GUARANTEED

Similarly, if you want to study naive participants, the field experiment may let you down. Former participants or talkative bystanders may talk about the experiment to potential participants and ruin everyone's naiveté. To illustrate this point, consider a field experiment conducted by Shaffer, Rogel, and Hendrik (1975) in the Kent State University Library. A confederate of the researcher sat down at a table occupied by a naive participant. After several minutes of studying, the confederate walked away from the table leaving behind several personal items. Sometimes the confederate asked the naive participant to watch his belongings (request condition), other times he said nothing (no request condition). Shortly after the confederate left the table, a "thief" appeared, went through the confederate's belongings, discovered a wallet, and quickly walked away with it. The dependent variable was whether participants tried to stop the thief. Results showed that 64% of the participants in the request condition tried to stop the thief, compared to only 14% in the no-request condition.

Imagine you were one of Shaffer et al.'s participants. After watching a thief steal a man's wallet, perhaps after trying to foil a robbery attempt, would you tell anyone about it? Let's say you told a friend about the incident and that friend says that she has heard of a similar incident. One night, she goes to the library to study. Shortly after she sits down, she finds herself approached by the same victim she's heard about, and witnessing the very crime you told her about. Not only has she lost her naiveté, but when she tells her friends about this, the whole school will know about the experiment.

Or, put yourself in the place of a curious bystander, say the reference librarian. You are working at the reference desk and out of the corner of your eye you observe two students sitting at a table. One student gets up and walks away leaving behind his books and several personal items. You go about your work. But then you notice a different man go up to the pile of belongings, rummage through them, pocket a wallet, and walk hurriedly away. What would you do? As a responsible employee, you would try to stop the thief. At the very least, you would report the incident to the authorities. The campus police arrive to get your statement, perhaps even to make an arrest. To stop the police investigation, the researcher explains that it's only an experiment. Students in the library strain to overhear the conversation with the police, and students question you endlessly about the incident. Soon, everyone on campus knows about the experiment.

Thus, a field experiment may end up having no more construct validity than a laboratory study *unless you take appropriate precautions.* Therefore, if you were doing Shaffer et al.'s study, you would try to collect all the data in one night to reduce the chances of participants talking to potential participants. Furthermore, to reduce the chance of innocent bystanders destroying participants' innocence, you would inform the library staff about the experiment.

## INTERNAL VALIDITY IS NOT GUARANTEED

A carelessly conducted field experiment may not only lack external and construct validity, but internal validity. Although all field experiments should have internal validity, some do not because of failure to randomly assign participants to groups, and because of mortality: participants dropping out of the study.

***Failure to Randomly Assign***    Most experimental designs rely on independent random assignment for their internal validity. Unfortunately, random assignment is much more difficult in the field than in the laboratory. Random assignment is especially difficult when you are manipulating an important, real-life treatment. Often real-world participants and their representatives do not believe that people should be randomly assigned to important treatments. Instead, they believe that people should be able to choose their own treatment.

To imagine the difficulties of random assignment in the field, suppose you wanted to study the effects of television violence on children's behavior. You approach parents and tell them that you want some children to watch certain non-violent television programs (for example, "Mister Rogers," "Sesame Street") and other children to watch violent television programs, such as "TV wrestling," boxing, and violent action/adventure shows. You may find that few parents will let you randomly assign their children to *either* condition. If you say, "I want to be able to assign your child to either one of these conditions," many parents will object. Some will say, "You can show my child 'Sesame Street,' but you're not going to make my kid watch violence and trash!" Other parents will say, "You can make my kid watch wrestling. I watch it all the time anyway. But not those other shows. They're on the same time as my shows. You're not going to make me sit around and watch childish junk!" However, the hassles with the parents may be nothing compared with the hassles of getting the children themselves to agree to random assignment.

Yet, with enough persistence (and enough money), you could probably get people to agree to random assignment. But once you've done that, you face a huge problem: How do you know that participants will watch the television shows you assigned? You cannot go to everyone's house. You cannot trust young children to carry out your instructions. You cannot trust parents to supervise the children because they may be busy with other tasks. Therefore, the prospect of using random assignment to determine children's television diets seems intimidating.

In fact, the idea of randomly assigning children to television-viewing seems so intimidating that most investigators researching the effects of TV have often avoided field experiments. This is unfortunate because such experiments would provide the strongest evidence about the effects of viewing violent television shows.

Have these researchers given up too soon? Cook and Campbell (1976) claim that researchers often give up on random assignment faster than they should. Cook and Campbell argue that random assignment can often be used in the field—if the researcher is creative.

In the case of researching the impact of television on children's behavior, researchers may have given up too soon. Perhaps researchers should approach a nursery school. If the nursery school would cooperate and get informed consent from the parents and children, the television-viewing could take place at the school as part of the children's ordinary routine. In this way, you would know that participants were getting the treatment they were assigned to.

***Mortality***    Unfortunately, even after you assign your participants to condition, they may not stay assigned. Mortality may raise its ugly head. That is, participants may drop out of your experiment before you collect the dependent measure. For example, suppose that you are doing the television violence experiment with nursery school children. As the study progresses, you find that participants are dropping out of the violent television condition (perhaps the kids are getting too violent or the parents are having second thoughts). However, participants are not dropping out of the non-violent condition. The fact that participants in one group are more likely to quit than participants in the other group threatens the study's internal validity. That is, if the violent television group is more aggressive, we cannot say whether this is due to the less aggressive children dropping out of the violent television group or to television violence causing children to be aggressive.

Usually, losing more participants from one group than the other is due to one of two reasons. First, the treatment is too intense. In such cases, the treatment should be toned down or eliminated. To use a manipulation that leads to such a high drop-out rate is often unethical. To take an extreme case of using an unethical level of treatment, suppose the television these children were watching was X-rated violence. In that case, mortality from the treatment group would be high (although we would hope that an ethics committee would prevent such a study from being conducted). Second, mortality from the treatment group will be higher than from the control group if the control group is merely left alone to engage in their normal activities. For example, if the experimental group was to watch a prescribed set of programs at home whereas the control group was simply allowed to do whatever they normally did at home, mortality would be higher in the experimental group. Therefore, the control group should always get some kind of treatment, even a placebo treatment.

## POWER MAY BE INADEQUATE

Not only is it easier to create an internally valid experiment in the lab than in the field, but it is also easier to create a powerful experiment in the lab than in the field. In the lab, you can have impressive power by reducing random error and by using sensitive dependent measures. By leaving the lab, you may lose your ability to reduce random error and to use sensitive measures.

***Random Error***    In the laboratory, you can reduce random error by minimizing the degree to which irrelevant variables vary. You can reduce unwanted variation due to individual differences by using a homogeneous group of participants. You can reduce unwanted variation in the environment by running participants under identical conditions. You can reduce unwanted variation due to participants being distracted by putting participants in a soundproof, simple, virtually distraction-free environment. You can reduce unwanted variation in your procedures by rigidly standardizing your experiment. Thus, if you do your study in the laboratory, you can use many tactics to stop irrelevant variables from varying.

By leaving the lab, you may lose your ability to stop these variables from fluctuating. Sometimes you willingly give up the opportunity to control these variables so that you can generalize your results to the real world. For example, you may do a field experiment to get access to a heterogeneous group of participants. The advantage of having a wide range of participants is that you can generalize your results to a wide range of people. The disadvantage is that you are giving individual differences a chance to account for a sizable difference between your groups. Therefore, your treatment's effect might be obscured by those individual differences.

Sometimes, however, you unwillingly give up the ability to control irrelevant variables. For instance, you always want to standardize your procedures. However, it's hard to follow the same procedure every time if:

1. you have to conduct your study on the run (perhaps even approaching participants and saying, "Excuse me, may I talk to you for a moment?"),
2. without the benefit of equipment,
3. in a noisy, crowded environment.

Furthermore, even if you succeed in administering the treatment in the same standard way, your participants may fail to perceive the treatment in the same standard way. That is, distractions in the environment may prevent all your participants from attending to your entire manipulation. Indeed, a manipulation that is overpowering in the lab may seem almost invisible when taken into the field.

***Insensitive Measures***    You have seen that, in the field, you cannot always administer the same manipulations with the same degree of standardization as you could in the lab. Because your treatment manipulation is less standardized and less effective, your experiment is less powerful. Unfortunately, the same factors that impede your ability to administer your manipulation may also hurt your ability to use sensitive, powerful measures. To illustrate, let's say you are interested in whether getting an unexpected gift will increase happiness. In the lab, you would probably measure happiness by having participants rate how happy they are on a 1 to 7 scale. Even if you were to use a more indirect behavioral indicator of happiness, such as helping, you would measure helping with a high degree of precision. For example, you would either measure exactly *how long* it took participants to help a person, or *how much* they helped the person.

In the field, measuring happiness is much more difficult. You probably won't be able to have participants fill out a rating scale. Therefore, you will probably have to use a less sensitive behavioral measure, such as helping.

Furthermore, you may not even be able to measure helping with any degree of precision. Unlike in the lab, you cannot merely sit in your chair, gaze through a one-way mirror, and record how much or how long participants help. Instead, you may have to inconspicuously look around the corner, filter out urban distractions such as dogs barking, cars honking, and pedestrians walking, just to see whether your participants help. Under these conditions, you're lucky to see whether participants help—much less to see how much they help. Thus, in the field, you may be unable to collect much information about the participant's behavior. Rather than collecting detailed and precise information about how the person performed the key behavior, you may be limited to finding out whether the participant performed the key behavior. Consequently, the measure you use in the field may be less accurate and less sensitive than the measure you use in the lab.

But you do not have to settle for less sensitive measures when you go to the field. One way to avail yourself of more sensitive measures is to use a second experimenter who does nothing but record data. This leaves you free to put quarters (unexpected gifts) in phone booths, hide until a participant finds it, and make yourself a convenient person "in need" for your unsuspecting participants to demonstrate their good will. The second experimenter could observe and record things like how quickly participants responded and to what extent they responded. If you do not have a second experimenter, let such equipment as videotape cameras, tape recorders, and stopwatches, do the recording for you.

For example, Milgram, Bickman, and Berkowitz (1969) had confederates look up at a tall building. Their independent variable was how many confederates looked up at the building. Their dependent measure was the proportion of people walking by who also looked up. Actually, the confederates were looking up at a videotape camera. After the experiment was over, Milgram et al. were able to count the number of people looking up by replaying the videotape.

## Special Problems with Field Experiments That Use Intact Groups

Some field experimenters try to regain the power lost due to having high levels of random error and insensitive measures by using a large number of participants. To get large numbers of participants, some researchers do field experiments on intact groups. For example, they might use a few large classes or a work group.

### FAILURE TO ESTABLISH AND MAINTAIN INDEPENDENCE

Unfortunately it's hard to independently assign participants from intact groups, and once they're assigned, it's hard to maintain independence. For example, suppose a nursery school was willing to help you out with your study on the effects of watching prosocial television. Then you would have a large, convenient sample. However, there might be a catch: The nursery school might insist that

**TABLE G–1**
**Pros and Cons of Field Experiments**

| PROS | CONS |
|------|------|
| Power may be enhanced by access to many participants. | The increase in participants may be more than negated by the inability to control random variables and the inability to use the most sensitive of measures. |
| Like randomized lab experiment, has internal validity because participants were randomly assigned. | Random assignment is sometimes difficult in the field. Mortality may harm internal validity. |
| External validity may be enhanced by studying a wide variety of settings and participants. | Often, field experiments do not study a wider range of participants than those in the lab. It may take more effort to do a field experiment than a lab experiment. Ethical questions may arise, especially in terms of informed consent. |
| Construct validity may be enhanced by using participants that are not playing the role of participant. | Construct validity may be harmed if people learn of the study. Not telling participants about the study raises ethical questions. |

you keep the classes intact. Thus, although you might want to assign each student independently, you may have to assign one class to one condition and another class to the other condition. Consequently, no matter how many people are in your study, you only have two independent units—the two classes. Because any two classes will obviously differ from one another in many ways, your experimental and control groups would be very different before the experiment began.

Even if you are able to assign participants independently, you may be unable to *maintain* independence because participants interact with one another, thereby influencing each other's responses. If the children in the group influence each other, you do not have independent responses from 60 individuals. Instead, you have responses from two mobs. For example, suppose there is one very aggressive child in the control group. As any teacher knows, one misbehaving child can cause virtually everyone in the group to misbehave.

Violation of independence, whether due to faulty assignment or failure to maintain independence of responses, can have one of two consequences—bad and worse. The worst consequence happens if the researcher does not realize that independence has been violated. In that case, she would conduct her statistical tests as if she had more individual, independent units than she has. She would think that since each group is made up of 30 randomly assigned participants, the groups should be fairly equivalent. She would believe that since she has so many independent units, chance differences between groups should be minimal. However, since, in reality, she has only two independent units, chance could easily be responsible for substantial differences between groups.

Therefore, she is very likely to misinterpret a difference that is due to chance as a treatment effect.

The bad consequence occurs if the researcher realizes that she has only two independent units. In that case, the good news is that since she realizes that even large differences might be due to chance, she probably won't mistake chance differences for treatment differences. However, the bad news is that since she realizes that even large differences may be due to chance, she will tend to dismiss real treatment effects as being due to chance. In other words, her study will be powerless.

## THREATS TO CONSTRUCT VALIDITY

You can remedy the problem of too few independent units by using more classes. For example, you might have 10 classes in one group and 10 classes in the other group. However, violation of independence is only one problem with using intact groups. Using intact groups exposes your study to three serious threats to construct validity: demoralization, compensation, and diffusion of treatment.

*Demoralization*   Your study's construct validity is harmed the moment the classes talk to each other and find out about their differential treatment. Do not be surprised if the no-television group becomes demoralized. They may vent their frustration about missing out on television by being violent. As a result, the television-watching group may be better behaved, even though watching television did not improve their behavior. In this case, it's not that watching television reduces violence, it's that feeling deprived increases violence.

*Compensation*   On the other hand, upon learning of the experimental group's good fortune, *compensation* could occur. That is, the no-television class members might pull together and behave as best as they could so that they would be allowed to watch television. As a result of their efforts, the no-television group might behave better than the television group. Again, you would see a difference between your groups, but the difference wouldn't be due to the effects of the television.

*Diffusion of Treatment*   Finally, you might not observe any effect for treatment because of diffusion of treatment: Both your groups are getting the treatment. In your television study, members of the no-television class might be watching television. For example, their teacher may succumb to their begging to "watch television like the other class" and thus borrow the television from the other teacher. Or, if the classes are held in the same room, pupils in the no-television group might watch or overhear the other class's television shows. Consequently, the impact of the television shows would diffuse to the no-television group.

**TABLE G–2**
**Dealing with Problems Caused by Studying Intact Groups**

| PROBLEMS | PARTIAL REMEDIES |
|---|---|
| Groups are not independent | Use many groups. In analyzing data, do not consider each participant as an individual unit. Instead, consider each group as a single unit. Thus, for the purposes of analysis, rather than having 300 participants, you may only have 10 classes. |
| Demoralization (no-treatment group being depressed that they were not in the treatment group) | Use placebo treatments. Minimize opportunities to talk by doing the experiment in a short time span and by using groups that do not come into contact with one another. |
| Compensation (no-treatment group working harder to compensate for being denied the treatment) | Use placebo treatments. Minimize opportunities to talk by doing the experiment in a short time span and by using groups that do not come into contact with one another. |
| Diffusion of treatment (no-treatment group getting access to the treatment) | Use placebo treatments. Minimize opportunities to talk by doing the experiment in a short time span and by using groups that do not come into contact with one another. |

## MINIMIZING THREATS TO CONSTRUCT VALIDITY

How can you minimize demoralization, compensation, and diffusion of treatment? The steps to take are obvious once you realize that these threats usually result from participants finding out that their treatments differ. With this in mind, the first step is to make your conditions resemble one another as much as possible. Never use a treatment group and a no-treatment group. Instead, use a treatment group and a placebo treatment group, or two different kinds of treatments.

In the television study, you could have one group watch one kind of television program (violent) while the other watched another kind of program (nonviolent). Or, you could be even sneakier and show both groups the same shows—the only difference is that in one condition you have edited out some of the violence. In this way, participants might not notice that their conditions differ.

The second step is to give participants fewer opportunities to talk. For example, shorten the time between giving the treatment and collecting the dependent measure. Obviously, the longer the time between the introduction of treatment and collecting the dependent measure, the more likely the groups are to talk. Therefore, you might conduct the entire study in one day rather than having it last for several months.

If you want to look at long-term effects of treatment, you could reduce opportunities for participants to talk to one another by using participants who will not run into another. Thus, in the television study, rather than assigning different classes in the same schools to different conditions, you could assign different schools to different conditions. The chances of a toddler from Busy Bee Day Care comparing curriculum with a child from Lazy Larry's Day Camp are remote.

# GLOSSARY

**A–B design** The simplest single-n design, consisting of measuring the participant's behavior at baseline (A) and then measuring the participant after the participant has received the treatment (B).

**A–B–A reversal design** A single-subject or small-*n* design in which baseline measurements are made of the target behavior (A), then an experimental treatment is given (B), and the target behavior is measured again (A). The A–B–A design makes a more convincing case for the treatment's effect than the A–B design.

**Abstract** A short (fewer than 120 words long), one-page summary of a research proposal or article.

**Analysis of variance (ANOVA)** A statistical test for analyzing data from experiments. Especially useful if the experiment has more than one independent variable or more than two levels of an independent variable.

**Archival data** Data from existing records and public archives.

**Baseline** The participant's behavior on the task before receiving the treatment. A measure of the dependent variable as it occurs without the experimental manipulation. Used as a standard of comparison in single-subject and small-*n* designs.

**Between-groups variance (mean square treatment, mean square between)** An index of the degree to which group means differ. An index of the combined effects of random error and treatment. This quantity is compared to the within-groups variance in ANOVA. It is the top half of the F-ratio. If the treatment has no effect, the between-groups variance should be roughly the same as the within-groups variance. If the treatment has an effect, the between-groups variance should be larger than the within-groups variance.

**Blind** A strategy of making the participant or researcher unaware of what condition the participant is in.

**Blind observer** An observer who is unaware of the participant's characteristics and situation. Using blind observers reduces observer bias.

**Blocked design** Dividing experimental participants into groups (blocks) on a variable (such as low-IQ block and high-IQ block). Then, randomly assigning members from each block to condition. Ideally, a blocked design will give you more power than a simple, between-subjects design.

**Carryover effects (also called treatment carryover)** The effects of a treatment administered earlier in the experiment persist so long that they are present even while participants are receiving additional treatments. Often a problem with single-subject and within-subjects designs because you do not know whether the participant's behavior is due to the treatment just administered or to a lingering effect of a treatment administered some time ago.

**Ceiling effect** The effects of treatment(s) is underestimated because the dependent measure is not sensitive to psychological states above a certain level. The measure puts an artificially low ceiling on how high a participant may score.

**Central limit theorem** If numerous large samples (30 or more scores) from the same population are taken, and you plot the mean for each of these samples, your plot would resemble a normal curve—even if the population from which you took those samples was not normally distributed.

**Chi-square ($X^2$)** A statistical test you can use to determine whether two or more variables are related. Best used when you have nominal data.

**Coefficient of determination** The square of the correlation coefficient; tells the degree to which knowing one variable helps to know another. Can range from 0 (knowing a participant's score on one variable tells you absolutely nothing about the participant's score on the second variable) to 1.00 (knowing a participant's score on one variable tells you exactly what the participant's score on the second variable was).

**Cohort effects**    The effects of belonging to a given generation (for instance, the 60s generation). Sometimes, people mistakenly assume that a difference between people of different age groups is the result of biological aging when the difference is really due to the two groups having different backgrounds because they grew up in different eras.

**Compensation**    When participants in the control group try to make up for being deprived of a desired treatment. May be a problem in field research when the treatment is a training program or some other desired treatment.

**Conceptual replication**    A study that is based on the original study, but uses different methods to assess the true relationships between the treatment and dependent variables better. In a conceptual replication, you might use a different manipulation or a different measure.

**Concurrent validity**    Validating a measure by giving your participant the new measure and some established measures of the construct at the same time (concurrently). You then correlate performance on the established measures with performance on the new measure. Concurrent validity is to be distinguished from predictive validity, predictive validity is seeing how well your measure predicts scores on measures that you will administer to the participant at some future time.

**Confounding variables**    Variables, other than the independent variable, that may be responsible for the differences between your conditions. There are two types of confounding variables: ones that are manipulation-irrelevant and ones that are the result of the manipulation. Confounding variables that are irrelevant to the treatment manipulation threaten internal validity. For example, the difference between groups may be due to one group being older than the other, rather than to the treatment. Random as-

signment can control for the effects of those confounding variables. Confounding variables that are produced by the treatment manipulation hurt the construct validity of the study. They hurt the construct validity because even though we may know that the treatment manipulation had an effect, we don't know what it was about the treatment manipulation that had the effect. For example, we may know that an "exercise" manipulation increases happiness (internal validity), but not know whether the "exercise" manipulation worked because people exercised more, got more encouragement, had a more structured routine, practiced setting and achieving goals, or met new friends. In such a case, construct validity is harmed because we don't know how properly to label the "exercise" manipulation.

**Construct**    A mental state that cannot be directly observed or manipulated, such as love, intelligence, hunger, and aggression.

**Construct validity**    The degree to which a study, test, or manipulation measures and/or manipulates what the researcher claims it does. For example, a test claiming to measure "aggressiveness" would not have construct validity if it really measured assertiveness.

**Content analysis**    A method used to categorize a wide range of open-ended (unrestricted) responses. Content analysis schemes have been used to code the frequency of violence on certain television shows and are often used to code archival data.

**Content validity**    The extent to which a measure represents a balanced and adequate sampling of relevant dimensions, knowledge, and skills. In many measures and tests, participants are asked a few questions from a large body of knowledge. A test has content validity if its content is a fair sample of the larger body of knowledge. Students hope that their psychology tests have content validity.

**Control group**    Participants who are randomly assigned to *not* receive the experimental treatment. These participants are compared to the treatment group to determine whether the treatment had an effect.

**Convenience sampling**    Choosing to include people in your sample simply because they are easy (convenient) to survey. It is hard to generalize the results accurately from a study that used convenience sampling.

**Convergent validity**  Validity demonstrated by showing that the measure correlates with other measures of the construct.

**Correlation coefficient**  A number that can vary from −1.00 to +1.00 and indicates the kind of relationship that exists between two variables (positive or negative as indicated by the sign of the correlation coefficient) and the strength of the relationship (indicated by the extent to which the coefficient differs from 0). Positive correlations indicate that the variables tend to go in the same direction (if a participant is low on one variable, the participant will tend to be low on the other). Negative correlations indicate that the variables tend to head in opposite directions (if a participant is low on one, the participant will tend to be high on the other).

**Counterbalancing**  Any technique used to control order effects by distributing order effects across treatment conditions. Typically, it involves giving different participants the treatments in systematically different sequences in an attempt to balance out order effects.

**Covariation**  That changes in the treatment are accompanied by changes in the behavior. To establish causality, you must establish covariation.

**Criterion validity**  The degree to which the measure relates to other measures of the construct. Concurrent validity and predictive validity are types of criterion validity.

**Critical studies**  A study that sets up a contest between two competing theories to try to settle the question of which theory's view of the world is more accurate.

**Crossover (disordinal) interaction**  When an independent variable has one kind of effect in the presence of one level of a second independent variable, but a different kind of effect in the presence of a different level of the second independent variable. Examples: Getting closer to someone may increase their attraction to you if you have just complimented them, but may decrease their attraction to you if you have just insulted them. Called a crossover interaction because the lines in a graph will cross. Called a

disordinal interaction because it cannot be explained by having ordinal rather than interval data.

**Cross-sectional design**  Trying to study the effects of age by comparing different age groups at the same point in time. For example, today, you might compare a group of 5-year-olds with a group of 10-year-olds. Different from longitudinal designs where you study the same people at different times (for instance, study a group of 5-year-olds today, then return five years later and study them again when they are 10).

**Crosstabs**  Tables of percentages used to compare different groups' responses; allows for an examination of the relationships among variables.

**Crucial studies**  Studies that put two theories into competition.

**Curvilinear**  A relationship between an independent and dependent variable that is graphically represented by a curved line.

**Debriefing**  Giving participants the details of a study at the end of their participation. Proper debriefing is one of the researcher's most serious obligations.

**Deduction**  Apply a general rule to a specific situation.

**Degrees of freedom (df)**  An index of sample size. In the simple experiment, the df for your error term will always be two less than the number of participants.

**Demand characteristics**  Characteristics of the study that suggest to the participant how the researcher wants the participant to behave.

**Demographics**  Characteristics of a group, such as sex, age, social class.

**Demoralization**  An effect of participants knowing that they are being denied the preferred treatment. Participants may then feel victimized and give up. A problem in field research if some participants get training that may improve their promotability but others get no treatment at all.

**Dependent groups *t*-test**  A statistical test used with interval or ratio data to test differences between two conditions on a single dependent variable. Differs from the between-groups *t*-test in that it is only to be used when you are getting two scores from each participant (within-subjects design) or when you are using a matched pairs design.

**Dependent variable**   The factor that the experimenter predicts is affected by the independent variable. The participant's response that the experimenter is measuring.

**Diffusion of treatment**   When the treatment given to the treatment group is spread to the no-treatment group by treatment group's participants. For example, a professor hands out sample tests to one section of a class, but not to the other. Students who get the sample test make copies and give them to their friends in the no-treatment class. May result in a failure to observe any difference between groups and thus falsely conclude the treatment has no effect.

**Direct replication**   Repeating a study as exactly as possible, usually to determine whether or not the same results will be obtained. Direct replications are useful for establishing that the findings of the original study are reliable.

**Discriminant validity**   When a measure does not correlate highly with a measure of a different construct. Example: A violence measure might have a degree of discriminant validity if it does not correlate with the measures of assertiveness, social desirability, and independence.

**Discussion**   The part of the article, immediately following the results section, that discusses the research findings and the study in a broader context and suggests research projects that could be done to follow up on the study.

**Disordinal interaction**   See Crossover interaction.

**Double-barreled question**   A statement that contains more than one question. Responses to a double-barreled question are difficult to interpret. For example, if someone responds, "No," to the question "Are you hungry and thirsty?" we do not know whether they are hungry, but not thirsty; not hungry, but thirsty; or neither hungry nor thirsty.

**Double-blind**   A strategy for improving construct validity that involves making sure that neither the participant nor the person who has direct contact with the participant knows what type of treatment the participant has received.

**Empty control group**   A group that does not get any kind of treatment. The group gets nothing, not even a placebo. Usually, because of participant and experimenter biases that may result from such a group, you will want to avoid using an empty control group.

**Environmental manipulation**   A manipulation that involves changing the participant's environment rather than giving the participant different instructions.

**Ethical**   Conforming to the American Psychological Association's principles of what is morally correct behavior. To learn more about these guidelines and standards, see Appendix A.

**Experimental group**   Participants who are randomly assigned to receive the treatment.

**Experimental hypothesis**   A prediction that the treatment will cause an effect.

**Experimental (research) realism**   When a study engages the participant so much that the participant is not merely playing a role (helpful participant, good person).

**Experimenter bias**   Experimenters being more attentive to participants in the treatment group or giving different nonverbal cues to treatment group participants than to other participants. When experimenter bias is present, differences between groups may be due to the experimenter rather than to the treatment.

**Exploratory study**   A study investigating (exploring) a new area of research. Unlike replications, an exploratory study does not follow directly from an existing study.

**Ex post facto research**   When a researcher goes back, after the research has been completed, looking to test hypotheses that were not formulated prior to the beginning of the study. The researcher is trying to take advantage of hindsight. Often an attempt to salvage something out of a study that did not turn out as planned.

**External validity**   The degree to which the results of a study can be generalized to other participants, settings, and times.

**Extraneous factors**   Factors other than the treatment. If we cannot control or account for extraneous variables, we can't conclude that the treatment had an effect. That is, we will not have internal validity.

**F-ratio**  Analysis of variance (ANOVA) yields an F-ratio for each main effect and interaction. In between subjects experiments, the F-ratio is a ratio of between-groups variance to within-groups variance. If the treatment has no effect, $F$ will tend to be close to 1.0.

**Face validity**  The extent to which a measure looks, on the face of it, to be valid. Face validity has nothing to do with actual, scientific validity. That is, a test could have face validity and not real validity or could have real validity, but not face validity. However, for practical/political reasons, you may decide to consider face validity when comparing measures.

**Factor analysis**  A statistical technique designed to explain the variability in several questions in terms of a smaller number of underlying hypothetical factors.

**Factorial experiment**  An experiment that examines two or more independent variables (factors) at a time.

**Factor loading**  Tells us the degree to which a given question appears to be measuring a certain factor. Factor loadings, like correlation coefficients, can range from $-1$ to $+1$.

**Failure to follow protocol effect**  Contamination caused when investigators deviate from the study's "script."

**Fatigue effects**  Decreased performance on a task due to being tired or less enthusiastic as a study continues. In a within-subjects design, this decrease in performance might be incorrectly attributed to a treatment.

**Field experiment**  An experiment performed in a nonlaboratory setting.

**Fixed alternative items**  Items on a test or questionnaire in which a person must choose an answer from among a few specified alternatives. Multiple-choice, true–false, and rating scale questions are all fixed alternative items.

**Floor effect**  The effects of treatment(s) are underestimated because the dependent measure artificially restricts how low scores can be.

**Functional relationship**  The shape of a relationship. Depending on the functional relationship between the independent and dependent variable, a graph of the relationship might look like a straight line, might look like a "u," an "s," or some other shape.

**Grand mean**  The mean of all the scores in a study. Sometimes used when doing the calculations for an ANOVA.

**Hawthorne Effect**  When the treatment group changes their behavior not because of the treatment itself, but because they know they are getting special treatment.

**History**  Events in the environment—other than the treatment—that have changed. Differences between conditions that may seem to be due to the treatment may really be due to history.

**Hypothesis**  A testable prediction about the relationship between two or more variables.

**Hypothesis guessing**  When participants alter their behavior to conform to their guess as to what the research hypothesis is. Hypothesis-guessing can be a serious threat to construct validity, especially if participants guess right.

**Hypothesis testing**  The use of inferential statistics to determine if the relationship found between two or more variables in a particular sample holds true in the population.

**Hypothetical construct**  An entity that cannot be observed directly with our present technology (such as, love, motivation, short-term memory).

**Independence**  Factors are independent when they are not causally or correlationally linked. Independence is a key assumption of almost any statistical test. In the simple experiment, observations must be independent. That is, what one participant does should have no influence on what another participant does and what happens to one participant should not influence what happens to another participant. Individually assigning participants to treatment or no-treatment condition and individually testing each participant are ways to achieve independence.

**Independent random assignment**  Randomly determining for each individual participant which condition they will be in. For example, you might flip a coin for each participant to determine to what group they were assigned.

**Independent variable**  The variable being manipulated by the experimenter. Participants are assigned to level of independent variable by independent random assignment.

**Induction**  Creating a general rule by seeing similarities among several specific situations.

**Inferential statistics**    Procedures for determining the reliability and generality of a particular research finding.

**Informed consent**    If participants agree to take part in a study after they have been told what is going to happen to them, you have their informed consent.

**Instrumentation bias**    The way participants were measured changed from pretest to posttest. In instrumentation bias, the actual measuring instrument changes or the way it is administered changes. Sometimes, people may think they have a treatment effect, when they really have an instrumentation effect.

**Interaction**    When you need to know how much of one variable participants have received to say what the effect of another variable is, you have an interaction between those two variables. If you graph the results from an experiment that has two or more independent variables, and the lines you draw between your points are not parallel, you have an interaction.

**Inter-judge agreement**    The percentage of times the raters agree.

**Instructional manipulation**    Manipulating the treatment by giving written or oral instructions.

**Internal consistency**    The degree to which each question in a scale taps the same construct. Internal consistency is believed to be high if answers to each item correlate highly with answers to all other items.

**Internal validity**    The degree to which a study establishes that a factor causes a difference in behavior. If a study lacks internal validity, the researcher may falsely believe that a factor causes an effect when it really doesn't.

**Interobserver reliability**    An index of the degree to which different raters give the same behavior similar ratings.

**Interval data**    Data that give you numbers that can be meaningfully ordered along a scale (from lowest to highest) and in which equal numerical intervals represent equal psychological intervals. That is, the difference between scoring a "2" and a "1" and the difference between scoring a "7" and a "6" are the same not only in terms of scores (both are a difference of 1), but also in terms of the actual psychological characteristic being measured. Interval scale measures allow us to compare participants in terms of how much of a quality participants have—and in terms of how much more of a quality one group may have than another.

**Interviewer bias**    When the interviewer influences participant's responses. For example, the interviewer might verbally or nonverbally reward the participant for giving responses that support the hypothesis.

**Introduction**    The part of the article that occurs right after the abstract. In the introduction, the authors tell you what their hypothesis is, why their hypothesis makes sense, how their study fits in with previous research, and why their study is worth doing.

**Known groups technique**    Determining the validity of a measure by seeing whether groups known to differ on the characteristic you are trying to measure also differ on your measure (for example, ministers should differ from atheists on an alleged measure of religiosity).

**Latency (also called response latency)**    How long it takes the participant to respond. Perhaps the most familiar example is *how long* it takes participants to push a button on a reaction time task.

**Law**    A strong, consistent, documented relationship between two or more variables.

**Leading question**    Questions structured to lead respondents to the answer the researcher wants (such as, "You like this book, don't you?").

**Levels of an independent variable**    When the treatment variable is given in different amounts, these different amounts are called levels. In the simple experiment, you only have two levels of the independent variable.

**Level of significance**    The risk the researcher takes of making a Type 1 error. With a .05 level of significance, the researcher takes a 5-in-a-100 chance of declaring the results significant when the variables are not related.

**Likert-type items**    Items that typically ask participants whether they strongly agree, agree, are neutral, disagree, or strongly disagree with a certain statement. These items are assumed to yield interval data.

**Linear trend**    A relationship between an independent and dependent variable that is graphically represented by a straight line.

**Loose protocol effect**   Variations in procedure because the written procedures (the protocol) is not detailed enough. These variations in procedure may result in researcher bias.

**Main effect (overall main effect)**   The overall or average effect of an independent variable.

**Manipulation check**   A question or set of questions designed to determine whether participants perceived the manipulation in the way that the researcher intended.

**Matched-pairs design**   An experimental design in which the participants are paired off by matching them on some variable assumed to be correlated with the dependent variable. Then, for each matched pair, one member is randomly assigned to one treatment condition, the other gets the other treatment condition. This design usually has more power than a simple, between-groups experiment.

**Matching**   Choosing your groups so that they are similar (they match) on certain characteristics. Matching reduces, but does not eliminate, the threat of selection bias.

**Maturation**   Changes in participants due to natural growth or development. A researcher may think that the treatment had an effect, when the difference in behavior is really due to maturation.

**Mean**   An average calculated by adding up all the scores and then dividing by the number of scores.

**Median**   If you arrange all the scores from lowest to highest, the middle score will be the median.

**Median split**   The procedure of dividing participants into two groups ("highs" and "lows") based on whether they score above or below the median.

**Mediating variable**   Variables inside the individual (such as thoughts, feelings, or physiological responses) that come between a stimulus and a response. In other words, the stimulus has its effect because it causes changes in mediating variables which, in turn, cause changes in behavior.

**Method section**   The part of the article immediately following the introduction. Whereas the introduction explains why the study was done, the method section describes what was done. For example, it will tell you what design was used, what the researchers said to the partici-

pants, what measures and equipment were used, and how many participants were studied and how they were selected. The method section could also be viewed as a "how we did it" section. The method section is usually subdivided into at least three subsections: participants, apparatus, and procedure.

**Mixed designs**   An experimental design that has at least one within-subject factor and one between-subject factor.

**Moderator variables**   Variables that can intensify, weaken, or reverse the effects of another variable. For example, the effect of wearing perfume may be moderated by gender: If you are a woman, wearing perfume may make you more liked; if you are a man, wearing perfume may make you less liked.

**Mortality (attrition)**   Participants dropping out of a study before the study is completed. Sometimes, differences between conditions may be due to participants dropping out of the study rather than to the treatment.

**Multiple-baseline design**   A single-subject or small-$n$ design in which different behaviors receive baseline periods of varying lengths prior to the introduction of the treatment variable. Often, the goal is to show that the behavior being rewarded changes whereas the other behaviors stay the same until they too are reinforced.

**Multiple operations**   When several different measures of the same construct are included in the same study.

**Mundane realism**   Extent to which the research setting or task resembles real life.

**Naturalistic observation**   A technique of observing events as they occur in their natural setting.

**Negative correlation**   An inverse relationship between two variables (such as, number of suicide attempts and happiness).

**Nominal scale data**   Qualitative data; different scores do not represent different amounts of a characteristic (quantity). Instead, they represent different kinds of characteristics (qualities, types, or categories). Because larger numbers do not represent more of a quality than smaller numbers, nominal scale measurement is considered the lowest level of measurement.

**Nonequivalent control group design** A quasi-experimental design that, like a simple experiment, has a treatment group and a no-treatment comparison group. However, unlike the simple experiment, random assignment does not determine which participants get the treatment and which do not.

**Nonreactive measures** Measurements that are taken without changing the participant's behavior; also referred to as unobtrusive measures.

**Non-response bias** The problem caused by people who were in your sample refusing to participate in your study. Non-response bias is one of the most serious threats to a survey design's external validity.

**Nonsignificant results** See null results.

**Normal curve** A bell-shaped, symmetrical curve that has its center at the mean.

**Normal distribution** If the way the scores are distributed follows the normal curve, scores are said to be normally distributed. For example, a population is said to be normally distributed if 68% of the scores are within one standard deviation of the mean, 95% are within two standard deviations of the mean, and 99% of the scores are within 3 standard deviations of the mean. Many statistical tests, including the t-test, assume that sample means are normally distributed.

**Null hypothesis** The hypothesis that there is no relationship between two or more variables. The null hypothesis can be disproven, but it cannot be proven.

**Null results (nonsignificant results)** Results that fail to disconfirm the null hypothesis; results that fail to provide convincing evidence that the factors are related. Null results are inconclusive because the failure to find a relationship could be due to your design lacking the power to find the relationship. In other words, many null results are Type 2 errors.

**Observer bias** Bias created by the observer seeing what the observer wants or expects to see.

**Open-ended items** Questions that do not provide fixed response alternatives. Essay and fill-in-the-blank questions are open-ended.

**Operational definition** A publicly observable way to measure or manipulate a variable; a "recipe" for how you are going to measure or manipulate your factors.

**Order** The place in a sequence (first, second, third, etc.) when a treatment occurs.

**Order effects** A big problem with within-subjects designs. The order in which the participant receives a treatment (first, second, etc.) will affect how participants behave.

**Ordinal data** Numbers that can be meaningfully ordered from lowest to highest. With ordinal data, you know a participant with a high score has more of a characteristic than a participant with a low score. But you do not know how much more. For example, with ranked data, you know the top-ranked student has a higher score than the second-ranked student, but how much higher? You do not know if you only have ranked data. Furthermore, someone with a rank of 1 might be way ahead of the number 2–ranked scorer, but the number 2 scorer may be only slightly ahead of the number 3 scorer.

**Ordinal interaction** Reflects the fact that an independent variable *seems* to have more of an effect under one level of a second independent variable than under another level. If you graph an ordinal interaction, the lines will not be parallel, but they will not cross. Called an ordinal interaction because the interaction, the failure of the lines to be parallel, may be an illusion resulting from having ordinal data.

**Parameter estimation** The use of inferential statistics to estimate certain characteristics of the population (parameters) from a sample of that population.

**Parameters** Measurements describing populations; often inferred from statistics, which are measurements describing a sample.

**Parsimonious** Explaining a broad range of phenomena with only a few principles.

**Participant observation** An observation procedure in which the observer participates with those being observed. The observer becomes "one of them."

**Phi coefficient** A correlation coefficient to be used when both variables are measured on the nominal scale.

**Placebo treatment** A fake treatment that we know has no effect, except through the power of suggestion. It allows experimenters to see if the treatment has an effect beyond that of suggestion. For example, in medical experiments, participants who are given pills that do not contain a drug may be compared to participants who are given pills that contain the new drug.

**Population**    The entire group that you are interested in. You can estimate the characteristics of a population by taking large random samples from that population.

**Positive correlation**    A relationship between two variables where the two variables tend to vary together—when one increases, the other tends to increase. (For example, height and weight: The taller one is, the more one tends to weigh; the shorter one is, the less one tends to weigh.)

**Post hoc test**    Usually refers to a statistical test that has been performed after an ANOVA has obtained a significant effect for a factor. Because the ANOVA only says that at least two of the levels of the independent variable differ from one another, post hoc tests are performed to find out which levels differ from one another.

**Power**    The ability to find differences or, put another way, the ability to avoid making Type 2 errors. The ability to find significant differences when differences truly exist.

**Practice effects**    The change in a score on a test (usually a gain) resulting from previous practice with the test. In a within-subjects design, this improvement might be incorrectly attributed to receiving a treatment.

**Pretest-posttest design**    A before-after design in which each participant is given the pretest, administered the treatment, then given the posttest.

*Psychological Abstracts*    A useful resource that contains abstracts from a wide variety of journals. The *Abstracts* can be searched by year of publication, topic of article, or author. For more about the *Abstracts,* see Appendix B.

**Quasi-experiment**    A study that resembles an experiment except that random assignment played no role in determining which participants got which level of treatment. Usually, quasi-experiments have less internal validity than experiments.

**Quota sampling**    Making sure you get the desired number of (meet your quotas for) certain types of people (certain age groups, minorities, etc.) This method does not involve random sampling and usually gives you a less representative sample than random sampling would. It may, however, be an improvement over convenience sampling.

**Random assignment**    In random assignment, you divide your participants into different groups. Each subgroup starts off as a random sample of the same larger group. Because all the subgroups come from the same parent population, all the subgroups are similar to each other at the start of the study. However, because the subgroups are assigned to different treatments, the subgroups may differ from each other by the end of the experiment. Random assignment to experimental condition is what allows the simple experiment, the multiple-group experiment, and the factorial experiment to have internal validity. Note that random assignment does nothing for a study's external validity.

**Random error**    Variations in scores due to unsystematic, chance factors.

**Random sampling**    A sample that has been randomly selected from a population. If you randomly select enough participants, those participants will usually be fairly representative of the entire population. That is, your random sample will reflect its population. Often, random sampling is used to maximize a study's external validity. Note that random sampling—unlike random assignment—does not promote internal validity.

**Ratio scale**    The highest form of measurement. With ratio scale numbers, the difference between any two consecutive numbers is the same (see interval scale). But in addition to having interval scale properties, in ratio scale measurement, a zero score means the total absence of a quality. (Thus, Fahrenheit is not a ratio scale measure of temperature because 0 degrees Fahrenheit does not mean there is no temperature.) If you have ratio scale numbers, you can meaningfully form ratios between scores. If IQ scores were ratio (they are not; very few measurements in psychology are), you could say that someone with a 60 IQ was twice as smart as someone with a 30 IQ (a ratio of 2 to 1). Furthermore, you could say that someone with a 0 IQ had absolutely no intelligence whatsoever.

**Regression** The tendency for scores that are extremely unusual to revert back to more normal levels on the retest. If participants are chosen because their scores were extreme, these extreme scores may be loaded with extreme amounts of random measurement error. On retesting, participants are bound to get more normal scores as random measurement error abates to more normal levels. This regression effect could be mistaken for a treatment effect.

**Regression to the mean** See regression.

**Reliability** A general term, often referring to the degree to which a participant would get the same score if retested (test-retest reliability). Reliability can, however, refer to the degree to which scores are free from random error. A measure can be reliable, but not valid. However, a measure cannot be valid if it is not also reliable.

**Repeated measures design** See within-subjects design

**Replication factor** A factor sometimes included in a factorial design to see whether an effect replicates (occurs again) under slightly different conditions. For example, a researcher may decide to use stimulus set as a replication factor. In that case, the goal would be to see if the treatment has the same effect when different stimulus materials are used.

**Researcher effect** Ideally, you hope that the results from a study would be the same no matter who was running the participants. However, it is possible that the results may be affected by the researcher. If more than one researcher is running participants for a given study, researcher may be included as a factor in the design to determine if different researchers get different results.

**Researcher expectancy effect** When a researcher's expectations affect the results. This is a type of researcher bias.

**Research realism** A study that involves the participant so that the participant is less likely to play a role during the study.

**Response latency (also called latency)** How long it takes the participant to respond. Perhaps the most familiar example is *how long* it takes participants to push a button on a reaction time task.

**Response set** Habitual way of responding on a test or survey that is independent of a particular test item (for instance, a participant might always check "agree" no matter what the statement is).

**Restriction of range** To observe a sizable correlation between two variables, both must be allowed to vary widely (if one variable does not vary, the variables cannot vary together). Occasionally, investigators fail to find a relationship between variables because they only study one or both variables over a highly restricted range. Example: comparing NFL offensive linemen and saying that weight has nothing to do with playing offensive line in the NFL on the basis of your finding that great offensive tackles do not weigh much more than poor offensive tackles. Problem: You only compared people who ranged in weight from 285 to 300.

**Results section** The part of an article, immediately following the method section, that reports statistical results and relates those results to the hypotheses. From reading this section, you should know whether the results supported the hypothesis.

**Retrospective self-report** Participants telling you what they said, did, or believed in the past. In addition to problems with ordinary self-report (response sets, giving the answer that a leading question suggests, etc.), retrospective self-report is vulnerable to memory biases. Thus, retrospective self-reports should *not* be accepted at face value.

**Sampling (inferential) statistics** The science of inferring the characteristics of a population from a sample.

**Scatterplot** A graph made by plotting the scores of individuals on two variables (for example, each participant's height and weight). By looking at this graph, you should get an idea of what kind of relationship (positive, negative, zero) exists between the two variables.

**Selection bias** Apparent treatment effects being due to comparing groups that differed even before the treatment was administered (comparing apples with oranges).

**Selection by maturation interaction** Treatment and no-treatment groups, although similar at one point, would have grown apart (developed differently) even if no treatment had been administered.

**Self-administered questionnaire** A questionnaire filled out in the absence of an investigator.

**Semi-structured survey** A survey constructed around a core of standard questions; however, the interviewer may expand on any question in order to explore a given response in greater depth.

**Sensitivity** The degree to which a measure is capable of distinguishing between participants having different amounts of a construct or who do more of a certain behavior.

**Sensitization** After getting several different treatments and performing the dependent variable task several times, participants may realize (become sensitive to) what the hypothesis is.

**Sequence effects** Participants who receive one sequence of treatments score differently than those participants who receive the treatments in a different sequence.

**Simple experiment** A study in which participants are independently and randomly assigned to one of two groups, usually to either a treatment group or to a no-treatment group. It is the easiest way to establish that a treatment causes an effect.

**Simple main effect** The effects of one independent variable at a specific level of a second independent variable. The simple main effect could have been obtained merely by doing a simple experiment.

**Single-blind** To reduce either subject biases or researcher biases, you might use a single-blind experiment in which either the participant (if you are most concerned about subject bias) or the person running participants (if you are more concerned about researcher bias) is unaware of who is receiving what level of the treatment.

**Single-n designs** See single-subject designs.

**Single-subject designs** Designs that try to establish causality by studying a single participant and arguing that the covariation between treatment and changes in behavior could not be due to anything other than the treatment. A key to this approach is preventing factors other than the treatment from varying. Single-n designs are common in operant conditioning and psychophysical research.

**Social desirability** A bias resulting from participants giving responses that make them look good rather than giving honest responses.

**Spurious** When the covariation observed between two variables is not due to the variables influencing each other, but because both are being influenced by some third variable. For example, the relationship between ice cream sales and assaults in New York is spurious—not because it does not exist (it does!)—but because ice cream does not cause assaults and assaults do not cause ice cream sales. Instead, high temperatures probably cause both increased assaults and ice cream sales. Beware of spuriousness whenever you look at research that does not use an experimental design.

**Stable baseline** When the participant's behavior, prior to receiving the treatment, is consistent. Single-n experimenters try to establish a stable baseline.

**Standard deviation** A measure of the extent to which individual scores deviate from the population mean. The more scores vary from each other, the larger the standard deviation will tend to be. If, on the other hand, all the scores are the same as the mean, the standard deviation would be zero.

**Standard error of the difference** An index of the degree to which random sampling error may cause two sample means representing the same populations to differ. In the simple experiment, we hope that the difference between our experimental and control group means will be at least twice as big as the standard error of the difference. To find out the exact ratio between our observed difference and the standard error of the difference, we conduct a t-test.

**Standard error (of the mean)** An index of the degree to which random error may cause the sample mean to be an inaccurate estimate of the population mean. The standard error will be small when the standard deviation is small and the sample mean is based on many scores.

**Standardization** treating each participant in the same (standard) way.

**Statistical regression** See regression.

**Statistical significance**   When a statistical test says that the relationship we have observed is probably not due to chance alone, we say that the results are statistically significant. In other words, since the relationship is probably not due to chance, we conclude that there probably is a real relationship between our variables.

**Stooges**   Confederates who pretend to be participants, but are actually the researcher's assistants.

**Stratified random sampling**   Making sure that the sample is similar to the population in certain respects (for instance, percentage of men and women) and then randomly sampling from these groups (strata). Has all the advantages of random sampling with even greater accuracy.

**Straw theory**   An oversimplified version of an existing theory. Opponents of a theory may present and attack a straw version of that theory, but claim they have attacked the theory itself.

**Structured survey**   A survey in which all respondents are asked a standard list of questions in a standard order.

**Subject bias (Subject effects)**   Ways the participant can bias the results (guessing the hypothesis and playing along, giving the socially correct response, etc.).

**Summated scores**   When you have several Likert-type questions that all tap the same dimension (such as, attitude toward democracy), you could add up each participant's responses to those questions to get an overall, total (summated) score.

**Survey design**   A non-experimental design useful for describing how people think, feel, or behave. The key is to design a valid questionnaire, test, or interview and administer it to a representative sample of the group you are interested in.

**Systematic replication**   A study that varies from the original study only in some minor aspect. For example, a systematic replication may use more participants, more standardized procedures, more levels of the independent variable, or a more realistic setting than the original study.

**t-test**   The most common way of analyzing data from a simple experiment. It involves computing a ratio between two things: (1) the difference between your group means, and (2) the standard error of the difference (an index of the degree to which group means could differ by chance alone). If the difference you observe is more than three times bigger than the difference that could be expected by chance, then your results are probably statistically significant. We can only say "probably" because the exact ratio that you need for statistical significance depends on your level of significance and on how many participants you have.

**Temporal precedence**   The causal factor comes before the change in behavior. Because causes must come before effects, researchers trying to establish causality must establish temporal precedence.

**Testing**   Participants score differently on the posttest as a result of what they learned from taking the pretest. Occasionally, people may think the participants' behavior changed because of the treatment when it really changed due to testing.

**Test-retest reliability**   A way of assessing the amount of random error in a measure by administering the measure to participants at two different times and then correlating their results. If the measure is free of random error, scores on the retest should be highly correlated with scores on the original test.

**Theory**   An integrated set of principles that explain many facts and from which a large number of *new* observations can be deduced.

**Times series design**   A quasi-experimental design in which a series of observations are taken from a group of participants before and after they receive treatment. Because it uses many times of measurement, it is an improvement over the pretest-posttest design. However, it is still extremely vulnerable to history effects.

**Trend analysis**   A type of post hoc analysis designed to determine whether a linear or curvilinear trend in our data is statistically significant (reliable).

**Type 1 error**   Rejecting the null hypothesis when it is in fact true. In other words, declaring a difference statistically significant when the difference is really due to chance.

**Type 2 error**   Failure to reject the null hypothesis when it is in fact false. In other words, failing to find a relationship between your variables when there really is a relationship between them.

**Unstructured interview**  When the interviewer has no standard set of questions that he or she asks each participant. Virtually worthless approach for collecting scientifically valid data.

**Within-groups variance (mean square within, mean square error, error variance)**  An estimate of the amount of random error in your data. The bottom half of the F-ratio.

**Within-subjects design**  An experimental design in which each participant is tested under more than one level of the independent variable. The sequence in which the participants receive the treatments is usually randomly determined.

**Zero correlation**  When there doesn't appear to be a relationship between two variables. For practical purposes, any correlation between −.10 and +.10 may be considered so small as to be nonexistent.

# REFERENCES

Adams, J. (1974). *Conceptual blockbusting*. San Francisco: Freeman.

American Psychological Association. (1981a). Ethical principles of psychologists. *American Psychologist, 36,* 633–638.

American Psychological Association. (1981b). Guidelines for the use of animals in school-science behavior projects. *American Psychologist, 36,* 686.

American Psychological Association. (1994). *Publication manual of the American Psychological Association* (4th ed.). Washington, DC: Author.

Anderson, J. R. & Bower, G. H. (1973). *Human associative memory*. Washington, DC: V. H. Winston.

Anastasi, A. (1982). *Psychological Testing*. (5th ed.). New York: Macmillan.

Aronson, E. & Carlsmith, J. M. (1968). Experimentation in social psychology. In G. Lindzey & Elliot Aronson (Eds.), *Handbook of social psychology* (2nd ed.), *2,* 1–79, Reading, MA: Addison-Wesley.

Aronson, E. & Linder, D. (1965). Gain and loss of esteem as determinants of interpersonal attractiveness. *Journal of Experimental Social Psychology, 1,* 156–171.

Ayllon, T. & Azrin, N. H. (1965). The measurement and reinforcement of behavior of psychotics. *Journal of the Experimental Analysis of Behavior, 8,* 171–180.

Baltes, P. B. (1968). Longitudinal and cross-sectional sequences in the study of age and generation effects. *Human Development, 11,* 145–171.

Baltes, P. B., Reese, H. W. & Nesselroade, J. R. (1977). *Life-span developmental psychology: Introduction to research methods*. Monterey, CA: Brooks/Cole.

Bandura, A. (1977). *Social learning theory*. Englewood Cliffs, NJ: Prentice-Hall.

Barber, T. X. (1976). *Pitfalls in human research: Ten pivotal points*. New York: Pergamon.

Barber, T. X. & Silver, M. J. (1968). Fact, fiction, and experimenter bias effect. *Psychological Bulletin, 70,* 1–29.

Baron, R. A., Russell, G. W., & Arms, R. L. (1985). Negative ions and behavior: Impact on mood, memory, and aggression among Type A and Type B persons. *Journal of Personality and Social Psychology, 48,* 746–754.

Blough, D. S. (1957). Effect of lysergic acid diethylamide on absolute visual threshold in the pigeon. *Science, 126,* 304–305.

Blough, D. S. (1961). Animal psychophysics. *Scientific American, 205,* 113–122.

Bousfield, W. A. (1953). The occurrence of clustering in the recall of randomly arranged associates. *Journal of General Psychology, 49,* 229–240.

Brady, J. V. (1958). Ulcers in "executive" monkeys. *Scientific American, 199,* 95–100.

Brannigan, G. G. & Merrens, M. R. (Eds.). (1993). *The undaunted psychologist: Adventures in research*. New York: McGraw-Hill.

Broad, W. J. & Wade, N. (1982). Science's faulty fraud detectors. *Psychology Today, 16,* 50–57.

Buros, O. K. (Ed.). (1978). *The eighth mental measurements yearbook* (Vol. I). Highland Park, NJ: Gryphon Press.

Campbell, D. T. & Stanley, J. C. (1966). *Experimental and quasi-experimental designs for research*. Chicago: Rand McNally.

Campbell, J. P., Daft, R. L., & Hulin, C. L. (1982). *What to study: Generating and developing research questions*. Beverly Hills, CA: Sage Publications.

Chapman, L. J., & Chapman, P. J. (1967). Genesis of popular but erroneous psychodiagnostic observations. *Journal of Abnormal Psychology, 72,* 193–204.

Chlopan, B. E., McCain, M. L., Carbonell, J. L., & Hagen, R. L. (1985). Empathy: Review of available measures. *Journal of Personality and Social Psychology, 48,* 635–653.

Cohen, A. S., Rosen, R. C., & Goldstein, L. (1985). EEG hemispheric asymmetry during sexual arousal: Psychophysiological patterns in responsive, unresponsive, and dysfunctional men. *Journal of Abnormal Psychology, 94,* 580–590.

Cohen, J. & Cohen, P. (1975). *Applied multiple regression/correlation analysis for the behavioral sciences*. Hilldale, NJ: Lawrence Erlbaum Associates.

Coile, D. C. & Miller, N. E. (1984). How radical animal

activists try to mislead humane people. *American Psychologist, 39,* 700–701.

Cook, T. D. & Campbell, D. T. (1979). *Quasi-experimentation: Design and analysis for field settings.* Chicago: Rand McNally.

Dawes, R. M. (1994). *A house of cards: Psychology and Psychotherapy built on myth.* New York: The Free Press.

Dipboye, R. L. & Flanagan, M. F. (1979). Research settings in industrial and organizational psychology. *American Psychologist, 34,* 141–150.

Dutton, P. G. & Aron, A. P. (1974). Some evidence for heightened sexual attraction under conditions of high anxiety. *Journal of Personality and Social Psychology, 30,* 510–517.

Eron, L. D. (1982). Parent-child interaction, television violence, and aggression in children. *American Psychologist, 37,* 197–211.

Eysenck, H. J., & Eysenck, M. (1983). *Mindwatching.* Garden City, NY: Anchor Press/Doubleday.

Festinger, L. (1954). Theory of social comparison processes. *Human Relations, 7,* 117–140.

Frank, R. (1984). A half-life theory of love. Presented at the 92nd Annual Convention of the American Psychological Association in Toronto, Canada.

Garner, W. R., Hake, H. & Eriksen, C. W. (1956). Operationism and the concept of perception. *Psychological Review, 63,* 149–159.

Geller, E. S. (1983). Rewarding safety belt usage at an industrial setting: Tests of treatment generality and response maintenance. *Journal of Applied Behavior Analysis, 16,* 189–202.

Graziano, W. G., Rahe, D. F., & Feldesman, A. B. (1985). Extraversion, social cognition, and the salience of aversiveness in social encounters. *Journal of Personality and Social Psychology, 49,* 971–980.

Greenwald, A. G. (1975). Significance, nonsignificance, and interpretation of an ESP experiment. *Journal of Experimental Social Psychology, 11,* 180–191.

Greenwald, A. G. (1976). Within-subjects designs: To use or not to use? *Psychological Bulletin, 83,* 314–320.

Groves, R. M., & Kahn, R. L. (1979). *Surveys by telephone: A national comparison with personal interviews.* New York: Academic Press.

Guthrie, E. R. (1952). *The psychology of learning.* New York: Harper.

Hammond, K. R. (1948). Measuring attitudes by error-choice: An indirect method. *Journal of Abnormal and Social Psychology, 43,* 38–48.

Hays, W. L. *Statistics* (3rd ed.). (1981). New York: Holt, Rinehart, & Winston.

Hernstein, R. J. (1962). Placebo effect in rats. *Science, 138,* 677–678.

Hess, E. H. & Polt, J. M. (1960). Pupil size as related to interest value of visual stimuli. *Science, 132,* 349–350.

Holmes, D. S., & Will, M. J. (1985). Expression of interpersonal aggression by angered and nonangered persons with Type A and Type B behavior patterns. *Journal of Personality and Social Psychology, 48,* 723–727.

Huck, S. W., & Sandler, H. M. (1979). *Rival Hypotheses: Alternative interpretations of data based conclusions.* New York: Harper & Row.

Hull, C. L. (1952). *A behavior system.* New Haven: Yale University Press.

Jackson, J. M., & Williams, K. D. (1985). Social loafing on difficult tasks: Working collectively can improve performance. *Journal of Personality and Social Psychology, 49,* 937–942.

James, W. (1950). *Principles of psychology.* New York: Dover.

Johnson, V. S. (1985). Electrophysiological changes induced by adrostenol: A potential human pherome. Unpublished manuscript, New Mexico State University.

Jolley, J. M., Murray, J. D., & Keller, P. A. (1992). *How to write psychology papers: A student's survival guide for psychology and related fields.* Sarasota, FL: Professional Resource Exchange.

Kahneman, D., Slovic, P., & Tversky, A. (Eds.). (1982). *Judgment under uncertainty: Heuristics and biases.* New York: Cambridge University Press.

Kelley, H. H. (1971). *Attribution in social interaction.* Morristown, NJ: General Learning Press.

Kenny, D. A. (1979). *Correlation and causality.* New York: John Wiley & Sons.

Kerlinger, F. N. (1973). *Foundations of behavioral research* (2nd ed.). New York: Holt, Rinehart, & Winston.

Keyser, D. J. & Sweetland, R. C. (Eds.). (1984). *Test critiques.* Kansas City, MO: Test Corporation of America.

Kincher, J. (1992). *The first honest book about lies.* Minneapolis, MN: Free Spirit Publishing.

Kohlberg, L. (1981). *The meaning and measurement of moral development.* Worcester, MA: Clark University Press.

Kohler, W. (1925). *The mentality of apes.* New York: Harcourt.

Kramer, J. J. & Conoley, J. C. (Eds.). (1992). *The eleventh mental measurements yearbook.* Lincoln, NE: Buros Institute of Mental Measurements.

Kuhn, T. S. (1970). *The structure of scientific revolutions.* (2nd ed.). Chicago: University of Chicago Press.

Laird, J. D. (1984). The real role of facial response in the experience of emotion: A reply to Tourangeau and Ellsworth and others. *Journal of Personality and Social Psychology, 47,* 909–917.

Latané, B. (1981). The psychology of social impact. *American Psychologist, 36,* 343–356.

Latané, B. & Darley, J. M. (1968). Group inhibition of bystander intervention in emergencies. *Journal of Personality and Social Psychology, 10*, 215–221.

Latané, B. & Darley, J. M. (1970). *The unresponsive bystander: Why doesn't he help?* New York: Appleton-Century-Crofts.

Latané, B., Nida, S. A., & Wilson, D. W. (1981). The effects of group size on helping behavior. In J. P. Rushton, Y. R. M. Sorrentino (Eds.), *Altruism and helping behavior: Social, personality, and developmental perspectives*. Hillsdale, NJ: Erlbaum.

Latané, B., Williams, K., & Harkins, S. (1979). Many hands make light the work: The causes and consequences of social loafing. *Journal of Personality and Social Psychology, 37*, 822–832.

Lemon, N. (1973). *Attitudes and their measurement.* New York: Wiley.

Light, R. J., & Pillemer, D. P. (1984). *Summing up: The science of reviewing research.* Cambridge, MA: Harvard University Press.

Lykken, D. T. (1979). The detection of deception. *Psychological Bulletin, 86*, 47–53.

Lykken, D. T. (1981). *A tremor in the blood: Uses and abuses of the lie detector.* New York: McGraw-Hill.

McCann, I. L. & Holmes, D. S. (1984). Influence of aerobic exercise on depression. *Journal of Personality and Social Psychology, 46*, 1142–1147.

Maslow, A. H. (1970). Cited in S. Cunningham, "Humanist celebrate gains, goals." *APA Monitor, 16*, p. 16.

McDougall, W. (1980). *An introduction to social psychology.* London: Methuen.

Milgram, S. (1974). *Obedience to authority: An experimental view.* New York: Harper & Row.

Milgram, S., Bickman, L., & Berkowitz, L. (1969). Note on the drawing power of crowds of different sizes. *Journal of Personality and Social Psychology, 13*, 79–82.

Mitchell, J. V. (Ed.). (1983). Tests in print III: An index to tests, test reviews, and the literature on specific tests. Lincoln, NE: Buros Institute of Mental Measurements.

Mook, D. G. (1983). In defense of external invalidity. *American Psychologist, 38*, 379–387.

Morris, J. D. (1986). MTV in the classroom. *Chronicle of Higher Education, 32*, 25–26.

Myers, J. L. (1979). *Fundamentals of experimental design* (3rd ed.). Boston: Allyn and Bacon.

Neisser, U. (1984). Ecological movement in cognitive psychology. Invited address at the 92nd Annual Convention of the American Psychological Association in Toronto, Canada.

Nisbett, R. E. & Wilson, T. D. (1977). Telling more than we can know: Verbal reports on mental processes. *Psychological Review, 84*, 231–259.

Orne, M. (1962). On the social psychology of the psychological experiment: With particular reference to demand characteristics and their implications. *American Psychologist, 17*, 776–783.

Parsons, H. M. (1974). What happened at Hawthorne? *Science, 183*, 922–932.

Pennebaker, J. W., Dyer, M. A., Caulkins, R. S., Litowitz, D. L., Ackerman, P. L., Anderson, D. B., & McGraw, K. M. (1979). Don't the girls get prettier at closing time: A country and western application to psychology. *Personality and Social Psychology Bulletin, 5*, 122–125.

Phillips, D. P. (1985). Natural experiments on the effects of mass media violence on fatal aggression: Strengths and weaknesses of a new approach. In L. Berkowitz (Ed.), *Advances in experimental social psychology, 19*, Orlando, FL: Academic Press.

Pronko, N. H. (1969). "Are Geniuses Born or Made?" In *Panorama of Psychology.* Belmont, CA: Brooks/Cole, 215–219.

Ranieri, D. J. & Zeiss, A. M. (1984). Induction of a depressed mood: A test of opponent-process theory. *Journal of Personality and Social Psychology, 47*, 1413–1422.

Rinn, W. E. (1984). The neuropsychology of facial expression: A review of the neurological and psychological mechanisms for producing facial expressions. *Psychological Bulletin, 95*, 52–77.

Roediger, H. L. (1980). The effectiveness of four mnemonics in ordering recall. *Journal of Experimental Psychology, 6*, 558–567.

Roethlisberger, F. J. & Dickson, W. J. (1939). *Management and the worker.* Cambridge, MA: Harvard University Press.

Rogers, C. R. (1985). Cited in S. Cunningham, "Humanists celebrate gains, goals." *APA Monitor, 16*, p. 16.

Rosenthal, R. & Rosnow, R. (1969). *Artifact in behavioral research.* New York: Academic Press.

Rubin, Z. (1970). Measurement of romantic love. *Journal of Personality and Social Psychology, 16*, 265–273.

Ruchlis, H. & Oddo, S. (1990). *Clear thinking: A practical introduction.* Buffalo, NY: Prometheus.

Schachter, S. (1959). *The psychology of affiliation.* Stanford, CA: Stanford University Press.

Schachter, S. (1971). Some extraordinary facts about obese humans and rats. *American Psychologist, 26*, 129–144.

Schaie, K. W. (1977). Quasi-experimental designs in the psychology of aging. In J. E. Birren & K. W. Schaie (Eds.), *Handbook of the psychology of aging.* New York: Van Nostrand.

Seligman, M. E. P. (1975). *Helplessness: On depression, development, and death.* San Francisco: Freeman.

Shaffer, D. R., Rogel, M., & Hendrik, C. (1975). Intervention in the library: The effect of increased responsibility on bystanders' willingness to prevent theft. *Journal of Personality and Social Psychology, 5,* 303–319.

Shefrin, H. M. & Statman, M. (1986). How not to make money in the stock market. *Psychology Today, 20,* 52–57.

Shultz, K. S. (1994, July). Type I error and multiple hypothesis tests of correlation coefficients. Paper presented at the sixth annual American Psychological Society Convention, Washington, DC.

Skinner, B. F. (1938). *The behavior of organisms: An experimental analysis.* New York: Appleton-Century-Crofts.

Solomon, R. L. (1980). The opponent-process theory of acquired motivation: The costs of pleasure and the benefits of pain. *American Psychologist, 35,* 691–712.

Steele, C. M. & Southwick, L. (1985). Alcohol and Social Behavior I: The Psychology of Drunken Excess. *Journal of Personality and Social Psychology, 48,* 18–34.

Sternberg, R. J. & Grajek, S. (1984). The nature of love. *Journal of Personality and Social Psychology, 47,* 312–329.

Stevens, S. S. (1957). On the psychophysical law. *Psychological Review, 64,* 153–181.

Stone, P. J., Dunphy, D. C., Smith, M. S., & Ogilvie, D. M. (1966). *The general inquirer: A computer approach to content analysis.* Cambridge, MA: M.I.T. Press.

Sudman, S. & Bradburn, N. M. (1982). *Asking Questions: A practical guide to questionnaire design.* San Francisco: Jossey-Bass.

Tversky, A. (1985). Quoted by K. McKean, Decisions, decisions. *Discover,* pp. 22–31.

Tversky, B. (1973). Encoding processes in recognition and recall. *Cognitive Psychology, 5,* 275–287.

Ward, W. C. & Jenkins, H. M. (1965). The display of information and the judgment of contingency. *Canadian Journal of Psychology, 19,* 231–241.

Webb, E. J. (1981). *Nonreactive measures in the social sciences.* (2nd edition). Boston: Houghton-Mifflin.

Webb, E. J., Campbell, D. T., Schwartz, R. D., & Seechrist, L. (1981). *Unobtrusive measures: Nonreactive research in the social sciences.* Chicago: Rand McNally.

Williams, K. B. & Williams, K. D. (1983). Social inhibition and asking for help: The effects of number, strength, and immediacy. *Journal of Personality and Social Psychology, 44,* 67–77.

Williams, R. L., & Long, J. D. (1983). *Toward a self-managed lifestyle* (3rd ed.). Boston: Houghton-Mifflin.

Winer, B. J. (1971). *Statistical principles in experimental design.* (2nd ed.). New York: McGraw-Hill.

Wohlwill, J. F. (1970). Methodology and research strategy in the study of developmental change. In L. R. Goulet & P. B. Baltes (Eds.), *Life-span developmental psychology: Research and theory.* New York: Academic Press.

Zimbardo, P. G. (1975). Transforming experimental research into advocacy for social change. In M. Deutsch & H. A. Hornstein (Eds.), *Applying social psychology: Implications for research, practice, and training.* Hillsdale, NJ: Lawrence Erlbaum Associates.

Zuckerman, M., Klorman, R., Larrance, D. T., & Spiegel, N. H. (1981). Facial, autonomic, and subjective components of emotion: The facial feedback hypothesis versus the externalizer-internalizer distinction. *Journal of Personality and Social Psychology, 41,* 929–944.

# Index

A–B design, 352–357, 386
A–B–A reversal design, 357–359, 386
Abstract, 346, 502
   reading, 325
   writing, 492
Aggregate data, 404
American Psychological Association (APA)
   ethical principles, 23, 505–518
   style, 498–501
Analysis of Variance (ANOVA), 238
   computing, 228–229, 231–233
   interpreting significant results, 233–234
   overview, 225–227, 231–233
   post hoc trend analyses, 235–236
   using an F table, 233
APA (*See* American Psychological Association)
Archival data, 401–405, 432
Attrition (*See* Morality)

Baseline, 386
Bell curve (*See* Normal curve)
Between–groups variability, 225–227, 229–231
Between–groups variance, 229–234, 238
Blind, 73, 100
   single and double, 180
Bonferroni t-test, 235

Carryover effects, 304–305, 320, 386
Causality
   and descriptive methods, 393–395
   inferring, 156–157, 350–352, 353
   and surveys, 438–439
Ceiling effects, 270–272, 286
Central limit theorem, 190, 202
Chi-square test, 469, 472
Coefficient of determination, 423–424, 433
Compensation, 598
Computers
   and literature searches, 525–528
Conceptual replication, 342–343, 347, 503
   justifying, 485–486

Confidentiality of data, 544–545
Confounding variables, 219–220, 239
Construct, 34, 65
Construct validity, 17–20, 21, 34, 89–91, 100
   of archival data, 403–404
   and content validity, 90–91
   and convergent validity, 89–90
   and critiquing articles, 335
   and discriminant validity, 87–89
   of ex post facto research, 401
   of matched pairs design, 295
   of multi-level experiments, 221–222
   versus power, 179–181
Content analysis, 402–403, 432
Content validity, 90–91, 100
Control group, 164, 201
   empty, 180, 201
   and validity, 222–224
Covariation, 386
Convenience sampling, 461–462, 470
Convergent validation, 89–90, 101
   and known-groups, 90
Correlation coefficient, 80, 99, 410, 432
   calculating, 415–417
   making inferences from, 418–430
   types of, 413
Correlational methods (*See* Descriptive methods)
Counterbalanced designs, 306–313
Counterbalancing, 307, 321
Covariation, 350–351
Crossover interaction (*See* Disordinal interaction)
Critical experiments, 53–54, 66
Cubic trends, 218
*Current Contents*, 82–83, 520, 525
Curvilinear relationship, 214–216, 240

Data
   confidentiality of, 23
   transforming, 332
   writing up (*See* Results section)
Debriefing, 23, 524
Deduction, 66

Degrees of freedom (df), 204
Demand characteristics, 76, 100
    reducing, 76-77
Demographics, 458, 472
Demoralization, 598
Dependent groups t-test, 297-298, 320
Dependent variable, 108, 201
Descriptive methods
    and causality, 393-395
    need for, 396-399
    sources of data, 400-408
    summarizing data, 408-418
    uses of, 393-395
Designs
    choosing an experimental design, 313-318
Discriminant validity, 87-89, 101
Diffusion of treatment, 598
Direct replication, 337-339, 347, 503
    justifying, 484-485
Discussion section, 347, 503
    reading, 333-334
    writing of, 491, 496-497
Disordinal interaction, 272-276, 286
Double-barreled question, 455, 471
Double blind, 57, 65, 201
Duncan test, 234
Dunn test, 234
Dunnett test, 234

Empty control group, 180, 201
Error variance (See Within-group variance)
Ethical, 34
Ethics, 20-26, 61-64, 505-518, 529-533
    and power, 189, 533-535
Experimental group, 164, 201
Experimental hypothesis, 162, 201
Experimenter bias (See Researcher bias), 92,
    100
Exploratory study, 503
Ex post facto research, 400-401, 431
External validity, 20, 21, 39, 151
    of archival data, 404
    and critiquing articles, 335-336
    of ex post facto research, 400
    and internal validity, 148-149
    of matched pairs design, 294-295
    of testing research, 407
    versus power, 179
Extraneous factors, 131

F ratio, 233, 239
F table, 233
Face validity, 123

Factor analysis, 99
Factor loadings, 99
Factorial experiments, 244, 285
    between subjects, ANOVA table for, 266
    interactions, 248-252
    2 × 2, analyzing result of, 264-266
    2 × 2, expanding of, 276-384
    2 × 2, potential outcomes, 253-264
    2 × 2, using of, 276-284
Fatigue effects, 305, 320
Field experiment, 589-600
    construct validity, 589-590, 592, 598-600
    ethics of, 590-591
    external validity, 589-591
    with intact groups, 596-598
    internal validity of, 589, 596-598
    limitations of, 590-596
    power of, 590
Fixed alternative items, 447-451, 471
Floor effects, 272, 286
Fraud, and replication, 338
Functional relationship, 57, 65, 214-218, 239

Generalizability (See External validity)
Group(s)
    arbitrary assignment to, 131-132
    experimental and control, 164
    matching of, 132-139
    self-assignment to, 129-131

Hawthorne effect, 93, 100
History, 151
History effect, 141, 387
Hypothesis, 66
    deducing from theory, 50-54
    generating from intuition, 42-43, 44
    generating from reading, 55-59
    null (See Null hypothesis)
    refining, 59-64
    testability, 59-60
Hypothesis guessing, 221-239
Hypothesis testing, 466, 472
Hypothetical construct, 49

Illusory correlation, 432
Independence, 201
    in assignment, 164-166
    maintaining, 165-166
Independent random assignment, 164, 201
Independent variable, 163, 201 (See also Manipulating
    variables)
    levels of, 163-164

Inferential statistics, 185, 168, 201
  use with survey research, 466–469
Informed consent, 445, 590
Instructional manipulation, 100, 432
Instrumentation, 151, 387
Instrumentation bias, 142, 404
Interactions, 248–452, 285
  to find moderator variables, 278
  to study effects of similarity, 282
Inter-judge agreement, 100
Inter-observer reliability, 100
Internal consistency, 82–83, 100
Internal validity, 16–17, 21, 24, 128–149, 151, 202
  of correlational research, 393–395
  and critiquing research, 336
  and external validity, 148–149
  logic of, 128–129, 350–351
  threats to, 17, 129
Interval data (*See also* Scales of measurement), 124
  hypothesis-testing with, 466–468
  parameter estimation with, 466–467
  summarizing, 464
Interviews, 443–446, 472
Interviewer bias, 444, 472
Introduction, 346, 552
  reading, 325–329
  writing, 478–487
Investigator-administered questionnaire, 442

Journals, 526–527

Known-groups, 90, 101

Law, 66
Leading questions, 454, 471
Levels of the independent variable, 201, 234
Likert-type item, 448, 471
Linear relationship, 214
Linear trend, 239
Literature review, 519–528
Loose protocol effect, 537–538

Main effect, 247, 285
Manipulating variables, 91–98
  and experimenter bias, 92
  and standardization, 92
  and subject biases, 92–94
  types of, 95–98
Manipulation checks, 95, 100, 331, 495
Matched pairs design, 291–296, 319

analysis of, 295–296
  construct validity of, 295
  external validity of, 294–295
  matching, 299
  power of, 292–294
Matching, 131–139, 379–383
  on pretest scores, 135–139, 379–383
Maturation, 151, 387
  as bias, 140–141, 367
  as research focus, 375–376
Mean, 202
Mean square between subjects (MS between), 231–233, 238
Mean square error (MSE), 231–233, 238
Mean square within (MSW), 231, 233, 238
Measures
  reliability of, (*See* Reliability)
  and validity, 86–91
Median, 433
Median split, 422, 433
Mediating variable, 66
Method section, 346, 502
  reading, 329, 330
  writing, 486–490
Mixed design, 316–318, 324
Moderator variables, 51–52, 66, 278
Mortality, 145–146, 151, 367, 369, 387
Multilevel experiments, 210–236
  analysis of, 224–234
  construct validity of, 219–224
  and empty control group, 221–222
  external validity of, 218–219
Multiple baseline design, 387
Multiple group experiments
  analysis of, 224–234

Naturalistic observation, 405, 432
Negative correlation, 409, 432
Newman–Keuls test, 234
Non-equivalent control group design, 388
Nonreactive, 432
Normal curve, 188, 202
Normally distributed, 188, 202
Nominal data (*See also* Scales of measurement), 123
  summarizing, 464–466
  using inferential statistics with, 468–469
Nominal dichotomous items, 447–448, 471
Nonequivalent control design, 379–383
Nonlinear relationships, 214–218
Nonreactive measure, 401
Nonsignificant results (*See* Null results)
Null hypothesis, 60, 66, 162–163, 201
Null results, 204

critiquing articles with, 336
interpretation of, 169–170, 196, 428–430

Observational research, 405–407
Observer bias, 71–74, 99
    and reliability, 71–73
Open-ended items, 451–452, 471
Operational definitions, 34, 48, 65, 70, 100
Operationalism, of theory, 48–49
Order, 320
Order effects, 300–305, 320
Ordinal data, 123, 268 (*See also* Scales of measurement)
Ordinal interaction, 268–272, 286
Overall main effect, 247, 285

p < .05, 204
Parameter(s), 466, 472
Parameter estimation, 466–467, 472
Parsimonious, 46, 66
Participant observation, 405, 432
Pearson *r*, 411–418
    calculating, 415–417
    determining significant of, 422
Phi coefficient, 425–426
Pilot study, 111, 541
Placebo, 93, 100, 180, 200
    versus empty control group, 223–224
Population, 202, 470
Positive correlation, 408–409, 432
Post hoc tests, 234–236, 240
    trend analysis, 235–236
    Tukey test, 234
Power, 204
    and critiquing articles, 336–337
    and Type 2 errors, 173
    tradeoffs involving, 341
    versus construct validity, 179, 181
    versus ethics, 181
    versus external validity, 179
    ways to increase, 174–178
    of within-subjects design, 306
Practice effects, 298–299, 301, 306, 320
Predictions,
    and descriptive methods, 395
    testability of, 4–6, 10–11, 59–60
Pretest
    matching from scores on, 135–139, 369–371
Pretest-posttest design, 139–146, 369–371, 388
*Psychological Abstracts,* 346, 520–522
Psychological tests, 442–443
Psychophysics, 359–360

Quadratic trend, 218
Quasi-experiments, 366–384, 388
    nonequivalent control groups design, 379–383
    threats to validity, 366–369
    time series design, 371–379
Questionnaires, 472
    format of questions, 446–452
    framing of questions, 453–456
    sequencing of questions, 456–458
    types of, 441–442
Quota sampling, 462, 470

Random assignment, 202
    to more than two groups, 211
    to two groups, 159–161
Random sampling, 202, 459–460, 470
    stratified, 460–461, 470
Randomization
    and other effects, 304–305
Ratio scales (*See* Scales of measurement), 124
Reading research articles, 324–334
References, APA style, 493
Regression, 136–139, 143–145, 151, 367–369
Reliability, 77–86, 100
    inter-observer reliability, 79–80
    and random observer error, 79–80
    sources of unreliability, 79–83
    test-retest, 78–79
    and validity, 86
Repeated measures (*See* Within-subjects design), 320
Replication, 55
    conceptual, 342–343
    direct, 337–339, 484–485
    systematic, 339–342, 485
Replication factor, 277, 286
Research hypothesis (*See* Hypothesis)
Research journal, 476–477
Research paper, sample, 570–588
Research proposal, 476–501
    abstract, 492
    discussion, 491
    introduction, 478–487
    method section, 487–489
    references, 493
    results section, 490–491
Research realism, 540–541
Research summary, 480
Researcher bias, 536–539
Researcher effects, 538–539
Researcher expectancy effect, 538–539
Response latency, 124
Response set, 451, 471
Restriction of range, 429, 433

Results, 347
    null, interpretation of, 428-429
    significant, interpretation of, 425-428
Results section, 503
    reading of, 330-333
    writing of, 490-491, 494-496
Retrospective self-report, 471
Reversal design, 357-359

Sample research paper, 570-588
Sampling, in survey research, 459-462
Sampling statistics, 202
Scales of measurement, 112-121
Scatterplot, 408, 432
Scheffe test, 234
Science
    and psychology, 8-15
    qualities of, 2-8
    versus common sense, 14
Selection bias, 129-135, 151, 367-369, 387
Selection by maturation interaction, 135-136, 151,
    367-369, 380-381, 387
Self-administered questionnaire, 441-442, 472
Semistructured survey, 452-453, 472
Sensitization, 302, 330
Sensitivity, 107-112, 124
    and reliability, 108-109
    and validity, 107-108
    and pilot testing, 111
Sequence effects (*See* Order effects), 321
Significant results (*See* Statistical significance)
Simple experiment, 202
    analyzing data from, 181-196
    and causality, 156-162
    confounding variables in, 219-221
    hypothesis guessing in, 221
Simple main effect, 245, 247, 285
Single blind, 180, 200
Single-n designs, 386
Single subject design, 352-366
A-B-A reversal, 357-359
    construct validity, 363
    external validity, 364-365
    internal validity, 361-363
    multiple baseline, 360-361
    and within-subjects design, 364
Social desirability, 76, 100, 454-455
Social Sciences Citation Index, 523-525
Social Sciences Index, 522-523
Spearman's rho, 413
Spurious, 351, 386
Stable baseline, 386
Standard deviation, 186-188, 203

Standard error of the difference (between means),
    191-193, 203
Standard error of the mean, 188-190, 203, 472
Standardization, 101
Statistical considerations in designing an experiment,
    178-179
Statistical regression (*See* Regression bias)
Statistical significance, 168-169, 204
    errors in determining, 171-173
    meaning of, 168-169
Stimulus sets, 268, 287
Stooges, 100
Stratified random sampling, 460-461, 470
Straw theory, 49, 66
Structured questionnaire, 452, 472
Subject bias, 75-77, 92-94, 100
Sum of squared differences, 203
Sum of squares, 203
Summated scores, 448-458, 471
Survey research, 470
    administering the survey, 462-463
    analyzing data from, 463-469
    considerations in using, 437-441
    hypotheses, 438, 446
    inferring causality, 438-439
    major types of, 441-446
    planning, 446-459
    question format, 446-452
    sampling in, 459-462
    survey format, 452-453
    uses for, 436-437
    using inferential statistics with, 466-469
Systematic replication, 287, 337-342, 347, 503
    and construct validity, 341-342
    and external validity, 340-341
    justifying, 485
    and power, 339-340

t-distribution, 193-194
t-table, 194, 557-558
t-test, 204
    assumption of, 194-196
    and between-groups variance, 426
    with correlational data, 422, 426
    dependent groups, 297-298
    executing, 194
Telephone interview, 444-446
Temporal precedence, 351, 386
Testing, 387
Testing effect, 141, 151
Test-retest reliability, 100
Theory, 66
    deducing hypotheses from, 43-55

defined, 44–45
evaluating, 47–49
locating, 49
and manipulating variables, 94
qualities of good theories, 45–47
testability of, 47–49
Time series design, 371–379, 388
Trend analysis, 233–234, 240
Tukey test, 234
Type 1 errors, 171–172, 204, 337, 352
    and replication, 484–485
Type 2 errors, 172–178, 204, 338–339


Unobtrusive measurement, 70
Unobtrusive measures, 540
Unstructured survey, 467, 472
U-shaped relationship, 212, 213, 236


Validity,
    construct (*See* Construct validity)
    and ethics, 24–25

external (*See* External validity)
internal (*See* Internal validity)
Variables,
    confounding (*See* Confounding variables)
    dependent, 168
    independent, 163
    mediating, 53
    moderating, 51–52
Variance, 203
    between-groups (*See* Between-groups variance)
    comparing between- and within-groups, 231–233
    within groups (*See* Within-groups variance)


Within-groups variability, 227–229
Within-groups variance, 231–233, 238
Within-subjects designs, 296–313, 320, 322
    counterbalanced, 306–313
    pure, 296–306


Zero correlation, 418–432